PRAISE FOR
THE HUNTING OF THE PRESIDENT

"Absorbing."

—*Milwaukee Journal Sentinel*

"Its documentation and analysis offer a clearer, if imperfect, picture of the Clinton investigations."

—The Associated Press

"The story of the Clinton scandals is a tortuous, labyrinthine puzzle, and Conason and Lyons do their best to simplify it…. Readers…will nevertheless gain a considerably more balanced and complex picture of the road to impeachment."

—*Publishers Weekly*

"Their evidence is interesting."

—*The Economist*

"Carefully documented."

—*The Village Voice*

"After reading *The Hunting of the President,* it is no longer possible to believe that…Ken Star was even remotely impartial or that the Jones suit was anything more than a vehicle for the public humiliation of the president."

—*The New York Observer*

"Their reporting, thickly documented with citations…makes a firm case that the president and his wife have been pursued by many scoundrels."

—*Library Journal*

"Which to choose? The nod goes to Conason and Lyons [over Jeffrey Toobin]…. The proof of their hypothesis is found all through the text."

—*Newsday*

"Admirable and useful."

—*The New York Times*

"*The Hunting of the President.* … ng histories of the secret machinations tha … t [Conason and Lyons] write without the … of the hallmarks of American journalism … uthority and appeal."

—Janet Malcolm, author of
The Crime of Sheila McGough

ALSO BY GENE LYONS

The Higher Illiteracy

Widow's Web

Fools for Scandal: How the Media Invented Whitewater

THE
HUNTING
OF THE
PRESIDENT

The Ten-Year Campaign to Destroy
Bill and Hillary Clinton

Joe Conason and **Gene Lyons**

Thomas Dunne Books
St. Martin's Griffin
New York

THOMAS DUNNE BOOKS.
An imprint of St. Martin's Press.

www.stmartins.com

Designed by Michael Mendelsohn at MM Design 2000, Inc.

ISBN 0-312-24547-5 (hc)
ISBN 0-312-27319-3 (pbk)

First St. Martin's Griffin Edition: January 2001

10 9 8 7 6 5 4 3 2 1

For

Ellie and Red Conason

For

Fred K. Darragh, Jr., and

Elizabeth W. Blass

CONTENTS

Acknowledgments   ix

Preface   xiii

CHAPTER 1 | *The Ghost of Lee Atwater*   1

CHAPTER 2 | *"A Crazy Person like Larry Nichols"*   14

CHAPTER 3 | *Jean Lewis's October Surprise*   30

CHAPTER 4 | *The Larry Case Tapes*   46

CHAPTER 5 | *"Justice Jim" Rides Again*   67

CHAPTER 6 | *A Pig in a Poke*   83

CHAPTER 7 | *The Scandal Industry's Secret Sugar Daddies*   99

CHAPTER 8 | *"A Truly Independent Prosecutor"*   116

CHAPTER 9 | *The Reverend Jerry Falwell, Seoul Man*   136

CHAPTER 10 | *Inside the Arkansas Project*   160

CHAPTER 11 | *Senator D'Amato's Long Good-bye*   183

CHAPTER 12 | *"The President of the United States Is Not on Trial"* 216

CHAPTER 13 | *"All They Wanted to Talk About Was Women"*   256

CHAPTER 14 | *Spinning the Widow's Web*   277

CHAPTER 15 | *Impeachment for Fun and Profit*   308

CHAPTER 16 | *"The Bastard Should Be Exposed"*   323

                Afterword   369

                Sources   375

                Index   403

ACKNOWLEDGMENTS

A NY BLAME FOR ERRORS, omissions, or infelicities in these pages belongs to the authors alone, but any credit must be shared with many others.

We were fortunate to find at St. Martin's Press an independent-minded editor named Thomas Dunne, who understood so well what this book is about that he had conceived the perfect title before he knew that it was being written. He and his associates—notably Peter Wolverton, Matthew Herman, Amelie Littell, Terence Bailey, Adam Goldberger, Josette Haddad, Naomi Shulman, and Justine B. Gardner—maintained a commitment to professional standards that any author would find gratifying. The same is true of Celeste Phillips of Levine, Sullivan & Koch, who contributed improvements to the text that went far beyond her duties as legal counsel.

We were just as lucky to be represented by the Wylie Agency, where Andrew Wylie and Jeffrey Posternack displayed an abiding confidence in this project that sometimes surpassed our own. Without their perseverance, this book simply would never have been published.

Nor would it have been completed without the timely beneficence of Bill Moyers, Patricia McCarthy, and the directors of the Florence and John Schumann Foundation; Fred Darragh and the Darragh Foundation; Elizabeth W. Blass; and Ralph Nader and John Richard of Essential Information, Inc. To be sustained by citizens such as these did us honor.

No contribution was more vital than the hundreds of hours dedicated to research and analysis by Bonnie Simrell. Often working late into the night, she never failed to answer our requests with energy, creativity, alacrity, and wit. Her untiring diligence left us with an obligation we will never be able to adequately repay. Researchers at the *New York Observer,* the *Columbia Journalism Review, The Nation, Harper's, Boston Magazine, Penthouse, U.S. News & World Report,* and *Salon* also made important contributions.

Of all the colleagues to whom Joe Conason owes special gratitude, the first mentioned must be Arthur L. Carter, the publisher of the *New York Observer,* whose generous support has meant more than he may know. Arthur's perseverance and integrity have made the *Observer* a unique voice in American journalism and an exhilarating place to be a writer and editor. Thanks are owed as well to *Observer* editor Peter W. Kaplan for, among other things, his intelligence and kindness; and also to Mary Ann Giordano, Terry Golway, and Brian Kempner.

Significant portions of this book derive from articles and columns first published in *Salon,* which has proved that new media can expand free expression while serving the public good. The encouragement of *Salon's* courageous editor, David Talbot, and his talented colleagues David Weir, Joan Walsh, and Daryl Lindsey have been much appreciated.

It also has been a privilege to be associated with *The Nation,* America's most venerable political journal, and its exceptional editors Katrina vanden Heuvel and Victor Navasky. Like them, Hamilton Fish III of the Nation Institute gave enthusiastic support to the journalism that eventually inspired this book. So did Peter Bloch, the astute maverick who edits *Penthouse* magazine.

And whenever reporting required a visit to Washington, John and Symmie Newhouse welcomed Joe Conason into their home with the warmest hospitality—usually on short notice.

Much of the reporting and thinking that became the genesis of this book began as an article in *Harper's* magazine. Gene Lyons is particularly indebted to *Harper's* editor Lewis Lapham and publisher John R. MacArthur for their generosity, patience, and wise counsel; and also to Michael Lind, Ellen Rosenbush, and Louisa McCune.

We both relied heavily upon the previous work of others, most notably Murray S. Waas, whose intrepid investigations guided so much of our own reporting. Among the writers and correspondents whose work also informed and influenced us are Jill Abramson, Elise Ackerman, James Ring Adams, Renata Adler, Jonathan Alter, Steve Barnes, Wayne Barrett, Russ Bellant, Andrea Bernstein, Sidney Blumenthal, Rodney Bowers, John Brady, Taylor Branch, Max Brantley, Steven Brill, David Brock, Jonathan Broder, John Brummett, Kevin Buckley, Vincent Bugliosi, John Camp, James Carville, Frederick Clarkson, David Corn, Cynthia Cotts, Elias Demetracopoulos, Mollie Dickenson, Joan Didion, Robert C. Douglas, Jesse Drucker, Joan I. Duffy, Ernest Dumas, Joan Early, Eric Engberg, Roy Faulkenberry, Willard "Skip" Fox, Richard Fricker, Karen Fuller, Jack Gillis, Dan Goldfarb, Florence Graves, Frank Greve, Karen Gullo, Tom Hamburger, Burton Hersh, Mike Hoyt, Michael Isikoff, Mary Jacoby, Michael Kinsley, Howard Kurtz, the late great Jonathan Kwitny, Bob Lancaster, Susan Lehman, Suzanne Braun Levine, Anthony Lewis, Trudy Lieberman, Pat Lynch, David Maraniss, Deborah Mathis, Rudy Maxa, Jane

Mayer, Wilson Minor, Dan Moldea, James Morgan, Lars-Erik Nelson, Jack Newfield, Robert Parry, Leslie Peacock, Charles Peters, Walter Pincus, Skipp Porteous, Jane Prettyman, Harrison Rainie, Roy Reed, William Rempel, Carrie Rengers, James D. Retter, Frank Rich, Geraldo Rivera, Dennis Roddy, Alfred Ross, Karen Rothmyer, Robert Scheer, Bruce Shapiro, Bill Simmons, Glenn R. Simpson, George Stephanopoulos, Lynn Sweet, Stuart Taylor, Jr., Charles C. Thompson II, Craig Unger, Don van Natta, Jr., Douglas Vaughan, Ed Vulliamy, Mike Wallace, James Warren, Daniel Wattenberg, Tim Weiner, Philip Weiss, Garry Wills, Louis Wolf, Byron York, and Pete Yost.

Unfortunately, not all of those who assisted us can be named here, but we must also express appreciation to at least some of the individuals who gave us interviews or provided insights: Chris Andersen, Tamara Baker, Charles Banks, Richard Ben-Veniste, Robert Bennett, Joan Bingham, Diane Blair, Jim Blair, Stephen S. Boynton, Juanita Broaddrick, John Brown, Dale Bumpers, Joseph Cammarata, Larry Case, Charles Chastain, John Coale, George T. Conway III, Andrew Cooper, Jan Cottingham, Ann Coulter, Douglas Cox, Gilbert K. Davis, Matt Drudge, Terry Eastland, Ambrose Evans-Pritchard, Mitchell Ettinger, Garrick Feldman, Steve Fehr, Kenneth Fry, John Fund, Judy Gaddy, William Gaddy, Doris Garner, Mike Gauldin, Mark Geragos, Jeff Gerth, Kathy Gifford, Lucianne Goldberg, Kay Goss, Yale Gutnick, Laura Handman, Pat Harris, Sarah Hawkins, David W. Henderson, Nancy Hernreich, Rick Holiman, Harold Ickes, Laura Ingraham, Fletcher Jackson, Kitty Kelley, Chris Kelly, David Kendall, Victor Kovner, Kia Larsen, Kathy Lavinder, Eddie Mahe, Frank Mandanici, Caryn Mann, Mary Matalin, Bob McCord, Susan McDougal, Rex Nelson, Theodore Olson, P. J. O'Rourke, Max Parker, Bill Plante, Wesley Pruden, David Pryor, Weldon Ramey, Archie Schaffer, Beverly Bassett Schaffer, Ricki Seidman, Julie Speed, Bob Steele, Julie Hiatt Steele, Warren Stephens, Mark Stodola, Herb Swartz, Roy Talbot, Lee Thalheimer, Jim Guy Tucker, Marilyn Vessier, Michael Viner, William Watt, former governor Frank White, Judge William Wilson, Larry Wood, Judge Henry Woods, and Betsey Wright.

Close friends and family humored, tolerated, and cheered us, no matter how much our preoccupations and absences strained their affection. And of course we owe the deepest debts to Elizabeth Wagley and Diane Lyons, who endured it all for love.

PREFACE

D EMOCRACY IN AMERICA has always been played roughly by all parties, and political adversaries have indulged in harsh and sometimes vicious assaults on each other ever since the nation's founding. Leaders now as revered as Thomas Jefferson, Abraham Lincoln, and Franklin Delano Roosevelt were attacked with astonishing vituperation by partisan rivals and hostile journalists alike. What President Clinton has aptly termed "the politics of personal destruction" is merely a new name for a very old phenomenon.

But rarely in this century has the impulse to destroy dominated our national discourse the way it has during the past decade. No president of the United States and no first lady have ever been subject to the corrosive combination of personal scrutiny, published and broadcast vilification, and official investigation and prosecution endured by William Jefferson Clinton and Hillary Rodham Clinton. In historical terms, certain of the mechanisms necessary to inflict this kind of punishment—from the Office of Independent Counsel to the twenty-four hour news "cycle" and the Internet—are quite recent innovations. All have been brought to bear against the Clintons and their associates with stunning effect.

From the beginning, his enemies portrayed Clinton as unworthy to occupy the office of president of the United States. This assessment held firm despite his acknowledged intellect, industriousness, and charm, and also despite the fact that by almost every statistical measure, the American people and their government were in far better condition by 1999 than when the Arkansan took office in 1993. With his remarkable political skills, the president had broken the Republican "lock" on the electoral votes of the southern states, muted his own party's clamorous left wing, adapted portions of the Republican agenda to his own uses, restored fiscal discipline, and outmaneuvered his bitterest foes in the GOP leadership again and again. But the better the president and the country did, the more his adversaries appeared willing to endorse almost anything short of assassination to do him in.

*   *   *

Hardly anyone, and certainly not the authors of this book, liked what they learned about Bill Clinton during the Monica Lewinsky scandal. Yet it was almost impossible to imagine a document like the Starr Report being written about any other president during his term in office—and not because Clinton's behavior was egregiously worse. Little knowledge of human nature or American history was required to understand that men who ascended to the Oval Office had often displayed vigorous libidos and imperfect fidelity to the truth.

Ironically, many of the same commentators who not so long ago decried the "culture of scandal" and its contamination of American public life have applauded some of the most extreme assaults upon the Clintons. Even their young daughter has not been totally exempt from scrutiny. As a result, everything that conservatives once warned against when Republican presidents were embattled has since come to pass: the coarsening and debasement of democratic discourse; the abuse of criminal prosecution to resolve political disputes; and the diminishment of popular respect for the presidency, the Congress, the federal judiciary, the news media, and other vital institutions. Although Bill Clinton surely deserves his substantial share of blame, the ill effects of the campaign against him and his family appear all but certain to outlast the current occupants of the White House.

In the authors' view, the conventional narrative of the "Clinton scandals" reveals very little about this ugly political era. Behind that flat, condensed presentation of reality lies a story that is far richer, more amusing, and considerably more troubling.

It is the story of a loose cabal, if not quite a "vast conspiracy," involving longtime Clinton adversaries from Arkansas and elsewhere: an angry gallery of defeated politicians, disappointed office seekers, right-wing pamphleteers, wealthy eccentrics, zany private detectives, religious fanatics, and die-hard segregationists who went beyond mere sexual gossip to promote rumors of financial chicanery, narcotics trafficking, and even politically motivated murder. Some were energized by spite, others by ideological zeal, and more than a few by the prospect of personal profit. Some shared all three motives.

It is also the story of the most successful and long-running "dirty tricks" campaign in recent American history, fomented by a handful of professional Republican operatives and corporate lawyers, and funded by a network of wealthy conservatives. Swept up in their movement's anti-Clinton fervor, these respectable figures sometimes eagerly joined forces with persons of considerably lesser repute. Indeed, the effort to destroy Clinton began early on in the highest councils of the Republican National Committee, and included aides to former president George Bush. Arguably, not even the chief justice of the United States held himself entirely aloof from the great crusade.

It is also the story of important journalists and news organizations succumbing to scandal fever, credulously and sometimes dishonestly promoting charges against the Clintons in heavily biased, error-filled dispatches, columns, bestselling books, and TV news specials, and thus bestowing "mainstream" prestige upon what was often little more than a poisonous mixture of half-truth and partisan malice. Some conducted themselves as if their mission were less to inform the public than to guard their institutional prestige by protecting their own erroneous reporting from correction.

There can be little question that Clinton's Arkansas origins had much to do with the suspicion with which establishment Washington greeted him. No sooner had he been inaugurated than reporters began descending upon Little Rock from such havens of clean government as New York City, Chicago, New Jersey, and the nation's capital itself to describe the president's native state as uniquely corrupt. Under the tutelage of local Clinton adversaries—whose motives, identities, and agendas were usually well concealed—these journalists quickly reduced the complicated history and politics of a small, little-known state to a simple morality play. There is even less doubt that the White House's panicky, defensive, and occasionally less-than-perfectly-honest responses to these and other "scandal" stories made matters still worse.

Having reached the direst conclusions from very limited (and often inaccurate) information, leading figures in the national media came to regard Bill Clinton as unfit to hold the office to which he was twice elected. (They developed a similarly jaundiced view of Hillary Rodham Clinton.) Too frequently, this assessment found expression in false analogies between Whitewater and Watergate, with all the career-building self-interest such a comparison implied.

However disproportionate to Clinton's alleged offenses this hostility may have been, the terms were set early on. "What threatens this President," wrote Michael Kelly in an influential 1994 profile in the *New York Times Magazine,* "seems to be much larger than mere partisanship. There is a level of mistrust and even dislike of him that is almost visceral in its intensity. In Washington, where power is generally treated with genuflecting reverence, it is no longer surprising to hear the President spoken of with open and dismissive contempt. . . . Clinton is routinely depicted in the most unflattering terms: a liar, a fraud, a chronically indecisive man who cannot be trusted to stand for anything—or with anyone."

It would later emerge that Kelly had spent much of his time in Arkansas in the company of political operatives employed by a reactionary Pittsburgh tycoon named Richard Mellon Scaife, although his article featured liberal activists who scolded Clinton from the left. By way of discounting Clinton's six election victories there, the article went so far as to claim that "Arkansas is not really a democracy." Rather, it was a benighted rural fiefdom where a tiny, incestuous elite "holds sway over a small and politically-disorganized middle class and a large, but well-beaten population of the poor." The article exemplified a journalistic attitude which the authors call "naive cynicism." In that mood, complexity and inconvenient fact are ignored while melodrama is crafted from ordinary political behavior.

Four years after Kelly's article appeared, on the day before Election Day 1998, Washington writer and social arbiter Sally Quinn spoke in almost identical terms for herself and many in her circle when she complained that "Establishment Washingtonians . . . can't abide it that the rest of the country might think that everyone here cheats and lies and abuses his subordinates the way the president has. . . . And many are offended that the principles that brought them to Washington in the first place are now seen to be unfashionable or illegitimate."

Anybody who had read her husband Ben Bradlee's disarmingly frank autobiography *A Good Life* had to smile at the notion of Quinn, a talented journalist who once wrote knowingly about "the Washington Affair," expressing outrage over the president's sexual misconduct. Like so many of Clinton's critics, she was hardly in a position to cast the first stone. Hypocrite or not, however, she accurately reported the views of a group she designated "the so-called Beltway Insiders," those who "call the capital city their 'town.'" Acting upon an exaggerated sense of outraged propriety, many if not most of the capital's journalistic elite had tacitly aligned themselves with independent counsel Kenneth Starr.

For reasons that will become clearer as the narrative proceeds, the mainstream media have—with some honorable exceptions—been reluctant to explore that element of the story. Suffice it for the moment to observe that, as George Seldes said, "the most sacred cow of the press is the press itself."

To the immense frustration of its various sponsors, the persistent campaign to ruin Bill Clinton failed to defeat him in the elections of 1992 and 1996. His success in twice leading his party back into the White House, after twelve years of exile, only hardened the determination of his opponents to wreck him and his administration. And despite his electoral victories, their efforts had a profound impact that went well beyond injury to the Clintons themselves, distracting and discrediting the White House and thus contributing heavily to the Republican congressional victory in the 1994 midterm elections. Greatly assisted by the president's own extravagant folly, the campaign to destroy Bill and Hillary Clinton eventually culminated in the Republicans' failed impeachment of him.

The yearlong crisis that followed the unveiling of Monica Lewinsky on January 21, 1998, is still fresh in the memories of most Americans and will not be retraced in any detail in these pages. Rather, this book simply endeavors to tell the story of how and why it all happened.

Chapter One

THE GHOST
OF LEE ATWATER

THE CHANCES ARE that hardly anyone noticed the two political operatives from Arkansas who slipped in and out of Republican national headquarters on an autumn day in 1989. Neither had a famous face, unlike the man they had come to visit. They had flown in from Little Rock to meet secretly with Lee Atwater, the chairman of the Republican National Committee.

Discretion was of the utmost importance in this matter. No doubt that was why Atwater had brought his guests to Washington rather than traveling to Arkansas himself, much as he enjoyed pressing the flesh out in the hinterlands. But now he was a celebrity, often recognized in airports and on the street. As the outrageous party animal who ruled the Grand Old Party, Lee Atwater had been featured on the covers of national magazines and on countless news broadcasts. In Little Rock, he would have been spotted right away, and someone there might have realized what he was up to.

Honored traditions as well as party rules generally forbid the Republican National Committee and its chairman from taking sides in a state primary. But that was precisely what Atwater was preparing to do in Arkansas, where he was anything but neutral in the upcoming race for governor. The two operatives had come to discuss the prospects of Atwater's handpicked candidate, a flamboyant congressman and former county sheriff named Tommy Robinson.

Elected to the House as a Democrat, Robinson had switched parties only months earlier, and faced a serious challenge in the gubernatorial primary from a wealthy Little Rock businessman who had long been his benefactor. He needed the party chairman's advice and instructions.

Atwater was taking a risk in supporting Robinson. Any proof of his direct interference in the Arkansas primary might be used to embarrass him by rivals in the party hierarchy and the White House. More than a few powerful Republicans were irritated by his swaggering, Blues Brothers style and his lust for notoriety. Many also envied Atwater's close personal bond with George Bush, the president who had rewarded him with the power and prerogatives of the party chairmanship. But he had not become a national legend at the age of thirty-eight by obeying rules and avoiding risks.

In Arkansas he was trying to deal with a problem that dwarfed any nit-picking about neutrality. Though he would never say so publicly, he was worried about the future.

"Bush and this crowd are going to screw it up," he had told his former consulting partner Roger Stone a few months earlier. "Bush won't get reelected."

Atwater's clandestine meeting with J. J. Vigneault and Rex Nelson was informal but businesslike. He didn't pick up his guitar and start singing, as was his frequent habit in the daily staff meetings. There were no cigars or liquor, either, just Cokes brought in by Mary Matalin, Atwater's chief deputy. She remained in the room when the door was closed.

Atwater didn't know Nelson, whom he was trying to recruit to the Robinson campaign, nearly as well as he knew Vigneault, a longtime friend and associate who had overseen the successful Reagan and Bush campaigns in Arkansas. After Atwater had taken over as chairman early in 1989, he had brought Vigneault onto the RNC staff as a regional political director, based in Little Rock. It was a sign of Atwater's concern about the Arkansas race that his protégé Vigneault had abandoned a top party position so suddenly to manage an insurgent campaign in a small, overwhelmingly Democratic state.

Nelson, a former Little Rock political reporter who had signed on as Robinson's campaign press secretary, still remembers Atwater's blunt explanation of his interest in their candidate.

"You boys have to remember, I don't give a fuck who the governor of Arkansas is," he said. "My only job as chairman of the Republican National Committee is to get George Bush reelected. The media's full of talk about Mario Cuomo or Bill Bradley. We know how to paint them up as northeastern liberals like Dukakis. That's easy! What scares me is a southern moderate or conservative Democrat, and the scariest of all, because he's the most talented of the bunch, is Bill Clinton."

As Atwater understood, Clinton possessed qualities of mind and personality that could make him a formidable national candidate. During a political career that spanned two decades, the friendly young governor had established alliances across his party's ideological divide. Somehow, Clinton had sponsored the creation of the centrist Democratic Leadership Council without injuring his own long-standing ties to liberals, blacks, and women's organizations. Intellectually fluent in the public-policy issues that bored pols like Atwater, the ambitious, hardworking, opportunistic Arkansan also had the special unteachable gift for remembering the names, faces, and concerns of people he met that is characteristic of the most successful American politicians. For Bush's sake, it would be prudent to eliminate Clinton before he could exercise those talents in a presidential campaign.

"We're going to take Tommy Robinson and use him to throw everything we can think of at Clinton—drugs, women, whatever works. We may or may not win, but we'll bust him up so bad he won't be able to run again for years."

Rex Nelson was impressed by Atwater's political prescience. A native Arkansan with a shrewd knowledge of the game, Nelson understood and respected Clinton's political mastery. "Lee had his eyes on the prize. He saw Bill Clinton as the real hurdle to Bush's reelection. . . . He spotted Clinton way out ahead of anybody else in the national party. All we had to do was get Tommy into the general election." Atwater's commitment to this project was total, he told Nelson and Vigneault. "He promised us everything: top pollsters, consultants, media people, money."

The reference to Clinton's alleged "skirt problem" didn't surprise Atwater's guests. In Washington as well as Little Rock, insider gossip compared the young Arkansas governor with Gary Hart, another once-bright presidential prospect whose career had been ruined by exposure of an extramarital affair. Some even believed that Clinton would never run for president because he couldn't withstand the inevitable scrutiny of his personal life. "My friends in the Bush camp dismissed him with a single word whenever his name was mentioned," as consultant Ed Rollins, an Atwater rival, put it. "Women."

In the fall of 1989, Atwater's allusions to Clinton's misbehavior were more or less "generic," according to Rex Nelson. "There were no individual women mentioned at all." But when push came to shove, generic rumors wouldn't stop Bill Clinton, as Atwater probably understood; after all, they had never stopped him before.

Whether Clinton's rumored and real indiscretions came close to rivaling Atwater's own remained an open question. As early as 1984, the long-married Atwater's reputation for compulsive, reckless womanizing was so well known, at least among fellow Republicans, that George Bush's closest advisors had urged Bush to avoid him altogether. According to Atwater biographer John Brady, "He reveled in telling stories of conquests, sharing details with office colleagues. . . . Disposable sex without commitment was a huge piece of his ego, a badge of honor." Nothing changed after he was appointed Republican national chairman, wrote Brady, except that Atwater began using his new RNC credit card to pay for weekends with a girlfriend at a Virginia hotel. He told his wife he was traveling on business.

In late November 1989, Atwater weathered a brief crisis brought on by his flagrant misbehavior. A *Washington Post* reporter confronted him with photographs that showed Atwater at an apartment building where a female White House staffer lived. He was indeed having an affair with the woman, as he admitted to several senior RNC staff members—but the story never ran, Brady wrote, because Atwater "leaned on" the *Post* reporter with the plea that "innocent bystanders would be hurt." He thus escaped the same wound he was simultaneously planning to inflict on Bill Clinton. In the politics of sexual morality, hypocrisy was a common occupational hazard.

Lee Atwater's disreputable public image, however, owed nothing to his sexual adventures. He had cultivated a reputation as the meanest and most devious campaign strategist in the business, a man who would do anything to defeat an opponent. It was a persona he cherished, and he had no intention of changing his identity simply because he had reached the pinnacle of party leadership. "I don't want you to squeal on me," he once told an applauding crowd at a Republican cocktail fund-raiser, "but I'm not going to be kinder and gentler."

Kinder and gentler didn't win elections, a lesson Lee Atwater had learned well and taught the rest of the country by example. Born and raised in South Carolina, he had entered politics as an intern to Senator Strom Thurmond, the former Dixiecrat segregationist who was the first important southern politician to defect to the Republicans. Young Lee's introduction to national politics came with the 1968 presidential campaign of Richard Nixon, whose darkly negative approach to politics influenced everyone around him. The men who made Nixon president routinely resorted to vicious pranks, spying, and underhanded personal attacks against the Democrats, those dirty tricks that the boyish Watergate trickster Donald Segretti memorably called "ratfucking." During Nixon's second term Lee had served as executive director of the College Republicans, where the same ethos prevailed. Back then Lee had blurted out to Nixon's RNC chairman, George Bush, that he wanted to be the party chairman someday.

Nor was kinder and gentler the way Atwater had finally won that job after fifteen years in the trenches. Sometimes he exaggerated his own viciousness to burnish his image. He liked to brag about how he had destroyed one early opponent's morale by mentioning the man's psychiatric history to a reporter. "I understand he once had to get hooked up to jumper cables," Atwater had quipped. In 1988 that story echoed again in the Republican campaign against Michael Dukakis, when rumors that the Democratic nominee once suffered from clinical depression were traced back to the Bush campaign. This canard was first raised by followers of the fringe political organization of Lyndon LaRouche, at the Democratic convention and then at a White House press conference. But conservative columnists Rowland Evans and Robert Novak reported that as Bush's campaign manager, Atwater had been "investigating the details and trying to spread the findings without leaving any vice-presidential footprints." That the rumors were utterly false didn't mean they couldn't be used. It only meant that someone else had to take the blame.

The same principle applied to the ugliest cheap shot of the 1988 campaign—the television attack ad that featured a mug shot of Willie Horton, murderer, rapist, and escapee from a Massachusetts prison furlough. Its blatantly racial thrust was disavowed by the official Bush campaign, which pointed out that the commercials had been produced and aired by an independent committee called Americans for Bush. After a while, the Bush campaign counsel even sent a letter asking the commercial's makers to desist. By then, of course, all the damage had been done.

At least six months before Rex Nelson and J. J. Vigneault came to Washington, Atwater had begun formulating his plan to preempt Clinton's presidential campaign. In May 1989 he had stopped off briefly in Little Rock, ostensibly for other purposes, and dropped a hint during a press conference in the pillared and carpeted lobby of the downtown Capital Hotel, an elegantly refurbished establishment on the banks of the Arkansas River where President Ulysses S. Grant had sojourned in 1870. The Democrats would have to nominate a southerner for president if they were to have any hope of winning the White House in 1992, he told the rapt audience of local reporters. But, he warned, they had better not choose the governor of Arkansas—because unlike some of the region's other leading Democrats, Bill Clinton just wasn't a "good, solid Southerner."

Atwater didn't elaborate on Clinton's faults, but his tart observation elicited questions about the upcoming 1990 race for governor. Asked about growing speculation that Democratic representative Tommy Robinson might defect to the Republicans and run against Clinton, Atwater replied that the GOP would welcome Robinson. And if Robinson did run for governor, he added, the party had lined up an excellent candidate for the congressman's vacated seat. Atwater glanced over at Ron Fuller, a Republican state legislator of no particular distinction. Many months later, Fuller's name would come up again, along with that of J. J. Vigneault—on a surreptitious tape recording of a conversation between Bill Clinton and a former lounge singer named Gennifer Flowers.

Running Robinson against Clinton was an idea that appealed greatly to the Republican Party's most important patrons in Little Rock, eighty-year-old billionaire Jack Stephens and his second wife, Mary Ann Stephens. Unlike his older brother Witt, a traditional conservative southern Democrat who had run Arkansas like a country store during the six terms of segregationist governor Orval Faubus, Jack Stephens was quite literally a country-club Republican. He had long served as chairman of the nation's ultimate country club, the Augusta

National Golf Club in Georgia, annual home of the Masters tournament. With its downtown Little Rock headquarters, Stephens, Inc., the nation's largest investment bank outside Wall Street, represented only a fraction of the family's multibillion-dollar holdings in oil, natural gas, and coal across several western states and a half dozen countries. Their corporate empire included considerable newspaper and broadcast holdings as well.

For decades a decisive power in Arkansas politics, the Stephens dynasty had seen its influence sharply reduced under Governor Bill Clinton, who had thwarted its wishes on any number of issues. Having financed the campaigns of Frank White, a Republican banker who had defeated Clinton in 1980 but lost two subsequent elections to the charismatic Democrat, Stephens, Inc., would have been delighted to replace the governor with Tommy Robinson.

But it was Jack Stephens's wife Mary Ann, a glossy, vigorous brunette married to a man thirty years her senior, who had found a calling in the Republican Party. She had helped win Arkansas for Bush in 1988, and the experience apparently had awakened a desire for a bigger, more glamorous role. "Mary Ann's plan was to become the Pamela Harriman of the GOP," according to a Little Rock political consultant who knew her well. "After Jack was gone, she saw herself maybe living in the Virginia horse country, having the Bushes over for dinner, hosting high-society party functions. Even an ambassadorship wouldn't have been out of reach." For the moment, Mary Ann's ambitions were tied to those of Tommy Robinson.

From Atwater's point of view, Robinson would have seemed perfect even without the Stephens endorsement. A rabble-rousing orator with an instinct for publicity, Robinson appeared to have discovered the universal solvent of southern politics: how to stir up blue-collar whites without alienating blacks. Plucked from obscurity as a small-town police chief by Governor Clinton in 1979 and appointed director of the Department of Public Safety, he had swiftly become embroiled in dramatic, highly publicized feuds with every agency in his department. In 1980 he abruptly resigned to run for sheriff of Pulaski County, which encompasses Little Rock, and won.

The glib, handsome lawman had a natural television presence and an instinctive feel for the hot-button issues of crime and drugs. His "supercop" exploits led the evening news night after night, turning him into a cartoonlike populist hero. Robinson hid armed deputies in liquor stores and convenience marts with orders to shoot to kill. Peering down the barrel of a 12-gauge shotgun, he bragged to the cameras: "My basic policy is to kick the butts of criminals. If I have to use excessive force, I will." Robinson once settled a dispute with state prison officials by chaining a busload of mostly black inmates to the penitentiary gates, then placing armed deputies around the county jail and defying state police to try to return them. Soon known statewide simply as

"Tommy," the new sheriff often outraged judges, prosecutors, and other cops with his publicity-seeking antics.

What made "Tommy" a household word, however, was his prosecution of a Little Rock criminal defense lawyer named Bill McArthur for the murder of McArthur's wife. McArthur was ultimately cleared, but not before his life was shattered by Robinson's lurid and ultimately baseless accusations. Combining elements of murder mystery, soap opera, morality play, political crusade, and multimedia extravaganza, the McArthur case was all anybody in Arkansas talked about during 1982 and 1983. Playing an important bit part in the affair was a Little Rock municipal judge named David Hale, who did Robinson's bidding during one of the strangest court proceedings in the state's history. To law enforcement professionals and the majority of educated Arkansans, the outcome of the McArthur case revealed the sheriff as a demagogic buffoon and a menace. "May the Almighty save the people in Arkansas," prayed one newspaper editorial, "from themselves and their fascination with characters like the current occupant of the Sheriff's office in Pulaski County."

Still, most blue-collar Arkansans of both races embraced Robinson as the scourge of the lily-livered establishment. Few noticed that this populist's upward climb had been bankrolled by a consortium of wealthy backers with holdings in timber, banking, natural gas, and electric utilities. Dubbed "the Power Company" by local journalists, this elite group helped him win election to Congress as a Democrat in 1984. From the beginning, Tommy established himself as a "boll weevil" Democrat who voted on critical issues with the Reagan Republicans. Overtures from the other side of the aisle came soon enough, but Robinson resisted crossing over until, toward the middle of his third term, he responded to one from President Bush and Stephens, Inc. The former sheriff had never understood the appeal of Washington life. His family didn't relocate there. An ardent outdoorsman, he came home to his district to duck-hunt with his cronies at every opportunity.

On July 28, 1989, ten weeks after Lee Atwater's stopover in Little Rock, Robinson announced that he was changing parties at a nationally televised press conference in the White House Rose Garden with the president. At the time, such conversions were sufficiently rare to merit the same treatment as a visit by a foreign dignitary. The newest Republican congressman stood shoulder to shoulder with Bush as he explained his decision. "The hard fact is that there is and will be no room for conservative southern Democrats in today's national Democratic Party," Tommy declared. In the front row sat an applauding Mary Ann Stephens, resplendent in a Nancy Reagan red dress. Atwater stood to one side, grinning. The president praised the former sheriff as "a man of exceptional caliber."

Back in Little Rock, Clinton and other Democrats professed little sorrow over Robinson's departure from their ranks. But privately, many worried that with the backing of Lee Atwater and Stephens, Inc.—as well as his own undeniable knack for demagogy—the former sheriff might be virtually unbeatable.

The immediate obstacle to Atwater's anti-Clinton strategy was Sheffield Nelson (no relation to Rex Nelson), another former Democrat who had turned Republican in 1989. Nelson had coyly announced his candidacy for governor earlier that year without telling reporters under which party's banner he proposed to run. When he finally declared for the Republican primary, a fierce nomination battle was assured. A sharecropper's son who had risen from poverty under the tutelage of the Stephens family, Sheffield Nelson had grown accustomed to getting his way.

Blue-eyed, blond, and quite handsome, Nelson radiated a sartorial elegance and aristocratic bearing that belied hardscrabble origins. He had started out as a summer intern in Witt Stephens's office and worked his way up into a job as chief executive officer of Arkansas-Louisiana Gas Company, the state's largest natural gas utility. At Arkla he had demonstrated an unseemly independence by refusing to carry natural gas owned by the Stephens interests at what he deemed to be preferential rates, thus initiating a feud of Shakespearean malevolence with his onetime benefactors that played out in the 1990 election.

Sheffield Nelson had been an ally of Bill Clinton's, as well. In 1984, the governor had appointed him to head the Arkansas Industrial Development Commission, the state agency once used by Winthrop Rockefeller as a stepping-stone to the governor's mansion. But by 1990, Nelson had grown impatient waiting in the shadows for Clinton to move on. He believed Clinton had reneged on a deal they had made in 1986, when Nelson first considered running for governor but didn't in return for Clinton's promise to step aside four years later. He had expected the governor either to make a presidential move in 1988 or to run for the U.S. Senate in 1990. Clinton's decision to run for reelection instead apparently triggered Nelson's abrupt switch to the Republican Party.

If Nelson saw little chance of defeating Clinton in a Democratic primary, his chances against Robinson in a Republican race at first seemed little better. Following Atwater's advice, the former sheriff went negative early with a classic populist theme. The Robinson campaign portrayed Nelson as a corporate fat cat who had enriched himself and his millionaire friend Jerry Jones while cheating the state's humble "biscuit cookers."

The specific accusations revolved around a 1982 deal between Arkla and Jones's natural gas exploration firm, Arkoma. The deal had made Jones wealthy enough to buy the Dallas Cowboys football team, but had almost ruined Arkla. In essence, Nelson had ignored the advice of Arkla geologists by selling rights to what turned out to be one of the richest natural gas fields in

North America to Jones's exploration company for a paltry $15 million. Having also contracted to buy gas from Jones's company at what became ruinous rates after a worldwide glut sent prices plummeting, Arkla was ultimately forced to pay Jones almost $175 million in 1986 to buy the rights back—a transaction that drove the company's stock prices down sharply and left an enormous bill to be paid by the many thousands of households that cooked and heated with Arkla's gas.

Worse still, Nelson had retired from Arkla in 1984 and cashed out millions in stock options just before the roof fell in. Robinson charged that the Arkla-Arkoma disaster had been a corrupt sweetheart deal between Jones and Nelson. Observers more sympathetic to Nelson thought that Jones had simply won a huge gamble, and that Nelson, distracted by a contemporaneous family tragedy, had simply failed to predict the future and made an unwise business decision.

The corruption charges destroyed another longtime friendship. Tommy Robinson and Jerry Jones had been childhood pals in North Little Rock, and both Jones and Sheffield Nelson had been among the supporters of Robinson's early political career. For years, Tommy had been the high-salaried "manager" of a well-appointed duck-hunting club owned jointly by Nelson and Jones. Over the years the three men had hunted and partied together frequently, and they were the subject of rumors and tall tales as sensational as anything said about Bill Clinton until after he became president.

In the past, Jones had paid Robinson's children's medical bills and bought him life insurance. The grateful Robinson had hired Jones's daughter Charlotte, a recent Stanford graduate, to work in his congressional office. The twenty-six-year-old Charlotte was still on the job, earning $80,000 a year, on the day in November 1989 when the Robinson campaign launched its first public attack on Nelson and Jones over the Arkla-Arkoma deal. Jones reportedly became livid. "I paid that sumbitch's medical bills when his kids were sick!" he shouted at a Robinson adviser who had been sent to calm him. "Now he says I'm a crook?"

The inevitable payback was delayed to ensure the maximum effect on primary voters. A few weeks before the May 1990 primary, copies of Robinson's confidential medical records from the House of Representatives were leaked to the Little Rock news media. As a freshman member, Robinson had told the House's attending physician that he drank upwards of a pint of bourbon every day and used a powerful sedative suspected of causing paranoia in some patients. In a state whose two largest religious denominations, Baptist and Church of Christ, forbid alcohol and where forty-three of seventy-five counties remain dry by popular vote, this was a bombshell. Robinson accused Nelson of leaking the records, but his protests only kept the story alive.

The rancorous campaign took its toll on both Republicans, but a decisive factor may well have been the brain tumor that eventually killed Lee Atwater. Falling ill in March 1990, he could no longer provide guidance during the final crucial weeks as the May primary approached. Nobody in the Robinson camp paid sufficient attention to the fact that a significant number of Democrats were prepared to cross over into the Republican column for the sole purpose of ending Tommy Robinson's career. Under the state's open primary law, Republicans had been doing the same thing for decades—voting in Democratic primaries, then supporting Republican candidates in general elections. Statewide, Sheffield Nelson defeated Robinson by just over eight thousand votes out of eighty-six thousand cast.

Had the crafty Atwater not succumbed to cancer, he might have detected the plan in time to devise countermeasures. With well over five hundred thousand Democrats casting primary votes in 1990—across much of rural Arkansas, the Democratic primary is in effect the general election for most local offices—a populist appeal to Tommy's core constituency could have alerted them to their hero's peril. But it was not to be.

Clinton's Democratic primary opponent was an idealistic foundation executive and former Peace Corps volunteer named Tom McRae, whose greatgrandfather had once occupied the governor's mansion. Poorly financed, and no match for Clinton as a campaigner, McRae was discounted as a serious threat to the incumbent governor. But before the primary ended, Clinton's enemies on the right quietly approached McRae with a deal.

A man whom McRae declined to identify showed up in his campaign office one day with a generous check and a file of smutty opposition research on Clinton. The main topics were women and drugs. Under the distinct impression that the messenger had come from Stephens, Inc., McRae said he had no use for that kind of material.

"Then you don't want to win," said this would-be benefactor. Angrily, McRae asked, "Has it ever occurred to you that there might be something more important than winning?"

"That's why I can't work with you," the man replied as he stood up and left McRae's office. The check left with him.

On the morning after Sheffield Nelson's primary victory, all talk of converting Arkansas to "New South" Republicanism stopped at Stephens, Inc. To the Stephens family and their allies, Bill Clinton at his worst was vastly preferable to the detested Nelson. Even the governor's successful effort to break the Stephens, Inc., near-monopoly on Arkansas municipal bonds, which had cost the company millions in revenue, didn't matter anymore.

"The Stephens people had spent thousands on anti-Sheffield research," said a Republican who was there. "They stuck it in boxes and carried it over to Clinton headquarters on the morning after the primary."

Never one to miss a winning campaign tactic, Clinton seized upon Tommy Robinson's accusations about the Arkla-Arkoma deal. He ordered a special state Public Service Commission Panel, all of whose members he had appointed, to begin a highly publicized probe of the deal and its impact on Arkansas ratepayers. Not long after the November election, Clinton's regulators criticized Arkla's deal and ordered the company to refund $17 million to ratepayers.

By all accounts, Clinton's exploitation of the Arkla-Arkoma charges left Nelson feeling doubly betrayed: first by the governor's abandonment of his supposed pledge to step aside, and then by his campaign tactics, which portrayed Nelson as a corporate shyster whose hard-earned success was actually achieved through a scandalous fraud. He stood to lose not only the election, he told campaign aides, but his reputation as well. With his hated enemies at Stephens, Inc., suddenly taking Clinton's side, an infuriated Nelson apparently thought no blow against the governor would be too low.

As Clinton's politicized probe of the Arkla-Arkoma deal continued to create headlines, the Nelson campaign decided to respond in kind. With the Republican lagging thirty points behind Clinton in the latest polls, Nelson's aides produced a pair of negative television commercials aimed at the governor. The first, which lifted and distorted a phrase from a budget speech by Clinton, backfired badly. The second was a sex-and-drugs smear, questioning Clinton's "character and moral judgment." Although that ad never aired, it had the more lasting impact.

The budget commercial was crude but initially effective. Addressing the state's budget problems, Clinton had once given a speech pointing out that unlike the U.S. government, the state of Arkansas was forbidden by law from running deficits or printing more money. Rather, he said, the state was obliged to "raise and spend" all the funds needed during each fiscal year. With a bit of editing, Nelson's advertising team turned the phrase into a seeming call for ever-higher taxes. The state soon resounded with radio and TV ads that featured Clinton's voice, repeating the words "raise and spend" over and over like a trained parrot. In less than a week, Clinton's poll ratings sank by as much as ten points.

The second ad played on long-standing rumors about the governor's personal life. Three years earlier, the annual "Gridiron Show" put on by the Pulaski County Bar Association had featured a skit with two lawyers impersonating Bill Clinton and Gary Hart, singing a duet of the Willie Nelson classic "To All the Girls I've Loved Before." Most knowledgeable observers thought that whatever Clinton's availability to adventurous women early in his marriage and political career, he had cleaned up his act in the wake of his brother Roger's 1984 arrest for cocaine possession and an ultimatum from Hillary. But nobody really knew. In a mostly rural state like Arkansas, populated by large numbers of fundamentalist Christians, sexual gossip about prominent people is epidemic. A list of leading political figures who had never been the subject of lurid fantasy would have been very short. Neither Sheffield Nelson nor Tommy Robinson would have been on it.

One of the Nelson aides who saw the sex commercial described it as "an innuendo-type ad" which "never named any names or made any concrete charges. . . . The idea was to make people think, 'I wonder about all those rumors I've heard.'" It didn't even mention Clinton's name, but showed his face superimposed over shadowy silhouettes of anonymous women. The voice-over script asked voters to consider the "character and moral judgment" of the candidates. "They were scared to flat point a finger at Clinton," the Nelson aide said. "I thought it should have been a lot stronger."

Long after the 1990 election was history, Sheffield Nelson would tell ABC News correspondent Sam Donaldson that he had compiled evidence documenting Bill Clinton's moral lapses. Nelson's millionaire friend and backer Jerry Jones likewise boasted later to Texas reporters that he had hired private detectives, who uncovered a Clinton paramour. Neither ever released any documentation.

There are various explanations as to why the sex ad never aired. One is that the misleading "raise and spend" commercial did so much damage to Clinton that using the second ad was deemed unnecessary overkill. Another is that the Nelson campaign's internal polls showed that the ploy would backfire badly by emphasizing the ruthless image Nelson had earned during the primary fight against Tommy Robinson. A third is that Nelson's wife, Mary Lynn, vetoed the sex ad on the grounds that an attack on Clinton's family should be off-limits. There are no copies of the commercial, according to a former Nelson aide who said he had destroyed the videotapes.

Clinton reacted to the "raise and spend" ad with a last-minute ad blitz of his own. During the campaign's final week he took out an emergency $50,000 bank loan which he used to pay for TV and radio spots exposing the deceptive nature of his opponent's commercial. Clinton himself went into the studio and recorded ads telling voters that Nelson was trying to play them for suckers. On the Sunday before Election Day, he personally persuaded the Little Rock TV stations to replace previously scheduled spots with the new commercials, and spent an additional $100,000 on radio. Aides in borrowed single-engine planes dodged torrential thunderstorms that Sunday flying all over Arkansas to make sure the Clinton campaign's brand-new commercials aired everywhere. A last-minute loan was obtained from the Bank of Perryville, a tiny institution owned principally by former state Democratic Party chairman Herbie Branscum.

On November 7, the incumbent governor defeated the Republican challenger in a landslide with 59 percent of the vote. Sheffield Nelson had entered the 1990 gubernatorial race angry at Bill Clinton. Now his crushing defeat and personal humiliation left him seething. He would find sufficient opportunities for revenge.

Chapter Two

"A CRAZY PERSON LIKE LARRY NICHOLS"

O F ALL THE ODD INCIDENTS that marked the 1990 campaign, perhaps the most consequential, in the long run, was the reappearance of a raffish but persistent local character named Larry Nichols. Like Sheffield Nelson, he carried a personal grudge against Bill Clinton, and he apparently saw Nelson's campaign as a vehicle for retribution. Larry Nichols wasn't a country-club Republican and he certainly wasn't a millionaire. But he too had been humiliated by Bill Clinton.

In 1988, Nichols, a husky onetime high school football star from Conway, Arkansas, who recorded advertising jingles for a living, had landed a new job as a marketing consultant for the Arkansas Development Finance Authority (ADFA), the state's centralized public bonding agency. Created by Clinton-sponsored legislation over the strong opposition of Stephens, Inc.—which had enjoyed a virtual monopoly on the Arkansas bond market since the fifties—ADFA's purpose was to serve both as a conduit between Wall Street and the state's industries and municipalities and as an engine for local economic growth.

Nichols's brief career at ADFA was ill-fated from the start. When the governor's chief of staff, Betsey Wright, heard that Nichols had been hired by the agency's director, and that he had specifically invoked her name to get the job, she was furious. She had in fact instructed personnel directors at other agencies who asked her about Nichols over the years that he was a political opportunist and a "dangerous con artist," to be hired under no circumstances. For some reason the ADFA director hadn't thought to ask.

It soon became clear that Nichols was preoccupied with issues more global than the marketing of Arkansas municipal bonds. He started telling other ADFA employees that he was a CIA operative working on behalf of the Nicaraguan contras. The CIA bit was fiction, but the claim wasn't altogether phony because he had gotten involved with the Coalition for Peace Through Strength, an organization headed by retired general John Singlaub—one of marine lieutenant colonel Oliver North's secret money conduits in the Iran-contra affair.

In that capacity, Nichols accompanied Tommy Robinson, leader of the boll weevil congressional Democrats who sided with President Reagan on the issue of U.S. aid to the Nicaraguan rebels, on a "fact-finding" mission to Central America. (The mercurial Robinson, no stranger to eccentricity, later warned aides to keep their distance from Nichols, whom he regarded as "a nutcase.") Nichols subsequently teamed up with one Darrell Glascock, a roguish political consultant from Louisiana who had run campaigns for Tommy Robinson and former GOP governor Frank White. A notorious "dirty tricks" operative, Glascock had once gotten caught sending an imposter to attend court-mandated drunk-driving classes in his place. Glascock's deal with Larry Nichols was more straightforward. In what would eventually become a lucrative business strategy for Nichols, the two produced, appeared in, and sold videotapes for the touted purpose of raising money for the contra insurgency.

For five months, Nichols devoted himself to the contra cause while drawing a state salary, until the Associated Press discovered that he had taken his politics to work. In September 1988, the AP reported that since coming to ADFA, Nichols had placed 642 long-distance telephone calls, at state expense, to contra leaders and politicians who supported them, principally Tommy Robinson. He had also made 390 calls to his business partner Glascock. At first, Nichols claimed that the calls—including his conversations with contra leader Mario Calero—had somehow promoted Arkansas bond sales. That pretense collapsed after reporters called the same telephone numbers and made inquiries.

Although Clinton was traveling abroad on a trade mission when the phone-call story broke, Betsey Wright made sure he learned about it immediately. "I woke him up in Asia in the middle of the night and told him to fire Nichols." Asked by reporters about Nichols's pro-contra activities, the governor said, "It looks to me like he could hardly have been doing anything else." The next day state officials forced Nichols to resign. He left protesting his innocence and complaining about the "knee-jerk liberal reaction from Governor Clinton."

Nichols's embarrassment didn't end there, however. Days after his firing, the AP discovered that Nichols faced "theft by deception" charges in two Arkansas counties. He had allegedly taken payments from electronics dealers for satellite TV equipment he never delivered. He avoided felony prosecution by promising to make restitution, but later declared bankruptcy and never paid up.

So when Larry Nichols called a press conference at the Arkansas state capitol on October 19, 1990, his credibility was not particularly high among the assembled reporters. He stood on the capitol steps, handing out copies of a $3 million libel lawsuit against Bill Clinton. He complained that he had been wrongly fired from his state job as a "scapegoat," in order to conceal "the largest scandal ever perpetrated on the taxpayers of the state of Arkansas." The governor had misused ADFA funds for "improper purposes," his legal papers charged; appended was a list of five alleged Clinton mistresses upon whom those funds had supposedly been spent. Nichols planned to subpoena all of them to give depositions about their relationships with the governor.

Among the women listed was Gennifer Flowers, a forty-year-old cabaret singer originally from rural Brinkley, Arkansas, population four thousand (which also happened to be the hometown of Sheffield Nelson). Flowers turned out to be the only one of the five whom Nichols knew personally. They had recorded advertising jingles together and still used the same booking agent. And there was one more interesting coincidence: In early October, about two weeks before Nichols's press conference, Gennifer Flowers had called the governor's office seeking help in finding a state job.

Of all the women named, only Gennifer Flowers wasn't a well-known public figure. Two were former beauty queens: Lencola Sullivan, a former Miss Arkansas, and Elizabeth Ward Gracen, the 1983 Miss Arkansas and Miss America. Another was Clinton's press secretary, Susie Whitacre, and the fourth was Deborah Mathis, a Little Rock newspaper columnist and former anchor of the state's highest-rated television news broadcast. She and Sullivan were black, adding the spice of interracial sex to the charges. Well known to every reporter in town for her irreverent wit, Mathis joked about Nichols's allegation in private. "Hell no," she told friends, she had never gone to bed with Bill Clinton. "But if I did sleep with that fat white boy, he'd still be grinning."

Reporters who contacted the women heard vehement denials from all of them. Three of them hired lawyers and threatened to sue if their names were used. Considering Nichols's dubious reputation, every media outlet in Little Rock made the same decision: The women's names were not published, and the lawsuit was ignored or buried on the back pages.

Betsey Wright had heard about the Nelson campaign's last-minute "character" commercials attacking Clinton, and now she was certain that Nichols had inspired it. "Yes, I was aware of them, and I was involved in trying to make sure they didn't run." Through a back channel, she sent a warning to an influential businessman in the Nelson camp. "The message was that you can't believe Larry Nichols."

Though he had filed his lawsuit without benefit of counsel, reporters soon learned that Nichols had met several times with the Republican state chairman, lawyer Bob Leslie, a confidant of Sheffield Nelson. Leslie said he and Nichols merely had lunch together and had never talked about the lawsuit. Nichols later told the *Washington Post* that Leslie had advised him about the legality of making the women's depositions public.

Reprints of the Nichols complaint were readily available at Nelson's campaign headquarters. Faxed copies began appearing at out-of-town newspapers and radio stations all over Arkansas, but received almost no attention. After a right-wing talk show host at a small Little Rock station allowed a caller to read Nichols's list over the air, the station's owner received a brisk letter from one of the women's lawyers threatening a libel action. The incident was never repeated. Headed for a quick dismissal in state court due to lack of evidence, the lawsuit was quickly forgotten in the wake of Clinton's reelection.

Two days before Election Day, Nichols tipped his hand. At a meeting in a diner with Clinton press secretary Mike Gauldin, he offered to settle his lawsuit if the governor arranged to pay off the mortgage on his house and give him an additional $150,000. Gauldin brushed him off.

In December 1990, a supposedly distraught Flowers made the first of what would become a world-famous series of four telephone calls to Bill Clinton himself. She told the governor that the Nichols allegations were hurting her ability to get nightclub gigs, and that she was concerned about Republican efforts to smear Clinton. Unaware that she was taping him, he spoke freely.

"I think [Nichols's] suit will be dismissed now," Clinton told her. "So I don't think you need to worry about [being subpoenaed]."

"Well, I'm . . . actively looking for a job, and I don't need all that," she replied. "And I know you sure as hell don't need it."

"Sheffield's headquarters," Flowers reminded Clinton, "was making it known that anybody that wanted a copy [of Nichols's lawsuit] could come by."

"They passed it around here."

"Well, then how does he claim that he didn't have anything to do with it?" she said. "You know what I'm saying? . . . You know, that's absurd. He is exactly behind it."

"He's a creep," Clinton replied.

"But I want to tell you something. I hope that it's over, but I would watch it. Sheffield's got nothing to lose. . . ."

"That's why he called and started to cover his ass. . . . He thinks that I'm gonna come after his ass." Ribald tales about Nelson and Robinson were almost as common as stories about Clinton's womanizing. The Clinton campaign had turned down a couple of self-styled investigators hawking alleged smut about the governor's opponents, including an extremely dubious tape of a female prison inmate claiming she had participated in a cocaine and sex party with Nelson and Dallas Cowboys owner Jerry Jones.

"Frankly," Clinton assured Flowers, "unless they got one of the parties to admit to it and got pictures . . . You know, you can't hardly go to the press with it. . . . All right, my dear, I'll talk to you later. Keep your chin up."

On January 30, 1991, Flowers's attorney sent a curt letter to the radio station which had "wrongfully and untruthfully alleged an affair between my client . . . and Bill Clinton, Governor of the State of Arkansas." Claiming emotional and physical distress as well as an "inability to find gainful employment," the letter demanded cash compensation and threatened to sue. More than three months had passed since the offending incident.

Five years earlier, supposedly during their torrid affair, Flowers had written the governor a letter. It arrived at the governor's office in January 1986 in an envelope marked "Personal," but was kept in a file there and was eventually released after Gennifer Flowers had become a household word. The letter read: "Bill, I certainly enjoyed speaking with you by phone! Enclosed please find a business résumé and an entertainment résumé. Anything you can do is much appreciated!! Thanks, Gennifer."

On the bottom of Flowers's 1986 letter, somebody scrawled her parents' home phone number and noted that she was interested in "PR-marketing." Apart from that, there appears to have been no follow-up on either side.

In the wake of Larry Nichols's lawsuit, Flowers renewed her quest for state employment. The governor's office forwarded her name to an aide named Judy Gaddy, who handled up to fifty such inquiries every week. Flowers's inquiry was handled as a routine matter. Over the next few months, Gaddy sent Flowers notices of job openings for which she might qualify. In February 1991, Flowers interviewed at the Department of Arkansas Heritage for a $15,200 job as a "multi-media specialist." She wasn't hired.

Gennifer wrote Clinton again on February 25. "Since we were unable to connect by phone," the letter began, "I thought I should drop you a note." Flowers complained that Gaddy hadn't been very successful in helping her and that her financial situation was dire. She enclosed a copy of her lawyer's letter threatening to sue the radio station, and closed by asking Clinton to "Please, be in touch." Three months later, Gaddy sent Flowers to the Arkansas Merit System to be tested for an administrative assistant position that paid $17,524. This time she got the job, and she began work in June 1991.

For a sultry performer who had appeared in some of the best clubs in Dallas and done a stint as a TV reporter in Little Rock, the job seemed rather pedestrian. Subsequent accounts of her six-month sojourn in state government were distinctly mixed. Her supervisors later said that while she possessed competent clerical skills, she had none of the computer expertise she had claimed. And on more than one occasion, her supervisor said, Flowers had made tasteless and inappropriate sexual remarks.

"She asked if I knew she was one of the women named in the Larry Nichols lawsuit as having had an affair with Bill Clinton," the supervisor later told a reporter. "When I told her I didn't, she said it was all bullshit anyway."

During the late summer of 1991, Bill Clinton announced that he would likely seek the Democratic presidential nomination in 1992 if Arkansas voters would release him from his campaign promise to serve a full term as governor. In mid-August, he and Hillary began a statewide pilgrimage for the laying on of hands. They already had reached out to longtime friends and supporters around the country, who had encouraged Clinton to run, and now he set up an exploratory committee. There was an undercurrent of worry, however, as the Clinton insiders frankly discussed how to cope with rumors about the candidate's philandering and the state of his marriage. At a breakfast with political reporters in Washington that September, Clinton acknowledged that his twenty-year relationship with his wife had not been "perfect or free from difficulties."

Around that time, Clinton received a phone call from a Bush aide he had encountered occasionally at national conferences on education. The presidential assistant's unsolicited advice had nothing to do with charter schools or teacher training. He urged Clinton not to run for president in 1992, not to try to deprive George Bush of a second term. "We think you're the only one who can beat him. And if you run this time, you will never be able to run for anything again. . . ."

Meanwhile, with her tape recorder running, Flowers began a new series of phone calls to Clinton a few days after he revealed his presidential ambitions. The story she told him couldn't have been better calculated to bring out empathy for a woman down on her luck—especially, a cynic might note, an attractive woman with old, shared secrets. This time she said that because Larry Nichols had refiled his lawsuit, she was being harassed by tabloid newspaper and TV reporters.

"To be real honest with you," she told him, "I'm not completely surprised. I didn't think it would start this quickly. But I think, Bill, you're being naive if you think that these other shows like *A Current Affair* and . . . *Hard Copy* . . ."

"I thought they'd look into it," Clinton replied. "But you know, I just think a crazy person like Larry Nichols is not enough to get a story on the television."

"Right. Well, he better not get on there and start naming names," Flowers said.

Perhaps mindful of her previous threat to sue the Little Rock radio station that had broadcast her name, Clinton assured her that as long as all the women stuck with their denials there was no way even the tabloid programs could use their names. She asked whether he thought Nichols could be coaxed into naming Sheffield Nelson as his sponsor.

"I think he would, at least, you know, if somebody gave him some money."

"I'll tell you something," Flowers said. "He would take your money and turn around and double-cross you. . . . Somebody else you better watch is Tommy Robinson. I wouldn't trust him."

Clinton's next response is inaudible. Then he asked Flowers if she'd seen what Tommy Robinson had told reporters about him and Sheffield Nelson.

"He said, 'Well, I ran a security detail for two years and I don't know anything about it [Clinton's sex life], but I'll tell you one thing, Sheffield Nelson makes Clinton look like the pope.'" Meanwhile Nelson, Clinton continued, was "working overtime. He's sending handwritten notes to reporters coming down here from other states."

At that point, Flowers told him about an approach she claimed was made by Ron Fuller, a Republican state legislator and Robinson supporter who had worked closely with Lee Atwater during the Tommy Robinson campaign. Behind Fuller's cash proposition for her cooperation, she insinuated, was his close friend J. J. Vigneault, the Robinson campaign manager and Atwater acolyte.

"J. J. Vigneault is a good . . . you know J. J.? He's a big buddy of Ron's," she explained, "and I don't know if J. J. had anything to do with it or not, but [Fuller] said, 'They would be willing to pay you $50,000' along with, give me a job in California" to go public.

She brought up Vigneault's name because it was he, not Fuller, who had ties to national Republicans, and she speculated that he had access to money and jobs in other states—connections which might be rewarding if Flowers confirmed the rumors about her and Clinton. He remained an influential Republican consultant long after his mentor's death, serving in 1996 as southern states coordinator for the Dole campaign. (He also appeared at conservative political conferences to denounce the Clintons.) As for Fuller, his alleged role in the scheme, which he later denied, may have seemed plausible to Clinton because Fuller shared Vigneault's ideological zeal. A widely mocked example of Fuller's ultraconservative bent was his bill to imprison homeless women for stealing supermarket shopping carts.

What Flowers didn't mention to Clinton was that she had spent several weeks working in Ron Fuller's losing 1990 congressional campaign and given him a contribution of $1,000.

"And what did you say to him?" Clinton asked. "Did you ask him if [the alleged affair] had to be true?"

". . . I just said, 'Well, you know, that's ridiculous.'"

Clinton asked if she would be willing to sign an affidavit. "It'd be extremely valuable, if they ever do run anybody by me . . . ," he said, "to have an on-file affidavit explaining, you know, you were approached by a Republican and asked to do that."

Flowers never answered. Instead, according to her tapes, she replied with a coarse joke about what she would tell inquisitive reporters. "I'll just tell them you eat good pussy." Whether Clinton actually heard that remark is unclear; again, there was a glitch on the tape. Printed transcripts describe his next six responses as inaudible.

Clinton closed by telling Flowers not to hesitate to phone him at the governor's mansion if she had any more news about Republican plotting. He could always be reached after 11:00 P.M.

When Flowers called again some weeks later, a state trooper named Roger Perry who answered the telephone failed to recognize her name. "Gennifer Fowler?" he asked when she said she was returning the governor's call.

"Flowers!" she repeated loudly, obviously annoyed.

"Hang on just a second," said Perry, one of the four state troopers who later recounted the "Troopergate" tales about Clinton, Flowers, and other women to the *American Spectator* and the *Los Angeles Times*.

Each of the four taped conversations between Clinton and Flowers revolved around the same topics: Larry Nichols's accusations, Sheffield Nelson's treachery, and Flowers's purported fear and loathing of the tabloid press. In December 1991, the candidate returned one last late-night call from the campaign trail.

"Gennifer," he said, "it's Bill Clinton." His voice was muffled and, for a longtime lover, oddly formal. Flowers remarked that he didn't sound like himself. Did he have a cold?

"Oh it's just my . . . every year about this time I . . . My sinuses go bananas."

"Yeah, me too."

"And I've been in this stupid airplane too much, but I'm okay."

Clinton's allergies afflict him every spring and fall. His voice gets hoarse and his nose swells up and reddens like W. C. Fields's. (That, and Roger Clinton's 1984 cocaine conviction, kept alive the persistent rumors about the governor's own alleged drug use.) Anyone intimate with him for more than a decade, as Flowers would soon insist she had been, might be expected to know that.

Once again she launched into a tale of woe. Parties unknown, she said, had broken into her apartment and rifled the place. "There wasn't any sign of a break-in," she explained, "but the drawers and things. There wasn't anything missing that I can tell, but somebody had . . ."

"Somebody had gone through your stuff?" Clinton asked. "But they didn't steal anything."

"No . . . I had jewelry here, and everything was still here."

Possibly that's why Flowers never reported any break-in to the Little Rock Police Department. Years later, she would pin the rap for this alleged burglary on Clinton himself.

At no point on any of Flowers's tapes did Bill Clinton say anything that indicated a long-term sexual relationship with her. During one of their earlier talks, Clinton had told her about his joking response to Bill Simmons, a Little Rock AP reporter who read him Larry Nichols's bimbo list over the phone. "I said, 'God, Bill, I kinda hate to deny it. They're all beautiful women.' I told you a couple of years ago when I came to see you that I'd retired. Now I'm glad I have, because they [his Republican enemies] have scoured the waterfront. And they couldn't find anything."

On the eve of the 1992 New Hampshire presidential primary, Larry Nichols and Gennifer Flowers simultaneously sprang their traps. Clinton had emerged by then as "the Anointed," the candidate deemed most likely and most deserving to succeed by national reporters and pundits. In another seeming coincidence, Nichols and then Flowers both sold their stories to the *Star*, a major supermarket tabloid whose editor bragged that "this isn't Martians walking the earth." Rather, he insisted, it was hard-hitting journalism. Nichols reportedly received $50,000 but later said, "I gave it back." Flowers later testified that the *Star* paid her $150,000 for her account of a "twelve-year love affair" with Clinton.

Larry Nichols's version of Clinton's sex life shared the cover of the *Star*'s January 28 edition, along with Roseanne's current diet, Donny Osmond's new squeeze, and Sally Jessy Raphael's latest heartache. The headline was extravagant: "EX-AIDE CHARGES IN COURT DEM'S FRONT-RUNNER BILL CLINTON CHEATED WITH MISS AMERICA AND FOUR OTHER BEAUTIES." Although Nichols's 1990 lawsuit had been dismissed with prejudice by an Arkansas judge—barring further action in state courts—he had refiled it in the federal district court in Little Rock. That enabled the *Star* editors to do what the Little Rock media had refused to do fourteen months earlier: The names and photographs of the five women Nichols had named as Clinton's mistresses were spread all over its pages.

Susie Whitacre denied the allegation through her lawyer, and eventually got a retraction. The *Star* published no response from the two beauty queens and newspaper columnist Deborah Mathis. For her part, Flowers, described as "a thirtysomething singer . . . very attractive and well-endowed" sounded coy: "Contacted by the *Star*, Gennifer . . . wouldn't discuss the matter: 'I'm afraid of the repercussions if I talk about it,' she said in a halting voice." In reality, the "thirtysomething" Flowers was forty-two, and her fears, if any, had been conquered weeks earlier when she and the tabloid's editors had come to terms. By the time Nichols's accusations appeared in print, Flowers was already ensconced in a Manhattan hotel, at the *Star*'s expense, talking with the tabloid's staffers.

The Nichols story went beyond naming five names to lay out other allegations against Clinton. The tabloid repeated Nichols's charges that Clinton had looted a slush fund of public money to wine and dine his girlfriends; spent state funds to visit a beauty queen on "love trips" to New York; and misused state police cars to ferry him to and from his secret trysts. There was, of course, scant mention of Nichols's own past legal difficulties or his dispute with the governor who had fired him. Nichols claimed that a few months after he was fired, he had taken to shadowing Clinton in his car while the governor jogged around the streets of Little Rock, supposedly following him to Flowers's apartment building. "I wanted to confirm what I'd heard."

The *Star* suggested that "local newspapers have given their favorite son an easy ride." The tabloid quoted Sheffield Nelson, who had told Clinton he had nothing to do with the sex charges. Now he scoffed at the notion that Clinton's private behavior should be of concern only to Hillary. "That may work in Arkansas—in fact, it has so far. But it certainly won't satisfy the national press."

On the campaign trail in New Hampshire, Clinton called the *Star* report "trash . . . old news . . . an absolute, total lie." He mocked the tabloid's preoccupation with space aliens and humans with cow's heads. Hillary Clinton characterized Nichols's allegations as "absurd . . . the equivalent of a conversation with Elvis." Exactly one week later, the Gennifer Flowers torpedo hit the Clinton campaign. The fact that Bill Clinton had foolishly allowed himself to be taped while talking candidly with her handed the *Star* an irresistible opportunity to gloat. In a refrain that would later become all too familiar, Flowers insisted that she had made the surreptitious recordings only after friends told her she needed to protect herself.

"THE BILL CLINTON LOVE TAPES," shouted the *Star*'s front page. "DEMOCRATIC FRONT-RUNNER'S EX-LOVER RECORDS THEIR INTIMATE PHONE CALLS WHEN PREZ HOPEFUL TELLS HER 'THEY DON'T HAVE PICTURES. IF NO ONE SAYS ANYTHING, THEN THEY DON'T HAVE ANYTHING.'" According to Gennifer, her alleged affair with Clinton had been True Love. "Sex was wonderful with Bill," she confided. "He introduced me to things I'd never done before, like oral sex. . . . In the beginning, he'd talk about leaving Hillary for me, and I wanted so much for that to happen, but that was my heart talking. My head told me he'd never leave."

In a manner that would come to seem quaintly old-fashioned in hindsight, the press debated how to handle the story. Daily tabloids in New York and Boston went wild. But of the major TV networks only NBC initially broadcast her allegations. In New Hampshire, the conservative *Manchester Union-Leader* relegated Gennifer to an AP dispatch on page 11. The state's leading TV news program, however, played the story prominently. On January 23, *ABC News Nightline* spent a high-minded half hour fretting over how the media should cover such seamy stories. Gingerly, if at all, said commentator Jeff Greenfield, veteran of a contentious divorce. "Does this aspect of a candidate's life really tell us anything worth knowing?" he wondered. "Are voters entitled to know the most intimate details of a candidate's marital history?"

Polls showed that more than 70 percent of the public disapproved of the media's covering political candidates' intimate lives. Nevertheless, Clinton's chances of winning the New Hampshire primary suddenly seemed remote. Tracking polls appeared to show that Democratic voters tended not to regard sexual improprieties as a disqualifying issue, but doubted Clinton's viability because they believed other voters would.

The Clintons chose an unprecedented interview on CBS News's *60 Minutes* as their forum for a rebuttal. Hillary's closest friends say she never hesitated. Having sat in the kitchen of the governor's mansion listening to her husband's end of the tape-recorded conversations with Gennifer Flowers, she was outraged by what she regarded as a cynical and duplicitious attack upon her marriage.

As sheer performance, the Clintons' joint appearance was almost flawless. Bill Clinton described Gennifer Flowers as a "friendly acquaintance" whom he had met during the late seventies. When Larry Nichols's first lawsuit put the allegation in play, Clinton said, Flowers had told him, "I haven't seen you for more than ten minutes in ten years."

"She's alleging," correspondent Steve Kroft said, ". . . a twelve-year affair with you."

"That allegation," the candidate replied firmly, "is false."

Hillary described how she had met with two of the women named by Larry Nichols. "They were friends of ours. I felt terrible about what was happening to them. Bill talked to this woman [Flowers] every time she called distraught, saying her life was going to be ruined, and he'd get off the phone and tell me that she said sort of wacky things which he thought were attributable to the fact that she was terrified."

"You've said that your marriage has had problems," Kroft said. "What do you mean by that? . . . Does that mean you contemplated divorce? Does it mean adultery?"

"I'm not prepared, tonight, to say that any married couple should ever discuss that with anyone but themselves," Bill Clinton said. "I have acknowledged wrongdoing. I have acknowledged causing pain in my marriage. I have said things to you tonight that no American politician ever has. I think most Americans who are watching this tonight, they'll know what we're saying. They'll get it, and they'll feel we've been more than candid."

*   *   *

The next day Gennifer Flowers and the *Star* editors held a riotous press conference at the Waldorf-Astoria Hotel in midtown Manhattan. Standing at a podium bristling with microphones, before a shouting, jostling mob of reporters and TV crews, Flowers sobbed and dabbed at her eyes with a tissue as she spoke.

"Yes, I was Bill Clinton's lover for twelve years. And for the past two years I have lied about the relationship. The truth is, I loved him. Now he tells me to deny it. Well, I'm sick of all the deceit, and I'm sick of all the lies."

In her tight bright red suit, with dark roots showing through her blond tresses, Flowers looked the part of an icy gold digger. Amid the carnival atmosphere—someone in the crowd shouted a question about whether Clinton used condoms—she maintained that she had intended to keep their affair a secret until she learned the *Star* planned a feature on Larry Nichols's lawsuit. She played selections from her tape-recorded conversations with Clinton—including her own raunchy remark about "eating pussy," to which Clinton's next several responses were garbled and inaudible.

Asked at a Baton Rouge campaign stop the same day about Flowers's tearful tirade, Clinton said, "She didn't tell the truth. She hired a lawyer a year ago—a year and a half ago—to say that anybody who says that was a liar and would be sued. And she commented that she changed her mind for money. . . . My wife and I have said everything we have to say about this whole subject yesterday. As far as I'm concerned, it's a closed matter."

Back in Arkansas, the Flowers controversy displayed the ugly underside of the 1990 election all over again. Sheffield Nelson, now cochairman of the Arkansas Republican Party, told the *Arkansas Democrat-Gazette* that he knew Clinton was lying. "Gennifer Flowers," he revealed, "was one of the files we had that we could have used in the campaign if we had been willing to do so. There was a super commercial developed during the campaign and I declined to use it because it alluded to . . . morals and drugs."

Tommy Robinson charged that Nelson himself had "orchestrated" the Flowers story. As state director of public safety during the governor's first term from 1979 to 1980, Robinson had supervised Clinton's state police bodyguards. "Bill Clinton had no affair with Gennifer Flowers," he asserted. "I would've known about it. . . . Sheffield's been spreading the rumors." Over the following weeks, investigative work by Arkansas journalists demolished Flowers's credibility. Her allegation that Arkansas Republicans had offered her $50,000 to accuse Clinton was fully explored in the Little Rock press, with details about her involvement in Ron Fuller's state senate campaign and her $1,000 donation.

Musicians and club owners who had worked with Flowers described her as manipulative and dishonest. Her résumé falsely proclaimed her a graduate of a fashionable Dallas prep school she'd never attended. It also listed a University of Arkansas nursing degree she'd never earned and membership in a sorority that had never heard of her. Her agent told the *Democrat-Gazette* that contrary to her claims, Flowers had never opened for comedian Rich Little. A brief gig on the *Hee Haw* television program had come to a bad end, the agent would later confirm, when Flowers simply vanished for a couple of weeks with a man she'd met in a Las Vegas casino—and then concocted a tale about having been kidnapped. She had never been Miss Teenage America. Even her "twin sister Genevieve" turned out to be purely a figment of Flowers's imagination.

The account that probably came closest to the truth was a column by the *Democrat-Gazette*'s John Brummett, a respected political analyst and frequent Clinton critic. His sources said Flowers had mentioned to friends fifteen years earlier that she was "having a fling with Clinton," but "they say they heard nothing from her after 1979 about a relationship with Clinton and were surprised and skeptical upon reading her assertion in *Star* magazine of a twelve-year affair that ended only in 1989.

"They are also dubious about her assertion that she was in love with Clinton all those years, dreaming of marriage. They say that she had other relationships in Dallas and Little Rock during that time. . . . They speculate that she doesn't like or respect men generally and probably enjoys using them. . . . Their instinctive reaction to the [*Star*] article is that her vivid, detailed account probably contains truth, exaggeration and fabrication, not necessarily in equal parts."

A subsequent, sexually explicit *Penthouse* article (accompanied by a nude photo layout for which Flowers was paid an additional $250,000, pushing her total scandal earnings over $500,000) made Brummett's portrait appear relatively kind. Flowers boasted of the many married men she'd seduced for fun and profit. "I usually throw them back. I don't want to keep them. Let the wives have them back." Her ex-roommate Lauren Kirk told the article's author, CNN correspondent Art Harris, that she believed Flowers had lied for revenge and money. "She just can't accept the fact that he [Clinton] came, wiped himself off, zipped up, and left."

The agreement between Flowers and the *Star* stipulated that no one would ever be allowed to examine her original tapes. Consultants hired by the tabloid vouched that they were free of tampering. But a specialist hired by KCBS-TV in Los Angeles examined a copy of the tapes provided to him by the *Star* and determined that they had been "selectively edited" and were misleading at best. He also concluded that some of Flowers's remarks may have been dubbed in later.

Flowers never produced a single photograph, valentine, or birthday card as evidence of her twelve-year affair with Clinton; no witness ever came forward who had seen them together. Indeed, she would eventually write an entire book, *Passion and Betrayal*, without stating a specific time and place where she and her famous lover were together.

In Little Rock, much sport was made of her claim that they had enjoyed numerous trysts between 1978 and 1980 at Little Rock's Excelsior Hotel. At the time, most observers found it highly improbable that the governor would have an illicit assignation in a landmark downtown hotel two blocks from the state's largest newspaper. Particularly in view of the fact that the Excelsior Hotel wasn't built until 1983.

On the day of the New Hampshire primary—after enduring further scrutiny of his effort to evade the Vietnam draft and his shifting accounts of his deferment—Clinton finished a strong second to Massachusetts senator Paul Tsongas. Bereft of money and organization, however, Tsongas's campaign had reached its zenith. Clinton dubbed himself "the Comeback Kid," and headed for New York, Illinois, and California as the front-runner. He had outmaneuvered his Arkansas antagonists again, this time on a national stage. By surviving New Hampshire and Gennifer Flowers, Clinton had demonstrated resilience and poise in the face of adversity that would have sunk a less gifted politician—as well as a certain glib facility for shading the truth. His adversaries would respond with exaggeration and innuendo about his womanizing, but Clinton himself knew that even the less sensational facts about his personal weakness might well be sufficient to ruin him.

In the short run, the Flowers and Nichols broadsides had backfired. Besides endowing Clinton with nearly 100 percent name recognition, the New Hampshire episode introduced his formidable wife to tens of millions of Americans, most of whom admired her poise and tenacity. The late Lee Atwater's worst fears about Clinton were coming true. Here was a different kind of Democrat who fought back.

Still, due partly to the Clinton campaign's decision to respond on the networks, the trajectory between the *Star* and the front pages of the *New York Times* and *Washington Post* had been drastically shortened. (Several days after the *60 Minutes* broadcast, the *Times* found itself reporting Hillary Rodham Clinton's denial of accusations it had never printed in the first place.) For Clinton, though he may not have realized it at the time, this was an ominous development.

Even more ominous were the easy profits and political impact achieved by Flowers and Nichols. Through the agency of a paid story in a supermarket tabloid, a pair of rank amateurs with almost no credibility among journalists in their hometown were able to make national headlines, turn themselves into minor celebrities, and earn a substantial amount of cash in the bargain.

* * *

On the morning of the Clintons' *60 Minutes* appearance, a very curious item appeared on the front page of the *Arkansas Democrat-Gazette*. Larry Nichols announced that he was dropping the libel suit trumpeted in the *Star* only a week earlier. "The feud is over," he said. "I want to tell everybody what I did to try to destroy Governor Clinton." In a one-page statement distributed to the Little Rock press, Nichols claimed his only motive had been to avenge his wrongful firing four years earlier.

"The media has made a circus of this thing and now it's gone way too far," he wrote. "When the *Star* article first came out, several women called asking if I was willing to pay them to say they had an affair with Bill Clinton.

"This is crazy. One London newspaper is offering a half-million dollars for a story. There are people out there now who are going to try to cash in.

"I apologize to the women I named in the suit. I brought them into the public's eye and I shouldn't have done that. The less significant part of my case were those [*sic*] concerning the rumors. I have allowed the media to use me and my case to attack Clinton's personal life. . . .

"In trying to destroy Clinton, I was only hurting myself. If the American people understand why I did this . . . and that [it] was wrong, then they'll see there's not a whole lot of difference between me and what the reporters are doing today."

The Clinton campaign released a brief statement thanking Nichols for having the courage to admit he was wrong. In effect, however, his apology had succeeded in planting a front-page classified advertisement in a newspaper with statewide circulation. The subtext was a want ad for still more women to come forward with the promise of a six-figure payoff, causing some observers to consider his remorse to be as sincere as Gennifer Flowers's tears. Behind the scenes Nichols was again trying to squeeze a payoff of $200,000 from Clinton, and again he was rebuffed.

In May 1992 he filed yet another lawsuit, this time demanding Clinton's resignation as governor for allegedly reneging on his promise to serve a full term. The new legal papers accused Clinton of using a state car and state employees—meaning the governor's trooper bodyguards—to ferry him to "illicit" assignations.

In a 1998 interview, Nichols indicated that he had known about the Clinton tapes long before Flowers brought them to the *Star;* he refused to say whether he had arranged the deal or whether he had helped her edit them. As for withdrawing his lawsuit and apologizing, he cynically explained, "I had done what I intended to do. I know Clinton was running for president, so all I had to do was keep the court case alive, then the media would come in and take it."

Nichols's "apology" was accurate in at least one respect. There were indeed people, not all of them tabloid journalists, who were eager to pay tens of thousands of dollars for proof (or anything that might pass for proof) of Bill Clinton's lechery, dishonesty, and all-around lack of moral fitness for high office. By the time Clinton prepared to accept the Democratic presidential nomination, Republican operatives had entered the game and driven up the price of smut.

That was why, not long after Nichols's apologia appeared in the *Democrat-Gazette,* he found himself in a curious partnership with a private detective named Larry Case. A colorful, bearish figure who had formerly worked as an investigator for the state Alcoholic Beverage Control Commission, Case accented his linebacker physique with cowboy hats, dark glasses, and gold chains. He had excavated tons of dirt on public figures in Arkansas, but his information varied widely in quality. In the mid-seventies, for instance, he made a series of secret tapes that helped expose real corruption in the Little Rock Police Department. During the 1990 gubernatorial campaign, Case had approached the Clinton campaign with dubious tapes purporting to prove that Sheffield Nelson had consorted with prostitutes.

Over the strenuous objections of Betsey Wright, Case had gotten an audience with Clinton campaign aides. Nothing came of it. Clinton's people say they listened to his story but promised him nothing. Case told friends he had been promised the directorship of the Alcoholic Beverage Control Commission—a position that would give him authority over every honky-tonk and bar in Arkansas. When the job predictably failed to materialize, Case went away feeling double-crossed.

If people wanted derogatory material about Bill Clinton, he believed he knew where to find it: at state police headquarters, in raw police files and secret videotapes produced during the drug probe of Roger Clinton. He also knew lots of state troopers, and cops were always full of gossip. Like most in his trade, Larry Case took a dim view of human nature. Like Larry Nichols, he had never been accused of being fastidious about mere facts. With six-figure sums on the table, there was no limit to what an enterprising private eye might do. For that kind of money Case and Nichols could be very inventive.

Chapter Three

JEAN LEWIS'S OCTOBER SURPRISE

ALTHOUGH SHEFFIELD NELSON found Larry Nichols useful in promoting the sex angle against Clinton, it was Nelson himself, a savvy executive, who pried open the Clintons' personal finances. Rather than the *Star*, his preferred forum for this more tasteful and complex story was the nation's single most important newspaper, the *New York Times*. In this project he enlisted the couple's embittered former business partner, James McDougal, and a *Times* reporter he had known for several years. Whether by design or not, their timing was excellent. Investigative reporter Jeff Gerth's initial Whitewater story appeared on the *Times*'s front page on Sunday, March 8, 1992—two days before the "Super Tuesday" primaries in six southern states and just weeks before the crucial Democratic contests in New York and California.

"What mighty contests," wrote Alexander Pope, "rise from trivial things." The Whitewater property was not vast: it spread across roughly 230 wooded acres, at the confluence of two of the best fishing streams in the Ozarks—Crooked Creek and the White River. The sums involved were also comparatively small. In buying the property back in 1978, the Clintons and McDougals together had put a bit more than $200,000 in borrowed money at risk. Had the project succeeded as planned, each couple hoped to realize a profit of roughly $45,000. As it happened, the Clintons ended up losing a bit less than that, the McDougals somewhat more—although Jim McDougal's habit of commingling funds among his many real estate entities would make a precise accounting impossible. Even the washboard gravel roads bulldozed and graded by the Whitewater Development Corporation remained unpaved fourteen years after

Bill Clinton was first elected governor. Far from trivial, however, was the depth of McDougal's resentment toward the Clintons.

In time, McDougal would portray his former partners as a coolly cynical couple, "takers rather than givers . . . unwilling to jeopardize their political position for the sake of friends." Hadn't they turned their backs on him after the catastrophic events of the eighties—when McDougal had ruined his marriage; suffered a stroke and succumbed to manic-depressive illness; lost a bank he had bought as well as his insolvent thrift, Madison Guaranty Savings and Loan; forfeited his overleveraged, ramshackle real estate empire; and finally found himself facing a four-count federal bank fraud indictment in 1990? Undoubtedly they had. But he had given them plenty of good reasons for shunning him, not the least of which was his inept and self-serving management of Whitewater itself.

McDougal's colorful and increasingly erratic career—as old-time agrarian populist, campaign organizer, failed politician, college professor, real estate developer, banker, entrepreneur, promoter, salesman, savings and loan mogul, recovering alcoholic, mental patient, criminal defendant, raconteur, and sometime confidence man—had made him a familiar if rather untrustworthy figure to many Arkansas journalists. A largely self-educated country boy from Woodruff County, McDougal had grown up on the geological and historical boundary between the Arkansas cultures of hill country and Delta. He could recite Bible verses and quote lengthy passages from Shakespeare and James Madison from memory.

After a well-publicized trial, McDougal had been acquitted of the original fraud charges in Little Rock's federal district court. At the time, he had blamed the bias of Bush administration Republican prosecutors for his plight, but few observers took that charge seriously. Reporters who covered the trial attributed the verdict to a poorly organized prosecution and the spellbinding effect of McDougal's own testimony on the jury.

Sick, bankrupt, and living on Social Security disability payments in a borrowed mobile home on somebody else's land near the little town of Arkadelphia, McDougal had then petitioned the governor's office for a job. Wary Clinton aides made an inquiry to Arkansas securities commissioner Beverly Bassett Schaffer, a Clinton appointee who had quietly urged the FBI to investigate him in the first place. No way, Bassett Schaffer told them. In her view, McDougal was no innocent victim of the national savings and loan meltdown, but a reckless and devious man who should not be trusted.

This rejection maddened the desperate McDougal. Oddly, however, it was a grudge against Clinton's Democratic rival Jim Guy Tucker, more than his brewing feud with Clinton, that first prompted McDougal to seek out Sheffield Nelson in 1992. Like Nelson, Tucker also had lost a bruising political race to Clinton. A handsome Harvard-educated ex-marine and former prosecutor,

Tucker had given up a seat in Congress to challenge Clinton for the governorship in 1982. He had emerged from the Democratic primary a loser, deeply in debt and feeling angry.

Nelson, Tucker, and Clinton had been mutually antagonistic for years, but McDougal had entered into separate business dealings with all three during the real estate boom of the late seventies and early eighties. Only Nelson had profited from his dealings with McDougal, and then only by threatening lawsuit against Madison Guaranty Savings and Loan—which made it all the more strange that McDougal came to him seeking revenge against Tucker and Clinton.

Another irony was that Madison Guaranty's collapse had been triggered not by Whitewater, but by the failure of a major resort development on Campobello Island in New Brunswick, Canada, according to bank examiners. McDougal's chief investors in that doomed $3.73 million enterprise happened to be Sheffield Nelson and Nelson's friend Jerry Jones, the oil-and-gas magnate and Dallas Cowboys owner. It had been the nostalgic McDougal's conceit that wealthy New England vacationers and retirees would be moved by memories of Franklin Delano Roosevelt's summer retreat (location of the 1960 film *Sunrise at Campobello,* starring Ralph Bellamy as FDR) to purchase lots on the cold, foggy island north of Maine.

Unlike Whitewater, which placed none of Madison Guaranty's assets at risk, Campobello Properties Ventures was mentioned repeatedly in Madison audits as a costly boondoggle. Eventually the U.S. Treasury Department, which inherited the property after Madison went under, entered negotiations to sell it to the Canadian government for use as a national park. Nelson and Jones had invested a reported $225,000 each to purchase a 12.5 percent share in the enterprise. In 1988, the Federal Home Loan Bank Board (FHLBB), then supervising Madison Guaranty's assets, had bought their share for $725,000—a profit of $275,000.

"I can't believe it. It's an extraordinary event. It smells," said William Seidman, who supervised the savings and loan bailout for the Bush administration, to the *Fort Worth Star-Telegram.* "It could be legit, but I doubt it."

Jim Guy Tucker's ties to McDougal were similarly extensive. At one time, the two men had shared ownership of a small bank in tiny Kingston, Arkansas. Although Tucker had grown wealthy investing in cable TV properties after his 1982 election defeat, his real estate dealings with McDougal had ended in mutual recrimination. Not long before McDougal's 1990 trial, Tucker learned that McDougal had collected loan payments from buyers on a parcel the two had subdivided, but had failed to pay off the bank debt. McDougal nevertheless sent worthless deeds to their customers, bearing Tucker's forged signature. Tucker had had no choice but to make restitution. But when McDougal subsequently asked him to serve as a character witness, Tucker did have a choice and said no. Despite his acquittal, McDougal never forgave Tucker.

McDougal's ostensible purpose when he contacted Nelson in February 1992 was to find a Republican lawyer willing to sue Tucker. McDougal wanted Tucker to return $59,000 worth of promissory notes which Tucker had, in fact, bought from him some years earlier, but which McDougal claimed he had stolen. After Tucker was elected lieutenant governor of Arkansas in 1990, putting him in line to succeed Bill Clinton, McDougal may have imagined that he would settle rather than risk bad publicity. In the end, no lawsuit was filed.

None of this complicated history was reflected in the *Times*'s Whitewater reporting, which also omitted any mention of Nelson's role. Exactly how Whitewater came to bear the imprimatur of the newspaper of record always remained murky. Early on, Gerth said he had noticed a reference to the project in Clinton's state financial disclosure forms, and telephoned the only Arkansan he knew for an explanation. *Times* editors insisted that Nelson had supplied nothing more than McDougal's phone number.

Nelson, however, always proudly took full credit for putting the *Times* onto Whitewater. In his posthumously published memoir, *Arkansas Mischief*, McDougal confirmed that boast. "It was Nelson who passed the information on to Jeff Gerth," he wrote. "Nelson was gleeful. He wanted me to talk with Gerth, the *New York Times* reporter who had written a long investigative article about the Stephenses' extensive connections in Arkansas a few years earlier."

On two previous occasions, Sheffield Nelson and Stephens, Inc., had each used the *Times* as a weapon in their ongoing feud. Gerth's 1978 story about allegedly predatory natural gas pricing in Fort Smith was credited by Arkansas political observers with influencing enough votes to knock Witt and Jack Stephens's nephew out of a three-way Senate primary race. Several years later, Stephens, Inc., had retaliated by talking to *Times* reporter Wendell Rawls, Jr., who wrote a critical examination of the Arkla-Arkoma deal, which indirectly helped Clinton put an end to Nelson's political career.

After Nelson made the initial contact, McDougal recalled, Gerth drove down to Arkadelphia to visit him. McDougal plied the reporter with documents and canceled checks allegedly showing that the Clintons had taken improper tax deductions and had failed to pay their fair share of Whitewater expenses. According to McDougal, he subsequently came up to Nelson's Little Rock office and gave him damaging information about Tucker. Nelson, he claimed, was delighted. Within weeks, Jeff Gerth was sharing piles of documents he believed might implicate Tucker with Little Rock journalists. The *Times*, he explained, was only interested in Bill Clinton.

*   *   *

Gerth's original article won praise from the *American Journalism Review* for containing "80 to 90 percent" of what the press ultimately learned about Whitewater. Even some Clinton loyalists acknowledged that the story examined legitimate issues concerning the Clintons' finances and Hillary Clinton's law practice. Unfortunately, its mistakes began with the headline: "CLINTONS JOINED S & L OPERATOR IN AN OZARK REAL ESTATE VENTURE." Actually, when the Whitewater partnership was formed in 1978, McDougal hadn't been involved in the banking or thrift businesses at all. He was a political science teacher at Ouachita Baptist University who had done well investing in real estate. McDougal didn't acquire a controlling share in the small institution he renamed Madison Guaranty until five years later, by which time the Whitewater project was virtually defunct.

Judging by subsequent stern editorials in the *Times,* the rest of the story could be summarized more or less as follows: When he was governor, Clinton and his wife entered into a sweetheart deal with a crooked financier at no risk to themselves. When their benefactor got into trouble, Clinton dumped the sitting Arkansas securities commissioner and appointed a political ally named Beverly Bassett Schaffer. He and Hillary then pressured Bassett Schaffer to grant special favors to Madison, until vigilant federal regulators cracked down and thwarted their scheme. When exposed by Gerth, Bassett Schaffer claimed a convenient memory loss, denying complicity in events she had supposedly forgotten. "In interviews," Gerth had written, "Mrs. Schaffer . . . said she did not remember the Federal examination of Madison, but added that in her view, the findings were not 'definitive proof of insolvency.' . . . 'I never gave anybody special treatment,' she said.'"

The problem, as Bassett Schaffer had pointed out in twenty pages of memoranda she had provided to Gerth, was that this version of events was mostly false. First, the Clintons and McDougals were jointly and severally responsible for the Whitewater loan. Moreover, federal regulators did not determine that Madison Guaranty was insolvent between 1984 and 1986, the years Gerth's story covered. The Federal Home Loan Bank Board had formally accepted Madison's debt-restructing plan in a letter dated September 11, 1984— a full six months before Bassett Schaffer's appointment. Nor was her appointment connected to Madison's troubles. She had filled a vacancy created when her Republican-appointed predecessor (who described the *Times* story as "unmitigated horseshit") resigned to enter private legal practice.

More important, Arkansas had no authority to close state-regulated S&Ls without the concurrence of the federal agencies who held the real power. "It may be important for you to know," Bassett Schaffer had written Gerth, "that state law grants the savings and loan supervisor no emergency acquisition authority similar to that of the FHLBB and FSLIC (the Federal Savings and Loan Insurance Corporation)." Subsequent Senate hearings would establish that not one of the 746 institutions that failed during the S&L crisis of the eighties was shut down by state officials anywhere in the country. Bassett Schaffer had been an active participant in a July 1986 decision to remove Jim and Susan McDougal from control of Madison Guaranty S&L after auditors discovered his insider trading and other abuses. She had also directed the *Times* reporter's attention to her certified letter dated December 10, 1987, all but begging federal regulators to shut down Madison and two much larger Arkansas S&Ls. She had gotten no answer until the feds finally closed Madison's doors in February 1989, roughly a month after President George Bush's inauguration.

According to Walter Faulk, then director of supervision for the FHLBB in Dallas, "I never saw her take any action that was out of the ordinary. . . . To my knowledge, there is nothing that she or the governor of Arkansas did or could have done that would have delayed the action on this institution."

When the *Times* story appeared, Bassett Schaffer briefly considered filing a libel suit. "I provided you with a detailed account in writing of the facts," she wrote Gerth bitterly. "This information was ignored and, instead, you based your story on the word of a mentally ill man [McDougal] I have never met and documents which you admitted to me on the telephone on February 26, 1992, were incomplete." He never wrote back to her. "I subsequently had conversations with her in which I tried to explain the situation. I sought to come down and meet her," he said later. "I had hoped to explain what happened with the editing of the first piece. She never would agree to see me." Because his errors and inferences had appeared on the front page of the *New York Times*, they would be repeated as gospel by other reporters for years to come.

Jim McDougal was likewise stunned by Gerth's initial foray into Whitewater. The article suggested that McDougal had criminally misused Madison deposits to subsidize the development. Having set out to hurt Tucker and Clinton, he had inflicted the worst injuries on himself. Sam Heuer, the Little Rock attorney who had successfully defended McDougal during his 1990 bank fraud trial, issued a statement: "I am appalled and affronted by the allegations and reckless disregard of the facts by the *New York Times* and its reporter Jeff Gerth."

The Clinton campaign dispatched attorney Jim Blair, an old friend of the Clintons and McDougal alike, to remind their former partner that further unguarded comments to reporters could have consequences more harmful to himself than to anybody else. When an Associated Press reporter contacted McDougal a couple of days later, he sounded chastened. "I've never done anything illegal," he said, "and as far as I know Bill Clinton has never done anything illegal or unethical." He would later claim that Blair had threatened him with a lawsuit.

But McDougal's retraction meant little. According to McDougal, weeks earlier, Sheffield Nelson had secretly taped him making several rash allegations, and Nelson proceeded to copy and distribute the tape to every journalist who would listen. To Nelson, McDougal had asserted that the Clintons never lost money on Whitewater. "I could sink [that] quicker than they could lie about it if I could get in a position so I wouldn't have my head beaten off," McDougal had said.

Meanwhile, confronted by Clinton campaign aide Susan Thomases about the shortcomings in his work, Jeff Gerth was initially somewhat apologetic, she recalled. He had planned a more extensive, three-part series on the Clintons' finances, she said Gerth had told her, only to have his piece chopped down to fifteen hundred words by his editors. Thomases also remembered Gerth mentioning that his Washington bureau chief, a southerner named Howell Raines, disliked Clinton and was largely responsible for the story's tone. Gerth later denied blaming Raines, although he said he "was upset" by the way his original Whitewater copy was edited and did request changes after the paper's first edition appeared (including the addition of a quote from Bassett Schaffer denying she had favored McDougal). There was no plan for a "series," he added, and he thought it was "highly unlikely" that the Whitewater story actually had been edited by Raines.

Campaigning in the New York primary, former California governor Jerry Brown frequently denounced the sleazy appearance of Hillary Clinton's law practice. In response, the Clinton campaign commissioned an accounting of Whitewater overseen by a Denver attorney and Clinton friend named James Lyons (no relation to the author). Hillary also asked Webster Hubbell and Vincent Foster, her two closest associates at the Rose Law Firm, to help explain her work for Madison. A more ill-starred pair of defenders could hardly be imagined, although she had no way of knowing that. In the process of gathering information, Foster obtained a computer printout from the law firm of Hillary's Madison Guaranty billing records.

The Lyons report, released by the campaign in late March, concluded that the Clintons had lost about $65,000 on the project. Due to insufficient information given them by McDougal, the Clintons had improperly deducted a handful of interest payments from their income taxes, amounting to a tax savings of less than $2,000. Although the five-year limit had long passed, the couple made a point of paying the back taxes. But at least for the time being, the Clinton campaign's swift response had put the Whitewater issue to rest. How much scandal could there be in a gravel-road real estate development in which the Clintons had ultimately lost money?

One aspect of the story that would never receive much attention was Jim McDougal's psychiatric history. In his initial 1992 article, Jeff Gerth noted that McDougal suffered from manic-depressive disorder, but described him as "stable, careful and calm." Aside from that reassuring reference, McDougal's affliction and its effect on his turbulent business and personal life were rarely mentioned.

McDougal's illness had much to do with his problems. Among the symptoms psychiatric manuals list for a manic episode are the following: "inflated self-esteem (grandiosity, which may be delusional)" and "excessive involvement in activities that have a high potential for painful consequences which is not recognized, e.g. buying sprees . . . foolish business investments." It's common for manic individuals to succumb to "grandiose delusions involving a special relationship to God, or some well-known figure from the political, religious or entertainment world."

McDougal's attorney had gone so far as to file, and later withdraw, an insanity plea during his 1990 bank fraud trial. Given his financial situation during the 1980s—his heavily mortgaged real estate investments, his ownership of a small, unprofitable bank and floundering S&L—and the fact that McDougal suffered from manic-depressive illness, serious trouble was inevitable.

Jeff Gerth's Sunday article may have left little impression on most *Times* readers, but to L. Jean Lewis in Tulsa, Oklahoma, it was thrilling. She was not, as it turned out, alone in her excitement.

Lewis was an investigator for the Resolution Trust Corporation (RTC), the temporary federal agency created during the Bush administration to bail out the savings and loan depositors and liquidate the assets of institutions seized by the government. A thirty-eight-year-old former executive secretary in a failed Dallas thrift, Lewis was neither a lawyer nor a CPA. When she joined the RTC she had no previous law enforcement experience. Having grown up in a military family in Texas, Lewis proudly identified herself as a conservative Republican. (In a contemporaneous letter to a friend, she described Bill Clinton as a "lying bastard.")

She worked out of the RTC's Tulsa office, and her job was mostly routine: to sift through the records of failed Arkansas thrifts for evidence of fishy transactions. Consulting closely with the FBI's Little Rock office, Lewis had compiled a prioritized list of Arkansas institutions to be looked into. At the top, as of December 1991, she had placed the two largest failed thrifts in the state, Saver's Savings and First Federal, both headquartered in Little Rock. Saver's had collapsed at a cost of $650 million, First Federal at a cost of $950 million—both amid strong FBI suspicions of criminal fraud. First Federal alone had squandered roughly twenty times the amount lost by Jim McDougal's Madison Guaranty, which was listed, sensibly enough, near the bottom of Lewis's list.

All that changed, however, with the publication of Gerth's story three months later. The following morning, on March 9, the RTC's Tulsa field office got two calls from senior RTC officials in Washington inquiring about the accuracy of Gerth's allegations. The acting head of investigations looked over the Madison Guaranty file and responded with a memo stating that "the White-water Development loan was not specifically classified by Federal Examiners, and . . . [the record] does not show any losses related to the Clintons or White-water development. . . . Bill and Hillary Clinton are not named in any of the documents contained in our criminal referral files." In fact, neither Whitewa-ter nor the Clintons had ever borrowed from Madison Guaranty.

Nevertheless, Lewis and her supervisor, Richard Iorio, moved Madison Guaranty to the head of their investigative list. Lewis quickly headed to Little Rock to search out more documents stored in a downtown warehouse.

Did Hillary Rodham Clinton know about or suspect problems with Whitewa-ter that she didn't want the press to discover? Certainly what she had learned when she took over the tangled affairs of the Whitewater Development Cor-poration in 1988—after McDougal had left the hospital and moved to Cali-fornia—had given cause for concern. Piecing together the company's jumbled records had been almost impossible, and many documents were missing. Property taxes, in some instances, hadn't been paid for years. The owner of a lot financed personally by Hillary had gone into bankruptcy. (She had never been notified, and McDougal had made no payments on the note.) The cor-poration's state franchise fees hadn't been paid for several years, a potential disaster had Bill Clinton's political rivals ever uncovered it.

Given the depressed real estate market during the mid-eighties, Whitewa-ter probably would have lost money anyway. The site, though picturesque, had been badly chosen. The nearest towns with gas stations, grocery stores, a hos-pital, or a golf course were more than a forty-five-minute drive away over nar-row, steep, curvy roads. And Marion County, where Whitewater is situated, is also dry—no alcoholic beverages. Years later, when an objective accounting of the project became available, it became clear that as Whitewater's managing partner, McDougal turned a poor investment into something much worse. He had treated the Clintons' investment as if it belonged to him personally, abused their trust, sold the company's assets at a steep discount to the realtor who was supposed to be their agent, deceived his partners about it over a pe-riod of several years, and arguably committed several crimes in the process.

In 1985, without telling his partners, McDougal had liquidated Whitewa-ter's real estate assets for pennies on the dollar. He sold all of Whitewater's re-maining lots (twenty-four of the original forty-four) to one Chris Wade, the realtor charged with marketing and selling the development. The asking price for twenty-three of those twenty-four lots, according to a "Whitewater Estates" inventory list dated November 1984, had been $191,550. In return for the land, Wade paid down no cash. He agreed to assume $35,000 of the $96,000 still owed by the Clintons and McDougals on the original 1978 loan that had financed the project. (Wade was so slow to pay that the bank was still charging the Whitewater Development Company interest on the money until 1992.) McDougal also accepted from Wade a 1979 Piper Seminole airplane, worth $35,000, which he promptly pressed into service as Madison Guaranty's official corporate aircraft. Eventually he sold the airplane and kept the money.

Whitewater's real estate assets were gone, but the Clintons didn't know it. They wouldn't learn many of these details until years after the fact. Outwardly flush, in May 1985, Madison Guaranty put the Rose Law Firm on a $2,000-a-month retainer, and McDougal hosted a political fund-raiser for the governor in the lobby of the thrift's newly refurbished downtown Little Rock headquarters. It wasn't until she took over the company's records that Hillary and her accountants learned that the company had been all but formally defunct for more than four years. Although more than $134,000 had been deposited in the Whitewater account between 1984 and 1986 from other McDougal-owned companies, a similar amount had been paid out, much of it to individuals and companies having nothing to do with Whitewater.

In November 1986, McDougal had written the Clintons offering a deal. The letter arrived several months after the Rose Law Firm had dropped Madison Guaranty as a client, and regulators had forced his removal from the S&L. McDougal had also recently suffered a stroke, and he was hospitalized for manic-depressive illness. To spare them any public embarrassment, he proposed that they simply hand over their share of Whitewater. In essence, he was offering to buy their share of the corporation for half the amount of the $90,000 losses, which he planned to claim on his federal taxes. The problem was that the company still owed almost $90,000 to Citizens Bank, which refused to release the Clintons from liability. In effect, they were being asked to give up their share of what they mistakenly believed was an asset in return for assuming a $90,000 debt.

Not surprisingly, Hillary Clinton balked and demanded to see Whitewater's books, infuriating McDougal. In December 1986 he wrote the Clintons again. Despite current cash-flow problems, he claimed, Citizens Bank had agreed to reduced payments, and the Clintons didn't owe him any money. There was no such agreement with the bank. By 1988, after both McDougals had left for California, Hillary Clinton was forced to take over the management of Whitewater—finding an empty shell, its assets stripped, its debts and taxes unpaid, its records disordered and incomplete.

The Madison ledgers Jean Lewis pulled from the dusty Little Rock warehouse were as chaotic as the Whitewater documents Hillary Clinton had taken possession of four years earlier. Worst of all were the records of the checking accounts of McDougal's dozen real estate companies. What Lewis uncovered would have confirmed Hillary's worst fears.

Madison Guaranty had drifted into deep financial distress for the same reason hundreds of other thrifts did during the eighties. Forced by the Federal Reserve to pay ruinously high interest rates on deposits, their income was restricted by the long-term low-interest mortgages they held. Hemorrhaging money, they were encouraged by Congress and the Reagan administration to make up the difference by speculating in real estate. Those regulatory "reforms" had lured McDougal into the thrift business, but no sooner had he taken over Madison Guaranty than the same ruinously high interest rates sent the real estate market into a tailspin.

Faced with cash-flow problems, Lewis found, McDougal had begun a frantic fiscal juggling act, commingling funds and moving money back and forth among the corporations and partnerships he controlled. The Clintons and Jim Guy Tucker were by no means the only business partners whose trust he abused.

Following Gerth's lead, Lewis focused her attention on the last six months of 1985, when Beverly Bassett Schaffer had supposedly done favors for Madison Guaranty's owner. Finding evidence of Jim McDougal's fiscal shenanigans everywhere she looked, Lewis leaped to a conclusion well beyond the *New York Times* reporter's imagining. Everyone in Arkansas who had ever done business with Madison Guaranty, including the Clintons, was part of a huge conspiracy, she seemed to surmise in her criminal referrals. Every transaction that appeared to benefit McDougal must also have benefited his partners, according to her theory.

By August 1992, the Little Rock FBI agents assigned to investigate financial crime were growing impatient with Lewis. Her agency, having seized the records of bankrupt institutions across the country, controlled all the paperwork in thrift investigations. Without referrals from the RTC, law enforcement officials could not move forward on potential fraud cases. Lewis's months of work on Madison Guaranty struck the agents as a waste of time and money, and her motives seemed suspiciously political. On August 26, FBI special agent Steven Irons spoke with Lewis by phone. He took notes of the conversation.

According to his notes, Lewis informed Irons that she had been given a deadline of August 31 to file a referral on Madison Guaranty, and that there were "big names involved." Lewis claimed that she "gave up a job opportunity in D.C. just to do referral. She or it could alter history—very dramatic." Irons would later testify he had no doubt that Lewis's motive was to disrupt the 1992 presidential election in favor of George Bush. Later that day, his Little Rock supervisor, Special Agent in Charge Don Pettus, sent a telex to FBI Headquarters in Washington, expressing his professional frustration. Pettus sought permission to press ahead on the First Federal and Saver's Savings cases without the RTC's help.

On August 31, Lewis delivered as promised. She filed a criminal referral with the FBI and the U.S. attorney in Little Rock, naming not only James and Susan McDougal as felony suspects, but also each and every contributor to the 1985 Clinton fund-raising event held at Madison Guaranty. As "possible witnesses" she listed both Bill and Hillary Clinton, Arkansas lieutenant governor Jim Guy Tucker, and former U. S. senator J. William Fulbright, who had also invested with his former aide McDougal. She named no Republicans.

Normally, criminal referrals from the RTC took months to be processed. But within days, Lewis started pestering FBI agent Irons and the U.S. attorney's staff in Little Rock with demands for immediate action. After Irons stopped returning her calls, she left a taunting message with the office receptionist. "Have I turned into a local pariah," Lewis demanded, "just because I wrote one referral with high profile names, or do you plan on calling me back before Christmas, Steven?????" (She specifically dictated the five question marks.) Irons returned her call only to tell her to back off.

Word of Lewis's efforts filtered back to the Clinton campaign sometime between mid-September and early October, when longtime aide Betsey Wright got a phone call from a supporter in California. On a recent business trip to Kansas City, the man said, he had attended a cocktail party where a female RTC staffer boasted that she had "just sent a criminal referral up to the prosecutor in Little Rock . . . which would implicate the Clintons." (Three months earlier, the RTC had closed its Tulsa office and transferred Jean Lewis to Kansas City.) And although Wright had no way of knowing it, there were signs around the same time that the White House, the Justice Department, and the Bush campaign were taking a direct interest in Lewis's machinations.

William Barr, then serving as Bush's attorney general, later testified that White House cabinet secretary Edith Holiday asked him about the Lewis referral during a flight on Air Force One on September 17, 1992. At the time, Holiday was "chief liaison" between the White House and the 1992 Bush-Quayle campaign. Previously she had served as operations director of the 1988 Bush-Quayle campaign, and then as general counsel to the Treasury Department. That week, Barr asked his aides to contact the FBI, which informed them it had no record of such a case. He reported back to Holiday, who seemed surprised. Her demeanor made him wonder whether "she had better information" than he did, he recalled. (Under oath, Holiday later said she did not remember any conversations with Barr about Madison Guaranty and the Clintons.)

On September 18, Lewis turned up in Irons's Little Rock office after a meeting he did not attend. The agent told her that due to its sensitivity, no action would be taken on her referral until after the November election. She warned him that RTC officials in Washington expected action. Much to Lewis's eventual chagrin, Irons once again made contemporaneous notes of their conversation.

At the same time, Lewis made repeated calls to career prosecutors on the staff of U.S. Attorney Charles Banks. They too questioned both her motives and her referral's substance. Assistant U.S. Attorney Fletcher Jackson saw no point in pursuing McDougal again. "The prior acquittal," he told Banks, "would be used against you to make this look like a vindictive prosecution." What Lewis described as illegal "check-kiting" at Madison, Jackson regarded as a slightly different kind of scam, though he didn't quarrel with her terminology. Check-kiting usually involves writing bad checks among several banks to create illusory balances. Instead, McDougal was shifting money back and forth among several accounts within his own bank.

"From appearances," he would later testify, "it's just McDougal taking care of McDougal and McDougal's corporations. . . . What it appeared to be was that most of the manipulation Mr. McDougal was doing was to make the debt carry. In other words, he was doing all of these fraudulent transactions, in a sense, in order to make his interest payments and principal payments on debts that he had." If McDougal's actions were in fact crimes—and Jackson had his doubts—the Clintons and his other business partners appeared to be his victims, not his accomplices.

Around the end of September or the beginning of October, the White House also displayed a discreet interest in the Madison matter. Sometime during that period, White House counsel C. Boyden Gray called Albert Casey, the chief executive of the RTC in Washington. Casey later testified that Gray asked him what he knew about an RTC matter involving the Clintons. He knew nothing, Casey said he replied, but he promised to look into it and call Gray back.

Casey then called RTC vice president William Roelle, who confirmed the existence of Lewis's referral, and showed him a copy. Roelle later testified that he told Casey that he should not provide any information to the White House. Before Casey could reach Boyden Gray, however, the White House counsel phoned him again. "Al, forget my request," Casey remembered Gray saying. "I don't want you to tell me a thing." Gray himself would later deny any memory of those conversations with Casey. Any such call, he said, would have come from the Bush campaign, not the White House. Campaign officials echoed Gray's denial, saying they had no idea that Madison was being investigated in 1992, and that the campaign had a strict rule that "nobody . . . was to talk to anybody in the government about Clinton." Only a "third-level, junior person" would have done something like that, they insisted.

Attorney General Barr was considerably less cautious. After his conversation with Edith Holiday, Barr insisted that his aides check once again whether

Madison was the subject of a Justice Department probe. When a second inquiry to the Executive Office of U.S. Attorneys brought confirmation of the RTC referral, Barr became angry because he felt that Chuck Banks had "deliberately witheld information about the referral from me."

On October 7, the Little Rock office of the FBI responded with a lengthy telex to its superiors in Washington, expressing extreme skepticism about the validity of Lewis's referral. After summarizing Jim McDougal's 1990 trial and shaky psychological state, it added that despite "the referral's stated supposition that the activity was for the benefit of the McDougals, the further supposition that other people benefitted does not appear to be factually supported by the details that follow.

"It is the opinion of Little Rock FBI and the United States Attorney . . . that there is indeed insufficient evidence to suggest the Clintons had knowledge of the check-kiting activity conducted by McDougal . . . [who] was in charge of [Whitewater] records, just as he was with the records of other companies involved in the check-kiting, and does not suggest the Clintons had access to checking account statements that would have reflected the questionable transactions. . . . It was also the opinion of [Banks that] the alleged involvement of the Clintons in wrongdoing was implausible, and he was not inclined to authorize an investigation or render a positive prosecutive opinion."

On October 8, 1992, Barr sent one of his assistants to a top-level meeting attended by Robert Mueller, the head of the Justice Department's Criminal Division, FBI assistant director Larry Potts, and several senior FBI officials. At that point, the Madison Guaranty referral was definitely a matter of active interest at Justice. The next day, FBI Headquarters sent a telex to its Little Rock field office, ordering agents there to review Jean Lewis's criminal referral and report in writing by October 16—less than three weeks before the 1992 presidential election.

As far as Banks was concerned, that order sealed his decision. A native Arkansan, he had been a Republican congressional nominee in 1982 and had also served as general counsel of the state party. As such, he had once brought a lawsuit against Bill Clinton for what he considered the politically motivated firing of a Republican labor commissioner. Appointed by Ronald Reagan in 1988, Banks had been nominated to a federal judgeship in August 1992 by President Bush. His nomination was still pending in the U.S. Senate. If anybody in Arkansas had a personal interest in seeing George Bush reelected in 1992, it was Chuck Banks.

But Banks also had his limits. He would not be used politically. He had come to distrust Jean Lewis's motives, and believed that charging Jim McDougal again would be a cruel and unnecessary waste of his office's resources. Further, based on the documents Lewis had produced, he saw no persuasive evidence against the Clintons or Jim Guy Tucker. More than once Banks discussed the case with Don Pettus, the special agent in charge of the FBI's Little Rock office, who shared his misgivings.

As the October 16 deadline approached, Banks decided to put his objections in writing. Dictating a letter to Pettus, he began by repeating all the reasons he had turned down the RTC's criminal referral in the first place. Then he staked out an uncompromising position: "I am now advised that you have been ordered to do an immediate review to determine if an investigation is warranted. As part of same, you are required to send a prospective proposal for such an investigation by Friday, October 16, 1992. Such an order does not apply to this office.

"However, I do believe it might be helpful to reiterate what I have told you previously. Neither I personally nor this office will participate in any phase of such an investigation . . . prior to November 3, 1992. You may communicate this orally to officials of the FBI or you should feel free to make this part of your report.

"While I do not intend to denigrate the work of RTC," Banks added, "I must opine that after such a lapse of time the insistence of urgency in this case appears to suggest an intentional or unintentional attempt to intervene into the political process of the upcoming presidential election. You and I know in investigations of this type, the first steps, such as issuance of grand jury subpoenas for records, will lead to media and public inquiries [about] matters that are subject to absolute privacy. Even media questions about such an investigation in today's modern political climate all too often publicly purport to 'legitimize what can't be proven.'

"For me personally to participate in an investigation that I know will or could easily lead to the above scenario . . . amounts to prosecutorial misconduct and violates the most basic fundamental rule of Department of Justice policy. I cannot be a party to such actions."

Banks closed by promising to direct "any press inquiry from any source whatsoever" to the attorney general or the head of the RTC. Such a statement from Banks would, of course, have been devastating to the Bush campaign. Whoever won the November election, Chuck Banks's government career was probably over.

The FBI's Little Rock office dispatched its report to Washington on October 16 as ordered, stating that there was "absolutely no factual basis to suggest criminal activity on the part of any of the individuals listed as witnesses in the referral." The telex went on to complain again about the RTC's failure to provide criminal referrals on the two much larger thrifts, Savers' Savings and First Federal Savings, whose combined losses of $1.5 billion offered "much greater prosecutive potential" than Madison Guaranty.

*   *   *

Despite fervent denials from the Bush camp, evidence later emerged that the White House had indeed sought derogatory information about Clinton from government agencies—specifically, and unlawfully, from his passport files. To underline the theme that his antiwar activism had been unpatriotic, a White House aide had asked a political appointee in the State Department to verify a rumor that Clinton had once tried to renounce his U.S. citizenship. The charges were so serious that an independent counsel was named to investigate. The special panel of federal appeals judges that appoints such prosecutors picked a former Republican U.S. attorney, Joseph diGenova, to conduct the probe. (The judge with the most influence on the panel, David Sentelle of the U.S. Circuit Court of Appeals for the District of Columbia, was a conservative North Carolinian handpicked by William Rehnquist, chief justice of the United States.) A year later, diGenova concluded the investigation without filing a single indictment.

Aside from the daunting complexities of Whitewater, Boyden Gray's sudden loss of interest may have reflected worries that were closer to home for the Bush family. Certainly neither the White House nor the Bush campaign would have wanted to risk drawing attention to the business dealings of the president's sons—in particular, Neil Bush's role as director of a corrupt Colorado savings and loan whose bankruptcy cost taxpayers a billion dollars. That was a story several reporters were pursuing around the time of Gray's phone calls to Albert Casey. It was more prudent to forget about alleged financial misdeeds and focus instead on Clinton's draft evasion.

So there would be no "October surprise" in 1992 for Bill Clinton. Though not for want of trying, Jim McDougal and Sheffield Nelson's effort to damage his presidential candidacy had failed. And Jean Lewis's apparent attempt to use the criminal justice system to subvert the political process had also gotten nowhere.

And for the time being, there would be no Whitewater scandal either. But as the Clintons soon learned, new allegations could be promoted as quickly as old charges were discredited. Their enemies were not really daunted by this defeat, and they would be bringing more tales of Arkansas criminality to the keen attention of the *New York Times* before too long.

Chapter Four

THE LARRY CASE TAPES

Not LONG AFTER Larry Nichols told reporters about the enormous sums the tabloids were prepared to pay for smut about Bill Clinton, he took on an informal partner to help him earn his share. Nichols's new associate was Larry Case, the Little Rock private detective with a reputation for digging dirt on local public figures. The big, bearded Case was an inveterate gossip with a gleefully dim view of human nature; he operated on the assumption that everybody was guilty until proven innocent. He liked heavy-caliber handguns and microcassette tape recorders.

Between them, Nichols and Case quickly established ongoing relationships with the *Star*, the *National Enquirer*, and the TV programs *Hard Copy* and *A Current Affair*. Through Nichols's extensive connections with Sheffield Nelson and the Arkansas Republican Party, the pair also formed jolly, mutually beneficial ties with reporters and producers from the *Los Angeles Times*, the *Washington Post*, Cable News Network, and other mainstream outlets. What few of his sophisticated new friends ever surmised was that Case habitually recorded his telephone calls, and often went around wearing a wire. This is perfectly legal in Arkansas. At times, he can be heard on tape assuring people he's not taping them, when in fact he is. (Following a later dispute with Nichols, whom he derided as a liar, a fraud, and a cheat, Case decided to share his tapes with the authors.)

Case and Nichols hoped to get rich by derailing the Clinton campaign, a quest they began in early 1992 with great confidence. In Arkansas, private detectives are licensed and regulated by a division of the state police. Case had cultivated a few friendly troopers who slipped him copies of investigative materials, including surveillance videos from the 1985 drug case against Roger Clinton, the governor's younger brother. Those tapes became a featured part of his inventory. Typically, Case's potential customers from Washington and New York didn't know that portions of those tapes had been broadcast on local television years earlier. For the right price, he bragged, he could produce videotapes that showed Bill Clinton himself sitting next to a bowl of cocaine at a party thrown by a flamboyant Little Rock financier named Dan Lasater. Due partly to evidence provided by Roger Clinton, Lasater had also gone to prison for possessing cocaine and giving the drug away to his friends. Case's idea of this tape's market value was more than a million dollars.

He and Nichols soon found themselves occupied full-time, frantically interviewing women of all ages and descriptions who were willing to accuse Clinton of sexual impropriety. With Case's tape recorder silently running, the pair regaled each other with bawdy imaginings about everything from Hillary Rodham Clinton's alleged frigidity to what would later be called the "distinguishing characteristics" of her husband's genitalia. When Betsey Wright talked to the *Washington Post* about suppressing "bimbo eruptions," she was thinking primarily of Case and Nichols.

The Case-Nichols conversations are reminiscent of "the Duke and the Dauphin," those itinerant hucksters in Mark Twain's *Adventures of Huckleberry Finn* who flimflam Arkansas yokels with vulgar tent shows. In 1992, however, it was the Arkansas yokels who tried to con the big-city sophisticates. As the campaign heated up, several reporters cultivated Nichols and Case for leads, but their most oddly symbiotic relationship was with William Rempel of the *Los Angeles Times*. Betsey Wright sensed that the California reporter "had an obsession and a mission to destroy Bill Clinton, and had the resources of a big organization behind him. I had never known that there were reporters whose full-time mission in life was destroying people."

As he told Case and others, Rempel felt he was merely doing his job, that the public had a right to know whether a presidential candidate had a secret life. In that pursuit he seemed perfectly comfortable exchanging tips with a private detective trying to dig up scurrilous information for personal profit. (A regretful Rempel later said Case had dishonestly "duped" him into sharing information about allegations against Clinton. "I can say absolutely that nothing he told me in the weeks and months leading up to the 1992 election, nor in the months and years since, has ever influenced, informed or otherwise contributed to a single syllable of type in the *Los Angeles Times*," he added. "I must confess to wasting a fair amount of valuable time [talking to the Little Rock detective].") Acting on tips from Rempel, with whom he recorded scores of long, rambling conversations, Case spent a great deal of time and energy trying to persuade a thirty-eight-year-old Oklahoma woman to go public with her tale of an extended affair with Bill Clinton in the mid-1980s. As narrated to Case on the telephone, the story was improbable: Over a two-year period, the governor and his entourage of troopers slipped out of Little Rock forty to fifty times to meet her in a downtown Oklahoma City motel roughly four hundred miles from Little Rock, then nipped back without arousing undue curiosity. (State law requires the governor to notify the lieutenant governor whenever he leaves Arkansas.) How Clinton managed all this, Case never thought to wonder, possibly because the woman did mention a name familiar to him: Arkansas state trooper Larry Patterson.

According to the woman, who identified herself to Case as Michelle Purdom, Clinton used the alias "Bill Wilcox"; she'd thought her secretive lover might be in the Mob. Lately, she said, both the *National Enquirer* and the *Los Angeles Times* had been pestering her to go public with her charges. Both newspapers had been tipped off by a disgruntled former employee of a certain Louwanda Faye Mason, who was some relation to Michelle. Louwanda had since moved to Southern California.

But the disgruntled former employee—whose identity Case failed to weasel out of Rempel—identified not Michelle but Louwanda herself as Clinton's Oklahoma paramour. He was also said to have described a photograph of the nude or partially nude candidate, sufficiently revealing to give a clear view of those "distinguishing characteristics." Case desperately wanted to put his hands on this valuable item. But first he needed to get the cast of characters straight. Posing as a journalist, he phoned Michelle in April 1992, pretending to have seen a copy of the infamous photo.

"There's a lot of question about who the hell everybody is," Case told her. "Everybody thinks that Louwanda is you. Everybody thinks Louwanda is the one that was involved with Bill Clinton."

"That's not true. I'm not Louwanda, Louwanda's not me. She's a separate person," Michelle insisted. "As far as I know, she never saw him. I don't know how she ever could have. Him and I had a personal relationship. I didn't just have sex with him just for nothing. I cared about him. He cared about me. We had a personal relationship. I wasn't just a sex bunny to him. . . . I think he makes personal relationships with the people he sleeps with."

"Everybody thinks that everybody's somebody else." Case was becoming frustrated.

"That's just not true. Louwanda had nothing to do with this. Believe me. I don't like Louwanda," she said. "I wouldn't do anything to cover for her."

"Then why did she call you when I contacted her?" he asked.

Michelle launched into a complicated explanation, which boiled down to gossip from a third relative. When a *Los Angeles Times* reporter had presented himself at Louwanda's door, "she knew it was me," Michelle insisted. "Louwanda shut the door in the *L.A. Times* guy's face. But he came back again. And she told me, 'This is not gonna work, you're gonna have to talk with this guy.' Then he called me, and it's gone on from there."

Meanwhile the *Enquirer*, she told Case, had offered her $75,000 for her tale, and twice that if she could somehow corroborate her claims. "He's not gonna give me $150,000," she said, "if I can't prove it was me. . . . But see, if there is no proof, I don't want to talk for $500,000. Because one, I don't want to get on TV and be called a liar and be shredded apart. But if somebody has proof. . . ."

"I have seen it," Case fibbed. "But nobody seems to know who anybody is. Everybody's talked to a different Louwanda."

"But see, her and I kind of look alike," Michelle insisted. "We both have an oval kind of face. We both have large lips. We both have a small, puggy-type nose. We both have blondish-colored hair. We're both a little chesty. We're both short, about five-two, five-three."

"Is there anybody who remembers you?"

"Larry Patterson would. Does he still work for him? But he wouldn't say nothing."

"What name would he remember?" Case asked.

"I don't know," she admitted. "It wouldn't have been Michelle Purdom. It could have been Suzanne James. It could have been Michelle James. . . . See, I have some blockages in my mind. Some things I just don't remember real clear. It could have been that name, I don't know."

Michelle not only couldn't remember her own name, but at some points she said ledgers could exist that show a "Bill C." paying $30,000 for her services; at other times she insisted that theirs was an affair of the heart, and that while her famous paramour bought her little presents, money never changed hands. She did affirm, however, that as Gennifer Flowers had already told the world, the candidate was very good in bed. Although she claimed that Clinton had eventually revealed his identity, she hadn't realized he was married until she saw Hillary on TV. That upset her greatly, as she had a firm policy against dating married men. She wanted to know more about the mythical snapshot. "Was it a small woman or a large woman?"

"It was a busty woman," Case chortled.

"I'd like to see if it was me," she said. "Couldn't you get a driver's license picture flashed up on the screen? I'm very unphotogenic. I kind of look like a Barbra Streisand and a Goldie Hawn and a Suzanne Somers. I don't have Barbra's nose, but I do have her mouth, I have Suzanne Somers' facial shape, and Goldie Hawn's nose. You think of her when you look at me sometimes."

That was as close as Case ever got to the elusive photo. When Case tracked Louwanda down in California, she insisted that she'd never met Bill Clinton, never met anybody who said he or she knew Bill Clinton; indeed, she had never heard of the candidate until she'd seen him on TV. Louwanda also hinted that Michelle had what she called "problems" that might account for the inconsistencies in her story.

Several months later, Case and his fellow investigators learned the nature of Michelle's "problems." On July 25, 1992, Michael Isikoff wrote an article for the *Washington Post* detailing the Clinton campaign's success in quelling "bimbo eruptions." In it, he quoted Case saying he had been paid $500,000—a huge exaggeration—by "three separate news organizations" to investigate Clinton's sexual behavior. Isikoff also chronicled the work of San Francisco private investigator Jack Palladino on behalf of the Clinton campaign. According to Betsey Wright there had been nineteen new allegations from women purporting to be Clinton's ex-lovers, in addition to seven earlier ones, since the Democratic convention two weeks earlier. "Since the convention, the gold-digger growth is enormous," Wright told the *Post*.

She drew a distinction between rival candidate H. Ross Perot's reported use of private detectives to investigate business and political rivals, and the Clinton campaign's counterintelligence operation against tabloid journalists and Republican operatives. "I don't think I've used [Palladino] on anything except bimbo eruptions," Wright claimed, in a phrase that to her chagrin passed instantly into the political lexicon. "We're trying to do a self-defense thing." She described the $28,000 paid to Palladino as "legal expenses."

Isikoff cited as Palladino's greatest triumph his debunking of Larry Case's taped interview with "a 38-year-old Oklahoma City woman" who claimed to have had an affair with Clinton. "Shortly after the interview," he wrote, "Palladino flew to Oklahoma City and took a three-page affidavit from the woman flatly denying the account. The woman said in a recent interview that she told Palladino she had never met Clinton and that she had been 'tricked' by Case after she had had surgery to remove a brain tumor. The tumor had caused her to suffer from 'amnesia' and a 'multiple personality disorder,' accounting for her willingness to agree to Case's suggestions that she had had an affair with Clinton, the woman said."

Of all the bad things that had been written and said about Case, nothing irritated him like the notion that he'd badgered a woman into making up a phony story over the telephone. Clearly, he hadn't. The woman had eagerly volunteered her tale. "They make her look better than me," he moaned to Rempel, "and hell, she's the damn nut." Despite the fact that Isikoff had been spending a good deal of time with Larry Nichols, Case assured Rempel that the *Post* reporter was "a wiseass, and a big-time Clinton buddy."

More consequential than detectives or brain surgery in persuading Michelle to abandon her unlikely story, perhaps, was something Isikoff didn't report: the extensive history of arrests of both Michelle and Louwanda, under several pseudonyms, for prostitution.

Betsey Wright had been dealing with allegations like these for as long as she'd worked for Bill Clinton. Born and raised in Texas, Wright had first met Clinton in 1972, when he worked in Austin for George McGovern's presidential campaign. After managing his comeback campaign for governor ten years later, Wright remained in Arkansas to serve as both mother hen and political commando. Although it's been widely reported that she confronted Clinton with a "bimbo list" in 1988, persuading him to forgo a presidential bid, she insists that never happened.

"There was no list," she said. "I discussed the issue with him. I didn't see any opening in 1988. I thought it was a long shot. Even in 1992, I didn't think the race should be run, because of what would happen to Hillary and Chelsea. Listen, the guy represented generational change. He was a baby boomer. He'd been on campuses during the Vietnam War. He did not go to Vietnam. He had been on campuses when birth control pills were first invented, and, quote, free sex, unquote, became a big deal. He had a brother who had gotten in trouble with drugs, and he was on campuses when drugs were used. He was attractive to women. There were a million rumors, and there were lots of people who would be willing to make allegations.

"I just knew that there was no way we were going to make that kind of generational change in this country without a struggle. That was what was going to happen to the first baby boomer who got out there by himself."

Early on, Wright's reluctance had kept her out of the 1992 presidential campaign. But as a resident at Harvard's Kennedy School of Government during the early weeks of 1992, she found herself transfixed in the middle of the New Hampshire media market. Then, having tried in vain to alert the campaign to the dangers posed by the likes of Larry Nichols and Gennifer Flowers, she was recruited by campaign lawyer Mickey Kantor on the morning after the crucial primary. Within days, she was back in Little Rock, organizing counter-intelligence against Nichols, Case, and their journalistic allies.

Stifling Michelle and Louwanda wasn't Wright's only success. Another was Connie Hamzy, aka "Sweet, Sweet Connie," Little Rock's most notorious rock groupie. During the seventies, Hamzy had achieved minor national notoriety thanks to a song by a band called Grand Funk Railroad. According to the lyrics, "Sweet sweet Connie was doin' her act / Had the whole band, and that's a natural fact." An inveterate publicity seeker, Hamzy was once the subject of a *Cosmopolitan* profile marveling at her sexual escapades. (Her interview included evaluations of the penis sizes and copulative skills of various rock stars.) Nothing could keep Hamzy from running to tabloid TV with a tale about Clinton passionately pursuing her, but Wright prevented the story from appearing anywhere else.

It was much the same with Sally Miller Perdue, a fifty-three-year-old former Miss Arkansas. Regarded as kooky and unreliable by most reporters in her hometown of Pine Bluff, Perdue had once kicked off a quixotic campaign for mayor with a press conference strenuously denying that she was a lesbian—a charge nobody present had ever heard. Not long before the Democratic convention, the Clinton campaign learned, Lenora Fulani of the fringe New Alliance Party planned to launch her own presidential candidacy in a joint appearance with Perdue, who would detail what she claimed had been her own passionate love affair with Bill Clinton. The New Alliance Party was a strange, quasi-Marxist group based on Manhattan's Upper West Side, whose members were mostly psychotherapy patients of the party's leaders. (Eventually it dissolved into another group that was simultaneously allied to Louis Farrakhan and H. Ross Perot.) Behind the scenes, Nichols and Case had helped broker the deal between Perdue and the eccentric New York activists. In their phone conversations, the two Arkansans had a derisive nickname for the New Alliance Party: "the Snake Doctors."

Clinton denied ever having met Sally Perdue. Assisted by Wright, the Palladino firm lined up several relatives and former associates who agreed to talk to reporters about the woman's eccentricities. The tactic succeeded. Although Perdue made an appearance on the nationally syndicated *Sally Jessy Raphael* TV program, no major news organization gave credence to her account.

The *National Enquirer*, of all papers, derided Perdue's tale under the head-line "WEIRD CULT OUT TO DESTROY CLINTON."

Betsey Wright's success in stifling Clinton sex stories drove Case and Nichols crazy. Having been in close contact with an *Enquirer* reporter named David Duffy for several months, the pair could not understand the tabloid's motives for debunking Sally Perdue. "Tell me this world ain't upside-fucking-down," Nichols growled. "I'm still trying to fathom why Duffy put an unfucking story in the *Enquirer*."

"I know why he did it," Case said hopefully. "To shake some fucking people out of the bushes that know about the affair."

Nichols suspected darker motives. "What I think, and I talked to [Bill] Rempel and he agreed. I told him if you want to see the unstory of the fucking century. I told you Duffy told me he was waiting to get his orders from the top. And I'm gonna guaran-fuckin'-tee you it's gonna be . . ."

"A whitewash?" Case guessed.

"Yup."

"It's kinda terrible when you have a tabloid running a whitewash."

A more immediate setback involved the saga of yet another woman, named "Denise," who claimed that Bill Clinton had beaten her up during a sexual liaison at Little Rock's Excelsior Hotel. Partly at Case's insistence, the allegation had been previously investigated by the Pulaski County prosecuting attorney and found to be without foundation. The woman herself had filed no complaint. But Case had in his possession a photocopy of what purported to be a handwritten letter from Clinton to "Denise," apologizing "for getting rough with you last night," and signed: "Your friend, Bill."

Anticipating a big payday, the detective had flown to California at the behest of the tabloid TV program *A Current Affair* and surreptitiously used a hidden camera to videotape an interview with the woman. The program's decision not to broadcast his tape—or pay him—was exasperating. Case phoned producer David Lee Miller and accused him of having been bought off by Betsey Wright and Jack Palladino.

"I'll take it to the fuckin' FBI myself!" Case shouted. "I will bring this thing to a head. I'm not no wayward, dumb son of a bitch that don't know how to operate. And if I have to accuse people to get my work done, I'll do it. I want the truth put out about the fuckin' tape. I want the truth put out about the fuckin' letter. I don't know if the letter's right. Nobody knows if the letter's right."

"If I thought the letter was right, we'd do it," Miller replied coolly. "Larry, we paid handwriting experts a lot of money to look at the letter, and it came back bogus."

"Isn't it a story that somebody's out there trying to pass bogus letters? Put me on the air. Put Betsey Wright on the air. Ask Clinton to come on. Ask Jack Palladino to come on the air. Ask them all to take a fuckin' polygraph. If people can't see through what this man can do because he has the power and money, they're crazy."

"We looked at the story in good faith because we thought it might be true," Miller patiently explained. "We wouldn't have gotten into it if we didn't. We spent a lot of time and money, and we talked to a lot of people involved in the case. If the story can be confirmed and corroborated, we will run with the story. But right now it isn't, and we can't use it."

Ordinary news standards, honored in some respects even by tabloid media, confused and upset Case and Nichols. Yet they could sometimes see the humor in their situation: On one tape, Nichols can be heard telling Case about coaching yet another eager informant on how to present her story of a torrid love affair with Clinton to the press. Above all, Nichols laughed, he had warned her to avoid any mention of the "demons" that were haunting her.

Often frustrated by the media, the two Larrys were no more enamored of the Republicans who were feeding rumors to Nichols. He mentioned Sheffield Nelson and Cliff Jackson, a local Republican lawyer whose distaste for Clinton dated back more than twenty years. "God, those guys are sick," Nichols told Case on the day Isikoff's story appeared. "Jackson and Nelson. They want to stick it to Clinton so bad they can't hardly see straight." In the *Post* article, Betsey Wright had blamed local Republicans for the bimbo glut. "One of these days," Nichols chuckled, "I'm just gonna probably give Betsey a kiss, and tell her it is coming from them."

*　　*　　*

The tantalizing question of how the prostitute "Michelle" knew the name of Trooper Larry Patterson, a member of Clinton's security detail, was a mystery Case and Nichols never solved. Case spent hours cultivating acquaintances at Arkansas State Police headquarters who he thought could give him the low-down on the governor. At one point, Nichols convinced him that Clinton's bodyguards actually had placed a battery-operated radio transmitter in a vase somewhere inside the governor's mansion. All Case needed to do, said Nichols, was slip into the building and replace the batteries.

More to the point, Nichols believed that for the right inducement, some of the troopers might be persuaded to expose their employer. "The main ones I've been talking to are [Carl] Kirkland and Patterson. I think they'll talk," he said.

"One of them can retire," Case suggested.

"I think it's Patterson, the white guy," Nichols said. "He's obviously in the middle of it, but . . . I figured him to be like Buddy." Nichols was referring to Buddy Young, the head of the governor's security detail. "You know that sumbitch ain't gonna crack. You know, most policemen are trained liars."

"They better be, hadn't they," opined Case, "dealing in this kind of shit."

Significantly, Case also had extensive conversations with Bill Rempel about the possibility of "turning" Clinton's bodyguards. He told the reporter about the hidden bug in the governor's mansion, and discussed a scheme to slip into the building on some pretext to activate it. Supposedly, the device was located in the bathroom of the Clintons' living quarters.

"What would it have besides the sounds of the john?" Rempel asked. "Which is certainly not something I'm interested in."

"You've come up with some stuff before that I'm not interested in," retorted Case, "and that's the size of somebody's private parts. And I ain't figured that shit out yet. I know you ain't gonna write about that."

Rempel guffawed. "That's the kind of information I'm just going to have to keep to myself," he agreed. "A family newspaper is just not the place for that."

It was, however, the kind of information Rempel had gone out of his way to obtain. In another of their tape-recorded chats, Case badgered the reporter for information on that very topic. Rempel had told him that an anonymous source claimed to have seen a sexually explicit photograph of Clinton in bed with a woman. If he flew to California and managed to put his hands on the photograph, the detective wanted to know, how would he recognize the real thing?

Rempel replied that Clinton had a large mole "in an area that normally wouldn't see that light of day. . . . I have extensive descriptions, as you know."

"You say you don't want to use tabloidism," Case chided, "but this sounds like tabloidism."

"I'll gather it. I'll ask all the questions and get all the information," the reporter answered. "But what I put in the newspaper will always be less than what I know."

". . . . There's a face in it?"

"Yeah, there's no question about it. There's more than a face," Rempel laughed. "You know what I mean."

"You can get somebody's body," Case cautioned him. "I may have one on mine. I haven't looked lately. Haven't had the opportunity."

"But there's a face to go with the mole," Rempel insisted. "It's a full-body shot."

Neither man had ever seen this racy photo; neither ever would. As was his and Nichols's custom, Case had no compunctions about embroidering information he'd gleaned from Rempel and passing it along to other reporters. Soon after their discussion about this "distinguishing characteristic," CNN correspondent Art Harris showed curiosity about the same topic. He was reporting a rather damaging profile of Gennifer Flowers to accompany a photo layout in *Penthouse.*

"Did either of them [Michelle or Louwanda] describe Bill's equipment," Harris inquired, "and how big or little it was? Because I know from other sources . . ."

"I heard his equipment was rather dainty," Case laughed.

"Yeah, you got it." Harris laughed, too. "And that he makes up for it with a lot of oral sex."

"That's exactly what Michelle says," Case assured him. "She says that she agrees with everything Gennifer says because that's exactly how he is. She says that on the tape now!"

In fact, Michelle didn't say anything about oral sex or Clinton's penis. But then Harris had explicitly asked Case if he was taping their conversation, and been solemnly assured that he was not.

Not all of Case's conversations with Rempel were as friendly and jocular as those concerning the candidate's "equipment." Rempel was annoyed when he learned that Case and Nichols were passing his information to other reporters. Although Case pressed him repeatedly for the names of his sources, the reporter never relented. When the frustrated detective demanded to know what kind of proof would justify publishing a story about Clinton's alleged misconduct in Rempel's newspaper, the reporter categorically refused to tell him. Plainly, he suspected Case and Nichols might manufacture the required evidence.

Meanwhile, the continuing effort by Case and Nichols to persuade Clinton's state police bodyguards to accuse the governor of sexual misbehavior was also getting nowhere. All they had accomplished was to supply Rempel with the names of several troopers they thought might be amenable to persuasion. For the time being, none was yet willing to risk making public accusations against their boss, who might become president.

As the campaign summer wore on, in fact, it was beginning to look as if Case and Nichols would never make their big score. They had received minimal remuneration, if any, since Nichols's payment from the *Star* in January. In early August, however, Case got an exciting phone call from Little Rock lawyer Cliff Jackson.

A Fulbright scholar at Oxford while Clinton was a Rhodes scholar there during the late sixties, Jackson had developed an obsession with what he saw as Clinton's character flaws. Others speculated that the somewhat dour Jackson had always been jealous of his fellow Arkansan's seemingly effortless charm, and had resented traveling all the way to England only to find himself in Clinton's shadow. Back home, Jackson's own political career had never gotten off the ground. He had run for Pulaski County district attorney some years earlier and done poorly.

During the 1992 campaign, Jackson developed a national reputation in media circles as a principled Clinton opponent who knew his old rival all too well. A member of the fundamentalist Assembly of God church, he held political views that were roughly in accordance with those of the religious right. During the New Hampshire primary, an organization formed by Jackson called the Alliance for the Rebirth of an Independent America had taken out full-page ads in the *Manchester Union-Leader* and distributed circulars that assailed Clinton as an unpatriotic draft dodger.

Washington Post reporter and Clinton biographer David Maraniss, the author of *First in His Class*, took Jackson's opinions most seriously—despite the fact that, as his own careful reporting of the draft controversy proved, Jackson's accounts of his Oxford classmate's struggles with the Selective Service System were at least as self-serving as Clinton's.

Jackson had provided Maraniss with several contemporaneous, but not particularly reliable, letters he had written on the subject in 1967. Specifically, in his letters Jackson had exaggerated his own role in assisting the candidate's efforts to avoid induction. He had also provided an inaccurate chronology obscuring the fact that, partly out of guilt over the Vietnam combat death of a high school friend, Clinton had surrendered his draft deferment two months before drawing a high lottery number in December 1969. For all of Clinton's efforts to avoid the draft, surrendering his deferment had been unusual back then. (Jackson himself got a medical deferment.)

Now the high-minded Jackson wanted to offer Larry Case something less elevated: a photograph sufficiently explicit to doom Clinton's candidacy and end his political career. He wouldn't tell Case who had this picture, but he wanted the detective to broker a lucrative deal.

"Is the photo good?" Case asked. "I mean, is it better than what we've seen around here? Because I've seen a bunch of photos, but nothing that's really spicy."

"This one is spicy," Jackson assured him. "I haven't actually seen it, but I know what's in it. I don't want to say over the phone, because that'll identify her to the Clinton people if my phone were bugged. Or yours."

"Aw, they wouldn't do that," Case said in a mocking tone.

"Bullshit."

"Shit," Case laughed. "I can't go out this door that ol' Betsey Wright don't already know what I'm doing."

"I told them that I didn't want to get in the middle of this type stuff," Jackson said. "That I'd pass it on to someone who can say what the market is. I'd put them into direct contact. . . . Let me just tell you this. My perception of it? If it's what's been represented to me, it ought to be worth two million. . . . If this woman has what she says she has, it'd be totally incriminating. . . . I think it'd absolutely do in the campaign."

Jackson's client—a friend of a friend, he said—wanted cash; no checks, no wire transfers. The lawyer wanted his own fingerprints kept off the deal, but he also wanted it done. Before he took another step, Case called Rempel. "Did you have Cliff Jackson make a run at me?"

"No, I didn't," Rempel replied. "I was surprised to hear you guys got together."

"We didn't get together on my call. And I assure you, I can play you his call."

The reporter laughed. "I'm sure you could. You could probably play this call."

Case denied taping Rempel. "He initiated the call. I don't know if he was trying to trick me. But I wouldn't burn him."

"One thing about Cliff Jackson," said Rempel. "I've never known him to lie or exaggerate. He's about the straightest man I've met in this state." The reporter told Case he hadn't seen the photograph, but if Jackson vouched for it, that was good enough. Thus encouraged, Case phoned an editor at the *National Enquirer*. Like many tabloid journalists, David Duffy spoke with a brisk British accent. Having been falsely promised raunchy photos of Clinton by the detective on an earlier occasion, he was understandably leery.

"She might as well stick it in her left ear," Duffy said, "until we've satisfied ourselves that it's a picture we want to buy. And if it's the genuine article, Christ, you're right. 'There's Bill Clinton. He is in bed with a woman.' Then you start to negotiate, and it's a very straightforward piece of negotiation. . . . We would not part with any money until I get that picture. Unless she's an imbecile, she can get the phone number of the *National Enquirer* from the papers. She must be a real nutcase if she doesn't know how to make a telephone call." His doubts proved prophetic. The $2 million picture never materialized. And Rempel, though fully aware of Jackson's attempt at brokering this deal, continued to describe him as a principled, thoughtful critic of Clinton's character. "Jackson said he regretted making the call to Case and said it made his skin crawl to be involved even that much," the reporter explained. "I believed him."

A similar gamy project, of which Cliff Jackson also appears to have been aware, took shape around the same time. Back in February, a supermarket tabloid called the *Globe* had published a four-page layout headlined "BILL CLINTON'S FOUR-IN-A-BED SEX ORGIES WITH BLACK HOOKERS." By all accounts, the *Globe* story was the handiwork of one Robert "Say" McIntosh, an eccentric Little Rock restaurateur variously billed as "the Sweet Potato Pie King" and "The Black Santa." McIntosh had also put in a cameo appearance in Larry Nichols's story in the *Star* a month earlier as "Mr. Fixit," allegedly paid $25,000 by the Clinton campaign to keep scandals under wraps.

During the eighties, Say McIntosh had been Tommy Robinson's tag-team partner during a few of the colorful sheriff's more absurd publicity stunts. On one memorable occasion, McIntosh—dressed for obscure reasons in a red sateen devil costume with horns—had climbed onto a twelve-foot wooden cross in front of the Sheriff's Department; then Robinson had noisily cut it down with a chain saw. The luridly drawn handbills advertising his barbecue joint were filled with lectures against racism and rumors about the sex lives of public figures. Having frequently accused Bill Clinton of an unseemly lust for black women, McIntosh had outdone himself for the *Globe*.

According to the tabloid, not only had "Bill Clinton. . . . been with enough black women to cast a Tarzan movie"; he had fathered a child by a prostitute named Bobbie Ann Williams. A little round-faced black child's smiling photograph was identified as the candidate's illegitimate son. The child had supposedly been conceived during a series of wild sex and drug parties at the Hot Springs home of Clinton's mother, Virginia Kelley.

During Cliff Jackson's call to Larry Case, he'd asked the detective whether he had heard about a paternity suit filed on behalf of Bobbie Ann Williams. Jackson had it on good authority that such a scheme was in the works. Indeed, people claiming to be working with Jackson had been phoning around Little Rock trying to find an attorney who would handle such a complaint. What Jackson neglected to tell Case was that the plan had originated in the uppermost circles of the national Republican Party.

*　　*　　*

Peter Smith was a wealthy fifty-seven-year-old Chicagoan who headed his own investment bank, Peter Smith & Company. Regarded as "very conservative" in Illinois Republican circles, Smith was one of the top twenty contributors to Newt Gingrich's political action committee, known as GOPAC, and also gave heavily to the Republican National Committee, the Heritage Foundation, and Gingrich's personal foundation. In addition to the $150,000 he contributed to GOPAC and the RNC, Smith raised tens of thousands more. "What a lot of people don't know is that when Peter W. Smith talks," a Chicago business magazine noted in an admiring profile, "Newt Gingrich listens."

But in 1992, with Republican prospects fading, Smith felt an urge to do more than give and raise money. From his contacts in the party, he knew that reporters in Arkansas had tried and failed to confirm several potentially damaging stories about Clinton. Turning to Gingrich's closest advisers, Smith devised a plan to get those stories into print by paying for their publication.

He enlisted Eddie Mahe, top Washington political consultant and longtime Gingrich confidant; Hugh Newton, a prominent conservative public relations executive in Washington; Daniel Swillinger, a GOPAC lawyer and Gingrich confidant whom Smith hired to advise him on federal election law; and E. Mark Braden, another lawyer with ties to Gingrich who had formerly served as general counsel to the Republican National Committee. Especially close to Gingrich was Mahe, who had volunteered in the Georgian's first, unsuccessful congressional bid in 1974, and whose far-right allegiances were an important influence on the Republican maverick. Richard W. Porter, a Bush White House aide working on opposition research for the Bush-Quayle campaign, also consulted informally with Smith on his project. After the election, Porter would go on to a partnership at the Chicago-based law firm of Kirkland & Ellis, where he would continue assisting Smith on his projects—and where he would eventually play a role in both the Paula Jones lawsuit and the Monica Lewinsky affair.

Hoping to torpedo Clinton before Election Day, Peter Smith spent as much as $80,000 on an informal investigation of the Democrat's sex life. Mahe alone was paid $25,000 to assist with the scheme. The political consultant, who acknowledged his role in the private probe, later joked that "they should have just hired one good private eye." In early September, Smith called on David Brock, who had been recommended to him as a competent right-wing investigative journalist. The two had met earlier when Brock was working on a profile of James Baker III for the *American Spectator*.

"I suggested to Mr. Brock that he look into a number of topics in Arkansas relating to Governor Clinton that had not come to the attention of the electorate, despite diligent reporting efforts of several national media organizations," Smith told the *Chicago Sun-Times* years later, after his role in the Bobbie Ann Williams affair was revealed in the *New York Observer.*

"He called and said there were Republicans in Arkansas with information about Clinton's womanizing," according to Brock. "He wanted me to go to a meeting in Eddie Mahe's office on the Hill. They had articles from a supermarket tabloid, and they were going to put me in touch with someone who could help me find the [illegitimate] son. This contact was codenamed 'Mr. Pepper,' and he claimed to be an investment banker on Wall Street."

Brock thought the whole prostitute story was "farfetched, crazy and silly." Nevertheless, he took a $5,000 check from Smith, with the notation "for contemplated editorial product," in order to help research a possible book on Clinton. "Mr. Pepper" never delivered, and no paternity suit was ever filed. Nor did Say McIntosh ever produce Bobbie Ann Williams and her little son.

Another possible reason for the failure of Peter Smith's venture into sexual politics emerged some years later—after the *Arkansas Democrat-Gazette* printed Bobbie Ann Williams's name as part of a laundry list of Clinton's alleged lovers in the spring of 1998. (The article was a reprint from the *Washington Times.*)

The angry woman turned up in the newsroom later that same day. She had little difficulty convincing the *Democrat-Gazette* editors that the woman in the *Globe*'s 1992 "exposé" was an impostor who had borrowed her identity. The accompanying photograph was of her sister, who had been a prostitute but had no children. Bobbie Ann Williams had children, but insisted she had never met Bill Clinton. As Brock had suspected, the entire story was a hoax. The *Democrat-Gazette* printed a retraction.

Yet another sensational sex story that fizzled during the run-up to the 1992 election involved a Van Buren, Arkansas, nursing home executive named Juanita Broaddrick. It, too, began with Sheffield Nelson, in tandem with a Fayetteville businessman named Philip Yoakum. A fellow Republican partisan, Yoakum enlisted Nelson in an attempt to bring Broaddrick into the open with an allegation that Clinton had raped her during a 1978 nursing home convention in Little Rock.

According to an open letter Yoakum distributed to reporters, he and Clinton's 1990 Republican opponent had visited Juanita Broaddrick at Brownwood Manor, a nursing home facility owned by her and her husband David. Yoakum said he tape-recorded their meeting, although no tape ever materialized and he later said he had destroyed it. (Nelson has failed to respond to requests for interviews.)

"I was particularly distraught when you told me of your brutal rape by Bill Clinton," he wrote, "and details of how Clinton first approached you as being interested in the nursing home business; how, while during an Arkansas State

Nursing Home Association conference in Little Rock, Clinton invited himself to your hotel room ostensibly to discuss business; and how, when Clinton came to your room at the Camelot, he started trying to kiss you and ran his hands all over your body, how you resisted until he ripped your clothes off, and how he bit your lip until you gave into his forcing sex upon you."

While phrased somewhat confusingly, Yoakum's letter also suggested his understanding of why Broaddrick remained silent. "[Y]ou mentioned that, if you did not come forward," wrote Yoakum, "that it would truly convince David of your innocence in the matter and also it would help to set his mind at rest." The couple had been married to other people and carrying on a love affair at the time of the alleged 1978 incident with Clinton.

Yoakum also claimed to have recorded a phone conversation in which David Broaddrick announced that he planned " 'to ask Clinton for a couple of big favors' and that he 'would get them' and that 'Clinton owed it' to you all." Brownwood Manor was not a retirement village, but a medical facility housing severely disabled individuals. Regulated by the state, it derived most of its income from Medicare and Medicaid payments administered by the Arkansas Department of Human Services. Juanita Broaddrick had accepted an appointment by Clinton to the state's Nursing Home Advisory Board, but there was no indication that she or her husband had sought or received special treatment from the state. Indeed, the couple was involved in a long-running dispute with the state over Medicaid reimbursement rates, which a lawsuit resolved in their favor in 1994. No tape of David Broaddrick ever materialized either.

Had many people in Van Buren outside Juanita Broaddrick's immediate circle known about her contacts with Yoakum and Sheffield Nelson, it might have struck them as rather odd. Any personal ill will she may have harbored toward Bill Clinton was a well-kept secret in the northwest Arkansas town of fifteen thousand. The governor had made a well-publicized campaign stop at Brownwood Manor during his hard-fought 1990 campaign against Nelson. A photo of Clinton attentively taking advice at the Broaddrick facility from the county's oldest living citizen—Mrs. Mabel Stevenson, age 101—was prominently featured in the *Van Buren Press Argus-Courier* on October 22, 1990. To some Crawford County residents, Clinton's appearance at Brownwood Manor signaled a truce in one of the community's longest-running political feuds.

The governor's problem, however, wasn't with the nursing home owners. His difficulties were with Norma Rogers and Jean Darden, two sisters who managed Brownwood for the Broaddricks. Like their employers, both were lifelong Van Buren residents. Their father's murderer had been spared the electric chair by Bill Clinton ten years earlier, and their family had held a very public grudge against him ever since.

The Brownwood Manor event, scheduled partly as a favor to a Clinton campaign worker who cared for the elderly Mrs. Stevenson, was regarded by campaign officials as a "peacemaking mission." Arranged by a longtime Crawford County political ally named Brooks Treece, since deceased, the visit hadn't been undertaken spontaneously; advance permission had been sought and received.

The political dilemma that Clinton's visit to Brownwood Manor was partly intended to ameliorate had been largely of his own making. A few weeks after his 1980 election loss to Frank White, Clinton had commuted the death sentence of one Guy L. Kuehn, convicted in the 1971 stabbing death of Ray Trentham, a school custodian who had surprised the killer during a break-in. The commutation was one of 129 recommended by the state parole board and acted upon by Clinton during the closing weeks of his administration. Clinton's action also made Kuehn eligible for parole.

His timing couldn't have been worse. The largely rural county in western Arkansas had experienced a rash of recent murders, including the highly publicized slayings of a father and daughter in a jewelry store holdup. The result, said former Clinton aide Kay Goss, was "political devastation." Clinton's explanation that he hadn't grasped the brutal nature of Kuehn's crime and assumed that the Trentham family had no objection only made things worse. A stinging editorial in the *Van Buren Press Argus* (which later merged with another paper, the *Van Buren Courier*) argued that "either [because of] his innocence or inability to tell the truth . . . Clinton's being ridiculous again."

That editorial so alarmed Clinton that he and Hillary drove 150 miles from Little Rock to explain themselves to its author, Garrick Feldman. The Democrat had lost Crawford County more than two to one in 1980, in a vote widely interpreted as a reaction to President Carter's housing of Cuban refugees at nearby Fort Chaffee. If he were perceived as "soft on crime," Clinton might never win the county again. He promised Feldman that Ray Trentham's murderer would never be paroled from the penitentiary as long as Clinton was in Arkansas politics. (Kuehn served out his sentence and was released in 1993 at age 51.)

After being reelected in 1982, despite winning only 38 percent of the Crawford County vote, Clinton made a determined effort to identify himself with the "victim's rights" movement, and commuted no more death sentences. The Trentham family, however, wasn't satisfied. They circulated petitions to keep Kuehn in prison and told local reporters of their strong hostility to Bill Clinton. Nevertheless, the governor did slightly better in the county in each successive election. By 1990, Brooks Treece and other local Democrats thought they might carry Crawford County. Clinton made several appearances in Van Buren that fall. His visit to Juanita Broaddrick's nursing home on the afternoon of October 20 was the very last.

Very little of that ancient history was known to the *Press Argus-Courier*'s publisher Ken Richardson, who had arrived in the town only one year earlier.

All he knew, Richardson recalled, was that Juanita Broaddrick had phoned him that morning and asked that his newspaper cover the event. Richardson was confident of his memory—he recalled being rather irritated at the time, because Broaddrick was a local businesswoman who never advertised in his biweekly newspaper.

Photographer Kia Larsen also remembered being annoyed when asked to give up a Saturday afternoon to chase the governor to Brownwood Manor. She had already gotten all the shots of Clinton she needed at a political rally that morning.

Years later, Juanita Broaddrick denied having been aware of then governor Clinton's visit to her business until she saw the photo in the *Press Argus-Courier*. She insisted that Richardson's recollection was wrong. She also contended that Clinton had chosen to barge into the nursing home unannounced on a Saturday specifically in order to avoid her, and that she and her husband were shocked and angered that he'd dared set foot on their property. There is no indication that she was present during Clinton's visit, although she agreed that Norma Rogers and Jean Darden were.

How Clinton could have anticipated Broaddrick's whereabouts is unclear. If she didn't like his use of her nursing home as a political prop, she voiced no objections at the time. As for the Kuehn pardon, she acknowledged her friends' strong feelings and put herself firmly in their camp. Broaddrick said that Clinton's motive in commuting Guy Kuehn's death sentence had been "to get revenge on this county, that was what we had heard."

For the first time in his political career, Bill Clinton won Crawford County in his 1990 contest against Sheffield Nelson by a margin of 5,504 to 5,178. Whether the "peacemaking mission" to Brownwood Manor played any part in his victory is conjecture, but it certainly didn't hurt.

Nelson and Yoakum's attempt two years later to publicize allegations that Clinton had raped Juanita Broaddrick got nowhere. The closest the two came to persuading reporters to pursue the story appears to have been the result of a tip to the *Los Angeles Times*.

According to reporter Bill Rempel, there were several things wrong with the story from his newspaper's point of view: its partisan origins with Arkansas Republicans; the unwillingness of the alleged victim to talk; and the late timing. "We got the tip in October," Rempel explained. "It was the consensus of reporters and editors that even if the facts turned out to be well documented, reliably corroborated, and served up on a silver platter, there was no way we could fairly report such a sensational allegation on the eve of [an] election. Furthermore, we had no way of assessing the validity of the story, even on a gut level, without talking to the alleged victim. Without her cooperation, there was no way to even begin an investigation."

Author David Brock recalled that when he attempted to research the story in 1995, he was put off by Yoakum's request to be cut in on a book deal. Yoakum told Brock that he had destroyed his tapes. Later, a private detective to whom Sheffield Nelson had directed Brock claimed to know the whereabouts of copies of Yoakum's tapes, but also told the *Spectator* writer that the tapes failed to support the written allegations and weren't worth excavating. From his conversations with Nelson, Brock concluded that even Clinton's old enemy questioned the story's validity.

Nevertheless, with Broaddrick's name deleted, Yoakum's letter continued to circulate in right-wing circles for several years, and it was eventually posted on the ABCNews.com Web site as well as various other locations on the Internet. Seven years, two presidential elections, a sworn affidavit, and a civil deposition denying the allegation would all come to pass before Juanita Broaddrick changed her mind, accepted a grant of immunity from Kenneth Starr, and spoke out in early 1999 on NBC News. When she did, the only witnesses to whom she had told contemporaneous versions of the two-decade-old story turned out to be her husband David and her old friends Norma Rogers and Jean Darden.

FBI agents working for the Office of Independent Counsel eventually deemed the evidence concerning Broaddrick's terrible accusation to be "inconclusive."

As the November election drew nearer, Case and Nichols also spent extraordinary amounts of time pursuing several women linked to Clinton by rumor—including several public figures—interviewing ex-husbands and former lovers, pestering coworkers and acquaintances with their suspicions, even trying to obtain the birth records of the suspects' children. From time to time, they gave detailed progress reports to their contacts in the national press. But despite all their effort, the pair were unable to document Clinton's adultery. There were no compromising photos, videos, motel receipts, or love letters, only a few obvious fakes. All they had gotten was some bad publicity for themselves.

"Blackmailer, sleazy practitioner, con man," Case complained that September in one of his long talks with Nichols. "It sounds like something my ex-wife would say. Anybody in the line of work we're in right now is gonna be classified as a con man. But hell, the best investigators I know have been con artists. They've got to be to get stuff out of people."

"Bill Clinton's the damn con man," Nichols replied bitterly. "But if they want absolute documentation, a picture of him sucking a dick, it ain't coming. And what if it did come? You know what Clinton would say? And you know what the media would say? Just because you suck one dick don't make you a cocksucker. Let's talk about the economy!"

* * *

Approximately ten days before the election, an adventurous young traveler arrived at the North Little Rock bus station late at night. Andrew Cooper was a twenty-three-year-old New Zealander who had wangled a letter of introduction from a Wellington newspaper and set about covering the American presidential contest. Unaware that he'd have to pay for a seat on the press plane that followed the Clinton campaign, and equally innocent of the fact that candidates' schedules were made up only a few days in advance, Cooper had found himself madly chasing the candidate across country by Greyhound. Unable to afford the Excelsior or any of the other downtown Little Rock hotels, Cooper took the advice of a friendly marine he'd met on the bus and pitched his tent in a grassy area on the north bank of the Arkansas River. He was awakened in the morning by a man with a revolver who informed him that he was trespassing.

Rather than call the police, however, Cooper's new acquaintance offered him a job. Everett Ham, whom the young New Zealander came to call "Big Daddy," was a gruff seventy-year-old with a gray crew cut, a great swag belly, and an abiding hatred of Bill Clinton. He lived in a ramshackle houseboat floating only a few hundred yards from the high-rise office buildings and luxury hotels of downtown Little Rock, on the north side of the Arkansas River. If Cooper would help with odd jobs and cleanup projects around the boat, Ham would let him have a spare room. The older man clearly hoped to take the young foreign journalist under his wing.

"I'm going to give you a lesson in southern history and culture," Cooper recalled Ham announcing. "I'm going to teach you how politics in this country and this state really work. You're in North Little Rock. This is niggertown. We don't have conflicts with our niggers here. We keep them in their place." To the young New Zealander, Ham "was like somebody who walked out of a history book."

Appalled but intrigued as well as broke, Cooper decided to stay. Quite by accident, he had stumbled into the nerve center of Cliff Jackson's anti-Clinton group, the Alliance for the Rebirth of an Independent America. Virtually every square foot of the houseboat was strewn with Bush-Quayle posters, heaps of newspaper clippings, and bumper stickers reading "Smile if you've slept with Bill Clinton." Cooper's host had indeed walked out of a history book, or a footnote. Decades earlier, Everett Ham had been an adviser to Governor Winthrop Rockefeller, and he had later served as state chairman of the Republican Party. On the walls of his houseboat, Ham proudly displayed photographs of himself with Richard Nixon, Gerald Ford, Ronald Reagan, and other prominent Republican politicians. And how Arkansas politics really worked, in Ham's view, was conspiratorially.

Spending his days mingling with the Washington press corps at Clinton-

Gore headquarters across the river in Little Rock, Cooper would return to the houseboat to find private meetings in progress, devoted to Clinton's ruin. He was never allowed to meet any of the "conspirators," although he later recognized Cliff Jackson as one of those present. To Cooper's amazement, the reeking houseboat was a constant hub of activity. Together with a friend named Gene Wirges, the former editor of a newspaper called the *Petit Jean Country Headlight,* Everett Ham stayed almost constantly on the telephone, giving interviews to talk radio stations in far-flung corners of the United States, while he sent and received dozens of faxes. Drinking from big tumblers filled with vodka, Ham and Wirges railed ceaselessly against Clinton, whom they regarded as a skirt-chasing, drug-abusing draft dodger.

The young reporter filed a preelection feature about the Little Rock scene to his newspaper in Wellington, New Zealand, the *Dominion,* describing Ham as "the aptly titled 'Big Daddy' of the anti-Clinton faction" whose mildest epithet for Clinton was "scumbag, an intellectual scumbag." But Cooper didn't portray Ham and Wirges quite as unpleasantly as he might have.

"They were in it for the hate," he recalled years later. "They considered Clinton a traitor to his country. Everett was infuriated that 'niggers, feminists, Jews, faggots, and the liberal New York press,' as he put it, could force people like himself from power. They were absolutely intent upon Bill Clinton's personal destruction by fair means or foul. Everett gravely assured me that they had the means at their disposal to bring about the utter destruction of Bill Clinton, and whether it happened before or after the election was of little concern to them. Their thinking was clearly long-term."

Chapter Five

"JUSTICE JIM" RIDES AGAIN

A DECADE AS GOVERNOR had left Bill Clinton with a small but dedicated cadre of enemies who regarded his presidential campaign as a chance for revenge or profit. Larry Nichols, Gennifer Flowers, and Cliff Jackson sought publicity as well as money; Sheffield Nelson, who wanted to ingratiate himself with George Bush and run for governor again someday, preferred to remain in the background. In due course, others with similarly mixed motives would emerge to torment Clinton, including the state troopers who had once guarded him, and his former business partner Jim McDougal. All of them were more or less aiming for Clinton's demise, though each of them had once claimed to be a friend of Bill's.

But Clinton had another implacable adversary whose rancor was untainted by greed, a spectral figure who dated back a quarter century to Clinton's earliest involvement in Arkansas politics. Jim Johnson had never pretended to be his friend. Normally concealed behind a courtly public persona, Johnson's rage combined the personal frustrations of a lifetime with a profound ideological passion.

In 1992 Johnson was sixty-eight years old, which meant he was old enough to remember a different Arkansas, especially in the cotton-growing, pineywood flatlands down along the Louisiana border where he was raised, and where the word "nigger" was still a term used in public discourse, and those to whom it applied were often kept forcibly in their place.

For decades, Johnson had struggled to preserve what he revered as the traditional southern way of life. In youth his scowling dark brow and burning glare had given him a threatening appearance; now he looked harmlessly avuncular, his hair snowy white and his narrow eyes squinting behind wire-rims. Denied the power he desired, Johnson had seen the old Arkansas slowly fade away, along with segregated schools, "colored" water fountains, and burning crosses. Bill Clinton was the smooth, smiling face of the New South, where open racism was no longer respectable or even tolerable. Indeed, the governor prided himself on his friendships with blacks and had appointed dozens of black officials. Clinton was the emblem of all that Johnson had lost and of everything that he could not abide.

Their feud carried a sharp personal edge, too, as Johnson would candidly admit. "Clinton boasted that his first political employment was as a campaign worker against me in my campaign for Governor of Arkansas in 1966," he once told an interviewer.

Retired and living outside Little Rock on a farm he had named "White Haven," Johnson had plenty of time and energy to pursue his grudge, and a wealth of contacts amassed during forty years in southern politics. Those who shared his obsessive urge to ruin Clinton seemed drawn to him, as if he were the center of a strange negative universe.

Jim Johnson never achieved the national fame of racial demagogues such as George Wallace, Lester Maddox, and Ross Barnett, but there was a moment when he wielded enough oratorical and organizational power to shake the entire country. In his own misguided way, he was a historic personage. Behind the scenes, it was Johnson who precipitated the 1957 constitutional crisis over the admission of nine black students to Little Rock's Central High School.

Of course, most of the responsibility for the Central High crisis belonged to Orval Faubus, then the governor of Arkansas. After the Little Rock school board voted to integrate Central High, Faubus disregarded a federal court order and called out the Arkansas National Guard to surround the school with guns on September 3, 1957. His defiant action forced President Dwight D. Eisenhower to dispatch the 101st Airborne Division three weeks later to escort the nine terrified children past a mob screaming "Get the niggers!" Faubus pandered to that hatred and embarrassed the United States before the eyes of the civilized world. But it was Johnson, the state's leading professional segregationist, who baited and bullied Faubus into acting while he inflamed the gang of bigots outside the high school.

Without Johnson's incessant goading, Faubus might have accepted the Little Rock school board's token integration plan. Raised in the Ozark Mountains along the Missouri border, Faubus bore blacks no personal ill will. Moderation, however, was unacceptable to Johnson, who had run against Faubus the year before in the Democratic primary, assailing him as a "nigger lover" and advocate of "race mixing."

Johnson's electoral base was the White Citizens Council, a well-financed, middle-class counterpart to the openly violent Ku Klux Klan. He was its founder, its statewide director, and its most spellbinding speaker. In 1950 he had first run for office in his hometown of Crossett, becoming at twenty-six the youngest man ever to win an election to the Arkansas state senate.

Examples of the Johnson style can be found in yellowing copies of *Arkansas Faith,* the "official publication of the White Citizens Council of Arkansas," which he edited and published. Its April 1956 edition, for example, featured a cartoon depicting a tornado labeled "Mongrelization" bearing down on a frightened white mother and her infant child. Another showed Faubus in a butcher's apron, wielding a cleaver labeled "gradualism." On the cutting block in front of him sat a dog with three slices chopped from its tail, labeled "Hoxie," "Fayetteville," and "Charleston"—three northern Arkansas communities which integrated their schools voluntarily. "This will please the niggers and confuse the white folks," the Faubus figure says.

As the opening day of school approached in September 1957, Johnson's group began a deliberate campaign to convince the governor that blood would flow in the streets if a single black enrolled at Central High. Caravans of armed men were rumored to be heading toward Little Rock from all over the state. Decades later, an unrepentant Johnson boasted to Faubus biographer Roy Reed: "There wasn't any caravan. But we made Orval believe it. We said, 'They're lining up. They're coming in droves.'"

The governor's confrontation with Eisenhower transformed Faubus into an icon of resistance and Johnson, who had considered opposing him again in 1958, ran for and won a seat on the state supreme court instead. Thereafter he was known to friend and foe as "Justice Jim." In keeping with his folksy image, Johnson didn't let his lofty new job preclude socializing with old friends. In 1960, an FBI investigation revealed that the judge had met with two men implicated in a terrorist bombing of Little Rock's black Philander Smith College, on the day before they brought the dynamite from Memphis. The accused bombers were, Johnson told the *Arkansas Gazette* a bit defensively, "very fine people."

During his six terms as governor, Orval Faubus grew steadily more reactionary and closer to his old adversary Johnson. In an effort to cripple the civil rights movement and root out "subversives," Faubus sponsored the notorious Act 10, a measure requiring all state employees and schoolteachers to list every organization to which they belonged or contributed financially. Lest white citizens be "tainted" by nonwhite blood transfusions, another law required the racial labeling of blood supplies. And while the Arkansas State Police ignored wide-open casino gambling in Hot Springs, its Criminal Investigation Division became a veritable redneck intelligence agency, devoting extraordinary resources to spying for Faubus.

"In pursuit of its mission," Roy Reed recounts, "the CID infiltrated organizations, tapped telephones, secretly tape-recorded meetings . . . and collected damaging personal information on political opponents and seemingly ordinary citizens. The gumshoes were especially alert for signs of adultery and homosexuality." Sharing information with similar agencies like the Mississippi Sovereignty Commission, the Arkansas state police spies functioned, in effect, as an investigative arm of the White Citizens Council. The heirs of this apparatus would one day be employed to probe the private life of Bill Clinton, who was only eleven years old at the time of the Central High incident.

By the time Faubus stepped down in 1966, Clinton was old enough to take an active part in the election of his successor—a watershed event that permanently changed Arkansas politics. Jim Johnson was back, running as a "states' rights" candidate for the Democratic gubernatorial nomination. Early in the campaign, he made a point of refusing to shake black voters' hands. His speeches decried integration as a Communist plot and "a worse crime than rape or murder."

To a college student inspired by the civil rights movement, the notion of "Justice Jim" as governor was beyond appalling. Clinton rushed home from Georgetown University that summer to work for Frank Holt, Johnson's leading Democratic opponent and former colleague on the state supreme court. His job was to drive Holt's wife and college-age daughters to campaign stops. While traveling with the Holt women, Clinton was shocked to discover the continuing shadow of Jim Crow in Johnson's native region. As he wrote to a girlfriend back at Georgetown, "Now we are campaigning in the heart of cotton country, south and east Arkansas where Negroes are still niggers. And I couldn't believe my eyes when I saw restrooms and waiting rooms still marked in Colored and White. It made me so sick to my stomach."

More sickening to the young Clinton was Johnson's upset victory in a Democratic runoff against Holt. The Republicans nominated civic activist Winthrop Paul Rockefeller, a scion of one of America's wealthiest families, to face Johnson in the general election. For years, Johnson had been attacking Rockefeller in *Arkansas Faith* for "opening his big fat mouth in public with unwanted advice . . . on the great race-mixing experiment." Now he sprayed his rich Yankee opponent with pure poison. In stump speeches Johnson lashed out at Rockefeller as a "prissy sissy" and a "Santa Gertrudis steer." His campaign distributed pamphlets which depicted Rockefeller as a drunken thief and a pornographer who indulged in sodomy with black men. (That Rockefeller was a heavy drinker was well known; he had also been married three times.)

In the run-up to Election Day, Johnson was endorsed by the Grand Dragon of the Ku Klux Klan at a public rally in the southeast Arkansas town of Star City. Garbed in white robes and illuminated by a flaming cross, one speaker after another warned against the Jewish–Communist–civil rights conspiracy. "The Klan has come out for Lurleen Wallace [in Alabama], Lester Maddox [in Georgia], and Jim Johnson," the Klan leader bragged, "and we're electing them one by one." Johnson never did repudiate the Klan's support.

Aroused by the Johnson threat, moderate white Democrats and newly enfranchised blacks almost unanimously supported Rockefeller, making him the state's first Republican governor since the Civil War. An editorial in the *Arkansas Gazette,* which had survived a White Citizen's Council boycott and earned two Pulitzer Prizes for editorials urging obedience to federal law during the Central High crisis, hailed voters for rejecting "the vacuous demagoguery that Mr. Johnson brought in his campaign, with all the name-calling, innuendo, distortions, and appeals to fear. They have spurned the smear literature and character vilification."

Two years later, Johnson entered the Democratic primary against Senator J. William Fulbright. This time he yoked his candidacy to the populist, white-power crusade of George Wallace, who was running for president on the American Independent Party line. Johnson escorted the Alabama governor on his swings through Arkansas, while attacking Fulbright—"the pinup boy of Hanoi"—for his opposition to the war in Vietnam.

The 1968 campaign afforded Johnson his first glimpse of Bill Clinton, who after graduating from Georgetown came home again, this time to help Fulbright. The talkative young aide chauffeured the senator around Arkansas, much as he had done in the Holt campaign, and meanwhile forged a relationship with James McDougal, the veteran pol and charming raconteur who ran Fulbright's Little Rock office.

One afternoon, Clinton drove out into the countryside with a college buddy to hear Johnson address a group of farmers. Enraged by Johnson's racist rant, Clinton stayed to confront the former judge after his speech. When they shook hands Clinton blurted, "You make me ashamed to be from Arkansas." Many years later, at a conservative meeting in Washington, Johnson would express precisely the same emotion about Clinton in less delicate terms, voicing his regret that his beloved state had produced "a president of the United States who is a queer-mongering, whore-hopping adulterer; a baby-killing, draft-dodging, dope-tolerating, lying, two-faced, treasonist activist."

The venerable Fulbright defeated Johnson in the 1968 Democratic primary. And although George Wallace took Arkansas's electoral votes in a three-way contest with Hubert Humphrey and Richard Nixon, the segregationist bloc was isolated permanently below 40 percent. No overtly racist candidate ever won another statewide election in Arkansas, which meant that Johnson's political career was finished.

After Win Rockefeller lost his bid for a third term in 1970, the new dispensation belonged to moderate Democrats such as Dale Bumpers, David Pryor, and Bill Clinton, their dominance assured by broad support across racial lines. Johnson's crowd gradually faded from the scene; they toned down their rhetoric, and ultimately abandoned the Democratic Party for the Republican religious right. Like any subdued minority, they resented the winners, and because Clinton beat them more often than anybody else, winning six statewide contests between 1978 and 1990, they resented him most.

During Clinton's final term as governor, he erased Johnson's legacy forever by successfully campaigning for an amendment that stripped the last vestiges of statutory racism from the Arkansas lawbooks and the state constitution.

Legally sanctioned segregation vanished from the South, but the impulse behind it was slower to disappear. The politics of race baiting in America was a slightly more refined art by the time Jim Johnson encountered its foremost contemporary practitioner. Actually, Johnson had encountered Floyd Brown—auteur of the most inflammatory television spot in recent history—before the "Willie Horton ad" made Brown infamous. They had met several months earlier, during the 1988 presidential primary season, when Brown was organizing five midwestern and southern states for Bob Dole and hired Johnson's daughter-in-law to work for Dole in Arkansas.

The aging segregationist and the young conservative quickly formed a lasting bond. Even though Brown didn't endorse all of Johnson's poisonous racial opinions, he and the judge agreed politically more than they disagreed. Both relished the intrigue of opposition research and the combat of negative campaigning. And the candidacy of Bill Clinton brought them even closer.

Boisterous, barrel-chested, and six feet six inches tall, Brown earned his status as a political pariah during the final weeks of the 1988 presidential campaign, when the Horton ad was unveiled. Its appeal to white fear was so blatant that even Lee Atwater considered it embarrassing.

Produced by an independent political committee called Americans for Bush, which listed Brown as "senior political consultant," the ad only aired briefly in a few markets, but it became an instant classic of its genre. Just as Brown expected, the ad's mere existence drew saturation coverage from the mainstream media. The brash Brown loved to boast about this coup, and years later claimed credit for it in his official résumé on the Citizens United Web site.

As a video production, the Horton ad was as primitive as its message. It opened with head shots of George Bush and Michael Dukakis as the voiceover recited, "Bush and Dukakis on crime." Noting that Bush "supports the death penalty for first-degree murderers," the announcer then remarked, "Dukakis not only opposes the death penalty, he allowed first-degree murderers to have weekend passes from prison."

Up came the scary mug shot of a stereotypical urban marauder, sullen and scruffy-looking with a bushy, uncombed Afro. "One was Willie Horton, who murdered a boy in a robbery, stabbing him nineteen times. Despite a life sentence, Horton received ten weekend passes from prison." The Dukakis head shot appeared again as the solemn voice concluded: "Weekend prison passes. Dukakis on crime."

That mug shot was reproduced millions of times before Election Day, in print and on television. Brown's cheap, blunt thirty-second ad dealt a virtual deathblow to the inept Dukakis. As Brown put it gleefully, the Horton ad was the "silver bullet" that destroyed the Democratic nominee.

The Horton episode proved lucrative as well as lethal. Behind Americans for Bush was the National Security Political Action Committee, an outfit founded by conservative activist Elizabeth Fediay, daughter of a close associate of Senator Jesse Helms. Between 1986 and 1988, the NSPAC raised over $9 million through direct-mail and telemarketing appeals. Twice the Bush campaign complained to the Federal Election Commission that the NSPAC was misusing the Republican nominee's name to enrich the group.

Brown knew better than to take those complaints seriously. As he pointed out to a *New York Times* reporter, the Bush campaign officials had waited until the Horton commercial's run on cable TV was nearly complete before they requested that the NSPAC quit raising money under the name of Americans for Bush. "If they were really interested in stopping this, do you think they would have waited that long to send us a letter?" he asked sardonically.

Two years later, allegations of collusion between Americans for Bush and the official Bush campaign emerged. In February 1990, the *New Republic* reported that business associates of Bush media consultant Roger Ailes had worked on the Horton ad with Brown. Democratic Party officials quickly filed charges of unlawful cooperation between the NSPAC and Bush-Quayle '88 with the Federal Election Commission. Although Ailes and his former employees denied any collusion, the FEC opened a formal investigation. But the FEC's Republican members succeeded in killing the Horton probe two years later, just in time for the '92 election.

By then Floyd Brown was launching a new operation, called the Presidential Victory Committee—a subsidiary of Citizens United, the political action group he had set up in November 1988. Brown had seen what he could do at the NSPAC, and gone into business for himself.

Anyone examining Floyd Brown's background would hardly have predicted his career as a professional right-winger. He had grown up in the Pacific Northwest as the son of a Democratic sawmill worker and, more remarkably, the grandson of a member of the Industrial Workers of the World, those free-wheeling anarcho-socialists better known as the Wobblies. It was as a student at the University of Washington that Brown veered sharply rightward, becoming an activist in the ultraconservative Young Americans for Freedom. In 1983, he was arrested demonstrating in front of the Soviet embassy in Washington, D.C. A gifted, tireless organizer with a quick wit, he was elected national vice chairman of the YAF, which funneled bright young activists into the Republican Party and the conservative movement.

The managers of Bob Dole's 1988 presidential bid hired Brown to oversee their Midwest primary campaign. He produced victories in five states before Dole finally dropped out of the rough race against Bush, but Brown had been shunned by the Bush-Quayle campaign. Then Fediay brought him into the NSPAC.

In 1988 Brown also acquired a stocky, crew-cut young sidekick named David Bossie. Like Brown, Bossie had been a campus conservative, joining the College Republicans at the University of Maryland. As a freshman he had been an enthusiastic volunteer in Ronald Reagan's 1984 reelection campaign, and he eventually dropped out for full-time political work. He never went back to school.

Working nights and weekends as a volunteer fireman in suburban Montgomery County, Bossie slept at the firehouse and knocked around in the low-paid world of Beltway conservatism until 1991, when Brown brought him into Citizens United as "chief investigator." While both were clever and ideologically driven, the dogged, low-key Bossie complemented his articulate, publicity-loving boss, who sometimes spoke of himself in the third person.

Typically, Brown was full of ambitious ideas for the Presidential Victory Committee. He intended to create a Horton-style ad using the Gennifer Flowers tapes—only this time, the ad itself would generate money with a 900 telephone number. Callers would be charged by the minute to listen to suggestive excerpts of the tapes. Beyond that, Brown planned to write and publish *Slick Willie: Why America Cannot Trust Bill Clinton,* a 150-page paperback book about Clinton's personal life and his record as governor. When he and Bossie arrived in Arkansas seeking the silver bullet, their first stop was Jim Johnson's White Haven.

Johnson offered historical guidance while his son Mark, a former congressional aide who hosted a Rush Limbaugh–style local radio program in Little Rock, chauffeured Brown and Bossie around the state, dredging up tales of Clinton's alleged libertinism, radicalism, and corruption. They spent hours consulting with Sheffield Nelson at his Little Rock law offices, which became their informal headquarters in the city.

In April, just as Clinton secured the Democratic nomination by winning the New York Democratic primary, Floyd Brown received an anonymous letter from Texas about a woman named Susann Coleman. (The same letter was sent to many news organizations around the same time.) Coleman had committed suicide with a shotgun in 1977. At the time of her death she was almost eight months pregnant. According to the letter, the baby was Bill Clinton's: "She spoke of her husband and how he'd been destroyed by her infidelity . . . She spoke of her love for Bill Clinton. . . . She condemned herself for being an obstruction to Clinton's high ambitions. She died for them."

Bossie, the twenty-six-year-old amateur sleuth, took over the task of tracking down this tantalizing lead. As the investigation progressed, Bossie often relied on Jim Johnson, who knew one or two ancillary figures in the case. They did establish that Susann Coleman had been a student of Clinton's when he taught at the University of Arkansas Law School, but could find no evidence of intimacy, let alone an illegitimate pregnancy. Coleman's widower refused to discuss his wife's suicide or her suicide note. Members of her family wouldn't talk much, either. As Bossie suspected, they had been reached first by the Clinton campaign, whose detective Jack Palladino had been monitoring Citizens United.

In May, Bossie found Coleman's mother in Georgia, where she had gone to visit her second husband in an army hospital while he recovered from a stroke. He tailed her to the hospital, eluded hospital security, and burst into the sickroom firing questions. Susann's stunned mother said little, except that "Clinton is not the father of Susann's baby."

It was Susann's sister, Lorna Lindsey, who seemed most hostile, demanding proof of Bossie's identity when Bossie called her at her home in South Carolina. Lindsey informed Bossie that she intended to advise her mother not to speak with him or anyone else from the Presidential Victory Committee.

When he reached Lindsey again, she wasn't forthcoming. Growing angry, Brown blurted out a wild accusation about why there had been no police investigation of Susann's death. "Possibly because one of your cousins, who was a police officer at the time, took care of it? . . . I won't stop this investigation," he warned. If his suspicions proved true, Brown added, he would dispatch attorneys to "meet with Clinton and tell him to get out of the race."

Despite Brown's blustering, Bossie finally filed a report acknowledging that he could find "no proof to support this letters [sic] allegations . . . [T]his case is closed."

But it wasn't entirely closed. Lindsey had recorded her second conversation with Brown and turned the tape over to the Clinton campaign, which made it available to CBS correspondent Eric Engberg. In mid-July, as Brown began running his Gennifer Flowers infomercial, Engberg aired a blistering report on the *CBS Evening News* about the Presidential Victory Committee.

Calling the Coleman affair "an unusually brazen dirty tricks operation," Engberg reminded viewers about Brown's authorship of the "notorious Willie

Horton ad of 1988." On camera, he interviewed a friend of Susann's family who said that Bossie had "peered" into the windows of her home when she was out. He described the hospital intrusion and played excerpts from Brown's sneering phone call to Lindsey.

"The Bush campaign, referring to Brown and his associates as the 'lowest forms of life,' today branded their tactics as 'despicable,'" the correspondent intoned, noting, however, that Bush lawyers had yet to file a complaint against Brown's committee with the Federal Election Commission.

However repellent Brown's tactics may have seemed to Bush, the president had more pragmatic reasons for preferring not to dwell on the infidelity issue. When the Democratic convention delegates filed into Madison Square Garden to nominate Clinton in late July, they found on their seats the new issue of the cheeky *Spy* magazine—whose cover blared "1000 Reasons Not to Vote for George Bush; No. 1: He Cheats on His Wife." The article within didn't justify that sensationally conclusive headline, but examined in some detail the rumors and facts surrounding Bush's alleged relationships with other women. There were reasons why some might believe Bush had strayed, including his angry reply to a question about adultery during a mock debate in 1988: "None of your damn business!" In an exclusive convention interview with *Time*, Clinton pointed to the *Spy* article as an early warning to the Bush camp. In the weeks that followed, the *New York Post* and *Vanity Fair* also referred to the president's alleged extramarital affairs.

Floyd Brown didn't care what the Bush campaign said about him, his Flowers commercial, or his tasteless exploitation of the adultery issue, any more than he had cared what they said about his Willie Horton blitz. He feigned outrage at the CBS attack, but friends thought he was privately pleased to renew his reputation as a political hit man. By late July he and Bossie were trying to finish *Slick Willie,* although additions were still possible before publication in mid-September. An unwieldy farrago of fact, exaggeration, and sheer invention, the book charged Clinton with dodging the draft, raising taxes, coddling blacks, chasing women, corrupting state agencies, flip-flopping on abortion, awarding special privileges to gays, promoting secularism (and witchcraft!), wrecking the school system, flirting with socialism, and, in its stirring final chapter, blaspheming the Lord with his campaign slogan of a "New Covenant" between citizens and government. Readers who detected a whiff of earlier anti-Clinton campaigns would not be surprised to see in the acknowledgments a "special thanks" to "Judge Jim Johnson."

Included in the lengthy appendixes were carefully edited excerpts from the Gennifer Flowers tapes. The chapter on Susann Coleman substituted innuendo for evidence: "As long as her family refuses to enlighten the public . . . we won't know why this woman, seven months pregnant, had her head blown off. . . . Why was there no autopsy? And who was the father of that unborn child? These questions remain unanswered, but Bill Clinton's hirelings are working day and night to keep them a mystery."

Brown was too sophisticated to imagine that *Slick Willie*—a novelty item designed for marketing to far-right mailing lists—would sway more than a handful of voters. At $8.95 a copy, the little paperback might bring in some money, but it was loaded with blanks, not silver bullets. As he prepared the book for publication, he told Jim Johnson that more and better material would be needed to beat Clinton. Johnson suggested a meeting with Larry Nichols, the man who had first exposed the Flowers affair. In fact, Nichols had been pestering Brown for months—but it was only after Johnson vouched for him that Brown agreed to meet with the gravel-voiced huckster.

When Brown invited Nichols to come to Washington for a meeting, Nichols convinced him that Larry Case should come too. Case said he had damning videotapes from Roger Clinton's cocaine prosecution that the mainstream media wouldn't touch, an audiotape of a prostitute talking about an affair with Bill Clinton, and much more, all for sale.

On August 7, Case and Nichols flew to Washington first-class at Citizens United's expense. After spending the evening at a Georgetown "titty bar" that still excited Case months later, the two showed up at Brown's office in suburban Fairfax, Virginia, lugging bags of documents and tapes. Present at the meeting, along with Brown and Bossie, was Deborah Stone, sole editor and publisher of Annapolis-Washington Book Publishers, which had been set up specifically to bring out *Slick Willie.*

Stone was a blunt and sometimes abrasive woman in her mid-twenties who had found her way into Beltway conservatism via the *Dartmouth Review.* She had been the editor of the controversial monthly when its staff made national news in 1986 by taking up axes and sledgehammers to tear down an anti-apartheid protest shanty on campus. On another occasion, they had secretly taped meetings of Dartmouth gays and outed several fellow students. This breach of civility, as well as the *Review's* racially divisive editorials and cartoons, had drawn a suspension and sharp criticism from university officials— but Debbie Stone had never seen any reason to apologize.

The meeting could not begin until the arrival of a surprise guest: John Fund of the *Wall Street Journal* editorial page. An intense, mid-thirtyish devotee of Ayn Rand who served as the *Journal's* unofficial emissary to the Republican right, Fund was more activist than journalist. He ghosted one of Rush Limbaugh's books and spoke frequently at conservative events. Fund was a particular favorite of *Journal* editor Robert Bartley, whose approach to editorial policy could be politely described as dogmatic. Dissatisfied with the *Journal's* straight approach to reporting, Bartley created what his staff called "the reportive editorial," including long investigative essays free of the constraints that governed the news section.

Earlier that year, Debbie Stone had edited a book by Fund for Regnery Publishing, and he had been advising her on research for *Slick Willie*. (He came to the meeting solely for journalistic reasons, Fund later recalled, "to find out more about Bill Clinton.")

When Fund at last did show up, Nichols and Case began to present their wares. If Brown had known Case any better, he would have suspected that Case was secretly taping the meeting.

Possibly hoping to start a bidding war, Nichols suggested that he and Case might take their anti-Clinton material to the Republican National Committee or even directly to the Bush campaign, a notion Stone and Fund both dismissed as silly. "Larry, you're not going to get anywhere with the RNC or George Bush," said Stone.

"You can either believe us or not believe us," Fund chimed in. "They'll have more to do with Abu Nidal than with you."

Nichols and Case didn't seem to get Fund's joking reference to a notorious Palestinian terrorist. "What?" said Case. Fund repeated himself, provoking nervous laughter. Stone moved briskly on to business, eager to examine the merchandise. "What are the videotapes of?"

"I have one video," Case said in his Arkansas drawl, "where he's settin' up a bribe and a payoff between a contractor in Hot Springs and his brother. . . ."

"Roger Clinton?" asked Stone. "And his brother. . . . ?"

"Bill Clinton."

"Has anybody in the news media seen this?" Fund wanted to know. "Not this one," Case lied. He had been trying to peddle all his tapes to major media outlets and tabloid TV shows for months.

"And you have a tape," Stone broke in.

"I have a videotape of it. Now I've got the one of him doing the cocaine and all that stuff, but people have seen that. . . ."

"Is CBS gonna use this?" Stone asked.

"Nobody's seen this," Case said. "I've been runnin' it today to get it up, and I haven't got it yet, but it's on there."

"You mean it's not cued up yet?" Stone asked, a note of petulance creeping into her voice. "Can we cue it up now?"

"Sure."

But as the television droned on—the tape's sound and picture quality dismally poor, as is often true of surveillance tapes—the only thing getting clearer was that Case had no idea where to find the vaunted "bribe" segment.

Meanwhile, Stone sounded concerned about Case's contacts with other media organizations. The private eye said he had told "everything" to a TV reporter, prompting another peevish outburst. "What do you mean, everything?" cried Stone. "Not what you've been telling us—Michelle, Louwanda, Denise . . . ?"

She naturally wanted exclusive rights to "Louwanda and Michelle"—the pair of prostitutes Case had taped talking about Clinton—as well as "Denise," supposed recipient of the handwritten note bearing Clinton's signature that sought forgiveness for physically abusing her.

"I used her maiden name," said Case reassuringly.

Nothing interesting seemed to be happening on the videotape, and Stone grew impatient. "What are we looking for on this tape again? The bribe?" she demanded. "Yeah," said Case, "the bribe is on one of these tapes." He paused. "I have the bribe, but I don't remember which one it's on. . . ."

"And why is that significant?" Stone snapped. "What's the bribe?"

"I think it's significant because he's setting up a bribe between a contractor in Hot Springs, to sign a contract on a sewer deal, between him and his brother," Case answered smoothly.

The discussion turned to Roger Clinton's jail term, and Nichols's false allegation that the governor had pardoned Dan Lasater, an investment banker and Clinton contributor who also had been convicted of giving away cocaine at parties. Lasater in fact had been convicted of a federal crime; Clinton had no authority to pardon him. The governor had, however, approved a waiver allowing the state Game and Fish Commission to sell Lasater a deer-hunting license.

"I bet if he wins the election, he'll pardon his brother," Fund remarked.

The tape droned on. "Can you fast-forward this?" barked Stone. "I don't know what to look for," said someone else. That was when Case admitted, "I don't even know if [the bribe] is on this one or not."

For more than an hour, Stone, Bossie, Brown, and Fund listened patiently as Larry Nichols rambled on about his grievances against Clinton, his theories about Gennifer Flowers and other alleged paramours of the Democratic nominee, Clinton's rumored illegitimate children, Nichols's aborted lawsuit against Clinton, and his unsuccessful attempt to negotiate a cash "settlement" from the Clinton campaign. Among other absurdities, Nichols accused the Democratic candidate of complicity in the unsolved homicide of a Little Rock swimming pool manufacturer for which the man's wife was later arrested. His listeners weren't learning anything they needed to know, but they played captive audience to his passionate soliloquy. If treated with deference, Case and Nichols might produce something. From time to time, however, Stone couldn't stifle a yawn.

Finally, Nichols got around to mentioning a videotape of Bill Clinton entering Gennifer Flowers's apartment, made by her neighbor. His bored audience suddenly woke up. "There's also tapes from cameras at the front door," said Bossie hopefully. He wondered how the dim apartment hallway had been taped. "Because I was in that hallway where Gennifer Flowers lived . . ."

"And where's this tape now?" Stone inquired.

"Guy's got it and I can't get hold of it," admitted Nichols.

"Where is he? Can we talk to anybody?" asked Stone. That tape would never turn up either.

Case and Nichols returned to Arkansas without a firm deal, but Brown said they would be in touch.

The list of participants at the Virginia meeting puzzled Bill Rempel. Trying to check out his potential customers, Case had called his friend at the *Los Angeles Times* for advice.

"What were they all doing in the same room?" Rempel asked. "You've got journalists there, supposedly, you've got political operatives. . . ."

"You've got Dave, you've got Floyd," Case recited, "and John Fund, who, he said, works for the *Wall Street Journal*."

Rempel offered to perform a Nexis search on the names Case gave him to determine their identities. Later the same afternoon he called back with the results, which perplexed Rempel even more.

"John H. Fund is an editorial writer for the *Wall Street Journal*," he told Case. "That makes it all the more curious why he was there. Deborah Stone is spokeswoman for the Republican National Coalition for Life, which is, I presume, an antiabortion outfit. David Bossie is executive director of the Presidential Victory Committee, which is Floyd Brown's PAC. Floyd's the front man on it, that's for sure. . . ."

"Is there any truth to this Debbie Stone's being backed by the Republicans? Does this group of people sound legitimate to you?"

"Who knows? Certainly the Republican National Coalition for Life is a right-wing organization." (Actually, the Coalition is a pressure group founded by former John Birch Society leader Phyllis Schlafly to ensure party purity on the abortion issue.)

Case was confused. "What would she get involved in something like this for?"

"Well, that's the mystery. I don't get that either. What's the *Wall Street Journal* guy doing there?" Rempel asked.

"That would be borderline unethical as a journalist, I would think," Case ventured.

"Borderline ain't the word. It's right over the edge. It's in free fall," the reporter said.

Case perked up. "So who can I sell that story to?"

Rempel laughed. "I don't know that it has any monetary value. . . . Did Fund seem uncomfortable being there?" he asked.

"I don't know." Now Case was laughing. "If that sumbitch knew me, he should have been."

Irresistibly tempted by Louwanda, Michelle, and other possible victims of Clinton's lust, Floyd Brown and his colleagues finally made Case a cash offer. Unaware that the burly detective had already tried and failed to peddle the same tales to the *Los Angeles Times*, NBC News, and the tabloid TV program *A Current Affair*, Citizens United agreed to pay him $10,000 for access to the videotapes and the talkative hookers.

In early September, Stone and Bossie agreed to meet Case at the Little Rock airport. Together the trio would fly to Phoenix, Arizona, where, Case said, he had an associate who had the evidence about Michelle and Louwanda. In reality, he had been trying for several weeks to persuade Bill Rempel to give him the name of the *Los Angeles Times*'s original source on the Oklahoma City hookers. He did know that Rempel's source had also talked to a Phoenix TV station. Whether Case ever intended to lure the Citizens United crew all the way to Arizona on so thin a pretext isn't clear.

As they prepared to board the plane in Little Rock, however, a farcical fracas erupted. Case suddenly accused Bossie and Stone of trying to abscond with his bags. Shouting obscenities in the crowded airport, he demanded payment of the $10,000 immediately, rather than the following day as agreed.

"Get on the airplane," Stone urged, according to Case's later recollection. "I'll give you $1,000 if you get on the airplane." He wasn't going anywhere for less than $10,000. Case said later that he pushed Bossie aside to get his bags. Bossie claimed that Case punched him in the face, and swore out a police report seeking his arrest. Case told the cops that Stone and Bossie had stolen documents from him valued at $1.5 million and threatened to kill him. He then called various media outlets, Floyd Brown later wrote, "in an attempt to plant a story implicating Miss Stone's and Mr. Bossie's research tactics as scandalous."

When Brown hired a handwriting expert to examine the "Denise" note he learned, like the tabloids before him, that it was a cut-and-pasted fake. In the introduction to *Slick Willie* he suggested that Case was a double agent working for Clinton. In reality, Case was a double agent working for Case. Within days of the airport altercation, Case was bragging to reporters that he'd "slapped the shit out of Bossie," and brooding about how to turn a profit by "exposing" Citizens United.

As Floyd Brown fumed over Case's treachery, the detective and his partner paused to consider their options. By late September, with Clinton's victory over Bush seemingly assured, Nichols and Case were worried. What if Clinton were to exact vengeance upon his Arkansas enemies? In a phone conversation taped by Case, the pair discussed the grim prospect of President Clinton.

"Bill Clinton's got the short course to the White House," Nichols fretted. "Hell, he could stop right now and not do nothin' else. He ain't gotta spend another fuckin' nickel. All he's gotta do is just say he's still running, and I believe he's in."

"Yeah, and you know where we're at. We're behind the eight ball," said Case glumly.

"We're the people that when he gets in, he's gonna be pissed at us," Nichols agreed. "And we're the people that if he don't get in by some quirk of fate, we're gonna get blamed for it. Now if I'm gonna get blamed for something, I'd damn sure like to do it, is my problem. And it wouldn't hurt to be set up financially to where whatever they did couldn't affect me. Now that's just me talking, because it damn sure ain't gonna happen."

Case, however, was mulling a contingency plan. "What the hell would they do," he asked Nichols, "if you brought the Republicans in now? What would the Republicans do to you?'

"What the hell can they do? They ain't gonna be in power."

"You think you could roll Bob Leslie?" Leslie was then chairman of the Arkansas Republican Party.

"I know I could," said Nichols.

"You got a paper trail on everybody?"

"Sure do." Nichols proceeded to name as his collaborators in smearing Clinton virtually every important Republican in Arkansas, and claimed to have documentation to prove it. While reluctant to make new enemies, he'd consider turning for the right price.

"You'd be amazed at who I've got on that phone," he chortled. "You'd be amazed at the phone numbers on there."

"You got [Sheffield] Nelson on there?"

"You bet. Home and office."

"Well, we could sure tie them into it, from here on up to Washington, if we really wanted to," said Case. "The way I look at it, Larry, if you're gonna be blamed for it, get paid for it. Shit, it's to the point now where, you know, I'm open. I'm open for business. You and me both."

Chapter Six

A PIG
IN A POKE

SOMETIME DURING the late afternoon of July 20, 1993, deputy White House counsel Vincent Foster left his office, drove across the Potomac River to Fort Marcy Park, sat down on a grassy hillside, put an old revolver in his mouth, and pulled the trigger. His body was discovered at 5:45 P.M. by officers from the U.S. Park Service police, who treated the incident from the very first as a routine investigation, made politically sensitive only later by the identity of the victim. Despite the incessant promotion ever since of strange theories about Foster's death—ranging from a soured affair with Hillary Clinton to a hit by an Israeli spy ring—that initial Park Police report was eventually substantiated by five separate federal investigations, two performed by independent counsels Robert Fiske and Kenneth Starr. All concurred in a finding of suicide caused by clinical depression.

Still, the notion persisted that Foster had died because he "knew too much," as did speculation about the Little Rock lawyer's possible reasons for killing himself or being killed by someone else. Foster, a close confidant and former law partner of Hillary Clinton, had certainly endured a series of embarrassing events during the final few months of his life. A shredded note found in Foster's briefcase, apparently jotted down not long before his death, indicated how worried he felt about his role in the wholesale firing of the White House Travel Office staff two months earlier, and the criticism directed at him and the Clintons in that ugly incident's wake.

"I made mistakes from ignorance, inexperience and overwork," he wrote in small, neat longhand on a yellow legal pad. "I did not knowingly violate any law or standard of conduct. No one in the White House, to my knowledge, violated any law or standard of conduct, including any action in the travel office. . . . The FBI lied. . . . The press is covering up the illegal benefits they received from the travel staff. The GOP has lied and misrepresented its knowledge and role and covered up a prior investigation. . . . The public will never believe the innocence of the Clintons and their loyal staff. The (*Wall Street Journal*) editors lie without consequence. I was not meant for the job or the spotlight of public life in Washington. Here ruining people is considered sport."

Foster's terse, bitter note expressed the anguish of an administration embattled almost from the moment President Clinton took the oath of office. The Clinton White House had enjoyed no postinaugural honeymoon. Clinton and his novice staff suffered one stumble after another, to the grim delight of a Washington press corps perpetually suspicious of newcomers. That the Clintons came from Arkansas, a small state remote from the nation's centers of power and little known to most Washington journalists, did nothing to lighten the atmosphere.

Undoubtedly, the Washington press corps distorted the Travel Office story, and did so partly out of self-serving bias. They largely failed to report allegations of mismanagement and malfeasance by Travel Office director Billy Dale. His attempt to plea-bargain the criminal charges also received little press coverage, and his subsequent trial was completely ignored until he was acquitted. The prosecution's case against Dale, which offered evidence that over $50,000 in Travel Office funds had been funneled to his personal bank account, went unreported. As Foster's note suggested, many in the White House press corps had journalistic conflicts in covering a trial of a defendant from whom they had garnered past favors. A few, notably ABC News correspondent Sam Donaldson, went so far as to volunteer their testimony as character witnesses at Dale's trial.

Yet the defensive tone of Foster's note suggests he may have realized that the Travel Office furor was not altogether unjustified. The office's seven career employees were dismissed with undue haste, unnecessary clumsiness, and an unbecoming disregard for their rights. And while the stated desire of low-level Clinton aides was to "reform" the Travel Office, that hardly concealed their own patently selfish motives. Moreover, White House lawyers and communications officials, led by presidential assistant George Stephanopoulos, had compounded the damage by publicly announcing the FBI investigation of the Travel Office to justify the firings.

As Washington scandals go, however, "Travelgate" was a minor affair, too minor to make Foster take his own life. Not all suicides have rational causes, particularly when the victim suffers from depression. Doubts were nevertheless aroused by the discovery of an odd coincidence: On the same day Vince

Foster shot himself, the Little Rock office of the FBI obtained a search warrant for the premises of one David Hale, a local businessman and part-time municipal judge.

The Hale search warrant became an issue in the Foster investigation only long after the fact because of sensational charges later leveled by Hale against Clinton, whom he accused of having "pressured" him into making an illicit $300,000 loan to James and Susan McDougal in 1986. Those who drew a connection between Whitewater and Foster's death surmised that the deputy White House counsel, possessing intimate knowledge of the Clintons' tangled finances, feared whatever might be found in Hale's office. In sworn testimony before the Senate Whitewater committee, however, FBI officials testified that after investigating the matter, they "could find no reason to believe that there was information leaked with regard to the [Hale] search warrant." Nor did FBI agents ever find evidence to incriminate the Clintons in Hale's files.

But that didn't mean there was no reason to worry about David Hale.

Far from the Washington Beltway, the Foster suicide also aroused the investigative and pecuniary instincts of Larry Nichols and Larry Case. Unsurprisingly, they assumed the case was all about sex, specifically Foster's long-rumored love affair with Hillary Clinton.

This kind of sniping, explained Webster Hubbell in his memoir *Friends in High Places,* came with the territory Hillary had staked out for herself in Arkansas. Because Hillary was the first female partner in the upper-crust Rose Law Firm, her close professional and personal relationships with Foster and Hubbell provoked resentment in the tightly knit community surrounding the Little Rock Country Club. The governor's wife was an inevitable focus of gossip, and everything she did provoked idle chatter. If Hubbell and Foster were sometimes said to be her lovers, at other moments her friendships with other professional women provoked speculation that Hillary was actually a lesbian.

Nobody who knew the painfully reserved Foster well ever gave any credence to his supposed liaison with Hillary. Certainly his widow, Lisa, didn't believe it. But the skeptics didn't include detective Larry Case, who saw an opportunity to get back in business. He and Nichols had never acted on their preelection impulse to turn on their Republican sponsors, and their jitters about Clintonian revenge had proved unfounded. With Clinton in the White House, they were still hoping to make their fortunes by ruining his reputation.

Nichols had a theory of his own about Foster's death. He told Case he had heard it from Michael Isikoff of the *Washington Post,* who called to ask him whether it was true that two White House officials were trying to muzzle Nichols about a tape recording he had made in 1990 of Rose Law Firm employees gossiping about Foster and Hillary. Even Nichols knew the tape was worthless.

"Whoever you talked to at the Rose Law Firm," Case asked, "did they name Vince Foster and Hillary?"

"Yeah, they did," Nichols said. "Named troopers that took them over there. But again, if [Larry] Patterson and those guys [in the Clintons' former security detail] don't talk, then it don't mean nothing. . . . Isikoff, bless his heart, I was almost rude to him. I don't mean to be. But today, I just didn't need that shit. What Isikoff was telling me was that he knows for a fact from a senior White House official that they're trying to cool me. Now who else are they calling and cooling off? And if so, why?"

A few days later, Nichols was feeling a bit more sanguine. He claimed to have pieced together the inside story from conversations with Isikoff and Jerry Seper, an investigative reporter for the *Washington Times*. According to Nichols, Foster had taken his life due to a mistaken belief that the *Washington Times* was about to publish a story about his alleged affair with Hillary Clinton. In truth, the Moonie newspaper had no such story in the works.

"I just feel bad for Vince," Nichols said. "That was a stupid thing to do when nothing was happening. . . . Foster killed himself for nothing, and they went into all this damage control for a story that was never going to come."

Despite having spent a good deal of time with Isikoff during the 1992 campaign, Nichols didn't trust the *Post* reporter.

"I'm telling you," he warned Case, "Isikoff's a snake."

"Oh, I know what he can do."

"Everything Isikoff was telling me," Nichols said, "I was real guarded, because I figured he was just fishing for Clinton. But I'd sure like to be in the middle of this one. You and I can do shit the media can't do. We can lie, and get the information, and then give it to the media. I don't know why the media don't figure this out. You walk up to somebody and flash your *New York Times* ID, they're going to clam up. If you go out and get them drunk, you don't even have to wire yourself. Just take a little pocket recorder. You can get all you need. . . ."

At that moment, Larry Case had no way of knowing that the Foster suicide and its aftermath would soon provide his erstwhile partner Nichols with a means of transcending the niggling constraints of the news media and making real money. Isikoff would likewise go on to much greater things. But to his immense frustration, Case and his ever-present tape recorder would be left far behind.

When a squad of FBI agents burst into the offices of Capital Management Services (CMS) in downtown Little Rock on July 21, 1993, and started carrying out boxes of files, their arrival ended several weeks of suspense for the company's proprietor, David Hale. While sitting as a judge in the city's municipal court, Hale had continued to operate several enterprises, the most lucrative being Capital Management Services, a private small business investment company (SBIC) that made loans backed by the U.S. Small Business Administration. With SBA funding and a license obtained in 1979, Capital Management Services was originally chartered to lend to businesses owned by minorities and other "disadvantaged" entrepreneurs. Under the Reagan administration, however, those federal requirements had been loosened to the point where virtually anybody qualified for an SBA loan—a loophole Hale exploited to the fullest advantage.

Hale's angle was a federally subsidized variation on the classic "bust-out" scheme. In collaboration with prominent political figures and others, he had loaned millions of federal dollars to more than a dozen dummy companies he secretly owned. Having no cash flow and no assets, his companies had then defaulted on the loans after Hale siphoned off all the money. The ultimate accounting would show that he had walked away with as much as $3.4 million.

This kind of crude fraud could hardly continue undetected forever. (A rather obvious clue was that the dummy companies all listed the same address as Hale's office.) By the end of 1992, Capital Management had drawn the scrutiny of SBA officials. Attempting to qualify for increased federal matching funds, Hale had confided to an administrator at the agency's Washington headquarters that millions in noncash assets had been "donated" to the firm thanks to his political influence. When the SBA proposed an audit, Hale attempted to withdraw his application, which aroused immediate suspicions. As soon as SBA investigators started poring over Hale's records, they found fraudulent entries everywhere they looked. Of fifty-seven outstanding loans on Capital Management Services' books, thirteen had gone to dummy corporations controlled by Hale. Altogether, he'd advanced the phony companies about $2.04 million.

Perhaps the most cynical aspect of Hale's scam was his exploitation of SBA matching funds. For every dollar of operating capital CMS came up with, the taxpayers kicked in three. Hale would finance a loan to one of his dummy companies, default on it, and then use the embezzled funds to generate more operating capital on a three-to-one basis. He repeated this pyramid scheme many times. Hale also ran various real estate and insurance frauds to raise more operating capital. One of the SBA investigators later told Senate staffers that Hale's embezzlement scheme was the most brazen he'd encountered in his twenty-five years with the agency. The SBA's inspector general swiftly referred the case to the FBI. No later than May 1993, Hale knew that federal officials were taking a hard look at his operation.

The FBI's seizure of his records concluded a long and remarkable dual career for David Hale. Publicly, he was a pillar of the community; privately, he was an inveterate con artist. Though his record as a judge was undistinguished, Hale came from an old hill-country clan with a long history in state politics, and he had established himself in Little Rock at an early age. Friendly and personable, a backslapper and glad-hander, he had pledged the right fraternity at the University of Arkansas; as a young businessman he had joined the Junior Chamber of Commerce, and he was elected national president of the Jaycees in 1974.

Regardless of his family's strong Democratic background, Hale never allowed partisan loyalties to obstruct his personal interests. He carefully cultivated the powerful, Republicans and Democrats alike. Hale was a longtime associate of Sheffield Nelson, the president's bitterest GOP rival. Many news reports would identify him as a Clinton appointee, but in fact Hale's judicial robes were bestowed upon him in 1981 by Governor Frank White, the Republican who had defeated Clinton's first bid for reelection the previous year. White signed a bill creating the judgeship for Hale, including an unusual provision that permitted him to run for election to the bench after his appointed term expired, a circumstance normally prohibited by the state constitution.

The entire scope of Hale's crimes, extending well beyond Capital Management, would not be revealed for years after the FBI raid. A few Arkansans had gotten a glimpse of Hale's true character prior to his well-publicized disgrace. Though he professed to be a devout and happily married Baptist, Hale conducted a long-running illicit affair with his secretary. While romancing her, he managed to swindle her grandparents into signing over their family farm to him. They later sued the judge and won a $486,000 judgment. Years before Hale was caught, at least one business associate later accused of complicity in his crimes had made a trip to Washington at his own expense to warn SBA officials that Hale was corrupt. Unfortunately, those warnings were ignored. Also known as something of an eccentric, Hale was the only judge in Little Rock—his court handled misdemeanors and traffic cases—to have a bulletproof shield installed in front of the bench. Visitors were required to pass through not one but two metal detectors to enter his courtroom.

Hale would eventually proclaim on national television that he had once been a "close political friend" of Bill Clinton, at the same moment he accused the president of joining a felony conspiracy to defraud the United States government. Oddly, however, he had never donated significantly to any of Clinton's political campaigns. And the clearest indication of Hale's true loyalties was that in the raid's aftermath, he immediately turned for help to Clinton's bitterest adversaries.

To "guide him through the jungle" of federal law enforcement, Hale hired defense attorney Randy Coleman, the partner of Sheffield Nelson's former campaign finance chairman. His new lawyer quickly ascertained from prosecutors that Hale would soon face several felony counts for a multimillion-dollar fraud against the Small Business Administration. With a federal indictment only weeks away, Coleman placed a call to William Kennedy, an attorney in the White House counsel's office whom he had known in Little Rock.

During a brief conversation, Coleman outlined Hale's sudden legal difficulties and added that this "might pose some problems for our mutual clients." When Kennedy asked him to be more specific, Coleman mentioned that the Hale investigation was likely to include the president's Whitewater partners, James and Susan McDougal, who had received loans from Capital Management Services; also likely to be caught up in the case for the same reason was Arkansas governor Jim Guy Tucker. And because of the McDougal connection to Whitewater, Coleman hinted, the Clintons themselves might fall under suspicion.

When Kennedy asked what Coleman wanted him to do, the defense lawyer replied, "Well, I don't want you to do anything. I'm just trying to figure out where everybody is on this matter." Two days later, Kennedy called back to learn more details. Coleman read off a list of certain Capital Management transactions that were under investigation, mentioning the $300,000 loan to Susan McDougal. Would Hale allege any "face-to-face meetings"? Kennedy wanted to know. Taking this as a reference to Bill Clinton, Coleman said he would. Kennedy didn't press any further, and Coleman remarked that if Heidi Fleiss was the "madam to the stars," then David Hale was the "lender to the political elite in Arkansas." (There was some truth to this quip, except that Hale loaned much more to elite Republicans, including two former party chairmen, than to Democrats.) Thanking him for the "heads up," Kennedy said he might get back to Coleman, but never did.

As Coleman eventually admitted in Senate testimony, he hadn't phoned Bill Kennedy simply to chat about the Hale case. He had hoped to provoke the White House into a foolish overreaction, such as interfering with the investigation in an attempt to keep Hale quiet. "I thought if I just made a provocative phone call, who knows what might transpire? These folks over here'd shown a propensity to make an ill-advised phone call or two in times past in their travel office situation, and I could just hope maybe it might happen again."

No "ill-advised" action was taken by anyone in the White House, however, and Coleman entered into several weeks of fitful negotiations with the newly appointed U.S. attorney in Little Rock. Paula Casey, an active Democrat and former law student of Bill Clinton's, had just taken over the office from her Republican predecessor, Charles Banks. Coleman's bargaining position never changed from their first meeting, and Casey found it unacceptable, not to mention audacious. In exchange for unspecified information about possible crimes by unnamed members of the "political elite of Arkansas," Coleman said, his client should be allowed to plead guilty to a misdemeanor. That way he could retain his judicial position and law license, and stay out of jail, too.

Casey and her deputy, veteran federal prosecutor Fletcher Jackson, told Coleman that based on the evidence against Hale, they wouldn't even consider a deal unless he agreed to plead guilty to a felony—and made a written "proffer," in advance, of any incriminating information he possessed about others. The proffer would then be tested for its veracity before any deal was made. These conditions were simply standard law enforcement procedure in dealing with any criminal defendant, let alone a con man of Hale's magnitude. As career Justice Department officials later testified, approving a lenient plea bargain without a proffer from Hale would have been the legal equivalent of "buying a pig in a poke."

As Coleman's jousting with Casey dragged on, the defense lawyer tried to create a written record that would support Hale's demand for a special prosecutor. On September 15, he sent a blunt letter to Casey accusing her of withholding a plea agreement because of "the potential political sensitivity and fallout regarding the information which Mr. Hale could provide to the [U.S. attorney's] office." He added vaguely that Hale's information "would be of substantial assistance in investigating the banking and borrowing practices of . . . the elite political circles of the State of Arkansas, past and present." He then asked Casey to step aside in favor of a special prosecutor.

Casey answered him by mail the following day. Hale's veiled assertions posed no problem for her, she wrote, but his crimes were too serious to permit the free ride Coleman was demanding. Her insistence that Hale plead guilty to at least one felony count had been repeatedly rejected by his lawyer. "Therefore, our plea negotiations are at an impasse," she concluded.

In the absence of a reasonable plea bargain and a proffer of useful testimony, Casey and her associates moved forward. On September 23, the federal grand jury in Little Rock handed up a four-count felony indictment against Hale charging him with fraud against the U.S. government.

The friend whose counsel Hale relied upon most as he faced criminal indictment wasn't his attorney, but "Justice Jim" Johnson, the diehard segregationist and perennial Clinton nemesis. Although there was no indication that Hale shared Johnson's extreme political outlook, their relationship went back decades. "I have known his family for three generations," Johnson once recalled. "His deceased brother John was one of my strongest supporters." They were so close, in fact, that during the tense summer of 1993, Hale went to live with the retired justice and his wife for a while at their farm, White Haven. From Johnson's point of view, "David was a young man who was in some trouble, and it was because of things that he did with Bill Clinton. We wanted to see to it that they were not able to cover that up." Telephone records show that during the months immediately following the FBI raid, Hale called Johnson's office more than forty times.

It was under Johnson's tutelage that Hale finally made his "proffer" about Clinton—not to the U.S. attorney, but to right-wing activists in Washington, and then to the news media. "I told him that with the influence the Clinton Administration and their friends had in the Federal court system here in Arkansas, that the only chance he had to help himself and his country was to see that all the facts were made available to the major news outlets throughout the world. I helped him get that project in motion."

Johnson later tried to suggest that he hadn't contacted Hale until after he read about Hale's problems in the Arkansas newspapers, but in fact they had been in touch months earlier. He also spread misinformation about Hale's supposed relationship with Clinton. "The Hale family," he told the ultraconservative *Washington Weekly*, "was a meaningful part of the Clinton Administration when [Clinton] was Governor of Arkansas. Clinton appointed David to a municipal judgeship." Both assertions were false. In fact, as a close observer of state politics and a Republican himself, Johnson surely knew that Hale was no friend of the Clintons. Not only were most of Hale's business associates prominent Republicans, but he had helped manage the campaign of Clinton's opponent, Jim Guy Tucker, in the bitter 1982 Democratic gubernatorial primary. Hard feelings persisted on both sides following that contest, to the point that Clinton and Tucker could scarcely speak of each other without snarling.

Sometime in August, Justice Jim Johnson called David Bossie, his associate from the 1992 presidential campaign, at the Citizens United office in Washington, saying he had "a friend who was in trouble." He assured Bossie that Hale could implicate Clinton in his own financial misdeeds. Bossie promised Johnson he would call Hale, but he didn't have to. At Johnson's urging, Hale called Bossie instead within minutes.

For two hours, Bossie listened with mounting excitement as Hale recounted his tale of woe. He was being set up as "the fall guy" by the Clinton-appointed federal prosecutor, Paula Casey, because she didn't want to act on his accusations against the McDougals, Tucker, and Clinton. As governor, Hale claimed, Clinton had "pressured" him in early 1986 to make an illicit $300,000 loan from Capital Management to a firm controlled by the McDougals called Master Marketing. The purpose of that loan, said Hale, was to "clean up" the Democratic "political family" in Little Rock, a reference to Clinton, the McDougals, and Tucker. On the deal's other end, he continued, there was an inflated $825,000 Madison Guaranty real estate loan provided by McDougal, which allowed Hale to pocket hundreds of thousands of dollars.

Later, Hale would embroider his story to include various colorful details of his alleged meetings with Clinton, including one on the steps of the Arkansas capitol and another in a trailer where McDougal kept an office, when they discussed the loan. He never would offer any specific dates, and the files seized from his office provided no support for his charges against Clinton. Lack of documentation, however, didn't prevent Hale from telling people that damning evidence had once existed. In several interviews given during the fall of 1993, the former judge claimed that he had formerly possessed documentary evidence proving Bill Clinton's participation in the bogus Master Marketing loan, but that federal investigators had stolen it.

"The file on the $300,000 loan was three to four inches thick when the FBI took it," Hale eventually told an Associated Press reporter. "But when my attorney and I asked to see it a month or so later, the U.S. Attorney's office gave us maybe an inch of stuff." One of the supposedly purloined documents was a handwritten letter from Jim McDougal to Hale, promising that Bill Clinton would make good on the Master Marketing loan. Not that a letter from McDougal to Hale, both of whom would later be proven to have forged and altered scores of documents for their own benefit, would have established the truth of Hale's accusations. Interestingly, however, almost none of the reporters or political operatives to whom Hale told this improbable tale chose to share it with the public.

When Assistant U.S. Attorney Fletcher Jackson was deposed on the subject of Hale's purloined papers, he categorically denied ever seeing what he mocked as "the smoking gun letter," and expressed doubt that it ever existed. Hale had dispatched his attorney to Little Rock FBI headquarters to fetch a copy of the letter from the file in September 1993. Asked if the lawyer had said why he wanted it, Jackson responded sardonically: "No, but hell, we both knew why he wanted the letter. . . . It was something that might support the position that [Hale] had been taking. 'The devil made me do all this. I was a victim of all these high-powered political types who forced me to give away all of the money which left S.B.A. and me holding the bag.'"

Hale's account was further undermined by at least one more stark contradiction. Back in November 1989, FBI agents investigating the failure of Madison Guaranty had questioned Hale about his dealings with Jim and Susan McDougal, including the $300,000 loan. According to the agents' official memorandum of that interview, Hale described in some detail his dealings with Jim Guy Tucker (then an attorney in private practice), both McDougals, and several others, but never mentioned Governor Bill Clinton. Nor did Clinton's name come up when Hale testified at McDougal's 1990 trial, which ended in an acquittal. Such exculpatory facts were routinely omitted from the news accounts of Hale's sensational allegations against the president.

Randy Coleman's defense strategy was to launch his client's story into print and onto the airwaves, even as he stubbornly rejected any compromise with Paula Casey. It appeared to many as if Coleman and his client—with the help of Brown, Bossie, and Johnson—wanted to create a public uproar concerning

Whitewater, so they might bludgeon Casey into reconsidering a lenient plea bargain or force her off the case entirely.

Drawing national attention to Hale was difficult at first. When his indictment was announced, he dramatically related his story about Clinton and the McDougals to the *Arkansas Democrat-Gazette,* but the report that appeared in the Little Rock daily wasn't sufficiently pointed in its accusations to be picked up by any larger media outlets. At Sheffield Nelson's urging, however, Coleman already had taken his client to the most influential newspaper in the country, hoping that the *New York Times* would welcome a fresh angle on the Whitewater story it had broken the year before.

About two weeks before Hale's indictment was handed down, Coleman had contacted Jeff Gerth, the *Times* investigative reporter whose front-page article had caused a brief stir in March 1992. The lawyer had invited Gerth down to Little Rock to hear Hale's account in person at his law office. Gerth accepted, and over the course of two days questioning Hale, became sufficiently convinced to ask him to go on the record. After hesitating for a few days, Hale agreed.

Yet when Gerth found and interviewed his old source Jim McDougal, the ailing recluse said he had no memory of talking about the $300,000 loan with Hale and Clinton. Gerth got nothing useful from Casey or the Clinton White House, either. Stymied for the moment, he remained in touch regularly with Hale and Coleman, whose telephone records show almost two dozen calls to the *Times* reporter between September 19 and December 10. (Those records, of course, do not show the calls placed by Gerth to Hale and Coleman.) During roughly that same period, from September 27 to December 21, Hale also made at least twenty-eight calls to Jim Johnson.

The *Times*'s national editors at first declined to publish unverified charges against the president by a man under indictment for embezzling federal money. But in a display of solidarity with his new source, Gerth took some unusual steps to assist Hale and Coleman. He contacted an agent at the FBI's office in Little Rock to report Hale's story concerning Clinton and the $300,000 loan. He also informed the FBI agent about the impasse Coleman and Casey had reached during their plea bargaining. In that conversation, it would appear that Gerth suggested to the FBI that Casey was unwilling to take testimony from Hale that might implicate Tucker and Clinton. The *Times* reporter later said, "I don't remember speaking to the FBI guy, but maybe I did."

After hanging up with Gerth, the FBI agent immediately posted a teletype from Little Rock to the FBI director's office in Washington, which said in part: "Gerth alluded that this was why the United States Attorney Casey would not deal with Coleman when he was attempting to work out a suitable deal for his client."

Later that day, Gerth also called Irv Nathan, associate deputy attorney general, at the Justice Department's Washington headquarters. He told Nathan about Hale and Casey, prompting the Justice official to inform his superiors about Gerth's tip. According to the reporter, who considered Nathan a friend, "I told him what Hale was alleging and asked what he knew, what his reaction was." Nathan's concern quickly led to a meeting of top Justice officials to consider whether Casey should recuse herself from the Hale case because of her relationships with Clinton, Tucker, and other Arkansas Democrats.

Among those participating in the Justice Department deliberations over Casey's potential conflicts were John Keeney, the second-ranking official in the Criminal Division, and Gerald McDowell, the chief of the Frauds Section. Casey and her staff took the position that absent strong and persuasive evidence from Hale, she should not recuse, lest every white-collar criminal in Arkansas force special consideration by claiming that Bill Clinton had made them commit a felony. Under the circumstances, however, Justice Department officials decided that Paula Casey should step aside, as she soon agreed to do. But they also resented what they viewed as underhanded methods used by Hale's lawyer in attempting to coerce a favorable plea bargain. To McDowell, "it looked like Coleman was using Gerth to send messages to the FBI and the Department of Justice in Washington and telling them, giving them, in effect, proffers, but not in any useable form." Both he and Keeney regarded this maneuver as "totally inappropriate."

Even after Hale's indictment, Coleman continued to insist that his client wouldn't plead to a single felony count. He remained steadfast after Casey recused herself in early November and was replaced by Donald McKay, a career Washington prosecutor in the Frauds Section. Clearly, Coleman was no longer interested in dealing with the Justice Department, if he ever had been. Hale's advisers were openly pushing for an independent counsel, and the surest way to achieve that was through the media, not the Justice Department or the courts. During the fall of 1993, Hale's telephone records show that in addition to his contacts with the *Times*, he called reporters at the *Washington Post, Time*, and *Newsweek*, as well as conservative publications such as the *Washington Times*, owned by Unification Church leader Sun Myung Moon, and right-wing media magnate Rupert Murdoch's new magazine, the *Weekly Standard*.

Although Gerth had a head start, the *Post's* Michael Isikoff began chasing down Hale's allegations not long afterward. Someone aware of Isikoff's interest in Clinton and Whitewater had faxed the *Democrat-Gazette's* September 24 story about Hale's charges to him. Like Gerth, Isikoff interviewed Hale himself. Then he and his colleague Howard Schneider, assisted by Susan Schmidt, a reporter on the savings and loan beat, spent weeks trying to confirm Clinton's role in the $300,000 loan. But all they got was a firm denial from Jim McDougal, which for the moment meant no story.

What broke through the earlier editorial misgivings about Hale was a fresh rivulet of leaks from the Resolution Trust Corporation. A new set of criminal referrals regarding Madison had arrived in Washington from L. Jean Lewis, the investigator whose work on the same case in 1992 had been regarded by the FBI and the U.S. attorney as politically motivated and shoddy. Word of the referrals reached Gerth, Isikoff, and other reporters in early October, and they worked to confirm them over the following weeks.

Ignoring the FBI's repeated attempts to persuade the RTC to investigate Arkansas thrift collapses ten and twenty times larger, Lewis and her boss, Richard Iorio, had worked on almost nothing but Madison Guaranty during the first year of the Clinton presidency. RTC time sheets showed that the Kansas City office devoted 2,608 hours to Madison in 1993; by contrast, it spent only 13 hours on the $950 million First Federal Savings collapse. Lewis became particularly exercised after Paula Casey, citing analyses by Justice Department experts and former U.S. attorney Charles Banks, turned down her original 1992 referral for a second time.

On October 6, Lewis sent a peculiar E-mail message to Iorio. Completely unbidden, she wrote, *Washington Post* reporter Susan Schmidt had turned up on her doorstep. According to Lewis, she had heard Schmidt out, scolded her, and sent her away empty-handed. Wrote Lewis, "My parting comment was 'When you contacted me last Thursday I told you that I had no comment, and made every effort to be polite. . . . What you have done this evening is the most unprecedented breach of professional courtesy that I've ever witnessed, so I will say this one more time, and one more time only. Do not contact me again at my office, or my home. I have no comment on your investigation and will not answer any more of your comments. Do not waste any more of my time or yours."

Lewis added that the reporter had somehow gotten hold of her 1992 referral, and added a list of questions Schmidt had asked, including several about the late Vince Foster's role in the Whitewater affair. Schmidt had asked if Lewis suspected a cover-up, and warned her that Jeff Gerth was back on the story. "I thanked her for the heads up," Lewis concluded.

Susan Schmidt's article revealing the existence of the RTC criminal referrals, involving the president and first lady appeared on page A1 of the *Washington Post* on October 31. A similar story by Gerth followed in the *Times* a few days later. Within a week, RTC officials removed Lewis from the Madison probe and gave her another assignment. At most law enforcement agencies, passing out confidential financial documents to reporters would have constituted a firing offense, and could warrant criminal sanctions. Intense bureaucratic warfare over the leaks and related issues broke out inside the Kansas City office, a struggle that would eventually be resolved at the highest possible levels.

* * *

Among other things, Lewis's referrals charged that Madison Guaranty deposits had been illegally diverted to a Clinton campaign fund in 1986. The result was that reporters linked Hale's allegations to the RTC leaks, producing stories in both the *Post* and the *Times*. Schmidt's page A1 scoop resulted in her immediate transfer from the humdrum savings and loan beat to the paper's national staff, and then to a Whitewater "special project" team.

The *Times* and *Post* articles set off a competitive fray not only between the two major newspapers—reviving the old rivalry of the Watergate era—but at other papers and in the electronic media as well. Almost instantaneously, Hale was transformed from a recalcitrant embezzler into a credible source. Both newspapers downplayed his crimes, and their imitators did likewise. Gerth, having interceded with the Justice Department on Hale's behalf, now described him as "recently indicted on charges of misleading the Government about the condition of his lending company," an offense that sounded technical and almost innocuous. What Hale stood accused of misleading the government about, of course, was his conversion of more than $2 million in federal funds to his own uses.

The *Times* buried Gerth's first Hale story on an inside page, but Floyd Brown and David Bossie were still sufficiently encouraged to amplify Hale's voice wherever possible. The indicted judge appeared on Brown's radio broadcast for an "exclusive newsmaking interview" to air his accusations against the president. He told the same story in the November 1993 issue of Citizens United's *Clintonwatch* newsletter, in an article headlined "Clinton Fingered in Loan Coverup." Then Brown made certain that the newsletter showed up on the assignment desk of every news bureau in Washington.

Controlling access to Hale, plus additional materials provided by Sheffield Nelson and documents retrieved by Bossie, Citizens United suddenly became a central resource for every reporter assigned to Whitewater. In rapid succession, their version of the story was picked up by all of the nation's major media. Shepherding Hale through this sudden journalistic maelstrom was Bossie, who supervised his interviews and appearances.

On November 4, for example, Bossie arranged an on-camera session with Hale for NBC producer Ira Silverman at Coleman's office. According to Mike Narisi, the independent Little Rock cameraman hired to shoot the interview for Silverman, "Bossie greeted employees of the office by their first names and appeared to be well acquainted with Hale and Coleman before the taping of the interview began, was present throughout the interview, and prompted Hale during the videotaping."

The carefully coached Hale told NBC that federal prosecutors had brushed off his accusations against Clinton. "We want you to come over here and plead guilty and shut up," he claimed they had told him. That was a wholly false summary of the plea negotiations, but one that well suited the new objective of Hale and his allies: to promote the appointment of a Whitewater special prosecutor to investigate Bill and Hillary Clinton.

That same NBC interview, as Floyd Brown boasted later, demonstrated Citizens United's influence in an even more dramatic fashion. Broadcast on November 11, 1993, it tied Whitewater to Vince Foster's suicide for the first time in the national media. "Before his death in July," said anchor Tom Brokaw, "former White House lawyer Vince Foster also got involved, helping the Clintons sell their share of the [Whitewater] land company. . . . Now questions are being raised about the growing Arkansas investigation and Foster's death. . . . That same day in Little Rock, a judge signed a search warrant for the FBI to raid David Hale's offices. White House officials insist that Foster could not have been tipped off about the impending raid."

Hale's appearance on a network broadcast, with its linkage of Whitewater and the Foster suicide, sent a collective frisson through the Washington press corps. A few weeks later the *Washington Times* reported that White House counsel Bernard Nussbaum had moved the Clintons' personal legal files from Foster's office to their private living quarters a few days after his death, initiating a full-tilt media frenzy.

The transfer of the papers was of little significance. At the time of Foster's death, there was no Whitewater scandal. Nor had any investigative agency requested to see the files in connection with the probe into his suicide. Protected by lawyer-client privilege, they belonged to the Clintons. Although there had been some differences between Nussbaum and the Justice Department over the exact procedures for searching Foster's office on July 22, investigators were looking for a suicide note, not Whitewater tax returns. Had there been any reason to do so, examining the files would have required a subpoena from a federal judge. But none of the investigators, subsequent testimony showed, ever sought one.

In a December 26 editorial, the *Times* depicted the Clintons' possession of their own private papers, "presumptuously spirited from the office of the deputy White House counsel Vincent Foster, following Mr. Foster's suicide," as cause for profound suspicion. Much later, Michael Isikoff recalled the mood among the press corps during the period in an interview with PBS host Charlie Rose. "Whitewater started to take off as an issue in December 1993," he explained, "[with the news] that Whitewater documents were spirited out of Foster's office in the hours after his death by White House aides. . . . No single allegation seemed more troubling than to somehow link Foster's death to Whitewater. You know, is there any possibility that he was so worried about Whitewater that he killed himself because he was fearful about some damaging disclosure? Or is it even worse than that? Some people believe that Foster was murdered, even though there's really no evidence for that."

As they orchestrated Hale's media offensive and played up the bogus connection to Foster's suicide, Citizens United, Brown, and Bossie remained hidden in virtually every news account—often behind the phrase "independent sources." After a thorough review of the 1993 Whitewater scandal explosion, the *Columbia Journalism Review* later concluded that the national media had regurgitated Citizens United's "highly partisan" tips and interpretations "without identifying the group as the source of their information." Not until months later was the role of Brown and Bossie revealed—and even then nobody noticed their Clinton-hating mentor, Jim Johnson.

For his part, Johnson had no desire for his activities to become public. A shrewd political operative, he understood that given his past leadership of the White Citizens Council and dalliance with the Klan, discretion served him better than notoriety. He continued to make discreet contacts for his friend Hale in the world of Washington conservatism—contacts with power and money who would prove very useful to Hale, and who would in turn find him very useful for their own purposes.

Chapter Seven

THE SCANDAL INDUSTRY'S
SECRET SUGAR DADDIES

WHEN PETER SMITH called David Brock again in the middle of August 1993, almost a year had passed since their last encounter. Brock's controversial new book, *The Real Anita Hill,* was moving quickly up the bestseller lists, and the thirty-one-year-old writer's status was soaring with it. Liberals regarded Brock as an ideological assassin, but their outrage over his scathing portrait of Clarence Thomas's accuser only made him more of a hero on the right, where he made his living. And the emotional reaction to his work was pushing up circulation at the *American Spectator,* where he had been elevated from just another staff writer into a journalistic star. The dark-haired, intense, soft-spoken Brock was an instant celebrity among Beltway conservatives, constantly invited to cocktail parties, black-tie dinners, and events of all kinds. He commanded big speaking fees and had the ear of important Republican politicians.

Now, like any suddenly successful young author, he faced the pressing problem of how to surpass himself.

On that score, Brock didn't expect any brilliant suggestions from Smith. The Chicago investment banker's previous tip, in the fall of 1992, was to urge Brock to investigate whether Bill Clinton had fathered an illegitimate son with a black prostitute in Little Rock. Smith had brandished a clipping from *The Globe,* one of the wackier supermarket tabloids, as if it would provide useful leads. If this tale had proved true, Smith was ready to spend his own money to promote it; as one of the top funders of GOPAC, Newt Gingrich's political action committee, he had hired an impressive team of Republican lawyers and publicists to launch a devastating attack before Election Day. But just as Brock had expected, the "black love child" never materialized. Smith's consuming interest in that bit of southern gothic fantasy had struck Brock at the time as mildly ridiculous.

This time, however, Smith had a proposal that sounded more convincing. Through Cliff Jackson, Smith had learned that four of President Clinton's former bodyguards were ready to talk about their old boss's secret life of debauchery in Little Rock. Toward the end of the '92 campaign, Brock had heard scuttlebutt about state troopers who could embarrass Clinton, but none of them had come forward. According to Jackson, a group of them had decided to reveal Clinton's dark side in a book and were looking for a writer. As their lawyer, Jackson had asked Smith for recommendations.

The investment banker said he was willing to do more than merely recommend Brock, whose evisceration of Anita Hill he greatly admired. He would write a $5,000 check to support Brock's work on a book proposal—in advance of the large sum such a book would surely attract from a major publisher. Taking research money from interested parties was nothing new to Brock, an unabashed advocacy journalist. *The Real Anita Hill* had been partially funded by grants from the conservative Bradley and Olin Foundations.

Brock agreed to let Smith arrange a preliminary meeting with the troopers. "It was a coincidence that Peter called me, but after Vince Foster killed himself I was interested in that story," the writer recalled later. "I thought there was more to it than what we had all heard. And that had happened about three weeks before Peter called. I had been talking to Republicans on the Hill, setting up a trip to Little Rock anyway. So when Peter offered to pay my way, I took him up on it."

A few days later, Cliff Jackson picked Brock up at the Little Rock airport and drove him to a Holiday Inn just across the expressway. The lawyer told him that a reporter for the *Los Angeles Times* was already working on the trooper story, and had been in town just the other day to interview them. As the troopers' legal representative and media adviser, Jackson had devised a plan to maximize the impact of their revelations—and increase their potential value to publishers. He had selected Bill Rempel, whom Jackson knew well and trusted, to break the story first in a mainstream newspaper. The *Los Angeles Times* exclusive would light the fuse of a publicity explosion, setting up the troopers for a big book advance. In the meantime, Brock would prepare a book proposal.

Brock had spent most of 1992 working on the Anita Hill book. He hadn't covered the presidential campaign or even visited Arkansas before now. He had heard of Jackson, but knew him only by reputation from the draft controversy, as a corrosively angry former friend of the president who had attended Oxford while Clinton was a Rhodes scholar there. As a Fulbright scholar, Jackson had nurtured the same ambitions as his fellow Arkansan, charting a political career back home. "I'd never seen anyone so obsessed with power," Jackson said of his rival years later. "I was fiercely competitive; he was the first guy who was more competitive than me." In 1976 the tall, awkward, unprepossessing Jackson had failed badly in his sole attempt to run for local office, and then withdrawn from politics to practice law. People who knew both men thought Jackson's distaste for Clinton reflected lifelong jealousy.

His conversations with Brock did nothing to dispel that assessment. "Cliff talked for quite a while about Clinton's character flaws." Although he was an active Republican, Jackson emphasized that Clinton's ideology wasn't the issue for him. What bothered him was Clinton's dishonesty, and his mistreatment of women. To Brock, he sounded as if he was speaking from conviction. What Jackson didn't mention, then or later, was his own agreement with troopers Larry Patterson and Roger Perry, signed about a week earlier, which named him as their exclusive agent for book, magazine, television, and any other deals relating to their revelations. The contract also guaranteed the troopers jobs outside Arkansas for seven years at a reported $100,000 a year, should they lose their badges due to anything they said about the Clintons.

Brock spent the next couple of days at the Holiday Inn, hardly venturing out even for meals, as Jackson escorted the four troopers to his room for hours of group interviewing. Also accompanying them was Lynn Davis, a taciturn former FBI agent and state police officer who knew the troopers and was assisting Jackson. The most talkative and enthusiastic was Patterson, a trim, crew-cut cop in his late forties who had served on the force for twenty-seven years and didn't try to conceal his passionate hatred for both Clintons. A talented raconteur, Patterson confidently reeled off one anecdote after another, while the other three mostly nodded and added details as Brock filled his notebooks. The darker, beefier Perry, a few years younger than Patterson, mostly sat in glum silence, though he obviously shared Patterson's feelings. Danny Ferguson, an imposing six-footer with salt-and-pepper hair, was more forthcoming but seemed more conflicted about his old boss, while short, chubby Ronnie Anderson said almost nothing. Patterson and Perry both felt that Clinton had used them as governor, and then discarded them when he moved to Washington.

None of the troopers had spoken out during the '92 campaign, either out of fear or in the hope that Clinton might someday reward them with federal jobs. Now all four professed to be disappointed with Clinton's first year as president, and deeply concerned for the nation's future with him in the White House. Unaware that Brock himself was gay, they complained with particular disgust about his executive order lifting the traditional ban on homosexuals in the military. But they hadn't come to talk policy. For hours they regaled Brock with stories of Clintonian vulgarity, immaturity, and obsessive lasciviousness. They claimed to have been called upon constantly to arrange and then cover up Clinton's sexual encounters with countless women, at the governor's mansion, at various apartments and hotel rooms, and even in a junior high school parking lot. They described the violent rages of the wronged Hillary, who they insisted had engaged in her own adulterous affair with Vince Foster, making out with him at stoplights like a teenager and on one occasion allowing him to fondle her breasts in public. Recalling detailed scenes they said they had observed during their years of everyday intimacy with the Clintons, they portrayed the president, in Brock's words, as "a man of gargantuan appetites and enormous drive," and his wife as a selfish, foulmouthed, power-crazed shrew.

While this thorough stripping of the Clintons' dignity fascinated Brock, he worried about the troopers' motivations. But he returned to Washington convinced that they were essentially truthful. Still, he wasn't at all certain that their stories would make a compelling book, and after consulting with his agents, he knew he didn't want to be anyone's ghostwriter. "There was no way they could be cut in on a book deal with me, because then I would be paying them for the story." To split a book advance with the troopers could easily be interpreted as a violation of the journalistic taboo against paying sources, and Brock had many enemies in the press who would be eager to trumpet that accusation. He was troubled, too, by his uncertainty about the role of Peter Smith, who he feared might have pledged money to the troopers before they came forward. When asked, Smith reassured Brock that he had made no such commitment.

About a month later, Brock went back to Little Rock for a second round of meetings with Jackson and the troopers at the airport Holiday Inn. He explained that he didn't see himself as a ghostwriter, and warned that their credibility would be questioned if they seemed to be angling for money. "I explained to them the whole Gennifer Flowers problem—that her story was discounted because a tabloid paid her to tell it."

Instead of preparing a book outline, Brock said, he wanted to tell their story in the *Spectator,* more fully and colorfully than Rempel's editors would permit in a mainstream newspaper. "I said what they could do is, if there was going to be a book deal, let me and the *L.A. Times* publish and get whatever publicity we could, and they could sign up to do a book later." The meeting was inconclusive, and Brock flew home thinking he might have no story at all. Actually, based on his own conversations with Rempel, Jackson was not at all certain that the *Los Angeles Times* would ultimately publish the troopers' story in any form. If not, the *Spectator* would provide an alternative outlet, albeit one with considerably less weight. Jackson called Brock to say the troopers would go on the record the next time the writer came to Little Rock. Until then, Brock hadn't really told his editors what he had been doing in Arkansas.

*   *   *

The *American Spectator,* which began in 1967 as a conservative, off-campus sheet at the University of Indiana called the *Alternative,* had established itself by 1993 as the country's premier venue for right-wing muckraking, mostly thanks to David Brock. Its editors had discovered how popular such material could be when Rush Limbaugh delivered a bonanza of radio publicity for Brock's initial feature on Anita Hill in 1991, driving up circulation almost instantly. Until then, the monthly had generated little excitement outside a smallish coterie, with its heavy-handed japes at liberals, feminists, and environmentalists and its pretentiously Anglophilic cultural criticism. The magazine's founder and editor, R. Emmett Tyrrell, Jr., known as Bob, fancied himself the true heir to H. L. Mencken, and *Spectator* copy too obviously aped the late, great columnist's bombastic, slashing style, without his wit or erudition.

Tyrrell's inherited wealth enabled him to indulge such vanities full-time, but his trust fund wasn't rich enough to sustain a money-losing periodical for twenty-five years. Despite its strong editorial commitment to capitalist enterprise, the *Spectator* had survived only because Tyrrell and his partner, publisher Ronald Burr, had set up a nonprofit entity—the American Spectator Educational Foundation—to publish it. Besides avoiding taxes, this arrangement allowed them to seek grants from like-minded individuals and foundations.

At a time when left-wing and liberal publications like *Rolling Stone* dominated the youth market, Tyrrell and Burr had eagerly promoted the *Spectator* to certain philanthropists as a staunch critic of the counterculture and a literary venue for young conservative intellectuals. After moving from bucolic Bloomington, Indiana, to suburban Washington during the Reagan years, the "self-consciously outrageous" *Spectator* had found a niche, in the words of one liberal observer, as "the most important journal of the younger conservative generation." If it was taken less seriously than Tyrrell might have wished, after a quarter century it enjoyed the patronage of important conservative writers and political figures, including Robert Novak, Irving Kristol, Jeane Kirkpatrick, Robert Bork, and Jack Kemp.

With the arrival of a new Democratic administration in 1992 there had been much talk around the *Spectator* of going on the attack. But in the first blush of the Clinton presidency, many of the magazine's articles lacked investigative bite. Tyrrell seemed enervated rather than energized, or so Brock thought; indeed, the editor appeared to have disengaged from his creation, carousing in London and New York with his friend Taki Theodoracopulos, socialite, shipping heir, and sometime right-wing columnist, rather than tending to literary business. The job of running the *Spectator* had fallen largely to managing editor Wladyslaw Plesczynski. Initially, Brock hadn't bothered to inform his editors about his research in Little Rock in part because he wasn't sure the trooper story would even interest them.

*   *   *

Between early October and late November, Brock made three more trips to Arkansas to interview the troopers for the record and on tape. He had moved to a better hotel in town, the Excelsior. Anderson and Ferguson had dropped out earlier, apparently fearful of losing their jobs, but Patterson and Perry remained enthusiastic. Their gung-ho attitude was reassuring, though Brock was still disturbed about the possible incentives behind their cooperation. He now knew that Cliff Jackson and Peter Smith had spoken about a "fund" to compensate the troopers should they lose their jobs or incur legal expenses for speaking out, but the details weren't at all clear yet.

Just before Thanksgiving, Brock was staying at the Legacy Hotel in Little Rock while he conducted a few final interviews and meetings with Cliff Jackson, Lynn Davis, Larry Patterson, and Roger Perry. One afternoon when they were all in his suite, arguing about the troopers' financial arrangements with Smith, the telephone rang. Brock picked up the receiver to find Bill Rempel on the line, looking for Jackson. He took the phone in another room and confided to Rempel his concerns about Smith. "I thought the *L.A. Times* might be in the dark about this," Brock said later. But much to Brock's surprise, Rempel brushed him off. "It was a very terse, very short conversation." Rempel doesn't remember talking with Brock and doubts they ever spoke. While he and colleague Douglas Frantz were well aware that Jackson was negotiating with a "conservative financier," Rempel emphasized that "Doug and I had nothing to do with that plan, did not review its fine points, did not know who Jackson approached. We told Jackson that whatever he came up with would have to be noted in any story we published."

A few days later, over the holiday weekend, Brock reached Smith at an exclusive island resort off the Florida coast. The investment banker stubbornly refused to understand that if he paid the troopers and the press found out, "everything would be ruined" for Brock. Frustrated by Smith's ethical naïveté, Brock threatened to expose his role in the whole affair. "That made him pretty nervous." Smith assured Brock that he had promised the troopers nothing. But the writer knew from earlier talks with both Smith and Cliff Jackson that jobs, money, and legal expenses had indeed been topics of intense negotiation.

According to Brock, "I had been talking throughout this period with Cliff and Peter, keeping track of discussions about payments to the troopers, the various arrangements and deals they were discussing. The troopers and Cliff kept trying to get more from Peter. Whatever he offered was never enough."

Around the same time, Smith urged Brock to call Richard W. Porter, a friend of Smith's and partner in the Chicago home office of the Kirkland & Ellis law firm. Indicating that Porter knew all about his backing of Jackson and the troopers, Smith urged Brock to tell the lawyer about his concerns.

Brock didn't know Porter, but recognized his name as someone who had worked in the Bush White House. He later found out that Porter's friends there included White House counsel C. Boyden Gray and Lee Liberman, a young lawyer who had helped to found the Federalist Society. When Brock reached him at his office, "Porter didn't say very much. I explained why the payments would be problematic. He seemed nervous about being involved. Peter had told me it was okay to talk with him, that Porter had been involved in opposition research and knew the stories about Clinton's philandering, et cetera. He and Smith seemed pretty close, as if they didn't have any secrets from each other. I had kept bringing this issue up, and I think he told me to call Porter to calm me down."

Smith's reassurances left Brock ill at ease. In early December, the writer demanded and received what he later described as "written assurance from Jackson prior to publication that no money had been paid or promised to his clients by anyone for disclosing any information." Although this scrap of paper provided him with an ethical refuge, Brock continued to suspect that the troopers would be paid anyway, that they had been promised money from the beginning, and that the payments sooner or later would be exposed.

The scabrous details of the story made Brock anxious, too. The troopers claimed, for example, to have observed women performing oral sex on Clinton in a state car on two separate evenings. Patterson claimed he had seen Vince Foster openly pawing Hillary Clinton's breasts at a party in an expensive west Little Rock restaurant, while she purred and writhed against him like a cat in heat. Aside from the improbability of these tales, Brock couldn't help wondering whether his own reputation would suffer permanently from putting his byline on such smut. Unable to reach a decision, he finally sought confidential advice from two older, wiser friends. William Kristol, the Republican strategist and former adviser to Vice President Dan Quayle, cautioned Brock that he might indeed be damaged by writing about the president's alleged sexual misbehavior. But Laurence Silberman, a strongly conservative federal judge and former Reagan aide who made no secret of his antipathy to Clinton, urged Brock to go ahead. This was, Silberman said, the kind of story that comes along once or twice in a reporter's career.

That November, as Brock pondered whether to proceed with the trooper exposé, a much more ambitious and sustained anti-Clinton enterprise—subsidized by another conservative Republican far wealthier than Peter Smith—was beginning to take shape at the *Spectator*. Later, his editors would tell Brock that his "Troopergate" exposé had inspired this new undertaking. As he eventually realized, that was only a cover story. The true inspiration had come from David Hale. And unlike Brock's story, which would be flogged for publicity, the second scheme was kept entirely confidential.

Expense ledgers from the *Spectator* show that on November 12, 1993, an attorney named Stephen S. Boynton took a taxi from his home in Vienna, Virginia, to Washington National Airport and flew from there to Pittsburgh. Ten days earlier, David Hale's accusations about President Clinton's role in an illegal loan scheme had broken in the *Washington Post* and the *New York Times*. Only the previous evening, *NBC Nightly News* had explicitly linked Hale's allegations to the Vince Foster suicide, setting off a cascade of speculation in Washington newsrooms.

Traveling on confidential *Spectator* business, Boynton's destination was the Mellon Bank building downtown, and specifically the thirty-ninth floor offices of the Sarah Scaife and Carthage Foundations. That was where Richard Larry oversaw the charitable and educational interests of Richard Mellon Scaife, heir to the Mellon banking, oil, and steel fortune. Boynton knew Dick Larry well, as a friend and fellow sportsman. ("We've fished together many times," Boynton would explain much later, without apparent irony.) That same evening, Boynton flew home to Virginia.

A few days later, Boynton took another flight, this time to Little Rock. In Arkansas, he had dinner with Parker Dozhier, owner of a fishing resort and bait shop on the shore of Lake Catherine, near Hot Springs, and a longtime acquaintance of David Hale. The disgraced judge had once rented an apartment in a downtown Little Rock apartment building that Dozhier managed.

On November 22, according to telephone records, Boynton received a call in Virginia from David Hale himself. That was the first of a flurry of calls from Hale to the offices and homes of both Boynton and David W. Henderson, vice president and director of the American Spectator Educational Foundation. Simultaneously, Hale remained in almost daily telephone contact with Justice Jim Johnson. With the support of Johnson and Floyd Brown of Citizens United, Hale had parlayed a multicount indictment for fraud and embezzlement into national celebrity; a *New York Times* reporter had lobbied the Justice Department on his behalf; journalists representing the *Washington Post,* the *Wall Street Journal,* the *Washington Times,* and NBC News were hanging on his every word. Now, with Steve Boynton's help, Hale was about to find an even more powerful patron.

Boynton's trip to Pittsburgh paid off quickly. During the first week of December, the American Spectator Educational Foundation received a check from the Sarah Scaife Foundation for $60,000. The letter accompanying the check, signed by Richard M. Scaife and dated December 2, 1993, said it represented the first payment toward a grant of $120,000 approved by the foundation's trustees in response to an earlier request "and after various conversations with us." Within days a second check arrived with a similar letter signed by Scaife—this time on the letterhead of the Carthage Foundation, another charitable entity controlled by the Pittsburgh billionaire and his aide Richard Larry. The check from Carthage was made out for $200,000.

*   *   *

Richard Mellon Scaife had been among the first big donors to the *American Spectator* in 1971, and his foundations had consistently supported the magazine, granting millions more in the years since then. A somewhat reclusive man in his sixties, Scaife had made a rare public appearance at the twenty-fifth anniversary bash for the *Spectator* in 1992. Wherever he did show up, he was hard to miss—a tall, bulky man with white-blond hair and striking bright blue eyes. Scaife liked Bob Tyrrell's sassy attitude toward American liberalism, which Scaife had despised all his life. By then the Mellon heir had been one of the most influential figures in American public life for almost thirty years, though he was little known beyond the elite his money had fostered. Unlike some wealthy conservatives, notably the Coors beer dynasty, Scaife was more interested in influence than notoriety.

Entire books had been published about the rise of the New Right with barely any mention of Scaife and his foundations, although since the early 1960s, when he gained control of much of his family's huge fortune, they had spent as much as $300 million to steer the country toward his brand of hardcore conservatism. Of all the foundations whose well-coordinated patronage built the infrastructure of the modern American right—with its myriad think tanks, academic institutes, media centers, legal advocacy organizations, training programs, fellowships, and endowments—none has been as generous for as long as those run by Scaife and his chief associate, Richard Larry.

Yet outside his hometown of Pittsburgh—where he was always newsworthy because of his estimated billion-dollar fortune, his Mellon heritage, and his ownership of the *Tribune-Review,* a local daily newspaper—Scaife rarely attracted press coverage until the nineties. The secretaries who answered his office phone at the Mellon Bank building were always instructed to tell the few reporters who called that "Mr. Scaife doesn't give interviews."

The first sign that Dick Scaife would break with the Mellon family tradition of moderate Republicanism came in 1964, when he backed Barry Goldwater for president. After Goldwater's landslide defeat, Scaife transferred his political affections to Richard Nixon. In 1971, he handwrote 334 separate checks totaling a million dollars to the Committee to Reelect the President in order to avoid gift taxes. Nixon and his men considered Scaife so reliable an ally that they encouraged him to acquire the *Washington Post* from Katherine Graham. Deeply disappointed by Watergate, Scaife remained distant from most politicians for years, until Newt Gingrich appeared on the horizon. Although Scaife was not a major political donor, he gave substantial amounts to various Gingrich ventures and committees.

Like his former mentor Nixon, Scaife always loved espionage, propaganda, and other clandestine operations. During the cold war he cultivated ties with both private and government intelligence organizations, particularly the Central Intelligence Agency, whose media operations he helped to subsidize and conceal for several years.

In the early 1970s, the agency asked Scaife to serve as a front man for its London-based "news service," Forum World Features, whose covert activities were eventually exposed in the press and in congressional hearings on CIA abuses. Forum provided feature stories, often laced with propaganda themes, to newspapers around the world, including more than thirty outlets in the United States; it also gave journalistic credentials to CIA agents. Its own complex cover involved a Delaware holding company, originally headed by newspaper heir John Hay Whitney. Its day-to-day operations were supervised by Brian Crozier, an extremely conservative British political analyst. Managing its finances was Robert Gene Gately, a CIA officer who later became the agency's station chief in Bangkok.

In 1970, the money-losing Forum badly needed an additional infusion of cash. According to Crozier, who published a memoir in 1993, the CIA "arranged for me to meet the American businessman and philanthropist Richard Mellon Scaife." Crozier hastened to Pittsburgh, where he "formed an instant rapport" with Scaife. "Dick Scaife . . . took over the burden from the aging Jock Whitney," who had grown weary of subsidizing Forum. Five years later, just before Forum's CIA ties were exposed in British and American newspapers, Scaife abruptly shut down the press agency. Later still, a disillusioned British army intelligence officer came forward to charge that Forum had assisted in a right-wing "dirty tricks" operation, spreading "smear stories" about Harold Wilson and nearly a dozen other prominent members of Parliament, mostly affiliated with the Labor Party, in an effort to elect a Conservative majority.

Aside from his philanthropies, most of Scaife's personal energy and money were devoted to newspapering, a passion he had acquired as a child. In 1969, he spent $5 million to buy the *Tribune-Review,* a small daily serving suburban and rural areas south of Pittsburgh on which he spent many millions more to challenge the dominance of the mainstream *Pittsburgh Post-Gazette.* He quickly earned a reputation for using the paper to advance both his personal causes and his conservative ideology. His newspaper and his foundations both became instruments of the mission he adopted in 1993, which was to discredit and if possible destroy Bill Clinton.

Observing the 1992 campaign, Scaife developed an intense, almost obsessive enmity for Clinton. "He disliked Clinton's liberal politics and Clinton's cleverness at cloaking them in moderate and conservative-sounding policies," said one longtime friend. "To him, Clinton was the embodiment of the sixties antiwar leftist movement that is amoral through and through. He suspects Clinton was a serious drug abuser; thinks he's still a huge womanizer. He bought all the stories, including the tabloid stories about Clinton having illegitimate children." And like his old allies at the CIA, Scaife had the means to propagate them.

On December 2—the same day that Scaife sent the *Spectator* that $60,000 check—Steve Boynton and Dave Henderson flew down to Little Rock to meet with David Hale. Twelve days later, the two men flew from Washington to Pittsburgh, and on the same day took a second flight from Pittsburgh to Little Rock, where they spent two nights and met with Hale again. In the meantime, they had paid Parker Dozhier a consulting fee of $1,000—covered, along with all the costs of Boynton and Henderson's travels to Pittsburgh and Little Rock, by the *American Spectator.*

Sometime during that same period, Boynton and Henderson attended a meeting at the downtown Washington law offices of Gibson, Dunn & Crutcher. Their host was Theodore B. Olson, senior partner at the prestigious law firm, a figure of considerable renown in conservative legal and political circles, and a close friend of *American Spectator* editor R. Emmett Tyrrell. (Henderson later described Olson to Parker Dozhier as "an eight-hundred-pound gorilla.") Among his many blue-chip clients was former president Ronald Reagan, in whose administration Olson had served as assistant attorney general. According to friends, he had been transformed from a relatively moderate Republican into a combative partisan after enduring a costly four years as the target of an independent counsel inspired by congressional Democrats. Accused of lying to Congress about Reagan administration environmental decisions, Olson was never indicted by independent counsel Alexi Morrison. In the 1988 case of *Morrison v. Olson,* the U.S. Supreme Court affirmed the constitutionality of the independent counsel law in a seven-to-one decision. Following his return to private practice, Olson had become active in conservative politics—and had joined the boards of several Scaife-funded Washington conservative groups.

Also present at the meeting, in addition to Boynton, Henderson, and Olson, were Olson's law partner John A. Mintz, *American Spectator* publisher Ronald Burr, and Michael Horowitz, then a fellow at the Manhattan Institute, a conservative think tank also funded with Scaife largesse. According to one participant, the agenda focused on how the *Spectator,* using Scaife's money, could best mount a series of probes into the Clintons and their alleged crimes in Arkansas. That day Ted Olson agreed to join David Hale's defense team.

Although he wasn't actually present during that first meeting, Richard Larry's influence pervaded the discussion at Olson's office. He and Scaife had provided the grants for an ongoing probe into Clinton's Arkansas past on the condition that the *Spectator* would hire Boynton and Henderson—neither of whom possessed any journalistic credentials whatsoever—to oversee it. They, in turn, hired Parker Dozhier, whose premises in Hot Springs served as their local headquarters, and also as a "safe house" for David Hale to visit them, away from the prying eyes of the Little Rock press. Hale also had reason to avoid state investigators, who were probing a long-standing insurance-fraud case against the former judge.

At first glance, Boynton seemed an unlikely candidate for this kind of sensitive work, or, for that matter, to provide much assistance to the beleaguered Hale. He wasn't, like Ted Olson, a skilled criminal defense attorney. Instead, like many other lawyers in Washington, he spent most of his time representing a commercial interest group; and true to type, he maintained an office address on K Street and a home in suburban Virginia.

His field of expertise was environmental law, with a subspecialty in curtailing legislation aimed at protecting endangered species. An avid hunter and angler himself, Boynton combated environmentalist encroachments on behalf of trade associations such as the American Fur Resources Council and the International Shooting and Hunting Alliance. Among his most prestigious clients was the Republic of Iceland, which hired him to help overturn the international ban on whaling. He also served as general counsel to the Congressional Sportsmen's Caucus Foundation, a progun group that sponsored hunting junkets for legislators. And while he had sometimes dabbled in conservative politics, he was essentially a lawyer-lobbyist who possessed little influence outside his own narrow field.

But Boynton did have important connections, particularly through his hunting and fishing buddies Dave Henderson and Dick Larry. Boynton and Henderson had known Larry for well over a decade, dating back at least to the celebrated libel case brought by General William Westmoreland against CBS News in the early 1980s. Larry's boss Scaife had secretly funded the bulk of Westmoreland's $3 million legal expenses, including the cost of hiring Henderson to handle public relations for the retired general. Boynton had played a supporting legal role in the case, which ended in a victory for CBS. In the years since, Henderson and Boynton had often fished and hunted on Maryland's Eastern Shore with Dick Larry. Henderson had eventually joined Westmoreland on the American Spectator Educational Foundation's board of directors.

Equally significant were Boynton and Henderson's connections in Arkansas. Jim Johnson knew and trusted both men, having met them through Parker Dozhier years earlier. A burly, outspoken fifty-six-year-old fur trapper who had inherited the Lake Catherine bait shop from his father, Dozhier was among Johnson's oldest and closest friends. The old judge often referred to Dozhier, who had worked in his last-gasp segregationist gubernatorial campaign in 1966, as "my boy." Apart from running the bait shop and fishing resort, Dozhier had led a varied and colorful career, including stints as a local TV reporter. In yet another of those curious Arkansas coincidences, back in his days as a newspaper photographer Dozhier had dated a striking young TV reporter and nightclub singer named Gennifer Flowers.

Dozhier liked to call himself a "mountain man," a vocation increasingly hampered by state and federal regulation of trapping and hunting in the nearby Ouachita National Forest. He maintained almost constant low-level warfare with the Arkansas Game and Fish Commission. His political views, like Justice Jim's, tended toward the rightward extreme, and he often echoed the old judge's deep hostility toward blacks. His bait shop's counters displayed right-wing books and pamphlets alongside the fishing gear. Acquaintances of Dozhier said he harbored an abiding, and, some thought, irrational hatred for Bill Clinton. "If Parker got a flat tire," one acquaintance explained, "it was somehow Clinton's fault."

The fur trappers' trade group led by Dozhier had been represented in Washington for more than two decades by Boynton. The two had taken occasional hunting and fishing trips together. They had grown even closer since the bait shop owner and others living along Lake Catherine had hired Boynton in 1991 to sue the Arkansas Power and Light Company over a disastrous flash flood. The electric utility had been compelled to open the floodgates on a dam upstream from Dozhier's bait shop after an abrupt fifteen-inch downpour. Dozhier's lawsuit was dismissed, but Boynton's trips to Arkansas to argue motions at the federal court had cemented their friendship.

Through Boynton, Henderson too had met Jim Johnson and Parker Dozhier. Oddly, Henderson had known David Hale in a different context for many years. Back when Hale had presided over the national Jaycees in the early 1970s, Henderson had served as the civic group's executive director. Through Boynton and Dozhier, he said, they had renewed their old friendship. Completing this small, tight circle was Dozhier's own relationship with Hale, which he later told reporters dated back at least thirty years. They could all trust one another to keep a secret.

The money flowing from Scaife, the meeting at Olson's office, the recruitment of Dozhier, and the contacts with Hale represented the genesis of a covert operation that soon was known inside the *American Spectator* as "the Arkansas Project." It would become a four-year, $2.4 million attempt to gather intelligence leading to the political ruin of the president of the United States. For Scaife, the Arkansas Project was but one of several ongoing anti-Clinton efforts that he subsidized. Although the gentlemanly billionaire lived in a sphere of ease and privilege that Jim Johnson and Parker Dozhier could only imagine, he vehemently seconded their visceral fury toward Bill Clinton. More than once in the months to come, Scaife would tell friends and employees of his determination to "get that goddamn guy out of the White House."

Apparently it never occurred to this odd assortment of political adventurers that a confidence man like Hale, already under indictment for embezzling more than $2 million in taxpayer funds, might prove less than reliable. Nor did they seem fazed by the legal and ethical questions that might arise in using funds from nonprofit, tax-exempt entities to pursue partisan political goals. After all, the Arkansas Project wasn't supposed to become public knowledge.

David Brock and most of the *Spectator*'s editorial staff would not learn about the existence of the Arkansas Project for months. When it began he was still preoccupied with his trooper story. In 1998, Brock would admit that had he known more about the cast of characters of his "Troopergate" story, much less about Arkansas itself, he might never have written it. "As difficult as it may be for the general public to fathom," he wrote in *Esquire* magazine, "Arkansas political culture has a rich history of personal intrigue in which wild sex stories do feature prominently. . . . Sit in the Capitol Bar, in downtown Little Rock, for a few nights, and you can be told that virtually every prominent public figure in the state is a rapacious womanizer and also gay—including Clinton. Even Hillary Clinton was not spared this treatment: one can hear that she was having an affair with Vince Foster and also that she is a lesbian, often from the same lascivious gossips."

Back in 1992, however, Brock's initial misgivings were finally overcome by a series of calls from Cliff Jackson, describing efforts by Clinton and others to cajole the troopers and perhaps intimidate them. To Brock and to editors of the *Los Angeles Times,* the White House outreach to the troopers legitimized their stories despite the aura of sexual sleaze. To Betsey Wright and other Clinton loyalists, such reasoning would make it all but impossible for a public figure to defend himself. To them, the effort to contain what came to be known as "Troopergate" was yet another skirmish in the campaign by Jackson and his right-wing allies to smear the president. Fully aware of Bill Rempel's relationship with Jackson, Larry Nichols, and Larry Case back in 1992, Wright had anticipated that it was only a matter of time until they cut some kind of deal with the troopers.

Clinton's state police bodyguards had long been a contentious subject among his gubernatorial staff. Far from being the briskly efficient outfit Brock described, the guard detail included some problem cases nearing retirement, and politically ambitious officers eager to exploit their proximity to the governor. Indeed, a controversy involving misappropriated funds had been stirred up during Clinton's tenure involving a private lobbying group called the Arkansas State Police Association. Larry Patterson and Roger Perry had been instrumental in founding the organization. Patterson was said to harbor a grudge over Clinton's failure to deliver on a bill funding the association through mandatory dues withdrawals from troopers' paychecks. The pair had also expressed bitterness toward Clinton for going to Washington without setting them up in federal jobs.

But what had always bothered Betsey Wright most about certain troopers was their bad influence upon Clinton himself. She disliked their boozing and womanizing most of all. Keeping sexually adventurous women away from Bill Clinton had been a staff preoccupation for as long as he had been in public life.

"They exploited his sexual attractiveness to women," Wright said. "Their running around carousing at night was driving me crazy, because the stories always came back about how these guys working for the governor were out picking up women in bars."

Yet Clinton plainly enjoyed the troopers' tales of conquest. Wright sometimes thought he had a compulsive need to be accepted that stemmed from childhood insecurities. "He had a vicarious enjoyment of the good old boy games," she said. "He loved locker-room stories. There's a part of this guy who wanted to be a good old boy and he just never could be. . . . I do think his being a pudgy little guy who wasn't a football star at the time the hormones raged . . . is where a lot of his needing to be loved and absorbing the flattery comes from. So when Larry Patterson says that Bill Clinton would use this term or that term, it probably was in some locker-room story that Larry was telling him."

Patterson's former superior Buddy Young put it even more directly. Young, who supervised Clinton's state police bodyguards and got one of the cushy federal jobs other troopers wanted, as regional director of the Federal Emergency Management Agency, said in a 1998 deposition: "Most of the conversations that went on of that type came out of Larry Patterson . . . [whose] mentality and objective in life was to sleep with as many women as he could. You could not have a conversation with Larry Patterson more than five minutes that sex didn't enter into it and whose britches he was trying to get in. . . . If Bill Clinton had a meeting with a woman behind closed doors, Larry assumed it was for the purpose of sex, because that's what it would have been if he had been there."

Attempts by Wright, Young, and Clinton himself to stifle the troopers, however, only made matters worse by adding a new angle to the story. In deference to his friend Bill Rempel, Cliff Jackson tried to delay Brock's blockbuster as long as possible while the Los Angeles Times editors dithered, but as Christmas approached he could wait no longer. With Jackson's permission, advance copies of the Spectator, with the headline "His Cheatin' Heart" and a red-faced caricature of Clinton sneaking through the darkness on the cover, went out to media contacts in Washington and New York on December 20. The next day, CNN featured interviews with Perry and Patterson, kicking off a barrage of stories about the troopers' lewd allegations.

Struggling with Whitewater, the White House responded flaccidly to the Troopergate frenzy. Rebutting their story was all but impossible, since the troopers had specified few times and places, Vince Foster was dead, and all of the unnamed women approached by the *Los Angeles Times* had denied the allegations. About the best the president and first lady could do was to deny that any of these awful episodes had taken place.

Arkansas reporters did determine that the restaurant where Vince Foster allegedly pawed Hillary had never hosted a Rose Law Firm party like the one described; nor had the law firm sponsored one. A Little Rock AP reporter parked his car exactly where the troopers told David Brock they had watched Clinton have sex in a pickup truck one night on the grounds of the governor's mansion. Then the reporter walked to the guard shack and asked for a demonstration of the TV monitor which allegedly captured the action. He couldn't see a thing.

Next, it turned out that visitors' logs which Larry Patterson and Roger Perry alleged that Hillary Clinton ordered destroyed—ostensibly to hide Gennifer Flowers's visits—had never, in fact, existed. Few of these facts, however, made it into the national press accounts of Troopergate.

Some newspapers published an Associated Press account of an incident in 1990, when Patterson had wrapped a state police vehicle around a tree after midnight. He and Perry, a badly injured passenger in the vehicle, had told their superiors that they had been cold sober and doing public business, and had induced a female trooper and another woman who'd been along for the ride to cover for them. In a subsequent insurance case stemming from the accident, the two swore under oath that Patterson had in fact downed a half dozen Crown Royal cocktails at the Bobbisox Lounge, a singles bar located in the same airport Holiday Inn where they regaled Brock with obscene tales about the Clintons. They made and then withdrew, upon Cliff Jackson's counsel, an offer to take polygraph tests to support their allegations against the president.

But the most salient facts behind their decision to attack Clinton—the book they hoped to sell, and their secret sponsorship by a chief fund-raiser for Newt Gingrich—were lost amid the "news" about the president's adulteries and his wife's vulgarities. In Rempel's story, featured on his newspaper's front page on December 21, the existence of a mysterious "politically conservative financier" and Cliff Jackson's effort to have him "guarantee jobs and legal defense for the troopers" was glossed over in a few deeply buried paragraphs. The story merely quoted Jackson saying he had "not been able to secure a formal commitment from the unnamed financier"—who supposedly had not been contacted by Jackson until "weeks after the troopers began talking to the *Times*." (Yet Smith had called Brock before Rempel's first meeting with the troopers, so he must have spoken with Jackson even earlier.)

In the *Spectator*, Brock's allusion to Peter Smith was a vague footnote to his ten-thousand-word article. He failed to mention Smith's name or his offer to act as agent for the troopers' book proposal, or that the Republican financier had picked up the costs of his first two trips to Little Rock.

The *Los Angeles Times* made no apparent effort to discover the identity of the troopers' mysterious conservative benefactor. As the *Chicago Sun-Times* finally revealed in March 1998, Smith waited only three months before he wrote checks of $6,700 each to Perry and Patterson—a substantial gift to a state trooper making $40,000 a year. He also wrote a check for $6,600 to Lynn Davis. Smith told the *Sun-Times* that he had given them the money "on humanitarian grounds." David Brock later said he considered the payments a violation of his agreements with Smith and Jackson, but by then he had come to regret the entire experience.

Amid the usual hand-wringing that inevitably accompanies sex stories in the mainstream news media, Troopergate faded fast. But not before it made the president's goatish lust into a staple routine of late-night stand-up comics. None of the participants knew that Brock's story in the *American Spectator* would also set in motion a series of events that would plague Bill Clinton until the end of his presidency. The consequences of the magazine's secret Arkansas Project would similarly affect Clinton for years to come.

Chapter Eight

"A TRULY
INDEPENDENT PROSECUTOR"

T HE NATIONAL MEDIA DEBUT of David Hale prompted a growing chorus of Clinton adversaries to demand the appointment of a special prosecutor to investigate Whitewater. The first was Senator Lauch Faircloth, a very conservative North Carolina Republican and member of the Senate Banking Committee, who wrote to Attorney General Janet Reno in November 1993 urging her to act immediately to remove David Hale from the clutches of Paula Casey, the U.S. attorney in Little Rock. Similar messages and press releases issued in rapid succession from other Republicans on Capitol Hill until, two days after New Year's 1994, Senate Republican leader Bob Dole publicly accused Reno of an unseemly delay.

"There are dozens of questions that need to be answered," Dole said about Whitewater and Foster during a Sunday talk show appearance. "And I think it's in the president's interest," he added, to support an independent investigation. As for Reno, Dole insisted she should move quickly, "for the sake of the integrity of the attorney general's office. She's wasted a lot of time dragging her feet, and it's time she moved and appointed an independent counsel."

That same weekend, Clinton's mother, Virginia Kelley, died after a long illness. The president was outraged that Dole, who was already mulling whether to challenge Clinton in 1996, would assault him at a moment of such profound grief. Rebuked publicly by Vice President Al Gore for his insensitivity, Dole nevertheless continued the attack for several days, not pausing even for the Kelley funeral in Little Rock. Although Clinton later accepted Dole's private apology, resentment lingered.

Still, there were some in the White House who agreed with Dole's "advice," even if they doubted his motives and manners. The president's lawyers, how-ever, were not among them: White House counsel Bernard Nussbaum, for one, vehemently opposed the naming of a special counsel, or independent coun-sel, to use the precise legal term. In fact, Nussbaum opposed independent counsels in general, partly because he felt that once appointed, they followed an inevitable institutional mandate to indict *someone.* Other close advisers and many Democrats on Capitol Hill felt just as strongly that pressure for an in-vestigation would not abate—would in fact hinder any other business—until Reno did name a special prosecutor. That pressure was rising not only among congressional Republicans but at major media outlets, in particular the edito-rial pages of the *New York Times* and the *Washington Post.* It was another sig-nal that both papers had invested their own prestige in the Whitewater probe.

During November and December 1993, one accusatory article had fol-lowed another to the front pages of the nation's two most important newspa-pers, followed by indignant editorials bristling with rhetorical questions. Did Arkansas regulators scheme to keep Madison Guaranty S&L open? Did White-water losses cause the institution's failure? Did the Clintons corruptly benefit? There was little or no evidence that any of these things had happened. Never-theless, David Hale's accusations, combined with L. Jean Lewis's leaked second set of criminal referrals, contributed to an air of excited speculation. That the *Times* and *Post*'s Whitewater coverage coincided with the "Troopergate" story only served to heighten the sense that the press had the administration on the run.

The editorials in both papers took on a peremptory tone. Even the Clin-tons' possession of their own legal files following Vince Foster's suicide was portrayed as suspect. "It may be that there is nothing damaging or even em-barrassing" in the Clintons' legal files, conceded the *New York Times* on De-cember 23, 1993. "The White House's ongoing evasions over the past two years have left the impression that there's something untoward in those files. There is only one way to tell: Hand them over."

In early January 1994, the White House arranged to have the Clintons' Whitewater records subpoenaed by the Justice Department in a manner calcu-lated to make them available to investigators, but shield them from the press. The *Washington Post* reacted indignantly. "Someone said the other day that Washington may now have reached the state-of-the-art point of having a cover-up without a crime," the paper's editorial page mocked. The effect of the White House's action was "to make it appear as if the Clintons have something to hide. White House cuteness is damaging the President and elevating inter-est in the Clintons' Arkansas affairs far more than the 'runaway prosecutor' they are said to fear."

Time magazine may have summed up the Washington press's attitude best in a column by Michael Kramer, who wrote that since the president's presumptive wrongdoing happened long ago in Arkansas, "even if the worst were proved—and no one yet knows what that is—the offense might not warrant impeachment." Yet he wondered how it could be "that two respected lawyers like Bill and Hillary Clinton didn't possess a paper trail capable of proving their innocence."

Janet Reno, however, wanted no part of appointing an independent counsel, because to do so would eventually place her in an untenable position that could only harm her reputation. She explained why in a reply to Senator Faircloth on January 11, almost three months after he had first written to her. It would be pointless for the attorney general to name a special prosecutor to investigate the president. "Any such counsel appointed by me," she wrote, "would not be regarded as truly independent." And whoever was dissatisfied or dismayed by the prosecutor's performance, including the president, would blame her.

Reno's observations were prescient, but by then the Republicans had no choice except a counsel appointed by her or no independent investigation at all.

The Republicans in Congress had brought this paradoxical situation upon themselves. Reacting angrily to the seven-year Iran-contra probe of the Reagan and Bush administrations by independent counsel Lawrence Walsh, as well as a host of lesser independent counsel probes, the Republican leadership in both houses had resisted reauthorization of the Independent Counsel Act, which had expired in 1992. Many Republicans and some eminent legal scholars regarded the statute not as a post-Watergate reform but as an unconstitutional monstrosity, cleverly designed by partisan Democrats to harass Republican administrations. In the 1988 case *Morrison v. Olson* (whose losing plaintiff was Theodore Olson), the Supreme Court had upheld the law—but not without a sharp rebuke from Antonin Scalia, the Court's most respected conservative. Scalia blasted his colleagues for exposing the presidency to destruction by an unaccountable prosecutor. "The context of this statute," Scalia had written, "is acrid with the smell of threatened impeachment."

In what would become a classic dissenting opinion, he noted that "in the ten years since the institution of the independent counsel was established by law, there have been nine highly publicized investigations, a source of constant political damage to two administrations." Senator Dole, who had been a virulent critic of both Walsh and the law that empowered the independent counsel, agreed. When that law expired, Dole had decided he didn't want any more "political" indictments of public servants like his friend Caspar Weinberger, the former secretary of defense indicted by Walsh and then pardoned by President Bush.

Yet now, two years after they had shut down the mechanism for naming an independent counsel, the Republicans suddenly wanted one to investigate a

Democratic president. Under the Independent Counsel Act, all appointments had been made by a Washington-based panel of three federal appellate judges: the Division to Appoint Independent Counsels, better known as the "Special Division." The Special Division's purpose was to ensure that every prosecutor named would be seen as completely free of outside influence. After all, the aim of the independent counsel law was to create the perception as well as the reality of independence and integrity whenever high officials were suspected of criminality. But with the act no longer in force, the Special Division had gone dormant; the panel of three judges, left only with the power to supervise investigations already under way, no longer possessed the legal authority to name a new independent counsel. The Republicans had left no legal method for the appointment of a special prosecutor except action by the attorney general. This was the same situation that had obtained during Watergate, before the Independent Counsel Act was first signed into law in 1978 by President Carter.

The president resolved the dispute within the White House on January 12—the day after Reno's negative answer to Senator Faircloth. For all his skills, Clinton's greatest political vulnerability arguably lay in his eagerness to compromise with his enemies. Evidently confident that an objective Whitewater probe would put the issue to rest, and sure of his ability to finesse tomorrow's crisis as adroitly as today's, Bill Clinton made the worst blunder of his presidency. While traveling in eastern Europe, he asked the attorney general to name a Whitewater special counsel. Despite her earlier resistance, she had thought such a request from Clinton might be coming, and had instructed her assistants to prepare a list of prospective appointees. Selecting Robert B. Fiske of New York from a roster that included some of the country's most distinguished attorneys, she quickly reached agreement with Fiske on the investigation's scope and his prerogatives, and announced his appointment on January 20.

Unpretentious and taciturn, the sixty-three-year-old Fiske possessed every credential to make him an ideal choice to probe and, if necessary, prosecute a Democratic president and his associates. Though by then ensconced in a top Manhattan law firm, Davis, Polk & Wardwell, he had previously served as the United States attorney for the Southern District of New York, one of the most demanding posts in the Justice Department (and, years earlier, as an assistant prosecutor in the same office).

The consensus of Bob Fiske's peers, including many of his opponents in court, was that he had done a very difficult job exceedingly well. Appointed U.S. attorney by President Ford and kept in office by President Carter, he had successfully prosecuted several highly sensitive white-collar and organized-crime cases—indicting an important Democratic labor leader and a top drug informant—without a whisper of partisanship or misconduct. During his tenure, the office had won convictions in almost every case prosecuted.

Politically Fiske was a moderate, Manhattan-style Republican; professionally he was a respected leader of the American Bar Association, the sort of civic-minded attorney regularly appointed to commissions and committees by politicians of both parties. For a time, he had chaired the ABA's prestigious committee on nominees to the federal bench. So when Reno named Fiske to investigate Whitewater, the junior Republican senator from his own state, Alfonse D'Amato, praised him as "uniquely qualified for this position . . . a man of uncompromising integrity . . . one of the most honorable and most skilled lawyers anywhere." Bob Dole, echoing his friend D'Amato, cautiously welcomed the selection of Fiske, noting that "people who know him think he is extremely well qualified [and he] is independent." Few objections were heard from any quarter.

At a press conference with Reno, Fiske vowed to resolve questions about Whitewater "as quickly as I can, consistent with doing the job right." In response to a reporter's question, he added, "I would certainly expect, before this investigation is over, [that] I would question both the president and the first lady, and it would be under oath." Fiske took an immediate leave of absence from Davis, Polk to begin staffing his new office.

Three weeks later, Paula Corbin Jones made her public debut at the Omni Shoreham Hotel in Washington during the convention of the Conservative Political Action Committee, a major annual event for the capital's most right-wing Republicans. Paula and her husband, Steve Jones, had flown in from their home in Long Beach, California, to attend a press conference at the CPAC meeting, where Arkansas state troopers Roger Perry and Larry Patterson also planned to announce the creation of a "Troopergate Whistleblower Fund" (complete with a toll-free telephone number for contributors). Cliff Jackson, the attorney for Perry and Patterson, had graciously invited the Joneses to attach themselves as a sideshow to the February 11 announcement of the Troopergate fund. Ostensibly meant to defray the legal expenses of any future Arkansas informants, the fund's actual purpose was to line Perry and Patterson's pockets. Jackson would later admit to the *Arkansas Times* that the trio cleared $40,000. By packaging the troopers and Jones together for the national press at a right-wing Clinton-bashing forum, Jackson clearly hoped to revive the already waning interest in his own clients. The troopers' stories from the previous December were old news already, while Jones's allegations of sexual harassment by Bill Clinton were fresh.

Besides, it would cost Jackson nothing. From the very beginning, Clinton's right-wing enemies subsidized Paula Jones. All the costs of her trip—including a stay in the hotel's Presidential Suite—were picked up by the bland-sounding Legal Affairs Council. The council claimed to have raised $300,000 in support of Oliver North's Iran-contra defense. The night before the Jones press conference, troopers Perry and Patterson received a $1,000 check and appreciation plaques at an event sponsored by the council, where they also met Floyd Brown and David Bossie. Occasionally another right-wing celebrity such as North himself or G. Gordon Liddy approached the troopers to shake their hands and praise their patriotic gumption. So did Republican minority leader Newt Gingrich, destined to take over the House of Representatives by the end of the year.

Logistics for the next morning's press event were managed by Craig Shirley, a professional conservative publicist and consultant to the Republican National Committee. Nervous and mostly quiet, the twenty-seven-year-old Jones, dressed demurely with her long dark hair teased and poufed, sat behind the podium with her husband and the troopers. They listened while her short, portly Little Rock lawyer, Danny Traylor, and the rangy, angular Jackson recounted her woeful tale.

On May 8, 1991, Paula Jones had been doing her job as a clerical employee of the Arkansas Industrial Development Commission, helping to staff a state-sponsored "quality management" conference at Little Rock's Excelsior Hotel. Sometime that afternoon, Jones had been approached by state trooper Danny Ferguson, a member of Governor Clinton's security detail. Ferguson allegedly told her that she "made the governor's knees knock," and that he wanted to meet her in his suite at the hotel, then gave her Clinton's room number.

Viewing this invitation as a possible opportunity for career advancement, according to Jones's testimony, she and Ferguson had gone up in the elevator to Clinton's suite a few minutes later. There, she said, the governor had complimented her hair and figure before attempting three "unsolicited and unwanted sexual advances," each one "more aggressive" than the last. The governor also had asked her for "a type of sex," she said, although she and Traylor declined to be more specific at the Omni press conference. Jones insisted that she'd been so shaken by the encounter that she had left work almost immediately and gone straight home. As Paula told her story, the well-prepared Jackson gave out copies of affidavits Traylor had taken from two of Jones's friends, each swearing that Jones had complained at the time about Clinton's unwanted sexual overtures.

Jones had decided to speak out, after remaining silent for almost three years, Traylor said, upon learning about David Brock's Troopergate exposé in the *American Spectator*. She didn't claim to be a regular *Spectator* reader, but she had heard about the article during a January trip home to visit her family in Arkansas. To her dismay, a friend had showed Jones the passage in which Brock mentioned a woman identified only as "Paula," who had become one of Clinton's complaisant conquests in a one-hour hotel-room tryst. The *Spectator* piece said that this "Paula" had even told Danny Ferguson, the trooper who escorted her to Clinton's suite, that she "was available to be Clinton's regular girlfriend if he so desired." She had decided to go public, as she put it, "to clear my name."

As they recited Jones's troubles, Traylor and Jackson understandably omitted a few salient details. Traylor's version did not, for example, include his own effort a few weeks earlier to settle the matter quietly with a call to George Cook, a Little Rock businessman and Clinton supporter with whom he was acquainted. As Cook later explained in a sworn deposition that went essentially uncontradicted by Traylor, the Jones attorney had met with him to deliver an ominous message sometime in January 1994. According to Cook, Traylor recited his client's story about Clinton, saying that "if she did not get money . . . she would embarrass him publicly." The lawyer suggested that for $25,000 cash, Jones would go away. Traylor had also suggested that an acting job for Steve Jones, perhaps provided by the successful TV producer Harry Thomason, a close Clinton associate, "would help." Cook rejected this overture as "preposterous" and reported it to Clinton's lawyers. (Paula Jones later insisted that Traylor had contacted Cook without her knowledge or consent, that in fact she had no interest in money at all.)

Traylor, whose Little Rock solo practice mainly involved real estate transactions, also did not mention the fact that he and his client had agreed to split any proceeds from future movie, TV, and book deals based on her story. Nor did he bring up the doubts of Jones's older sister Charlotte and Charlotte's husband, Mark Brown, both of whom had attempted to dissuade Paula from pursuing her claims against Clinton, which they regarded as "a stupid lie." They believed that Paula had gotten herself in a lot of trouble out of simple greed. Just before Paula left for Washington, Charlotte Brown would later tell reporters, she had boasted that "either way it went, it smelled [like] money."

The prospect of money and a moment of fame were powerfully seductive for Paula Corbin Jones. She had grown up quite poor in a rural county outside Little Rock, under the strict religious discipline of her father, Bobby Gene Corbin, a garment factory worker and lay preacher in the Christian fundamentalist Nazarene sect. In the devout Corbin household many modern pleasures—movies, television, dancing, fashionable clothes and makeup, even bowling and skating—were held to be "worldly," probably sinful, and thus forbidden. Paula and her two sisters would accompany Bobby Gene Corbin to prayer meetings where they would sing hymns while he played the piano.

But when Paula was only nineteen, her father died of a heart attack; and her mother, Delmer Corbin, was unable to control her and her sisters as Bobby Gene had. Suddenly, Paula could wear short skirts and date men, staying out as late as she pleased and sometimes not coming home at all. Her brother-in-law Mark Brown, with whom she and her mother lived for several years after her father's death, worried about her flirtatious sexuality and her choice of boy-friends. Quite rightly, since one of them eventually sold seminude pictures of Paula to *Penthouse* magazine. (Even that came as no surprise to Mark and Charlotte Brown, who had seen the same photographs years before, when Paula boldly displayed them to the family.) In an accompanying article, several of Paula's former boyfriends described her as what southerners call a "wild child," promiscuous and bold.

Paula graduated high school but dropped out of the local community college before completing her first year there, moving on through a series of clerical jobs, sometimes quitting, sometimes getting fired, until she went to work as a receptionist for the Arkansas Industrial Development Commission, located on the state capitol grounds in Little Rock. A familiar figure around the capitol complex, her short, tight skirts, squeaky voice, and flirtatious manner earned her the nickname "Minnie Mouse." In the meantime she had met Steve Jones, a Northwest Airlines ticket agent and aspiring actor who bore a slight resemblance to Elvis Presley, at a Little Rock nightclub. By the spring of 1991 and her encounter with Bill Clinton, they were living together in a suburb north of the city. They married in 1992.

Former coworkers of Steve Jones recalled that he, too, liked to display pictures of Paula in various states of undress. They remembered as well his powerful animosity toward Clinton and his equally strong support for the Republican ticket in 1992. Jones put Bush-Quayle stickers on his locker and his gym bag, and had to be admonished to remove a Bush-Quayle button from his Northwest uniform. But none of his old colleagues had ever heard him say his wife had been harassed by Clinton. "Steve would have been screaming bloody murder if something happened to Paula," a friend told *People* magazine. "He would have made us aware that Clinton was a scumbag." People who knew Steve and Paula believed that he had pushed her into pursuing a vendetta against the president, to promote either his political views or his acting career, or perhaps both.

Whatever Paula Jones's initial motives, the reviews of her appearance in Washington were dismal where she got any coverage at all. By surrounding her with ultraconservative activists, Traylor and Jackson had ensured that her motives would be questioned and her story discounted, at least for the moment. Both that strategic blunder, and his failed effort to obtain a settlement, had demonstrated that Traylor lacked the skill and experience to handle an explosive case against the president.

The unveiling of her complaint in that highly political milieu also undermined Jackson's quiet effort to gain credibility for Jones, as he had done for the troopers a few months earlier, with mainstream news coverage. Instead of the *Los Angeles Times*'s Bill Rempel, Jackson had given the exclusive this time to

Michael Isikoff at the *Washington Post;* Jackson had arranged the paper's access to Jones and two friends who corroborated parts of her story, Pamela Blackard and Debra Ballentine. Isikoff met with Jones in Washington during her February visit, and had then overseen a team of reporters in Little Rock trying to confirm her accusations.

Isikoff had quickly become convinced that Jones and her friends—who swore she had tearfully told them of her humiliation by Clinton the day it occurred—were telling the truth. His superiors, however, took a more skeptical view, and before the Jones story finally ran three months later, Isikoff would go nose-to-nose with a doubting editor as they screamed at each other in a *Post* office. (That incident led to Isikoff's departure in May for *Newsweek,* also owned by the Washington Post Company.)

According to Ambrose Evans-Pritchard, the Washington correspondent for the London *Sunday Telegraph* who became a journalistic icon of the Clinton-hating right, Isikoff's failure to get her story in print spurred Jones into launching her lawsuit against the president. Traylor told the English journalist about his plan at a March 1994 meeting on Everett Ham's houseboat in North Little Rock (the same houseboat on which the fiercely bigoted Ham had so impressed Andrew Cooper, the young reporter from New Zealand, with his determination to destroy Clinton in 1992). Frustrated by Isikoff's exclusive access to Jones and wanting to interview her himself, Evans-Pritchard visited the houseboat to ask his friend Everett Ham and Ham's sidekick Gene Wirges for help. Immediately, Ham phoned Traylor, ordering the lawyer to "get your ass over here right away." And it quickly became clear that Traylor answered to this group, which was led by Cliff Jackson. Having refused several times before to give Evans-Pritchard his client's California phone number, Traylor quickly handed the number over when he was summoned to the houseboat.

After a few drinks, Traylor also confided that Jones might file a "tort of outrage" lawsuit against Clinton, but admitted he would need more skilled co-counsel to join a battle against the White House. Given the widespread belief among Clinton's Arkansas enemies that his campaign was in the practice of paying "hush money" to keep women quiet, Traylor may never have actually intended filing a lawsuit at all. Apparently convinced of Jones's veracity before he had even spoken with her, Evans-Pritchard suggested the name of Gerry Spence, a nationally famous attorney with a reputation for taking tough cases. Spence later declined Traylor's offer, but the search for a serious litigation team had begun. By early March, only eight weeks remained before the statute of limitations on Jones's claims against Clinton would expire. The point in suing Clinton was simple, Evans-Pritchard told his *Sunday Telegraph* readers. It doesn't "matter all that much whether Jones ultimately wins or loses her case," he wrote. "The ticking time bomb of the lawsuit lies elsewhere, in the testimony of other witnesses. Put plainly, the political purpose of the Jones lawsuit is to reconstruct the inner history of the Arkansas Governor's Mansion, using the legal power of discovery."

Apparently word went out in right-wing circles that Jones needed help, because at some point that spring Stephen Boynton and David Henderson, the duo directing the Scaife-funded Arkansas Project, tried to find her better legal assistance. Their eagerness to assist her was a sign that Traylor's threat to sue the *American Spectator* had been hollow. The Little Rock lawyer, in over his head, hadn't realized that his client's right-wing sponsors would never approve such a lawsuit.

It was during a fishing trip on the Chesapeake Bay that Boynton and Henderson—joined by their associate Parker Dozhier and their benefactor Richard Larry, the Scaife Foundation executive—placed a series of calls to Republican lawyers and conservative organizations seeking additional counsel for Jones. Dozhier's ex-girlfriend, Caryn Mann, recalled that on the fishing trip, "they wore out the batteries on six cell phones trying to find someone," but didn't do much fishing.

Exactly how Paula Jones finally found her way to Gilbert Davis and Joseph Cammarata, the Virginia attorneys who filed her complaint against Clinton on the deadline date of May 8, 1994, was then unclear. Reporters who asked about their sudden alliance with Traylor received vague answers or no answer at all. The Landmark Legal Foundation, a conservative legal advocacy group that received hundreds of thousands annually from Scaife, played some matchmaking role at the beginning. (Landmark attorneys reportedly convinced Jones not to sue the *American Spectator,* which of course was also funded by Scaife.)

A more direct role in the talent search was played by Richard Porter of Kirkland & Ellis—the Chicago attorney who had consulted with financier Peter Smith and Cliff Jackson on a compensation deal for the Arkansas troopers.

Either Smith or Jackson had approached Porter, a former aide to both President Bush and Vice President Dan Quayle, to represent Jones. Porter had turned the case down and instead called Nelson Lund, a law professor at George Mason University with expertise in employment discrimination and civil rights law. Lund, too, had worked in the Bush administration, serving as a lawyer in the White House Office of Legal Counsel; and like Porter, he was a Federalist Society stalwart with ties to Newt Gingrich.

Lund also declined the Jones case. But it was he who put Davis and Cammarata in touch with Danny Traylor, through a mutual friend and sometime associate of Davis named Frank Dunham, a Republican lawyer who also taught at George Mason. (Davis's friend Oliver North, whose benefactors at the Legal Affairs Council had paid for Jones and her husband to visit Washington, also encouraged Davis to take the case.) With only weeks to go before the statutory deadline, Traylor twice announced and then postponed the filing of Jones's lawsuit until the last day possible. Independent analysts surveyed by

Legal Times, a Washington legal publication, derided the complaint as poorly drafted and "dismissable on its face." That didn't discourage the flock of reporters and TV crews who had come to the federal courthouse in Little Rock to make Paula Jones a celebrity. Early media coverage was balanced with skepticism. On May 23, 1994, *Newsweek* interviewed several people around the Arkansas state capitol who scoffed at her claims. Jones was described as an unreliable, self-dramatizing person who had made a pest of herself hanging around the reception desk outside the governor's office, prattling about Clinton's sex appeal like a starstruck teenager. Nevertheless, with her lawsuit officially begun, she broke out of the right-wing ghetto and into the mainstream media.

Only by contrast to Traylor would Gilbert Davis or Joseph Cammarata seem like Washington insiders. Both were solo practitioners in the Washington area, well respected by their colleagues but of no great distinction. A former assistant United States attorney, the heavyset fifty-one-year-old Davis specialized in personal injury lawsuits, though he was known to take a drunk-driving case when business was slow; while Cammarata, a brisk, dark-haired, intense New York native of thirty-six who had once worked in the Reagan Justice Department, usually handled routine tax matters. Genial but sharp, Davis had been deeply involved in Virginia Republican politics since the early seventies, first as chairman of the Young Republican Federation, then running unsuccessfully for state attorney general in 1975. He regularly attended the annual state GOP conventions and had volunteered as an election lawyer in the 1988 Bush campaign.

Still, no one who knew the two lawyers believed they had accepted the Jones case to make a political point. By Virginia standards Davis was a moderate conservative, and Cammarata, until recently a Democrat, seemed to have little political commitment of any kind. They thought that the president, rather than see his personal life opened up in the process of legal discovery, would offer a substantial settlement.

They were well aware that Clinton wouldn't surrender without a fight, however, and probably thought they were overmatched by his attorney, Robert Bennett, a Washington eminence who commanded fees of $450 an hour. Already, Bennett had vowed to go to the Supreme Court if necessary to seek immunity from the Jones lawsuit. And they no doubt had assessed the weaknesses of their client and her allegations. "What stirs a warrior's blood is battle," Davis told the *Washington Post* in June, relishing the pose of David to Bob Bennett's Goliath.

But in fact he and Cammarata also knew they could rely upon a brain trust of hotshot conservative attorneys, all affiliated with the Federalist Society, from some of the country's most eminent firms and law schools. Included among these advisers, in addition to Richard Porter, were George T. Conway III, a tobacco litigator at Wachtell, Lipton, Rosen & Katz, one of the biggest New York corporate firms; Jerome Marcus, a young partner at the Philadelphia firm of Berger & Montague; and Ronald Rotunda, a distinguished professor of constitutional law at the University of Illinois, who would also coauthor an amicus brief to the Supreme Court supporting Jones.

The sole public hint of the hidden legal network accessible to Davis and Cammarata came in the presence of Kenneth W. Starr, who appeared on television and in the newspapers several times during the spring and summer of 1994 to argue that the Jones lawsuit should be permitted to proceed against Clinton without delay. "Our system is premised on the proposition not only that we're all subject to the rule of law," he told CBS News, "but secondly, that we will proceed as expeditiously as we can to get to the bottom of things."

In Washington, Starr carried at least as much clout as Bennett, maybe more. He had stepped down from the bench of the U.S. Court of Appeals for the District of Columbia in 1989 to serve as solicitor general in the Bush administration. He had long nursed hopes of a Supreme Court appointment, but when Clinton took office he had been exiled into the private sector. Since 1992 he had been earning roughly a million dollars a year, handling appeals for major corporate clients in the tobacco and auto industries as a senior partner in the Washington office of Kirkland & Ellis—the same firm that housed Richard Porter.

Starr took a personal interest in the Jones case, speaking frequently with Gil Davis about the constitutional issues raised by Clinton's claim of immunity. Early that summer, he even considered filing an amicus brief for Jones on behalf of the Independent Women's Forum, a conservative group funded by Richard Mellon Scaife as a counterweight to liberal feminist organizations. One of his younger partners told the *Washington Times* that Starr felt so strongly about the Jones case that he was willing to forgo his usual $400-an-hour fee and write the brief for free.

By the end of June, only five months after his appointment as Whitewater independent counsel by the attorney general, Robert Fiske had thoroughly infuriated his fellow Republicans. Their disenchantment with him had started to grow as early as March, when he told congressional leaders that any hearings on Whitewater ought to be postponed until he completed his investigation. He had issued subpoenas to presidential advisers George Stephanopoulos and Harold Ickes and Assistant Treasury Secretary Roger Altman, seeking to question them about their contacts concerning the Resolution Trust Corporation's investigation of Whitewater. Among the matters Fiske intended to explore was whether Stephanopoulos had tried to reverse the appointment of Republican attorney Jay Stephens and his firm, Pillsbury, Madison & Sutro, to prepare a report for the RTC about Madison Guaranty Savings and Loan, the Clintons, and other aspects of the alleged scandal.

Although Senate Republicans were eager to hold hearings about allegations that the White House had interfered with the probe or received an illicit warning about it, Fiske didn't want any of the Clinton officials scheduled to appear before his grand jury to testify at public hearings. If they obtained grants of congressional immunity, any chance to prosecute them later might be lost. Similar conflicts had virtually crippled the Iran-contra investigation run by Fiske's longtime friend and mentor Lawrence Walsh. Congressional immunity bestowed on Iran-contra witnesses had led to several criminal convictions, most notably Oliver North's, being overturned on appeal.

Led by New York senator Alfonse D'Amato, the ranking Republican on the Banking Committee, the Senate minority pushed ahead anyway, intimidating enough Democrats into voting for hearings in mid-March. The resolution did promise that the Senate "would not interfere" with Fiske, adding specifically that no witnesses would be granted immunity. The House Banking Committee planned to hold its own limited inquiry in late July.

But this compromise didn't placate Fiske's increasingly irritable critics in the press, notable the *Wall Street Journal* editorial writers and *New York Times* op-ed columnist William Safire, both of whom had accused Fiske of complicity in a White House "cover-up." Possibly mindful of Fiske's moderate reputation, the *Journal* had raised the specter of conflicts of interest between Fiske's law practice and his prosecutorial role. "Mr. Fiske has taken a full leave of absence, which means something other than resignation," huffed a February editorial. "Davis Polk is a sprawling firm with sprawling clients. . . . Seems to us there's a potential for conflict of interest with practically the whole world. . . . When the special counsel gets around to learning something about Whitewater, he will discover its largest single transaction was a land deal with International Paper Co.," a Davis, Polk client. Even Fiske's successful negotiation of a plea agreement with David Hale around the same time won him no friends in the anti-Clinton camp, perhaps because he required Hale to accept not one but two felony counts.

On March 24, Hale appeared before U.S. district judge Stephen M. Reasoner and admitted to "deceit, craft, trickery and dishonest means to defraud the United States" by falsely inflating the assets of Capital Management Services in order to secure federal matching funds, and by lying about the status of several government-backed loans. The judge, a Reagan appointee, asked Hale a series of pointed questions. Specifically, Reasoner wanted to know what had happened to some $900,000 in Small Business Administration matching funds.

"It was loaned out to various entities," Hale answered.

"Were any of the entities [ones] that you had an interest in?" the judge asked. In other words, had Hale stolen the money twice, once when he fraudulently obtained it as working capital, and a second time by lending it to one of the shell corporations he'd set up to funnel government money directly into his pockets?

"I don't believe so," Hale said.

Fiske and his assistants stood mute. Given the extraordinary complexity of Hale's schemes and his willingness to plead guilty, they may have been unaware that he was telling something less than the whole truth. Money the ex-judge never admitted stealing, he couldn't be forced to pay back. Hale had made a proffer to Fiske of allegations against Jim McDougal, Governor Jim Guy Tucker, and Bill Clinton. His sentencing would be postponed until its usefulness could be assessed. In the meantime, the independent counsel placed Hale under FBI supervision. Long prone to worries about his safety, Hale professed to believe that his life was in danger.

Hysteria over the circumstances of Vince Foster's death was being fanned daily on talk radio that spring, the most notorious example being Rush Limbaugh's repetition of a rumor that "Vince Foster was murdered in an apartment owned by Hillary Clinton." Citing an obscure investment newsletter as his source, Limbaugh contended that a fake crime scene had been fabricated at Fort Marcy Park. A hitherto little-known reporter named Christopher Ruddy began an extended series of articles that was ultimately published in the Scaife-owned *Tribune-Review* attempting to cast doubt on the findings of suicide. Encouraging the wild speculation about Foster, Senator Bob Dole referred to his death as an "alleged suicide," while Newt Gingrich also rejected the findings of the FBI and the Park Police, remarking ominously: "There's a lot there that is weird." The ranking Republican on the House Banking Committee, Representative Jim Leach, whose staff had been consulting regularly with Floyd Brown and David Bossie, insisted that Foster's death was somehow linked to Whitewater.

The cool, professional Fiske ignored his critics, proceeding expeditiously with investigations of both the Foster case and the RTC matter. On June 30, five months after his appointment, he released two reports. Regarding Foster, Fiske found that the late White House deputy counsel had "committed suicide by firing a bullet from a .38-caliber revolver into his mouth," and that "there is no evidence to the contrary." Furthermore, he "found no evidence that issues involving Whitewater" or the Clintons had led to Foster's suicide. The true cause was Foster's untreated clinical depression, which according to Fiske had been exacerbated by the harsh editorials about him in the *Wall Street Journal*.

As for whether White House aides had attempted to impede the RTC's probe of Whitewater, Fiske concluded that "the evidence is insufficient to establish that anyone within the White House or the Department of the Treasury acted with the intent to corruptly influence an RTC investigation." He would issue no indictments in either matter.

The special counsel's interim findings predictably outraged Clinton's critics, notably Safire, Floyd Brown, Republican leaders on Capitol Hill, and of course the *Journal*'s editors. Not only was Fiske coming to the wrong conclusions, he was moving much too fast.

By a curious coincidence, the president provided the means for retribution against Fiske on the same day that Fiske's reports were released, when he signed the newly reauthorized Independent Counsel Act that had been approved by the Senate several weeks earlier. With a Democrat in the White House, most Republicans had dropped their long-standing objections to the law. And now Clinton heard no objection from Bernard Nussbaum, the White House counsel who had argued so strenuously in January against appointing a Whitewater special counsel, and denounced the institution of the independent counsel as biased and "evil." Nussbaum was gone, forced to resign months earlier over a spate of bad press resulting from his alleged interference with the investigation of Vince Foster's death. Clinton himself felt misgivings about the Independent Counsel Act, though he had long since committed to renewing it. As he put pen to paper in the Oval Office, he muttered, "I may be making a terrible mistake."

With his signature, the president returned the power to choose and supervise independent counsels to the Special Division, the panel of three federal appeals judges selected by William Rehnquist, the chief justice of the United States. Once appointed, an independent counsel ultimately answered to no one else, regardless of his or her excesses—not even to the attorney general. The final authority to apply disciplinary sanctions, including dismissal, rested with the Special Division. Judges served on the panel for two-year terms, after which they could be reappointed or replaced by the chief justice. In an era of scandal politics, few appointments were more critical than those of the judges who held the ultimate legal weapon of the independent counsel. It was a serious mistake indeed for any Democratic president to cede control over that lethal mechanism to Rehnquist, a committed Republican and conservative ideologue.

During his two decades on the high court, memories of the fierce battle over Rehnquist's original 1971 nomination to the Supreme Court had faded, although the chief justice hadn't changed much. He had come to Washington from a western extremist milieu, associated with Barry Goldwater and the John Birch Society, as had many of the lawyers in Nixon's White House and Justice Department, where Rehnquist had served as assistant attorney general. When he had clerked at the Supreme Court in the early fifties, Rehnquist had composed a memorandum arguing for continued school segregation that later returned to haunt him. His spotty record at Justice, where he had approved covert army surveillance of antiwar protesters, became an issue in 1986, after

President Reagan nominated him as chief justice. Reagan surely knew, as Nixon had, that Bill Rehnquist would faithfully reflect his own political disposition.

The chief justice fulfilled those expectations on many occasions, and he did so again when he kept the Special Division stacked with two Republican judges and one Democrat. Had he wanted to avoid the appearance of partisanship, the chief justice could have rotated the three positions so that no party had a majority of the three judges for more than two years at a time. But Rehnquist erred in the other direction, going so far as to appoint David Sentelle, a protégé of Senator Jesse Helms and former Republican Party chairman in North Carolina's Mecklenburg County, to preside over the Special Division in 1992, and then reappointing him to the same position again in 1994. Few commentators seemed to notice at the time that Sentelle, who had risen so swiftly from a federal judgeship in 1985 to a seat on the D.C. Circuit Court of Appeals only two years later, lacked the best credentials for such a sensitive political position.

A loophole in the Independent Counsel Act permitted Rehnquist to appoint the relatively inexperienced and partisan Sentelle. The statute's pertinent clause clearly directed the chief justice, "in assigning judges or justices" to the Special Division, to give "priority" to "senior [i.e., semiretired] circuit judges and retired justices." But it didn't explicitly *require* him to appoint senior judges. Sentelle's two colleagues on the panel fit that description: John Butzner, seventy-six, a Johnson appointee, and Joseph Sneed, seventy-four, a Nixon appointee whose selection also presumably satisfied Rehnquist's implicit criteria. Like the chief justice himself, Sneed was a veteran of the Nixon Justice Department. A reliable conservative from Texas, Sneed had served as deputy attorney general, with broad responsibility for political and policy issues. Nixon trusted Sneed so much that early in the Watergate investigation—when then attorney general Richard Kleindienst recused himself from overseeing the probe—the president and his aides briefly considered asking Sneed, Kleindienst's deputy, to deal with the scandal. They discarded that idea because Sneed would have been seen as an obvious pawn of the White House. A few months later, in August 1973, Nixon named Sneed to the U.S. Court of Appeals' Ninth Circuit.

Neither Sneed, based in San Francisco, nor Butzner, whose chambers were in Richmond, Virginia, satisfied the law's sensible requirement that one of the three judges on the Special Division must come from the D.C. Circuit Court of Appeals, where the panel is headquartered. Sentelle's presence in the capital's federal courthouse was his sole visible qualification.

When Rehnquist first named Sentelle to head the Special Division in 1992, the North Carolina native was just forty-eight years old and had served only seven years on the bench. Widely regarded as one of the federal judiciary's most extreme conservatives, he was so enamored of the president who had first appointed him that he named one of his daughters Reagan. Though a competent attorney, he had earned his appointment after much political fundraising and campaigning for Reagan and Helms. Even after his elevation to the U.S. appeals court, Sentelle continued to write articles laced with strident partisanship, often couched in religious terms. In one 1991 article Sentelle accused "leftist heretics" of scheming to turn the United States into "a collectivist, egalitarian, materialistic, race-conscious, hyper-secular, and socially permissive state."

To choose such a figure to preside over the Special Division appeared to mock the appearance of impartiality that the Independent Counsel Act was supposed to guarantee. Besides, there were at least a dozen judges in the D.C. circuit who were senior to Sentelle and thus better qualified to oversee the independent counsel. Some believed Rehnquist had selected him not because of any particular qualification, but to do exactly what would be expected of a conservative ideologue: that is, to engineer the appointment of reliable Republican lawyers to investigate Democratic officeholders. First, however, Robert Fiske had to be removed.

From the moment that Fiske issued his findings about the Foster death and the RTC inquiries, Republican leaders and influential conservatives began maneuvering to eliminate him. William Safire, who had criticized Fiske early on for seeking to preserve his investigation from congressional interference, made a particularly blunt recommendation. Attacking Fiske's interim report, Safire wrote that he "cheerfully sees no evil. . . . What's with this non-independent counsel who helps Democrats avoid oversight? Find a way to get rid of him." The *Times* columnist was echoed by Floyd Brown and ten Republican members of Congress who wrote to the Special Division asking for Fiske to be replaced.

On July 1, Attorney General Reno wrote to the panel with the opposite request, suggesting that the three judges officially name Fiske as independent counsel so that his probe could continue with their sanction. That same afternoon, however, Senator Faircloth gave a speech on the Senate floor, asking the Special Division to appoint "a new, truly independent counsel." Among other complaints, the North Carolina senator mentioned Fiske's cooperation in an unrelated matter with Robert Bennett, the president's lawyer in the Paula Jones case, as well as his firm's representation of International Paper Company, which many years earlier had sold a parcel of land to Jim and Susan McDougal. To Faircloth, these were all serious conflicts of interest.

The sequence of events that followed Faircloth's speech left a permanent taint on the Whitewater investigation. In mid-July, he met with Judge Sentelle for a luncheon where they were joined by Sentelle's political sponsor and Faircloth's Senate colleague, Jesse Helms. Both of the North Carolina senators would later insist that they had spoken of nothing related to Fiske or Whitewater, but had merely engaged in friendly chatter with Sentelle about old acquaintances, western-style clothing, and prostate problems. Eventually, however, Sentelle himself would admit in public testimony that the subject of a new independent counsel might have come up.

On August 5, the Special Division unanimously rejected Reno's request that Fiske be reappointed and instead chose Kenneth Starr to continue the Whitewater probe. Explaining its decision, the panel's order said that allowing Fiske to continue "would not be consistent with the purposes" of the Independent Counsel Act, "though this reflects no conclusion on the part of the Court that Fiske lacks either the actual independence or any other attribute necessary to the conclusion of the investigation. . . . It is not our intent to impugn the integrity of the Attorney General's appointee, but rather to reflect the intent of the Act that the [independent counsel] be protected against perceptions of conflict. . . . The Court therefore deems it in the best interest of the appearance of independence . . . that a person not affiliated with the incumbent administration be appointed."

It did not take long for the irony of these assertions to become obvious. Within two weeks, Sentelle's lunch with Helms and Faircloth was reported in the press, raising eyebrows even among observers who professed little sympathy for the White House (which prudently issued no statement on the matter). In an editorial headlined "Mr. Starr's Duty to Resign," the *New York Times* recalled that in removing Fiske, the Special Division had cited "the need for the appearance, as well as the reality, of impartial justice." But, said the *Times,* "it is now clear that the chairman of that panel, Judge David Sentelle, violated the court's own standard for purity of appearances by meeting with a Senator eager to have the court dump Mr. Fiske as counsel," which the *Times* described as an example of "flamboyantly bad judgment." Five former heads of the American Bar Association also publicly urged Starr to step aside. None of this appeared to faze Starr, who ignored the editorial's call for him to step down immediately, lest his sterling reputation be impaired. Nor did it trouble Sentelle, who knew he had nothing to fear from the *Times*'s advice to Rehnquist that Sentelle ought to likewise stand aside or be replaced.

From the perspective of his fellow Republicans, Kenneth W. Starr must have seemed a nearly perfect choice as independent counsel. He was that rare combination of a deeply committed conservative and an esteemed stalwart of the bipartisan Washington establishment. As proclaimed years later by Sally Quinn, that establishment's self-styled doyenne, Starr had long been included as a capital insider. The forty-eight-year-old lawyer had started his career as a clerk for Warren Burger, then the chief justice of the United States; had gone on to work in the Reagan Justice Department; and had been named at a surprisingly early age to the U.S. Court of Appeals, without the slightest demurral from anyone. As President Bush's solicitor general he had managed to avoid arousing the ire of liberals and Democrats, to a point where some hard-line conservatives regarded him as a bit "soft."

His reputation for reasonableness was matched by a mild, ingratiating manner that didn't quite conceal his intense ambition but did set him apart from the cruder partisans on his end of the spectrum, who didn't get invited to Georgetown dinner parties. More importantly, Starr had earned the deference of the *Washington Post* when, as an appeals judge in 1987, he handed down a landmark First Amendment decision in a libel suit brought against the newspaper by a Mobil Oil executive. Among editors and executives at the *Post*, Bob Woodward was hardly alone in regarding that opinion as one of the most important moments in the paper's history, freeing it from inhibiting strictures on its tradition of aggressive investigative reporting, not to mention a multi-million-dollar jury verdict in favor of the plaintiff.

With his record of personal achievement and million-dollar salary, Starr had risen far from his rural Texas roots. His father had been a Church of Christ minister, renowned for severe interpretations of Scripture, and he had indoctrinated young Kenneth in biblical inerrancy and the dangers of drinking, dancing, playing music, and other worldly distractions. (In those details, Starr's strict upbringing resembled the grimly devout youth of Paula Jones.) His religious background may help to account for Starr's almost mystical confidence in his own righteousness. "We really did feel like we were special, like we were right and everybody else was wrong," an old high school friend of Starr's once explained to a reporter.

Politically, the Church of Christ elders gravitated toward the far right, particularly when Starr was growing up in the fifties. After graduation he attended Harding College, a church-affiliated institution in Arkansas that barred black students and maintained ties to the John Birch Society. But after two years there, Starr grew restless and moved on to George Washington University, where he met his future wife, a Jewish woman from New York named Alice Mundell.

By the time of his appointment as independent counsel, Starr's conservatism had taken on a more sophisticated corporate tinge. His firm's biggest clients were tobacco and auto companies seeking to minimize government regulation and avoid liability lawsuits, as well as the Republican National Committee and a host of wealthy right-wing foundations. Starr himself looked forward to a new Republican administration, as he told *Time* magazine, perhaps headed by his good friend from the Bush administration, former vice president Dan Quayle. Relatively young and vigorous, Starr still hoped to serve on the Supreme Court someday. Living in suburban Virginia, he remained active in Republican politics, cochairing the campaign of a GOP congressional candidate and quietly promoting himself as a potential nominee for the U.S. Senate in 1994.

He was, in short, a respectable figure, still known around Washington by the honorific "Judge Starr." At the same time he was an ambitious partisan, whose powerful personal interest in bringing down the Clinton administration, preferably in time for the next election, was bolstered by an equally strong ideological hostility to Clinton's policies. In his own brief public comment about his appointment, Starr expressed confidence in his own "complete fairness." Then he announced that while serving as independent counsel, he intended to continue as a partner at Kirkland & Ellis, drawing a million-dollar salary from a firm involved in litigation against the federal government and as counsel to the president's political adversaries.

The *New York Times* found Starr's evident conflicts of interest objectionable, particularly his advocacy on behalf of Paula Jones. So did many congressional Democrats, who bitterly protested the apparent influence-peddling by Faircloth and Helms that had led to Starr's appointment. But as Justice Scalia's 1988 dissent had predicted, the law left little recourse against such abuses. "An independent counsel is selected, and the scope of his or her authority prescribed, by a panel of judges. What if they are politically partisan, as judges have been known to be, and select a prosecutor antagonistic to the administration . . . ?" he had asked prophetically. "There is no remedy for that, not even a political one."

Chapter Nine

THE REVEREND
JERRY FALWELL, SEOUL MAN

A S HARD AS HE AND HIS SPONSORS in the Arkansas Republican Party had worked to prevent it, the election of President William Jefferson Clinton turned out to be the best thing that ever happened to Larry Nichols. By then, his lawsuits against Clinton had been dismissed with prejudice by both state and federal courts. Peddling his tales of Clinton's lechery to the *Star* tabloid during the presidential primaries had netted Nichols a mere $30,000. He and his fellow scandalmonger, private eye Larry Case, had not only failed to realize their dreams during the 1992 general election campaign, but had ended up talking about changing sides and ratting out their Republican sponsors.

The Clinton presidency and its myriad controversies, however, provided Nichols with an opportunity far beyond any he had hitherto imagined. In early 1994, the former high school football star, rock musician, state bureaucrat, jingle writer, and small-time operator was poised to turn himself into a nationally known celebrity on the Clinton-hating talk radio circuit.

The immediate agencies of Nichols's good fortune were a California-based outfit called Citizens for Honest Government and the Reverend Jerry Falwell, the famous Baptist preacher and right-wing politico from Lynchburg, Virginia. Like many another organ of the political right—the American Spectator Educational Foundation, for example—the innocuous-sounding Citizens for Honest Government was registered with the IRS under Section 501(c)(3) of the tax code as a nonprofit educational organization, theoretically nonpartisan, tax-exempt and free to solicit tax-deductible charitable contributions. (Actually, Citizens was set up under the aegis of another nonprofit organization that Matrisciana already had qualified with the IRS under the name Creative Ministries.)

In practice, the new organization had two main purposes: to propagate the political and religious nostrums of the extreme religious right, with which its founder and sole proprietor, Pat Matrisciana, was closely allied; and to promote and distribute videotapes produced by Jeremiah Films and Integrity Films, two for-profit corporate entities he owned.

Until 1993, Jeremiah Films produced slick, melodramatic videos on themes mainly of interest to Christian fundamentalists. In 1988, for example, Matrisciana unveiled *The Evolution Conspiracy,* a documentary exposing the organizing principle of modern biology as a scientific hoax and religious heresy used by "atheists, hindu mystics and The New Age" to subvert Christianity. *Halloween, Trick or Treat?* warned American parents that lurking behind such "seemingly innocent symbolism" as black cats and jack-o'-lanterns lay a satanic plot to seduce their children into "Pagan Occultism." The spread of AIDS, according to a 1989 production, had resulted from "a homosexual cover-up" of the disease's actual causes. And a sequel titled *Gay Rights, Special Rights* revealed the hidden purpose of civil rights laws forbidding discrimination by sexual preference: to enable homosexuals to "procreate" in "public classrooms where they recruit and propagandize the innocent."

The advent of Clinton offered theological entrepreneurs like Matrisciana an eschatological thrill. With the millennium almost nigh, it seemed possible that Americans were living in the End Times and had fallen under the sway of the Antichrist, as predicted in the Book of Revelation. It also seemed possible to make money and advance right-wing Republicanism by stirring up millennial anxieties.

Jeremiah Films' initial response to the Clinton presidency was a 1993 production titled *The Crash: The Coming Financial Collapse of America.* By 2000, this video predicted, the U.S. Treasury would default on the national debt. Hyperinflation would render the dollar worthless, placing the nation at the mercy of Japanese bankers. Inner-city riots, breadlines, and fear of chaos would lead Americans to abandon democracy in favor of a Hitlerian strongman. Narrated in part by such GOP stalwarts as former attorney general Edwin Meese III, former California representative William Dannemeyer, and Mississippi senator Trent Lott, it urged a "spiritual revolution" and recommended stockpiling food. (Somewhat paradoxically, Citizens for Honest Government simultaneously offered a course in "Christian Investment Counseling" for a mere $19.95, Visa and MasterCard accepted.)

What Jeremiah's doomsday video neglected to note was that almost everyone involved in making it, including Matrisciana himself, belonged to a tightly guarded political organization known as the Council for National Policy. Founded in 1981 by the Reverend Tim LaHaye, the CNP's roughly five hundred members include virtually everybody who is anybody on the evangelical far right. Its thrice-yearly meetings are members-only events, strictly closed to press and public. Even the organization's membership list is supposed to be confidential, although the Institute for First Amendment Studies and other liberal critics have obtained the roster and even posted it on the Internet.

Along with Meese, Dannemeyer, and Lott, other Republican politicians then affiliated with the CNP included North Carolina senators Jesse Helms and Lauch Faircloth, Don Nickles of Oklahoma, and John Kyl of Arizona. Former Southern California representative Bob Dornan is a longtime CNP stalwart, as are House Majority Whip Tom DeLay, Dick Armey of Texas, and Dan Burton of Indiana. No Democratic senator or representative is a member.

On the pastoral side, televangelists Pat Robertson and James Dobson belong to the CNP, as do Falwell and many others. So do the leaders of virtually every far-right foundation and think tank in the country, including Gary Bauer of the Family Research Council, Paul Weyrich of the Free Congress Foundation, Phyllis Schlafly of the Eagle Forum, Floyd Brown of Citizens United, Larry Klayman of Judicial Watch, and political consultant Ralph Reed. Television commentator Oliver North has been a member for many years. But what really enhances the organization's political significance are its connections with major sources of wealth, such as the Coors and DeVos families and rich individuals such as Colorado investor Foster Friess.

In essence, the CNP functions as the central committee of a theocratic "popular front"—an alliance of individuals and groups who set aside their differences for the sake of fighting a common enemy. Abstractly stated, that enemy appears to be America's constitutional separation of church and state; more concretely, the CNP's targets are liberals, most Democrats, and "secular humanists" of all sorts, including moderate Republicans. Many influential CNP members adhere to a doctrine known as "Christian Reconstructionism," which essentially argues that the U.S. Constitution derives its earthly legitimacy from the Bible as interpreted by Protestant fundamentalists.

The intellectual underpinnings of Christian Reconstructionism derive largely from the writings of a California theologian (and CNP member) named R. J. Rushdoony. In an eight-hundred-page tract published in 1973 entitled *Institutes of Biblical Law,* he wrote, "The only true order is founded on Biblical law. All law is religious in nature, and every non-Biblical law-order represents an anti-Christian religion." Accordingly, he prescribes the death penalty for a wide variety of sins, including adultery, homosexuality, abortion, atheism, heresy, and blasphemy. Among those most heavily influenced by Rushdoony is his fellow CNP member John Whitehead, founder of the Rutherford Institute (and, by late 1997, one of the lead attorneys for Paula Jones).

The more pragmatic evangelicals disdain Rushdoony's extremism. CNP member Ralph Reed, former executive director of the Christian Coalition, has criticized Christian Reconstructionism as "an authoritarian ideology that threatens the most basic civil liberties of a free and democratic society." Still, there is one Reconstructionist idea that unites the American religious right. "Most Reconstructionists," writes scholar Frederick Clarkson, believe that the United States should be a "Christian Nation" and that they are the champions and heirs of the "original intentions of the Founding Fathers."

If that vision of a Christian America stirs powerful emotions among conservative evangelicals, their fundamentalist theology can also predispose them to a conspiratorial mind-set. "The view of history as conspiracy," Rushdoony has written, "is a basic aspect of the perspective of orthodox Christianity." Those who view history as an all-encompassing struggle between God and the Devil may find it natural to regard political opponents as agents of Lucifer.

Reed's former boss, the televangelist and Christian Coalition founder Pat Robertson, plainly shares that perspective. "There will never be peace," Robertson wrote in 1992, "until God's house and God's people are given their rightful place of leadership at the top of the world. How can there be peace when drunkards, drug dealers, communists, atheists, New Age worshippers of Satan, secular humanists, oppressive dictators, revolutionary assassins, adulterers and homosexuals are on top?"

In other words, the "culture war" declared by Robertson, Falwell, Pat Buchanan, and Representative Henry Hyde was doctrinally unavoidable. And Clinton's election galvanized the culture warriors of the Council for National Policy. Even the relatively cautious Christian Coalition called Clinton's inauguration "a repudiation of our forefathers' covenant with God." Such rhetoric implied a divine mandate to bring down an unfit president.

As soldiers of fortune in that crusade, Pat Matrisciana and Larry Nichols were destined to do business. If Citizens for Honest Government was in the market for conspiracies involving Bill Clinton, Nichols had plenty to sell. They were introduced in late 1993 by a former NBC News cameraman named John Hillyer, who had been hired by Matrisciana to scout Arkansas for anti-Clinton material. Nichols's antics during the 1990 and 1992 campaigns had made him a well-known figure in Little Rock newsrooms (where reporters knew better than to use him as a source for anything that couldn't be independently confirmed).

"More than anything else, Larry just loves to talk," said one Little Rock journalist who understood his raffish appeal. "He's literally a bullshit artist. . . . If Bill Clinton has this amazing charm, Larry has a similar ability to sit down with somebody—maybe not a smart, skeptical person—but, say, a small-town banker or a right-wing radio talk show host, and persuade them to believe almost any damn thing he comes up with. He's witty. He can make you laugh."

Nichols and Matrisciana's first joint venture was a thirty-minute video called *Circle of Power*. Distributed nationwide by Falwell's Liberty Alliance early in 1994, the video opens with Nichols sitting in a cozy parlor, wearing a red cardigan like Mister Rogers and earnestly telling of "countless people who mysteriously died" after running afoul of Clinton's political ambition.

Few on the right had accepted independent counsel Robert Fiske's verdict that Vincent Foster had committed suicide for reasons that had nothing to do with his job at the White House. "Fiske was appointed by Janet Reno at the suggestion of Bernard Nussbaum," Falwell told reporters. "It's like putting Hillary Clinton in there." Pat Robertson, Rush Limbaugh, and the editors of the *Wall Street Journal* had expressed similar doubts.

Taking Foster's death as a starting point, *Circle of Power* tied the president to a series of suicides, accidental deaths, and unsolved homicides. Few of these smears were original; most of the video's content was identical to a list appearing on an Internet Web site—"The Clinton Body Count: Coincidence or the Kiss of Death?"—run by an Indianapolis lawyer named Linda Thompson. Thompson had quit her one-year-old law practice in 1993 to run the American Justice Federation, a for-profit group that indulges in conspiracy theories and progun agitprop through a shortwave radio program, a computer bulletin board, and sales of newsletters and videos. Updated biweekly, by mid-1994 the list included thirty-four names of Clinton-linked people the Web site said had died under suspicious circumstances, including four federal agents killed in the Branch Davidian shoot-out in Waco, Texas; four army crewmen who died in a helicopter crash in Germany; a Democratic campaign strategist who died of a heart attack; a friend of White House adviser Mack McLarty who perished in a ski accident; a seventy-two-year-old Little Rock lawyer who crashed a single-engine airplane on a foggy airstrip; and so forth.

Almost simultaneously with the release of the video—promoted on national TV as "Jerry Falwell Presents Bill Clinton's Circle of Power"—former representative William Dannemeyer, a founding member of the Council for National Policy, sent an open letter to his former colleagues in the House of Representatives citing the list of mysterious deaths and demanding a congressional investigation.

But it was *The Clinton Chronicles,* Falwell and Matrisciana's second, more ambitious production, that reached the widest audience after it was released that spring. Although Falwell has since denied subsidizing the scurrilous video, the financial records of Citizens for Honest Government prove that its production costs were underwritten by Falwell's Liberty Alliance. Those same documents also show that nearly every individual interviewed in what was ostensibly a work of documentary journalism was paid a substantial fee or royalty.

Even more disturbing were the allegations, in court records obtained by former *Newsweek* reporter Robert Parry for his on-line publication *I.F. Magazine*, that suggest that Falwell may have been subsidized by the Korean evangelist Sun Myung Moon.

Those court papers, filed in a lawsuit in the Circuit Court of Bedford County, Virginia, claim that Falwell and two associates made a seven-day "secret trip" to South Korea on January 9, 1994, to meet with representatives of the Unification Church, accompanied by *Washington Times* executive Ronald N. Godwin, formerly the director of the defunct Moral Majority, Inc., and a conservative direct-mail entrepreneur named Daniel Reber. According to the same documents, two former business associates of Reber's claim that the trio had met a few months earlier at Falwell's Liberty University in Lynchburg with Dong Moon Joo, the president of the *Washington Times* and the Korean preacher's chief American representative.

Moon, the self-proclaimed messiah whose theology is rejected by evangelical Christians, has lavished millions on right-wing political causes in the United States for well over two decades. His church's ownership of the *Washington Times*, as well as affiliated publications like *Insight* magazine, whose combined losses are subsidized at an estimated rate of $100 million per year, have lent Moon legitimacy in conservative circles. Indeed, former presidents Reagan and Bush both have accepted enormous honoraria for their speeches at Unification Church events despite the fact that Moon has repeatedly denounced America as the "Kingdom of Satan."

On July 26, 1994—in the midst of his promotion of *The Clinton Chronicles*—Falwell showed up at Moon's side for a dinner honoring a new allied group called Youth Federation for World Peace. His willingness to publicly associate with Moon, whom Southern Baptists consider heretical, appeared to have at least one clear motive: money.

Falwell's own right-wing sympathies dated from the early sixties, when he had defended segregation from the pulpit and denounced the civil rights movement as an instrument of Communism. As a mainstay of evangelical Republicanism, he had been particularly close to both Ronald Reagan and George Bush. But like other TV evangelists, Falwell had seen contributions drop in the wake of the Jim Bakker and Jimmy Swaggart scandals; public opinion of Falwell himself was negative as well. After being forced to abandon the Moral Majority, Inc., for financial reasons in 1986, he was virtually buried beneath a mountain of institutional debt. By 1993, his Liberty University owed $73 million to the bondholders who had financed its construction, and was badly in danger of a default.

*   *   *

The Clinton Chronicles made Larry Nichols a star. Cinematically, the video resembled the anti-Communist films churned out at Arkansas's Harding College during the fifties and early sixties, when the young Kenneth Starr matriculated there, with a pseudodocumentary format, a deep-voiced narrator warning of impending doom, and a musical score evocative of *Bride of Frankenstein*. As in those old movies about the totalitarian Communist conspiracy, the new video depicted the "Clinton machine" as achieving "absolute control" over the state of Arkansas and misusing that power for sinister purposes.

The video's intellectual style would be familiar to any student of historian Richard Hofstadter's classic essay, *The Paranoid Style in American Politics.* "The typical procedure of the higher paranoid scholarship is to start with . . . a careful accumulation of facts or at least of what appear to be facts and to marshal these facts toward an overwhelming 'proof' of the particular conspiracy that is to be established."

Preceded by a notice that "all information in this video is documented and true," the tape was narrated principally by Nichols and the ubiquitous Justice Jim Johnson. According to Johnson, a white-haired eminence identified only as a retired state supreme court judge, the evidence of Clinton's crimes was "more credible than the evidence of 90 percent of the people who are confined on death row across America."

The challenge facing Arkansas journalists was to find a single "true" or "documented" statement in *The Clinton Chronicles.* Veteran reporter Carrie Rengers drew the assignment of reviewing the Citizens for Honest Government opus for the resolutely Republican *Arkansas Democrat-Gazette.* ("Apparently," she commented tartly, "honesty isn't necessary in videos.") She painstakingly debunked its most absurd assertions. Had Governor Clinton really failed to balance Arkansas's state budget even once? In fact he had done so every year because state law forbids deficit spending. Had he, as the video alleged, issued a full pardon to a political supporter named Dan Lasater who was convicted of giving cocaine to his acquaintances? Impossible, because Lasater had pleaded guilty to a federal crime.

Had all the financial records of Clinton's political campaigns mysteriously vanished? No, they were duly on file with the Pulaski County clerk and the Arkansas secretary of state. Had poultry mogul Don Tyson, of Tyson Foods, donated some $700,000 to Clinton's 1992 presidential campaign? Neither he nor his firm had donated a penny to the Democrat or his party in 1992. Had Tyson Foods received a low-interest $10 million state loan which it failed to repay? Although a version of this fable also had appeared under Jeff Gerth's byline on the front page of the *New York Times* (which ran a correction), the poultry giant had never borrowed a dime from the state of Arkansas. As far as Rengers could determine, the whole story was invented.

Unsurprisingly, the largest volume of fabrications in *The Clinton Chronicles* concerned the Arkansas Development Finance Authority (ADFA), the state agency from which Nichols had been fired in 1988. As presented by him, the ADFA's purpose wasn't to help Arkansas cities and businesses finance sewage projects, schools, and industrial parks. Rather, it was designed to help Clinton's cronies loot the public treasury and launder billions in drug-smuggling profits—and to finance Clinton's out-of-state partying with loose women.

Again, every allegation that could be checked was phony. Contrary to Nichols, Webb Hubbell had played no role in writing the ADFA's enabling legislation. His father-in-law's company P.O.M. (which manufactured parking meters, not hollow airplane nose cones for stashing cocaine) had once qualified for a $2.8 million loan, but far from making no repayment, the firm had retired the debt on time.

The Clinton Chronicles asserted that the Rose Law Firm had a monopoly on ADFA businesses, and that the governor personally signed off on all ADFA loans. In reality, the *Democrat-Gazette* found, a half dozen Little Rock law firms competed vigorously for ADFA work; the governor's office played no active role in the agency's lending process. One of the video's silliest charges was that the ADFA had laundered $100 million per month (or $1.2 billion per year) in illicit cash. In the agency's nine-year existence, it had made loans totaling only $1.7 billion.

These errors and falsehoods didn't discourage Falwell from promoting *The Clinton Chronicles* as if it were *The Ten Commandments.* For four successive weeks in May 1994, viewers of the Virginia evangelist's syndicated TV program, *The Old-Time Gospel Hour,* saw not sermons and spirituals but excerpts from *Circle of Power* and *The Clinton Chronicles,* along with a half-hour infomercial touting the videos for a donation of $40 plus $3 for shipping and handling. A few of the more than two hundred TV stations that carried Falwell's program deemed the episodes political rather than religious, and refused to broadcast them without payment, but most showed them on schedule.

Toward the end of the thirty-minute infomercial, Falwell interviewed a figure in silhouette, identified only as an "investigative reporter."

"Can you please tell me and the American people why you think that your life and the lives of the others on this video are in danger?" the reverend asks.

"Jerry, two weeks ago we had an interview with a man who was an insider," the dark figure replies. "His plane crashed and he was killed an hour before the interview. You may say this is just a coincidence, but there was another fellow that we were also going to interview, and he was killed in a plane crash. Jerry, are these coincidences? I don't think so."

The silhouette's voice was recognized by investigative reporter Murray Waas, who finally got Pat Matrisciana to admit he was the mystery man. "Obviously, I'm not an investigative reporter," Matrisciana confessed, "and I doubt our lives were actually ever in any real danger. That was Jerry's idea to do that. . . . He thought that would be dramatic."

A few months later, Falwell's Liberty Alliance sent out a direct-mail solicitation to thousands of supporters, asking for contributions to help him "produce a national television documentary which will expose shocking new facts about Bill Clinton." But the letter didn't reveal why Falwell needed to finance yet another edition of the anti-Clinton exposé. In keeping with Larry Nichols's allegiance to Sheffield Nelson, *The Clinton Chronicles* had made several dubious allegations against Nelson's lifelong enemies at Stephens, Inc., the Arkansas investment house.

It charged that a Little Rock commercial bank owned by the Stephens family had reaped illicit profits from its dealings with the ADFA and other state accounts, and had in return made an illegal $3.5 million loan to Clinton's 1992 presidential campaign that was never repaid. But the Stephens family no longer owned a controlling share in Worthen Bank; it had lost, rather than gained, state business as a result of the ADFA's creation; and it had played no part in the perfectly legal Worthen loan to the Clinton campaign, which had been repaid in full. Although Stephens, Inc., would be forced to defend itself in print against hurtful inaccuracies in both the *Wall Street Journal* and the *New Republic* on several occasions during Bill Clinton's first term, it had more direct means to deal with Jerry Falwell.

The investment firm had long underwritten bond issues for religious colleges across the South—one of which happened to be Falwell's own insolvent Liberty University. "We had first claim on Liberty University to pay the bonds we owned," explained chief executive Warren Stephens. "After they went into default, we could have taken the first dollar of tuition payments to satisfy the debt. We could have shut the place down, but we didn't. Then lo and behold, here came *The Clinton Chronicles*—all lies."

Rather than foreclose, Stephens took a gentler approach. He flew to Lynchburg in a corporate jet and explained the facts of life to the portly Virginia evangelist. "There was no pressure, no threat," Stephens recalled. "It was more like, 'Hey, you know us. You absolutely know from a character standpoint that these things aren't true.' Falwell acted like he was shocked. They took it out of *The New Clinton Chronicles* and sent out a letter to the people who'd ordered the video explaining that there had been a mistake. But I don't mind telling you, he's a bizarre guy. Flat spooky."

With President Clinton's popularity edging toward record lows during the spring and summer of 1994, *The Clinton Chronicles* became an underground sensation. Citizens for Honest Government would later claim sales of more than 150,000, with perhaps double that number of bootleg copies in circulation. The Council for National Policy bulk-ordered copies for all its members, and Matrisciana sent tapes to all 435 members of Congress and to influential Washington journalists. Indiana congressman Dan Burton—a Foster conspiracy buff who achieved a degree of notoriety by conducting an amateur ballistics test in his backyard involving a .38 revolver and a watermelon—invited Larry Nichols to Washington and introduced him to like-minded House members. Evangelical churches, particularly across the South, showed the video during services. Conservative talk radio amplified its ominous message to an audience of millions. Nichols's gravelly baritone soon became a familiar feature of the nationally syndicated Michael Reagan radio talk show, where he took to claiming that his life was in danger and that he was being forced into hiding. He solicited donations to finance his life as a political fugitive.

In real life, Nichols cruised around his hometown of Conway, Arkansas, in a brand-new white Lincoln Continental. He and his wife, whose state job as secretary to the president of the University of Central Arkansas remained unaffected by her husband's activities, moved into a large new home with a swimming pool on a winding street.

He set up his own Internet Web site, began a shortwave radio program, and became a favorite speaker among "patriot" and militia groups nationwide. On May 11, 1994, he spoke at a Colorado rally sponsored by a group called the "Boulder Patriots." A videotape of the proceedings was later turned over to the Secret Service, probably because at one point during his manic monologue, Nichols pulled a nickel-plated semiautomatic handgun from his pants and provoked cheers by waving it in the air. "I made a deal with Bill Clinton," he shouted. "In 1994, we're gonna meet at high noon, and one of us is gonna get out of town!" Voices in the crowd could be heard yelling, "Shoot the bastard!"

Although Nichols's actual military experience consisted of four months duty as an electrician in the Arkansas National Guard, he boasted of his extensive record as a Special Forces combat infantryman. "Everything I did," he roared, "I did for God and country. And when you're playing with commies, it ain't easy. In the old days before Clinton took over, communists were bad guys and I was trained—I was taught—to get in the other man's world and beat him at his game. I'm in Bill Clinton's world now, and there's not ever gonna be the day when the draft-dodging, lying, woman-chasing, dope-smoking, cocaine-using womanizer that exposes himself will be the president of this country!"

Eventually, the president was forced to defend himself. He gave an interview to the *Minneapolis Star-Tribune* on April 8, 1994, complaining about the right-wing media. "There's something that those of us who are Democrats have to contend with. The radical right have their own set of press organs.

They make their own news and then try to force it into the mainstream media. We don't have anything like that. We don't have a *Washington Times,* or a Christian Broadcasting Network, or a Rush Limbaugh, any of that stuff."

Interviewed in June on KMOX, a St. Louis radio station, Clinton complained again about the "constant, unremitting drumbeat of negativism." A KMOX reporter asked Clinton if he was referring to the Reverend Jerry Falwell and *The Clinton Chronicles.* "Absolutely," he said. "Look at who he's talking to. I mean, does he make full disclosure to the American people of the backgrounds of the people that he has interviewed that have made these scurrilous and false charges against me? Of course not."

Falwell responded by inviting the president to prove his innocence. He told the *New York Times* that Clinton should be angry not at him but at those who made the accusations. If Clinton were to "tape a personal and direct rebuttal" to the video indictment, the reverend promised to broadcast it unedited on *The Old-Time Gospel Hour.* Floyd Brown, author of *Slick Willie,* publisher of the *Clintonwatch* newsletter, and previous employer of the talents of Larry Nichols and Justice Jim Johnson, commented that the Clintons were very "thin-skinned."

The president's complaints caused a flurry of front-page stories in newspapers like the *Times* and the *Philadelphia Inquirer* that inevitably focused on the more sensational accusations and observed that the videos offered no proof that Clinton was a drug-smuggling murderer. These articles provoked an oddly defensive editorial in the *Wall Street Journal* on July 20, 1994. While conceding that many of *The Clinton Chronicles* accusations made no sense, the *Journal* editors still insisted that "the Falwell tape and the controversy around it get at something important about the swirl of Arkansas rumors and the dilemma it presents a press that tries to be responsible. The 'murder' accusation, for example, is not made by Mr. Falwell or Mr. Nichols, but by Gary Parks, whose father was gunned down gangland style on a parkway near Little Rock last September."

The elder Parks had run a private security firm that supplied guards outside Clinton's Little Rock headquarters during the 1992 campaign. The anti-Clinton clique, including the London *Sunday Telegraph*'s Ambrose Evans-Pritchard, deduced that he had been killed because he knew too much about Clinton's sex life. The *Journal* acknowledged that there was no evidence, and speculated that "Jerry Parks had plenty of reason to have enemies, and his family may be overwrought." That was how Little Rock police viewed the still-unsolved crime. (Gary Parks eventually apologized for accusing Clinton and expressed regret about his involvement with the video.)

The *Journal* editors stipulated that they could not "for a minute imagine Bill Clinton knowingly involved, even tangentially, in plots of violence." Yet even in criticizing Falwell, they published the names of several more putative

Clinton "victims" previously listed in the British press. Then, chafing against the niggling constraints of responsible journalism, they went further.

Rumors about Clinton were "old news to any of the journalists covering Arkansas scandals, but few of us have shared any of this knowledge with readers. . . . Finding no real evidence of a Clinton connection, and feeling that the President of the United States is entitled to a presumption of innocence, we decline, in the name of responsibility, to print what we've heard. And then it is left to less responsible sources to publish the first reports, and the disclosure of basic facts adds credibility to their sensational interpretation, especially among those losing trust in the mainstream press."

The performance of the mainstream press did leave much to be desired as far as knowledgeable Arkansans were concerned. Highly influential articles about the president and his home state continued to appear in prominent publications with information that was scarcely more accurate, if less luridly presented, than the *Clinton Chronicles*. Taken together, they strengthened the Washington-press elite's impressions of Bill and Hillary Clinton's scandal-ridden past.

The *Journal* first betrayed its own impatience with journalistic restraint during a farcical episode that had occurred earlier in 1994. That incident, too, involved Larry Nichols, along with a writer named L. J. Davis. At issue was a cover story that ran in the April 4, 1994, issue of the *New Republic*. Headlined "The Name of Rose," it purported to be an exposé of Arkansas's "colorful folkways" and corrupt political culture. With the venerable Washington magazine's imprimatur, Davis introduced the worldview of *The Clinton Chronicles* to an influential, sophisticated elite that would scoff at the Falwell videos.

His article, which had been rejected by *Harper's* magazine, sketched Arkansas state government as a "Third World" criminal conspiracy among Bill and Hillary Clinton, the Rose Law Firm, and Stephens, Inc. Assisted by "sinister Pakistanis" and "shadowy Indonesians," this cabal had looted the president's home state and now menaced the nation.

Considering that Larry Nichols and a Republican political consultant named Darrell Glascock were the writer's two primary sources, it was unsurprising that he erred so badly. (Some months after the Davis article appeared, Glascock copped a plea in a scam involving a fraudulent state purchase of fifty thousand nonexistent U.S. flags, and gave testimony that sent his co-conspirator to jail for seventeen years.)

Employing no fact checkers at the time, the *New Republic* was helpless against Nichols and Glascock's inventions. Two examples should suffice: "With the stroke of a pen and without visible second thought," Davis wrote, "then-Governor Clinton . . . gave life to two pieces of legislation inspired by his wife's boss [i.e., the Rose Law Firm]—revising the usury laws and permitting the formation of new bank holding companies." Supposedly by abolishing the constitutional 10 percent limit on interest rates, Clinton had enriched Stephens, Inc., which owned Worthen Bank, then the state's largest. In return, Worthen had hired Hillary's law firm as its outside counsel, in exchange for which Clinton had made it "a major depository of the state's tax receipts." Next, Worthen had given the Clinton presidential campaign a $3.5 million line of credit, and so on—much the same tale told in *The Clinton Chronicles*.

In reality, the usury law was changed not by Bill Clinton, but by a constitutional amendment enacted in the 1982 general election. It was placed on the ballot by the legislature, at the urging of Republican governor Frank White, a banker, and became law before Clinton became governor. Furthermore, Stephens, Inc., didn't own Worthen Bank either when the amendment was enacted or when Davis's article was written twelve years later. The Rose Law Firm had been Worthen's outside counsel for fifty years. And as Arkansas's largest bank, Worthen had been the major depository of state money since Bill Clinton was a little boy.

Davis's central premise was that Stephens, Inc., and the Stephens family had pocketed vast ill-gotten wealth through shady bond deals with the Clinton administration. As he put it, "The intimate connection between Rose, Stephens, Inc. and the Governor's office may help explain how the Stephens family made a huge amount of money when its most visible enterprises were doing no such thing." Passing over the fact that the Stephens interests had bankrolled every GOP gubernatorial nominee (except the hated Sheffield Nelson) in recent Arkansas history, the notion that Clinton had made the family rich provoked helpless laughter in Little Rock. The value of Stephens, Inc., comprised just under 7 percent of the Stephens family's $1.7 billion net worth. Besides vast natural gas reserves in Arkansas and four western states, they owned huge soft coal reserves, banks, gas and electric utilities, newspapers, and scores of other concerns. During Clinton's tenure, Stephens, Inc.'s underwriting fees on Arkansas bonds came to less than 1 percent of the firm's total revenues.

But what really made L. J. Davis temporarily famous wasn't the *Wall Street Journal*'s endorsement of his sinister view of Arkansas politics, but its account of an alleged act of violence against him. In covering Clinton, lamented *Journal* editors the week Davis's article appeared, the "respectable press . . . has shown little or no appetite for publishing anything about sex or violence," a taboo they would no longer observe.

On the evening of February 13, the same editorial recounted, Davis "was returning to his room in Little Rock's Legacy Motel about 6:30 after an interview. . . . The last thing he remembers is putting his key in the door, and the next thing he remembers is waking up face down on the floor, with his arm twisted under his body and a big lump on his head above his left ear. The room door was shut and locked. Nothing was missing except four 'significant' pages of his notebook that included a list of his sources in Little Rock. . . . Mr. Davis says his doctor found his injury inconsistent with a fall, and that he'd been 'struck a massive blow above the left ear with a blunt object.'"

The *Journal* concluded that Arkansas was "a congenitally violent place, full of colorful characters with stories to tell, axes to grind, and secrets of their own to protect." In this climate, the editors concluded, "the respectable press is spending too much time adjudicating what the reader has a right to know, and too little time with the old spirit of 'stop the presses.'"

The near-martyrdom of Davis fit perfectly with the Foster "murder" and the *Clinton Chronicles* death list. Rush Limbaugh and his imitators on right-wing talk radio professed shock and horror. Rumors spread among the Washington press corps that the phones in Little Rock's Capital Hotel, owned by the Stephens interests, were bugged, and that Bill Clinton employed thugs and gumshoes to shadow reporters in Arkansas.

Oddly, L. J. Davis himself soon discovered that the crucial four pages weren't missing from his notebook after all, merely torn and wrinkled. Still, the *Democrat-Gazette*, alarmed that a colleague had been assaulted in downtown Little Rock, sent reporters out looking for the perpetrator. They didn't take long to find a suspect.

According to Legacy Hotel records, the assailant appeared to be a half dozen straight gin martinis. During the same four hours that Davis reported having spent facedown on his hotel-room floor, he'd actually been seated upright on a barstool. Hotel officials showed a copy of his bar tab to Little Rock police, and the bartender distinctly remembered refusing Davis a seventh drink. The writer denied drinking more than his usual ration of martinis, although he didn't specify how many that was. "I might have been a little happy, but so what?" he told reporters. "I have never made any charge about that, and why am I going to call the cops if I don't know what happened?"

Inside the downtown Little Rock headquarters of Stephens, Inc., the *New Republic* article caused severe annoyance, but what generated fury was the *Wall Street Journal*'s embrace of it. Warren Stephens's semiretired father, Jackson T. Stephens, wasn't merely a Republican, after all. Having donated more than $100,000 each to the campaigns of Ronald Reagan and George Bush, he was a card-carrying member of the GOP's Team 100.

The younger Stephens had been raised on the *Journal*'s conservative verities. Now he found his firm and family accused of imaginary improprieties and crimes by *Journal* editors who appeared contemptuous of facts. Following an earlier disagreement, Jack Stephens had paid editor Robert Bartley a visit at the newspaper's New York headquarters to protest the newspaper's coverage, but that cordial meeting had gotten him nowhere. Nor did a series of increasingly exasperated letters Warren Stephens wrote to Bartley regarding the Davis piece.

"In your rush to tar and feather Mr. Clinton," he urged, "don't damage the authority of the *Wall Street Journal* to be a conservative voice. Your praise of such a disjointed, incorrect piece will not serve you well in the long run." By return mail came a curt note essentially accusing Stephens, Inc., of complicity with the corrupt Bank of Credit and Commerce International, echoing another *New Republic* charge.

The Stephens interests were not the only important economic power in Arkansas to draw attention from the scandal-seeking national press. Among the state's largest and most controversial enterprises was the poultry industry, dominated by Tyson Foods.

It was perhaps inevitable that Tyson became a hot topic when, in January 1994, editors of the *New York Times* convened an unusual meeting of the paper's entire investigative staff to advance the Whitewater story. Like their counterparts at the *Washington Post*—indeed, like many national journalists—the *Times* editors thought they might be on to another Watergate, and they didn't want to be beaten this time.

Among Jeff Gerth's previously unexplored leads was an offhand remark by Jim McDougal about profitable commodity futures trading by Hillary Clinton. Returning to Arkansas, he and his colleagues soon found Robert "Red" Bone, the trader who had handled Hillary's account at the behest of a corporate attorney named James Blair. And Blair, whose wife, Diane, happened to be one of Hillary's oldest personal friends, had later gone to work for Tyson. The *Times* reporters uncovered considerable detail about Hillary's trading, which had over time netted a profit of about $100,000 on a marginal investment of $1,000. But the initial article about her trading was played on the *New York Times* front page on March 18, 1994, partly due to an erroneous suspicion about Blair's motives for helping Hillary. His client Tyson Foods, Gerth wrote, had benefited "from a variety of state actions, including $9 million in government loans."

In fact, those alleged loans were imaginary. Arkansas had no state loan program for Fortune 500 companies, and more than a month later the *Times* conceded in a published correction that there were no such loans to Tyson. Rather, it said, Tyson had enjoyed $7 million in state income tax credits—investment incentives available to every corporation, as the correction failed to mention. By then the fictive $9-million loan had been featured in scores of accusatory editorials and columns.

Handled judiciously, the cattle futures story need not have done the Clintons much harm. In essence, they had been done a favor by a shrewd friend who had little to gain apart from something he already had: the new governor's ear. Stung and defensive, however, Hillary Clinton instructed her White House spokesperson to claim that while Jim Blair had indeed given her tips, she had done most of the trading herself, based upon her study of the *Wall Street Journal.*

That claim, as reporters quickly determined, was not supported by the evidence. Blair had done most of the successful trading. Mrs. Clinton had briefly managed a second commodities account on her own, but without much success. Had she not gotten uneasy and quit trading before the cattle futures market plummeted, she might have ended up along with Blair and several others in federal court, suing the broker who had failed to make timely margin calls until their losses had become ruinous. Still, her explanation, which she withdrew weeks later, was at best a half-truth and at worst a falsehood. There was less to the commodities story than the sensational coverage implied, but the first lady's foolish attempt to mislead permanently injured her credibility.

As governor, her husband's relationship with Tyson Foods had been more troubled than chummy. In 1980 and 1982, the firm's CEO, Don Tyson, had supported Republican Frank White. The Clinton administration's ongoing conflict with the potent poultry lobby had been one of the two or three most persistent stories in Arkansas politics during his tenure. Few governors set out to alienate themselves permanently from their state's largest private employer and fastest-growing industry, but Clinton and the chicken growers had repeatedly found themselves at odds over such mundane but critical issues as highway truck weight limits, waste disposal, water quality standards, sales taxes on animal feed, and corporate income taxes to support community colleges.

Some battles Clinton won, and sometimes the poultry lobby defeated him; most often they cobbled together legislative compromises. But when Michael Kelly came to Arkansas in 1994 to write a Clinton profile for the *New York Times Magazine,* all that complicated history yielded to the need for melodrama. Populist voters who thought they were choosing reform, he wrote, invariably ended up being defrauded by politicians who were wholly owned by a handful of cynical corporate tycoons. Clinton emerged in this account as the quintessential product of a corrupt system.

According to Kelly, Clinton's first major gift to the poultry giant was supposed to have been the increase in highway truck weight limits to eighty thousand pounds in 1983 (a full five years after Hillary Clinton's commodities trades). He mentioned that Clinton had linked the weight increase to a "ton-mile" tax hike on eighteen-wheel truck trailers. But he didn't note that Arkansas was the last of the fifty states to accede to the eighty-thousand-pound standard, leaving its shippers at a disadvantage.

Pursuing the Tyson connection, Kelly also recounted a dispute over tainted groundwater in an Ozarks community. The state had reacted passively, he wrote, after "the sewage system in the town of Green Forest, which had been for years overloaded by Tyson-produced animal waste, dumped so much sewage into Dry Creek that a giant sinkhole formed," polluting local wells. (Kelly did not mention that the acccident had taken place during Governor Frank White's tenure.) Although Clinton declared a "disaster emergency" within months of assuming the governor's office again in 1983, Kelly noted, "the state failed to levy any fines against the company or to sue it for damages."

True, but woefully incomplete. Until Clinton pushed environmental legislation through a recalcitrant legislature in 1985, the Arkansas Department of Pollution Control and Ecology had no power to levy fines or file lawsuits. Passed in reaction to the Green Forest incident, the new law could not be made retroactive to 1983. Town officials also bore considerable blame for failing to upgrade the town's sewage treatment facilities, as they had promised to do when Tyson Foods proposed to build a processing plant there. Any fair account of the subsequent lawsuit against Tyson Foods and the city of Green Forest, filed in federal court by a citizens group, also would have noted that Arkansas state officials testified on behalf of the plaintiffs.

Kelly's skewed account of the relationship between Clinton and Tyson was a perfect example of "naive cynicism," in which a reporter remains naively ignorant of basic information while cynically assuming the prevalence of corruption. In a joint letter to the *New York Times Magazine*, both of Arkansas's senators made a similar point. Democrats Dale Bumpers and David Pryor, both former governors, explained that in a one-party state, the chief executive "must form a new coalition on each issue. The resulting bartering and negotiations may look slick to the unpracticed eye, but the novice should try it before judging. . . . In his twelve years as Governor, the President alienated every large interest group in the state at one time or another: utilities, timber, building contractors, the Chamber of Commerce, the Arkansas Medical Society, the Education Association, the poultry industry, the Farm Bureau, the National Rifle Association," and so on.

But this complex reality wouldn't have supported Kelly's own darkly simplistic conclusions about Clinton's character, shared by many of his Washington colleagues, which in turn justified the gathering momentum of scandal coverage during that spring and summer. Tyson Foods and Stephens, Inc., were merely outsized props in a political morality play that was to have a long and profitable run in the national media.

Ironically, Jerry Falwell's urgent need to revise *The Clinton Chronicles* to edit out accusations against Stephens, Inc., afforded Larry Nichols another opportunity. Although the video came advertised as a documentary, many who appeared in it got paid. Citizens for Honest Government ledgers show that the organization paid out more than $200,000 to individuals featured in the Clinton videos between 1994 and 1996. Nichols repeatedly claimed to have received no money but was in fact paid over $89,000 according to the ledgers, and probably made far more selling the tapes. Justice Jim Johnson was given a new pickup truck, while Paula Jones and her husband received a paltry $1,000 for their appearance in *The Clinton Chronicles* (although Falwell paid Matrisciana $5,000 for the privilege of broadcasting the Jones segment on his *Old-Time Gospel Hour*).

Also appearing on Matrisciana's pay sheet was Jane Parks, widow of the slain security-firm owner whose son blamed his death on Bill Clinton. Over a two-year period, Mrs. Parks received a bit more than $22,000 from Citizens for Honest Government. "We did not pay people to tell lies," Matrisciana told *Salon* magazine reporter Murray Waas. "We paid people so that they would no longer have to be afraid to tell the truth."

Over the next few years Jane Parks did quite a bit of talking. Shortly before the 1996 presidential election, she was quoted by *American Spectator* editor R. Emmett Tyrrell, Jr., to the effect that she had personally overheard Bill Clinton snorting cocaine with his brother Roger through a flimsy wall at an apartment complex she managed. She later told Ambrose Evans-Pritchard that her husband had been murdered because he was involved with Vince Foster in a massive drug-smuggling ring at the rural airport in Mena, Arkansas—the locus of numerous Clinton conspiracy tales. She also claimed she had once found hundreds of thousands in cash hidden in the trunk of her late husband's car. She didn't say what happened to it.

Another Arkansan who joined up with Citizens for Honest Government was a former Saline County deputy sheriff named John Brown. Over a two-year period, between 1994 and 1995, Pat Matrisciana paid the ex–homicide detective $28,000 for "investigative work" on the anti-Clinton videos, and Brown himself appeared in two of them. He took the money but soon came to take a jaundiced view of Matrisciana's operation. During his tenure in Saline County, a rural and suburban area roughly thirty miles southwest of the state capital, Brown had been the lead investigator in one of Arkansas's most disturbing unsolved crimes. Dubbed "the boys on the tracks" case, it involved the 1987 murders of two teenage boys whose dismembered bodies were found on the Union Pacific railroad tracks.

The case first drew notice due to a foolish error by the state medical examiner. Dr. Fahmy Malak, a British-trained Egyptian seemingly unfamiliar with the intoxicating properties of marijuana, had initially ruled the deaths accidental. Young Kevin Ives and Don Henry, the doctor hypothesized, had smoked twenty-five joints, fallen asleep on the tracks, and been run over by a freight train. Greeted by widespread derision, Malak's verdict was eventually proved false by an outside pathologist, who showed that the victims had been beaten to death before being placed on the railroad tracks. Whether the over-worked medical examiner—deemed overly solicitous of law enforcement by some observers, incapable of admitting error by almost everybody—had simply misplaced a decimal point was hard to say. But because Malak served at the governor's pleasure, the first edition of *The Clinton Chronicles* had little difficulty linking Bill Clinton to the "cover-up."

John Brown's suspects in the slayings were all Saline County residents involved in drug dealing. Meanwhile, Brown was also engaged with the FBI in an undercover investigation, probing corruption in the local district attorney's office. Despite the *Chronicles*' ludicrous suggestion that the Ives-Henry murders somehow involved Clinton, its citations of evidence did suggest a familiarity with sensitive investigative materials. Brown's superiors urged him to find out how that information had leaked by meeting with representatives of Citizens for Honest Government. He did so, then briefed two FBI agents about what he discovered. Thus began his two-year sojourn in the hermetic world of Larry Nichols and the professional Clinton-haters.

At the outset, the young, idealistic cop found himself in sympathy with the organization's stated goals. As an investigator in one of Arkansas's most corrupt judicial districts—where ex-prosecutor Dan Harmon has since been convicted by U.S. Attorney Paula Casey on federal narcotics charges—the notion of fighting for "honest government" appealed to him. He thought Bill Clinton had done a poor job of dealing with local corruption during his twelve years as governor, although under the archaic 1837 state constitution, there was little Clinton could have done to curb locally elected district attorneys. No statewide prosecutorial authority exists.

Eventually Brown regretted his involvement with Matrisciana. Although he appeared on *The New Clinton Chronicles* and a second video titled *Obstruction of Justice,* he contends that his remarks were scripted, electronically altered, and placed in a context that entirely changed their meaning. Moreover, he says the same is true of virtually all the law enforcement officers who appear on Matrisciana's videos.

In August 1999 Brown testified as a witness in a federal court case on behalf of two Pulaski County detectives, Lieutenants Jay Campbell and Kirk Lane, who brought a libel and defamation suit against Matrisciana, Citizens for Honest Government, and Jeremiah Films. At the trial, FBI agent Michael Smith confirmed Brown's account of how he came to be involved with Citizens for Honest Government.

The *Obstruction of Justice* video had claimed that "eyewitnesses have implicated several people in the [Ives-Henry] murders and subsequent cover-up." It then proceeded to list Prosecutor Dan Harmon and the two police officers as the killers. During his own testimony, Brown said that he had repeatedly and pointedly warned Matrisciana not to name Campbell and Lane and that no credible evidence existed against them. Far from being Dan Harmon's associates, they too had been engaged in the effort to bring the corrupt prosecutor to justice. The jury found unanimously for the two officers, awarding them a $598,750 judgment.

Afterward, Matrisciana told reporters that "in Arkansas, I believe it's almost impossible for me to have a fair trial." Explaining that Citizens for Honest Government is "a little mom-and-pop operation," he claimed that it would be impossible for him to pay the verdict.

"If they'd been halfway honest," Brown explained to a Little Rock reporter, "they'd have called themselves Citizens Against Democrats. Basically, they just wanted to play a game of connect the dots. Except that every picture had to show Bill Clinton's face. They'd take somebody like Dan Harmon or Dan Lasater, or even Roger Clinton, and find a way to tie everything they'd done wrong to Bill Clinton."

On August 5, 1994, the same day that the Special Division announced the removal of Robert Fiske and the appointment of Kenneth Starr as Whitewater independent counsel, Brown traveled to Washington, D.C., at Matrisciana's expense. Also along on the trip were Matrisciana, Larry Nichols, and an Arkansas lawyer named Jean Duffey who promoted a conspiratorial view of the Henry-Ives case. In the Capitol Hill offices of Representative Bob Livingston of Louisiana they met with prominent Republicans such as Representative Bill McCollum of Florida, and staffers of several others, including Jim Leach of Iowa, chairman of the House Banking Committee, and Senator Lauch Faircloth of North Carolina. The lean, white-maned Matrisciana videotaped the proceedings as Nichols regaled the politicians with tales of Clintonian skullduggery. Though unnoticed by the press, Livingston's cameo role in *The New Clinton Chronicles* gave an air of authority to the production.

Soon after Kenneth Starr arrived in Little Rock that fall, the FBI agent who had asked Brown to look into Citizens for Honest Government moved on and the agency appeared to have lost interest in local corruption. Frustrated at being told to put the Henry-Ives case aside after seven years, Brown resigned to run as the Republican nominee for county sheriff. After a narrow defeat, he served as police chief in the town of Alexander and opened his own security and investigative firm. Against his better judgment, Citizens for Honest Government became one of his clients.

Brown says he remained curious about the organization's tactics and motives. What intrigued him was the presence of former military intelligence figures with extreme right-wing views, such as Lieutenant Colonel Tom McKenney, a retired marine who appeared in several of Matrisciana's videos and contributed a column to the group's bimonthly newsletter. Brown also needed the business.

The more Brown saw of Nichols, the more it amazed him that Matrisciana kept Nichols around. According to Brown, Nichols came up with the notion to dispatch Brown to Chicago to investigate Hillary Clinton's supposed membership in an underground clique of lesbian dominatrices. On another occasion, Brown took Nichols and *Pittsburgh Tribune-Review* reporter Christopher Ruddy to the Sherwood, Arkansas, police department to look into what the pair deemed a suspicious death.

Ruddy had become nationally famous for a series in the Scaife-owned newspaper that questioned the suicide verdict in Foster's death. It would later appear that among his many anti-Clinton projects, the reclusive Pittsburgh billionaire may have been subsidizing Matrisciana's Citizens for Honest Government as well. By 1997, internal documents indicate, Citizens for Honest Government maintained a bank account in the name of Jeremiah Films that had an average balance of over $3 million.

The death that brought Nichols and Ruddy to Sherwood was that of Kathy Ferguson, ex-wife of Danny Ferguson, the Arkansas state trooper who was Clinton's codefendant in the Paula Jones lawsuit. Despondent over a failed love affair, she had called 911, then turned a gun on herself. The funeral was hardly over before Ferguson's name was added to the growing list of Clinton-connected deaths. John Brown's connections in Arkansas law enforcement persuaded Sherwood detectives to open their files to him and the Citizens for Honest Government sleuths. After hearing the 911 tape and examining the crime scene photos and forensic evidence, Brown had no doubt that the official verdict was correct: Kathy Ferguson had died of a self-inflicted gunshot wound. His companions, however, could not be persuaded.

"Aw hell," Nichols argued, "they just doctored them pictures."

"No they didn't," replied Brown, noting how unlikely it was that Clinton's tentacles extended into the Sherwood, Arkansas, police department, and also that many of the photos were Polaroids, virtually impossible to fake.

"Let them prove they didn't," Nichols said.

Although Christopher Ruddy had been unable to examine the graphic photos without getting sick, he nevertheless wrote a story for the *Tribune-Review* indicating that in his professional opinion, the Ferguson suicide, too, looked fishy.

One possible explanation for Nichols's erratic behavior, and ironic in view of his oft-repeated accusations about Bill Clinton's drug use, was his own addiction to the painkiller Dilaudid. A derivative of the opium family, Dilaudid is similar in its physiological and psychological effects to heroin. It is a Schedule II narcotic with potentially fatal side effects, including suppressed respiration, mood disturbances, and impaired judgment. Nichols may have first been given the drug after suffering a hang-gliding accident, although his doctor later testified to a state medical board hearing that he had prescribed the pills to ease Nichols's pain from a rare viral affliction. In any event, by the time John Brown got to know him, the *Clinton Chronicles* star was gobbling pills by the handful and staggering around in a daze much of the time.

In a strange incident, Brown insisted he saw Nichols demonstrate his toughness by emerging from the bathroom having run an electric guitar string through his scrotum. "That was it for me," Brown exclaimed. "I got up in his face and told him if he ever came around me pilled-up like that again, I would kick his ass and turn him in." From that point forward, the former detective's relationship with Citizens for Honest Government deteriorated rapidly.

Nichols already had found other friends in Arkansas law enforcement. For agreeing to appear in *The New Clinton Chronicles,* he signed a contract to pay state troopers Larry Patterson and Roger Perry a $1-per-video royalty for yet another project, tentatively titled *Nichols vs. Clinton.* According to an interview Trooper Perry gave to Murray Waas, Nichols bragged that he had earned more than $150,000 in royalties by selling *The Clinton Chronicles,* and persuaded the troopers that they could share the wealth. These protagonists of David Brock's original Troopergate story also agreed to appear in a Matrisciana-Ruddy production about the death of Vince Foster. But Perry claimed the only check Nichols ever wrote him bounced.

Nichols and Patterson, however, appeared to get along well. According to Waas, records he obtained showed that the pair opened a joint checking account in a Conway bank from which cash payments were made to several individuals who appeared in anti-Clinton videos. Living rent-free in a west Little Rock house owned by Republican lawyer and professional Clinton-basher Cliff Jackson, Patterson also joined Nichols on the far-right lecture circuit, earning up to $1,000 per appearance.

By September, two months before the 1994 midterm congressional elections, *The New Clinton Chronicles* was ready for distribution. All references to Falwell's creditors at Stephens, Inc., were deleted and replaced by spooky intimations about narcotics trafficking at the Mena, Arkansas, airport. Again, Pat Matrisciana turned to his comrades at the Council for National Policy to promote his new product.

Free copies were shipped to all CNP members from the organization's Arlington, Virginia, headquarters, along with a cover letter urging them to circulate the tapes as widely as possible among public officials and members of the media: "As many Americans as possible should become informed about the evil which infests the Clinton administration. Contact Senators and Congressmen with whom you have influence. Insist that when the Whitewater hearings resume . . . they look into the operations of the Arkansas Development Finance Administration (ADFA) and the other matters mentioned on the tape. Larry Nichols, who was Director of Marketing for ADFA, should be called to testify. Bill Clinton must be held accountable for his actions."

On Monday, October 31, Jerry Falwell spoke before a Baptist preachers' gathering in Little Rock. Originally scheduled to be held at Immanuel Baptist Church, where the president had worshiped during his years as governor, Falwell's appearance had to be moved after pastor Rex Horne refused to allow his church to be used for the event. Having watched *The Old-Time Gospel Hour* on cable TV, Horne felt that Falwell had blatantly violated the Ninth Commandment's prohibition against bearing false witness. "I happened to tune in on a Sunday morning," he explained. "I saw Falwell promoting the tapes that have proven to be scurrilous and full of innuendo and falsehoods directed against not just Clinton but other Arkansans. I could not, with good conscience, go along with it any longer."

Falwell's speech excoriated Madonna and Michael Jackson along with Clinton, but he didn't mention the videos until afterward. Questioned by a reporter about his relationship with Citizens for Honest Government, the reverend claimed, "I have not associated with or [had] any relationships with [those] people."

One week later, Democrats suffered stunning defeats in the midterm elections, losing control of both the House and Senate for the first time in forty years. Universally regarded as a repudiation of the Clinton presidency, this seismic turnover was attributed to three factors: Newt Gingrich's catchy "Contract with America," the failure of the administration's national health insurance proposal, and the cumulative weight of the "Clinton scandals," including Whitewater, Troopergate, the Paula Jones lawsuit, Foster's suicide, and *The Clinton Chronicles.* Like his fellow southerner, the hapless Jimmy Carter, President Clinton appeared all but certain to be a one-term wonder. As 1995 began with the elevation of Gingrich to Speaker of the House, many pundits were advising the Democrats to dump Clinton in 1996.

On January 28, 1995, about a year after his alleged trip to South Korea for an audience with Sun Myung Moon, Jerry Falwell informed his television flock on *The Old-Time Gospel Hour* of heaven-sent good news. Two Virginia businessmen named Dan Reber and Jimmy Thomas had come to his rescue. Their nonprofit Christian Heritage Foundation had bought up almost half of Liberty University's $73 million in bonded debt at a bankruptcy sale for the bargain price of $2.5 million. Then they had agreed to forgive the debt. After years of financial crisis, Falwell's domain was saved.

"They had to borrow money, hock their houses, hock everything," the ebullient preacher told his audience. "Thank God for friends like Dan Reber and Jimmy Thomas." He told reporters that the bailout was "the greatest day of financial advantage" in the fundamentalist school's history. Left unmentioned in the celebration was the identity of Falwell's benefactor.

Clues to this mystery were unearthed later quite by accident. While researching an article on how much a Unification Church group called Women's Federation for World Peace had paid former president Bush for a series of 1995 speeches in Asia, journalist Robert Parry noticed a $3.5 million "educational" grant to the Christian Heritage Foundation. Women's Federation vice president Susan Fefferman told Parry that the grant's proceeds had gone to "Mr. Falwell's people" for the benefit of Liberty University. Although the $3.5 million stipend was by far the largest issued by the organization that year, Fefferman could tell the reporter nothing about its purpose. Another Unification Church official to whom she directed Parry failed to return his calls, as did Falwell himself.

Dan Reber, who had joined Falwell on his January 1994 pilgrimage to Korea, ran a Virginia company called Direct Mail Communications. According to court records, more than a third of its income came from a direct-mail subscription drive for Moon-sponsored organizations (and the rest mostly from Texas governor George W. Bush, Oliver North, the National Rifle Association, and the Republican National Committee). It seemed that Reber's only sacrifice in acting as Falwell's financial savior had been to give the evangelist's various enterprises large discounts on direct-mail solicitations.

The real losers in the bailout were 2,500 small bondholders who had invested with the Texas-based Church & Institutional Facilities Development Corporation and who owned millions of the school bonds, which were sold to Reber and Thomas for 20 percent of value. Doug Hudman, a lawyer for the bondholders, told Parry that his clients mostly were "Moms and Pops cashing in their IRA money because their local minister and Falwell's letters said they'd be doing God's work. . . . All it was doing was going to fund Mr. Falwell's continued indebtedness. It's kind of sickening."

Chapter Ten

INSIDE THE ARKANSAS PROJECT

F ROM ITS INCEPTION in November 1993, the Arkansas Project was kept so quiet that even senior staff members of the *American Spectator* had little notion of what the project was intended to do, let alone what Stephens S. Boynton and David Henderson actually were doing in the magazine's name. The funds flowed reliably every six months or so from Richard Mellon Scaife's office in Pittsburgh to the American Spectator Educational Foundation, as they had for many years. But from there, most of the money now went directly into an account controlled by Boynton, with virtually no oversight by Ronald Burr, the magazine's publisher, or anyone else.

Not unlike the arrangements used to conceal CIA involvement in Scaife-financed press agencies during the Pittsburgh billionaire's earlier adventures, this method of obscuring the purpose of Scaife's money skirted the edges of propriety. Certainly it violated the transparency intended by the tax laws governing nonprofit and allegedly charitable or educational organizations like the Spectator Foundation. On the foundation's internal documents and on the annual tax forms it filed with the Internal Revenue Service, the payments to Boynton were reported as "legal fees." But Boynton was performing no legal services for the magazine. Internal Spectator Foundation tax documents recorded far lower total legal expenses, for services provided by other law firms (including Ted Olson's firm, Gibson, Dunn & Crutcher).

Moreover, the amounts transferred to Boynton were substantial. By January 1995, the sum advanced to the Virginia lawyer-lobbyist (usually in checks of $40,000 or more) totaled nearly $500,000. Nor did that include additional tens of thousands spent on expenses for telephone calls; books and office supplies; fees paid to writers, researchers, and other attorneys; and travel costs, along with the $800 monthly rent paid to Parker Dozhier for a house that was meant to serve as quarters for visiting *Spectator* personnel.

Meanwhile, the specific results of Scaife's half-million-dollar investment during the Arkansas Project's first year remained unknown to the magazine's regular staff. Most assumed that Bob Tyrrell was running the operation himself. That was definitely the view taken by managing editor Wladyslaw Plesczynski, who regarded the project as Bob's plaything, not to be confused with the normal business of the *Spectator,* which Plesczynski actually ran on a daily basis.

In a confidential memorandum written a few years later, Plesczynski recalled his own pointed skepticism about the Arkansas Project. "Initially Boynton and Henderson would occasionally mention a few things to me about the situation in Arkansas, but I wasn't impressed by what they had to say. They seemed to have a source or two—David Hale, Parker Dozhier—but not much more than that. There always seemed to be lots of hush-hush and heavy breathing, but it never amounted to anything concrete enough for a story. In any event, I got the sense [that] Henderson spent most of his time with Bob when dealing with someone at the magazine, and Bob never asked me to pay any attention to Boynton and Henderson's work. He seemed completely content to have them all to himself."

As the sardonic memo conceded, Boynton and Henderson's constant trips to Arkansas did bring some results, particularly in articles by James Ring Adams, one of four *Spectator* staff writers. Early in 1994, Adams produced a lengthy feature titled "Beyond Whitewater," recounting the sad story of one Freddie Whitener, an otherwise obscure victim of James McDougal's financial chicanery at Madison Guaranty. Apart from that article, which made few waves, and several contacts provided to Adams, Plesczynski and other top *Spectator* personnel were only dimly aware of what Boynton and Henderson did during their sojourns in Little Rock and Hot Springs. But as his passing reference to Hale and Dozhier indicates, Plesczynski seemed aware that the Arkansas Project maintained a close connection with the independent counsel's key Whitewater witness.

Indeed, a significant portion of the project's energy during its first year was directed toward the care and feeding of Hale, whose cooperation agreement with Robert Fiske, the first Whitewater independent counsel, was negotiated in the spring of 1994. From that point onward, Hale became a virtual ward of the U.S. government, from which he received a tax-free annual stipend of $60,000 for his services as a federal witness. In the meantime, however, he had lost or forfeited the ill-gotten assets from the frauds that had led to his indictment, along with his salary as a municipal judge. To all appearances Hale was a hard-up loser, a busted con artist with rapidly growing legal bills. In subsequent testimony, Hale would claim that he was so destitute that he and his wife were forced to sell their furniture to buy food. Questioned about how he paid Ted Olson's fees, however, Hale boasted that he paid cash.

The ledgers kept by Boynton showed not only frequent visits to Arkansas, but numerous meals with Hale and his friend Dozhier, as well as airfare for Hale to Washington and expenses for sending packages to Hale's Little Rock attorney, Randy Coleman. According to the testimony of Caryn Mann, who lived with Dozhier between late 1994 and early 1996, Hale spent much of his time residing in a cottage near the Hot Springs bait shop. "From August '94 on, Hale was there two to three weeks a month, three or four days a week," she recalled. "Under Fiske, he'd been in protective custody under the FBI. When Starr took over, they took that away. That was when he stayed there the most, after that."

Accompanied much of the time by FBI special agent David F. Reign, who conducted more than forty interviews with him between March 1994 and November 1995, Hale was theoretically inaccessible to the press during the period—although he spent many hours with the *Spectator* team. Other frequent visitors to Dozhier's compound on the banks of Lake Catherine included luminaries of the right-wing press, among them Ambrose Evans-Pritchard of the London *Sunday Telegraph* and the *Journal* editorial page's "investigative columnist" Micah Morrison.

Until Hale entered a federal prison in 1996, Dozhier also loaned a car to him and his wife. In 1995, Hale had an auto accident in Shreveport, Louisiana, where the Office of Independent Counsel (OIC) maintained a "safe house" for him. After the former traffic judge misidentified himself to investigating officers as Parker Dozhier, it was decided to add him and Mrs. Hale properly to the vehicle's insurance policy. In addition, Caryn Mann and her teenage son, Joshua Rand, also recalled a steady stream of modest cash payments, in amounts ranging from $40 to $200, from Dozhier to Hale—an assertion that Dozhier, Henderson, and Hale's attorneys hotly denied when Mann went public in 1998.

A native of Chicago's South Side, Caryn Mann made her way to Hot Springs, Arkansas, by way of a failed marriage. She was working there as a funeral home administrator when she met Parker Dozhier in the process of making arrangements for his mother's burial in February 1994. Initially, Mann found the talkative bait-shop proprietor energetic and likable. After a few dates, she and her son moved into a mobile home on Dozhier's lakeshore property east of town.

A big-city girl from a large Italian American family, Mann felt slightly out of place at the fishing camp in the woods. But it was more than the rustic surroundings that caused her discomfort. According to Mann, Dozhier's fascination with guns, his overt racism, his flirtation with political extremism—he wrote strident articles for a militia publication in New Mexico about an alleged government conspiracy to confiscate firearms—and his obsession with Bill Clinton gradually began to disturb her. Although a Democrat, Mann was unfamiliar with Arkansas politics. She was initially alarmed by stories about the president's alleged involvement with embezzlement, drug smuggling, political assassination, and other crimes. "I believed Dozhier at first," she said. "I thought, oh my God, what terrible things the president did."

The more she saw of Dozhier and his Arkansas Project colleagues, however, the less credible she found their stories. (No stranger to speculation, Mann was something of an amateur astrologer.) To her there appeared to be a strong element of paranoia and make-believe among Dozhier's crowd. Although the guns frightened her, she also found it faintly comical to watch Dozhier's buddies swaggering around the fishing camp, carrying the semiautomatic pistols Dozhier furnished them on the pretext that their lives were in danger. Micah Morrison, she said, was prone to making noisy displays of his dislike for Clinton in Hot Springs restaurants and other public places. Between themselves, she and her son Josh began to refer to the Washington duo of Stephen Boynton and David Henderson as "Cisco and Pancho."

At the beginning, the whole point of the Arkansas Project seemed to be to protect Hale from the consequence of his crimes. Dozhier even had a shelf of champagne bottles on the wall of the bait shop labeled with the names of Hale's enemies—U.S. Attorney Paula Casey, Governor Jim Guy Tucker, Little Rock prosecutor Mark Stodola, and Hillary Rodham Clinton among them. Both Mann and her son described activities suggestive of the "source" relationship mentioned in Plesczynski's Arkansas Project memo. Escorted by FBI agents, they said, Hale brought documents to be copied by Dozhier in an office he kept behind the bait shop, spending many evenings in intense discussion with his benefactors about developments in the Whitewater case.

"Once Kenneth Starr started dealing with David Hale," she said, "he was dealing with P. D. whether he knew it or not. I don't think they were sure of Starr until after Hale and Dozhier went to Washington to talk to Ted Olson. After they came back, there was a whole new level of confidence in what was going to happen."

"Did Starr's people know? They called there for him," according to Mann. "The independent counsel's office would call and ask for David Hale. How could they not know? One night during the summer of 1995, Hale came back from OIC with stacks of documents. He and Dozhier stayed up copying until 2 A.M." Afterward, Dozhier told her "they had what they needed to bring Hillary down." Stories began to appear in the national press to the effect that the first lady would soon be indicted. Testimony at Susan McDougal's 1999 trial for contempt of court would reveal that Deputy Prosecutor Hickman Ewing, Jr., had drafted an indictment of Mrs. Clinton around the same time—a document the independent counsel never presented to the Whitewater grand jury.

As Caryn Mann's doubts about Dozhier's activities grew, their personal relationship also deteriorated. Dozhier's bullying of her son, to which Josh responded defiantly, only made things worse. By the time she determined that she and the boy would have to leave, Mann had become badly frightened. She was privately of the opinion that what Dozhier and his associates were up to was tantamount to "treason."

The Arkansas Project's money also helped the *Spectator*'s editors to cultivate a relationship with yet another former state trooper named Larry Douglass Brown, usually called "L. D." Between 1983 and 1985, L. D. Brown had served in the security unit at the governor's mansion in Little Rock. Better-educated and more articulate than the other bodyguards, he had developed an unusually close relationship with Bill and Hillary Clinton. Then in his late twenties, Brown looked up to the sophisticated couple as friends and mentors. For him, the mansion's atmosphere was intimate and familial. It was while he was in their orbit that he met his wife, Becky, who lived and worked at the mansion as Chelsea Clinton's nanny. Becky's mother, Ann McCoy, eventually became the mansion's administrator (and went on to work in the White House). Until he fell out with the Clintons, mainly over state police politics, Brown was known as the governor's "fair-haired boy."

Like Patterson and Perry, the officers featured in Brock's Troopergate story, Brown was known to be disgruntled and had been pursued by reporters since the 1992 presidential campaign. He had been a confidential source of derogatory information about alleged Clinton paramours for Sheffield Nelson (and, he claimed, Jim Guy Tucker, who denied receiving any smut from Brown) as early as 1990.

The reporter who finally persuaded L. D. Brown to talk was *Spectator* staff writer Daniel Wattenberg, author of a lengthy profile featured on the magazine's May 1994 cover. "Love and Hate in Arkansas" was Troopergate's sequel. In semiconfessional mode, Brown told how he too had solicited women for the governor; how he had enjoyed sexual "residuals" in the process; and how he had become disillusioned with the Clintons, describing them as monstrously selfish, foulmouthed snobs who secretly despised police officers and other regular folks. Openly displaying the same animus toward Hillary as the other troopers, he repeated their claims about her supposedly torrid love affair with Vince Foster. (Former Clinton aides in Arkansas insisted that Brown had been embittered by Hillary's attempt to warn his future wife that L. D. was an incorrigible skirt chaser.)

In any case, Wattenberg forthrightly acknowledged the malice of his talkative new informant. Brown had broken bitterly with Clinton in 1985 after the governor reneged on a personal promise to appoint him assistant director of the state crime laboratory. When Clinton withdrew the offer, the furious trooper stormed out and quit his position in the security detail. He rarely spoke to Clinton after that, but they continued to feud publicly for years, mostly over what he believed to be another failed promise to support a bill funding the Arkansas State Police Association. He believed that Clinton was behind his eventual removal as the organization's president, and had later instigated a criminal probe of the alleged misuse of association funds which led to Brown's resignation. Portraying himself as a victim of the Clinton political machine, to many Brown appeared to be pursuing a mission of vengeance.

That mission continued long after Wattenberg's story was forgotten. The *Spectator* crowd, as Brown discovered, had money and spent it freely; and the state trooper quickly found himself being courted by Boynton, Henderson, and especially Tyrrell, who brought Brown to Washington for wining and dining at his mansion in suburban Virginia. Between early February and late March, while Wattenberg worked on "Love and Hate," the magazine paid Brown more than $10,000, listed as "travel expenses" in the Arkansas Project files.

Tyrrell in particular befriended Brown, who must have been impressed by the editor's obvious wealth and connections. Brown had no way of knowing that the high-living editor—despite his own substantial inheritance and his frequent complaints about the Clintons' alleged failure to pay their fair share of income taxes—had long misused the magazine's tax-exempt funding to subsidize his extravagant tastes. The Spectator Foundation had paid one-third of the purchase price of Tyrrell's lavish home in McLean, Virginia; had covered his large liquor bills and many other domestic expenses; had rented an apartment in New York City occasionally used by Tyrrell; had paid for his memberships at the New York Athletic Club and Washington's exclusive Cosmos Club; and had reimbursed him for hotel and airfare on costly and frequent trips to London—all in addition to a salary that amounted to well over $250,000 a year plus the more usual benefits. No doubt Brown was awed by Tyrrell's constant patter about London and New York nightlife, and the personally inscribed photographs of Ronald Reagan and Richard Nixon that hung on the walls of his big brick house. (He might have been surprised, however, to learn that the editor's frequent drinking buddy, the right-wing Greek gossip columnist Taki Theodoracopulos, had served three months in an English prison for cocaine smuggling.) It wasn't too long before Tyrrell discovered that Brown could tell impressive stories, too, about matters far more intriguing than Bill Clinton's extramarital exploits.

*   *   *

In the fall of 1994, Brown made the stunning assertion that he could corroborate David Hale's testimony about pressure from Clinton to lend $300,000 to Susan McDougal. Although he had never mentioned Hale to Danny Wattenberg during numerous interviews earlier that year—when the Little Rock embezzler's name was constantly in the news—Brown now claimed to have witnessed a meeting between Clinton and Hale outside the state capitol sometime in 1985 or 1986 where the governor said, "You're going to have to help us out. We're going to need to raise some money."

This incriminating memory was suddenly recovered by Brown after a year of fruitless searching by the independent counsel for any evidence connecting Clinton to the fraudulent $300,000 loan. Lacking such evidence, Starr would never be able to prove the central allegation of the Whitewater case. Even a biased source like Brown might prove useful, and investigators from Starr's office took a statement from him, which was promptly leaked to the *Washington Times*. Citing "federal law enforcement sources," the conservative daily reported on October 19 that Brown had told the independent counsel of overhearing Clinton press Hale to make the loan. Susan Schmidt followed up the next day in the *Washington Post* with her own interview of Brown.

The trooper's account, which he said he had withheld until then out of fear that he would lose his job, was almost as vague as Hale's. Exactly how vague may be deduced from the headlines of two stories which appeared side by side in the *Arkansas Democrat-Gazette* on October 23, 1994: "ARKANSAS TROOPER SAID HE SAW CLINTON PRESSURE JUDGE FOR MONEY" and "TROOPER DENIES STORY ON SBA LOAN." Brown told the *Post*'s Schmidt he couldn't recall whether he was still on the governor's security detail or had already left to head the state police association. But Hale had placed the date in late 1985 or early 1986, well after Brown's angry departure from the mansion. It seemed unlikely that Clinton would have conducted illicit business in front of a disgruntled former employee. When Schmidt called Hale's lawyer, Randy Coleman, he wouldn't confirm or deny Brown's assertions. "You've got to save something for the wedding," Coleman told her teasingly. Clinton lawyer David Kendall dismissed Brown as a liar with "an ax to grind against the president."

Ultimately, Starr placed no more confidence in Brown's claim than Kendall. But according to Caryn Mann, Parker Dozhier told her that he and Henderson had tried to bolster this fresh support for Hale. She claims that Dozhier told her they had debriefed Brown in a motel room while Hale sat in an adjacent room, providing questions as Dozhier went back and forth. Unable to offer a specific date for that meeting, Mann cannot be certain whether Henderson and Dozhier were trying to prepare Brown for his testimony.

"Parker said that it was important that L. D. and Hale never speak directly because it might appear like they were colluding with one another to put a story together," recalled Mann. "But Parker said that Brown probably knew that Hale was in the room next door, because Brown made jokes about it. L. D. said, 'If I didn't know better, I'd say you guys know David Hale.'"

It is also unclear why L. D. Brown would submit to such an interrogation by agents of the Arkansas Project, except for his own growing commitment to their anti-Clinton crusade and the opportunities it presented him. Brown appears to have become convinced over time that Bob Tyrrell would believe almost anything the trooper told him. Eventually, he drew the *Spectator* editor into a story of international intrigue far more fantastic than his implausible but rather modest attempt to buttress Hale. Brown said he possessed direct, personal knowledge of Bill Clinton's connection with a legendary CIA-sponsored narcotics-smuggling cabal, at a rural airport in the western Arkansas town of Mena.

The earliest rumors about the smuggling of weapons and cocaine at Mena Intermountain Regional Airport appeared in 1987, emanating from liberal and leftist opponents of the Reagan administration's support for the Nicaraguan contra rebels. Outside Arkansas these rumors drew little attention, gaining wider circulation only when Reagan's most fervent admirers, without a trace of self-consciousness, picked them up a few years later to discredit Bill Clinton.

Although the Mena story developed a baroque complexity with the passage of time, its essential outline was simple: The CIA had used the rural airfield as a transshipment point and staging area for its secret contra support activities, and had tolerated (or in some versions, encouraged) the importation of cocaine on planes returning from weapons drops in Central America.

A central figure in this scenario was Adler Berriman "Barry" Seal, a legendary pilot and drug smuggler who had indeed became a government informant in 1983 after being busted by the Drug Enforcement Administration. In 1984, Seal had participated in a CIA scheme to film Nicaraguan officials and Colombian drug kingpin Pablo Escobar unloading cocaine from his plane in Managua. Seal was murdered in New Orleans two years later by hit men working for the Medellín cartel. Three Colombian gunmen were eventually convicted of the killing. On October 5, 1986, that same C-123 transport plane (known as the "Fat Lady") crashed in the Nicaraguan jungle and set off the explosive revelation of Washington's covert contra resupply operation. By that time, however, Barry Seal was already dead and the "Fat Lady" had long since been sold to a CIA front company.

Much additional evidence eventually emerged about the byzantine entanglement of arms purchases with cocaine smuggling during the contra war, an embarrassment that the CIA understandably tried to conceal as long as possible. Two federal grand juries in Arkansas had probed the goings-on at Mena without returning any indictments; the second grand jury was led by then U.S. attorney and later Republican representative Asa Hutchinson. Local law enforcement officials, such as IRS investigator Russell Welch and state attorney general Winston Bryant, believed that their efforts to prosecute suspected crimes at Mena had been frustrated by federal officials in Washington as part of the cover-up, "despite a mountain of evidence," as Bryant said in 1990. As the contra war receded into history, however, the Mena story faded too, until it reappeared as an accusation against Clinton.

Revived by Clinton critics in *The Nation* magazine and other left-leaning outlets during the 1992 presidential campaign, but never pursued by mainstream reporters, the story proved fascinating to conservatives who previously had ridiculed all the charges of contra drug smuggling. Their belated acceptance of the Mena story necessarily implicated such right-wing icons as Oliver North, George Bush, and Ronald Reagan, of course, along with the contra leaders, in a vast narcotics enterprise.

That troubling aspect of the Mena conspiracy didn't seem to alarm its new promoters, so long as most blame fell upon the former Arkansas governor. Reagan and Bush were history, after all, while Clinton was president; Reaganite complicity in contra drug trafficking could be treated as a footnote to garish headlines about the former Arkansas governor. In this convenient refurbishing of the Mena story, it was Clinton who had tolerated the illicit guns-for-drugs operation, enforced the cover-up, and, in the most outlandish versions, siphoned off a tidy profit from "billions" in narcodollars passing through the backwoods airstrip.

As the original popularizer of Clinton mythology, Larry Nichols naturally had concocted his own variation on the Mena theme, cleverly tying it into the Arkansas Development Finance Authority—the state agency from which Clinton had fired Nichols—to lend an air of authority. His narration of the *Clinton Chronicles* video suggests that Dan Lasater, the Arkansas investment banker, Clinton contributor and convicted cocaine user, was involved somehow with smuggling at Mena, using the ADFA as a money-washing machine. Nichols went so far as to claim that he had seen cargo planes loaded with cocaine at the airfield (although apparently he never bothered to report these blatant felonies to anyone in law enforcement).

Thousands of credulous viewers no doubt accepted all this creative yarn spinning, but Nichols's wild accusations were unlikely to convince a wider and presumably more sophisticated audience. The daunting task of verifying them was taken up by the agents of the Arkansas Project.

Bob Tyrrell seems to have been particularly captivated by Nichols's assertions. His interest was further piqued by the small-press publication that spring of *Compromised: Clinton, Bush and the CIA* by Terry Reed and journalist John Cummings. According to Reed, a pilot, machinist, and former air force officer who claimed to have worked with Seal, he had been recruited by Oliver

North to assist a secret contra-training operation in Arkansas. A highlight of Reed's seven-hundred-page memoir, which sold well thanks to heavy promotion by Floyd Brown and the right-wing talk-radio circuit, is his account of an alleged 1986 meeting at a "bunker" somewhere outside Little Rock.

Gathered to clean up the Mena operation at this clandestine conclave were Reed himself, North, former CIA agent Felix Rodriguez, Bush's future attorney general William Barr (traveling then under the name "Johnson"), and of course Governor Clinton and Clinton's ADFA director, Bobby Nash. As Reed tells it, they squabbled Hollywood-style over whether the 10 percent skimmed from smuggling proceeds by the state of Arkansas should be taken from the profit or the gross. Speaking as the representative of CIA director William Casey, Barr concluded the meeting with this soothing advice for the ambitious governor: "Bill, you are Mr. Casey's fair-haired boy. But you do have competition for the job you seek. We would never put all our eggs in one basket. You and your state have been our greatest asset. The beauty of this, as you know, is that you're a Democrat, and with our ability to influence both parties, this country can get beyond partisan gridlock. Mr. Casey wanted me to pass on to you that unless you fuck up and do something stupid, you're No. 1 on the short list for a shot at the job you've always wanted. That's pretty heady stuff, Bill. So why don't you help us keep a lid on this, and we'll all be promoted together." A few pages later, Reed meets with Clinton in a parked van outside a Mexican restaurant to discuss Barry Seal's assassination, while the governor of Arkansas casually smokes a joint: "He took a long, deep drag. After holding it in until his cheeks bulged, he then exhaled slowly and deliberately."

Terry Reed found his way to Boynton and Henderson. Arkansas Project records show numerous meetings that Boynton and Henderson held with Reed and his lawyers in New York City (at the time Reed was involved in at least two lawsuits, both of which he would later drop). Early on, they also brought Reed to the *Spectator* offices to tell his amazing revelations. The bedazzled Tyrrell introduced him to Wlady Plesczynski, David Brock, and other staff members, all of whom found his story unbelievable. Later, Plesczynski bluntly rejected Henderson's suggestion that the *Spectator* publish an excerpt from *Compromised*—the first of a series of skirmishes at the magazine over Tyrrell's Mena fixation.

Convinced that proof of a link to drug-smuggling could finish Clinton, Tyrrell became a Mena enthusiast. But the amateur sleuths of the Arkansas Project couldn't be expected to crack such a formidable case without professional assistance. For this and other tasks requiring investigative expertise, Boynton and Henderson had engaged the services of Rex Armistead, a sixty-five-year-old private detective recommended by their trusted adviser, Justice Jim Johnson.

*   *   *

After more than three decades in and around Southern law enforcement, Armistead had acquired a high profile and a decidedly mixed reputation. In 1983, the Jackson, Mississippi, *Clarion-Ledger* described him as "a flamboyant policeman who worked hard and sometimes took a few shortcuts during his thirty-five-year career." A tall, bulky, bald-headed figure usually sporting gold jewelry and sunglasses, he flew his own airplane and sometimes arrived at a crime scene driving a Lincoln Continental. He was renowned for his underworld contacts, particularly in the so-called Dixie Mafia, and had killed at least nine people "in the line of duty." Testifying in a 1985 lawsuit the veteran cop explained, "I never shot anybody that was not armed. I sleep very well at night."

Though he was the scion of a wealthy Delta cotton-growing family, and surely was bright enough to enter college, Armistead instead opted for a job as deputy county sheriff of rural Coahoma County at the age of eighteen. Several years later, after serving as the local constable, he obtained an appointment as an investigator for the Mississippi Highway Patrol, where he continued working, frequently undercover, until 1975. That year he moved on to head the Regional Organized Crime Information Center, a federally funded coordinating office based in New Orleans, where he simultaneously participated in the Justice Department's Organized Crime Strike Force, pursuing cases against the crime family of New Orleans Mafia boss Carlos Marcello. When the ROCIC moved to Memphis in 1978, he went with it. Armistead retired from police work in 1982 to set up shop as a detective and security consultant in West Memphis, Arkansas, where his primary clients were in the oil and trucking businesses.

For the unique needs of the Arkansas Project, Armistead possessed important connections—especially his ties to federal law enforcement through the ROCIC and his stint in New Orleans, which had once served as the headquarters of Barry Seal's smuggling network. His expertise in organized crime might also prove useful in a major narcotics investigation such as the Mena case.

But at least as significant as Armistead's professional credentials was his political pedigree, reflected in his endorsement by Jim Johnson, the old segregationist and perennial Clinton opponent. They had met while Armistead served under John Bell Williams, the last openly racist governor of Mississippi.

Their paths had crossed again in 1992, when Johnson tried to find a letter that Clinton had written to a Mississippi draft board in the sixties endorsing conscientious-objector status for Paul Parish, a fellow Rhodes scholar from the Magnolia State. As Johnson later told an interviewer, he asked Mississippi senator Trent Lott for help in retrieving the Clinton letter. After his request to Lott, Johnson said, "I was subsequently contacted by Colonel Rex Armistead of

Lula, Mississippi. Colonel Armistead was the head of the Mississippi State Police when my friend, former Congressman John Bell Williams, was Governor of Mississippi." The letter never turned up, but within a year or so Armistead was working for Johnson's friends in the Arkansas Project.

The "colonel"'s notoriety dated back to the infamous rioting against integration at the University of Mississippi in the fall of 1962, when Armistead is reputed to have flown retired general Edwin Walker to the Ole Miss campus from Dallas. Walker had resigned his commission after being suspended for ultraright propagandizing within the army and turned to agitating full-time for the John Birch Society and similar organizations.

Hoping to spark a rebellion at Ole Miss, the paranoid general helped to rally more than three thousand angry whites to prevent the court-ordered enrollment of a lone black student named James Meredith. In a radio speech, he cried: "Bring your flags, your tents, and your skillets! It is time! Now or never!" (He was later arrested, along with about two hundred others, and charged with federal offenses, including "insurrection.") Before army units arrived to quell the mob, scores of federal marshals and National Guardsmen were wounded by rocks, Molotov cocktails, and shotgun pellets; a British journalist and a civilian bystander were killed by rifle fire.

While Armistead's cameo appearance in the Ole Miss disturbances may be apocryphal, there is no doubt that his earliest patron was Paul Johnson, Jr., the lieutenant governor who physically blocked Meredith from entering the university campus. The following year, Armistead flew Johnson around the state during his successful run for governor. (The candidate displayed his qualifications to succeed Ross Barnett by referring publicly to the NAACP as "Niggers, Alligators, Apes, Coons and Possums.")

Upon taking office, the new governor rewarded Armistead with an appointment to the highway patrol as a plainclothes investigator. In that capacity Armistead worked mostly at the direct command of the governor, in particular as his official liaison with the Mississippi Sovereignty Commission—an official propaganda and police outfit that spied on civil rights workers, prominent blacks, white liberals, and other suspected "subversives," while funding and promoting the White Citizens Councils.

Armistead rose to prominence in the Mississippi police apparatus during an era of wanton official terrorism and repression against blacks and civil rights workers. One of the worst incidents occurred two years after he was appointed chief investigator of the highway patrol by Governor Williams. In May 1970, Armistead was present at predominantly black Jackson State College when city and state police officers opened fire on unarmed student protesters, killing two and wounding twelve. After the gunfire ended, the police picked up hundreds of shell casings to prevent ballistics identification of their weapons, in an obvious obstruction of justice. A congressional investigation of the Jackson State incident rejected Armistead's claim that "sniper" fire had provoked the deadly fusillade aimed at a women's dormitory.

Two years later another new governor took office and promptly demoted Armistead, who quit the highway patrol in 1975 and moved to New Orleans. His tenure at the ROCIC created further controversy, with the American Civil Liberties Union accusing him of conducting unlawful surveillance of law-abiding citizens. (Law enforcement officials in Memphis and Little Rock complained that Armistead had little to show for the $2 million budget his organization received annually from the Justice Department.)

Within a year after he entered the private sector, Armistead provoked a searing political scandal back in his home state. Bill Allain, the Democratic candidate for governor, charged in October 1983 that the hulking detective had masterminded a Republican plot to smear him as a homosexual. As a former assistant attorney general for the state of Mississippi, Allain had encountered the ex–highway patrol officer on other occasions. "If you know Rex Armistead like I know Rex Armistead," he told the *Jackson Daily News*, "this is his bag, this is his kind of thing."

Armistead denied that he had done anything more than interview a few police officers about the allegations against Allain. But he had made the mistake of bringing the charges to the attention of Charles Thompson, a producer for *20/20*, the ABC News magazine program. Thompson and correspondent Geraldo Rivera went down to Jackson to investigate the story, and quickly uncovered a clumsy scheme by prominent Mississippi Republicans—notably including Armistead's personal attorney and longtime friend, William Spell, Jr.—to pay three black transvestite prostitutes to falsely implicate Allain. Under questioning by Rivera on camera, all three recanted their slurs against the Democrat.

Waving off any notion that he was the "instigator . . . behind this plot," Armistead insisted that he had merely helped out as a favor to Bill Spell. He seemed to regard the Republican dirty trick as a kind of civil duty. "If the man is a homosexual, the public has a right to know," he said of Allain, who passed a lie detector test and went on to win the election.

Armistead's costly investigate efforts for the Arkansas Project focused largely upon Mena and the death of Vince Foster, according to David Brock, who met with the detective at an airport hotel in Miami during the winter of 1995. For two days the young writer sat listening and taking notes as Armistead, Henderson, Boynton, and Tyrrell discussed their theories about the Foster and Mena cases. The short version was that Armistead had spent a small fortune, traveling as far as Belize and Costa Rica, without producing evidence that implicated Clinton in any wrongdoing at the rural airport or anywhere else. As they talked, Brock recalled, Armistead occasionally dropped a racist remark. Henderson and Boynton didn't seem to notice. They thought Armistead "was great," but "he struck me as a shady character. Actually, I thought they were all putting on a show for Bob, to make the money they were spending look worthwhile."

As a conservative, Brock also found it strange that the *Spectator* would lend credence to a contra-cocaine story, with all its obviously ugly implications for Republican heroes like Reagan, Bush, and North. But as he learned in Miami, Tyrrell planned to spin the contra-cocaine allegations not only against Clinton but also Senator John Kerry, the Massachusetts Democrat who had first exposed evidence linking the contras to the drug trade back in 1986. The editor wanted Brock to prepare an exposé, based on Armistead's research, that would affect Kerry's reelection chances in 1996. Its proposed thesis was that the senator, a highly decorated Vietnam War veteran, had aided Communists in Central America and covered up drug dealing by leftists in the region. According to Brock's notes of their meeting, Armistead claimed to have a source who could place Kerry and the president of Costa Rica together at a fishing resort that was also "a big drug transfer point."

Soon after the Miami conference, Brock quietly decided to avoid the Kerry piece and any assignments related to the Arkansas Project or Rex Armistead. He and other staffers later tried to convince Tyrrell that using Mena against Clinton made no sense, that Reed's allegations were ridiculous, and that publishing this kind of dubious material would damage the *Spectator*'s reputation. There were many angry arguments at the magazine and at least one resignation prompted by disagreement over Tyrrell's obsession. Brock came to feel that arguing with his boss about Mena was a waste of time: "Bob never made a coherent case for any of this stuff. If it would damage Clinton, that was the bottom line. Bob had no regard for the credibility of these sources."

If Brock, Plesczynski, and most of their colleagues weren't buying Armistead's goods, other journalists were. Ambrose Evans-Pritchard of the London *Sunday Telegraph* and Micah Morrison of the *Wall Street Journal* editorial page both spent considerable time at Parker Dozhier's bait shop, picking up leads and documents. (Evans-Pritchard quotes Armistead at length on the Dixie Mafia in his 1997 book, *The Secret Life of Bill Clinton*.) The few *Spectator* staffers like Brock who spent any time in Arkansas eventually realized that the project's material was turning up in other publications. Had the *Spectator* writers been aware of the dollar amounts being spent on Boynton, Henderson, and Armistead, they probably would have been even more appalled. (Adding insult to injury was the bureaucratic description of the Arkansas Project in correspondence between the Spectator Foundation and Scaife's office. In those letters it was formally designated the "Editorial Improvement Project.") Boynton's ledger shows that before the project ended in 1997, the Mississippi detective collected more than $375,000 in monthly fees and expenses.

A separate document from the *Spectator*'s files shows that Boynton and Henderson were even more generous with themselves. Starting with monthly compensation of $12,500 for Boynton and $10,000 for Henderson, and adding on the annual raises they awarded themselves, their combined draw from Scaife's tax-exempt "charitable" largesse totaled well over $1 million (excluding expenses) between January 1994 and June 1997. Boynton's share came to nearly $600,000, while Henderson got just over $475,000.

With such loose financial controls, it may never be known how much of Scaife's cash, if any, ended up with David Hale. But there are numerous entries in the ledgers that don't seem to correspond with actual expenses—such as "article fees" paid to Brock, who got a biweekly salary check and said he received no such fees.

Neither Tyrrell nor the *Spectator*'s publisher, Ronald Burr, received any regular accounting of the project's expenditures. Parker Dozhier, however, was at least dimly aware that his $1,000 monthly stipend compared poorly with the money being lavished on Rex Armistead, according to Caryn Mann. "He was very jealous and angry about Armistead, because when Rex was hired, P. D. went into rages, [saying] Armistead was getting money he should be getting."

The frenetic efforts of the Arkansas Project took on a greater political salience when the Republicans gained control of Congress in 1995. Newt Gingrich, the incoming Speaker of the House, had warned before the midterm election that he planned to use "subpoena power" to wage war against the White House. In a private speech to business lobbyists at the Capitol Hill Club, he envisioned as many as twenty congressional committees simultaneously investigating the Democratic administration, which he called "the enemy of normal Americans." The new chairmen of the House and Senate Banking Committees both announced that they intended to resume investigating the Clintons under the rubric of Whitewater.

This power shift immediately enhanced the influence of Floyd Brown and David Bossie, the Citizens United duo who had served as the early impresarios of Whitewater. "People who answer our phone calls now have 'Chairman' before their names," Brown bragged to *The Nation* magazine, which described him as "elated by the prospect of a swarm of subpoenas flying off Capitol Hill toward 1600 Pennsylvania Avenue." Brown said he was urging the new congressional leadership to "reopen the probe into the death of White House counsel Vince Foster and to investigate the drug smuggling in Mena, Arkansas."

Justice Jim Johnson, Brown's Arkansas mentor, also viewed Mena as an urgent matter. With characteristic hyperbole, he told an interviewer in February

1995 that there was "absolutely no doubt in my mind that the government of the United States was an active participant in one of the largest dope operations in the world, and that the [former] Governor of Arkansas enjoyed a benefit from its success."

It was hardly a coincidence that Floyd Brown's announced priorities for the new Congress mirrored Justice Jim's concerns and Rex Armistead's investigation. Brown and Bossie had remained in close contact with Johnson and the *Spectator*'s team while cultivating members and staff on Capitol Hill who might make use of the Arkansas Project. The Senate Banking Committee, with jurisdiction over the revived Whitewater investigation, had several receptive members, including its new chairman, Alfonse D'Amato, and the implacable North Carolina conservative Lauch Faircloth (who hired Bossie as a full-time committee aide in 1996).

Whitewater also topped the agenda of the House Banking Committee, taken over by ranking Republican James Leach of Iowa. Leach had a reputation for fairness and moderate, almost liberal, politics, making him an unlikely ally of Clinton's enemies. But the Iowan had been close to President Bush and strongly disliked the man who had displaced him; almost from the beginning, he had adopted Whitewater as a personal crusade. (His zeal may also have been encouraged by the growing power of the religious right in his home state's Republican Party. During the 1992 Iowa GOP caucuses, delegates loyal to the Christian Coalition had controlled forty-two of forty-six precincts.)

As early as March 1994, Leach had declared on the House floor that "Whitewater is about the arrogance of power," accusing Clinton of "Machiavellian machinations of a single party government" that had virtually caused the entire savings and loan crisis. He compared Bill Clinton's Arkansas to Huey Long's Louisiana. The basis for that and other Leach speeches had been furnished by Citizens United, with information funneled from David Bossie to Leach's press secretary, Joe Pinder. And Pinder, worried that his respectable boss would be tainted by proximity to those disreputable right-wingers, took care to keep his relationship with Bossie a secret. They never left their full names in phone messages, and met to exchange information in restaurants far from the Capitol.

Unsurprisingly then, the press releases handed to reporters by Pinder were virtually indistinguishable from Citizens United materials. A "preliminary briefing" prepared by Pinder in August 1995 for the committee hearings starred L. Jean Lewis, the Resolution Trust Corporation investigator who would testify about "events that suggest an effort by RTC Washington and highly placed political appointees at the Department of Justice to suppress or at least control her criminal referrals" regarding Madison Guaranty. Featured in villainous supporting roles were Hillary Clinton; Beverly Bassett Schaffer, the former Arkansas securities commissioner who allegedly helped Madison at Hillary's behest; and an RTC attorney named April Breslaw, who Lewis claimed had tried to kill the Madison probe in February 1994 (and whom Lewis had "accidentally" taped during a meeting in her office).

Around the same time, Citizens United distributed a "Whitewater's Most Wanted" poster with caricatures of Bassett Schaffer (over the phrase "AT LARGE" in red) and Breslaw ("RTC FLUNKY"). Over the protest of committee Democrats, Leach had decided to call none of these women to dispute Lewis's accusations, nor any of the relevant officials from the Arkansas Securities Commission or the Federal Home Loan Bank Board whose testimony would contradict Lewis. Along with Bassett Schaffer and Breslaw, the first lady would be tried publicly in absentia.

The most important media outlets in Washington continued to play up the burgeoning scandal. Led by the *New York Times*'s Jeff Gerth and the *Washington Post*'s Susan Schmidt, both recipients of the November 1993 leaks of L. Jean Lewis's criminal referrals, the press overwhelmingly took the Citizens United line in previewing the upcoming House hearings. Doing so required some real creativity. With the hearing scheduled to begin on Monday, August 8, GOP staffers made a preemptive leak late on the previous Friday afternoon. Anticipating that Democrats would attack Lewis's motives, they released a number of documents damaging, if not downright devastating, to her credibility. Among them were former U.S. attorney Charles Banks's letter refusing to pursue her allegations against the Clintons on the basis of weak evidence and political bias, and internal FBI cables and Justice Department appraisals that concluded: "No facts can be identified to support the designation of President Bill Clinton [or] Hillary Rodham Clinton . . . as material witnesses to the allegations made in the criminal referral."

The Associated Press distributed a story quoting and summarizing those documents over the weekend. The *New York Times*, however, did not. No mention of their existence ever appeared in the newspaper of record. The broadcast media as usual followed the *Times*'s lead. The *Washington Post* buried a brief version of the AP story on an inside page.

Burying exculpatory material about Whitewater was becoming routine. On June 26, *Wall Street Journal* reporter Ellen Joan Pollock had published details of a preliminary report prepared for the RTC by the San Francisco law firm of Pillsbury, Madison & Sutro. So closely was the firm identified with its principal Washington partner, Jay Stephens, the former Reagan and Bush administration U.S. attorney for the District of Columbia, that White House aide George Stephanopoulos had bitterly protested its selection to probe the Clinton's Whitewater investment. But the Pillsbury Report's preliminary findings could hardly have been more favorable to the White House.

"A long-awaited report on the collapse of Madison Guaranty Savings & Loan," reported the *Journal,* "corroborates most of President and Mrs. Clinton's assertions about their Whitewater real estate investment." Specifically, Pollock wrote, the Pillsbury Report "shows that the Clintons were passive investors in Whitewater Development Corp. and weren't involved in its financial transactions until 1986 [when state and federal regulators removed Jim McDougal from control of the institution]. . . . That is significant because of allegations that funds transferred from Madison to Whitewater before 1986 contributed to the thrift's collapse." The report also verified the amount lost by the Clintons on their investment with McDougal—just over $43,000. To any reporter who took the time to read it carefully, the report's 143-page history of the Whitewater Development Corporation (with 768 footnotes) completely refuted the conventional wisdom. Without the Clintons' knowledge, their deranged partner had looted their investment. "More and more," the Pillsbury Report noted, "the McDougals lacked the money to pay their personal debts, so increasingly they transferred money between entities they owned or controlled to cover their obligations to third persons." One of those entities was Whitewater. But few reporters did read it, and those who did managed to ignore McDougal's chicanery. By the time the New York Times got around to it weeks later, reporters Jeff Gerth and Stephen Engleberg told readers that the Pillsbury Report's real significance was that the Clintons had failed to pay "their half of Whitewater's losses." That Jim McDougal had deceived his partners did not strike the Times as worth reporting.

The House hearings that began on August 8, 1995, hardly lived up to their advance billing. In his opening remarks, Leach portrayed Jean Lewis as the protagonist of "an uplifting and indeed heroic story of middle Americans, public servants in obscure government agencies who refused to be cowed by the power structure." And as predicted on page A1 of that morning's *New York Times* by Jeff Gerth, Lewis made sweeping charges of a conspiracy to "obstruct" her Madison probe at the highest levels of government. When asked by Democrats to identify any of these officials by name, however, she couldn't. She also failed to provide any evidence that Whitewater had helped to sink the ailing thrift. The "obstructions" turned out to be two delays, of one and two weeks respectively, by RTC and Department of Justice lawyers examining her referrals.

When the tape of her recorded conversation with RTC lawyer April Breslaw was played aloud, it became obvious that Lewis had significantly misconstrued their conversation. During her prepared testimony, Lewis had stated boldly: "It is clear that Ms. Breslaw was there to deliver a message that, quote, The people at the top would like to be able to say Whitewater did not cause a loss to Madison, close quote. Of course, Whitewater did cause a financial loss to Madison, and Madison's failure cost the American taxpayer millions of dollars."

But Lewis, it turned out, did not accurately recount Breslaw's words. First, the statement attributed to the RTC lawyer simply did not appear in her tape-recorded remarks. What she had in fact confided to Lewis was a bureaucratic truism: If they could do so honestly, the RTC's top officials would be relieved to be left out of a high-stakes political probe. Even so, the tape also showed Breslaw pressing Lewis for definitive evidence that Whitewater had helped sink Madison Guaranty. Despite her categorical statements to that effect, Lewis provided none. Nor, it turned out, had she troubled herself to read the RTC's own Pillsbury Report, dated four months earlier.

None of these weaknesses in her testimony appeared in the pages of the *Times* or the *Washington Post*—where Susan Schmidt reported that "Lewis gave a detailed description of how [her] investigation . . . was thwarted by [RTC] and Justice Department officials after Bill Clinton was elected president." Schmidt was the reporter whom Lewis claimed to have banished empty-handed from her doorstep in November 1993. Only the *Wall Street Journal* reported that FBI and Justice documents belied Lewis's allegations and noted that Lewis "didn't seem wholly credible . . . [and] struck many as ready to draw the most incriminating conclusions from ambiguous circumstances."

Two days later, Leach reversed himself and allowed April Breslaw to testify. Expressing shock at her treatment by Lewis and Leach, the RTC attorney pointed out that she couldn't have tried to quash the Whitewater probe, which by the time she and Lewis had spoken in February 1994 was already in the hands of independent counsel Robert Fiske. To his credit, the chairman apologized for tarring Breslaw without first listening to her side of the story. Leach wasn't as kind to Beverly Bassett Schaffer, who was never permitted to testify in the House despite Democratic protests.

The fizzling of the August hearings appeared not to discourage Leach, who clearly was determined to pursue the Clintons into the following election year. David Bossie and Joe Pinder had plans, too. Before summer's end they had moved on to Mena, a fresher and sexier topic that had suddenly resurfaced in the pages of the *Spectator* and the *Wall Street Journal* thanks to the ever-improving memory of a compelling new eyewitness: Trooper L. D. Brown.

According to Tyrrell's account in his disparaging biography, *Boy Clinton*, L. D. Brown first unburdened himself about Mena in late 1994 or early 1995, a few months after he spoke out publicly in support of David Hale. An interview concerning Hale that Brown gave to ABC News never made the air, Tyrrell writes, because Clinton attorney David Kendall filled the ears of network executives with invective against the trooper, calling him a "pathological liar." Infuriated, Brown confided in Tyrrell, telling his eager listener a sensational tale that the editor finally convinced him to reveal in the pages of the *Spectator*. Having failed to interest any other writer on the magazine's exasperated staff to write it up, Tyrrell published Brown's story under his own name in the July 1995 issue.

It was a conspiratorial blockbuster. Brown claimed that in the spring of 1984, with Clinton's eager help, he had applied for employment with the CIA. Five months later, even before the trooper had been interviewed by the spy agency, a clandestine operative (whom he later identified as Donald Gregg, the former ambassador to South Korea and national security adviser to Vice President Bush) lured Brown into "moonlighting" as a CIA contract employee. His first assignment, on October 23, 1984, was to accompany Barry Seal on a covert flight from Mena to Central America aboard a C-123K transport plane, the famed "Fat Lady." The mission consisted of parachuting pallets of M16 rifles to the contras and picking up some "duffel bags" at a Honduran airport before flying home. According to Brown, Clinton behaved as if he knew about Brown's adventure. "You having any fun yet?" he asked playfully at the mansion.

Brown told Tyrrell how he discovered the terrible truth at the end of his second trip with Seal on Christmas Eve. After they returned to Mena, the pilot reached into a duffel bag in the back of his car, pulling out $2,500 in cash and a kilo of cocaine, which he handed to Brown. The shaken trooper immediately confronted Clinton when he got home to Little Rock.

"Do you know what they're bringing back on those planes?" he demanded. "They're bringing back coke." Clinton took this news quite calmly. "That's Lasater's deal," he supposedly said, casually implicating a campaign contributor who also employed his brother Roger Clinton.

At this point, Brown recalled yet another incriminating tidbit he had neglected to mention a year earlier to Danny Wattenberg. As the governor's bodyguard, he now recalled, he had accompanied Clinton to parties given by Dan Lasater where the entertainment had included "young girls" and "plenty of cocaine." In this completed scenario, everything fit together exactly the way Larry Nichols had explained it in *The Clinton Chronicles*.

(A year later, only weeks before the 1996 election, Brown added yet another new element to his narrative: Felix Rodriguez, a Cuban exile and longtime CIA operative, allegedly had showed up at the governor's mansion in January 1985 and, in brief summary, tried to entice Brown into assassinating one of the Mena accomplices in Puerto Vallarta, Mexico. The target, Brown claims to have discovered later, was none other than Terry Reed, whose book also fingers Rodriguez, a well-known associate of Oliver North in covert airdrops to the contras. Brown's saga ended with him ditching an unfired weapon, flying home conscience-stricken from Mexico after a few days in the sun with his wife, and rejecting all further overtures from Rodriguez.)

Tyrrell professed amazement that his interview with Brown received so little media attention. The only significant response appeared on the *Journal* editorial page, which had published lengthy articles on Mena and related Arkansas drug arcana by Micah Morrison. Under the headline "Investigate Mena," the newspaper's lead editorial on July 10, 1995, declared that "a congressional committee with resources [and] subpoena power should look into this. If some chips fall on the Republican side, so be it."

Evidently Jim Leach agreed. On July 11, the House Banking Committee chairman wrote to Vice Admiral John McConnell, the director of the National Security Agency, to request an immediate briefing on any information gathered by the supersecret intelligence agency about "money laundering in Arkansas in the late 1980s." The Iowa Republican admitted he was pursuing "tales" from the press and the Internet, and had a list of specific allegations in mind, including "the laundering of drug money . . . through Mena, Arkansas"; "any covert activities by the U.S. government or any private parties (the so-called private benefactors) in or around Mena in the late 1980s"; and "any contractual or other relationship [of NSA] with the late Adler Berriman 'Barry' Seal."

Appearing on C-SPAN a month later to talk about Whitewater, Leach hinted that he would investigate Mena. "There are activities at an airport that have been ruled outside the scope of these hearings," he told host Brian Lamb. "But it is possible that we can hold later hearings to address those issues."

Although Leach eventually spent more than a year (and an untold sum of his committee's budget) delving into Mena, he never held any public hearings on the subject. But the congressman's interest in the topic was sufficient to excite scandal buffs in the right-wing press, notably at the *New York Post,* where financial columnist John Crudele published frequent updates on the everwidening probe, beginning with this dispatch on July 28: "Leach's recent hearings on the Whitewater scandal will probably be expanded to look into the operations of the Arkansas Development and [*sic*] Finance Authority (ADFA) as well as the events that took place at Mena."

To the dismay of his staff, Bob Tyrrell also continued to chase the Mena story for many months. He hired another detective to work the same beat in the fall of 1995. This second gumshoe was William T. "Tom" Golden, a former military intelligence officer who sometimes introduced himself as a Hollywood producer named "Tom Spielberg." Golden had showed up in an army intelligence sideshow of the Iran-contra affair known as "Operation Yellow Fruit." In 1983, after a stint as assistant military attaché in the U.S. embassy in Managua, a spy post, he was assigned to Yellow Fruit to learn how the project's managers had spent huge sums of money advanced by the Pentagon for covert operations. What he discovered was that roughly $324 million intended to benefit the Nicaraguan contras and various other secret operations had been stolen by the officers in charge of Yellow Fruit. Golden turned his findings over to the Army's Criminal Investigation Division, which spent years prosecuting his leads. After his retirement, Golden had set up shop as a private investigator in the southwest Arkansas town of Glenwood, not far from Mena itself.

Golden's invoices, marked "Arkansas Project," went directly to Tyrrell. More detailed than Boynton's records, they trace a peripatetic two-year search for documentation of the Mena story in Louisiana, Texas, Tennessee, Mississippi, Florida, Missouri, and Arkansas. Some expenditures indicate work on other leads, such as his entry of $110 for "dinner and drinks with Independent Counsel source regarding Hillary Clinton possible indictment." (Another entry documents "dinner with Garland County prosecutor, Karen Fuller." But Garland County has no prosecutor, and the district of which it is a part has never employed anyone named Karen Fuller. The best-known Arkansas citizen with that name is the evening news anchor on KATV, the ABC television affiliate in Little Rock. That Karen Fuller said she has never heard of Tom Golden or "Tom Spielberg.")

The former army spy also provided some research on the Vince Foster case and for articles by James Ring Adams. And at one point in March 1997, Golden paid $5,000 for unspecified services to L. D. Brown, who had also established his own investigation business. By that time, the Arkansas Project's pursuit of Mena had come full circle, with a payment to the story's original source. Golden later conceded to a producer for CNBC that despite all the strenuous legwork, he had found no credible evidence of Clinton's involvement in any illegal activities at Mena.

In the meantime, Rex Armistead's activities had taken an ugly turn, reminiscent of his role in the Bill Allain smear. He had commenced a side investigation of Cable News Network correspondent John Camp. The CNN correspondent learned that Armistead was trying to discredit him when Patricia Byrd, his former wife, called with a warning in the fall of 1996. The two had been divorced for twelve years but maintained a friendly relationship. Byrd told her former husband about a distressing telephone call she had received from a man who identified himself as Rex Armistead. The detective had called her at home, asking about their marriage and Camp's personal life, obviously looking for dirt. "I said that I didn't know anything derogatory," said Byrd, an assistant district attorney in Louisiana. "But he still persisted and kept trying to ask me questions."

Armistead prepared a report on Camp and members of his family that turned up in the files of the House Banking Committee. A spokesman for the committee later admitted to reporter Murray Waas that its investigators had frequently spoken with Armistead, although he denied that the Mississippi detective had provided any information about John Camp. The spokesman didn't explain why Leach's aides had compiled personal information about a journalist.

There was no mystery, however, as to how Camp had attracted the attention of the Arkansas Project operatives. Beginning in 1994, the award-winning CNN correspondent had filed a number of reports casting doubt on the premises of the Whitewater scandal. After spending several days poring over documents in pursuit of an angle, he once told a National Press Club forum sponsored by *Harper's* magazine, "I emerged with a huge dilemma. Was I going to believe the *New York Times,* or was I going to believe my lying eyes? And my choice . . . was to believe my lying eyes, because the documentary evidence did not support the premise of the initial story in March of 1992."

Besides filing a sympathetic interview with beleaguered Arkansas securities commissioner Beverly Bassett Schaffer, Camp had profiled Dan Lasater, the Little Rock investment banker whom Larry Nichols and L. D. Brown had designated as the chief malefactor in the Mena story. Camp showed him as a reformed drug abuser who had found religion in prison. But what may really have turned the ire of the Arkansas Project upon the CNN veteran was his debunking of L. D. Brown's tale of flying from Mena, Arkansas, to Central America on October 23, 1984.

Barry Seal's C-123 did in fact make a flight that day, one of two days it left the ground that year—according to Arkansas State Police surveillance files that may well have been available to L. D. Brown. But it turned out that Seal had a different passenger on that particular date, namely John Camp himself. Then working for TV station WBRZ in Baton Rouge, Louisiana, Camp and his crew were making a film documentary about Seal's career as smuggler turned DEA informant. The Peabody Award–winning program was broadcast in November 1984. Camp and his crew had flown up from Baton Rouge with Seal before dawn that morning, spent the entire day shooting film, and returned with him to Louisiana late that night.

They had flown nowhere near Central America, and they had picked up no guns, no cocaine, and nobody resembling L. D. Brown.

Chapter Eleven

SENATOR D'AMATO'S
LONG GOOD-BYE

O N JUNE 7, 1995, independent counsel Kenneth Starr indicted Arkansas
governor Jim Guy Tucker, his attorney, and a former business partner
from San Francisco on three counts of conspiracy to commit bankruptcy and
tax fraud in Little Rock. The charges grew out of Tucker's 1987 acquisition of
cable TV companies in Florida and Texas. Highly technical in nature, the
charges brought by the Office of Independent Counsel struck local criminal
defense attorneys as curious in two ways. First, Tucker and his associates were
not accused of actually evading taxes—only of concocting a sham bankruptcy
that would theoretically have made such evasion possible. (The relevant
statute had been enacted to deal with so-called drug kingpins.) Second, the indictments had no connection of any kind with Whitewater, Madison Guaranty
Savings and Loan, or Bill and Hillary Clinton.

To Arkansas journalists it was well known that Bill Clinton and Jim Guy
Tucker were more enemies than friends. Although generational contemporaries
with Ivy League degrees, they were of two entirely different breeds. Having
grown up in Little Rock, Tucker had enlisted in the Marine Corps immediately
after graduating from Harvard University in 1964. Discharged due to a chronic
liver disorder, he had nevertheless found his way to Vietnam by taking a job as
a correspondent for the military newspaper *Stars & Stripes*. He subsequently
earned a law degree from the University of Arkansas, served as Little Rock's
prosecuting attorney, preceded Clinton as state attorney general, and won
election to the U.S. House of Representatives in 1976.

Unlike the ingratiating Clinton, Jim Guy thrived on confrontation, tended
to resist compromise, and was not averse to making enemies. As a prosecutor,

he sometimes accompanied police on drug busts. Critics called him arrogant. He and Clinton first crossed swords politically during the 1978 Democratic primary race for the U.S. Senate, in which Clinton supported the eventual winner, David Pryor. Four years later, Clinton defeated Tucker in a rough contest for the gubernatorial nomination. The campaign left Tucker badly in debt and both men with bruised feelings. Tucker had consoled himself by earning a considerable fortune in real estate and cable TV. As recently as 1990, he had publicly contemplated running against Clinton again, only to back off in the face of the incumbent's superior funding. Settling for the position of lieutenant governor, Tucker had succeeded to the governorship at last after Clinton left Arkansas to become president in 1993. He had been easily elected to a new four-year term in 1994 in a race against Republican Sheffield Nelson.

During the 1994 campaign, Nelson had repeatedly charged that Tucker was about to be indicted. His campaign ran TV commercials showing a cell door slamming, a tactic that served mainly to reinforce the Republican candidate's reputation as a sore loser whose machinations had led to the widely resented Whitewater investigation. Although they clearly backfired, Nelson's efforts to portray Tucker as a corrupt politician got a strong boost from an extraordinary four-part "investigative report" in the *Arkansas Democrat-Gazette* titled "Whitewater: The Tucker Connection." The newspaper was so proud of its work that it issued a special reprint less than two months before the election.

When reporters examined Madison Guaranty and David Hale's Capital Management Services, the *Democrat-Gazette* editors explained, they found themselves wondering "which governor of Arkansas is really at the center of the story?" As the series made clear, Tucker had done a great deal of business with both David Hale and Jim McDougal during the eighties. Less obvious, amid the welter of details about long-ago real estate transactions, was exactly what, if anything, the governor had done wrong. Tucker compared his role in the newspaper series to the hero of the Tom Hanks film *Forrest Gump*, as the ultimate innocent bystander. Hale was not a named source for the *Democrat-Gazette* series; just how closely its premises were tied to his version of events would become evident only with time.

Tucker's response to Starr's indictment was characteristically combative. He accused the OIC of blatant partisanship, and attacked what he called the "sickening mendacity" of a prosecutor who publicly pledged to respect his targets' dignity while covertly leaking hurtful accusations to Republican members of Congress and the press. In the course of its yearlong investigation, the OIC had subpoenaed more than fifty thousand documents from Tucker and his wife, Betty, including his credit records, bank records, military records, college and law school transcripts, passports, and every business and personal check the couple had written since 1978.

Starr's answer to Tucker's defiance was a second indictment, handed down on August 17, 1995, charging him, Jim McDougal, and his ex-wife, Susan McDougal, with a total of twenty-one counts of bank fraud. At an angry press conference, Tucker accused the OIC of a "politically driven . . . taxpayer-funded invasion of Arkansas." He complained that he had learned of the second indictment, like the first, from a reporter. "If you throw enough mud at somebody," Tucker said, "maybe you can make something stick. You file enough indictments against a whole bunch of people, some who are in fact culpable, and include someone who is not, maybe you'll get one of those to stick." He vowed to ignore Sheffield Nelson's call for his resignation.

Starr's initial indictment of Tucker for bankruptcy fraud was assigned by lot to U.S. district judge Henry Woods. On September 5, 1995, Judge Woods handed down an opinion dismissing the three-count indictment on the grounds that the independent counsel had exceeded his lawful authority. "The subject matter of the indictment at issue," Woods wrote, "bears no relation whatsoever to the Clintons or James McDougal or their relationship with Madison Guaranty Savings and Loan Association, Whitewater Development Corporation, or Capital Management Services, Inc." Woods's decision took sharp issue with a rhetorical question in Kenneth Starr's brief: " 'What is the harm if the Independent Counsel handles this investigation rather than the Attorney General?' What difference does it make? It makes a great deal of difference if the statute and the Supreme Court plainly state that only matters related to the Independent Counsel's original prosecutorial jurisdiction are to be handled by him. . . . To gloss over and shortcut the requirements of criminal statutes is the first step toward tyranny."

Woods quoted the words of the late Supreme Court justice Robert Jackson on the dangers of prosecutorial abuse, previously cited by Justice Scalia in his dissent in *Morrison v. Olson*. "Therein is the most dangerous power of the prosecutor; that he will pick people that he thinks he should get, rather than cases that need to be prosecuted. With the law books filled with a great assortment of crimes, a prosecutor stands a fair chance of finding at least a technical violation of some act on the part of almost anyone. In such a case, it is not a question of discovering the commission of a crime and then looking for the man who has committed it, it is a question of picking the man and then searching the law books, or putting investigators to work, to pin some offense on him."

The eighty-year-old judge and former FBI agent could hardly have administered a more stinging rebuke to Starr. But if Woods's opinion angered the independent counsel, it outraged the *American Spectator*'s Arkansas Project team. Jim Guy Tucker's indictment had been greeted with popping cham-

pagne corks down at Parker Dozhier's bait shop in Hot Springs. Its dismissal
had Dozhier and his associates, including one in particular, vowing revenge.
An appointee of President Carter, Henry Woods had been an outspoken opponent of Arkansas governor Orval Faubus's racist policies during the fifties
and sixties—and a bitter foe of arch-segregationist Jim Johnson.

The Arkansas Project's first strike against Woods had come earlier, in the
form of a lengthy attack on the *Washington Times* op-ed page written by Johnson himself. It described Woods as a corrupt Clinton crony who had narrowly
escaped indictment for misusing highway funds in the fifties. The late Orval
Faubus, Johnson wrote, had once commented in Shakespearean tones that
"Henry was measured for prison stripes, and now he wears the purple." The
accusation of cronyism appeared to stem from the fact that Woods had once
appointed Hillary Clinton to a panel overseeing integration of the Little Rock
public school system, which Johnson had long denounced as a Communist
plot. Woods had also earned Justice Jim's eternal enmity in 1991 by voiding the
notorious "Johnson Amendment" to the Arkansas state constitution, in response to a lawsuit filed by black state legislators. The 1956 measure, authored
by Johnson, empowered the governor of Arkansas to resist what it called the
U.S. Supreme Court's "unconstitutional" 1954 *Brown v. Board of Education* decision banning school segregation.

Johnson's accusations of financial impropriety against Judge Woods had
been disproved forty years earlier. The remaining charges in his *Washington
Times* essay came straight from *The Clinton Chronicles,* among them the hoary
myth that Stephens, Inc., described as Woods's benefactor as well as the nation's largest commodities broker, had made an improper $3.5 million loan to
the 1992 Clinton presidential campaign. In reality, Woods had no financial ties
to Stephens, Inc. (which has never traded commodities at all).

Once again, Warren Stephens found it necessary to defend his company's
honor against its ostensible Republican allies. He wrote a letter to *Washington
Times* editor Wesley Pruden describing himself as "surprised and appalled"
that any newspaper would lend credence to Jim Johnson, "one of Arkansas'
most prolific and least credible conspiracy theorists. . . . When the facts do not
support his theories, he simply distorts them or makes up events that did not
occur. . . . [Y]ou do yourself and your readers a disservice by printing anything he has to say on any subject." But Stephens knew he was wasting his time.
Wesley Pruden was a Little Rock native whose father had been the chaplain of
Johnson's White Citizens Council.

Despite their manifest inaccuracies, Johnson's attacks upon Woods were
extensively quoted in a subsequent article in the *Arkansas Democrat-Gazette*
and parroted on the editorial page of the *Wall Street Journal* by investigative
columnist Micah Morrison, a regular at Dozhier's bait shop.

A page of contemporaneous notes from Dozhier's files shows numerous references to Judge Woods and "JJJ," for Justice Jim Johnson. The notes say, "Woods' charge is to protect the president by taking care of Tucker." Another page shows Johnson's Conway, Arkansas, phone number along with the notation "Wesley Pruden told me Wesley sent material to M.M.," presumably Micah Morrison. Pruden acknowledged meeting with Johnson on many occasions, but denied any knowledge of the Arkansas Project. (Morrison refused comment.)

The Arkansas Project documents also include a derogatory memo about Woods, written by Parker Dozhier, that was faxed to the office of Senator Lauch Faircloth, the North Carolina Republican, on August 28, 1995. Markings on the fax indicate that it was routed to Faircloth's office through Stephen Boynton, the Virginia attorney who held the Arkansas Project purse strings. The Dozhier memo, addressed to Faircloth aide Jim Highland, claimed that Woods plotted with President Clinton to fix the Tucker case in order to hamper the independent counsel's investigation. "Tucker," it claimed, "is in the position of offering testimony [that] would send the President to prison."

Only days before Woods was scheduled to hear oral arguments on Tucker's challenge to Starr's indictment, the judge was notified that Faircloth's office had requested fifteen years' worth of his financial disclosure statements. The request came from David Bossie, the Citizens United sleuth only recently hired as a full-time aide to the senator.

Upon learning of the request, the judge summoned all parties to the Tucker case to his chambers and informed them, he later wrote, of what he considered "a crude attempt to intimidate me, since it was well-known that Senator Faircloth had more than a passing interest in the Whitewater investigation. I assured counsel that such an attempt would in no way affect my handling of the Tucker case." At that meeting, neither Tucker nor the OIC requested that the judge recuse himself.

But Starr's attitude changed soon after Woods ruled against him. Following a second vitriolic attack upon the judge by Jim Johnson in the *Washington Times* (which described every Democratic-appointed federal judge in Arkansas as a member of Bill Clinton's "corrupt machine"), the independent counsel filed an appeal with the Eighth Circuit Court of Appeals in St. Louis. In it, Starr urged not only that the Tucker bankruptcy indictment be reinstated, but that the appeals court take the almost unprecedented step of removing Woods from the case due to his friendship with Hillary Rodham Clinton and others in the "Arkansas political establishment." Conceding that the Tucker indictment accused the Clintons of no wrongdoing, Starr nevertheless argued that "information in the public domain" created "an unmistakable appearance of bias by Judge Woods."

*   *   *

In Washington, meanwhile, the burden of promoting the "Clinton scandals" had fallen to the Senate Banking Committee, chaired by Alfonse D'Amato. The notion of the ethically tarnished junior senator from New York leading a clean-government crusade against the president struck many as an absurdity. Al D'Amato had endured a lengthy and still-secret investigation by the Senate Ethics Committee in 1991 before escaping with a mere reprimand for allowing his lobbyist brother Armand to misuse his Senate office. (Armand had been indicted and convicted of fraud and conspiracy in a related matter involving a crooked defense contractor, only to have his conviction overturned on appeal.) The ethics probe had covered many additional accusations against D'Amato, involving alleged misuse of his office and illicit fund-raising. Literally dozens of the senator's friends and associates had cited the Fifth Amendment and refused to testify before the committee. After his reprimand, he had refused to unseal his executive-session testimony before the Ethics Committee, which couldn't release it without his permission under Senate rules. Without the least embarrassment, D'Amato would demand "full disclosure" from the White House—while falsely claiming that his own testimony was "classified," as he put it in his 1995 memoir, *Power, Pasta and Politics.*

After fifteen years in office the New York senator was best known for his many and varied ethical transgressions, which had won him the title "Senator Sleaze." D'Amato had once appeared as a character witness for a Mob-connected Long Island disco owner who raised money for his first Senate campaign. He had twice approached Rudolph Giuliani, then the United States attorney for Manhattan, seeking leniency for Mafia gangsters then represented by Roy Cohn, the late attorney who had been a close D'Amato friend. Many times he had sought campaign contributions from the businesses whose interests he assiduously served, prompting the *New Republic* to give him another nickname: "Senator Shakedown."

There was an old D'Amato scandal, from his first Senate campaign in 1980, that closely paralleled the Whitewater accusations about Clinton getting favors from Madison Guaranty. For years, as a town official on Long Island, D'Amato had placed public funds in interest-free accounts in a local bank (a practice investigated and harshly criticized by a Nassau County grand jury). When he ran for the Senate, D'Amato had turned to the same bank for loans that totaled more than a million dollars—and had gotten the money on very soft terms, at an interest rate below prime.

Episodes like that typified D'Amato's career. There were so many that few observers could recall them all in detail. The impression he had left was clear enough, however. Many New Yorkers found it hard not to laugh when D'Amato railed against the ethics of the Clintons, and many Republicans wished that some other senator could lead the Whitewater investigation. But Bill Clinton's luck held firm when Al D'Amato insisted on his prerogative to delve into Whitewater as the Banking Committee chairman.

The Senate Whitewater hearings opened with a flourish on July 18, 1995, with Alaska Republican Frank Murkowski upending Vince Foster's empty brief-case—duly sent over for use as a stage prop by the Office of Independent Counsel—to dramatize the senator's view that there had been something ter-ribly suspicious about the belated discovery of the White House aide's torn suicide note several days after his death. Starr's own reinvestigation of his pre-decessor Robert Fiske's finding that Foster had killed himself due to clinical depression was then almost a year old, with no end in sight.

Despite that dramatic beginning, D'Amato's hearings soon settled into a predictable pattern: Amid the glare of TV lights and the clicking of camera shutters, one Republican senator or another would level broad changes of cor-ruption and cover-up against the Clintons and their allies, in Arkansas, the White House, or both. Reporters for the *New York Times,* the *Washington Post,* and their followers at the TV networks would gravely repeat each accusation, warning of shocking evidence to come. Subsequent testimony would either fail to support or actually disprove the damning charge. Accusers would then either harangue the witnesses for testifying falsely, or pretend that the point had been proved and move on.

Led by *Times* columnist William Safire, media commentary followed this same pattern with utter regularity. Safire notched numerous false predictions, most notably a January 1996 column declaring Hillary Clinton a "congenital liar" who would soon be indicted for perjury. Senator Christopher Dodd, the Connecticut Democrat, captured the mood of the hearings precisely. "If you get a witness who says, 'Oh, I don't recall,'" Dodd said, "the immediate accusa-tion is 'You're being disingenuous.' If you have witnesses with conflicting testi-mony, the allegation is 'Someone's lying.' And if you have witnesses that have consistent statements, 'It's a conspiracy.'"

The committee Republicans devoted weeks to probing the Clintons' al-legedly incriminating possession of their own financial records. During the first months of the new administration, Vince Foster had done the job of putting the president and first lady's assets into a blind trust. A few days after his suicide, their tax returns (including Whitewater records) were returned to the Clintons pending their selection of a private attorney. At Hillary's instruc-tions, her chief of staff, Maggie Williams, had stored the documents tem-porarily in a closet in the upstairs living quarters at the White House. Five days later, they were sent to Robert Barnett, a Washington attorney who repre-sented the Clintons.

Even the fact that there simply was no Whitewater investigation on July 20, 1993, and hence no reason to hide the files, failed to deter suspicion. Protected by lawyer-client privilege, the files in Foster's office couldn't have been examined without a subpoena from a federal judge who believed there was "probable cause" that evidence bearing directly upon his death would be found in them. No investigator who testified to the Senate had ever considered seeking such a subpoena.

At the Senate hearings, Republicans accused a succession of White House aides of stripping Foster's office of incriminating Whitewater evidence and conspiring to lie about it under oath. The scheme was allegedly coordinated by Hillary Clinton via telephone from her mother's home in Little Rock, and carried out by Maggie Williams, Hillary's friend Susan Thomases, and White House counsel Bernard Nussbaum. A July 24 column by Safire alleged that a White House lawyer named Steve Neuwirth "told congressional investigators that Susan Thomases, Hillary's confidante, told Nussbaum that the Clintons wanted the search [of Foster's office] strictly limited."

Neuwirth opened his Senate testimony on August 3 with a prepared statement explaining that the information in Safire's column was categorically false. He read aloud questions and answers from his deposition, in which he had explicitly denied the premise of a question implying any knowledge of what Hillary Clinton or Susan Thomases wanted. He explained that every lawyer in the White House was concerned about how to balance the legitimate interests of law enforcement, lawyer-client privilege, and the institution of the presidency. In a time of tremendous grief and confusion, Hillary Clinton's views had never been consulted. Neither Safire nor Susan Schmidt, whose byline appeared on a similarly themed news article in the *Washington Post,* ever corrected themselves.

During his testimony on August 9, former White House counsel Bernard Nussbaum attacked the very premises of the Senate hearings. With no precedent to follow, Nussbaum had made himself responsible for sorting through the contents of Vince Foster's office in the presence of investigators from the Park Police and the Justice Department. In so doing, he had missed noticing the torn-up note in the bottom of Foster's briefcase, which bitterly expressed the dead man's lament that in Washington, "ruining people is considered a sport." Although none of the witnesses believed that he had done anything unethical, Justice Department officials had warned Nussbaum that suspicious minds could misconstrue his actions.

Nussbaum, however, insisted that "what prompted these hearings is something different. It is the unfair linking of two separate, disparate events. The first event involved the transfer, in July 1993, of personal files—including a Whitewater file—to the Clintons' personal attorneys following Vince's death, a transfer which was totally proper and, indeed, known to Justice Department officials. The second separate, disparate event involves the emergence in the fall of 1993 of the Whitewater investigations and the resulting media frenzy. Linking these two events is illogical, unwarranted and unfair. They are totally unrelated."

Senator Richard Shelby, an Alabama Republican, was not persuaded. He compared Nussbaum's actions to "the fox guarding the henhouse." Shelby scolded the former counsel: "You did it your way and the American people will never really know what was in there. . . . You didn't want the people to know, including the Justice Department of the United States of America."

Another southern politician who generated lots of accusatory sound bites during the Whitewater hearings was Lauch Faircloth. The North Carolina Republican lavished particular attention upon Maggie Williams, then Mrs. Clinton's chief of staff. He found it incredible that Williams could have forgotten the details of a two-year-old phone conversation with the first lady, someone she spoke with several times each day. Faircloth scoffed at Williams's tearful denials, buttressed by two lie detector tests—including one administered by the Office of Independent Counsel—that she had removed a stack of files from Vince Foster's office during the hours immediately after his body was found in Fort Marcy Park. Her testimony was contradicted by a career Secret Service agent who swore that he had seen her take the files, although he could not be certain of the exact date. (Williams had admittedly transferred the files after investigators finished with Foster's office.)

With David Bossie whispering frequently in his ear, Faircloth was equally scathing toward Susan Thomases, who had exchanged a number of phone calls with the first lady and Bernard Nussbaum on the morning after Foster died. He openly mocked her protestations that she and Hillary were sharing their grief, consoling each other, and discussing funeral arrangements. At one point, Faircloth read aloud from a media account quoting James Carville to the effect that "Susan Thomases has the juice," meaning strong influence. "And then we go back to the calls to Bernie Nussbaum," Faircloth drawled. "I mean call, call, call, call, call, call. And you were discussing the weather, his general feelings, politeness, niceness, and all of a sudden you spill the juice, according to you. You no longer had it. Is that right?"

Thomases tersely said that was correct. She hadn't discussed the search of Foster's office with the first lady, and didn't know what Hillary Clinton's opinion was.

By the time the Senate Whitewater hearings went into summer recess, opinion surveys showed that whatever the level of suspicion among the Washington press corps, the public didn't share it. A Louis Harris poll released on August 13 showed that only one in four adults who had followed the Congressional probes thought less of President and Mrs. Clinton as a result. Just 8 percent of Democrats thought Whitewater a damaging issue, compared with 35 percent of Republicans. D'Amato's investigation appeared to be getting nowhere, and very slowly.

Possibly it was frustration over his committee's inability to deliver that caused D'Amato to throw in temporarily with the Vince Foster conspiracy theorists. The senator probably didn't realize that he had stumbled into yet another Larry Nichols production.

By 1995, Nichols and his friends at Citizens for Honest Government were busily seeking another vehicle to follow upon the success of *The Clinton Chronicles* and its sequels. After Nichols signed a contract to pay Arkansas state troopers Larry Patterson and Roger Perry a flat $1-per-video royalty for a new project tentatively titled *Nichols vs. Clinton,* the trio began searching their memories for important (and potentially marketable) revelations.

The first bombshell they came up with involved Vince Foster's death, still quite a popular subject on the talk-radio and Clinton-conspiracy circuits. It debuted April 9, 1995, in the London *Sunday Telegraph* under the byline of Ambrose Evans-Pritchard. The White House, his startling article alleged, had falsified both the time and place of Foster's demise. According to the troopers, a young woman named Helen Dickey had telephoned the governor's mansion in Little Rock at 6:00 P.M. on July 20, 1993, to inform Governor Jim Guy Tucker of the terrible news. Roger Perry had been on duty in the guard shack and had taken the call.

At the very least, Evans-Pritchard extrapolated, that meant somebody in the White House had known about Foster's death hours before the Park Police had relayed the bad news to the Secret Service at 8:20 P.M. (Little Rock is in the central time zone, one hour behind Washington.) Even more ominously, it appeared that Foster's body had been moved. Helen Dickey, recalled Perry, "was kind of hysterical, crying, real upset. She told me that 'Vince got off work, went to his car in the parking lot, and shot himself in the head.'" Perry's account was confirmed by his friend and fellow trooper Larry Patterson, whom he had phoned at home immediately after taking Dickey's call. The chain of corroboration extended to Lynn Davis, whom Patterson said he had called the same evening. Davis was an attorney and former trooper who, along with Cliff Jackson, had negotiated payments from Chicago financier Peter W. Smith at the time of the Troopergate episode.

Oddly, Davis, Patterson, and Perry all had neglected to mention Dickey's suspicious phone call to David Brock of the *American Spectator* or Bill Rempel of the *Los Angeles Times* back in the summer and fall of 1993, just after it allegedly happened. This discrepancy did not prevent the excited Evans-Pritchard from drawing dire conclusions. "Dickey, a former nanny to Chelsea Clinton," the *Sunday Telegraph* explained, "is a member of the tight-knit 'Arkansas Group.' She refused to answer queries about the alleged call to the

Governor's Mansion. . . . If the White House received an early warning about Foster's death, why would it have been covered up? One explanation is that a tip-off would have provided a window of time for pre-emptive moves."

Within days, the Western Journalism Center, a Scaife-supported outfit in California, paid for a full-page ad in the *Washington Times* reprinting Evans-Pritchard's article. The advertisement also urged readers to purchase a Citizens for Honest Government videotape titled *Unanswered: The Death of Vincent Foster*, by "award-winning journalist Christopher Ruddy." A compilation of largely irrelevant questions supposedly not addressed by investigators, the video was an all-out attack on the integrity of the Fiske Report. To the tiny fraction of Americans familiar with the forensic evidence, the video was silly. One example of Ruddy's methods should suffice. His video portrayed as a mystery the fact that the .38 revolver Foster used to take his life was found in his hand. Impossible, Ruddy and an "expert homicide investigator" protested.

Fiske's investigators had shown otherwise. "After firing," the report concluded, "the trigger of Foster's gun rebounds forward. Based on analysis of scene photographs and an autopsy photograph showing a mark on Foster's right thumb, the Pathologists Panel and FBI ballistics experts concluded that Foster's thumb was 'trapped and compressed' between the trigger and the guard of the gun. This conclusion is corroborated by the statement of Park Police Technician Peter Simonello who removed the gun from Foster's hand. He stated that Foster's knuckle initially prevented him from removing the gun from Foster's hand. As a result, Simonello half-cocked the gun causing the trigger to be pulled back. Only then could Simonello remove the gun."

On June 15, Ruddy weighed in with his own version of the Arkansas troopers' new story in the Scaife-owned *Pittsburgh Tribune-Review*. Already the Internet was abuzz with fanciful conspiracy scenarios. Letters and faxes began to pour into the offices of senators on the Whitewater committee. By August, columnist John Crudele of the *New York Post* took it upon himself to offer D'Amato some advice on how to revive the flagging Whitewater hearings by bringing the troopers to Washington: "Perry telling his story, followed by [Arkansas first lady] Betty Tucker confirming it, followed by Helen Dickey explaining the call, would make a great closing act to an otherwise tedious melodrama." Next the *Wall Street Journal* editorial page, stung by the Fiske Report's endorsement of the lament in Foster's suicide note that "WSJ editors lie without consequence," seized upon the trooper tale.

In a September 13 interview with WCBS radio in New York City, D'Amato vowed to get to the bottom of the Foster case. His Whitewater committee, the chairman announced, planned to subpoena Helen Dickey. Echoing Newt Gingrich, D'Amato insinuated that Foster had been murdered. "It's impossible for that gun to be found in his hand after the discharge," the senator said. "It would have been kicked back and the gun would have jumped out. Yet here it is in his hand by his body. How do you explain that?"

The White House released a sworn affidavit from Helen Dickey to the effect that she had, indeed, phoned Little Rock and spoken briefly with trooper Perry on the night of Vince Foster's death—except that the call had been made after 10:00 P.M., three hours later than the troopers claimed. Nor had she mentioned anything about any White House parking lot.

Almost as if on cue, independent counsel Kenneth Starr sent FBI agents to search Fort Marcy Park with metal detectors for the third time. The OIC made sure that reporters and TV cameras went with them. The inability of investigators to locate the bullet that killed Foster was another "unanswered question" that much impressed conspiracy buffs, although little knowledge of the range and velocity of a .38 revolver was required to know that the chances of finding it had never been good. Starr was merely grandstanding.

The second round of Senate Whitewater hearings, which began in November 1995, went very much like the first. Armed with detailed telephone records, the Republicans took another pass at Maggie Williams and Susan Thomases. According to a detailed chart dutifully printed by the *New York Times*, the two women, Hillary Clinton, and Bernard Nussbaum had exchanged some forty-three phone calls between the discovery of Vince Foster's body and the searching of his office, although many were clearly taken by answering machines.

"It's difficult to believe," D'Amato said, "[that] all of these calls were the result of touching, feeling, holding." Senator Faircloth denounced Williams's and Thomases's testimony—both had professed inability to remember in detail many of the calls—as "an insult to this committee." Suspicions, however, aren't evidence—and the hearings produced none of the latter.

By late November, the stage was set for the triumphal return to Washington of L. Jean Lewis. Given her incoherent performance several months earlier before Representative Jim Leach's House Whitewater committee—where her misquotation and mischaracterization of her own tape-recorded conversations with an RTC attorney named April Breslaw had been disclosed—the Republican senators were courting disaster by asking her back.

To anyone familiar with her House testimony, Lewis's opening statement on November 29 was remarkable. Seemingly undaunted by her previous experience, she told almost precisely the same story in virtually the same words. Waving the flag of her military upbringing, she recounted how RTC lawyers had "obstructed" her Whitewater investigation for seven long days. (One RTC attorney, Democrats later forced Lewis to admit, had delayed her probe by pointing out the futility of seeking an indictment against a Madison Guaranty official who had died some years earlier.) She complained that Clinton-appointed U.S. Attorney Paula Casey had stalled two entire weeks before rejecting her criminal referral naming the Clintons—as she put it, "in direct conflict with information I had received from the Justice Department in Washington."

Once again Lewis charged that RTC attorney April Breslaw had visited her office "to deliver the message that 'the people at the top would like to be able to say that Whitewater did not cause a loss to Madison'"—the same inaccurate quote that Lewis had unpersuasively relied upon during her House testimony. Once again, she stated bluntly that the Whitewater project had caused a loss to Madison and that the Clintons had earned illicit profits, statements for which she had provided no evidence, nor ever would. "But if the committee wants to know what the Clintons knew about the corrupt activities resulting in losses to Madison," she smirked, "why not invite the Clintons to testify as I am today and have in the past? Why not invite them directly?"

Perhaps unbeknownst to Jean Lewis, both Clintons had already answered detailed written interrogatories from RTC investigators, under oath. The White House had released those answers to the press back when the House and Senate hearings opened in August 1995. The Clintons had also testified under oath about Whitewater to the Office of Independent Counsel.

Subsequent testimony revealed that there were many things about the Whitewater investigation that L. Jean Lewis didn't know. She didn't know, Lewis swore, that Little Rock U.S. attorney Chuck Banks had rejected her 1992 referral. She didn't know that the Justice Department and FBI had exchanged letters and telex reports debunking her evidence, and pointing out her ignorance of the law and her political motives. She didn't know, although the details had been reported by the *Wall Street Journal* and the Associated Press months earlier.

Unfortunately for Lewis, Senate Democrats had a few nasty tricks waiting for her. Her political bias and her high-handed treatment of her colleagues had not gone unnoticed in the RTC's Kansas City office. More than a year earlier, a two-week preliminary inquiry into Lewis's conduct had resulted in her being placed on administrative leave pending an investigation by the RTC inspector general. Among the charges forwarded to Washington were improper handling and disclosure of confidential financial documents, secret tape-recording of her colleagues, and frequent use of her government office for personal gain. Her supervisor, Richard Iorio, was charged with failing to take action regarding her leaks, allowing her to take Madison Guaranty documents home and thus hide them from RTC lawyers, condoning her surreptitious recordings, and helping her defy orders to investigate larger thrift failures to keep working on Madison.

One of Kenneth Starr's little-noticed first acts as independent counsel had been to assume control of the RTC investigation of L. Jean Lewis and turn it against her supervisors. At the same time, Starr's law firm, Kirkland & Ellis, was negotiating a highly sensitive legal settlement with the very same RTC officials Starr proposed to investigate.

Ironically, the settlement had involved Kirkland & Ellis's longtime representation of a bankrupt thrift in Colorado. Considering that the three judges of the Special Division had removed Robert Fiske as independent counsel on the grounds that his law firm had represented a timber company that once sold a piece of land to Jim McDougal, Starr's behavior seemed almost reckless. Yet no one noticed his extraordinary conflict of interest until much later, an early sign that Starr would exercise with impunity great liberties as independent counsel.

The Senate Democrats, however, had done their homework with regard to L. Jean Lewis. Hardly had she finished her prepared remarks at the November 29 hearing when minority counsel Richard Ben-Veniste confronted her with Little Rock FBI agent Steven Irons's contemporaneous notes showing that—contrary to her sworn deposition—she had begun pushing him to act upon her 1992 referral only days after filing it. Lewis had also made what the agent called "very dramatic" statements about altering history. There had been similar testimony from former U.S. attorney Chuck Banks's staff. Altogether, the evidence showed Lewis had made a minimum of eight determined attempts to prod her ill-conceived referral along in the two months before the 1992 election. In her deposition, Lewis claimed she had made none.

Next, Ben-Veniste produced a personal letter retrieved from the hard drive of Lewis's computer. It mocked "the illustrious Gov. Bill Clinton" as a "lying bastard" who had put his mistress Gennifer Flowers on the state payroll. Senator Barbara Boxer questioned Lewis about a November 1993 letter in which she had proposed to market "Presidential BITCH" T-shirts and coffee mugs bearing Hillary Clinton's likeness. (She had listed her RTC office as her business phone.)

Lewis testified that to her, the word "bitch" signified no disrespect, and that she personally had no objection to being called a bitch.

Ben-Veniste also questioned her closely about her tape-recording of April Breslaw. He asked if she hadn't, in fact, bought a brand-new tape recorder for the specific purpose of ambushing the RTC attorney.

Nothing, Lewis insisted, could be further from the truth. "I purchased that new recorder well after I had that conversation with Ms. Breslaw," she said. "As I have previously testified, the old one worked sometimes. It didn't sometimes. It was eight years old. . . . I did not deliberately set out, which I believe is your inference, to tape Ms. Breslaw."

But the real drama took place after Democrats laid out documents casting doubts on Lewis's behavior. Maryland senator Paul Sarbanes read to Lewis from U.S. Attorney Banks's letter refusing to act on her 1992 referral, on the grounds that to do so would constitute "prosecutorial misconduct." Next, Sarbanes brought up a 1993 Justice Department appraisal pointing out Lewis's woefully inadequate understanding of federal banking law. It noted in acid terms that what she called Jim McDougal's "check-kiting"—shifting money back and forth among his own corporate accounts inside the same bank— simply wasn't a crime.

But Sarbanes had scarcely begun when a remarkable thing happened. Lewis began to tremble visibly. Tears suddenly welled in her eyes, and she fainted dead away at the witness table. After being revived, she had to be assisted from the Senate chamber, hospitalized overnight, and treated for high blood pressure. L. Jean Lewis's career as Whitewater heroine had come to an abrupt and seemingly ignominious end. Her appearance before D'Amato's committee had been a complete disaster.

Yet while many thousands of citizens watched Lewis live on C-SPAN, neither of the newspapers that had received stacks of confidential RTC documents two years earlier reported her swoon. Both the New York Times and the Washington Post failed to mention her sudden collapse. Just as both newspapers had ignored U.S. Attorney Banks's letter and other documents casting doubt on Whitewater's factual and legal premises, so they elided the contradictions in Lewis's testimony. No "Presidential BITCH" coffee mugs— nothing. To the Times's Stephen Labaton, the most significant event of the day had been the mention of Gennifer Flowers. "SENATE HEARING TOUCHES ON CLINTON'S INTEGRITY," read the headline. "A LINE OF INQUIRY BACKFIRES ON THE DEMOCRATS." Only a few days later, on December 6, a Times editorial stated without a particle of irony that "Jean Lewis, a star witness . . . and a government investigator into Madison's practices, repeated her charge that there had been a deliberate effort at both the Justice and Treasury departments to obstruct her inquiry. Ms. Lewis has said flatly that the Clintons knew about and improperly benefited from Madison's freewheeling practices. . . . Why not come forward with the complete story?"

Later that same day, December 6, minority counsel Ben-Veniste read into the hearing record a few salient facts about Lewis's allegedly defective tape recorder. It turned out that receipts submitted to the committee to support her contention that she had bought a new recorder only after accidentally taping April Breslaw hadn't told the real story. Records subpoenaed by the committee from the Office Depot store showed that Lewis had in fact purchased an Olympus Pearlcorder Model S-924 two weeks before her meeting with Breslaw. It seemed that Lewis had deliberately misled the committee. Ben-Veniste announced that the tapes had been submitted to independent counsel Kenneth Starr with a request that FBI experts determine whether the new recorder had made them. This challenge to Lewis's credibility was again ignored by both the New York Times and the Washington Post.

Evidently, Starr felt free to ignore the Senate Democrats' request as well. Nothing was ever heard of the issue again.

With the congressional budget process at an impasse and the Republican leadership vowing to shut down the federal government rather than compromise with a seemingly crippled president, the Senate Whitewater hearings droned on into December. Apart from reporters, the hearing room was almost devoid of spectators. The demand for transcripts was so small that the Federal News Service quit providing continuous overnight coverage.

Typical of the investigation's many blind alleys was a much-hyped legal confrontation between the White House and the Whitewater committee over a few pages of handwritten notes taken by Clinton aide William Kennedy on November 5, 1993. With the *Washington Post* and *New York Times* then featuring front-page stories about Whitewater and David Hale, the White House lawyers had met with the Clintons' private counsel to decide how to cope with the burgeoning scandal. White House attorney Kennedy, a former law partner of Hillary Clinton, had kept notes on that meeting.

Accompanied by heavy rhetoric about "cover-ups" and "smoking guns," D'Amato demanded to see Kennedy's notes. The White House agreed to surrender the notes, but only if the committee would stipulate that by so doing, the Clintons hadn't given up attorney-client privilege altogether.

The dispute remained unsettled for a couple of weeks, amid grave commentary about a "constitutional crisis." Finally, just before Christmas, the White House got its way on the privilege issue and turned over the Kennedy notes. They turned out to contain little of interest. A sheaf of clippings released along with the notes made it clear that the lawyers had mainly talked about how to respond to media accusations. But in television interviews, Senator D'Amato charged that the phrase "Vacuum—Rose Law Firm files" was proof of a cover-up. Kennedy said he had used "vacuum" to describe the paucity of available information. To conclude otherwise—that he had meant "vacuum" as a verb—it was necessary to assume that a half dozen top Washington lawyers (three from the White House, three from Williams & Connolly), meeting for the first time, had hatched a conspiracy to obstruct justice, taken notes on the conspiracy, and kept the notes in case any investigator might want them in the future.

A second entry that provoked speculation read "VF suicide—David Hale investigation—same day." Here at last was evidence that the White House had secretly worried about the alleged link between Foster and Whitewater. The actual meaning of that notation only emerged when William Kennedy testified a month later. Had the lawyers discussed the fact that Vince Foster killed himself on the very day the FBI raided David Hale's Little Rock office? They hadn't, because it wasn't true. The earlier press accounts were erroneous. Foster died on July 20, 1993; Hale's office was not searched until July 21. What Kennedy had set down in his notes was the lawyers' discussion of Whitewater coverage in the media—and how much of it was driven by a conspiracy theory based upon a simple factual error.

A moment of truth intruded in the midst of D'Amato's hearings on December 13, 1995, with the release of the second volume of the Resolution Trust Corporation's $3.6 million Pillsbury Report. The remainder of the study was to appear over the ensuing weeks. With the RTC due to go out of existence at the end of 1995, the San Francisco law firm of Pillsbury, Madison & Sutro was obligated to deliver its conclusions about the Clintons and Whitewater by December 31. In an embarrassing incident that led to his appearance before the grand jury, White House aide George Stephanopoulos had vigorously protested to a Treasury Department aide about the RTC's decision to hire the San Francisco firm because he feared the partisan bias of Pillsbury partner Jay Stephens, the former Reagan and Bush administration U.S. attorney for the District of Columbia, who had been fired by Clinton in 1993.

Stephanopoulos's much-publicized fears had proved baseless. The firm's findings could hardly have been more favorable to the White House. Based on the Clintons' sworn interrogatories, interviews with forty-five other witnesses, and some two hundred thousand documents, the report concluded that the president and first lady had told the truth about their Whitewater investment: The Clintons were passive investors who were misled about the actual status of the project by Jim McDougal almost from the start. The report failed to challenge their account on a single substantive point. As Charles Banks had anticipated back in 1992 when he was the U.S. attorney in Little Rock, every one of L. Jean Lewis's incriminating assumptions regarding the Clintons was shown to be wrong.

The Pillsbury Report found no evidence that Whitewater's losses had been subsidized by taxpayers in the savings and loan bailout. But even if they were, it concluded, the Clintons were not at fault: "There is no basis to assert that the Clintons knew anything of substance about the McDougals' advances to Whitewater, the source of the funds used to make those advances, or the sources of the funds used to make payments on the bank debt. . . . There is no basis to charge the Clintons with any kind of primary liability for fraud or intentional misconduct. This investigation has revealed no evidence to support any such claims. Nor would the record support any secondary or derivative liability for the possible misdeeds of others. . . . There is evidence that the McDougals and others may have engaged in intentional misconduct. There are legal theories by which one can become liable for the conduct of others—e.g. conspiracy and aiding and abetting. On this evidentiary record, however, these theories have no application to the Clintons."

Over the ensuing weeks, the RTC released several more volumes of the report, plus appendixes, clearing both the Rose Law Firm and Arkansas state regulatory officials of all accusations of wrongdoing. Far from coddling Jim McDougal, the report found, "if anything, Arkansas regulators took a more aggressive position toward Madison Guaranty than did the FHLBB [Federal Home Loan Bank Board]." It noted that in December 1987, Arkansas securities commissioner Beverly Bassett Schaffer "wrote a letter to Stewart Root, Director of the Federal Savings and Loan Insurance Corporation, stating that Madison Guaranty (and two other Arkansas thrifts) are 'unquestionably insolvent and have been for a long time . . . We must request that these associations be transferred immediately to the FSLIC.'" She wanted Madison shut down, which "did not happen for reasons that had nothing to do with Bassett."

In its hundreds of minutely detailed pages, thousands of footnotes, and documentary exhibits, the Pillsbury Report demonstrated that the premises of the Whitewater "scandal" had no factual foundation. On December 18, the *Wall Street Journal* ran a straight, clear summary of its findings, written by Viveca Novak and Ellen Joan Pollock. But other newspapers with a substantial investment in Whitewater virtually buried news of the report. The *Washington Post* stuck a brief mention of the report's existence into a story devoted to the battle over William Kennedy's notes. The *New York Times* waited until Christmas Eve, then hid Stephen Labaton's perfunctory summary on page 12. Judging by his article's dismissive tone, no reader could imagine that the Pillsbury Report answered every one of the accusatory rhetorical questions the *Times* had urged the president and first lady to come clean about for years (most recently in a December 6 editorial). Labaton's story ignored the passages pointedly exonerating the Clintons, and focused upon the fact that the report's "authors had been unable to interview a number of important witnesses, some of whom have been cooperating with the independent counsel." Specifically, neither David Hale nor the McDougals had been interviewed by the Pillsbury lawyers.

The major television networks predictably followed the *Times* and the *Post*. For the great majority of the Washington press corps, and thus for their national audience, the Pillsbury Report and the facts and conclusions its authors had painstakingly assembled didn't exist.

Within the Office of Independent Counsel, meanwhile, a plan was taking shape to indict Hillary Rodham Clinton for perjury—or, at the very least, to persuade the press that such a headline-grabbing event was about to happen. Behind this effort was deputy independent counsel Hickman Ewing, Jr., the head of Kenneth Starr's Little Rock operation and a veteran federal prosecutor from Memphis.

Ewing enjoyed a well-earned reputation as a crusader against political corruption and something of a religious zealot. After being appointed U.S. attorney in 1981 by Ronald Reagan, he specialized in public integrity, gambling, and pornography prosecutions; many of his cases involved state, county, or federal officials—including two controversial attempts to win a conspiracy conviction against Harold Ford, a black Democratic congressman from Memphis who was ultimately acquitted.

During nearly a decade as U.S. attorney, though, Ewing won dozens of important victories, including felony convictions of former Tennessee governor Ray Blanton, banker Jay Butcher, a top judge, a few state senators, and several west Tennessee sheriffs. He was renowned for pursuing his quarry doggedly, unfazed by a mistrial or two. The theme of his legal career, which began several years after a navy tour in Vietnam, was the punishment of those who violated positions of public trust—and whose transgressions often resembled those of Ewing's father, a county court clerk who pleaded guilty to stealing $43,000 and was sentenced to three years in prison. He sometimes said he blamed his father's criminality on excessive drinking.

Hick Ewing's combination of piety and pugnacity made the prosecutor widely popular in his home state, but he also acquired some powerful enemies. When George Bush entered the White House, Don Sundquist, Tennessee's most influential Republican member of Congress, asked the new president to seek Ewing's resignation—possibly because he had targeted Sundquist's former campaign manager and her husband on tax charges. Another Sundquist friend and Ewing target was Dana Kirk, the Memphis State University basketball coach, whom Ewing sent to prison in 1988 on charges of tax fraud and obstruction of justice in a wide-ranging sports-betting probe.

Whenever questions arose about his motives, the congressman blandly insisted that he had no personal quarrel with Ewing and merely believed it was time for a change in the U.S. attorney's office. Sundquist eventually succeeded in removing Ewing, but not without an embarrassing struggle. A newspaper advertising campaign and petition drive to keep Ewing as U.S. attorney was led by his close friend Ed McAteer, a leading Memphis Republican and chairman of the Religious Roundtable, a national organization of Christian conservatives. "I supported Ewing from the first day he went into office and I haven't changed my position one iota," vowed McAteer, a senior figure on the religious right who in the seventies pioneered the effort to mobilize evangelical Christians as a political force. After the campaign to save Ewing's job failed, he was celebrated at a June 1991 luncheon tribute featuring speeches by the mayor and local religious right leaders.

In praise of the departing prosecutor, the *Memphis Commercial Appeal* quoted Mark Wardell, a representative of the Reverend Donald Wildmon's American Family Association, which promotes "morality in media." "He has made Memphis a place where pornographers didn't feel comfortable doing business," Wardell said. "What we have here is a man whose faith is not separate from his work. We appreciate that." John Bramlett, a former pro football player turned evangelist, agreed. "I'm thankful today we had a man in office who obeyed God rather than obeyed man" (a peculiar description of a federal law enforcement official). Ewing modestly insisted that he had been merely an instrument of God's will. His future plans were uncertain. "I'm trusting the Lord for the next step." But as he left government, he was said to be considering full-time church work with the Campus Crusade for Christ, or a "quasi-legal position" with a "pro-family organization such as the Rutherford Institute."

Instead, after a few years in solo law practice, Ewing got a call in late August 1994 from Kenneth Starr, who had just been appointed Whitewater independent counsel. They met at a McDonald's restaurant in Brinkley, Arkansas, and Ewing quickly accepted the position as Starr's senior deputy, even though it meant living in Little Rock during the week and commuting home to his family in suburban Memphis on weekends. He had the right attitude for the Office of Independent Counsel, guided always by his trained ability to sense guilt, as he told the *New Yorker*'s Jeffrey Toobin years later.

As early as the spring of 1995, Ewing testified years later, he had drawn up a draft indictment against Hillary Rodham Clinton and circulated it to other lawyers in the OIC. He said the document was based upon a sworn statement she had given that April "about her representation of Madison Guaranty when she was at the Rose Law Firm: How the business came in, what work she performed, and how the retainer was returned." During his testimony at Susan McDougal's contempt trial in 1999, Ewing also admitted that he had taken to making quasi-public pronouncements about the first lady's guilt. He recalled, "We were eating dinner one night, and somebody said, 'How do you grade them?' I think the President was about a 'C' and Mrs. Clinton was about an 'F'."

On December 19, 1995, the morning after the *Wall Street Journal*'s comprehensive news summary of the Pillsbury Report's findings absolving the Clintons, a front-page article appeared in the *New York Times* indicating that the first lady was in serious trouble. Written by Stephen Labaton, the story appears likely to have relied upon Ewing or other Starr deputies as sources. It confidently laid out a case for two possible felony courts against Hillary: perjury and obstruction of justice. Labaton repeated Jim McDougal's account of Bill Clinton jogging over to Madison Guaranty's office in the summer of 1984 to solicit legal business for Hillary because the couple needed cash. But the real bombshell in the *Times* article was the supposed contradiction between Hillary's account of how her law firm came to represent Madison Guaranty and that of a former colleague named Rick Massey.

"Mrs. Clinton said in a sworn statement this year," wrote Labaton, "that Mr. Massey, then a first year associate at the Rose firm, had been contacted by a friend at Madison, John Latham, with a request for legal help. . . . Mr. Massey, who is now a partner at the Rose firm, told Federal investigators he 'does not know how or why Madison selected the Rose Law Firm,' according to a summary of his October 1994 interview with the Federal Deposit Insurance Corporation."

Even more damning was a *Nightline* report broadcast that same evening. The segment came very close to branding Hillary Clinton a perjurer. In his introduction, host Ted Koppel spoke pointedly about "the reluctance of the Clinton White House to be as forthcoming with documents as it promised to be." He then turned to correspondent Jeff Greenfield, who posed a rhetorical question: "Hillary Clinton did some legal work for Madison Guaranty at the Rose Law Firm, at a time when her husband was governor of Arkansas. How much work? Not much at all, she has said."

Up came a video clip from Hillary's April 22, 1994, Whitewater press conference. "The young attorney, the young bank officer, did all the work," she said. "It was not an area that I practiced in. It was not an area that I know anything, to speak of, about." Next the screen filled with handwritten notes taken by White House aide Susan Thomases during the 1992 campaign. "She [Hillary] did all the billing," the notes said. Greenfield quipped that it was no wonder "the White House was so worried about what was in Vince Foster's office when he killed himself."

What the audience didn't know was that the ABC videotape had been edited so as to create an inaccurate impression. At that press conference, Mrs. Clinton had been asked not how much work she had done for Madison Guaranty, but how her signature came to be on a letter dealing with Madison Guaranty's 1985 proposal to issue preferred stock. ABC News had seamlessly omitted thirty-nine words from her actual answer, as well as the cut, by interposing a cutaway shot of reporters taking notes. The press conference transcript shows that she actually answered as follows: "The young attorney [and] the young bank officer did all the work *and the letter was sent. But because I was what we called the billing attorney—in other words, I had to send the bill to get the payment sent—my name was put on the bottom of the letter.* [Emphasis added.] It was not an area that I practiced in. It was not an area that I know anything, to speak of, about."

ABC News had taken a video clip out of context, and then accused the first lady of prevaricating about the very material it had removed. Within days, the doctored quotation popped up elsewhere. ABC used the identical clip on its evening news broadcast; so did CNN. The *New York Times* editorial page used it to scold Mrs. Clinton, as did columnist Maureen Dowd. Her colleague William Safire weighed in with an accusatory column of his own: "When you're a lawyer who needs a cover story to conceal close connections to a crooked client," he began, "you find some kid in your office willing to say he brought in the business and handled the client all by himself." Safire predicted the first lady's imminent indictment.

What really made the story take off, however, was White House aide Carolyn Huber's belated discovery of missing Rose Law Firm billing records that had been under subpoena by the OIC. The time sheets had been used by the 1992 Clinton campaign to respond to reporters' questions, and then disappeared. For weeks, Republicans on the Senate Whitewater committee had spoken darkly of obstruction of justice. On January 4, 1996, Huber found the missing documents in a box in her office at the Old Executive Office Building. She called the Clintons' lawyer, David Kendall, who immediately made copies and sent the originals to Kenneth Starr. Actually, the documents Huber found weren't themselves originals, but photocopies of computer printouts made in 1992. Nobody who wanted to hide them could have any way of knowing how many additional copies might be floating around. Nor was Mrs. Huber, an Arkansas loyalist who supervised the Clintons' personal correspondence, certain where she had found the documents, at least according to Kendall.

In her subsequent Senate testimony, however, the former office manager at the Rose Law Firm was unequivocal. Huber recalled coming upon the time sheets in August 1995 in the "book room" on the third floor of the White House, inside the Clintons' private quarters. Without looking to see what they were, she had stuck them in a box and taken them to her office for later filing. Then in January 1996, she had opened the box and gotten scared.

How she could be sure they were the same papers without having examined them in the first place was never clear. Putting the 1992 campaign records in order and storing them was one of Huber's secondary tasks at the White House. Kendall later testified that when Huber first contacted him, "She said a number of different things that were inconsistent. She was flustered. She was upset. Her hands were shaking. She said that she had brought the documents over from the residence at some earlier point. She said she thought it was maybe three months ago. A little while later in the conversation, she referred to bringing them over ten months ago. She was very confused about the timing. . . . She was unclear about where she had found them. . . . Her stories were extremely vague." Kendall's co-counsel Jane Sherburne remembered the same thing. But the lawyers hadn't pressed Huber on the issue because they didn't want to be accused of trying to influence her testimony.

Here at last was a dramatic Whitewater event that even the dullest voter could grasp. Kenneth Starr lost no time hauling the first lady before a Washington grand jury in the most public manner possible, prompting press commentary about a "smoking gun." The irrepressible Safire predictably saw Nixonian skullduggery: "Can you imagine the sinking feeling in the 'Someone,' when he or she came back to the Book Room and found the records gone?" *Newsweek*'s Michael Isikoff went further. "The printouts were covered with the late Vince Foster's handwriting," he wrote, continuing, "it is Foster's suicide that lends Whitewater its aura of menace."

Hillary Clinton emerged from Starr's grand jury to say that she had no idea where the billing records had come from, but was glad they had turned up—perhaps because they provided only exculpatory evidence. Along with Vince Foster's handwriting, FBI fingerprint analysts found his fingerprints, as well as those of the first lady. Hers were found only on those pages dealing with issues discussed during the 1992 campaign—but not on topics of more recent interest, such as the ill-fated McDougal real estate development and shopping center known as "Castle Grande." All the forensic evidence suggested that the billing records had in fact been misplaced ever since the 1992 election.

The records' contents also supported Hillary's testimony and public statements in detail. In her sworn statements to RTC investigators, she had recalled only a single phone conversation with Securities Commissioner Beverly Bassett Schaffer regarding the Madison Guaranty preferred stock issue. The records showed exactly one, on April 29, 1985.

Asked whether she had done any work on McDougal's "Castle Grande" development, she had replied no. Republicans charged that an unused 1985 real estate document she had prepared for Webb Hubbell's father-in-law contradicted her. But the billing records, like all internal Rose Law Firm documents, referred to that transaction not as Castle Grande but as "the IDC matter."

A small part of a large parcel of land Madison Guaranty bought from a company called the Industrial Development Corporation later became known as "Castle Grande"—but not the part described in the document Hillary Clinton had prepared. Her answer was accurate. After studying the newly found billing records, the investigators at Pillsbury, Madison & Sutro came back with an even stronger conclusion that nobody at the Rose Law Firm had done anything unethical or illegal in their representation of McDougal's savings and loan. Regarding the unused real estate contract, the report stipulated that "while Mrs. Clinton drafted the May 1, 1986 option, nothing proves she did so knowing it to be wrong, the circumstances of the work point strongly toward innocent explanations, and the theories that tie this option to wrongdoing . . . are strained at best."

Starr's investigators would spend years seeking evidence to the contrary, with no success.

In January 1996, however, such exculpatory facts received no attention in the press. To hype their excerpt from James B. Stewart's forthcoming Whitewater book *Blood Sport,* the editors of *Time* magazine ran a cover photo of the first lady that looked like a post office "Wanted" poster. *Time* columnist Richard Stengel opined that "Hillary Rodham Clinton now faces a crisis that even the most artful public relations may not be able to fix." Stengel predicted that the stage was set for high drama at the Whitewater hearings. "Mrs. Clinton has stated that the lion's share of the work on Madison was done by a 'bright young associate' named Richard Massey. Mrs. Clinton also implied in a sworn statement to the RTC in May 1995 that Massey brought Madison's business to the firm. Committee sources tell *Time* that Massey will testify this week that he did not bring Madison in as a client, and that he assumed Mrs. Clinton was involved."

And in the *New York Times*, William Safire advised the president that the time had come to hire himself a separate criminal defense lawyer, because his wife was going to jail.

All such expectations were dashed when the first lady's soft-spoken, balding former partner Rick Massey appeared before the D'Amato committee on January 11. Not only did Massey fail to contradict Hillary's testimony; any tighter fit between their recollections would have been suspect. As a twenty-six-year-old associate at the Rose Law Firm, Massey said, he had taught a night course in securities law at the University of Arkansas in Little Rock. Among those enrolled was a Madison Guaranty officer named John Latham, whom Massey had known in college. During the semester, Latham began staying after class to ask Massey's advice about raising new capital for the thrift.

"I should say for the record," Massey testified, "that I asked him to lunch one day and I pitched the business, asked for their work. They were a growing S&L. We liked working for companies like that, so I pitched the work. . . . I think the pitch was basically, 'Gee, you're asking me all these questions. Why don't you hire us and put us to work on these things?'"

The only problem had been Jim McDougal's tardiness in paying the bills for legal work that the Rose firm had done for him several years earlier. Certain partners objected to taking him on as a client again without a prepaid retainer. So the firm had sent Hillary Clinton to meet with McDougal on April 23, 1985, to see whether such an arrangement could be made. Madison Guaranty agreed to a $2,000 per month advance against billings, and the work arrived on Rick Massey's desk the next day. What Massey had been unable to remember, eleven years after the fact, was whether he had first approached Hillary about taking up the payment issue with McDougal, or whether she had approached him— a question of no consequence. Such was the pretext upon which deputy independent counsel Hickman Ewing, Jr., proposed to indict the first lady of the United States for perjury.

As to who had done all the work on the preferred stock matter, Massey was unequivocal. Based upon his review of the billing records, he told Senator Connie Mack of Florida that "these were primarily one-man jobs, and I did primarily all of the research, writing, drafting, and so forth. Mrs. Clinton had a role in these matters. I view it as a supervisory role. In terms of who was in the trenches and doing the work, Senator, it was me."

Concerning the preferred stock deal itself, the allegedly illicit transaction the *New York Times* had placed at the center of the "scandal," Massey's explanation was simple. As Arkansas state officials had tried to show reporter Jeff Gerth four years earlier, the idea of selling stock in thrift institutions was first proposed by the Federal Home Loan Bank Board. "Sir, there is no better form of capital than cash," said Massey, "and we were trying to raise cash for the institution."

Not much of this was conveyed by the same journalists who had failed to notice L. Jean Lewis's fainting spell. "AT WHITEWATER SESSION, A STRUGGLE TO RECALL," read the headline in the *New York Times*. "In five hours of testimony before the Senate Whitewater committee," wrote Stephen Labaton, "a lawyer for Hillary Rodham Clinton's law firm said today that he could not remember events of 11 years ago clearly enough to support the First Lady's account of how the firm came to represent a troubled Arkansas savings and loan association." The *Times* account did mention Massey's luncheon pitch to his college friend, but concluded by pointing the finger of suspicion back at an implicitly corrupt bargain between Jim McDougal and Bill Clinton to funnel cash into Hillary's pocket.

A similar account appeared in the *Washington Post* under the byline of Susan Schmidt. Massey, she wrote, testified "that he does not believe that he was responsible for signing up Madison as a client, as [Mrs. Clinton] has asserted. . . . She has said Massey came to her with a proposal for a stock plan to help Madison raise capital after meeting with Madison president John Latham. She said he asked her to work as the firm's billing partner and work with James B. McDougal, the S&L's owner, to resolve a past billing dispute Rose had with him. 'I don't believe it happened that way,' Massey said."

When investigators for Pillsbury, Madison & Sutro issued their final report on February 25, they concluded that the minor discrepancies between the recollections of Rick Massey and Hillary Clinton weren't worth quibbling over. Moreover, "the purported recollections of Jim McDougal are inconsistent with those of the others and upon analysis make little sense." Contrary to McDougal's story, the retainer agreement didn't begin until work on the preferred stock issue started—almost a year after the purported "jogging" incident. "Most significantly," the report concluded, "the alleged economic motivation makes no sense. . . . There is no evidence that the Clintons ever received anything like $2000 a month from this engagement, and every reason to believe that they never received more than a trivial sum of money. . . . Even if all the retainer had been earned in fees, Mrs. Clinton's share would have been less than $20 a month."

*   *   *

On the evening of Massey's testimony, *Nightline* aired key portions that made its real import clear. This time Ted Koppel made a point of emphasizing that few, if any, of Senator D'Amato's dire predictions had turned out to be accurate. On Saturday, January 13, the *New York Times* ran an "Editor's Note" stipulating that Stephen Labaton's story on Massey's appearance "should have included testimony that seemed to support" Hillary Clinton—a halting clarification, but a clarification all the same.

The manifest failure of the monthlong assault on Hillary Clinton to yield evidence of wrongdoing was not ignored everywhere. *New York Times* columnist Anthony Lewis became the first important voice at his newspaper to break ranks. "Three years and innumerable investigations later," he wrote on January 15, "Mrs. Clinton has not been shown to have done anything wrong in Whitewater. One charge after another has evaporated."

Lewis compared D'Amato's performance to that of Senator Joseph R. McCarthy during the anti-Communist witch-hunts of the fifties. But Lewis noted one major difference. "On Whitewater, the press too often seems an eager accomplice of the accusers. . . . Some of the coverage of Whitewater reads as if the reporters or editors were committed to finding something wrong—as if they had an investment in the story."

Still, other celebrated journalists continued to predict the first lady's probable indictment as the election year began, most notably Pulitzer Prize–winning author James B. Stewart. Published by Simon & Schuster in early 1996 to the accompaniment of a multimedia publicity campaign, Stewart's book *Blood Sport* claims to be the inside story of "the president and first lady as they really are." Set forth as a sweeping narrative, it includes dramatized scenes and imaginary dialogue purporting to represent the innermost thoughts of individuals whom the author had in some cases never met, much less interviewed.

"Scenes that Mr. Stewart could never have observed firsthand," complained *New York Times* reviewer Michiko Kakutani, "are recounted from an omniscient viewpoint. Mr. Stewart rarely identifies the sources for such scenes; nor does he take into account the subjectivity and often self-serving nature of memory. The reader never knows whether the quotes Mr. Stewart has put into the mouth of an individual . . . are from a first or secondhand source."

Kakutani also noticed that everybody who served as a source for Stewart got gentle treatment, while those who did not were treated harshly. (After considering Stewart's request, both Clintons decided not to cooperate.) Yet neither the *Times* reviewer nor the thousands of others who read *Blood Sport* had any way of protecting themselves against the author's chronic inaccuracy. The book is filled with telling errors from beginning to end. It opens with a dramatized scene purporting to render the first lady's reaction to a phone call informing her of Vince Foster's death at "the Rodham home in Little Rock, where Hillary was visiting her mother and father, who was ill." In fact, Hugh Rodham had died three months earlier, in April 1993.

Another pivotal early scene has the young Bill Clinton traveling to the college town of Arkadelphia in 1975 to seek "kingmaker" Jim McDougal's advice about running for David Pryor's U.S. Senate seat. A gripping moment, except for the fact that Pryor was governor of Arkansas between 1975 and 1979. Stewart also seemed unaware that the "crusty country lawyer" and "Democrat-turned-Republican" Jim Johnson had hardly "veered steadily to the right," but had won the 1966 endorsement of the Ku Klux Klan.

Other errors are more significant. Not only does *Blood Sport* describe the "devout Baptist" David Hale as having been appointed by Bill Clinton, rather than Republican governor Frank White, as history records, it also misreports what got Hale in trouble with the Justice Department. According to Stewart, Hale's crime was that he "fraudulently misrepresented the kinds of loans he was making . . . to what Hale, quoting McDougal, described as his Democrat 'political family.' " Hale in fact made more loans to Republicans than Democrats. His crime was embezzling over $2 million.

Stewart's worst blunders appear to stem from his decision to accept Jim McDougal's word as truth and his disinclination to offend any important Washington reporter. Thus a Pulitzer Prize–winning financial journalist whose previous book had pilloried junk-bond savant Michael Milken somehow failed to see any problems in McDougal's handling of Whitewater. He ignored the Pillsbury Report's findings altogether, along with McDougal's secretive sale of Whitewater's assets for pennies on the dollar, his elaborate fiscal juggling act, his misleading assurances and deceptive letters to the Clintons. Stewart portrayed Hillary Clinton as the embittered McDougal saw her: a greedy, coldhearted shrew.

The book's key scenes depict her coolly refusing to sign over the Clintons' Whitewater stock to McDougal without also being released from the company's debt. "While Hillary was technically correct about the mortgage," wrote Stewart, "from McDougal's point of view, he didn't see that there was a problem." But Stewart doesn't mention that had she agreed to McDougal's terms, the Clintons would still owe the bank roughly $100,000, but no longer own a share of the company. Not until two years later did her accountant inform Hillary that the Whitewater stock was worthless, another point that escaped Stewart.

Stewart began his whirlwind publicity tour telling interviewers that his book hadn't uncovered any actual crimes by the president and his wife, merely bad character and political opportunism. But surely, Ted Koppel pressed during Stewart's March 11, 1996, appearance on *Nightline,* there was some problem that "will still come back to haunt the Clintons." Stewart affirmed that there was indeed, though the charge wouldn't be murder, perjury, fraud, or obstruction of justice. What Stewart had discovered at the root of Whitewater was "the Clintons' refusal to abide by financial requirements in obtaining mortgage loans." He told Koppel that in filling out a personal financial statement for a 1997 Whitewater loan, Hillary Rodham Clinton had "vastly inflated" the value of the property. "It is a crime," he added gravely, "to submit a false loan document." The first lady's guilt was "a question for a prosecutor and a jury to decide."

Again Stewart was badly mistaken. Down at the bottom of the allegedly felonious loan document, thoughtfully reproduced in *Blood Sport*'s appendix, was the following warning, which Stewart apparently hadn't noticed: "(BOTH SIDES OF THIS DOCUMENT MUST BE COMPLETED.") And on the document's reverse side, available from the first lady's private attorney, was all the information the author had accused Hillary of omitting, written in her own quite legible hand. Stewart had simply failed to notice that his set of papers was missing that second page.

Meanwhile, the Senate Whitewater hearings continued to grind on relentlessly toward Election Day. Before Senator D'Amato and his Banking Committee colleagues finally quit, they held more than seventy days of hearings—far more than were necessary to investigate either Watergate or Iran-contra. Former Arkansas securities commissioner Beverly Bassett Schaffer finally got her chance to testify on January 25. Ever since she had agreed to speak with Jeff Gerth four years earlier, her life had been devastated. "I provided you with a detailed account in writing of the facts," she had written the *Times* reporter bitterly after his first article portraying her as a corrupt hack appeared in March 1992. "This information was ignored and, instead, you based your story on the word of a mentally ill man I have never met [McDougal] and documents which you admitted to me on the telephone on February 26, 1992 were incomplete."

In December 1993, Bassett Schaffer had found herself pursued through the streets of Fayetteville, Arkansas, by an NBC News crew guided by Citizens United's David Bossie. Her name and caricature had appeared on "Wanted" posters circulated by his group. During the House Whitewater hearings in August 1995, she had been accused of suspicious behavior by witnesses she had never met. Despite Democratic protests, Chairman Jim Leach had refused to let her testify in her own defense. But she had been called to Little Rock to testify before the Whitewater grand jury numerous times.

The endless media pressure and resulting emotional distress had forced Bassett Schaffer to abandon her law practice and deal with Whitewater full-time. Her husband, Archie Schaffer, a public relations executive for Tyson Foods, had been indicted by independent counsel Donald Smaltz for the crime of writing a letter to Agriculture Secretary Mike Espy, inviting him to the annual meeting of the Arkansas Poultry Federation—which coincided with chicken mogul Don Tyson's yearly birthday bash.

In the interim, Bassett Schaffer and her department had been vindicated. After multiple FBI and grand jury interviews, the Office of Independent Counsel had notified her that she was not a target of its investigation. The recently released Pillsbury Report had concluded that her department had acted more aggressively with regard to Madison Guaranty than had the federal thrift regulators. Only because Democrats insistently pressured Senator D'Amato was she called to testify at all. At the Washington hearings, Bassett Schaffer was amused to notice that David Bossie, then an aide to Senator Faircloth, carefully avoided her and her husband.

D'Amato's chief counsel, Michael Chertoff, tried to make an issue of the fact that Bassett Schaffer had informed the governor's office back in 1986 that state and federal regulators intended imminent action against Jim McDougal. She replied that aside from her duty to warn Clinton of an impending action apt to bring both press inquiries and calls from anxious Madison Guaranty depositors, she had sought to ensure that McDougal couldn't involve Bill Clinton in his troubles.

And why would she think that might happen? inquired Chertoff. "Because of Mr. McDougal's history of bragging about his relationship with Bill Clinton," she answered. "Because of his having told people over the years that he was friends with Bill Clinton. . . . I believe that Jim McDougal abused his relationship with Bill Clinton, and might again."

"And he abused it in order to get influence?" Chertoff pressed. "Is that what you're saying?"

"Well, he didn't get any," she snapped. "But he certainly tried."

From the perspective of her friends and neighbors in Arkansas, Bassett Schaffer's best moment may have come when Senator Paul Simon, the professorial Illinois Democrat, asked why she found Whitewater so distressing. "It's personal," she told him. "I don't think it's been very fair to me—actually, to the whole state of Arkansas. It's really been very personal, very vicious. It's been an effort to vicariously destroy Bill Clinton piece by piece by ruining the people that he trusted, that worked for him—good people, who didn't do anything wrong. The job's been done very well. And a lot of people have been hurt unnecessarily for the purpose of winning an election. And I just think there's something wrong with that."

The Senate hearings, having opened with theatrical flair in August 1995, eventually faded out, having proved none of the Republicans' initial accusations. Despite all the insinuations about perjury and obstruction, not a single witness was ever charged with any offense. To the extent that the hearings had any real effect, it appeared to be the opposite of what the sponsors had intended. Senator D'Amato's habit of promising horrors and proving nothing, to paraphrase Anthony Lewis, caused him severe political damage among his own constituents. His ratings dropped precipitously in New York opinion polls, and he was soundly defeated by Democrat Charles Schumer in 1998. A similar fate retired Lauch Faircloth, the even more obstreperous Republican from North Carolina.

But the real climax of the Senate Whitewater hearings may have come during the February 14, 1996, testimony of White House aide Helen Dickey. Only twenty-five years old, she had practically grown up in the Arkansas governor's mansion, and had at one time been Chelsea Clinton's nanny. Her mother was Robyn Dickey, the former mansion administrator who moved on to oversee the White House Social Office.

It was Helen Dickey who, according to Arkansas state troopers Roger Perry and Larry Patterson, had allegedly phoned the governor's mansion hours before Vince Foster's death was announced, crying hysterically because the lawyer had killed himself in his car on a White House parking lot. Working with Larry Nichols, the troopers and their attorney Lynn Davis had filed sworn affidavits to that effect with the D'Amato committee. Trumpeted by British journalist Ambrose Evans-Pritchard in the London *Sunday Telegraph,* and then amplified by the American right-wing media, the troopers' story eventually persuaded Senator D'Amato himself to endorse its dubious premises.

All that came to an abrupt end during Helen Dickey's tearful appearance before the committee. She explained that a White House usher had told her of Foster's suicide shortly after she had watched President Clinton being interviewed on *Larry King Live* on the terrible night of July 20, 1993. "Vince Foster was very close to our family," she explained. "[We] lived next door to them in Little Rock. It was a very personal thing to me. I immediately began to cry, and become hysterical." She phoned her mother, then her father with the news. Telephone records obtained by the Senate showed that those calls were made shortly after 10:00 P.M.—several hours later than the troopers' affidavits claimed.

She had then wandered around the White House living quarters in a daze until she encountered the president, who told her the exact circumstances in which his boyhood friend's body had been found. Only then did she think to call the Arkansas governor's mansion; she didn't want Foster's friends there to learn about his death on television. As for the troopers' testimony that Foster had shot himself in a White House parking lot, she swore, "That's absolutely not true. . . . I never heard that. I never would have said that because that's not the facts as I knew them at the time. I'm absolutely certain of the timing of this."

To his credit, Senator D'Amato apologized to Helen Dickey. He explained that Senate officers had been deluged with letters and phone calls from citizens who had bought the conspiracy theories about Foster's death. "Senator Sarbanes," said D'Amato, "suggested that we attempt to deal with this in a public way. So I would think that what we've attempted to do is to bring some facts and less of this wild speculation—the kind of thing that, you know, fuels the fire."

After examining telephone records and hearing Helen Dickey's testimony, Republicans on the committee decided they didn't need to hear from the troopers. Within twenty-four hours, Larry Patterson was nevertheless narrating his version of the saga to a shocked Pat Robertson on his TV news program, *The 700 Club*. Because the conclusion of the Dickey episode went virtually unreported, hardly anybody in the national media confronted its implications about the Arkansas troopers' motives and credibility. (One who did was David Brock, who ultimately made a public apology to the president for all the trouble his Troopergate article had caused.)

In contrast, Kenneth Starr, in a footnote to his subsequent report endorsing Robert Fiske's conclusions about the Foster suicide, blandly suggested that Patterson and Perry were merely mistaken.

It was during the government shutdown of November 1995 that Bill Clinton first made the acquaintance of an attractive, dark-eyed twenty-two-year-old White House intern named Monica Lewinsky. On Capitol Hill, triumphal Republicans behind the leadership of Speaker Newt Gingrich had decided to inflict further humiliation on the scandal-weakened president. They confronted Clinton with an ultimatum: Sign the Republican budget bill as written, or they would close the United States government until such time as he did. Perhaps understanding the wishes and priorities of the American people better than his overconfident opponents, Clinton accepted the dare. For the first few days of the shutdown, Republican spokesman were breathing fire. On conservative talk radio, Rush Limbaugh demanded to know just who needed the federal government, anyway.

Still the Whitewater hearings lumbered onward, having been deemed essential by Congress and exempted from the shutdown. Well-placed leaks had the Washington press corps abuzz with rumors that Hillary Rodham Clinton would soon be indicted. In Little Rock, the Paula Jones case was in temporary hiatus, while Judge Susan Webber Wright's order postponing trial until after President Clinton left office was considered by the Eighth Circuit Court of Appeals in St. Louis. Dominated by conservative Reagan appointees, the court was expected to overrule Wright. Almost as certain, however, was a White House appeal to the Supreme Court that would have the effect of delaying the decision until after the presidential election. Deputy independent counsel Hickman Ewing was proceeding with plans to try Arkansas governor Jim Guy

Tucker, Jim McDougal, and Susan McDougal on bank fraud charges early in 1996.

As she remembered it, Monica Lewinsky first caught Bill Clinton's eye along a rope line at a departure ceremony on the South Lawn of the White House in early August 1995. They made "intense eye contact" that Lewinsky found thrilling. On November 15, the buxom brunette intern succeeded in getting herself invited to a West Wing party for an aide named Jennifer Palmieri. She made eyes at the president again and, when she was sure nobody else was looking, lifted her jacket to show him the top of her thong panties.

Around 8:00 P.M. that evening, Lewinsky was walking past George Stephanopoulos's office when she saw the president inside, alone. Clinton beckoned to her to come in. Determined not to miss her chance, Lewinsky blurted out that she had a crush on him. "We talked briefly," she would eventually testify, "and sort of acknowledged that there was a chemistry that was there and that we were both attracted to each other, and then he asked me if he could kiss me."

"And what did you say?" she was asked.

"Yes."

Behaving rather gallantly for a man accused of dropping his pants in front of an unwilling stranger, Clinton asked Lewinsky to come back ten minutes later, at which time he escorted her to his private study off the Oval Office. According to her account (though disputed by his subsequent testimony), they began to make out like high-school kids, quickly advancing to what was euphemistically called "heavy petting" when the fifty-one-year-old president was her age. Lewinsky assured him that she had been involved with a married man before and understood the rules.

For his part, the president later swore that the intern's oral endearments didn't begin until two months after that first encounter. Two nights later, on November 17, according to Lewinsky, she contrived at Clinton's suggestion to deliver a pizza to the private study, where their furtive grappling resumed. Altogether, Lewinsky was able to recall with great particularity nine separate occasions over a period of several months when she and her new boyfriend conspired to steal a few crazy moments together.

For the romantic Monica, it was puppy love from the start. "We enjoyed talking with each other and being with each other," she was later forced to explain to Starr's Washington grand jury. "We were very affectionate. . . . We would tell jokes. We would talk about our childhoods, talk about current events. I was always telling him my stupid ideas about what I thought should be done in the administration, or different views of things. I think back on it and he always made me smile when I was with him. . . . He was sunshine."

To the president, a seemingly sentimental lecher, it quickly became clear that he had made an extraordinarily reckless and foolhardy mistake. "I formed an opinion early in 1996, once I got into this unfortunate and wrong conduct," he would explain during his own grand-jury testimony, "that when I stopped it, which I knew I'd have to do and which I should have done a long time before I did, that she would talk about it. Not because Monica Lewinsky is a bad person. She's basically a good girl. She's a good young woman with a good heart and a good mind. I think she is burdened by some unfortunate conditions of her upbringing. . . . But I knew that the minute there was no longer any contact, she would talk about this. She would have to. She couldn't help it. It was part of her psyche. So I had put myself at risk."

Chapter Twelve

"THE PRESIDENT
OF THE UNITED STATES
IS NOT ON TRIAL"

O N DECEMBER 12, 1995, the Eighth Circuit Court of Appeals in St. Louis
heard oral arguments in independent counsel Kenneth Starr's attempt to
save his three-count bankruptcy fraud indictment of Governor Jim Guy
Tucker. Two months earlier in Little Rock, U.S. district judge Henry Woods
had thrown out Starr's indictment on the grounds that the governor of
Arkansas was not a "covered person" under the Independent Counsel Act (and
therefore not within Starr's jurisdiction); and that Tucker's alleged offenses
were in no way related to Whitewater Development Corporation, the Clintons,
the McDougals, Madison Guaranty Savings & Loan, or their dealings with
David Hale's Capital Management Services. In seeking to overturn the lower
court's decision, Starr had also petitioned the court to remove Woods from the
case because "information in the public domain" created "an unmistakable appearance of bias" on the judge's part.

The stakes in this legalistic dispute were far higher for the Office of Independent Counsel than they might have appeared. Arriving in Arkansas in August 1994, Starr and his team had formulated a typical white-collar prosecution:
Based largely upon the testimony of confessed embezzler David Hale, the OIC
would indict both Jim and Susan McDougal, Jim Guy Tucker, and several others. If a Little Rock jury convicted them, the OIC would then try to "flip" those
initial targets into testifying against Bill and Hillary Clinton.

"This approach," Starr later told Congress, "was the time-honored and
professional way to conduct the investigation." But from the outset, the OIC's

targets complained that Starr and his deputies had turned the criminal justice system upside down. The prosecutors were investigating not crimes but individuals—and they were doing so for political reasons. By citing Justice Scalia's prescient warning in 1988 against precisely that danger, Judge Woods had given credence to those claims. If his ruling was upheld, every defense lawyer who opposed the OIC could be expected to cite the judge's opinion in his or her opening and closing arguments.

More importantly, the OIC's evidence against Tucker in the surviving indictment that did deal with Madison Guaranty, Jim McDougal, and Capital Management Services was weaker than the number of counts suggested. Most, if not all, depended entirely upon the veracity of David Hale. The documentary evidence against Tucker, as subsequent events would make clear, was ambiguous at best. According to *New Yorker* legal analyst Jeffrey Toobin (himself an ex-prosecutor for former independent counsel Lawrence Walsh), Starr's deputies had been sharply divided over indicting a sitting governor on such shaky premises. Should the Eighth Circuit refuse to give Starr his way over Judge Woods, there was every possibility that the OIC would come up empty in Arkansas.

Starr had voiced no objection to Woods's original assignment by lot to the Tucker case—not even after the judge informed all parties of what he regarded as Senator Lauch Faircloth's highly partisan and improper attempt to intimidate him. Normally, that would have doomed the OIC's attempt to have Woods removed; courts frown upon litigants who lose a pretrial motion and then demand a new judge. Indeed, Starr's request to remove Woods was highly unusual. But the Tucker case would prove unique. Originally assigned to a panel of three judges, two of whom were Democratic appointees, Starr's appeal was taken by an all-Republican panel chaired by Judge Pasco Bowman. A former dean of the Wake Forest University Law School and a protégé of Senator Jesse Helms, Bowman was regarded as the most ideologically conservative jurist in the Eighth Circuit.

During the December 12 oral argument, lawyers for the independent counsel referred to newspaper and magazine articles connecting Woods to the Clintons. The court then asked Starr to produce those articles in a supplemental brief. Within hours, the OIC delivered an indexed, annotated file of newspaper and magazine articles that obviously had been assembled earlier.

Starr's team was shrewd enough not to include any of Justice Jim Johnson's shrill essays about Woods from the *Washington Times*. But the clippings did include a *Wall Street Journal* column by Micah Morrison and articles from the *Arkansas Democrat-Gazette* that quoted Johnson's charges. In the clips proffered by Starr, heavy emphasis was placed upon Woods's friendly relationship with Hillary Clinton, in particular the judge's 1994 visit to the White House. Given that all federal judges are either Republicans or Democrats, and that the Clintons were in no way parties to the Tucker case, the OIC's brief revealed its own political agenda as much as that of Judge Woods.

But the Eighth Circuit didn't see it that way. On March 11, 1996, the appeals court summarily granted both of Starr's requests. In *Morrison v. Olson* the Supreme Court had ruled that to be prosecuted by an independent counsel, a case had to be "demonstrably related" to the factual circumstances which led to the counsel's appointment. Writing for the Eighth Circuit, however, Pasco Bowman's opinion ruled that "the term 'related' is undefined and without parameters." So Tucker's business dealings didn't have to be factually connected to Whitewater or the Clintons to make the governor vulnerable to prosecution by Starr. A procedural connection was sufficient: The OIC had come upon the evidence against Tucker through David Hale. In effect, Bowman said, Starr could prosecute virtually any citizen he chose to prosecute.

In removing Judge Woods, Bowman's opinion specifically cited both articles quoting Johnson's smears, including Morrison's opus in the *Journal,* which he characterized as "a daily periodical with national—actually international circulation." The court said it acted "not because we believe Judge Woods would not handle the case in a fair and impartial manner, we have every confidence that he would, but only because we believe this step is necessary in order to preserve the appearance as well as the reality of impartial justice."

In a dissenting opinion, two judges on the Eighth Circuit panel warned of the dangers of permitting "the perceived impartiality of a judge to be held hostage by the writings or reporting of the media without concern for the accuracy of those reports or potential explanation," adding that "relying on newspaper and magazine reports as proof of substantive fact has no support in the rules of evidence." Judge Woods remarked to the *Los Angeles Times* that "I have the distinction of being the only judge in Anglo-American history, as far as I can determine, who was removed from a case on the basis of newspaper accounts, magazine articles, and television transcripts."

In Little Rock, U.S. district judge William R. Wilson, a Clinton appointee, fired off an angry letter to the Eighth Circuit's chief judge. "This case, when the fundamental facts are known," he wrote, "graphically illustrates the vice of allowing points to be raised for the first time on appeal." Wilson protested that no factual hearing was ever held. "Disqualification of an honorable trial judge is a most serious matter—at least as viewed from down here in the valley—and should never be based upon hearsay, hearsay on hearsay, and triple hearsay contained in media reports."

Two years later, after a reporter for *Salon* magazine showed Judge Woods a sheaf of Parker Dozhier's handwritten notes revealing the Arkansas Project's covert effort to discredit him during the summer of 1995, the elderly jurist released a written statement: "I have now been shown documents indicating that . . . closed-door meeting were held during the summer of 1995 at the Dozhier Bait Shop in Hot Springs. These alleged meetings involved, among others, Mr. David Hale (the government's chief witness in the Whitewater investigation), Mr. Parker Dozhier . . . and other persons with ties to Mr. Richard Mellon Scaife (who is, among other things, a financial backer of *The American Spectator*).

"[These] notes and memoranda reflect communications with Mr. Jim Johnson (a long-time foe of mine from the 1950s, when he led the segregationists in Arkansas while I worked on the other side). . . . There are also references to Mr. Wesley Pruden, a native Arkansan who is now the editor of *The Washington Times*. (Mr. Pruden's father was the chaplain to the White Citizens Council in the 1950s and an ally of Mr. Jim Johnson.)

"Mr. Johnson wrote an op-ed piece which appeared in *The Washington Times* on June 23, 1995, in which he accused me, as well as a host of prominent Arkansas judges and officials, of having improper ties, communications and connections. . . . [T]hat op-ed piece was subsequently quoted in other newspapers. Then a collection of . . . articles formed the basis of the 'documentation' used by the Independent Counsel to ask the Court of Appeals to remove me from presiding over the Tucker case. . . . Such actions strike at the heart of the judicial process. I want this matter thoroughly investigated."

Woods made it clear that he did not trust Kenneth Starr to oversee any probe of the Arkansas Project. "If it remains in the hands of the Independent Counsel," he added, "I am not sanguine."

The existence of the Arkansas Project and Dozhier's sub-rosa "advocacy" in the Tucker case remained secret until 1998. As of March 11, 1996, the important news for Starr was that thanks to the Eighth Circuit's ruling, the OIC was not only back in business on the Tucker bankruptcy indictment, but had secured an enormous expansion of his office's powers. So long as it presented its evidence to a "Whitewater" grand jury, the OIC could indict almost anybody—inside or outside Arkansas—for almost any crime in the federal code.

The crucial locus of Starr's effort, meanwhile, had shifted back to Arkansas. During the previous week, jury selection had been completed at the federal courthouse in Little Rock for the Tucker-McDougal "Whitewater" trial in U.S. district judge George Howard's court. A black Democrat appointed by President Carter, Howard was nevertheless considered to be strongly pro-prosecution. As the pastor of a small church, the judge held strong religious beliefs that were also well known to lawyers who practiced in his court. During pretrial hearings, Kenneth Starr made a point of arriving early in Howard's courtroom, where he would pass the time by reading his Bible.

During the Tucker-McDougal trial itself, though, Starr was nowhere to be found, devoting most of his time to his private appellate practice at Kirkland & Ellis. The bulk of the prosecution was handled by the husband-and-wife team of Ray and LeRoy Jahn, both assistant U.S. attorneys from San Antonio. A former winner of the Justice Department's John Marshall Award, Ray Jahn had first gained attention by prosecuting drug conspiracy cases in south Texas. His most famous case had been the conviction of Charles Harrelson, father of the film star Woody Harrelson, for the 1979 contract murder of U.S. district judge John Wood in San Antonio. Jahn would later testify under oath that he was a registered Democrat who had told Kenneth Starr when he was hired that he hoped to find evidence exonerating President Clinton—a claim not easily credited in light of his actions. A heavyset, mustachioed man with a reddish complexion, Jahn reminded Jim McDougal of a "Poland China pig," or so the defendant claimed in one of his bombastic media performances on the sidewalk in front of the courthouse.

During pretrial motions, Judge Howard had consistently ruled for the prosecution. From Tucker's point of view, the single most damaging decision may have been the judge's denial of his motion to be tried separately from the McDougals. The entire Whitewater imbroglio had begun because of Jim McDougal's irrational belief that Tucker had cheated him. McDougal's book, *Arkansas Mischief,* says that what drove him to take his tale of woe to Republican partisan Sheffield Nelson in 1992 was less the deterioration of his friendship with Bill Clinton than "the betrayal by one of my best friends, Jim Guy Tucker." Tape transcripts of his talks with McDougal that Nelson made available to the *New York Times*'s Jeff Gerth and other reporters consisted largely of McDougal railing against Tucker.

Formerly partners in several successful real estate ventures, the two had parted bitterly in the late eighties after Tucker learned that McDougal had pocketed buyers' payments on some properties they had sold in northwest Arkansas, failed to pay off the bank loans, and then sent out bogus warranty deeds with Tucker's forged signature. To avoid a messy situation, Tucker made good on the loans out of his own pocket. He knew that McDougal had been mentally ill at the time. The Jim McDougal who emerged from the catastrophic events of 1986—the year when he had suffered a stroke, been hospitalized for manic-depressive illness, and then been removed from Madison Guaranty by regulators—was not the man Tucker had known.

But Tucker had also refused to testify as a character witness at McDougal's 1990 bank fraud trial. He had explained to McDougal's lawyers that being forced to tell the story on cross-examination could be devastating to Jim's chances. The lawyers understood, although McDougal himself never did.

Being forced to stand trial for conspiracy along with McDougal severely limited the affirmative defense Tucker could offer. Judge Howard also ruled for the prosecution on two critical defense motions concerning the OIC's star witness, David Hale. In January, Tucker's attorneys had filed a motion to compel the prosecution to disclose all its arrangements with Hale. The OIC had replied by revealing $56,000 in cash payments made to Hale since his 1994 guilty plea. Tucker and his lawyers were convinced that there was much, much more.

Specifically, his attorneys wondered whether the Pulaski County (Little Rock) prosecutor had been "asked, requested, coerced or threatened to not bring charges" against Hale for violating state law. About the same time the FBI raided Hale's office in 1993, state insurance regulators had initiated a fraud investigation. Hale had bought a company which sold burial policies mainly to poor black families, and allegedly looted its assets. If the OIC was keeping Hale out of the Arkansas penitentiary, the jury had a right to know it.

Starr's office replied that its only contact with state officials had been strictly informational, and thus it was not required to turn over any evidence. Once again, the judge agreed. As governor, however, Tucker was not without resources. Somebody gave the defense a copy of a letter written to Kenneth Starr by Little Rock police chief Louis Caudell, which Tucker's lawyers promptly released to the press. "The investigative portion of this case," Caudell had written, "has been completed for some time; however, at your office's request we have postponed presenting this file for prosecutorial decision. . . . I am now requesting any advice you have in how to proceed in this matter."

Evidently, Chief Caudell had no intention of taking the blame if Starr's protection of Hale became public. Thus caught, the OIC sent out its "ethics counselor," Sam Dash, to explain. The longtime Washington insider, who had served as Democratic counsel during the Senate Watergate hearings, told reporters that Little Rock prosecutor Mark Stodola was under political pressure to press charges against Hale. He implied that Stodola could be charged with obstruction of justice for prosecuting Starr's chief witness. The *Washington Post*'s Susan Schmidt wrote a timely story also quoting former attorney general Griffin Bell to that effect.

Schmidt's story omitted two salient facts: The state charges against Hale had preceded Starr's case, and the Little Rock prosecutor had agreed to postpone action until the OIC was finished with Hale. Nor did the *Post* account mention a letter Stodola had sent to Starr and copied for Schmidt, pointing out that he saw "no overlap between Hale's felony state insurance law violation and his crimes against the federal government." Having promised Hale leniency, Stodola wrote, Starr could hardly safeguard the state's interest. "The two legal positions are hopelessly in conflict with each other." He also noted that parallel state and federal prosecutions went on in his jurisdiction all the time.

In Washington, conservative pundits led by Robert Novak set up a clamor that it was all a dastardly plot by Arkansas pols to protect President Clinton. In an appearance on the Michael Reagan radio program, Larry Nichols asserted that Stodola's real goal was to have Hale murdered in the Little Rock city jail.

Tucker's lawyers were most curious about who, other than the OIC, might be taking care of Hale. They asked Judge Howard to compel Starr to disclose "any meetings or conversations" involving Hale and a long list of individuals and organizations, including the "Republican Party or . . . Republican candidates . . . The Free Congress Foundation; *American Spectator* magazine; William Kristol; The Landmark [Legal] Foundation," and so on.

In a brief signed by Ray Jahn, Starr's team responded caustically. "Tucker also seeks disclosure of myriad alleged contacts, between Hale and various persons and organizations apparently associated in Defendant's mind with 'the right,'" Jahn wrote. "The United States has no independent knowledge of such contacts. Plainly, the government cannot 'disclose' information that it does not possess." But the word "independent" required an explanatory footnote: "We understand that Hale has evidently had contact with certain of the persons or entities Tucker lists, e.g., that he has been interviewed by the *American Spectator* magazine; we presume Tucker seeks information that is not in the public record."

Despite its scathing tone, the OIC's brief now appears evasive. It never denies all knowledge of Hale's links to the *Spectator*'s Arkansas Project, only "independent" knowledge. Judge Howard denied Tucker's motion. For the time being, the Arkansas Project and its relationship with Hale remained under cover.

The pretrial motion that meant the most to Tucker's lawyers concerned Hale's FBI interviews and grand jury testimony. Disclosed to the defense just days before trial, the FBI document, dubbed a "302" in law enforcement jargon, consisted of a sixty-page single-spaced narrative summarizing forty separate meetings with Hale over a two-year period. Its author was FBI special agent David Reign, subsequently identified as Hale's "keeper" during his many visits to Parker Dozhier's Hot Springs compound.

Transcripts of Hale's grand jury testimony offered more of the same. Rather than answering questions, the OIC's star witness had been put before the Little Rock grand jury with a written statement, which he read aloud. Tucker's lawyers thought they had a right to the FBI's raw interview notes, in order to search for inconsistencies, as well as to determine how Hale's story had evolved over time. Once again, however, Judge Howard sided with the prosecution. In response to a motion by the OIC, the judge also forbade the defense from presenting evidence or arguments as to the prosecution's motives for bringing charges against Tucker and the McDougals.

In other words, there would be no "political" defense.

*   *   *

The essence of prosecutor Ray Jahn's opening argument on March 12 came directly out of David Hale's FBI 302 form. It alleged that in a meeting in Jim Guy Tucker's kitchen on an unspecified date in late 1985, a conspiracy had been hatched among Tucker, Jim McDougal, and David Hale to engage in a series of "bogus real estate transactions" in order to raise money for Hale's Capital Management Services. All the other alleged crimes derived from that conspiracy. The concept was to book a paper profit by falsely inflating the value of a piece of commercial property that Hale sold to a friend, then use the fake proceeds to secure matching funds from the Small Business Administration. Those funds, in turn, would enable Hale to make loans of up to $300,000 each to Tucker and McDougal.

"David Hale will testify," Jahn informed the jury, "that he told both Jim Guy Tucker and Jim McDougal that this property isn't worth anywhere near enough to generate the money [he] need[ed] because they were after a target figure. David Hale needed to come up with $500,000 to put into his CMS so the government would give him a matching million and a half dollars. If we can come up with $500,000 we end up with $2 million to play with. So that's what he says. He tells them I don't have enough property, and the response to that from Jim McDougal is, 'Let me worry about that.'"

Jahn stipulated that it hadn't been the intention of any of the defendants to steal the money. The conspirators had intended to pay the loans back. "These, ladies and gentleman, were going to be, the evidence will show, perfect crimes."

Why would Tucker—a highly successful businessman who had borrowed and repaid literally millions of dollars in business loans from banks all over the United States—conspire with Hale to defraud the government of money so that he could then borrow it and pay interest? Tucker's motives aside, it took the prosecutor almost an hour and a half to reach the point in his opening argument that the national press had crowded into the Little Rock courtroom to hear. President Clinton was neither a defendant nor an "unindicted co-conspirator," but Jahn nevertheless managed to mention his alleged role in Hale and McDougal's schemes. According to Hale, Clinton had appeared—on another unspecified date early in 1986—at a meeting during which the three men had discussed a $300,000 loan ostensibly intended for Susan McDougal.

"David Hale's recollection," said Jahn, "is President Clinton, then Governor Clinton, was present at that particular conversation. . . . The testimony will be that they wanted to get a loan and they needed to get a loan in the name of something other than themselves. There was a desire expressed that Bill Clinton's name not appear on any of the loan papers, that Bill Clinton's involvement be kept secret in this particular matter. . . .They obtained this $300,000 by using Susan McDougal's name, by representing that it was being made to her, that as a woman she would be obviously qualified to borrow money as far as being a Small Business Administration–type loan that would be encouraging to her, and a document was created."

If the OIC actually had such evidence, though, why wasn't the president on trial too? One answer came from Susan McDougal's court-appointed lawyer, Bobby McDaniel, during his opening argument the following day. The "Master Marketing" loan had been examined during the original FBI investigation of Madison Guaranty back in 1989. Not only had his client not been indicted back then, said McDaniel, but Hale had told federal investigators a completely different story—in which Susan had stated the purpose of the loan was to promote Madison Guaranty and develop real estate. In 1989 Bill Clinton's name had never come up.

"But then something changed," the balding Jonesboro lawyer contended. "What changed? David Hale was raided in the summer of '93, caught red-handed defrauding the SBA innumerable times. And one other critical thing happened. Bill Clinton was elected President of the United States. And David Hale, as you've heard mentioned, in his scheming, plotting way that the evidence will show he was a master at, found a way to try to exonerate himself." Although the president was not a party to the case, McDaniel noted sarcastically, his name had been mentioned, by the lawyer's count, eighteen times during Ray Jahn's opening statement.

Little Rock traffic judge Bill Watt took the witness stand on Tuesday, March 26. A compact, energetic man, Watt had been immunized from prosecution by the OIC in July 1995, leaving a widespread impression that he must have something to hide. A former business partner of David Hale, Watt was also known to be a political ally of Bill Clinton. No sooner had Hale's indictment been announced in September 1993 than speculation began that Watt would be next. Few were astonished when the judge was named an "unindicted co-conspirator" and given immunity in exchange for his testimony. The assumption was that he would be used to bolster Hale's shaky credibility.

During the trial's first two weeks, virtually every prosecution witness had described Hale as a con man and manipulator of surpassing skill. "If he told me a rooster could pull a freight train, I'd have hooked it up," admitted Dean Paul, a former business partner who Hale had made the pigeon in the $825,000 real estate scam that lay at the center of the OIC's case. Hale had persuaded Paul to borrow that amount from Madison Guaranty to buy a property worth far less, then used the bogus $500,000 profit to cheat the SBA out of $2 million in federal matching funds. After hearing many unkept promises from Hale, Paul was left holding the empty bag—while facing a lawsuit and an FBI investigation.

"Does he present a persuasive picture when he talks?" asked Tucker's lawyer on cross-examination.

"About as good as I've ever seen," Paul said.

"And he can paint a picture and make you believe it, can't he?"

"He did me."

"And Mr. Paul, you are not by any means a stupid man, are you?"

"I don't know," Paul answered. "I feel pretty stupid sitting up here today."

Though a prosecution witness, Bill Watt had nothing good to say about Hale's credibility either. He had become so angry with Hale's chicanery at one point in the late eighties, Watt testified, that he had challenged his fellow judge to a fistfight. Watt was granted immunity even though his ties to Tucker and Jim McDougal, and his knowledge of the charges against them, were quite limited. Watt had done much of the legal work on the Dean Paul loan; he testified that the amount of the appraisal struck him as much too high, but that the responsibility for making that decision lay with Madison Guaranty's loan officer.

What appeared to be the true purpose of Watt's appearance finally emerged from a sidebar conference at the bench. He was there to give evidence against the president. Around the time Hale was pressuring Watt to get a quick appraisal on the Dean Paul property, Hale had intimated to him that Governor Clinton had an interest in getting the deal done. Defense lawyers protested that Clinton was neither a defendant nor a co-conspirator, and that Watt's testimony would be double hearsay at best. Prosecutor Jackie Bennett managed to convince Judge Howard that Watt's testimony wasn't being submitted as factual evidence, but merely to prove David Hale's "state of mind." The issue wasn't whether Clinton actually had any interest in the deal, only that Hale thought he did.

The result was precisely what Starr seemed to want. The headline in the next morning's *Washington Post* read "Trial Witness Indicates Clinton Sought to Expedite Loan; Hale Told Associate That Governor Urged Approval of $825,000 Transaction to 'Help My Friends.'" For Starr's prosecutors to have given Watt immunity for so small a point appeared to signal weaknesses in their case. Meanwhile, columnists for the *Arkansas Democrat-Gazette* and the weekly *Arkansas Times* asked how so compromised a figure could continue to sit on the bench, with the result that Watt was forced to resign from his $90,000-a-year judgeship. Pulaski County officials subsequently took actions effectively stripping the judge of his $45,000 pension.

What few realized at the time was that Watt hadn't been granted immunity so much as he had won it, emerging battered but intact from a yearlong legal skirmish with the OIC. David Hale had implicated Watt in several felonies, just as he had Jim McDougal, Jim Guy Tucker, Bill Clinton, and a number of prominent local Republicans the OIC had chosen not to pursue. Faced with the threat of multiple felony indictments, Wyatt was pressured to testify against Tucker and Clinton. What they didn't know was that Watt had suspected Hale was a crook long before federal investigators caught on. Moreover, he had taken decisive action to extricate himself and his clients from Hale's schemes, and to bring the plots to the attention of the proper authorities.

If he had failed to deter Hale's criminal career, Watt at least had been clever enough to create a documentary record of his efforts. That record helped Watt win immunity. But it didn't help anyone else indicted by Starr, partly because Tucker had been either too wary or too arrogant, Watt said much later, to agree to a meeting he had proposed. Watt claimed FBI agents and prosecutors had instructed him to put the exculpatory documents he showed them in his attic. The OIC would send for the papers when they were needed. That day never came. Instead, Watt's 302s were written by the FBI, and did not include the information Watt believed could help clear both Tucker and Clinton.

Around the time in 1986 that Hale had boasted of Bill Clinton's interest in his business deals, Watt had two chance encounters with the then governor, as he told FBI agent David Reign. Both times he had deliberately mentioned Hale, he recalled, to observe Clinton's reaction. There was none.

"David would drop names," Watt told *Salon* magazine reporter Murray Waas years later. "He would lie and manipulate people. He was a pathological liar. He was trying to convince me to do something. And in my mind I knew that I've been with Clinton on at least two occasions where nothing was said . . . about Hale. Nothing was said about the deal. Nothing was said about the people involved."

But Watt never got to tell the Tucker-McDougal jury about his two conversations with Clinton because, he and his attorney said, the FBI neglected to mention them in its report. Nor did Starr's prosecutors ask Watt about them in front of the grand jury, with the result that the defense lawyers never learned about them either. Watt had tried to warn Tucker's attorneys that they were in a street fight against what he regarded as a ruthless and determined foe, and needed to combine forces. After Tucker refused to meet with him, however, Watt decided that it was every man for himself. He liquidated a couple of real estate investments, put aside enough cash to fight a criminal prosecution, and dared the OIC to indict him. He won immunity instead.

The documents kept by Watt included certified mail showing that as early as February 1988, he had alerted title companies and clients that David Hale was essentially "kiting" bogus loans from Capital Management Services to shell companies he controlled. He stopped doing business with Hale altogether. In July 1988, Watt had flown to Washington at his own expense and met with Small Business Administration officials to alert them to Hale's fiscal juggling. He kept the airline tickets, hotel bills, and copies of his follow-up letters to SBA administrators. Somehow Hale persuaded the SBA that Watt was merely a disgruntled debtor.

When the OIC's investigators arrived on his doorstep in 1995, Watt greeted them with all of those documents, as well as the results of three poly-graph tests regarding his dealings with Hale, given by an FBI-trained expert. Watt's papers could have been used to show that David Hale had tried and failed to set Bill Watt up as the fall guy for his schemes, precisely as the gover-nor's lawyers were trying to prove he had used Jim Guy Tucker. But the jury never saw that evidence.

All the defense lawyers could do was call attention to the fact that the day after Watt first testified to the Whitewater grand jury on August 17, 1995, was the day it voted to indict Tucker. They also solicited his evaluation of Hale's manipulative skills.

"You didn't consider yourself a naive, weak person, did you, Judge?" asked McDaniel.

"No, sir."

"But yet he rolled your pants leg up, didn't he?"

"A figure of speech," Watt answered. "A way of putting it."

"You know what I mean by that, don't you?"

"Yes, sir," Watt said, "unfortunately, I do."

Whitewater had cost Bill Watt his job, his pension, and his reputation. But as he saw it, he hadn't backed down, and he hadn't pleaded guilty to a crime he didn't commit. Not everyone in Arkansas who had dealt with Kenneth Starr's prosecutors could say that. What Watt didn't know, as he walked out of the courtroom, was that the OIC hadn't finished with him yet.

David Hale finally took the witness stand on April Fools' Day, 1996, at the be-ginning of the trial's fourth week. The somewhat epicene Hale had none of the swagger of a wheeler-dealer. A plump, soft-spoken man of medium height, the fifty-five-year-old former judge gave an impression of mild geniality. Under Ray Jahn's direct examination, his story varied not at all from his grand jury testimony. The $825,000 Dean Paul loan had been dreamed up by Jim Guy Tucker and Jim McDougal at a meeting in the kitchen of Tucker's downtown Little Rock house. Its purpose was to generate an inflated $502,000 profit, in order to raise another $1.5 million in federal matching funds for Capital Man-agement Services. That increased funding would in turn raise Hale's lending limit to $300,000—exactly the amount needed to clean up some debts for what McDougal supposedly called his "political family."

"Did you have an understanding or did you have an opinion," Jahn asked, "as to what Mr. McDougal meant by the 'political family'?"

After Judge Howard overruled a long series of defense objections, Hale replied that he did.

"What was your opinion, sir?"

"That it involved Bill Clinton and maybe some of his aides, and some of Jim's political associates, and Jim Guy Tucker."

Susan Schmidt's lead in the next day's *Washington Post* needed no embell-ishment: "David Hale, a onetime Arkansas political insider who has spent the past two years in hiding, took the witness stand in federal court today and be-gan describing a financial fraud scheme whose players included President Clinton's former business partners, his successor as governor of Arkansas—and, Hale has claimed, Clinton himself."

During his second full day as a prosecution witness, Hale helpfully nar-rated the story of a meeting that had supposedly taken place one evening dur-ing January or February 1986. Participants in this clandestine gathering were Hale, Jim McDougal, and Clinton. The scene was McDougal's temporary of-fice in a trailer at the Castle Grande shopping center construction site, several miles southeast of downtown Little Rock. McDougal had insisted upon that location, Hale recalled, because he had lent his office at Madison Guaranty to federal bank examiners who were conducting an audit. When Hale drove up, McDougal's Jaguar was already parked outside, and the two men were dis-cussing Clinton's campaign against former governor Frank White. Clinton wore a jogging outfit, although Hale didn't know whether or not the governor had arrived on foot. Nobody else was around.

"And we visited a minute, visited about cars a minute," Hale said, "and then Jim said we ought to get our business done. So we sat down and Jim said, 'You know, what I want to do is, we're going to put this in Susan's advertising company.'"

"Okay, which is a conversation then about a loan?" Jahn asked.

"Yes, sir. It was about a loan for Jim and the Governor. . . . And I said, 'Well, that will be fine.' And we were discussing it, you know. He was talking about getting the proposal ready, the proposal for the loan ready, and then I don't remember just exactly how the discussion came about, but security was mentioned and—or the loan, and the Governor mentioned that they could provide a security interest in some raw land in Marion County. . . .When the Governor brought up about the security interest in the land, McDougal said that his and Susan's financial statement was strong enough to handle it and that it wouldn't need any additional security for the property. . . .[T]he Gover-nor said, 'Be sure'—he said, 'My name cannot show up on this,' and McDougal said, 'I've already taken care of that.'"

Whitewater, which Hale claimed he had never heard of back then, was lo-cated in Marion County. Because Hale's 302 and his grand jury testimony both avoided mentioning his earlier accusation that FBI agents or federal prosecu-tors had stripped his files of a letter guaranteeing that Clinton would repay the loan, Ray Jahn was able to tiptoe around that touchy topic. If the OIC actually believed Hale, it was hard to understand why the president was not a defen-dant—or at the very least an "unindicted co-conspirator."

What struck the defense attorneys was that Jahn seemed to be eliciting

Hale's story in a disjointed and elliptical manner. Was he parceling out daily "revelations" for their value as headlines? On Hale's third day of testifying, Jahn again asked whether he had spoken with Bill Clinton regarding the $300,000 loan. Instantly, Tucker's attorney George Collins rose to object. A heated debate took place out of the jury's hearing.

"A conversation by Mr. Clinton where Clinton is the speaker and Hale is the listener out of the presence of McDougal or Tucker or Watt or whoever, an unindicted co-conspirator, would be the purest of hearsay," Collins argued. "I object to any such [testimony] unless they said Clinton is a co-conspirator, and they have never said that. . . . The BBC carried this story this morning that they were claiming that Clinton was an unindicted co-conspirator, and it's all over the world. . . . I do want to respect the office of the President of the United States. I think that's offensive and, therefore, I object *in limine* specifically to any conversation, any mention of any conversation, to which Mr. Clinton is a party."

Put up, Collins seemed to be saying to the prosecution, or shut up. Jahn quickly backed down.

On cross-examination, Hale appeared querulous and argumentative. Several times the judge warned him to answer the question and quit making speeches. Sam Heuer, a veteran Little Rock trial lawyer whom Judge Howard had appointed to represent Jim McDougal, walked Hale through the $825,000 Dean Paul loan to show the jury that every illicit dime had gone directly into his pocket. Also, there was no independent evidence that any of the conspiratorial conversations he described had ever taken place. Early in 1986, moreover, loan officers for Madison Guaranty had turned down two applications Hale had submitted to the savings and loan.

"So your co-conspirators are turning you down," Heuer observed sarcastically. "There is no reciprocity in your deal, is there? . . . Why didn't you call McDougal, and say, 'McDougal, dad gum. Here I'm doing all of this for your political family, you are turning your back on me.' Did you ever make that call, Mr. Hale?"

"I didn't see the need for it," Hale answered.

Hale's penchant for filing falsified documents with banks and government agencies neither began nor ended with the alleged conspiracy. Scarcely a piece of paper that had passed through Capital Management Services in a decade or more could be taken at face value. Yet the prosecution had filed felony counts against all three defendants on the basis of Small Business Administration 1031 forms Hale had filled out, incorrectly reporting the purpose of loans he had made.

"You did everything at the SBA to try to make it fit your story, didn't you?" Heuer challenged. "You sent in false 1031s when *you* were actually receiving money from loans, you sent in false letters . . . saying people had paid their loans when they hadn't?"

"That's correct," Hale admitted. "I did that."

Sam Heuer rattled Hale with an attempt to uncover his partisan bias. Yes, he had exchanged more than forty phone calls with Jim Johnson in the months after his indictment in 1993, Hale admitted—but he hadn't known of Justice Jim's hatred of the president. He hadn't realized that Floyd Brown and David Bossie were political operatives; he had never heard of Citizens United and had assumed that the two men were journalists. Heuer questioned him extensively about the November 1993 interview with Bossie and NBC producer Ira Silverman that had done so much to revive the Whitewater story.

"Do you have any idea what your story has done to this nation?"

"I hope it helps clean up some corruption," Hale retorted. "I do."

"I guess you ought to be commended by somebody on that," said the sarcastic Heuer.

When his turn came to question Hale on April 5, Tucker's lead attorney, George Collins, poked a few more holes in the prosecution case. For example, the crucial Castle Grande meeting during which Bill Clinton had offered to put up Marion County real estate as collateral for Susan McDougal's $300,000 loan was supposed to have taken place between January 10 and February 28, 1986—the date that the Dean Paul loan closed. According to Hale, Jim McDougal had met with him and Clinton in a construction trailer out in the boondocks rather than at Madison Guaranty, a few blocks from the governor's mansion, because federal bank examiners had temporarily taken over McDougal's office. Hale looked surprised to learn that the federal officials hadn't arrived at Madison Guaranty until March 4. But he quickly explained that he only knew what McDougal had told him.

It wasn't until the afternoon of Monday, April 8, that Collins caught the witness in what sounded like a thunderous contradiction. The defense lawyer spent a couple of hours walking Hale through the intricate details of his crimes against the SBA, seemingly to impress the jury with the deviousness and complexity of his schemes.

"Now, do you remember that you went before Judge Reasoner to plead guilty?"

"Yes, sir."

"And do you remember that you were placed under oath so they could ask you questions about what you had been doing?"

"Yes, sir."

"And you were represented by counsel and [the] Independent Counsel was in there with you, is that correct?"

"Yes, sir."

"Did the court say, 'What happened to the money [$900,000] that you obtained from the SBA by this plan?' And did you say, 'It was loaned out to various entities'?

"And then the court said 'Were any of the entities entities that you had an interest in?' And then you said, 'I don't believe so.' Do you recall that's what you said to Judge Reasoner when you pleaded guilty?"

"I was scared to death," Hale answered. "I really don't remember."

What the sentencing judge had wanted to know, in effect, was whether or not Hale had stolen the money twice: once when he obtained it as capital by fraudulent means from the SBA, then a second time by lending it to one of his nonexistent shell companies.

"But you had used part of that money," Collins continued, "to lend it out to Arkansas Commercial Realty, to lend to Little Rock Clothiers, isn't that correct? . . . And those are your entities, weren't they? You just said that they were? . . . And what you said to Judge Reasoner when you were pleading guilty was not true, was it?"

In fact, Collins showed, more than $178,000 of the money had been diverted to Hale's shell companies and was never repaid.

"Like I said when he asked me," Hale replied, "I did not know I was going to have to say anything, and when you are standing up there—I was scared to death and I don't even recall what I said except it's recorded."

"Do you lie when you are scared?"

When Collins noted that the OIC had done nothing about Hale's lying at his March 1996 sentencing hearing, Ray Jahn objected. "Now he's trying to say that the government stood by while the witness misled the court," the prosecutor complained. "And that obviously is a misstatement. He's testified as to the circumstances. To now go on and attack the government based upon this is clearly an improper line of cross-examination." Judge Howard agreed, but the damage to Hale's credibility was done.

Jahn was more successful, however, in preventing any detailed examination of Washington attorney Theodore Olson's role in protecting Hale. Collins was reading aloud a list of twenty attorneys who had represented Hale in some capacity when the mention of Olson's name made Jahn leap out of his chair to object as if he had been stung.

"Now, going into what Mr. Olson does for practice, what Mr. Olson does before the Supreme Court or anything else is completely irrelevant to the issue. A man named Olson represented him at one point during the course of his life." The judge allowed Collins to proceed.

Hale said he had retained Olson to represent him in December 1993 and had paid him out of his own pocket—although he had earlier testified that after the FBI raided his office, he and his wife had been forced to sell furniture to buy food. Twice, said Hale, Olson had helped him avoid testifying before Congress.

"And were you aware of his background when you hired him, of his fame, how well known he was?" Collins asked.

"When we went up there in December he was just a lawyer to me."

"Who referred you to Mr. Olson?"

"Randy Coleman found out there was a fellow down here who worked in Democratic Senator Hollingsworth's office," Hale answered smugly, "that knew him and recommended him."

No such senator has ever existed in Little Rock or Washington, although Collins couldn't be sure of that at the time. He returned to the subject a few moments later.

"Did you know," he asked, "that Theodore Olson was a former partner of Kenneth Starr?"

Jahn jumped to his feet again.

"Your Honor, Your Honor, that is outrageous. Counsel is engaging in unscrupulous conduct at this point. . . .The Court has already sustained an objection to this line of questioning."

"I think I'm entitled to know that he's personally represented by—"

Jahn angrily cut him off. "They live in the same city," he snapped. "So what? We object to it, Your Honor. We object to it."

The dispute continued at the bench, out of the jury's hearing. Jahn argued that the defense was trying to get into the prosecution's political motives, which the court had ruled out of bounds. "Years and years and years ago Mr. Olson belonged to a firm which later on Mr. Starr joined," Jahn protested, giving a rather diminished picture of Starr's continuing close friendship with Olson. "He's trying to make it seem that Mr. Olson is there now and it's unethical conduct on the part of Mr. Collins and Mr. Collins knows that."

"If Your Honor please, the fact that Mr. Hale, their main witness, winds up being represented by the former partner of Kenneth Starr—I think that is material to how he came to have such a story about the President and perhaps others," said Collins. "Things can happen, Judge, and I think I'm entitled to let the jury draw that inference."

Judge Howard sent the jury out of the courtroom and let the lawyers argue it out. Jahn contended that Hale had no idea of any relationship between Olson and Starr. Hale swore that he had never heard of Kenneth Starr in December 1993, and Jahn's objection was sustained. Any opportunity to uncover the Arkansas Project or the looser cabal of political operatives, journalists, and lawyers that had choreographed the Whitewater affair since September 1993 was lost.

*   *   *

A final point was scored by Bobby McDaniel, who brought up a November 1993 interview with ABC News in which Hale had alleged that $110,000 of the Master Marketing loan had benefited the Clinton's Whitewater investment.

"Got any documents to show $110,000 of that money went into Whitewater Development Company?" McDaniel challenged.

Hale admitted he didn't, then turned around and claimed that documents furnished to his attorney by a reporter for the *Washington Post* showed that the money had gone to another McDougal company called Flowerwood Farms. The OIC would eventually endorse Hale's logic—arguing, in essence, that because Jim McDougal had moved money back and forth among his various real estate entities, any cash transfer that appeared to benefit any one of his companies also benefited the Clintons.

Yet the most significant aspect of that exchange was its potential to illuminate Whitewater's murky origins, because documents leaked to the *Washington Post* had made their way into the hands of an embezzler under indictment—an embezzler who then utilized them, in concert with unscrupulous political operatives, to concoct charges against the president on national TV.

Many observers at the trial felt that Hale's nine days of testimony had been disastrous for the prosecution. For her part, conservative columnist Meredith Oakley of the *Arkansas Democrat-Gazette* had seen enough. A longtime Clinton critic who had written a highly unflattering biography of the president titled *On the Make,* Oakley was appalled by David Hale.

"Frankly," she wrote on April 15, "I'm glad the lawyers finally got this guy off the witness stand in the latest round of so-called Whitewater litigation. I wish they'd get him out of the country. He is a shame and a disgrace to Arkansas, and his treatment at the hands of profligate federal 'protectors' is a shame and a disgrace to America. . . .[The] case against Gov. Jim Guy Tucker and Jim and Susan McDougal . . . is so full of holes and so full of lies admitted to by Hale that it's become more of a laughingstock than the Arkansas political system it seeks to discredit."

That same day, Professor Stephen Smith was called to testify. An aide to Bill Clinton during his ill-fated first term as governor from 1979 to 1981, Smith had also engaged in business partnerships with Jim McDougal and Jim Guy Tucker, making him a prime target of the OIC. He and McDougal had once shared ownership of a tiny bank in Smith's native Madison County. Like several other Arkansans caught up in Kenneth Starr's dragnet, Smith had pleaded guilty to a crime he didn't think he had committed. Based upon an accusation by David Hale, Smith had been charged with conspiring to divert the proceeds of a $65,000 loan from Capital Management Services. Hale's records indicated that Smith had borrowed the money as working capital for a political consulting firm but had used it to pay off a real estate debt.

Smith had borrowed the money from Capital Management Services at McDougal's urging, in place of renewing a long-standing loan from Worthen Bank. His understanding had been that Hale had contacted McDougal actively seeking lenders. Hale himself had filled out the application, and had been fully aware of the loan's actual purpose. Nobody had told Smith that Capital Management Services was an SBA-financed company or that SBA policies forbade real estate loans. Listing an inaccurate purpose for the loan was for Hale's convenience, not his. In fact, Smith had never met Hale until he drove down to Little Rock to sign the application and pick up a check in January 1986. Nevertheless, Smith's attorney had persuaded him to plead guilty to a misdemeanor rather than spend upwards of $250,000 he didn't have fighting felony charges in federal court.

Although such purely technical charges are rarely prosecuted, and juries normally refuse to convict so long as the loan is repaid, Smith couldn't afford to risk a trial. He had one child in college and another about to start. A misdemeanor plea would not affect his job as a communications professor at the University of Arkansas; a felony conviction would lead to dismissal. Smith's guilty plea in June 1995 had led to a four-column front-page headline in the *Arkansas Democrat-Gazette*—probably a state record for a misdemeanor.

Smith's plea bargain with the OIC had come with two conditions: that he refrain from speaking with the media, and that he testify against Tucker and McDougal. He had no chance to tell the whole story until he testified in the same courtroom during Susan McDougal's contempt-of-court trial in April 1999.

After Smith had agreed to testify in 1995, he had arrived at the OIC's Little Rock headquarters and been handed a written script that purported to be his testimony. He was expected to read it to the Whitewater grand jury the following day.

"There were charges in there," Smith testified years later, "that involved things that I had told them were not true, things that I had repeatedly told them I had no knowledge of. They asked me to implicate other people in a criminal conspiracy. . . . It was one of the most intimidating things I had ever experienced, I think. At this time I had already pled guilty to a misdemeanor and was awaiting sentencing. . . . On one hand, I thought maybe it was a trick that they had put this false testimony in there and were asking me to read it to the grand jury so they might charge me with perjury. On the other hand, if I refused to read that and incriminate other people, they might argue that I wasn't cooperating, or at least, you know, the story I was telling—what I knew the truth to be—wasn't the story they had in mind."

Gathering his courage, Smith told deputy prosecutor Amy St. Eve that many statements in the script were untrue and that he refused to read it as written. A tense all-day negotiating session ensued. At one point, tempers flared. "It was a discussion generally about whether or not Governor Tucker had been involved in a criminal conspiracy with regard to the loan which I had pled guilty to," Smith later testified. "And at one point, [deputy prosecutor Bradley] Lerman started yelling at me saying, 'Tucker is a millionaire. Why are you protecting him?' I mean, [it was] just sort of bizarre. I was testifying truthfully about everything I knew, and he seemed to have another story in mind that I should be telling."

Lerman subsequently apologized for his part in the "good cop–bad cop" routine, and Smith reached an accommodation with the OIC that eased his fear of a perjury rap. Still, his time on the witness stand in the Tucker-McDougal trial was a humiliating and emotionally harrowing ordeal. He scarcely knew Jim Guy Tucker, who had owned only a 5 percent share in their real estate venture in the Ozarks, and he felt terribly sorry for Jim McDougal. At the time Smith agreed to the 1985 loan from Hale, Smith's father—who owned a quarter share—had been hospitalized in intensive care with a cerebral hemorrhage. The professor came close to tears on the witness stand describing the circumstances of his one-day trip to Little Rock to sign for the loan.

After Jim McDougal suffered a stroke and had to be hospitalized for manic-depressive illness in 1986, Hale had filed a lawsuit for repayment of the loan. On cross-examination by Tucker's attorney, Smith tried to explain how he had driven the two hundred miles to Little Rock in an attempt to straighten things out, but had found McDougal too feeble and confused to be of any help. Prosecutors immediately objected. They argued that McDougal's health in 1986 had nothing to do with the conspiracy to defraud the government that he, Stephen Smith, and David Hale had plotted in 1985. Their real concern, it appeared, was that the jury not feel sympathy for the defendant.

Judge Howard sustained the objection, and Stephen Smith's ordeal ended.

The OIC presented its final prosecution witness, FBI special agent Michael T. Patkus, on May 3. An accountant by training, Patkus spent the better part of the morning tracing with great particularity exactly how Jim and Susan Mc-Dougal had spent the proceeds of the $300,000 Master Marketing loan. Defense attorneys complained that given Jim McDougal's habit of transferring money as needed among his various enterprises, Patkus's tightly focused analysis was rather like substituting a snapshot for a motion picture. But the truly significant aspect of the FBI agent's testimony was that the *New York Times* misreported both its factual content and its meaning within the larger Whitewater saga. As usual, the *Times*'s version became the official version of the truth.

Exactly how that happened would remain a bit of a mystery. According to an astringent article later published in Harvard University's journalism quarterly, *Nieman Report,* by former *Des Moines Register* editor Gilbert Cranberg, the Associated Press moved an accurate summary of Patkus's testimony on

May 4. "Prosecutors rested their case against Gov. Jim Guy Tucker and President Clinton's former business partners Friday," the AP story began, "*without showing how Clinton benefited* from a $300,000 loan as another witness had claimed." [Emphasis added.] The AP dispatch added that while David Hale had testified that the Clintons had benefited, "an FBI agent's testimony Friday made no direct link between the loan proceeds and Clinton, leaving the issue hanging after nine weeks of testimony. . . . Prosecutor Ray Jahn said it was not important to link Clinton to money from the $300,000 loan, even if the omission might undermine Hale's credibility."

The AP story correctly pointed out that Special Agent Patkus had not mentioned Bill or Hillary Clinton.

Although it appeared under an AP byline, the *Times*'s May 4 story turned the wire service version inside out. It claimed that the prosecution had rested "after presenting testimony that money from an allegedly fraudulent loan went to benefit the Whitewater development. . . . [J]urors heard an FBI agent testify that nearly $50,000 from a $300,000 loan was used to cover Whitewater expenses."

The *Times* version specified that Jim McDougal had used $25,000 of the loan proceeds to buy a parcel of land on behalf of Whitewater and had deposited another $24,455 to cover the corporation's earlier payments to a realty company. The property at issue was the eight-hundred-acre "Lorance Heights" tract McDougal had purchased from International Paper in October 1986 without the Clintons' knowledge or permission.

Yet according to the Pillsbury Report, "That transaction did not benefit Whitewater or the Clintons; in fact, it left Whitewater with a large mortgage but no corresponding asset." Actually, Patkus never mentioned Whitewater, either—probably because McDougal had transferred the Lorance Heights property to his Great Southern Land Company within two weeks of closing.

Patkus hadn't even suggested that the $24,455 deposit into Whitewater's account came from the proceeds of the suspect loan. To begin with, that deposit had been made in 1985, a full year earlier than the Master Marketing loan, rendering the alleged connection "impossible, absent a time warp," Cranberg wrote. And as Patkus made clear, the deposit repaid not a valid Whitewater obligation, but a McDougal debt of uncertain origin. The *Times* editors did not respond to Cranberg's requests for an explanation.

The *Times* error had no impact on the Tucker-McDougal jury. But once again, the imprimatur of the newspaper of record turned a mistake into a cliché that would color dozens of subsequent articles about Whitewater. Over the next two years, the apocryphal "$50,000 benefit" to the Clintons would become the focus of accusatory articles by the *Times*'s own William Safire, Michael Kelly and James B. Stewart of the *New Yorker*, a PBS *Frontline* documentary—and several public speeches by independent counsel Kenneth Starr.

*　　*　　*

After a lengthy hearing on May 6, Judge Howard dismissed four of nine indictments against Jim Guy Tucker for lack of evidence—specifically those relating to the Stephen Smith loan and the acquisition of the Castle Sewer and
Water Company. The judge also threw out four of eight counts against Susan
McDougal, including all of the conspiracy charges, ruling that she had played
no role in the $825,000 Dean Paul loan. Howard denied Susan's motion for
severance and a separate trial, promising to instruct the jury not to hold the alleged deeds of others against her.

Everybody involved with the trial who had Jim McDougal's best interests at
heart begged him not to testify. His attorney Sam Heuer believed that McDougal's best chance for acquittal was to play the president's videotaped testimony,
recorded at the White House on April 28, and then send the case to the jury.

McDougal was a very sick man. His doctors, too, had pleaded with him to
stay off the witness stand. A clogged carotid artery was blocking blood flow to
his brain, affecting cognitive function, and his heart was very weak. Twice during the course of the trial he had required overnight hospitalization, most recently on May 3. McDougal wasn't listening. He had glorious memories of
testifying in his 1990 bank fraud trial, and thought he could easily best Ray
Jahn in a battle of wits.

Susan McDougal had seen all these symptoms before. Never fully compli-
ant with his psychiatric treatment, her ex-husband was now on a manic high,
self-medicating and gobbling pills at random. She regarded him as actively
delusional, obsessed with the notion that it was his destiny to save the Clinton
presidency from Republican scalawags. She pleaded with Heuer to seek a com-
petency hearing to prevent Jim from testifying.

With his shaved head, Panama hat, Colonel Sanders white suits, and walking stick, McDougal had turned himself into a walking caricature of the
"southern gentleman" for Yankee reporters he considered too obtuse to get the
joke. Despite his infirm health, he put on a daily performance for the TV cameras outside the courthouse, debunking the evidence against him and ridicul-
ing the prosecutors by name. He routinely promised to "kick Kenneth Starr's
butt up between his shoulder blades." He even handed out business cards identifying him as "Capt. James B. McDougal, Cotton Factor"—an obscure occupation that scarcely existed anymore, and certainly not in his hometown of
Arkadelphia.

On the morning of May 8, Jim McDougal stepped up to the witness stand.
Heuer led him through a brief history of his small-town Arkansas childhood,
his early political career as an aide to Senator J. William Fulbright, his marriage
to Susan, and his career as a populist banker and land developer. Jim had only
good things to say about his codefendants. Although they were no longer hus-

band and wife, he and Susan still loved each other. His ex-wife had never done a dishonest thing in her life. As for Tucker, "like all relationships, it's been a little bumpy. I think that I've been furious enough with him to hit him over the head with my walking cane if I could catch him, but whatever differences we have have been resolved . . . so I have nothing but warmest personal feelings for Jim Guy today."

The conspiratorial meetings described by David Hale, McDougal swore, were purely figments of Hale's imagination. There had been no gathering in Jim Guy Tucker's kitchen, and no 1985 Thanksgiving Eve meeting at Madison Guaranty. (McDougal said he had been out of town that night, although he offered no proof.) Hale had never visited the Castle Grande sales office at all, and certainly not with Clinton, who had played no role whatsoever in the Master Marketing loan. McDougal had said nothing to Hale about helping his "political family." Madison Guaranty had never lent a dime to Bill or Hillary Rodham Clinton.

Sadly for McDougal, however, on cross-examination his battle of wits with Ray Jahn swiftly turned into a rout. Handed an opportunity to salvage his case, the veteran prosecutor launched into the confused defendant, catching him in numerous contradictions and outright falsehoods. Shown signed contracts of real estate deals of which he had claimed no knowledge, McDougal accused the OIC of forgery. Moments later, he broadened the accusation to include Representative Jim Leach and Senator Alfonse D'Amato. They too, McDougal asserted, had manufactured Whitewater documents in their investigations.

At the next break, Susan McDougal bolted from the courtroom, took an elevator downstairs to a room where she could be alone, and wept. Everything she had feared was happening. Jim's testimony could end up convicting them all. She couldn't believe that a man who had been found totally disabled ten years earlier and had survived on Social Security payments ever since would be allowed to testify. Watching Jahn destroy him was more than she could bear.

The longer McDougal testified, the worse it got. Desperate to use the president as a shield, McDougal even denied telling the foolish but widely reported tale about how Bill Clinton had jogged by his office in 1985 whining about money and implored him to hire Hillary to represent Madison Guaranty. After Jahn showed him attorney Jim Blair's handwritten notes documenting the allegation, McDougal insisted that Blair was a "notorious liar." Confronted with FBI 302s that told the same story, McDougal claimed that the agents had misunderstood him.

By his second day of testimony, McDougal's credibility was shot and Jahn continued to hammer away. If the OIC failed to win convictions, Whitewater would be history and Kenneth Starr would be out of business. The jury hadn't yet seen the videotape of the president's testimony, but Jahn knew what it would show—and it wasn't helpful. Not only had Clinton denied the Castle Grande meeting, he had denied ever having had a substantive conversation with David Hale anywhere at any time. With no evidence to the contrary, Ray Jahn's blustering attempts to force Clinton to admit otherwise had made the prosecutor look foolish.

"As far as your adamancy as far as pressure is concerned," Jahn had asked Clinton for at least the fourth time, "what is that based on, sir?"

"Based upon the fact that it didn't happen, sir."

"Well, is it based on your recollection of all your conversations with Mr. Hale?"

"It's based upon the fact that I know that I never pressured David Hale to make a loan, just like I never ran in my jogging shorts out to 145th Street to see him in the cold. I know that I never did that. . . . I never jogged to any of [Mc-Dougal's] real estate offices, and certainly not to 145th Street, which was twelve miles or so, or ten miles, from downtown Little Rock."

The prosecutor had tried taunting Clinton. How could he know Hale felt no pressure? Was he clairvoyant? No, but he had never talked business with David Hale. Next, Jahn had tried to draw the president into a debate about whether it was theoretically possible for him to have visited Castle Grande in McDougal's car. When Clinton declined to speculate, Jahn accused him of ducking the question.

"All I'm asking you to do is admit to the jury, sir," Jahn said, "that there is no physical law, no spiritual law, no inconsistency that would prevent you from getting in McDougal's car and driving anywhere that you wanted to back in 1985 and 1986. That's all I'm asking you."

"I wasn't in handcuffs and chains," said Clinton, "if that's what you are asking. No, I could have physically done it."

"Is there a reason that you didn't want to answer that question?"

"I didn't understand it," the president answered. "I still don't."

Cross-examining McDougal, however, gave Jahn another chance to win the case by turning Clinton into a witness for the prosecution. Having methodically walked the president through the real history of the Whitewater Development Corporation, Jahn shrewdly set out to turn McDougal's own complaints against his former business partners back upon him. He showed McDougal the 1985 contract in which he had swapped all of Whitewater's remaining real estate assets to realtor Chris Wade for a twin-engine airplane. After putting the plane to his own uses for a time, McDougal sold it and put $25,000 in his pocket. Had he ever told Bill and Hillary Clinton that he had practically given Whitewater's assets away for pennies on the dollar?

McDougal admitted he had not. Had he told Susan McDougal? He doubted that he had. Whitewater, Jim explained, had simply been an "albatross around my neck." How about when he had approached Bill and Hillary Clinton later in 1985 to renew the Whitewater bank loan, Jahn probed. Had he informed his partners that they were paying for property they no longer owned? And that the Whitewater Development Corporation was essentially a shell?

"I never informed Bill about anything about the company," McDougal said. "I tried once or twice, and his disinterest in it was so marked that I never attempted further to do it. He simply wasn't interested."

Jahn moved on to the purchase of the Lorance Heights property from International Paper. He produced the 1986 contract bearing Jim and Susan McDougal's signatures. "Did you, sir," he asked, "on March the fourth of 1986, tell Bill Clinton about this development in the name of Whitewater Development Corporation?"

"No, sir."

"And can you tell us why not, sir?"

"There was no need to tell him."

"Well, at this particular time," Jahn persisted, "was Mr. Clinton interested in the future of Whitewater Development Corporation?"

"It's my understanding at that time that they had withdrawn from the corporation, and it was my understanding that they had assigned their stock to Susan and me, and . . ."

"How did you gain that understanding, sir?"

"Primarily from Susan, who prepared the stock transfers and took them, I think, to the Governor's mansion," McDougal claimed. "And we were under the misapprehension that they had been delivered, that they had been executed and that we were the sole owners of Whitewater Development Corporation."

"When did this event occur, sir?"

McDougal didn't know. The correct answer was 1993, when Jim Blair lent him $1,000 to purchase the Clintons' stock—long after Bill Clinton had become president and the press had turned Whitewater into a national issue.

"Were you being honorable to Mr. and Mrs. Clinton, your business partners," Jahn demanded, "in continuing to conduct business in the name of Whitewater Development Corporation?"

McDougal said that he was, then abruptly reversed course, claiming that he had, in fact, notified the Clintons that he had sold Whitewater's assets prior to the Lorance Heights purchase. "I think I called him on the phone."

"I'm trying to pin down a time, sir, trying to ask you if you can to assist us in locating a time when you informed Mr. Clinton that you didn't want to do business with him anymore?"

McDougal couldn't supply a date. On videotape the president had already testified that he and Hillary had never been told about the bargain-basement sale of Whitewater's assets, knew nothing about the Lorance Heights purchase, and thus had never agreed to surrender their ownership in the company unless they could also be released from its debts. Clinton's account was fully backed by the documentary record in the Pillsbury Report. Still, the president had refused to blame McDougal for the investment's failure.

"Mr. McDougal," said Clinton, "never promised me any money. He asked me if I wanted to take a risk with him, a business venture, an investment. There is no such thing in the free enterprise system as a risk-free investment. We took a chance. We made what I thought was a prudent investment, and it didn't make money. I'm sorry about that, but he didn't violate any promise."

By late on the afternoon of May 9, with Jim McDougal contradicting himself every few sentences and Sam Heuer complaining to the judge that the prosecutor was wearing down an obviously confused witness, Jahn still had one high card to play. McDougal's catastrophic performance had made him look like a liar and a cheat; Susan, too. Apparently thinking he was helping her, he had bragged about his ex-wife's terrific business sense, making her look like his accomplice.

But what about Jim Guy Tucker? On the first morning of his testimony, McDougal had spoken of his warm personal regard for the governor. The Whitewater scandal had begun in the first place due to a grudge McDougal held against Tucker. At a time when he had been desperate for cash in 1986, Jim had begged Tucker to buy $100,000 worth of promissory notes from him at a steep discount. Later, McDougal had demanded that Tucker return the notes; when he had refused, Jim had accused him of stealing and then taken his complaint to Sheffield Nelson in 1992.

"Mr. McDougal," Ray Jahn asked after the judge overruled a lengthy objection from Tucker's attorneys, "isn't it a fact on June 30, 1995, you told [FBI] Special Agent Norris that Mr. Tucker was a, quote, thief who would steal anything that wasn't nailed down, end quote?"

"I don't think that's exactly what I said," came the answer. "I think I said 'like most lawyers, he would steal anything that wasn't nailed down.'"

To the astonishment of many in the courtroom, defense lawyers played the videotape of Clinton's testimony on the afternoon of May 9, then rested their case. Sam Heuer told reporters that Clinton's categorical denial of Hale's allegations made the jury's decision an easy one. "The president," he declared. "You can't ask for a better witness than that. You can't ask for better credibility."

Outwardly, the defense lawyers presented a unanimous front: The jury couldn't possibly believe David Hale, and without Hale, there was no conspiracy. Therefore, the OIC had clearly failed to prove its allegations. "If the heart and soul of their case is not there," Sam Heuer asked reporters, "why go on?"

Behind the scenes, the decision had been more complicated.

Susan McDougal was praying that the judge's dismissal of the conspiracy charges against her would outweigh her ex-husband's ruinous performance on the witness stand. She could only defend herself by telling the jury how she and Jim had separated in 1985, and that she had moved in with Pat Harris, a former Madison Guaranty employee, several years before her divorce. Following Jim's stroke and nervous breakdown in 1986, she had signed whatever he asked her to sign, partly out of guilt. Privately Susan feared that if they learned all that, the nine middle-class white women on the jury would punish her for being a "fallen woman."

Tucker and his lawyers thought that Judge Howard's dismissal of four counts ought to have sent a strong signal to the jury that the OIC had brought a weak case. But at least one of Tucker's attorneys thought he was making a terrible mistake. Darrell Brown, an expert criminal defender who had played a key role in some of the most politically charged cases in recent Arkansas history, believed that Jim Guy simply had to testify. A fighter by nature, Brown had been the first black player to wear an Arkansas Razorback football uniform back in the sixties. He also thought Tucker badly underestimated the public's suspicion of politicians. Regardless of what the judge told them, Brown thought, an Arkansas jury would want to hear their governor tell them he was innocent. If he didn't they might well assume it was because he couldn't.

In his younger days, people said that Jim Guy Tucker would "argue with a fence post if he thought he was right." But the stress of the trial had taken a terrible toll on his health. While too proud to let it show, he was virtually bedridden outside the courtroom. His confident smile and apparent vigor were illusions produced by steroid injections. The governor's chronic liver disease was nearing an acute stage; without a transplant, he wouldn't have long to live. Furthermore, should he testify, prosecutors could be depended upon to raise the issue of his bankruptcy fraud indictment. Jahn had already questioned Hale about it. Putting on a complete defense could extend the trial by a month to six weeks. Tucker didn't feel he had the strength to endure it.

Closing arguments in the Tucker-McDougal case began on Monday, May 14. Ray Jahn spent two hours rehashing David Hale's allegations and defending Hale's truthfulness. Jahn put heavy emphasis on Bill Watt's testimony that Hale had hinted to him about Bill Clinton's financial interest ten years earlier. Did the defendants expect the jury to believe that Hale had picked "the future President of the United States to incriminate" years before Hale had gotten into trouble? He reminded them that Judge Howard had said, "[Y]ou can believe some of what he says, you can believe all of what he says, or you can completely disbelieve what he says. . . . As far as the documents themselves are concerned, the documents are there."

Just as predictably, all three defense lawyers tried to destroy Hale's credibility. Scarcely mentioning the president, Tucker attorney Buddy Sutton, a veteran Little Rock trial lawyer handling his first criminal case in years, pointed out that his client hadn't seen a dime from the Dean Paul loan at the heart of the OIC's conspiracy theory. Sutton led the jury through a detailed accounting of Hale's embezzlement schemes, emphasizing that Tucker had no role in any of them.

Sam Heuer, however, did his best to turn the trial into a swearing contest between Hale and Bill Clinton. Hale, he argued, was "involved in his last and biggest and greatest con game.... What has that done to our nation? What has that done to our President? What has that done to our state? David Hale's greed has grown so big that he doesn't care.... He'll tear this nation to shreds, he'll tear this state to shreds to save himself from going to the penitentiary."

Representing Susan McDougal, Bobby McDaniel took a similar line. "Deceitful David pulled it off," said McDaniel. "He got an independent counsel appointed. But do you know what? The President of the United States testified under oath that he never pressured David Hale to do anything. He did not pressure him to make a loan to Susan McDougal.... Is there any evidence that President Clinton benefited [by] a dollar? No. Not a dollar. Who is telling the truth here? Bill Clinton."

The next day, Ray Jahn shrewdly switched tactics in his rebuttal. Producing a colorful flowchart that featured unflattering photographs of the defendants, he too suddenly defended Bill Clinton's veracity. "The President of the United States," he reminded the jury, "is not on trial. Why isn't the President of the United States on trial? Why isn't he on trial? Because he didn't set up any phony corporations to get employees to sign for loans that were basically worthless. He didn't get $300,000 from Capital Management Services like Jim and Susan McDougal did by falsely claiming their use.... The President didn't backdate any leases. He didn't backdate any documents. He didn't come up with phony reasons not to repay the property. He didn't lie to any examiners, he didn't lie to any investigators. It's another act of desperation, ladies and gentlemen. The defendants are trying to drag the President of the United States into this courtroom and set up a defense, hide behind the President by claiming that you must in some way make a bad judgment concerning the President to convict them, and I submit to you that's not true."

In a stunning reversal of more than four years of accusations—many of them obviously leaked by the OIC to eager Washington reporters—Jahn took the jury step by step through the Whitewater maze, showing that Jim McDougal had abused the Clinton's trust, absconded with their investment, and lied to them for years. He suggested that the president had merely forgotten about meeting Hale and McDougal at Castle Grande because it had been a trivial event of no importance to him. "The President basically admits that he does not recall." Although directly at odds with Clinton's actual testimony, this rhetorical ploy permitted Jahn to argue that it wasn't Hale who had lied about the president, it was Jim McDougal. At great length, Jahn showed how Mc-Dougal had repeatedly lied to the Clintons about the giveaway sale of White-water's real estate assets to the realtor who was supposed to be their agent. Then McDougal had told three mutually contradictory stories to the jury.

Precisely the same thing was true about the Clintons' surrender of their Whitewater stock and the Lorance Heights deal. Jim McDougal had deceived Bill and Hillary Clinton, deceived International Paper about the ownership of the company, then lied repeatedly to the jury. "Ladies and gentlemen, who is contradicting the President of the United States?" Jahn thundered. "It's not David Hale. It's Jim McDougal. . . . The office of the Presidency of the United States can't be besmirched by people such as Jim McDougal!"

If anybody in the national press corps understood the significance of what had just taken place in Little Rock, nobody covering the trial reported it. In a manner of speaking, it had been necessary to destroy the Whitewater scandal in order to save it. With Ray Jahn's closing prosecution argument, any hope Kenneth Starr and his deputies may have entertained of bringing criminal charges against President Clinton with regard to the Whitewater Development Corporation or Madison Guaranty Savings & Loan were defunct. Absent powerful and unambiguous new evidence of wrongdoing by Clinton—evidence that didn't depend upon the credibility of David Hale or Jim McDougal—the Whitewater scandal was over.

The jury stayed out for almost two weeks before returning stunning verdicts of guilty against all three defendants on Tuesday, May 28. Jim McDougal was convicted on eighteen of nineteen counts of conspiracy and fraud. Susan McDougal was found guilty on four counts involving misuse of SBA funds and making false statements in connection with the $300,000 Master Marketing loan. Evidently her apprehension about the jurors' opinion of her was not mistaken.

Strangely, the jury found Jim Guy Tucker innocent of wrongdoing in the $825,000 Dean Paul loan that was supposed to be the cornerstone of the entire scheme, yet guilty of one count of conspiracy and one count of mail fraud. The mail fraud involved Hale's submission of an inaccurate 1031 form to the SBA, describing an otherwise legal corporate business loan Tucker had used for the acquisition of Castle Sewer and Water. The form said the loan's purpose was to repair a water tower. No evidence had been presented that Tucker had seen the document or assisted in its preparation. It almost looked as if the jury had decided that Tucker, having done legal work for both Hale and McDougal, simply must have known something crooked was going on.

The stunned governor announced that he would resign effective July 15. "Although I am innocent of the charges made," he told reporters standing in bright sunlight outside the courtroom, "I must accept the verdict of the jury while I appeal. But I cannot, and should not, allow our people or our state to bear any part of that burden." Tucker's resignation placed the governor's office in the hands of Lieutenant Governor Mike Huckabee, a Baptist minister who would become the third Republican to occupy that office since the Civil War.

Within minutes of the verdict, television pundits were informing the nation that the verdict meant more trouble for President Clinton because the jury had taken David Hale's word over his. That impression was rapidly dispelled, however, after jurors told reporters that they had believed Clinton's testimony but had agreed with the prosecution that it had little or nothing to do with the charges. Forewoman Sandra Wood, a nurse, told ABC's *Nightline* that "the president's credibility was never an issue. . . . I just felt like he was telling us to the best of his knowledge what he knew."

The next day, Stephen Labaton's account in the *New York Times* quoted jurors who believed Hale had fabricated his allegations against Bill Clinton. Juror Colin Capp stated that jurors thought Hale "an unmitigated liar . . . [who] perjured himself. . . . David Hale invoked the President's name for one reason: to save his butt. We all felt that way."

Capp told the *Arkansas Democrat-Gazette*, "I wasn't going to take away anyone's freedom on the testimony of David Hale. . . . He's one of the greatest con men whom I've ever seen. I think it was an absolute travesty that Hale got sentenced to [only] 24 months."

The second "Whitewater" trial of 1996 got started on June 17 in the Little Rock courtroom of U.S. district judge Susan Webber Wright. A Bush appointee who had studied under Bill Clinton at the University of Arkansas Law School, Wright had previously ordered the Paula Jones sexual harassment lawsuit postponed until Clinton left office, only to be reversed by the Eighth Circuit. That decision was on appeal to the U.S. Supreme Court. The Arkansas legal community tended to regard Wright as somewhat pedantic, but not particularly ideological.

The defendants in the OIC's latest set of indictments were a pair of small-town bankers from rural Perryville, a county seat of roughly eleven hundred souls about forty-five miles west of Little Rock. Herbie Branscum, Jr., and Robert W. Hill faced eleven felony counts for illegally funneling cash from their small bank into Bill Clinton's 1990 and 1992 campaigns. Branscum was a longtime Clinton ally who had formerly been chairman of the state Democratic Party; in 1991, Clinton had appointed him to the politically powerful state highway commission. Clinton had reappointed Hill to the state bank board that same year.

The case centered around the Perry County Bank's failure to report cash withdrawals by Clinton's 1990 gubernatorial campaign to the Internal Revenue Service. Nobody disputed that the money belonged to the campaign or that it was spent legally. At issue was Branscum and Hill's violation of a Treasury Department regulation requiring banks to report cash transactions of more than $10,000. The chief purpose of the law is to hinder narcotics syndicates and other criminal organizations that launder illicit cash through legitimate accounts.

Neither the bank nor the Clinton campaign had anything to gain by the admitted oversight; it was, the defense argued, a purely technical violation. The defense attorneys could find not a single instance of the Treasury law being used to prosecute any transaction that did not involve "dirty" money.

Branscum and Hill were also charged with illegally using bank funds to reimburse themselves and family members for contributions made to Clinton and other Arkansas politicians—an equally curious accusation, since they owned a controlling share of the bank and could have awarded themselves increased salaries or bonuses at will. In effect, they stood accused of stealing from themselves.

With perfect predictability, *New York Times* columnist William Safire drew dire conclusions in advance of the trial. Safire had reacted triumphantly to the Tucker and McDougal convictions. Proceeding from his own newspaper's erroneous account of the "benefits" to Whitewater from the Master Marketing loan, he declared that "if the Clintons knew about this abuse . . . then they would be accomplices in stealing $50,000 from the poor." (The columnist somehow had confused David Hale's lending company with an antipoverty agency.) And now the convicted Jim Guy Tucker held the key "to the looming case against the Clintons."

The president's handpicked successor, Safire surmised, "knows too much" to languish in jail covering up for Bill Clinton. In a follow-up column titled "Jail to the Chief," Safire speculated that the Branscum-Hill trial would prove Clinton had "accepted $7000 in perhaps-stolen cash . . . from bankers who wound up with a political plum." He even pondered the prospect of an election-year presidential impeachment.

Another aspect of the case that made the president's enemies salivate was Starr's inclusion of deputy White House counsel Bruce Lindsey as an "unindicted co-conspirator." Dubbed a "notorious consigliere" by Safire, Lindsey was one of Clinton's oldest and closest associates. Besides playing endless games of hearts with the president on Air Force One, the quiet, bespectacled Little Rock attorney was trusted to deal with ticklish personal matters. Most suspicious of all, perhaps, Lindsey had a rule against talking to reporters. As treasurer of Clinton's 1990 gubernatorial campaign, he had withdrawn some $52,000 in cash from the Perry County Bank in the last days of that heated race against Sheffield Nelson for a "get out the vote" effort—a Democratic euphemism which meant reimbursing black preachers in the cotton-patch counties of east Arkansas for driving their poor and elderly parishioners to the polls.

In pursuit of its case, the OIC had vivisected the defendants and their families. Besides issuing the usual wall-to-wall subpoenas for complete financial and tax records spanning the entirety of Branscum and Hill's adult lives, Starr's investigators had interviewed every past and present employee of the Perry County Bank, as well as numerous associates and family members. Branscum's ailing seventy-six-year-old mother had been called in for questioning. FBI agents even showed up at Perryville High School to serve a subpoena on Robert Hill's teenage son. (The school principal expelled them.) Branscum later estimated that the cost of defending himself had exceeded $500,000. As wealthy bankers and political insiders, Branscum and Hill were not universally beloved. Yet in a country town like Perryville, the OIC's actions provoked great resentment.

More than in the first Whitewater case, the Branscum-Hill prosecution rested upon the testimony of a single witness. Even before the OIC found him, Neal T. Ainley had been fired as president of the Perry County Bank: a disgruntled former employee who might have borne a grudge. Indicted on five felony charges, Ainley pleaded guilty to two misdemeanors and agreed to testify against his former employers. He alleged that Bruce Lindsey had asked him not to file the IRS forms, and that Branscum and Hill had instructed him to comply. Lindsey acknowledged asking bank officials to keep the withdrawals a secret from the public, lest Sheffield Nelson use them as ammunition for a last-minute radio ad blitz. But hiding the withdrawal data from the IRS made little sense. The reports are strictly confidential; disclosing their contents is itself a crime. Besides, the Clinton campaign had documented the same transactions in its state campaign finance filings.

The president again testified, by videotape, on Thursday, July 18. If the prosecutors were hoping to shock the public with the revelation that politicians appoint their friends rather than their enemies to patronage jobs, they failed. Clinton said that his appointment of Herbie Branscum to the Arkansas Highway Commission and Robert Hill to the bank board had nothing to do with campaign contributions. Not only were both men highly qualified, Clinton pointed out, but in appointing them he had passed over others who had contributed considerably more. In words that would later sound ironic, he argued that campaign fund-raising doesn't have to be sleazy. "I think it's an act of good citizenship," he said, "for people to get involved."

What appeared to turn the Branscum-Hill trial, however, was the testimony of witnesses dubbed the "three amigos" by defense lawyers Jack Lassiter and Dan Guthrie. The trio testified that star witness Neal Ainley had admitted being browbeaten into singing for the independent counsel. A carpenter named Gary Butler told the jury about a conversation with Ainley at a Little

League baseball game. "He said, 'Butler, when the big boys get a hold of you, you'll tell them anything they want to hear,'" the carpenter testified. "He said he was going to cooperate one hundred percent, and if Herbie and Rob [Hill] wouldn't, they were going to make it hard on their butts."

Deputy independent counsel Hickman Ewing, Jr., did his best to rattle the defense witnesses, questioning whether they hadn't tailored their testimony to benefit Perry County's most powerful businessmen. "Where in this affidavit did you say anything about 'big boys'?" he challenged.

"Well, it's not typed up here, but that's what he said, that's what he told me," Butler answered. "He said he was a little fish and they were after the big fish."

Bobby Hammonds, a convenience store manager, testified that Ainley harbored great resentment against the burly Branscum, frequently calling him "Boss Hogg" and other derisive nicknames. "I remember the comment that the right information in the right hands could bring them down," Hammonds said. "I said, 'What do you mean?' and they [Ainley and a friend] said, 'Lie to the FBI or to Sheffield Nelson.' I felt like they were going to contact somebody."

On August 1, the jury returned innocent verdicts on four felony counts against Branscum and Hill. The two were acquitted on charges that they had conspired to defraud the IRS. Jurors deadlocked on the accusation that the pair had stolen campaign contributions from their own bank. "This was a strictly political prosecution from the start," Hill said outside the courtroom. Branscum's Dallas lawyer Dan Guthrie remarked, "This is a $30 million prosecution machine that has been stopped dead in its tracks in Little Rock, Arkansas, by a jury that exercised good common sense."

Ewing promised that, following interviews with the recalcitrant jurors, the OIC would almost certainly move for a new trial. On September 14, however, Kenneth Starr announced that his office was giving up on the case. After publishing numerous articles hinting that Branscum and Hill's imminent conviction would lead prosecutors directly into the Oval office, the *Washington Post* neglected to cover the case's demise. According to a poll released by the Pew Research Center, only 14 percent of Americans were following Whitewater closely, most of them already holding a dim view of the Clintons. William Safire didn't say so, but suddenly it seemed quite unlikely that the election-year impeachment of President Clinton was going to happen.

Though it went largely unnoticed outside Arkansas, Jim Guy Tucker had attempted at the last minute to renege on his resignation on July 15. To his amazement, Tucker had learned only days before that one of the jurors who voted to convict him of conspiracy and mail fraud was married to a man whose sentence for cocaine trafficking he had twice refused to commute. On top of that, Charles Marvin Hayes, the juror's husband, was also the nephew of

Little Rock black activist and frequent Tucker critic Robert "Say" McIntosh. The self-styled "Sweet Potato Pie King" had been ubiquitous in and around the courthouse during the Tucker-McDougal trial, distributing luridly illustrated handbills charging the governor with crimes and immoral acts. He had been heard to boast that he "had one on the jury."

On the day of the governor's conviction, the irascible McIntosh—relatively quiet for some time after peddling the "Clinton's Black Love Child" myth to the *Globe* tabloid during the 1992 presidential campaign—made headlines by punching out a television producer. Terry Frieden of CNN had tried to prevent McIntosh from disrupting a live shot on the courthouse steps. Frieden pressed charges, and McIntosh was subsequently convicted of assault.

The idea that Say McIntosh had a relative on Tucker's jury sounded wrong, even in Arkansas. Still more disconcerting was the fact that the juror, Renee Johnson Hayes, had not responded when jurors were asked during the selection process if any of Tucker's actions as governor had affected them. Tucker filed an immediate appeal of his conviction on July 12. Three days later, he phoned his Republican successor just as Mike Huckabee finished rehearsing a television address and was preparing to depart for the state capitol to be sworn in. Tucker invoked a clause in the state constitution permitting him to step aside until such time as he was no longer "disabled."

But Huckabee was not to be denied. He met with Democratic legislative leaders, who dispatched a delegation to tell Tucker he risked impeachment. He responded defiantly, saying he would resume the powers of governor. Handed the letter during a press conference, Huckabee called it evidence of Tucker's inability to serve. "We fully believe the governor is not acting in accordance with the constitution," Huckabee said. "I have no intention of turning the reins over to Governor Tucker at this time." He gave Tucker an ultimatum: resign by 5 P.M. that evening or face impeachment. Only after Democratic attorney general Winston Bryant filed a lawsuit to oust him did Tucker relent, sending a brief, handwritten letter of capitulation to Huckabee.

On August 19, U.S. district judge George Howard rejected Kenneth Starr's recommendation that Tucker be sentenced to ten years in prison. After hearing testimony from the former governor's doctors about the gravity of his illness, the judge sentenced Tucker to probation and eighteen months of home detention. On Christmas Day, Tucker underwent a successful liver transplant at the Mayo Clinic in Minneapolis. He continued to maintain his innocence, vowing to fight both of Starr's indictments to the end. He further insisted that he had no knowledge of wrongdoing by Bill or Hillary Clinton. Following a series of hearings on the tainted-juror issue in 1998 and 1999 by the Eighth Circuit Court of Appeals and Judge Howard, Tucker's conviction remains on appeal.

*   *   *

On July 15, 1996, the *New Yorker* published a lengthy "Letter from Little Rock" by James B. Stewart. The *Blood Sport* author's article was widely assumed to represent Starr's latest thinking. A telltale sign was his portrayal of the Tucker-McDougal trial as "a test of [David] Hale's credibility against the President's." After perusing the trial transcript, Stewart reported that "contrary to White House assertions, the case was far from having nothing to do with the President."

Ignoring Ray Jahn's closing argument, which had repeatedly portrayed Bill Clinton as an unwitting victim of Jim McDougal's manipulations, Stewart contended that prosecutors had gone to "great lengths in [their] questioning of the President—lengths that may not have been necessary simply for the conviction of the McDougals and Tucker." Apparently Stewart had forgotten that both Clintons had submitted comprehensive written answers to interrogatories from the Resolution Trust Corporation years earlier. So Jahn had known in advance how the Clintons would answer every question he asked.

The *New Yorker* article suggested that the president had very likely been complicit in the $300,000 Master Marketing loan. "Clinton's motive," suggested Stewart, "would have been simple: he would have gained co-ownership of a potentially valuable asset [the Lorance Heights property] without putting up any additional money. Should this theory be borne out, it would implicate Clinton in a crime: conspiracy to defraud a financial institution." He hinted that Starr was actively contemplating an indictment.

But Stewart's piece also dealt for the first time with documentary evidence omitted from *Blood Sport*. A recent review in *Harper's* magazine had scolded the author for telling only half the Whitewater story—specifically Jim McDougal's self-serving half; now the author seemed to be conceding the point.

"Clinton's testimony that he did not know that McDougal had sold Whitewater's real estate to [realtor Chris] Wade," Stewart wrote, "is plausible. The Clintons' refusal to give up their stake suggests that they still thought it was something worth holding on to . . . [and] the available documentary evidence supports them."

He acknowledged, too, that "there is also good reason to believe that McDougal didn't tell either of the Clintons he had unilaterally taken the [Lorance Heights] land out of Whitewater and put it into a company owned solely by Susan and Jim. . . . In other words, McDougal, his finances shattered, may have attempted to cheat his business partners."

In reality, as the Pillsbury Report had concluded and the trial testimony affirmed, there was no evidence that the Clintons had any knowledge of the Lorance Heights property at all.

Blood Sport, by contrast, had portrayed McDougal as the innocent victim of Hillary Clinton's greed. How then, in Stewart's view, did Kenneth Starr pro-

THE HUNTING OF THE PRESIDENT | 251

pose to indict the president for scheming to acquire eight hundred acres about which he had no knowledge? The author hinted that McDougal might have withheld material damning to the Clintons. Once more, the incriminating evidence lay just over the horizon.

Meanwhile, Starr's deputies were doing all they could to bring Jim and Susan McDougal around. With their sentencing in Judge Howard's court scheduled for August 24, both were subjected to extreme pressures. At maximum, Jim's eighteen-count conviction could result in a sentence of up to eighty-four years in the penitentiary. While nobody imagined that would happen, for a man as sick as McDougal, any prison sentence might well be a death sentence. Having temporarily taken up residence again in a borrowed trailer on his old friend Claudia Riley's land in Arkadelphia, McDougal told everybody how desperately he feared dying in jail.

As Jim McDougal told the story in his ghostwritten book, *Arkansas Mischief*, he had gotten a call one day in early August from Amy St. Eve, one of Starr's youngest, most attractive assistants. A petite brunette with a girlish voice and a perky demeanor, St. Eve asked McDougal if he would mind if she and another young woman in the office drove down to Arkadelphia to pay him a visit. The two arrived on a Saturday afternoon carrying a copy of *Blood Sport* for the old promoter to autograph. Flattered, he invited them to the Western Sizzlin' steak house for lunch. According to his book, St. Eve told McDougal she hoped there were no hard feelings, that she admired him and had merely been doing her job.

McDougal told Susan that St. Eve had confided that she was a Democrat, regretted what had happened to him, and would like to help him write his memoirs. "He said that he thought it would be a great thing to do for her, for him to cooperate with Amy St. Eve," Susan later testified. "It would look good for her career. And he said, 'You know, that would really be a big boost to her. And I like her a lot. And I would like to do that.'"

Another important influence on McDougal's decision, according to *Arkansas Mischief*, was ABC News producer Chris Vlasto, who had befriended Jim early in the Whitewater saga. (Vlasto had produced the December 19, 1995, *Nightline* broadcast, in which Hillary Clinton's statement was electronically altered.) Vlasto, McDougal wrote in his book, convinced him that he had been convicted only because his defense lawyer Sam Heuer sold him out. "'Sam wasn't representing you,' Chris said. 'He was representing the Clintons.'" Vlasto further advised McDougal that he didn't have to die in jail: "If you walk in to see Ken Starr," the producer urged, "he'll greet you with open arms."

Actually, Starr did better than that. A few days later, the independent counsel himself arrived in Arkadelphia in a two-car caravan, along with Amy St. Eve, Ray Jahn, and a pair of FBI agents. Discerning in Starr's eyes "a trustworthy look . . . the same determined glint I once saw in the eyes of my early political patrons, Wilbur Mills and John McClellan," McDougal changed sides again. He told his visitors that Bill Clinton had, indeed, discussed the Master Marketing loan with him and David Hale at Castle Grande one afternoon during the winter of 1985–86, and later proffered a series of failed polygraph examinations to prove it. (The logic appeared to be that proof of McDougal's lying in the past somehow confirmed his truthfulness in the present.) Unfortunately for Starr, the story as McDougal eventually told it still differed in several significant particulars from Hale's version.

All at once, McDougal felt like a new man. He bragged to Susan that Starr had promised him a lenient sentence and his choice of federal medical facilities. The independent counsel had also agreed, he chortled, to tell Judge Howard what a fine Christian gentleman he was. Susan was angry and appalled. Jim had always mocked her religious beliefs. "Jim McDougal had consistently, throughout our marriage," she would eventually say, "always made fun of religion and belittled it and said that . . . if you were a person who could manage your own life, you never should have to call on God, [that] it was just all made up. There he was on the phone laughing and kidding that Kenneth Starr was going to come and tell the judge that Jim was a religious man so he could get leniency."

At first, Susan had trouble taking Jim's conversion seriously. She too was staying in Arkadelphia at the home of Claudia Riley, the widow of former Arkansas lieutenant governor Bob Riley. A much-decorated hero of World War II, Riley had been an old friend of Susan's father. The Rileys had first introduced Jim and Susan during her undergraduate years at Ouachita Baptist College. She had always been grateful to Claudia Riley for giving Jim a place to live.

"Jim would come up periodically in the next few weeks," Susan would later testify. "He would say to both Mrs. Riley and myself, 'I've got a whole new twist on that story that I'm going to tell them. Listen to this. What do you think about the way I say this? I've been thinking about this story.' And this went on where he would come up and tell different stories to us and different ways that he was thinking about telling it, and did this sound more believable or did this sound more believable? And I remember that Claudia and I were talking about it and saying, 'They're never going to believe him. This story is just so incredible.' I really thought that the story was getting so outlandish that they would . . . look at it as we did and say there's nothing to it."

At Susan's 1999 contempt trial, Claudia Riley testified that while she didn't recall any of McDougal's stories, she agreed he was too irrational to be taken seriously. "Jim weaved lots of webs depending upon his mood," she said. "I frankly never attached too much significance to the things that [he said]. Jim would come in, like [he was] delivering a message . . . delivering a statement. I just really didn't place too much emphasis on what he was saying."

The OIC saw their new witness differently. They moved Jim to Little Rock, set him up in a comfortable apartment, and showed every sign of taking his stories very seriously indeed. The pressure on Susan increased. "He told me that it would be a lot of fun," she recalled, "that we could have fun together, we could be together again, and they would pay for a place for us to stay, and that we would be able to pay the Clintons back for their not being good friends to us, and it would be something we could do together. And he said it wouldn't be hard at all. We'd be a team again. And he acted as if it would just be a lark to do it together."

Devastated by her conviction, Susan didn't think so. Two aspects of her experience with Starr's prosecutors had made her cynical about their motives. She believed they knew she'd had no real knowledge about her ex-husband's dealings with David Hale. And it especially galled her that Hale's wife, whose signature appeared on scores of documents used by her husband for felonious purposes, had never been charged.

The OIC's treatment of a former Madison Guaranty employee named Sarah Hawkins also persuaded Susan McDougal that Starr's prosecutors had no honor. Hawkins, once a federal bank examiner, had been the thrift's "compliance officer," responsible for ensuring compliance with state and federal regulations. Threatened by Starr with eighty felony counts, the black single mother had maintained her innocence and refused to roll over. After a year-long legal struggle, the OIC finally notified Hawkins and her attorney that she was no longer a target.

After she was subpoenaed to testify on Susan's behalf at a pretrial hearing, however, the OIC told Hawkins that she was once more a criminal suspect. In open court, Ray Jahn advised her attorney that a wise defense lawyer would urge his client to plead the Fifth Amendment. Hawkins did so, thus depriving Susan McDougal of an important exculpatory witness. A month later, Hawkins, her career already ruined by the OIC, was informed that she was again free of suspicion.

A conference call McDougal and her attorney had with the OIC on August 15 only heightened her apprehension. In what she considered no uncertain terms, Ray Jahn let her know that he was aware of her legal problems in California. A former employer, the wife of symphony conductor Zubin Mehta, had accused McDougal of embezzling. Partly because Mrs. Mehta had brought similar allegations against other employees in the past, for which no charges were filed, the Los Angeles County district attorney had at first taken no action against McDougal.

After Starr became independent counsel the California authorities had changed their attitude, and Susan didn't believe that was a coincidence. According to her, Jahn also indicated she might soon encounter difficulties with the IRS. The OIC had also issued subpoenas to two of Susan's brothers, both previously cleared of wrongdoing in connection with Madison Guaranty. All those problems could be made to disappear, the prosecutor observed, if she would cooperate with Kenneth Starr. McDougal never claimed that Jahn said he wanted her to lie. He mentioned Bill and Hillary Clinton's names. "You know who the investigation is about," she recalled Jahn saying, "and you know what we want." (Under oath, Jahn emphatically denied making any such statements.)

Afterward, Claudia Riley, who had accompanied her to Bobby McDaniel's office, asked whether there wasn't some way to give Starr what he wanted. "I'm going to tell you, Susan," said Riley, "if you were Megan, my daughter, I would tell you to tell them what they want to hear. It is too good a deal to pass up. You should just do it."

Susan's fiancé, Pat Harris, was of a contrary persuasion. Born in Arkansas and educated at the University of Michigan Law School, Harris was a public defender in Nashville. He warned Susan that it wasn't a matter of just one lie.

"A lie isn't for that day," he said. "You don't just tell it once. You will have to go before many grand juries, you will have to go into many courtrooms, and if you lie right now it will never be over. Your whole life will be lying and buttressing that lie, and you will be doing it over and over and over again, and it's not that easy."

Susan's mother agreed, for other reasons. She had come to America from Belgium as a war bride after enduring the Nazi occupation of her homeland. Decades later, she told her daughter how that had been. "When they wanted to put somebody in prison," Susan remembered, "the Nazis would go to their children or to their families and they would say just give us information on them or we will get you. And my mother said to me that night, 'If I can stand up to that, you can stand up to this. We'll do it together.'"

Susan talked to Jim McDougal on the telephone one more time before their sentencing. She told him she couldn't go through with his plan. With characteristic ingenuity, Jim had an alternate proposal, according to his ex-wife. "He said, 'You don't have to say that Clinton pressured David Hale to make the loan,'" she testified. "'You can just say you had a sexual affair with him. The election is coming up. That would be enough to destroy him. It would be enough to win the election. There's a man named Hickman Ewing who works in the independent counsel's office, and he believes he can get Clinton on a sex charge before the election. If you will come in and do this, you can write your own ticket. You can have anything you want.'"

Susan resisted his entreaties. "He said, 'If you don't do this thing, Susan, I don't think I ever want to speak to you again,' and he hung the phone up."

She never spoke to Jim McDougal again.

*   *   *

On August 20, Susan McDougal appeared in Judge George Howard's court-room for sentencing. The OIC presented evidence concerning two job résumés she had used: Seeking employment as a secretary, in Ann Arbor, Michigan, and then in Nashville, she had understated her actual educational and work experience. Another time, she had applied for a credit card in her sister's name to avoid having to explain the history of Madison Guaranty Savings & Loan. Portraying her as a habitual liar, the OIC sought the maximum penalty. Judge Howard sentenced her to two years.

Shackled hand and foot by U.S. marshals, she was led past TV cameras to a waiting prison van. At the Pulaski County jail, her temporary place of incarceration, she was stripped naked, given a full body cavity search, and doused with delousing chemicals. Susan McDougal's strange pilgrimage through the American penal system had only just begun.

On September 4, she was brought before the Whitewater grand jury meeting in Little Rock. Her attorney notified the OIC in writing that Susan would refuse to testify. She said she feared that unless she told Ray Jahn what he wanted to hear, he would indict her for perjury. She had come to believe that anybody who would pretend to believe David Hale and Jim McDougal was capable of that and worse.

Jahn asked her three questions: "Did you ever discuss your loan from David Hale with William Jefferson Clinton?" "Did you ever discuss Lorance Heights with William Jefferson Clinton?" and "To your knowledge, did William Jefferson Clinton testify truthfully during the course of your trial?"

After refusing to answer, Susan McDougal was cited for civil contempt, and led once more before the TV cameras in chains.

Chapter Thirteen

"ALL THEY WANTED TO TALK ABOUT WAS WOMEN"

THE SECOND INAUGURATION of William Jefferson Clinton was not quite the triumphal occasion that might have welcomed the first Democratic president since Franklin D. Roosevelt to win reelection. Almost daily since the final weeks of the presidential campaign, the country's major media had been trumpeting evidence of fund-raising practices by the president and his party that skirted the edges of legality and decency.

After achieving a victory once widely deemed impossible, Clinton would be returning to a White House not elated but increasingly besieged—by stories of illicit contributions from foreign sources (including donors who also had given hundreds of thousands to his legal expense trust), of importuning calls made by him and Vice President Al Gore to wealthy donors, of "sleepovers" in the Lincoln Bedroom and presidential "coffees" for those who gave, of unsavory businessmen whose donations had won access to the president, of big-donor junkets organized by an official in the Commerce Department.

Whether illegal or merely gross, these were dismaying displays of money's influence at the highest levels; and if the Republicans behaved similarly, raising far more by equally dubious methods, the odor of impropriety remained pungent. In his first inaugural address, after all, it was Clinton who had urged an effort "to reform our politics, so that power and privilege no longer shout down the voice of the people. . . . Let us give this capital back to the people to whom it belongs." Four years later those words returned to haunt him with stinging irony, as the media recited the names and donations of wealthy Americans (and foreigners) whose voices had been amplified by their checkbooks. Never one for unilateral political disarmament, Clinton had augmented Reagan-era fund-raising techniques with a few innovations of his own after the Republican congressional leadership stifled meaningful campaign finance reform.

Yet, the Republicans had outraised and outspent the Democrats in 1996 by hundreds of millions of dollars, as they always did. Some of their cash had been raised from illicit sources too. One of Bob Dole's finance vice-chairmen went to prison after pleading guilty to laundering millions into the Dole campaign's coffers, and Republican Party chairman Haley Barbour had cleverly siphoned $2 million into the national campaign through a complex loan scheme with a Hong Kong investor. But Republicans at least had the consolation of ideological consistency. Many conservatives argue that limitations on campaign donations are contrary to the First Amendment's guarantee of free political speech, and that there should be no limit to the ability of rich donors to influence the political process. Democrats are at least supposed to believe in limiting the influence of corporate interests and the wealthy.

Perhaps that was why the Clinton fund-raising stories originated largely from the initiative of the Washington press corps, rather than the president's right-wing adversaries. Following the media exposés, congressional committees chaired by Republicans would hold well-publicized hearings on the fund-raising scandal, struggling to maintain the media focus exclusively on Democratic rather than Republican abuses. With some success, the Republicans did their best to portray Clinton and Gore as uniquely brazen. In uglier moments, some Republicans played upon the prevalence of Asian and Asian-American names among Democratic donors to inflame latent nativism, encouraging talk radio hosts to charge that Clinton had treasonously "sold out" the country to Indonesia or China.

Public anger, however, was limited by two factors: the failure to prove any specific instances of corrupt favors, and a widespread perception that the Republicans were no better.

Nevertheless, the steady flow of postelection embarrassments kept Clinton's enemies energized. Many still seethed over Dole's refusal to exploit the "character issue" during his doomed campaign. (They may not have realized that the Republican candidate's reluctance was at least partly based upon his own moral vulnerability. Had Dole attacked Clinton as an adulterer, the *Washington Post*, which elected not to run a story during the 1996 campaign on the GOP nominee's own extracurricular love life, might have decided differently. The story did emerge in *Vanity Fair* magazine, which probably was warning enough.) Growing public outrage over campaign-finance issues would, the Republicans hoped, spark a renewed interest in the familiar accusations about Whitewater, the White House Travel Office, and the FBI files flap. A synergy of scandal might finally overtake Clinton during his second term.

The more sincerely the Clinton critics believed that the White House was covering up serious crimes, the more difficult it was for them to imagine how little evidence of those supposed offenses had been assembled after more than two years of costly investigation by the Office of Independent Counsel. Despite a steady media drumbeat suggesting that Starr's probe had reached "a critical turning point" or "a crucial phase," the truth was that OIC prosecutors had already taken their strongest shot during the election year with mixed results: convictions of the McDougals and Tucker, acquittals of Branscum and Hill.

Despite the illusion of a vast web of criminality, the independent counsel hadn't found much in the way of credible testimony or documentation. The June 1995 plea bargain of Assistant Attorney General Webster Hubbell had come as a result of offenses unrelated to Whitewater that implicated nobody but himself. As his former law partner, Hillary Clinton was actually a victim of Hubbell's overbilling and expense-account padding, not to mention of his inexplicable decision to accept a sensitive position in the Justice Department despite his crimes. Lying to the president about his guilt for months after the scandal broke and allowing ill-advised White House officials like Erskine Bowles to solicit legal work for him were equally wrong. But little of it was anybody's fault but Hubbell's.

Concerning the Travel Office and FBI files fiascoes, the OIC had found insufficient evidence to support indicting anybody on the White House staff, let alone Bill or Hillary Clinton. Although Starr steadfastly concealed his lack of progress until November 1998, no proof emerged that any felonious acts had occurred in either case. Starr's investigators could find no evidence showing that anyone more senior than Craig Livingstone and Anthony Marceca, the two lower-level White House security officials responsible for issuing credentials and passes, had so much as glanced at the FBI files of former White House employees.

Starr also knew by January 1997 that he would sooner or later have to endorse the conclusions of his predecessor, Robert Fiske. Despite feverish speculation and elaborate conspiracy theories on the crackpot fringe, Fiske had swiftly completed grand jury probes of the Foster suicide, and of alleged obstruction of the Whitewater investigation by administration officials, without issuing a single indictment.

Then there was Whitewater, the progenitor of the independent counsel's probe. Press speculation notwithstanding, anyone familiar with the several thick volumes of the RTC's Pillsbury Report, not to mention the testimony and exhibits that emerged at the Tucker-McDougal trial, knew that Starr's probe of the land deal had reached a dead end. The OIC could encourage as many stories about the imaginary "$50,000 benefit" to the Clintons as the media were willing to publicize. That wouldn't change the pile of documentary evidence contradicting them.

With Susan McDougal refusing to cooperate, Starr had two witnesses against the president: David Hale and Jim McDougal. Both had been convicted of multiple crimes involving fraud, deception, and forgery. Not only did both men have obvious reasons to lie, but jurors at the Tucker-McDougal trial had been unanimous in disbelieving their testimony. And there was the problem of Ray Jahn's closing argument, specifically exonerating the president of White-water crimes.

These facts and judgments might be kept off television and out of the newspapers, but they would inexorably surface in an American judicial pro-ceeding. Any legal action against the president premised on Whitewater would be far more dangerous to Kenneth Starr than to Bill Clinton. His ideological zeal and personal ambition didn't blind the canny Starr to all that.

Rather than disclose his dispiriting failure to all the politicians and pun-dits who were depending on him to ruin the Clintons, Starr quite naturally preferred to continue "investigating." He allowed his supporters and friends to believe that indictments and perhaps even impeachment were yet in the off-ing. Meanwhile, he considered how best to escape from what had become a frustrating and fruitless endeavor.

Evidently Starr's closest friends and allies didn't know how unproductive his probes of Whitewater, Travelgate, and Filegate had been. On the political right and among the Washington press corps, hope still abounded that somehow the independent counsel would inflict a mortal wound on the president and vindicate the moral equivalence between Clinton and Nixon. That was plainly the theme of "RICO, Anyone?"—the title of Theodore Olson's latest screed in the January 1997 issue of the *American Spectator,* penned under the pseudo-nym of "our legal counsel," Solitary, Poor, Nasty, Brutish & Short. Olson's wheezing satire again cataloged felonies potentially chargeable to the Clintons and their supporters, now including alleged fund-raising offenses, to support his conclusion that "comparing Clinton to Nixon may underestimate the scope of the administration's problems . . . [when] the appropriate compari-son for Bill Clinton may well turn out to be Don Corleone."

If any single figure in Washington embodied the effort to undermine Clinton it was Ted Olson, the former Reagan aide turned Republican power lawyer. Olson didn't seek publicity (leaving his name off his *Spectator* essays, for example) but he had played a part in almost every assault on the president, as an attorney for David Hale, as counselor to the Arkansas Project, as friend and defender of Kenneth Starr—and as a secret adviser to the lawyers for Paula Jones as well.

The Jones lawsuit, stalled in the appellate courts for more than a year, had reached a crucial showdown at the beginning of 1997. On January 13 the plaintiff's lawyers of record, Gilbert Davis and Joseph Cammarata, were scheduled to appear before the Supreme Court. They had prevailed a year earlier at the Eighth Circuit Court of Appeals, which had overruled Judge Susan Webber Wright's decision postponing the case until the president left office. In response, Clinton's attorneys had filed a writ of certiorari to the Supreme Court, successfully holding Jones off until after the election. Now at last the nine justices would hear the arguments of both legal teams and decide when her case would go to trial.

Behind Davis and Cammarata as they prepared for that momentous day was the same trio of youngish lawyers who had first assisted their representation of Jones—Jerome Marcus, of the Philadelphia firm Berger & Montague; George Conway III, a partner a New York's Wachtell, Lipton, Rosen & Katz; and Richard Porter, the former Quayle aide who had joined Kenneth Starr's firm, Kirkland & Ellis, in its Chicago home office. During the early eighties Porter and Marcus had attended the University of Chicago Law School, coming under the influence of its strongly libertarian faculty.

Jones's case had been sustained by conservatives from its very beginnings, less out of any concern for the legal rights of women than from a keen perception of its potential to make trouble for Clinton. Davis and Cammarata hadn't taken the case for ideological reasons, although both were Republicans, and Davis, at least, nurtured an ambition for elected office in Virginia, where he had long been active in party affairs. (In 1997 he would run unsuccessfully for state attorney general.) They hoped to make money and win a measure of fame for themselves; and while they didn't mind battling with the president, that wasn't their prime objective. As events unfolded, however, the two lawyers wielded less influence over their client than others whose purposes were frankly political.

Davis and Cammarata had decided early on to protect their own reputations by keeping the fund-raising and public relations aspects of the Jones case separate from their own legal work. They had authorized a friend, Republican activist Cindy Hays, to oversee the Paula Jones Legal Fund. That way, the lawyers could say they didn't know the identities of those who had contributed money to their client's cause. They were aware, of course, that right-wing figures had raised funds for Jones; Davis knew that the Legal Affairs Council and some antiabortion activists had made early donations totaling several thousand dollars. As the case proceeded, however, he preferred to keep his distance from the Jones fund, whose contributors were in any event kept secret for reasons of privacy as well as politics.

Hays hadn't been able to raise vast sums of money, but at least one major contribution had come from a close associate of Richard Mellon Scaife. Washington attorney William Lehrfeld, a tax specialist who advised Scaife's foundations as well as the *American Spectator* and the Arkansas Project (in addition to a host of other conservative institutions), had sent a check for $50,000 to the Paula Jones Legal Fund in September 1995. That check was drawn on the account of a little-known nonprofit group controlled by Lehrfeld and registered with the Internal Revenue Service as the Fund for a Living American Government (FLAG). Asked for more detail about FLAG and this contribution by reporters for *Salon* magazine in 1998, Lehrfeld at first claimed that he was FLAG's sole funder. Then he refused to permit them to examine its tax documents until he could delete the names of FLAG's other funders. But other IRS records show that one of Scaife's foundations contributed directly to FLAG.

Money from the Pittsburgh billionaire's foundations also supported three conservative organizations prominently associated with the Jones case. Between 1988 and 1996, nearly a million dollars in Scaife funds had been lavished on the Landmark Legal Foundation, an organization based in Kansas City and Washington which litigated on behalf of right-wing causes. Well over half a million dollars had been doled out to the Independent Women's Forum since 1994, when its leaders engaged Starr to write a brief on Jones's behalf.

Another million or so had subsidized the Federalist Society, established as a national legal fraternity during the Reagan era. It acted as a clearinghouse for clerkships with conservative judges, policy forums, and a right-wing political network. Its roster of members and patrons included many of the most prominent Republican judges, attorneys, and legal scholars, including Kenneth Starr and Judge David Sentelle, the presiding judge of the Special Division that had appointed Starr. (In the first few months of 1998, Sentelle spoke at no fewer than six Federalist events.) Certain of its members, including Starr, had provided a great deal of high-priced legal advice to Jones for free.

Gil Davis and Joe Cammarata weren't the sort of attorneys attracted to the highly ideological Federalist milieu. But Richard Porter and George Conway were among the group's active members, and they had mobilized its resources during the early days of the Jones lawsuit to lend additional respectability to her claims. At the urging of Conway and Marcus, a group of Federalist-affiliated law professors and constitutional lawyers had signed "friend of the court" briefs in 1994 supporting her right to proceedings against the president while he was still in office.

Now, as the date for argument on that issue in the Supreme Court approached, the young Federalist attorneys in the Jones camp called upon two of the organization's legal eminences to help prepare Davis and Cammarata. During the first week of January, they brought Davis and Cammarata to the Army-Navy Club for a coaching session with Robert Bork, who had addressed the founding conference of the Federalist Society at Yale in 1982, and Ted Olson, the chairman of its powerful Washington chapter.

Bork had lost his own chance to sit with the nation's top judges during an exceptionally bitter confirmation battle in 1986, an experience that had left him furious at the liberal Democrats he believed had blocked him and blackened his name unfairly. Aside from his legal acumen, Bork could offer informed personal opinions about the court's most influential justices. He regularly played poker with Chief Justice William Rehnquist and Associate Justice Antonin Scalia.

Less renowned than Bork, Olson too had a brilliant reputation as an appellate lawyer. He and Gil Davis had met once before, during the late summer of 1995, when Davis was preparing his successful argument on the same constitutional issues before the U.S. Court of Appeals for the Eighth Circuit. The easygoing Davis didn't mind taking advice from Olson, whom he viewed as a "very smart" attorney with substantial Supreme Court experience. Besides, Olson had graciously hosted their last session at the downtown offices of Gibson, Dunn & Crutcher, the giant law firm whose Washington operations he managed.

According to Davis, George Conway had wanted to run the coaching session as a "moot court," with Bork and Olson barking out the kind of sharp questions Davis could expect from the justices. But the scowling, opinionated Bork—possibly self-conscious about mimicking "the Brethren" he would never join—preferred a less formal approach, and everyone else deferred to him.

The atmosphere was businesslike. For two hours the lawyers sat around a table eating sandwiches as Olson and Bork advised Davis how best to present his brief urging that the case against Clinton proceed immediately to trial. To the justices, Olson emphasized, the most pressing problem would be whether the president should be distracted from his elected job to cope with a civil lawsuit, and how the lower court could address his special needs as a defendant. He urged Davis to convince the high court that Jones would accommodate the president in terms of court dates, depositions, and other infringements on his schedule.

As they all prepared to leave, Davis thanked his distinguished tutors and said, "Someday somebody will ask me who was present at this meeting." Did anyone mind his name being mentioned? Olson didn't seem to care, and neither did Bork. But Conway and Marcus, who had kept their participation in the Jones case from their law partners—some of whom were Democrats close to the White House—continued to insist upon complete anonymity.

A week later Davis, Cammarata, and their small entourage strode through a noisy gaggle of reporters and television crews and into the hushed marble corridors of the Supreme Court. The confrontation between the Jones team and the president's lawyers, led by Bob Bennett and Solicitor General Walter

Dellinger, was the biggest news story of the week leading into Clinton's inauguration.

Ted Olson wasn't there, but his prediction about the Court's concerns quickly proved accurate. Davis recalled that the justices "asked me what happens if the president says, 'I have to attend a NATO session and I can't be in court.' Scalia got a laugh out of it." Following Olson's cues, Davis responded that the lower court couldn't "force the president to show up at pain of going to jail," like an ordinary civil defendant. The court would have to grant the presidency a presumption of goodwill and work more or less at his convenience.

Conway later told others that he thought the Virginia attorney's lack of experience in the high court had showed when Justice Sandra Day O'Connor upbraided a fumbling Davis for seeming to abandon the Eighth Circuit's hardline opinion. When the tense morning of argument ended, however, Conway presented Davis and Cammarata each with a gracious memento. It was a miniature copy of the cover of the brief they had constructed together, encased in a plastic paperweight.

On January 20, Chief Justice Rehnquist administered the oath of office to the president, who then turned to the cameras and extended a classically Clintonian offer of reconciliation to his enemies. Noting that his inauguration coincided with the birthday of civil rights martyr Martin Luther King, Jr., the president said, "His quest is our quest, the ceaseless striving to live out our true creed. . . . To that effort I pledge all my strength and every power of my office. I ask the members of Congress here to join in that pledge. The American people returned to office a President of one party and a Congress of another. Surely, they did not do this to advance the politics of petty bickering and extreme partisanship they plainly deplore. No, they call on us instead to be repairers of the breach, and to move on with America's mission. . . . Let us remember the timeless wisdom of Cardinal Bernardin, when facing the end of his own life. He said: 'It is wrong to waste the precious gift of time on acrimony and division.'"

While House Speaker Newt Gingrich and the other Republicans present at Clinton's address dutifully applauded those fine sentiments, the president privately maintained few illusions about "repairing the breach" with his enemies. Since assuming office in January 1995, the Speaker had fulfilled his threat to mount an endless serial of investigations of the administration. Having been outmaneuvered and politically neutralized by Clinton ever since the government shutdown of 1995 had only deepened Gingrich's enmity. Like many in the Washington press corps, the congressional Republicans saw the president as fundamentally illegitimate, an ideological changeling who had stolen their strongest issues—welfare reform, crime control, a balanced budget—and made them his own. Gingrich had already begun to make good on a promise to seize the new opportunities presented by the campaign-finance scandals.

Less than a month after the inaugural festivities, however, Clinton and his supporters rejoiced in an astonishing announcement from the OIC. On February 17, Starr said he had tendered his resignation as independent counsel, effective August 1. He had accepted an unusual dual appointment at Pepperdine University—a conservative institution closely affiliated with the Church of Christ and beautifully situated on acres of Malibu oceanfront—as dean of both its law school and a new school of public policy.

This strange turn seemed even odder because, only a week earlier, the OIC had opened an aggressive new media campaign. First came an article in the *New Yorker* by James B. Stewart. Granted an audience with Jim McDougal, Stewart detailed the ailing rogue's new story: Contrary to his previous testimony, Bill Clinton had, indeed, attended a meeting at Castle Grande where the $300,000 Master Marketing loan to Susan was discussed. Like Hale, McDougal supplied no date, leaving the allegation impossible for Clinton to disprove. As told in Jim McDougal's book, *Arkansas Mischief,* the story differed in several particulars from Hale's rendition. Most significantly, McDougal said Clinton hadn't worn jogging attire but a business suit. Moreover, Clinton's solitary arrival in the dusk at a construction site outside Little Rock had come as a complete surprise to McDougal. To him it could mean just one thing: that Susan had asked Clinton to intervene on her behalf with Hale because the two had resumed their love affair. Only Susan had known that Jim was meeting Hale to discuss the loan.

Stewart reported that McDougal claimed to have discovered Clinton's affair with his wife in 1982, when he phoned her from out of town and was accidentally patched into a conversation while the two whispered suggestively. Even Stewart acknowledged the improbability of that scenario, which local telephone company officials described as technologically impossible. Stewart also traveled to California, where Susan was retrieved from solitary confinement in the Los Angeles County jail to meet her unexpected visitor. Having been shipped there to face the long-postponed charges brought by Nancy Mehta, Susan was being kept in lockdown twenty-three hours a day, ostensibly for her own safety. She was also required to wear a red uniform—marking her as a child molester or an informant—for the same reason. The OIC insisted that it had no control over the conditions of her incarceration. However, Stewart wrote, "After I decided to seek an interview with her, the office of Kenneth Starr was instrumental in arranging my visit."

Astonished that anybody would believe her desperate and mentally ill exhusband's tales, she told Stewart that she had never been intimate with Bill Clinton, although Jim had wanted her to be. After their own sexual relationship ended in the early eighties due to Jim's ill health, she said, he had often urged her to seduce others; it was, she believed, a symptom of his illness. Stewart also wrote that the OIC had told him about telephone records indicating that Susan had spoken with someone in the Arkansas governor's office in 1986 and 1987. (In *Blood Sport* he had reported Susan's efforts to persuade the Clintons to give up their Whitewater stock during that time.) The White House refused comment. Stewart made several TV appearances promoting his *New Yorker* article, bringing a touch of *Jerry Springer* to *Meet the Press.*

Two other important stories had appeared in the weeks before Starr's surprise resignation, both casting the OIC's probe in a more dubious light and neither receiving the publicity accorded to Stewart's. One was an account of a seven-hour interview with David Hale, conducted inside the Texarkana Federal Prison by Associated Press reporter Pete Yost. As with Stewart, Yost couldn't have gotten the interview without Starr's permission. Like much of his testimony in the Tucker-McDougal trial, Hale's stories were cast in classic con-man terms. His accusations against others invariably depended upon unverifiable hearsay conversations to which only he was a party. He told Yost, for example, of a supposedly incriminating telephone chat between himself and Hillary Clinton on an unspecified date.

Hale took his fabulizing a step too far, though, when he told Yost a story that OIC prosecutors had previously worked carefully to conceal. "Hale says some of his own records on the $300,000 loan that he says he was pressed to make by Clinton have disappeared—including a handwritten note by Jim McDougal suggesting that Clinton would help make good on the debt," Yost wrote.

" 'The file on the $300,000 loan was three to four inches thick when the FBI took it, but when my attorney and I asked to see it a month or so later, the U.S. Attorney's office gave us maybe an inch of stuff,' Hale says."

Few in the national press seemed aware of this rather shocking assertion by the OIC's star witness. By carefully omitting this allegation from Hale's FBI 302s, as well as from the scripted testimony he read to the grand jury, Starr's prosecutors had avoided any cross-examination about it at the Tucker-McDougal trial. Were Hale to testify against either of the Clintons, however, this accusation was sure to be explored. A parade of FBI agents and federal prosecutors would step forward to deny it, including agents still working for Starr. The odds against persuading a rational jury to believe David Hale had just increased by an order of magnitude.

What was potentially the most damaging blow to the OIC came in an almost unnoticed article in the *Arkansas Democrat-Gazette* on February 13—four days before Starr resigned. Written by veteran reporter Rodney Bowers, the story said that four mock juries, convened by outside consultants hired by the OIC, had returned innocent verdicts against Bill and Hillary Clinton. Us-

ing actors to impersonate the witnesses, Bowers wrote, the closest Starr's prosecutors had come to a conviction in mock trials held both in Little Rock and
Washington, D.C., was an 8–4 vote to acquit Hillary Clinton.

The disappointing results, wrote Bowers, "showed Starr and his attorneys
that they needed to 'fine-tune' their investigation." According to Bowers's
source, that meant interviewing Arkansas state troopers Roger Perry, Larry
Patterson, and L. D. Brown on a "'broad range of topics,' including alleged sexual encounters, drugs and money laundering, state purchases, meetings with
politicians and political favors." A state police source confirmed the trooper
interviews. Starr was less interested in Clinton's "alleged sexual escapades,"
Bowers's source told him, than in the purpose of his reputed late-night visits
to the Quapaw Towers apartment building in Little Rock, residence of Gennifer Flowers as well as several Clinton staffers and prominent state legislators.

Whether the mock trials actually took place was not certain. Starr's office
flatly denied it, and a week later Bowers's source told the newspaper's editors
that he had been mistaken. The *Democrat-Gazette* ran a retraction. *Washington
Post* media columnist Howard Kurtz sniped that the Arkansas paper's "Deep
Throat turned out to have shallow knowledge." Bowers himself privately believed that the OIC had simply pressured his source to recant.

Lost in the mock-jury dispute was the more significant news in Bowers's
story, which the OIC was unable to deny. Beginning late in 1996, Starr's investigation had veered off onto a new and gamy tangent. The *Democrat-Gazette*
confirmed what many Arkansas journalists had been hearing but had been unable to persuade anyone to confirm on the record. The OIC was calling in state
troopers and women whose names had been linked to Bill Clinton by rumor,
and questioning them about sex.

Much of this unpleasant work, moreover, was being done not by FBI
agents loaned to Starr's operation by the Justice Department, but by private investigators. Provided with business cards identifying them as agents of the
OIC, several were retired FBI agents who had worked with Hickman Ewing,
Jr., during his tenure as U.S. attorney in Memphis. Altogether, General Accounting Office records later showed, the OIC expended some $2.45 million
on private investigators between 1996 and 1999. Some of the expenditure
probably occurred in response to complaints from the special agent in charge
of the Little Rock FBI office that Starr had drained his office of manpower. But
one advantage of hiring private eyes answerable to Ewing rather than using career FBI agents on these assignments was obvious: he knew he could trust
them to do as he asked and keep quiet about it.

By calling in the troopers and tracking down sex rumors, the OIC was headed
toward what Clinton's most dedicated Arkansas enemies like Sheffield Nelson
and Larry Nichols always considered his greatest vulnerability. But what would

it mean for Starr's own reputation to follow the likes of Nichols down that well-trodden path?

That Kenneth Starr had a political "tin ear" even his closest friends conceded. Tactics such as parading Susan McDougal in chains before TV cameras had backfired badly. Yet Starr did seem keenly aware of the damage Whitewater had already done to his image as a fair and judicious man, particularly during the past year. He could scarcely give a speech without references to his own "civic virtue." Public criticism of Starr had grown almost continuously since March 1996, when *The Nation* magazine published an article by Joe Conason and Murray Waas revealing that Starr had investigated the same RTC officials who were negotiating the settlement of a million-dollar federal lawsuit against Kirkland & Ellis, his own law firm. Questions about Starr's partisanship and conflicts of interest in representing tobacco companies, right-wing foundations, and other Clinton adversaries were raised in scores of publications. On the very day that the Tucker-McDougal verdict was announced, Starr was in New Orleans, representing the Brown & Williamson tobacco company. The former Clinton campaign consultant James Carville's scorched-earth media crusade against Starr was succeeding, largely due to the independent counsel's own mistakes. To leave the OIC might mean preserving what remained of his good name.

The choking rage of conservatives at the news of Starr's resignation was best expressed by William Safire. In a February 20 column headlined "The Big Flinch," the *New York Times* columnist accused Starr, a man with "a warped view of duty," of fearing partisan attacks by Carville and of shirking his responsibility "just before the moment of prosecutorial decision." Heaping on the invective, Safire accused Starr of bringing "shame on the legal profession by walking out on his client—the people of the United States—leaving us alone at the courthouse door." Better that Starr should leave immediately, to be replaced by his chief deputy, Hickman Ewing, or even Robert Morgenthau, Manhattan's Democratic district attorney (and a very close friend of Robert Fiske, whose removal Safire had urged and then cheered).

Excitable and influential, the former Nixon speechwriter regularly filled his space on the op-ed page with ruminations about the Clintons' "cover-ups," "stonewalling," "conspiracy," and "obstruction of justice," forever echoing the terrible phrases that drove his old boss from the White House. Now, even as he denounced the "craven counsel" Starr, Safire again predicted the imminence of "stunning indictments" of Clintonites and "a series of detailed reports of wrongdoing" by them. "We can hope that Starr, having looked history in the eye and flinched, will get out of town and let someone else finish the job he misled the nation he was prepared to do," Safire concluded.

The *Times* editorial page was more forgiving than Safire if somewhat less consistent. Having strongly urged Starr to step down in an April 1996 lead Sunday editorial because of his conflicts of interest and appearance of partisan bias, the institutional voice of the *Times* now urged him to forsake Pepperdine and stay on to finish the job.

Safire's fury was understandable. Only two months earlier, *Newsweek* had featured Starr on its cover, hyping a profile of "The Most Dangerous Man in Washington." During an exclusive three-hour interview with Daniel Klaidman and Michael Isikoff, Starr had hinted at big things soon to come. "We are very far along," he had confided, leading Klaidman and Isikoff to suggest eagerly that "Starr . . . is promising to deliver." In fact, they added, "*Newsweek* has learned that within the next three months, he plans to decide whether to bring indictments that could very possibly alter the course of Bill Clinton's second term." This revelation was accompanied by a list of potentially criminal acts attributed to Bill and Hillary Clinton and their aides.

The only thing nobody leaked to *Newsweek* was Starr's plan to decamp for Malibu. Well before his interview with Isikoff and Klaidman, he had commenced discussions on that subject with David Davenport, the beachfront university's president. But how was *Newsweek* to know, when even Starr's best friends seemed unaware of his intentions? Ted Olson and former U.S. attorney Joseph diGenova, the OIC's most frequently quoted defenders, both professed total surprise. Olson, the author of those smirking, anonymous prophecies in the *Spectator,* sounded especially disheartened. Brushing off Starr's insistence that his departure implied nothing about the Clinton investigation, Olson told reporters: "If he was about to embark on a prosecution of historic proportions, then he wouldn't at the same time be planning on leaving."

The blast of anger at his resignation, from his own staff and deputies as well as from the likes of Safire, reportedly shocked Starr. He had assured Davenport there would be little fuss about the announcement. With both Safire and Carville mocking him as "a quitter," he began to realize that his reputation would be permanently stained by resigning. What came next only compounded Starr's predicament. Two days after he announced his resignation, the *Washington Post* reported that the single most generous donor to the Pepperdine School of Public Policy was the Sarah Scaife Foundation, which had given $1.35 million to establish the new school thanks to lifetime Pepperdine regent Richard Mellon Scaife.

The revelation of Scaife's connection with Pepperdine, and by extension with the university's new Dean Starr, gave fresh currency to some old suspicions. By a curious coincidence, the White House press office had been forced to defend itself against charges of "paranoia" about the conservative philanthropist only five weeks earlier. This minor Beltway controversy had been ignited by the reappearance in early January of a 332-page report on the anti-Clinton network of foundations and media outlets. First distributed quietly in 1995 to major news organizations, the report had been prepared by junior aides at the White House and the Democratic National Committee, and rather infelicitously titled "Communication Stream of Conspiracy Commerce." It documented the circulation of conspiratorial rumors concerning the Vince Foster case and Whitewater from right-wing activists and writers in the United States to conservative tabloids in England and then back into the mainstream American media.

Organizations and media outlets associated with Scaife figured heavily in the report. It also featured a 70-page section subtitled "Richard Mellon Scaife: The Wizard of Oz Behind the Foster Conspiracy Industry," which consisted mostly of clippings about him, his various enterprises, and his connections with Newt Gingrich.

There was nothing new in any of this—except that the *Wall Street Journal* editorial page and the *Washington Times,* both excoriated in the "Conspiracy Commerce" report, had learned of its existence from an inquiring freelance journalist. The two newspapers ran long, indignant articles and editorials about the document. Reporters then peppered presidential press secretary Mike McCurry with furious questions about the use of government funds to "target" Clinton critics. The contretemps put the White House on the defensive while renewing a sense of solidarity among mainstream reporters and their less reputable right-wing colleagues.

That righteous consensus was also reflected by another *Newsweek* cover story in early January about Paula Jones, in which assistant editor Evan Thomas offered his personal apology for having doubted her story three years earlier. Based largely upon a tendentious article by Stuart Taylor, Jr., in the *American Lawyer,* the *Newsweek* article, written by Michael Isikoff, was a new departure from the magazine's previously evenhanded coverage of the Jones case.

Specifically ignored was *Newsweek*'s own May 23, 1994, article interviewing people around the Arkansas state capitol who remembered Jones as a state employee and scoffed at her claims. Her former coworkers told *Newsweek* reporters that although Paula kept them entertained with detailed soap opera accounts of her love life, she had never mentioned her encounter with Clinton. Describing her as a "Dogpatch Madonna," that story portrayed Jones as an unreliable, self-dramatizing person who had made a pest of herself hanging around the reception desk outside the governor's office for months following the allegedly horrifying incident at the Excelsior Hotel, prattling like a starstruck teenager about Clinton's sex appeal and his hair. "I remember her because when she was there," former Clinton press aide Mike Gauldin said, "I had to listen to hours and hours of beauty shop inane conversation—she was a groupie."

Newsweek's shift helped ensure that other mainstream press outlets ignored her story's glaring inconsistencies. One of those many problems was the fact, later highlighted in James D. Retter's book *Anatomy of a Scandal,* that her initial legal pleading described her encounter with Clinton as taking place around 2:30 P.M. This time frame was consistent with her claim to have left the Excelsior Hotel in tears immediately afterward, as she'd stayed on duty until late afternoon, but conflicted with the fact that Clinton had given an 8:30 A.M. breakfast speech at the Excelsior that day and left the hotel not long afterward. An afternoon function at the governor's mansion precluded his return to the hotel that day. In Jones's later pleadings, the time of day was not explicitly mentioned.

To Stuart Taylor's credit, he wrote a second piece in *Legal Times* partially documenting how Jones's account of her adventure at the Excelsior had become steadily more lurid over time and had varied according to her audience. Jane Mayer of the *New Yorker* also did some careful reporting along the same lines. Most of the Washington press corps, however, followed *Newsweek*'s lead. The result was that a nuisance lawsuit funded and inspired by Clinton's political enemies, one that had little chance of prevailing on its merits, came to be seen as a grave threat to the president's political survival.

With Richard Mellon Scaife showing up as Starr's benefactor, albeit indirectly, the White House looked less paranoid, and the questions about Starr's partisanship became more salient. The same news organizations that had mocked the "Conspiracy Commerce" report in early January were consulting its section on Scaife by late February. Most accounts mentioned the same Scaife-funded groups that had promoted Foster murder theories: Accuracy in Media, the National Taxpayers Union, the Western Journalism Center, and Scaife's newspaper, the *Pittsburgh Tribune-Review.* Some noted Scaife's financial support of the *American Spectator*—but the Arkansas Project would remain secret for another year.

If Starr's resignation had looked bad, the uproar over Scaife looked worse, despite swift denials by Scaife and Pepperdine that the philanthropist had influenced the university's decision to hire Starr. Thus, four days after his initial announcement, the independent counsel hurriedly summoned reporters to his Washington office to hear him change his mind. "My commitment is to the American people and to the pursuit of the truth, and I will seek to fulfill that commitment to the best of my ability and for as long as it takes," he told them. "I deeply regret any action on my part that may have called that commitment into question." Pepperdine would have to wait. The investigation would continue, he vowed, "full speed ahead."

*   *   *

Just before the Jones case was argued before the Supreme Court in January, Joe Cammarata had received a peculiar telephone call in his office. The caller was a woman who insisted on remaining anonymous. She had seen Cammarata's name and photo in *Newsweek*. She told him that when she worked at the White House in 1993, she had suffered "a similar thing" to what had allegedly happened to his client Paula Jones.

As Cammarata took notes, the caller explained that she and her husband had raised money for Clinton in 1992. The following year she had worked in the White House, as a volunteer in the Social Office and then as a secretarial assistant in the Office of Legal Counsel. When her husband got into "legal trouble" that autumn, she had gone to see Clinton in the Oval Office to explain that she needed a permanent job. The president had taken her into a smaller office next door, where their meeting "got physical." Clinton, she said, had kissed her, felt her breasts, and placed her hand on his crotch. His advances had only stopped when an aide knocked on the office door.

The woman refused to give Cammarata her name, but she offered several clues about her identity: Her husband had killed himself with a revolver the day after her encounter with Clinton, and his name had later showed up on lists of "mysterious deaths" published by the president's right-wing critics, including a newsletter called the *Guarino Report*. She had worked in the White House counsel's office after the incident and had later traveled on two State Department junkets to Denmark and Indonesia. And she had told a friend who also worked in the White House about Clinton's groping of her on that day in November 1993.

Cammarata hadn't had the time or resources to pursue this tantalizing caller. He did nothing about it until a few days after the Supreme Court argument, when he received a casual phone call from Isikoff. After Cammarata mentioned his anonymous caller, the reporter perked up. He came by Cammarata's office the following day to get the details.

As he describes at length in his 1999 book *Uncovering Clinton,* Isikoff skillfully proceeded to trace the mystery woman by following the road map she had laid out for Cammarata. He looked up the name of her deceased husband in an old issue of the *Guarino Report.* Using Nexis searches and computer databases, he learned that the dead man, a lawyer named Edward Willey, Jr., had lived in Richmond, Virginia—and that he had shot himself not because of any connection with the president, but because he had been caught embezzling hundreds of thousands of dollars from a client. His widow showed up as a former White House employee in the *Federal Staff Directory* and still lived near Richmond. Her name was Kathleen.

At first Kathleen Willey seemed reluctant to talk when Isikoff contacted her. But in late March she agreed to tell her story at the Richmond office of her attorney, Daniel Gecker. The interview would remain off the record unless and until Willey permitted Isikoff to publish it. As he tells it, Isikoff found her "calm" and "convincing" as she explained that Clinton had started flirting with her back in 1992, when he had visited Richmond for a debate with George Bush and Ross Perot. Nancy Hernreich, a Little Rock campaign worker who later became one of the president's Oval Office aides, had gotten Willey's phone number after Clinton spotted her during an airport rally. They had only met once before, in 1991, but she and her husband had become strong Clinton supporters. On the afternoon before the debate, Clinton had called. He was obviously suffering from laryngitis, and asked Kathleen—flirtatiously, she thought—to bring him some chicken soup.

Though she said she had gotten "the drift" of Clinton's amorous intentions back then, she continued to back him enthusiastically. A few months after his first inauguration, she had joined the White House Social Office as one of many volunteers. According to Willey, she had maintained a friendly relationship with Clinton until the week after Thanksgiving, 1993. Distraught over her husband's growing legal and financial troubles, she had asked Hernreich for an appointment with the president, hoping to get his assistance in finding a permanent paid position in the White House. On the afternoon of November 29, Hernreich called her in and said she could see Clinton in the Oval Office.

After some small talk, Clinton had taken her back into a hideaway office and poured her a cup of coffee. She had explained her dire situation to him, burst into tears, and started to leave. Before she could exit, she said, he had grabbed her in a tight embrace and kissed her. Taken aback, Willey had asked, "Aren't you afraid there are people around here?"

She said she had tried to rebuff him, but he had just clung to her more tightly. "I've wanted to do this ever since the first time I laid eyes on you," she recalled him saying as his hands roamed over her hair and breasts, then up her skirt. Pressed by Isikoff, she also said he had placed her hand on his erect penis.

His alleged assault had ended as abruptly as it had begun, said Willey, when the president's personal assistant Andrew Friendly knocked on the door and called out, "Mr. President!" Fleeing through the Oval Office, Willey had noticed Treasury Secretary Lloyd Bentsen, budget director Leon Panetta, and Laura Tyson, chair of the Council of Economic Advisers, all waiting outside to meet with the president.

Asked by Isikoff whether anyone could corroborate her story, Willey said she had told two people that same day what had happened. One was Julie Hiatt Steele, a close personal friend who also lived in the Richmond area. The other was a former friend and White House colleague, to whom Willey had confided the shocking incident immediately. Her name was Linda Tripp, and the last Willey had heard, Tripp was working at the Pentagon.

*   *   *

During the spring of 1997, not long after Kenneth Starr renewed his commitment to the Office of Independent Counsel, the investigation of the president took yet another peculiar turn. On April 14, Starr appeared at the Little Rock federal courthouse for the sentencing of his latest key witness, Jim McDougal. Only a few days earlier, Hillary Rodham Clinton had made headlines on a call-in radio program in Washington by dismissing Whitewater as "a never-ending fictional conspiracy that honest-to-goodness reminds me of some people's obsession with UFOs."

Starr told Judge George Howard that McDougal had "truthfully and substantially aided" his investigators by providing information "which could only be known to a few insiders." While conceding that Hale's and McDougal's testimonies would be insufficient to bring charges against the president and first lady, *New York Times* reporter Stephen Labaton wrote that "all outward signs indicate that the investigation has moved into a higher orbit." A photograph of Starr arm in arm with a broadly grinning Jim McDougal dominated the *Times* front page the following day.

Starr's deputies continued to pressure both Webster Hubbell and Susan McDougal for damaging testimony about the Clintons. After serving a year at the federal prison camp in Cumberland, Maryland, Hubbell had been released to a halfway house in August 1996, where he had remained until completion of his twenty-one month sentence in February 1997. Although Starr could never prove it, he suspected that friends of Clinton, including Vernon Jordan, had arranged hundreds of thousands of dollars in legal fees as "hush money" payments to Hubbell between the time he resigned from the Justice Department in March 1994 and his indictment the following December.

Subpoenas flew out to the White House and to all the individuals and firms that had hired Hubbell. His friends and members of his family were repeatedly interviewed by FBI agents, all in a vain effort to elicit the incriminating information Starr believed Hubbell had withheld during many interrogations by the OIC prosecutors. He continued to insist that he knew of no wrongdoing by Bill or Hillary Clinton.

Exactly what it was Hubbell was supposed to be hiding remained unclear. Despite an accusatory *New York Times* editorial complaining that Hubbell "never cooperated with the Whitewater investigation," the fact was that he had answered questions posed by Starr's investigators repeatedly over a period of more than two years. He had made several appearances before Whitewater grand juries in Little Rock and Washington, and testified at several congressional hearings.

Susan McDougal's ordeal was far worse. Despite being encouraged to cooperate with the OIC by Isikoff, who personally vouched for an old friend on Starr's staff, and by ABC producer Chris Vlasto, Susan remained defiant. She believed that the independent counsel had everything to do with her California prosecution, and with her being incarcerated with drug dealers and murderers as well. Starr's willingness to publicize Jim McDougal's latest addition to his repertoire of stories—namely that Susan had engaged in an adulterous affair with Clinton during the Whitewater era—was for her the final indignity.

With Jim McDougal cast as repentant informer, the Whitewater story line was becoming increasingly baroque and hard to credit. By April 29, one important Republican could no longer pretend to believe it. Senator Alfonse D'Amato, up for reelection in 1998 with his approval ratings among his New York constituents having sunk into the mid-twenties, told reporters that Starr's investigation had "dragged on too long. . . . The American public has just grown sick and tired of it." Observing that Starr's flirtation with Pepperdine University had done tremendous harm to his credibility, "I don't have too much faith in the whole thing," D'Amato confessed. "People come up to me and say, 'Why are we still doing this?' It goes on and on and on. . . . It's become very politicized. People don't have any great confidence in it."

Starr's response to his critics came in the form of an extraordinary profile in the June 1 edition of the *New York Times Magazine.* Depicting the independent counsel in familiar terms as a "deeply religious man . . . who reads the Bible every morning," author Jeffrey Rosen ran down an equally familiar laundry list of Whitewater allegations, including the mythical "$50,000 benefit" to the Clintons' investment from the Master Marketing loan and suspicions that Hillary Clinton had hidden her billing records, plus the newer insinuation that Susan McDougal was covering for Bill Clinton. "I'm not sure she has publicly said he testified truthfully," said OIC spokesman John Bates.

Illustrated by a dramatic black-and-white photograph of Starr, Bates, Hickman Ewing, and Jackie Bennett scowling fiercely into the camera, Rosen's article outlined a series of Whitewater "victims," including the Clintons and "taxpayers, who have paid more than $28 million to finance the investigation of a $300,000 loan." But Whitewater's most "sympathetic person," Rosen suggested, might be "Kenneth Starr himself, who, after setting up a professional team of prosecutors, tried to move on, only to find he could disentangle himself no more easily than his targets."

In an angry letter he released to the press, Clinton lawyer David Kendall protested that "grand jury secrecy rules are aimed at preventing precisely this kind of leak-and-smear damage. . . . What conceivable right do representatives of the [OIC] have to speculate like this?"

*   *   *

The *Washington Post*'s discovery of Starr's sudden, intense interest in all of Clinton's alleged ex-girlfriends put the OIC's tactics under a national spotlight. A June 25 front-page story by Bob Woodward and Susan Schmidt reported that eight current and former Arkansas state troopers from Clinton's old security detail had been summoned to interviews at the Office of Independent Counsel between March and June 1997. Roger Perry and Ronnie Anderson, two of the troopers who had been sources for David Brock's "Troopergate" story in 1993, told the *Post* they had been interrogated by FBI agents and prosecutors about Clinton's personal affairs. Some had been interviewed before, but only about Whitewater. "This last time, I was left with the impression that they wanted to show he was a womanizer," said Perry. "All they wanted to talk about was women." Perry said he had been asked whether "I had ever seen Bill Clinton perform a sexual act. The answer is no."

Anderson had refused to answer the independent counsel's questions about Clinton's alleged extramarital liaisons. "I said, 'If he's done something illegal, I will tell you. But I'm not going to answer a question about women that he knew because I just don't feel like it's anybody's business.'" Both troopers claimed that Starr's investigators had showed them a list of women's names and asked whether Clinton had been involved in affairs with any of them. Perry, who had been one of Brock's two named sources, identified "seven or eight" names of women whom he or other troopers had taken Clinton to meet when the governor's wife was away or asleep. The investigators asked whether one of the women on the list had given birth to Clinton's illegitimate child, and "whether the child looked like Clinton."

Inevitably, the name of Gennifer Flowers had come up, according to Anderson. Perry said he had been questioned about Susan McDougal. And, he added, "They asked me about Paula Jones, all kinds of questions about Paula Jones, whether I saw Clinton and Paula together and how many times."

Remarkably, one of Starr's top aides confirmed the new area of investigation. Deputy independent counsel John Bates termed the questions "perfectly appropriate" to establish the relationship between an investigative target and a possible witness. "We are continuing to gather relevant facts from whatever witnesses, male or female, who may be available. Our obligation is to acquire information from friends, business associates, or other acquaintances or confidants." An unnamed source "familiar with the investigation" elaborated on this point. The investigators were seeking out people who were close to Clinton during his years as governor, hoping to find a friend or lover in whom he might have confided secrets about Whitewater or Madison Guaranty. In that vein, they had also interviewed several of the women on their list. The source didn't explain how Paula Jones, who claimed to have met Clinton one time in a hotel room, would possess any knowledge about his business dealings with the McDougals.

*   *   *

On May 24, four weeks before the *Post* article about the troopers appeared, Bill Clinton finally put an end to his fitful adolescent sexual trysts with Monica Lewinsky. Aside from whatever feelings of guilt plagued him, he had grown wary of the former intern, having learned that he had good reason for concern about her discretion. Walter Kaye, the insurance executive and Democratic contributor who had placed Lewinsky in the White House, had heard rumors about the affair and mentioned it to someone on the president's personal staff. This unwelcome news had reached Clinton.

At a meeting in the Oval Office, he tried to soften the rejection in the usual manner, telling Monica he hoped they could remain friends and that he could do much to help her. These bromides gave little comfort to the infatuated Lewinsky, who later referred to the date as "Dump Day."

Clinton's attempt to distance himself from his young girlfriend was futile anyway. Too many people already knew abut his brainless behavior with the intern. And three days after Dump Day, the Supreme Court awarded his most implacable adversaries a license to hunt down every sexual sin Clinton had ever committed.

In a unanimous opinion handed down on May 27, 1997, the nine justices ruled that the president enjoyed no immunity, even temporarily during his term of office, from a civil lawsuit. The matter of *Jones v. Clinton* was immediately remanded to the federal district court in Little Rock, where Judge Wright would schedule the next phase of the proceedings, known in legal parlance as "discovery." With what would come to seem extraordinary naïveté, the high court urged the judge to take care to conduct the proceedings with maximum concern for the dignity of the presidency.

Chapter Fourteen

SPINNING
THE WIDOW'S WEB

AFTER FIVE YEARS INVESTIGATING Bill Clinton's private life and three years on the Paula Jones case, Michael Isikoff faced a frustrating problem in the spring of 1997. The indefatigable *Newsweek* reporter believed that Clinton had harassed Jones and had made crude, unwelcome sexual overtures to other women, perhaps many other women. Indeed, he had come to regard Clinton as a dangerously pathological personality, whose secret misbehavior and public lying had infected his entire career and needed to be exposed.

But the few women who had spoken to Isikoff about encounters with Clinton refused to go on the record or couldn't corroborate their accusations; at least one of them would remain entirely anonymous; and in any case, most of the alleged events had taken place before Clinton became president. At one point, Isikoff had gone so far as to pass a few names along to David Brock over drinks at a Washington hotel, hoping that they might appear in the *American Spectator* if nowhere else. It might be a nasty job, but someone had to do it somewhere.

Now the discovery of Kathleen Willey promised to break that dismal pattern. What she had said about Clinton forcing himself on her in the White House went beyond anything the reporter had heard before in several respects. The pretty, upper-middle-class widow from Virginia was no right-winger. She had been a dedicated Clinton supporter, giving enough money and time to his campaigns to attain a position in the White House. Most significantly, the incident she described had taken place in the office of the president. And it seemed quite possible that sooner or later, she would be called as a witness in the Paula

Jones case—since Isikoff had gotten the tip about Willey, although not her name, from Jones lawyer Joe Cammarata.

At their first formal interview on March 19, conducted in the Richmond, Virginia, office of her lawyer, Daniel Gecker, Willey wasn't prepared to go on the record with Isikoff. Yet although Gecker assured him that she would never confirm her story publicly, there was still more than a hint that she might eventually do so.

At the very least, Willey seemed to want Isikoff to pursue her allegations. She had provided him with the names of two "contemporaneous corroborative witnesses," friends with whom she said she had discussed the Oval Office incident shortly after it had occurred. She was so eager to help, in fact, that she arranged for Isikoff to meet one of the witnesses immediately, so that he could avoid another long trip down from Washington. From Gecker's office Willey called Julie Hiatt Steele, a longtime friend who also lived near Richmond, and asked whether Steele could meet with Isikoff right away.

When Isikoff reached Steele's suburban home later that afternoon, he found a cordial, talkative divorcée in her early fifties, with curly blond hair and a six-year-old son. According to Isikoff, Steele "had quite a bit to say" about the events of November 29, 1993. She told him that Willey had showed up at her house unexpectedly that evening, terribly distressed about the disappearance of Ed Willey the day before, and stunned by Clinton's groping assault that afternoon. Willey "told me he had his hands up her skirt, in her hair, on her breasts, all over her," Steele is quoted recalling in *Uncovering Clinton*. Isikoff's account also quotes Steele recalling that Willey "was humiliated, scared, embarrassed and in major disbelief. I said to her, 'You're kidding.' I couldn't believe it." Steele has sworn an affidavit saying she never said that to Isikoff.

The morning after the alleged incident with Clinton, Willey learned that her husband was dead. The police had found his Isuzu Trooper deep in the woods with his body nearby, dead from a self-inflicted bullet wound. Within days Willey had fallen into a state of mental and emotional breakdown, Steele told Isikoff, and Steele had been forced to place her friend in a hospital for care. Steele had done so, but insists she never told Isikoff.

Isikoff later wrote that he drove home from Richmond that day somewhat perplexed. Although Julie Steele had "basically confirmed Willey's version of events," as promised, he was troubled during the hourlong interview by "her vagueness about some details." He considered the news about Willey's hospitalization slightly disturbing, too. Steele and her attorney say that Isikoff's accounts are largely fiction. In a lawsuit against him and *Newsweek,* she states that the reporter never pressed "for details about her independent recollection of Willey's story and Willey's reaction at the time." Instead, she charged, Isikoff asked her "leading questions," using an "interview technique [that] made it easy for Ms. Steele to hide the fact that she had no independent knowledge or awareness" of the 1993 incident. In fact, Steele insisted, she had first heard about the alleged sexual assault from Willey on the telephone only minutes before Isikoff arrived on her doorstep. But she didn't mention that Willey had asked her to lie until Isikoff called her again, four months later.

Back in Washington, the resourceful, well-connected journalist soon located a document that confirmed part of Willey's story. She had told Isikoff that waiting outside the Oval Office as she fled the groping president were the members of the National Economic Council: Lloyd Bentsen, then the treasury secretary; budget director Leon Panetta; and economic adviser Laura Tyson. From an old source, Isikoff learned that the retired Bentsen had donated his government papers to a library at the University of Texas in Austin. Several calls later, he reached a diligent archivist who agreed to check Bentsen's old calendar. It showed a 3 P.M. meeting with Clinton in the Cabinet Room on November 29, 1993, matching Willey's account almost to the minute.

Encouraged by that piece of hard evidence, Isikoff began looking for the second "corroborative" witness, Linda Tripp. She and Willey were no longer in touch; Willey only knew that when Tripp had left the White House staff three years earlier, she had moved to a job in the Pentagon. On March 24, accompanied by *Newsweek*'s defense correspondent, Isikoff wandered through the corridors of the enormous military complex until they found someone who knew Tripp and directed them to the basement. There, in the offices of the Joint Civilian Orientation Conference, Isikoff found a "somewhat annoyed-looking, heavy-set woman with disheveled hair."

When Kathleen Willey had first mentioned Linda Tripp, Isikoff had remembered hearing her name during the Whitewater hearings a couple of years earlier. In 1995 the Senate Whitewater committee called Tripp to testify about the Foster suicide and its aftermath because she had worked as a secretary to White House counsel Bernard Nussbaum at the time. She had a way of turning up wherever the Clintons had trouble.

As she recalled dramatically in her public testimony, she was the last person at the White House to see Foster alive in his office on the afternoon he shot himself. (A Secret Service agent may have seen him later in the parking lot as he left.) She dropped a few hints about her own doubts regarding the circumstances of Foster's death, saying she had observed him removing onions from a hamburger he ate for lunch that day, and she wondered why he would worry about his breath if he were planning to kill himself. (It apparently didn't occur to her that he just didn't like onions.) She noted also that the usually fastidious Foster hadn't taken his briefcase with him. And he had told her on the way out, "I'll be back."

Before appearing at the committee's public hearings, Tripp had given confidential depositions on three afternoons in July to the Whitewater committee's Republican and Democratic lawyers. Behind closed doors in the Dirksen Senate Office Building, she had recalled that Foster "seemed to spend an inordinate amount of time being the President's and the First Lady's personal attorney as opposed to what I perceived the role [of White House lawyers] had historically been." She had even asked Nussbaum about that. At one point, she told the committee lawyers, she became aware that Foster had been working on "private real estate matters" for the Clintons, although that information had been kept "exclusive to certain individuals who had a need to know."

Evidently Tripp had her own need to know everything she could find out about the president and first lady. The only work she had ever done for Foster, she testified, was when she had volunteered "to make photocopies of the Clintons' tax returns" in 1994. Foster's own secretary had been very busy, and Tripp had stepped forward helpfully to lighten her load.

In fact the divorced Tripp, then forty-three, had a reputation as a snoop and busybody, and if Clinton's aides had examined her background carefully they might have worried about her far sooner than they did. Her federal civil service career had begun in the military, after she married an army officer named Bruce Tripp. Following him around from one base to another as a secretary, she gradually moved into higher pay grades and more responsible positions. For more than two years she served as personal assistant to a major general at the headquarters of the Allied Forces for Central Europe, which according to her résumé required a "top secret security clearance due to the preponderance of highly classified and sensitive material involved."

In 1987 she was a secretarial assistant in army intelligence at Fort Meade, Maryland. A year later she transferred to the operations group of the Army Intelligence Command based at the Pentagon, where she "prepared and maintained intelligence case dossiers," served as liaison with the FBI and other federal agencies, and again had access to exceptionally sensitive data. Toward the end of 1988, her husband took command of the Signal Corps Battalion at Fort Bragg, North Carolina, where Linda Tripp became the secretary to the deputy chief of staff for personnel of the special operations unit. The Green Berets are based there, as is the supersecret Delta Force special operations unit. In 1989, Tripp was "handpicked to fill a position with the Delta Force," meaning a job as personal assistant to the chief of the security operations training facility.

By the summer of 1990, her twenty-year marriage to Bruce Tripp was falling apart. Both had been reassigned to the Pentagon again, she as an office manager for yet another high-ranking army official. An old friend working in the Bush White House suggested that Tripp take a job as a "floater" there, and she transferred over in April 1991. Given her background in military intelligence, she must have seemed an excellent prospect to serve under a president who had once been director of the CIA. Whoever decided to hire Linda Tripp probably thought that a secretary cleared to handle highly classified documents would be able to keep the president's secrets.

Assigned to the Office of Media Affairs as the Bush staff prepared for the 1992 presidential campaign, Tripp loved her new job. She edged even closer to the center of power when she was named executive assistant to Robert Zoellick, then Bush's deputy chief of staff. There she stayed until Election Day.

In the wake of Bush's defeat, Tripp took a few weeks off before returning to face the incoming Democrats. She liked the Bushes and had dedicated herself to the reelection effort. "During the Bush '92 campaign I had been working, as most people in the West Wing had, from seven in the morning till midnight during the entire campaign, six and sometimes seven days a week." When she came back she was "refreshed, ready to face a new administration and welcome them." Before long, she heard that she had been "name-requested" by the president to work in his immediate office area. "Someone on the [Bush] transition team had recommended me to them." For the first three chaotic months of the Clinton Administration, Tripp helped out around the Oval Office, getting to know Bruce Lindsey, Nancy Hernreich, and other top presidential aides. Better than her novice employers, she understood how to get things done, like getting the White House telephone system to function properly. Hoping to keep her job despite her dislike of the Clintons and their entourage, Tripp made herself indispensable. After a few months she was offered a permanent secretarial job by Bernie Nussbaum, who believed that her institutional knowledge would prove useful.

As Linda Tripp told the Senate Whitewater committee counsel about her recollections of the White House counsel's office, she could not entirely conceal the bitterness she still felt. She seemed to go out of her way to accuse a former coworker of suffering from "a drinking problem," and added that this same woman had been kept on the White House staff despite obvious incompetence. Another "low-level, very low-level staffer" kept on in the White House had been given "more responsibility of which I'm not certain she is capable." Tripp claimed to revere her boss Nussbaum—but then an E-mail message turned up in which she referred to him and two colleagues as "the Three Stooges." More than a year after leaving the White House, Tripp still resented her exile from the epicenter of Washington power and gossip. That experience had hardened her feelings toward the Clintons, but then she had never like them much.

The most intriguing exchange in her Whitewater deposition came on the afternoon of July 12. Minutes before Tripp was dismissed, Democratic counsel Lance Cole very briefly opened a new line of inquiry. He asked Tripp whether she had "granted any interviews" about Whitewater, Vince Foster, or her experiences in the White House counsel's office to anyone in the press.

"No," Tripp replied. It was a deceptive answer, though Cole had no way of knowing that. Years later, Tripp conceded that in March 1994 she had leaked news of Webster Hubbell's resignation from the Justice Department to the media.

"Does the word 'Deepwater' mean anything to you?" he continued.

"You know, I've heard it," said Tripp. "But I don't know if I've heard it in a song. So, I don't know how to answer that."

"So you don't know," Cole asked, "if anyone has ever referred to you as 'Deepwater'?"

"Good Lord," she exclaimed. "You are serious? This is a question?"

"It's a serious question, yes."

"Absolutely not. And, I guess I'm shocked."

"Have you ever heard of something called the Center for American Values?"

"No."

"And so, you've never provided information about this matter to—"

"No," she answered, evidently miffed.

"I'm just asking the questions," Cole said innocuously. "I'm not implying what the answer may be. But if I don't ask the questions, I don't know the answers."

There the odd questions ended as abruptly as they had begun. Robert Giuffra, the Republican counsel, thanked Tripp for her time, and she was excused. She didn't ask Cole what "Deepwater" and the Center for American Values were, or what he thought they might have to do with her.

Clearly, the Democratic counsel suspected that Tripp might indeed be "Deepwater"—the code name used for "an inside White House source" interviewed by Deborah Stone and Christopher Manion in their 1994 book *Slick Willie II: Why America Still Cannot Trust Bill Clinton.* This was of course the same Deborah Stone who, in partnership with Floyd Brown and David Bossie, had published the original scurrilous paperback *Slick Willie* in 1992. By 1994, Stone was still operating Annapolis-Washington Book Publishers as well as a nonprofit called the Center for American Values, described as "a grass-roots group committed to truth and fairness in government and the media."

Although relegated to an appendix, the "exclusive" interview with Deepwater was the most sensational feature of what was otherwise a rather dull collection of previously published negative material about Waco, Vince Foster, Travelgate, Whitewater, health-care reform, and assorted conservative complaints. "For the first time, an inside White House source describes an administration amok," the paperback's cover blurbed, with a quote from Deepwater saying, "I question the authenticity of the [Foster suicide] note."

Inside, the authors explain that in March and April 1994 they conducted interviews with Deepwater, who had to remain behind a scrim of anonymity "to ensure job and personal security." By the time *Slick Willie II* was published that May, any knowledgeable person who read the remarks of Deepwater would have had reason to suspect that Linda Tripp was the anonymous insider. Whoever hid behind that code name possessed intimate knowledge of the White House counsel's office and its personnel. Under Nussbaum and Foster only four people worked there, and only one was ever considered disloyal.

Deepwater recounted conversations with Foster's former executive assistant, Betsy Pond, and had apparently witnessed various events that only someone with regular access to that office could have seen. Many of the themes in the Deepwater interview—the supposed immorality and sloppiness of the Clinton White House, the suspicious aftermath of the Foster suicide, the cuts in White House personnel—mirrored the concerns expressed repeatedly by Tripp after her name became a household epithet.

At one point Deepwater remarked, "I know a lot about Travelgate, but let's save that." Tripp has claimed extensive knowledge about the Travel Office case since her national debut, both publicly and privately. She has gone so far as to say on national television that she witnessed "potentially criminal activity on a daily basis" in the White House. (In an FBI interview in January 1998, she complained that the OIC prosecutors presenting information about the Travel Office to a Washington grand jury in 1996 had failed to ask her "the proper questions" about relevant documents in the counsel's office.)

Deborah Stone reused portions of the Deepwater interview in 1995, when the Center for American Values published a pamphlet called *Why Did Vincent Foster Die?* Three years later, Stone (by then an associate producer at ABC News) told a reporter for the *Wall Street Journal* that she "did not recall" whether she had interviewed Tripp. Through her lawyer, Tripp denied to the *Journal* that she was Deepwater. But her conservative fans at the *Washington Weekly,* which marketed both *Slick Willie* volumes for Stone, weren't persuaded. "It now seems exceedingly likely," they editorialized, "that Linda Tripp is in fact the 'Deep Water' source interviewed in 1994 by Deborah J. Stone and Christopher Manion . . . even though she has denied it."

Aside from Tripp there were few others in the White House who knew as much about the counsel's office as Deepwater did. One was Gary Aldrich, an FBI agent who served in White House security from 1990 to 1995, then retired and wrote a sensationalized, fantastically exaggerated memoir titled *Unlimited Access* for Regnery Publishing. Subsidized by Scaife through the Southeastern Legal Foundation, his book caused a stir in 1996 over its repetition of a false rumor about Clinton slipping out for late-night trysts at the Washington Marriott Hotel.

Aldrich, who eventually joined the religious right's Council for National Policy, was a hard-line twenty-five-year FBI veteran and faithfully reflected the worldview of the late J. Edgar Hoover. His White House responsibilities included frequent contact with the counsel's office, where he became a close confidant of Tripp. In those days they regularly shared horror stories about the behavior of the Clintons and their staff.

Both Tripp and Aldrich belonged to a tiny, informal cabal of anti-Clinton White House staffers held over from the Bush administration. For a short time that disgruntled group included Phil Larson, longtime director of civil service personnel, until he quit in 1993. Larson immediately joined the Republican minority staff of the House Government Operations Committee as an investigator, but remained in touch with Aldrich. Tripp has testified that she secretly spoke with Larson in 1994 about her observations concerning the Travel Office firings and the alleged misuse of FBI files—both of which became topics of investigation by the House committee after the Republicans took control of Congress in 1995. According to David Brock, it was Aldrich who introduced Tripp to Larson.

Tripp was also communicating regularly during that period with Tony Snow, a conservative columnist and Fox News television host. They had become friendly soon after Tripp first joined the White House Staff and was assigned to the Office of Media Affairs, where Snow then worked as a speechwriter and as the president's deputy assistant for media relations. (Prior to accepting his own government post, Snow had been the editorial page editor of the *Washington Times*.) He and Tripp remained close after Snow returned to the private sector and began appearing as a regular substitute host for the Rush Limbaugh radio program. About once a month, she would call him to complain about her new Democratic bosses.

"I discussed some of my observations with Tony Snow during the time that I was still on the White House staff, in confidence," she later testified. "I was free to say to Tony things like, 'Oh, you won't believe what's going on in here. I can't take it.'" She fed Snow so much salacious gossip that he was soon urging her to write a tell-all book. She was unreceptive at first. "No, it's ridiculous. Who'd read it?" But by early 1995 Tripp had begun to change her mind. It was Snow who arranged her first contact with another of his friends, the conservative literary agent Lucianne Goldberg.

Tripp's superiors in the Clinton White House weren't aware of the hostile milieu in which she was privately immersed. During her tenure there, and long afterward, she maintained a self-protective facade of loyalty. She "kept working and kept quiet" and "took great care to conceal her attitude" toward the administration, as Gary Aldrich explained much later.

Her dissembling wasn't entirely effective, however. White House officials were increasingly troubled by rumors that Tripp had leaked negative information to the press. More than rumors, there were "repeated complaints" to the White House ethics office by colleagues about Tripp's leaking. "We had had some experience with her when she was in the Counsel's Office," Lindsey testified, "in which we believed . . . that she was talking to members of the press around the time that Bernie Nussbaum was leaving." Although Tripp would portray herself as an upright and trustworthy employee even after all her machinations against Clinton came to light, she finally admitted to federal agents that she had been a White House media source. She confessed that during the weekend before Webster Hubbell officially quit as assistant attorney general in March 1994, she had leaked word of his impending resignation to contacts in the press. She also said that was the only time she had done such a thing.

Just how duplicitous Tripp could be is illustrated by her attempt—around the same time she admittedly put out the word about Hubbell's resignation—to convince Lloyd Cutler, who succeeded Nussbaum as White House counsel in April 1994, that he should keep her on as one of his executive assistants. Cutler, a sophisticated insider who had also served as counsel to President Carter, met with Tripp at his Washington law office before he even began work at the White House. She had taken it upon herself to visit him, along with her friend Kathleen Willey, to propose that he hire both of them.

From early in 1993, Willey had been volunteering in the White House Social Office. She had struck up a friendship with Tripp, who conceived the notion in the spring of 1994 that together they should ask for jobs with Cutler. He initially agreed to keep Tripp on, and she continued to lobby him on behalf of Willey. "And he was agreeable to all this and warm and friendly," Tripp later said of Cutler, "and then all of a sudden it stopped. It just came to a complete stop." A month after Tripp began working for Cutler, she was essentially fired. Joel Klein, the deputy counsel who had replaced Vince Foster, called her into his office and told her, "There's just no role for you here right now." Klein offered no further explanation. It may not have been entirely coincidental, however, that the suspected leaker was told to find a new job in May 1994—the same month that *Slick Willie II* appeared with the Deepwater interview.

Klein suggested that she try returning to the Correspondence Office, where she had worked before as a floater. But Marsha Scott, the old Clinton friend who was then in charge of correspondence, said she could only offer a position at a much lower salary; she obviously didn't want Tripp in her shop either. For the next several weeks, the unemployed secretary was given a desk in the Old Executive Office Building next door, to work on her résumé and look for posts in other agencies. So eager was the Clinton administration to remove Tripp from the executive mansion that presidential aide Bruce Lindsey, deputy chief of staff Philip Lader, and Jim King, the director of the Office of Personnel Management, all assisted her job search. For top officials to get involved in such a trivial matter was extraordinary. By August, Lindsey and Lader had arranged her new assignment at the Defense Department, just as she had requested. That was how Tripp ended up as deputy director of the Pentagon's Joint Civilian Orientation Conference, arranging VIP tours of defense facilities and earning almost $70,000 a year, an increase of $20,000. No longer a mere secretary, Tripp was in line for promotion to JCOC director and another large raise.

Yet Tripp was anything but grateful for her enhanced status and income. Her unceremonious removal from the White House, the pinnacle of her climb through the civil service, was rankling. What infuriated Tripp still more was that in the meantime, Cutler had decided to hire Willey as an assistant in the counsel's office. The Richmond widow was attractive and poised but disorganized; she plainly possessed none of Tripp's skills or effectiveness. But Willey had caught the president's eye and possibly more, as Tripp knew to her disgust. Jealous and hurt, she blamed Willey for her own dismissal. The women's once intimate friendship ended in angry recriminations as Tripp prepared to leave the White House. Her last day ended with a loud warning to Willey: "I will get you if it's the last thing I do."

Tripp's recollection of her initial meeting with Michael Isikoff is somewhat different from his. They both remember going out to a courtyard so they wouldn't be overheard, while Tripp smoked a cigarette. In *Uncovering Clinton,* Isikoff writes that he then told Tripp he wanted to talk about Kathleen Willey "and a meeting she was supposed to have had with the President on November 29, 1993." He refused to answer when Tripp uneasily asked what Willey had told him. "I didn't want to color her comments if I could help it. What I really wanted to know, I said, is what she told you." Tripp declined to speak with him at all until after she had a chance to talk to Willey, he recalls.

But according to Tripp's testimony to the Starr grand jury, the reporter told her: "I am doing a story which I intend to publish either this week or next about a case of sexual harassment alleged by Kathleen Willey on the part of the President of the United States." Tripp was dumbfounded, she told the grand jurors. "And she has named you," Isikoff continued, "as a contemporaneous corroborative witness who can verify everything she says." Tripp said she shot back, "That is absolutely completely inaccurate." Actually, Tripp admitted under oath, Isikoff was right about everything—except for "Kathleen's state of mind at the time." But she told him again, "That's all completely inaccurate and I'm not talking to you."

That day or the next, Tripp told Monica Lewinsky, likewise exiled to the Pentagon, about the visit from Isikoff. As Lewinsky later testified, she urged her friend to alert the White House about the reporter's inquiries. Over the next several days, Tripp called Bruce Lindsey's office, asked his secretary to page him, and sent him messages via electronic mail. Without naming names or mentioning the subject, she warned Lindsey that she needed to discuss "an urgent matter of potential national media significance." Lindsey, who no longer trusted Tripp, didn't call back, and Lewinsky observed that Tripp seemed "deflated" and "insulted" by the presidential adviser's implicit rejection.

When she got home on the evening of Isikoff's visit, Tripp called Willey for the first time in almost three years and bluntly accused her of lying to the *Newsweek* reporter. "Kathleen, what are you doing?"

Without a hint of doubt, Tripp recalled, Willey coolly rebuffed Tripp's objections. "You must be misremembering, Linda. . . . Of course it was sexual harassment. I don't know why you're now saying that I wanted it."

"Kathleen, because we talked about it for months before it happened, because you chose your outfits, because you positioned yourself, because you flirted, because you looked for every reason to get in [to see Clinton privately]," Tripp remembered saying, when she described their conversation later. "Why are you now saying that this came as a huge surprise and he assaulted you?"

As Tripp testified in vivid detail, Willey's sudden claims of indignation didn't remotely resemble the truth about her feelings toward Clinton in 1993. Not only had she been "happy" after the president's allegedly feverish embrace in the Oval Office, but she and Tripp had been scheming together for months to stage her seduction of him. Tripp claimed her marriage to Ed Willey was loveless, on the verge of divorce. She wanted to move to Washington and have an affair with Clinton. "Kathleen [felt] that it had the potential to be a relationship that would be agreeable to the two of them." (Tripp's portrait of Willey was corroborated in sworn testimony by Harolyn Cardozo, another friend of Willey's and wife of Michael Cardozo, a Washington attorney and the former director of the President's Legal Expense Trust. Cardozo recalled Willey boasting that she might become "the next Judith Exner" [one of President Kennedy's mistresses] and pondering how to advance the relationship. "We've got to get Hillary out of town!" Cardozo recalled her saying, only half in jest.)

Well before the Oval Office incident, Willey had taken Tripp on as her secret romantic adviser, calling to chat in the evenings about her obsession with the president. Tripp admittedly encouraged the infatuation, because in her view both Clinton and Willey were stuck "in not very good marriages, and it just seemed to be as consenting adults." She also enjoyed the intrigue, helping Willey gain access to the president's daily schedule so the pretty matron could arrange to bump into him, always dolled up "to catch his eye." The two friends would talk about creating the conditions for a tryst, escaping the Secret Service, and "the logistics of how this could work," Tripp testified. They had even discussed a specific location. Debbie Siebert, a mutual friend whose husband had been named ambassador to Sweden, had quite innocently invited Willey to use their empty house on the water in Annapolis. Tripp thought that would be just perfect.

After she had finally met with Clinton alone in the Oval Office, Willey had hurried to find Tripp, and met her coming upstairs in an elevator. Right away Tripp noticed her usually immaculate friend's red face, bare lips, and mussed hair. "Do you have a lipstick? Come down with me." Flushed and breathless, Willey dragged her outside to a parking lot and told her about Clinton's ardent, "forceful" embrace in graphic terms. Willey praised him, Tripp recalled, as "a great kisser," and said she had kissed him back despite her fear that someone would walk in on them.

The next day, Willey learned that her husband was dead. To Tripp, however, she seemed oddly disengaged in the aftermath of his suicide, even from the practicalities of arranging his funeral. She "didn't cry, she didn't dwell or even speak much about Ed," according to the testimony of Tripp, who spoke with her frequently around that time. Instead, Kathleen talked "almost obsessively" about her encounter with the president. Willey worried that her late husband's suicide "would be enough to spook [Clinton] for at least a year, that . . . he would not have anything to do with her on a personal level after this because of the tragedy.

"And I remember she received a call from Nancy Hernreich saying that the President wanted to call at an appropriate time to extend his condolences, and Kathleen called back because she apparently had had people at the house helping her and left a message [for the president]: 'You can call anytime.'"

But as she and Tripp argued over the telephone many months later, Willey kept insisting that Clinton had subjected her to an unwanted mauling. And to Tripp's astonishment, she ultimately realized that Willey "believed everything she was telling me that night." Willey also confided that what she had really wanted from Clinton was lucrative employment. And although Tripp didn't realize it that night, Willey's financial desperation was an important clue to her behavior.

Her late husband's Richmond law practice had provided what prosecutors often call a "big lifestyle": designer clothes, luxury sports cars, first-class travel, exciting political and social events, and the leisure to enjoy it all. As major donors and fund-raisers, they had cultivated close relationships with top Democratic officials; that was how they had met Clinton in 1991. Unfortunately Ed Willey, the well-liked and outwardly successful son of an influential state legislator, was quite the opposite of what he seemed. On an evening a few days before he killed himself, he had sat down with Kathleen and confessed embezzling nearly $250,000 from two clients, a brother and sister named Anthony Lanasa and Josephine Abbott. The defrauded clients had discovered his thefts, and that night he had prevailed upon Kathleen to cosign a note promising to repay the money by November 30. He left his widow to fend off the litigation that ensued when Lanasa and Abbott moved to recoup their losses. His total debt the day he died was nearly $1 million.

The job in the White House counsel's office that had ruptured Willey's friendship with Tripp ended less than a year later. After being laid off in 1995 Willey had importuned Clinton and his aides for two years, by mail and phone, to find her another position. She boldly requested an ambassadorship but would gladly have signed on as a paid campaign fund-raiser. While all her chatty notes had been answered quite cordially by the president himself, she had gotten nothing but a couple of nonpaying junkets to Europe and the South Pacific and an honorary post with the USO. Early in 1996 she was offered a fund-raising job with Clinton-Gore '96, only to turn it down because the $30,000 salary was too low. That July, she wrote an angry letter to Nancy Hernreich about her employment travails and Clinton's failure to help her find well-paid work. "I am appalled at the way in which I have been trifled with," it said.

Meanwhile, Willey had transferred the proceeds from her late husband's life insurance policy to her children, and then borrowed up to $4,500 a month from them to cover her living expenses. This maneuver shielded the money from creditors, including Ed Willey's furious former clients. She eventually took menial jobs at a bakery and a beauty salon in Richmond. She still had huge debts and legal bills, owing mainly to Lanasa and Abbott's continuing litigation against her.

While maintaining occasional contact with the White House, she had apparently decided by the spring of 1997 that her old and unconsummated flirtation with Clinton might yield a financial dividend after all. That was why she and her attorney, Daniel Gecker, started to play the Jones camp against the Clinton camp. By early summer Willey was simultaneously identifying herself to various interested parties as a faithful, steadfast Friend of Bill; a reluctant but possibly devastating witness for Paula Jones; an off-the-record *Newsweek* source about the president's peccadilloes; and the potential author of a White House tell-all bestseller.

Tripp finally agreed to talk with Isikoff a few weeks after their initial encounter at her office. Over drinks and at her home in Columbia, Maryland, the Pentagon official let him in on her own jaundiced view of the lawless and immoral Clinton administration, which mirrored Aldrich's. The president had had many mistresses, she insisted, many of whom worked in the West Wing of the White House and were known as "the graduates." There was even a current girlfriend, only twenty-three years old, who had been an intern and then moved to another federal agency—although she wouldn't give him a name or say where this young woman, a "friend" of Tripp, now worked. According to Tripp, this unnamed paramour had performed oral sex on Clinton several times in his private study off the Oval Office and had engaged in phone sex with him as well. One night, she silently beckoned Isikoff to the telephone to hear this woman's voice. He listened for a few moments to Monica Lewinsky complaining about Marsha Scott's refusal to bring her back to the White House.

But without knowing the young woman's identity, Isikoff couldn't very well pursue that angle. What if she were just a "disturbed stalker" concocting a fantasy to impress a friend? Besides, as he wrote much later, the relationship between the former intern and the president as described by Tripp "was entirely consensual. If anything, the young woman was the pursuer." He wanted to write about Kathleen Willey, whose possible testimony about a presidential grope "was squarely relevant to the Jones case."

Unfortunately, that story was complicated rather than confirmed by his interviews with Tripp. She explained that Willey's November 1993 encounter with Clinton had involved "no harassment whatsoever." Afterward, she had asked Tripp's advice about what the sudden embrace meant and how she might advance the relationship. Willey had been chasing Clinton—as Tripp explained to Isikoff in the same terms she later used before the grand jury— from the day she arrived in the White House. Moreover, Tripp had a kind of proof that her version was true.

Tripp showed the reporter a book proposal she had written eight months earlier, titled "Behind Closed Doors: What I Saw at the Clinton White House." Tony Snow had put her in touch with Lucianne Goldberg, the New York literary agent provocateur, and Goldberg had set Tripp up with Maggie Gallagher, a conservative newspaper columnist willing to serve as ghostwriter. Together, Tripp and Gallagher had quickly prepared the proposal for Goldberg to take to Regnery Publishing, a well-established right-wing house based in Chicago. Its president, Alfred Regnery, had served in the Reagan administration and still played a role in national Republican politics. With Aldrich's scurrilous tome still on the bestseller lists, Regnery had been eager to rush Tripp's memoir into print as a sequel; indeed he had hoped to get it into bookstores before the 1996 election.

Despite Goldberg's vision of a $500,000 advance, Tripp ultimately had backed out of the deal, fearing the possible loss of her government job and pension if it was discovered that she was the pseudonymous author (under the name "Joan Dean") of this work. But Tripp still had a copy of the proposal, which she showed to Isikoff, who later confirmed with Gallagher that it had been written in 1996. In a planned chapter called "The President's Women," Tripp and Gallagher had outlined the Willey story, calling her "Brenda" and describing her as a woman "always dressed to kill" to further her "mission" of seducing the president. It used some of the same phrases Willey had spoken to Isikoff in recalling her alleged encounter with Clinton.

With the sudden embrace in the Oval Office, Brenda had seemed on the verge of fulfilling her mission—until her husband had walked out and killed himself. "The publicity apparently scared the President off," the would-be authors had written, "which frustrated Brenda to no end." Tripp and Gallagher left no doubt about whether Willey had desired Clinton's attentions. The result, for Isikoff, was the blurring of his clear-cut story of presidential sexual harassment into "a muddle."

The *Newsweek* reporter might have put aside the confusing tale of Kathleen Willey, at least temporarily, except for the intervention of the Supreme Court. After the justices ruled unanimously on May 28 that the Jones case should proceed, Isikoff realized that Willey might be the plaintiff's most valuable witness in discovery and, if necessary, at trial. Jones's attorney Joe Cammarata was already aware of her existence if not her identity, and was likely to find her sooner or later. Isikoff had to move quickly. His editors urged him to keep reporting until he had enough to publish.

Isikoff called Willey again in early June, hoping to convince her to go on the record. "Your story is going to have to come out," he told her. "It's inevitable." She still refused.

Her apparent reluctance may have been a sham, although Isikoff had no way of knowing that. She too may have realized that the Supreme Court decision had increased her market value. The same week that she rejected the reporter's entreaties to go public with her story, she was attempting—as Tripp had done before her—to sell it as a tell-all book. Her literary model was Faye Resnick, the friend of Nicole Brown Simpson whose potboiling account of the events leading up to the O. J. Simpson murder trial had been a quickie bestseller, and a Kathleen Willey favorite.

Willey's telephone records show that during the second week of June she made several calls to top New York literary agencies. She called both International Creative Management and Janklow & Nesbit on June 6. (That same day she also called *Publishers Weekly* and *New York* magazine; her three calls to *New York*, she eventually testified, concerned her subscription to the glossy weekly.) She called both firms again on June 11. While she received little encouragement at either agency, she did get to make her pitch to Lynn Nesbit's associate Tina Bennett. Under oath, Willey later explained these calls as attempts to seek public relations advice, because she anticipated that Isikoff's article about her experiences would soon appear in *Newsweek* and cause a media explosion.

As Nesbit recalled their conversations, however, Willey only mentioned *Newsweek* as the curtain-raiser to a book deal. "She was trying to get ready," Nesbit told freelance journalist Florence Graves. "She said *Newsweek* would be breaking her story, she was trying to get ready. She thought she ought to look into a book deal. She was trying to sell a memoir based on Ed's death and the Clinton grope." Nesbit felt that Willey seemed "desperate for money," but the renowned agent didn't think such a book was viable. "Everyone thinks they've got a bestselling memoir."

Rejected by the New York publishing elite, Willey turned back to the White House a few weeks later, hoping to convince Clinton aides that she remained a loyal friend of the president. During the last week of June she placed a cryptic call to Nancy Hernreich, the overseer of the Oval Office and someone who had befriended Willey during her White House sojourn. Michael Isikoff had been calling her, she told Hernreich. The president ought to know. That day Hernreich informed both Clinton and Lindsey about Willey's call.

With permission of the nation's highest court, the Jones lawyers now set out to investigate the sex life of the president. They hadn't had the resources or time to research the many leads suggested to them by Clinton's enemies while the appeals were pending. For much of the month following the Supreme Court decision, the attention of Cammarata and Davis had been engaged in quiet discussions with the president's lawyers, whose client's concern had been aroused by the ruling against him. Even though Jones continued to insist on a public "apology," Clinton had directed Robert Bennett to try to reach a settlement, if possible, and thus avoid the embarrassment of depositions, subpoenas, and all the other potentially unpleasant aspects of the discovery process. Three days after losing in the Supreme Court, Bennett had announced publicly that he was willing to recommend "some kind of financial resolution" of the matter.

By the end of June, however, with the negotiations at an impasse, the Jones lawyers resumed their effort to gather compromising evidence. Cammarata was preoccupied with the mystery woman who had contacted him almost five months earlier. When he passed along that tip to Isikoff—whom he seems to have considered an honorary member of the Jones team—he had expected the reporter to share information with him. He found out differently when he called the reporter a few days after the Supreme Court issued its ruling. Yes, Isikoff had found the woman; no, he couldn't tell the Jones lawyers her name. Nor would he arrange for Cammarata to speak with her. Cammarata, a sharp native of the Bronx, had assumed that he and Isikoff had reached some unspoken arrangement. Isikoff's sudden silence irritated him.

*   *   *

On July 1, Cammarata placed a call to John Brown, the former Saline County deputy sheriff and part-time consultant to Citizens for Honest Government, producers of *The Clinton Chronicles*. The Jones lawyers had hired Brown to assist them in Arkansas as a process server and investigator. Now Cammarata wanted a favor. According to Brown's notes of their conversation, the lawyer said he needed to find the name of an "attorney who killed himself after he and wife went to Washington—she worked in white house—fund-raisers." He didn't tell Brown why this information was important, but suggested that the ex-cop might have a "friend" who knew the answer. After talking with Cammarata, Brown immediately phoned a Little Rock man of his acquaintance named Larry Wood.

Brown had known Wood for a while by then as a man with connections at the highest level of the Office of Independent Counsel—specifically, to deputy independent counsel Hickman Ewing, Jr. Wood's exact background is vague. Wood has claimed to be a former Nashville and Memphis police officer, although no record of anybody by that name exists in either department. In recent interviews, Wood said he once ran "topless and bottomless" joints, managed slot machines, and distributed drugs, bootleg liquor, and pornography all over the mid-South. Indicted for police corruption and other offenses, Wood also said that he became a confidential informant for Ewing, then the U.S. attorney in Memphis, after turning state's evidence in two major federal organized crime and political corruption cases in Tennessee.

Like Ewing, he became a "born-again" Christian, and the two men became close friends, attending church together, having frequent lunches and dinners, and traveling to out-of-town religious revival meetings. Like his police career, Wood's account of his experiences as a government witness cannot be corroborated. Of his relationship with Ewing, however, there is no doubt. An extremely large man with a prosthetic leg, Wood makes a memorable impression. According to Wood, he moved back to the Little Rock area, where he had grown up as "Baron Woods," around the time of Clinton's election in 1992. When he heard that Ewing had joined Starr's Arkansas office, he called his old friend and volunteered his free assistance. Ewing took him up on the offer. He brought information and witnesses to Ewing, he claimed, but the Starr deputy told him nothing in return.

But Brown surmised that Wood "was getting specific assignments" from Starr's office. "One week he'd be looking into this. Next week he'd be looking into that. It was kind of odd, but Wood knew every woman they [the Office of Independent Counsel] ever talked to."

Perhaps more significantly, Wood also served as Ewing's unofficial liaison to certain members of the press. "You won't believe this," he boasted, "but I would sometimes get hundreds of phone calls a day." Among the most frequent callers was Christopher Ruddy of the *Pittsburgh Tribune-Review*, best known for his conspiratorial writings on the suicide of deputy White House counsel Vincent Foster. It was Ruddy, while working closely with Citizens for Honest Government, who first introduced John Brown to Larry Wood. Other journalists who acknowledged using Wood as a source included John Crudele of the *New York Post*, then a frequent purveyor of sensationalized "scoops" about the Starr investigation, and Ambrose Evans-Pritchard, U.S. correspondent of the London *Sunday Telegraph* and perhaps the most indefatigable of all the "Clinton scandals" chroniclers.

By his own account, Wood played a central role in connecting various anti-Clinton activists with the OIC. He said he was acquainted with the cast of characters in the Arkansas Project, including its local manager, Parker Dozhier, the bait-shop owner. He also said he knew the two private detectives hired with Scaife foundation money, former Mississippi state police official Rex Armistead and former army intelligence specialist Tom Golden. According to Wood, he helped facilitate several meetings with Ewing for Golden and Armistead. (Expense reports submitted by Golden to the *American Spectator* show at least four "confidential" meetings with members of Starr's staff. On October 23, 1995, for example, Golden reported having "Dinner and drinks with independent counsel source regarding Hillary Rodham Clinton's possible indictment." The same records also claim meetings with OIC staffers on July 1–3, 1997, and August 27, 1997.)

In their early meetings, Brown said, he thought Wood alarmingly indiscreet about his connections with the Office of Independent Counsel. But he also had no doubt that Wood's insider status was real. "Wood tried to imply that he was part of [Starr's] office," the former deputy sheriff recalled. "When I asked him directly, he said no. But he did tell me all about his friendship with Ewing." Wood also boasted of helping Ewing to compile "whole file cabinets full of information about Clinton," much of it personal and highly derogatory. Wood confirmed that somebody he identifies as a "highly placed Arkansas elected official" had provided him with an annotated list of Clinton's alleged paramours, and that he shared the list with the Office of Independent Counsel. Brown said he saw the same list.

That was why Brown had called Wood about Cammarata's request. After listening to him, according to Brown, Wood promised to call Ewing. Minutes later, Wood phoned Brown with an identification for the deceased lawyer. Wood has denied calling Ewing about this but Brown's notes state: "Possible it's Ed Willey. 11/30/93 suic." Brown dialed Cammarata's number in Washington. He had no idea of the significance of the information he passed along to the lawyer. And Cammarata had no idea, he said later, that his investigator might have gotten Ed Willey's name from Hick Ewing. (Ewing declined requests for an interview.) The entire transaction had taken half an hour, Cammarata recalled. With additional help from a former FBI agent in Virginia, the lawyer traced Kathleen Willey to her home in Richmond within a few days.

On the morning of July 4, the telephone rang at the Willey residence. Kathleen Willey glanced at the caller ID and instantly recognized the name of Joe Cammarata. She waited for the phone to stop ringing and called her attorney, Daniel Gecker.

That same morning around nine o'clock, Monica Lewinsky was passed through the guard post at the White House and into the West Wing. The day before, she had sent over a handwritten three-page letter which, in essence, complained at length about Clinton's failure to bring her back to the White House and threatened to expose their affair if he didn't do so. It was the latest in a long series of querulous demands for attention from the immature Lewinsky, but this time she had gone too far. Addressing him as "Dear Sir," she reminded him that she had gone quietly, like a "good girl," to the Pentagon in April 1996 after being ousted from his presence by the adults who protected Clinton's reputation, notably deputy chief of staff Evelyn Lieberman. If she wasn't brought back soon, she would have to explain the reason to her parents.

According to Lewinsky, Clinton tried to be stern with her as they sat down in his office that morning. Brandishing her letter, he said, "It is illegal to threaten the president." He lectured her. They bickered. She cried. He comforted her and she became convinced again that he loved her (although what he may have been thinking at any time during their tormented relationship is impossible to imagine). Then, before she left, Lewinsky imparted a bit of information that had been worrying her. A friend of Lewinsky's at the Pentagon was being hounded by Michael Isikoff, the *Newsweek* reporter. He was asking pointed questions about Kathleen Willey and an alleged instance of sexual harassment by the president. Lewinsky also offered her opinion that the problem would "go away" if the White House just found Willey a decent job.

Clinton listened and, instead of asking for more details about Lewinsky's Pentagon friend, told her about Willey's call to Hernreich concerning Isikoff. No neophyte at sexual intrigue, Lewinsky thought this sounded suspiciously as if the Richmond widow somehow was playing both sides for her own interest. She knew that Willey had sent Isikoff to Tripp in the first place. She warned Clinton against Willey's duplicity, but he seemed to shrug off the entire problem with a vulgar aside about Willey being too "flat-chested" to attract his interest. As was her habit, Lewinsky went home and briefed Tripp about her visit.

The president paid little heed to another sign of impending danger on that Fourth of July. It arrived in a form that would come to symbolize the journalistic perils in the "new information age" he liked talking about so much. Among cyber-sophisticates on both coasts, the *Drudge Report* was just beginning to become very popular.

Proprietor Matt Drudge, a quirky, thirty-year-old former gift-shop clerk with a high school education, had an ear (and an eye) for hot gossip. More than that, he perceived that the Internet was open territory for an outlaw like him, that the product put out by the giant media conglomerates was too safe, too homogenized, too predictable. While his copy tended to be comically over-heated and sorely deficient in grammar, spelling, and punctuation, he could and would report items that the "dinosaur" media wouldn't touch. Significantly, his home page was among the first to offer dozens of handy links to other useful sites, another attractive feature for thousands of new and uncertain surfers of the World Wide Web.

Obsessed with getting the story first and untrained in journalistic rudiments, Drudge disdained standard news practices such as editing and fact checking. He defined himself as "a reporter, not a journalist. I'm not a member of the media club." He brushed off his most grievous errors (such as his "exclusive" about the bald eagle tattoo on Clinton's nether parts and his prediction that Hillary would be indicted) by pointing to his numerous scoops. Yet if he sometimes lacked judgment, he did possess a natural instinct for the news his audience of media junkies and would-be hipsters wanted. Whenever challenged about his sloppiness, he gleefully retorted that the big newspapers and networks made big mistakes too. He could recite the worst of them from memory, in detail.

From among his fast-growing readership he cultivated a corps of sources in Hollywood, in Washington, and in New York. Some were staffers at major publications and networks who delighted in sending tips via E-mail about breaking stories, feuding executives, and other gossipy tidbits. When Drudge got word of tomorrow's big headline in a newspaper or magazine, which was quite often, he could post it a few hours early and notch another "scoop." And he did it all from a one-bedroom apartment in Hollywood.

The proprietor of the *Drudge Report* consciously styled himself as a computer age simulation of gossip pioneer Walter Winchell—right down to the trademark fedora that Drudge usually refused to take off even indoors. Self-consciously or not, he also mimicked Winchell's politics, which veered sharply to the right in the fifties when the columnist served as a mouthpiece for J. Edgar Hoover and Senator Joe McCarthy. Drudge was no ideologue—on some days he was a patriotic populist, on other days a prankish nihilist, but every day an enemy of the media establishment, which he regarded as snobbishly liberal. Most political issues didn't interest him much; his attention span was too short for policy debate. He liked Republicans because, with Democrats in the White House, it was the right-wingers who had scandals to peddle. Besides, Drudge really didn't like the Clintons. He proudly identified himself as a "Clinton crazy."

The *Drudge Report*'s Independence Day exclusive was vague but searingly hot: *Newsweek* sleuth Mike Isikoff was building a major story about a "mystery woman" who had been harassed by the president "on federal property." With characteristic aplomb, the Web gossip had posted "exclusive" and "must credit Drudge" over an item featuring another reporter's work. For quite a while afterward, Isikoff would wonder how Drudge—whom he had met for the first time at *Newsweek*'s Washington offices only a week earlier—got inside his supersecret investigation. The problem would get much worse before anyone figured out the answer, and by then it was too late.

There was more bad news for Isikoff on July 7, the Monday after the holiday. Unbidden, he received a call from Linda Tripp, who no doubt took pleasure in telling the reporter that her ex-friend Willey had betrayed him to the White House. It was an occasion not only to expose the duplicity of someone Tripp hated, but a chance to prove that her young friend the ex-intern really did know the president intimately. That, said Tripp, was how she had learned about Willey's chat with Hernreich.

What Isikoff bemoaned as "a bizarre game of telephone" continued when he called Willey to complain. If Clinton had harassed her, why was she protecting him now? he demanded. She admitted speaking with Hernreich and offered no real explanation. But, she reassured Isikoff, her story was true. When they hung up, Willey again called Hernreich to ask how Isikoff could have known she had alerted the White House.

The strange, circular flurry of meetings and phone calls resumed on the evening of July 14, when Lewinsky was again summoned to the White House by Betty Currie, the president's secretary. Once more Clinton greeted her coldly when she arrived at his office. They went into Hernreich's office, where he kept a physical distance from her and didn't bother with small talk. Her friend at the Pentagon, the one who knew about Willey and Isikoff—was that Linda Tripp? In conversations with Bob Bennett, Willey's lawyer Gecker had complained that the White House was "trashing" his client to Isikoff. Understandably, Gecker was disturbed that the reporter knew all about Willey talking to Hernreich—which Isikoff had learned from Tripp. Of those who knew about Willey's call, only Monica would have blabbed. Hernreich knew that Willey and Tripp had been close when they worked together in the counsel's office. The missing link among Lewinsky, Isikoff, and Willey had to be Tripp.

Having made a smart deduction, however, Clinton suddenly asked a dumb question. "Do you trust this woman?" Lewinsky insisted that she did, assuring Clinton that Tripp was among his greatest admirers, an impression Tripp had falsely encouraged for more than a year with displays of jumbo-sized photographs of the president in her Pentagon office. Had Lewinsky told "this woman" about their relationship? No, she lied; she had cleverly duped Tripp by claiming she had heard about the Willey call from her old friend

Betty Currie. Apparently satisfied with these answers, Clinton asked Lewinsky to convince Tripp to talk with Bruce Lindsey about the Willey matter. Lewinsky agreed to try.

Subjected to Lewinsky's cajoling, Tripp finally did call Lindsey. She admitted having spoken with Isikoff, but denied responsibility when the Clinton aide asked whether she had informed the reporter about Willey's White House phone call. Lindsey urged her to meet with Robert Bennett, and an appointment was arranged. But at the last minute, Tripp didn't show up. She feared and distrusted Bennett. Her excuse to Lewinsky was that her own attorney, Kirby Behre, had advised her to remain "neutral."

On July 25, Cammarata and Davis moved to subpoena Kathleen Willey. Although their settlement negotiations with Bennett had progressed slightly, both sides remained stuck on what kind of statement Clinton might issue to satisfy Paula Jones's need for an "apology." The Jones lawyers hoped to strengthen their bargaining hand with the threat of a devastating new witness. The mercurial Bennett reacted to the subpoena by threatening to withdraw from the negotiations. Any exposure of Willey's claims, he warned darkly, would be a deal breaker.

Like his client, Willey's lawyer Gecker had been cultivating both sides, talking to both Cammarata and Bennett. With Cammarata he had discussed ways to "preserve Willey's testimony" without a subpoena, such as obtaining her affidavit. From Bennett he had sought a promise that the White House wouldn't publicly attack Willey if she resisted testifying for Jones. Still insisting that she was a "reluctant witness," he filed motions to quash the subpoena, claiming that she had no information relevant to Jones's complaint.

Under additional pressure from the two insurance companies that were paying most of Clinton's legal costs, the settlement talks intensified. There was one scenario where everyone could minimize their losses: Jones and Clinton would settle, Willey would remain silent, and the White House would release no derogatory information about her.

The worst mistake Davis and Cammarata made was to confide all those sensitive details to their behind-the-scene advisers, a little group of committed conservatives led by Philadelphia lawyer Jerome Marcus. (It was Marcus's name that appeared most often on the time sheets kept by the Jones lawyers, although they frequently spoke and communicated with George Conway in New York, and less often with Richard Porter in Chicago.) Both men valued the assistance donated pro bono by the group, though they had believed from the beginning that Conway, Marcus, and Porter all were motivated more by hatred of Bill Clinton than by any desire to rescue Paula Jones. Yet Davis and Cammarata, although Republicans themselves, wouldn't countenance the misuse of their lawsuit to advance a partisan agenda. They took their duties as officers of the court seriously, and consistently placed their client's interest ahead of politics. They had also assumed that the advisers would behave honorably despite the fact that all three had insisted upon keeping their work in support of Jones secret from their own law partners.

Cammarata and Davis treated the group with absolute trust, faxing internal documents to them and often including them in strategic discussions as negotiations with the president's legal team proceeded. According to Davis, both Conway and Marcus knew about Kathleen Willey, and they certainly understood that public exposure of her allegations would badly complicate any prospects of a settlement. He simply expected them to keep their mouths shut. "There were many times back then that they were both on the phone with us on conference calls," he said. "We talked as lawyers. They did good, workmanlike work and we just assumed that they would keep all information confidential." In Davis's view, "Working with us, they were ethically required to do that, just as if they were attorneys of record on the case."

If Conway or Marcus did not feel bound by such strictures because they weren't in fact Jones's attorneys of record, neither ever said so to Davis or Cammarata. They did urge the Jones lawyers, more than once, to keep quiet about their own identities. "We didn't put Conway's name on our time records, but we talked with him extensively," recalled Davis. "There were numerous times when he and Marcus were both on the phone with us in conference calls."

Those calls provided useful guidance and consultation to the Jones lawyers, as Davis would readily admit (although he understandably took umbrage later when Isikoff suggested that he and Cammarata were small-time practitioners who would have been lost without all the outside help). Youngish hotshots who had gone to better schools and made partner early at important law firms, Marcus and Conway both exhibited a brash self-confidence.

Marcus's own wife had thought him "arrogant" from the day they met. At the University of Chicago Law School, where he had been friendly with Richard Porter, Marcus had been the kind of student who needed to shout out answers before the professor called on him. After graduating in 1987, he had eventually joined Berger & Montague, a heavily Democratic firm specializing in the kind of corporate tort lawsuits that Republicans have long tried to stifle. (Both name partner Daniel Berger and his son, also a firm partner, were personally friendly with Clinton; together, they donated almost $175,000 to the Democratic Party during the 1996 election cycle.) A registered Democrat married to an "inveterate liberal" and living in a Philadelphia suburb, Marcus was an unlikely anti-Clinton conspirator. But he despised Clinton profoundly, had voted for Bush in 1992, and had made his views known in articles for the *Washington Times*. It was Porter who brought him into the Jones clique early on, as a specialist in the constitutional separation of powers. Having helped put together the Jones legal team, Porter had foreseen the need for expert advice to counter Bennett's argument that the president cannot be sued while in office.

Though a few years younger than the others, George T. Conway III was even more successful and considerably higher profile. In his early thirties, he had made partner at New York's Wachtell, Lipton, Rosen & Katz, one of the biggest and richest litigation shops in the country. His primary occupation was defending the major tobacco companies, and he reportedly made as much as $1 million a year doing it.

With his name and Yale Law School degree, Conway looked on paper like a scion of old wealth; he was in fact the middle-class son of an electrical engineer from suburban Boston. Short, dark, slightly overweight, and painfully shy, he was also, at the age of thirty-three, unmarried and without a regular girlfriend at the time. He aspired to date tall blondes, preferably of the conservative persuasion. Laura Ingraham, the woman he was pursuing in 1997, epitomized that desire. The willowy Ingraham had become a budding celebrity early in 1995 when the *New York Times Magazine* profiled young Washington conservatives, featuring her on the cover in a fetching leopard print miniskirt. For Conway and other right-wing males of his generation, she was an intellectual pinup.

He began to pursue her several years after both had clerked for Ralph Winter, a federal judge and leading patron of the Federalist Society. Conway's magnanimous courting behavior included inviting Ingraham on all-expense-paid ski trips and island holidays. On a Caribbean trip they once ran into Bob Bennett, an embarrassing moment for Ingraham. Before commencing her television career, she had been an associate at Skadden, Arps, Slate, Meagher & Flom—the firm where the president's lawyer was a partner and her friend.

Evidently it was Ingraham who connected Conway with Matt Drudge during the summer of 1997, though she and the tobacco lawyer insist they played no part in the Internet gossip's Willey scoops. Fascinated by the *Drudge Report,* as so many in Washington were, Ingraham had befriended its author after they met at the White House Correspondents Association spring awards dinner. In late June, she and David Brock hosted a gala dinner party at Brock's Georgetown townhouse, with Drudge as guest of honor.

About two weeks later, when Drudge returned to spend the Fourth of July weekend at Ingraham's home in northwest Washington, she presented him with a new source and a valuable scoop. Two knowledgeable sources affirm that on the evening of July 3, Ingraham took down the details about Kathleen Willey from Conway over the telephone while she and Drudge composed his stunning holiday "exclusive" about Isikoff's investigation of alleged sexual harassment in the White House. He headlined it "Ants in the Picnic Basket."

But Ingraham, who was working as a commentator for CBS News at the time, said she hadn't brought Conway to Drudge. "Believe me, if I had been a player or a source that first helped expose the lengths to which the President would go to save his own skin, I would have already claimed credit for it."

And Conway was just as emphatic in an August 1999 letter to the authors: "I never received any confidential information from Mr. Davis and Mr. Cammarata; nor did I ever provide such information to Mr. Drudge." He also insisted that he had never tried to "scuttle any settlement discussions" in the Jones case, because he had believed that settlement "was strongly in the interests of both sides. . . ."

Nevertheless, there is reason to believe the source's account of that July 4 weekend.

Drudge's July 4 blind item about Kathleen Willey and the issuance of a subpoena to her had shaken up the president's lawyers, who now pressed for a deal. Then, on July 28, Drudge posted a "World Exclusive" that Gil Davis believes was planted to disrupt the delicate negotiations.

"WILLEY'S DECISION: White House Employee Tells Reporter That President Made Sex Pass," the headline proclaimed. The brief item had just enough detail to infuriate Bennett—and to sharply prod Isikoff, whom Drudge accused of "holding back" the "explosive story." It explained that Willey still refused to go on the record with the "*Newsweek* ace investigative reporter" about her allegation that Clinton had "fondled" her. In the week that followed, Drudge posted four additional stories. On July 29, he confirmed that Willey had indeed worked in the White House, and added in his own peculiar language that "the President made sexual overtones towards her as she made her request [for a job], according to intelligence familiar with her conversations with a reporter." Two days later, Drudge had the Willey subpoena, as did CBS News and several other news organizations, adding, "If Willey tells lawyers the same story she has told Isikoff—Washington will be rocked." Meanwhile the Web gossip had demoted his new rival to "*Newsweek*'s once ace reporter."

On August 1, Drudge featured Gecker's public announcement that Willey intended to resist the Jones subpoena. In an aside, he attacked Isikoff again, blaming the reporter for the leak of the Willey story and suggesting that the story wouldn't have appeared without Drudge's intervention. He seemed to mock Isikoff for talking too much: "Reporter shares, he likes to have friends on all sides so he'll seem all-knowing for stories that he'll probably never print."

As he scrambled to get into print with the story Drudge had purloined, Isikoff naturally wondered how this disaster had befallen him. Tripp thought he had leaked Willey's name himself, and she wasn't entirely alone in that suspicion. That insinuation enraged Isikoff, who insisted he had told no one but his editors and a couple of trusted colleagues. Maybe, he thought, Drudge had hacked into the magazine's computer system.

Or else someone had gotten impatient waiting for *Newsweek* to publish the Willey story. Someone with both the inside knowledge and the motive to disrupt a negotiated settlement of *Jones v. Clinton*.

By the time he wrote *Uncovering Clinton,* Isikoff had deduced the source and motive behind the Jones leaks. In the book he quotes Ann Coulter—another blonde conservative attorney, media figure and, also like Ingraham, a member of George Conway's circle—about the dread inspired among Jones's advisers by the prospect of a settlement.

An outspoken enemy of the Clintons who consulted on political strategy with Conway, Coulter admitted that they had given various journalists the story of the "distinguishing characteristic" of Clinton's penis, supposedly observed by Jones when he exposed himself to her in 1991. The reason, as she eventually explained to Isikoff: "We were terrified that Jones would settle. It was contrary to our purpose of bringing down the President." (Later still, in confirming that leak to the *Hartford Courant,* she remarked that her work with Conway and his colleagues had amounted to "a small, intricately knit right-wing conspiracy—and I'd like that clarified.")

Coulter claims that she helped Conway and Marcus with legal research in the Jones case, but according to Gil Davis neither he nor Cammarata ever heard of her while they were working on the lawsuit. Both felt that there was no permissible reason for any of the attorneys to have revealed confidential information to Coulter.

In addition to Coulter's boasting, there is documentary evidence that Conway operated in such a way as to frustrate a settlement—even after Davis and Cammarata had resigned from the case. On October 8, 1997, Conway sent a long E-mail message via America Online to Matt Drudge.

"Subject: Your Next Exclusive" is the caption on that message. "Remember me?" it begins. "I'm Laura's friend. We talked once about Kathleen Willey. . . . This is being given to you, of course, subject to your not disclosing the source." (Conway forwarded the same message to Ingraham the following day.)

The main topic of the October 8 message was not Willey but the "distinguishing characteristic," a matter nearly as sensitive as the Willey allegations. Like Coulter, Conway must have realized that with the leak of its details to Drudge, any further settlement negotiations could again be disrupted.

Davis certainly thought so. "Conway's leaking of this stuff certainly jeopardized a settlement," said Davis after examining the Drudge E-mail in 1999. "I had no concept, no idea that they did or would do such a thing [as to leak Willey's name]."

With his exclusive blown by Drudge, Isikoff moved fast to capitalize on his inside information about the Willey matter. Her lawyer Gecker told him to forget about Willey going on the record, and added that it was "a horrible injustice and invasion of privacy" for the press to explore his client's personal life. Worse still, when Julie Steele returned Isikoff's call on the morning of July 31, she administered a crippling blow to her friend's credibility. According to her sworn affidavit in a lawsuit she filed in 1999 against *Newsweek* and Isikoff, Steele told the reporter that Willey had asked her to lie about the alleged incident when he first interviewed them both in March 1997. In truth, Willey hadn't "mentioned her so-called encounter with the President in the White House on the day that it had allegedly occurred or at any other time." She apologized to Isikoff for lying and said she didn't want him to have "egg on his face" for publishing her friend's phony story.

Steele contended that he called her back in the afternoon, telling her that their morning interview was going into his story with quotes from her. That stunned Steele, she later said, because he had agreed earlier that their conversation was "off the record." She recalled Isikoff explaining that "there's so much pressure to get this out . . . I have to do it." (Isikoff and *Newsweek* have denied he ever agreed not to quote Steele.)

The following day, Isikoff contacted Tripp to get her version on the record. Meeting in a coffee shop, she told the reporter he could quote her saying that when she ran into Willey that day in the White House, the Richmond widow was "disheveled. Her face was red and her lipstick was off. She was flustered, happy and joyful." She also wanted Isikoff to state that she had come forward "to make it clear that this was not a case of sexual harassment."

Bob Bennett, who had been trying without success to speak with Tripp, wasn't grateful to her for making that distinction. Denying that Clinton did anything "improper" with Willey, he declared that Tripp "is not to be believed."

Isikoff's story, "A Twist in *Jones v. Clinton*," appeared in the edition of *Newsweek* dated August 11, which actually came out on August 4. It plumbed the "complicated and murky" background of Willey's accusations, her marriage, and her tenure in the White House. It presented Steele's confirmation and recantation. (However, the *Newsweek* version is different from the version in *Uncovering Clinton*. In *Newsweek*, Steele was said to have admitted actually hearing about the incident from Willey "weeks after it happened." That detail is excised from Isikoff's book.) But what Isikoff omitted entirely from his story were Tripp's allegations that Kathleen Willey was conniving to seduce the president. Almost two years later in his book, Isikoff drops his mask of neutrality long enough to suggest a reason. He states clearly, more than once, that he believes Willey—in part because of an anonymous phone call he got from another woman who told him a similar story about being groped by Clinton.

Linda Tripp was frightened and angered by Bennett's cutting remark about her, taking it as a veiled warning that she could lose her Pentagon job. (Some of her friends felt she was also excited by the attention focused on her in

Newsweek.) Tripp's fury in turn scared Monica Lewinsky, who worried that her friend would someday make good on a muttered threat to "write a tell-all book" about the Clinton White House. Linda would never reveal her relationship with the president, would she? Lewinsky asked. "Of course not," Tripp replied. Together, they decided that Tripp should send a letter to the magazine correcting any impression that she was a disloyal employee.

That letter, which Tripp allowed both Lewinsky and Isikoff to edit, noted that the reporter had showed up in her office uninvited by her. "I was compelled to respond when he asserted that Ms. Willey had given him my name as a purported contemporaneous witness who could corroborate her new claim of 'harassment' or 'inappropriate behavior' on the part of the president." That charge was "completely inaccurate," she wrote. Moreover, "her version in 1993 and her version in 1997 were wholly inconsistent." As for "the comment made by the president's attorney about me, which appeared in the same article, I am acutely disappointed that my integrity has been questioned."

The letter didn't run, and Isikoff later dismissed it as "quibbling." Certainly it would have amplified questions and facts about Willey that *Newsweek* had chosen to downplay. And what no one seemed to notice then was the letter's blunt confirmation that this supposedly silent, reluctant witness had been guiding Isikoff all along. In addition to protecting Willey's fragile credibility, the suppression of Tripp's letter allowed the double game being played by the Richmond widow and her lawyer to continue.

The uproar over Kathleen Willey eventually died down long enough for the lawyers on both sides of *Jones v. Clinton* to resume their negotiations. Within a couple of weeks, they had reached an understanding. If Jones would forgo an explicit apology, Clinton (or his legal fund and insurance policies) would pay her $700,000—the full amount her lawsuit had originally demanded. Furthermore, the defendant would issue a statement that she had engaged in no "sexual or improper conduct" at the Excelsior Hotel that day, and would express regret at the damage Jones had suffered to her character and reputation.

Not only did Davis and Cammarata regard this outcome as a "complete victory" on the merits for Jones, but they knew that the president never would offer a humbling statement along with the money. They also knew, as they indicated to her, that their client had a terribly weak case. If it finally got to trial, which was by no means certain, they would be hard pressed to show that Jones had suffered any loss of income or status in her state job as a result of her encounter with Clinton. Her claims of defamation and false imprisonment had already been dismissed. So even if the jury believed her remaining claims, the absence of provable damages was sure to leave her with a money judgment far lower than the offer on the table.

In long telephone conferences and meetings, as well as a twelve-page, painstakingly detailed letter, they strongly recommended in mid-August that she accept the deal and move on. But with Jones so strongly influenced by her husband, Steve, who had always wanted to use the lawsuit to punish Clinton, as well as by her overbearing spokeswoman Susan Carpenter-McMillan, there was no chance of making a deal.

For the lawyers back east, the flashy, bleached-blond activist had meant trouble virtually from the moment she took up Paula Jones's cause full-time in the spring of 1997. At the urging of a religious-right radio personality in Los Angeles, Susan Carpenter-McMillan had befriended Jones in 1994. The lawyers had liked the idea of a "minder" for the inarticulate Jones and her excitable husband, who needed to be kept from making public statements that might jeopardize their case. What Davis and Cammarata didn't anticipate was that the two women would form a personal bond that ultimately eclipsed the lawyers' authority.

It wasn't difficult to see why Jones came to idolize her new mentor, who, on the surface at least, was everything she was not but might wish to be. Jones lived in a small condominium apartment and was married to an airline ticket agent making $37,000 a year. Carpenter-McMillan lived in a million-dollar French-style "chateau" and her husband earned a fortune as a successful personal-injury lawyer. The daughter of a poor rural family, Jones had graduated high school with minimal literacy. Carpenter-McMillan had grown up in an affluent suburb, attended private schools and the University of Southern California, and for three years had appeared on a network-affiliate TV station as a political commentator. Paula shopped at Wal-Mart; Susan shopped on Rodeo Drive.

To those who knew Carpenter-McMillan, however, it was equally clear why she would be attracted to Jones, a powerful generator of the media attention that she had always craved. Long before she assumed her role as Paula's alter ego, Carpenter-McMillan was a battle-hardened veteran of the antiabortion movement, having begun her public career in 1980 as a spokeswoman for the Right to Life League of Southern California. She was by temperament an absolutist who berated foes as "lesbians" and "antimoral parasites" and tolerated no exceptions to her pro-life position, not even in cases of rape or incest.

Tough and quick-witted, she gradually became a minor celebrity in her hometown, although her hunger for celebrity was growing faster than her fame during the eighties. She got an unwelcome taste of what fame could bring in 1990, when the *Los Angeles Times* discovered that beneath her strident militancy lay a rather embarrassing secret. Carpenter-McMillan had undergone not just one but two abortions. The second, a therapeutic abortion to terminate a "failed pregnancy," had occurred in 1983—while she was leading the local pro-life movement. "It was my own private life and I don't consider myself a public figure," she said at the time. "You can go through 13 years of absolute denial where you don't even remember the fact, hardly, that you ever had an abortion."

No longer viable as a pro-life leader, she stepped down to form her own multi-issue, "conservative feminist" organization, the Pro-Family Media Coalition, bankrolled by her husband. Within a year she got what she had always wanted back when her hobby was calling up radio talk shows: a job on KABC-TV replacing a male conservative pundit. That gig was about to end four years later when Carpenter-McMillan latched on to Paula Jones and a chance at national prominence.

She was a boon to reporters and talk-show bookers, but her habit of berating Bennett and referring to the president as "that little slimeball" clashed with Davis and Cammarata's settlement strategy. She didn't think much of the lawyers either, feeling they had surrendered in the face of vicious attacks on Paula from the likes of James Carville. "She's crying and she says, 'Look what they're doing to me.' And I said, 'Oh, no, it's your lawyers allowing this to happen to you,'" Carpenter-McMillan recalled. "And I called up [the lawyers] and said, 'I'm on board. You don't have to like it, you don't have to approve of it. I'm here, I'm going to defend her.'" In the spring of 1997 she took over as official spokeswoman and administrator of the Paula Jones Legal fund (a for-profit sole proprietorship that collected some $250,000 from donors who believed they were paying the plaintiff's legal bills). At last she was getting the attention she needed, appearing regularly on television and finally winning a job as a regular cohost on CNBC's *Equal Time*. The spokeswoman's star was still rising while the lawyers were struggling toward a settlement. Behind their backs, she constantly urged Paula to hold out for more money and "a real apology."

On August 29, Davis and Cammarata informed Paula Jones that they intended to ask Judge Wright to permit them to withdraw from the case at the beginning of September. Unless she reconsidered her rejection of Bennett's offer over the Labor Day weekend, they were getting out. "We cannot ethically pursue expensive, time-consuming litigation where a settlement now would achieve every legitimate goal, and where continued litigation would be perceived (rightly or wrongly) as primarily a matter of political hatred or spite," they wrote in a final plea for reason. The two lawyers had always believed Jones was telling the truth, and that her motives were above suspicion. They had tried to keep her clear of the right-wing forces which sought to abuse her case as a propaganda weapon against Clinton. That had been difficult with Jones living on the other side of the country, under the daily influence of a woman they regarded as a self-serving ideologue. Now that Jones had rejected a remarkably generous deal, Davis and Cammarata no longer thought that her lawsuit was about justice rather than politics. At a press conference in front of her house, Carpenter-McMillan triumphantly announced their exit. Until further notice, her husband, Bill McMillan, would be handling Paula's legal affairs.

Unaware that Linda Tripp had almost sold a scandal-mongering book about the White House a year earlier, Monica Lewinsky assumed that her friend's "tell-all" threat had been mere angry talk. Lewinsky resumed her fruitless quest for a job in the White House, meeting with the president on August 16 to give him a costly 1802 edition of a biography of Peter the Great and some other gifts for his birthday. He was going to turn fifty-one a few days later. They argued as usual and then kissed, but the president rejected any sexual celebration. "I'm trying to be good," he said.

It was much too late to be good as far as his dealings with Lewinsky were concerned. The excitement and worry of the Willey episode had pushed Tripp into a decision. She called Tony Snow, the former Bush White House aide turned conservative columnist, and asked him to put her in touch with Lucianne Goldberg again.

Chapter Fifteen

IMPEACHMENT
FOR FUN AND PROFIT

IN JUNE 1997, people across the country who had purchased *The Clinton Chronicles* had received an urgent telephone call from Infocision, a Christian telemarketing firm located in Akron, Ohio. "Good evening," the callers' script began. "I'm calling on behalf of Citizens for Honest Government. Former congressman Bill Dannemeyer has recorded an urgent message on the impeachment of Bill Clinton. I will go ahead and play it for you, okay?"

If the "potential donor" answered yes, he or she was urged to stay on the line after the tape ran. If he or she replied no, the telemarketers were instructed to say, "If you are concerned about illegal activities going on in the White House, then you'll really want to hear how Bill [Dannemeyer] plans to bring charges against Bill Clinton. I'll go ahead and play that message for you, okay?"

Those who agreed to listen then heard the stentorian rumble of Dannemeyer, a retired Republican member of Congress from Southern California and longtime stalwart of the religious right:

"I'm calling you because I'm concerned about the future of America. We were once led by great men like George Washington, Thomas Jefferson, and even Ronald Reagan. But now the office of the president is held by a liar and a criminal. . . .

"Well, my friend, I have just about had enough. I have talked with other congressmen and they will consider a vote for impeachment, but they're waiting to hear from . . . people like you and me. That's why I'm calling on you to show your support for the impeachment of Bill Clinton. . . .

"My friend, Representative Henry Hyde, is already studying the law on impeachment, but it up to us as voters to pressure congressmen, especially

Clinton's Democratic cronies. . . . I'm calling for committees of impeachment to be formed across the United States to lead concerned citizens and help them rise up in the name of democracy. . . .

"And I want you to serve with us."

When the tape ended, the telemarketers would return. "Hi . . . As you heard, former congressman Dannemeyer feels the crimes at the White House are so serious he asked Citizens for Honest Government to distribute hundreds of thousands of petitions all across America, demanding that Congress begin the impeachment procedure immediately. Can we send a petition for you to sign?"

And if so, the telemarketers would continue, "Bill also wanted me to mention that this is going to be the most expensive fight we've ever faced! That's why we are forced to go to the American people directly. Tell me, can you help Citizens for Honest Government get the petitions into the hands of five million concerned Americans, with a gift of . . ." The suggested dollar amounts ranged from $10 all the way up to $250 or more, depending on how much the listener had spent or given on previous occasions.

Upon encountering resistance, the Infocision telemarketers pushed forward with certain well-tested techniques for getting donations. Potential donors who immediately said they couldn't afford to give, for example, were mildly admonished: "But I sense that you are deeply concerned about Bill Clinton's illegal and immoral activities." Plucking at certain common resentments, the telemarketers usually added that "the reason we're calling is we expect fierce opposition from the radical feminist and homosexual activist groups who have gained influence with the Clinton White House." And to all the skeptics who inquired, "What about Al Gore?" there came this instant reassurance: "Right now, we are in the process of impeaching Bill Clinton. We are planning the same process for Al Gore."

Thousands of such calls, followed by an even larger volume of direct-mailed impeachment petitions to his organization's eighty-thousand-name database, represented the vanguard of what Pat Matrisciana and his comrades at the Council for National Policy hoped would become a stong impeachment movement based in the religious right during the coming year. Sales of *The Clinton Chronicles* and Matrisciana's other Jeremiah Films products had dropped off considerably since their initial vogue a few years earlier. Now, as the CEO of both Citizens for Honest Government and Jeremiah Films, Matrisciana hoped that this latest revival of the anti-Clinton campaign might improve his business in the wake of the president's overwhelming 1996 victory.

Matrisciana and his allies had been planning their crusade to remove Clinton from office since no later than his second inauguration. Back then, the citizens for Honest Government's January 1997 newsletter—which featured on its roster of contributing writers such figures as Ambrose Evans-Pritchard,

Christopher Ruddy, and Jim Johnson—had featured Dannemeyer on its front page, arguing "Why Congress Must Impeach Bill Clinton."

The ex-congressman's essay rehearsed many familiar themes from the Matrisciana video archive, from drug smuggling to Whitewater, Filegate, Travelgate, and, of course, the death of Vince Foster. "I for one believe that both Bill and Hillary Clinton know where, when, why and by whom Foster was killed," Dannemeyer wrote, "and it was no suicide. . . . And he has been accused publicly of being responsible for the September 1993 murder of Little Rock private investigator Luther 'Jerry' Parks, and possibly involved in covering up other murders." Any day now, Dannemeyer warned, former White House counsel Bernard Nussbaum and former personnel director Craig Livingstone "are likely to be indicted . . . for perjury and obstruction of justice."

Matrisciana's chatty essay in the same newsletter—headed "Slaying the Clinton Dragon in 1997"—reluctantly acknowledged that Clinton had been reelected a few months earlier. "I was heartsick on the night of last November 5. As the election returns came in, I realized that the unthinkable had happened once again. . . .

"Personally, I don't believe that America can survive four more years of a Bill Clinton presidency. His ungodly, globalist, socialist agenda is deadly. . . . The good new is, he'll never get away with it. You see, Bill Clinton can be impeached."

Matrisciana, too, looked forward with eager anticipation to the "likelihood" that officials Bernard Nussbaum, Margaret Williams, Craig Livingstone, and Hillary Clinton would be indicted soon by the OIC.

"My top goal," he continued, "for 1997 is to raise the groundswell of public opinion that eventually will result in the impeachment of Bill Clinton. . . . Will you stand with me, either with a onetime gift of $1,000 or more, if you are able, or as a monthly supporter of this organizing work, or both?"

Aside from some elderly patriots on fixed incomes who were willing to sacrifice for their country, Pat Matrisciana had found some very well-heeled conservative backers by 1997. Just before the 1996 election, for example, the widow of the late former CIA director William Casey had sent Citizens for Honest Government a check for $10,000.

More significantly, perhaps, Matrisciana had joined forces financially as well as ideologically with Christopher Ruddy, the journalist and entrepreneur associated with Richard Mellon Scaife. Together Ruddy and Matrisciana were preparing to distribute a new video in early 1997 titled The "60 Minutes" Deception, a counterattack on the popular CBS magazine show and its venerable correspondent Mike Wallace for debunking Ruddy's book on the Foster suicide. It portrayed Wallace and CBS as liars and liberal Clinton shills. Ruddy and Matrisciana had mapped out an entire promotional campaign for the spring, including discounted advertising in the *Washington Times;* a special call-in premiere on National Empowerment Television, the conservative satellite network; and extensive appearances by Ruddy and others on talk radio.

With Ruddy came various other Scaife-funded entities, including Accuracy in Media—which paid part of the production cost of the *"60 Minutes"* video and would help to sell it nationwide—and the Western Journalism Center, as well as Paul Weyrich's Free Congress foundation, which operated National Empowerment Television. And Ruddy apparently brought a substantial bankroll, too, to his partnership with Matrisciana. As Murray Waas later reported in *Salon,* Matrisciana and Ruddy controlled a Citizens for Honest Government bank account, separate from the other, depleted accounts of Citizens for Honest Government and Jeremiah Films, that had at one time a balance of roughly $3 million. Although Matrisciana always portrayed Citizens as a "bootstrap" nonprofit operation, that $3 million cash cushion was far more than the small average balance in the organization's accounts a couple of years earlier.

By late spring, the impeachment drive was under way. The May issue of Matrisciana's newsletter prominently displayed a call for a congressional "inquiry of impeachment" beneath a photo of its author, Representative Bob Barr, a backbench Republican whose Georgia district abutted that of House Speaker Newt Gingrich. Barr, too, had long-standing ties to Scaife through the Southeastern Legal Foundation, a conservative litigation outfit based in Atlanta which Barr had formerly headed and which received annual infusions of money from Scaife's foundations. The short, mustachioed Barr, best known until then for his alliance with the National Rifle Association and other firearms interests, would become the point man for impeachment advocates in the House for a year before there was any realistic prospect of impeaching the president.

Matrisciana's associates at the Council for National Policy were on the move, too. When the CNP met in June 1997 at a hotel in Montreal, Canada, impeachment was high on the agenda. Exact details of what the religious right leadership planned at that meeting are not known because, as always, the CNP meeting was closed to the press. But the text of an "impeachment organizer's kit" later sent out by Citizens for Honest Government revealed that the drive had been encouraged by "an impeachment panel discussion" during that CNP gathering, as well as by "a follow-up [CNP] discussion in South Carolina." Presiding over the Council for National Policy at the time was Edwin Meese III, the former Reagan administration attorney general, whose enthusiastic endorsement of Citizens for Honest Government ("doing important work on behalf of the American people") appeared on every newsletter and fund-raising plea mailed out by the organization.

Ed Meese's own career in government had ended with his resignation in disgrace from the Justice Department, while an independent counsel pursued corruption allegations that resulted in indictments of several Meese associates but not the former attorney general himself. Yet this personal history in no way inhibited Meese from entering the political arena once more on behalf of impeachment. Memories were short, and Meese's problems had concluded a decade earlier.

In June, Meese agreed to appear with Barr as the featured speaker at a Washington press event to announce that the Georgia congressman had sent a three-page letter urging Hyde, the House Judiciary Committee chairman, to open an inquiry of impeachment. The sponsor of this event was Floyd Brown, still the chairman of Citizens United (not to be confused with Citizens for Honest Government) and not incidentally a fellow member of the Council for National Policy. In reality, Hyde and Gingrich weren't quite ready for such an ambitious undertaking. As Brown complained in a letter to his supporters that summer, "just before the news conference was scheduled to take place, the Republican congressional leadership pressured Barr to back out and cancel." That scarcely discouraged Brown, whose organization had first proposed impeaching Clinton as early as the summer of 1994.

The same political fever had also raised temperatures at the *American Spectator,* where editor Bob Tyrrell was toiling over the manuscript of a paperback "political docu-drama" for Regnery Publishing titled *The Impeachment of William Jefferson Clinton.* Its foreword was provided by the busy Barr, who also doubled as the hero of Tyrrell's speculative fiction—on which Tyrrell was collaborating with a "secret source," according to the jacket copy, who was "giving him 'Deep Throat' style information." Tyrrell's purported coauthor was dubbed "Anonymous" (evidently in homage to Joe Klein, the journalist whose novel *Primary Colors* under the "Anonymous" byline had been a major bestseller).

Tyrrell's satire relied heavily, as always, on the metaphor of Watergate. His plot envisioned congressional impeachment hearings in 1998, sparked by a vaguely explicated "Starr report" on Whitewater. He imagined Henry Hyde filling the role of the wise, avuncular Sam Ervin, the late Democrat who once chaired the Senate Watergate committee. In the book's denouement, Tyrrell depicted a heroic Bob Barr discovering a set of secret, damning White House tapes—one of which records the guilty Bill and Hillary Clinton squabbling over their bribery of Webster Hubbell. Unoriginal, certainly, but no doubt satisfying to the Washington conservatives who had yearned so long to avenge Nixon.

For the *Spectator* editor, such fantasies may have provided a happy refuge from the realities of the Arkansas Project, which over the summer had suddenly taken an unpleasant turn. Months earlier, Tyrrell's own personal Arkansas

Project obsession—the Mena narcotics story—had proved to be little more than an entertaining myth. After two years of investigation, House Banking Committee chairman Jim Leach conceded that his investigators had found nothing to implicate Clinton in any illicit business there.

Still, the money had continued to flow from Scaife's foundations, with a check for $150,000 from the Carthage Foundation on June 3 and another from the Sarah Scaife Foundation for $75,000 on June 5 (with a note accompanying the latter from Scaife himself, promising an additional $75,000 "during the third quarter of 1997").

But not long after those checks arrived, Scaife Foundation president Richard Larry made an ugly accusation about the vast sums expended on the Clinton investigations overseen by Larry's friends, Stephen Boynton and David Henderson. He said that *Spectator* publisher Ronald Burr was responsible for the misuse of $1 million in Arkansas Project funding. In response to that charge, Tyrrell, Burr, and other top Spectator Foundation officials had gathered at attorney Ted Olson's downtown Washington office on July 10.

At the meeting, according to a furious letter that Burr dispatched to Larry four days later, Tyrrell had stated: "I am here to announce an audit. Dick Larry said that Ron [Burr] has misallocated $1 million of the Arkansas Project funds and we are going to have a complete audit of the project." That incensed Burr, who believed that Larry was trying to deflect blame for the project's shortcomings from his pals Boynton and Henderson, who were responsible for squandering hundreds of thousands if not millions of dollars. Burr had raised questions about where the money had gone, and also about the creation of a full-time job for Henderson at the *Spectator*.

Firing back, Burr demanded that Larry either repudiate his unfounded accusation or make a formal written apology. Moreover, he added, "I look forward to a complete audit of the Arkansas Project. . . . I have asked Messrs. Boynton and Henderson to provide us with their accounting records in order to give the auditors a basis to verify how they spent the funds we paid them." Burr copied the letter to Tyrrell and Olson.

Tensions had been growing between Burr and Tyrrell for months because in late 1996 the publisher had started questioning his old friend's habit of spending foundation moneys on himself—his house, his dinner parties, his liquor bills, and myriad other unauthorized personal expenses. In an effort to conform with tighter IRS regulation of nonprofit organizations, Burr had been scrutinizing Tyrrell's lavish spending and suggesting some changes.

When Richard Larry neither apologized nor withdrew his accusation of mismanagement, Burr didn't let the matter rest. He felt that his personal honor and the integrity of the magazine were both at stake, and he continued to press for a full audit of the Arkansas Project after Tyrrell and Larry dropped the subject. He solicited proposals for an audit, first from the *Spectator*'s own longtime accountants in Indianapolis, where the magazine had been founded, and then from Arthur Andersen LLP, the huge worldwide accounting company. The Andersen firm delivered its proposal on September 17, promising to complete a review of approximately $2.4 million in Arkansas Project expenditures between October 5 and early November, for a fee of $50,000. Among the Andersen partners on the proposed audit team was a white-collar-crime specialist from the firm's "business fraud consulting practice."

Preoccupied with completing and promoting his impeachment book, Tyrrell was in no mood for such ominous distractions. On September 9, he sent Burr a peremptory memo, telling him to buy costly advertising time on the Rush Limbaugh radio program in mid-October for his book—yet another expenditure of foundation funds that Burr considered dubious, since profits from the book would accrue to Tyrrell, not the *Spectator*. The editor was also impatient with Burr's insistence on referring to the proposed examination of the Arkansas Project accounts as a "fraud audit."

The two old friends were no longer on speaking terms. Indeed, Tyrrell had made it perfectly plain that he wanted Burr to vacate the post he had held for thirty years. Burr knew that Tyrrell had the authority to fire him, and was hesitantly dickering over severance terms. He didn't want to leave, but he refused to back down on the audit. He thought a fraud had been committed, and he knew he wasn't culpable.

On September 30, Tyrrell sent Burr another terse memo. "No one has accused anyone at The American Spectator with fraud. I do not want a 'fraud audit' of any project. I do not want any further audits until I have examined our accounting of the Arkansas Project. I want to review our accounting to familiarize myself further with it.

"This issue is now closed."

Burr didn't think so. On October 6 he sent Tyrrell a long memo, insisting that the only way to "close" the issue was "to hire Arthur Andersen to do a complete fraud audit." What Burr evidently didn't realize yet was that he had been officially dismissed the day before. At a special meeting of the Spectator Foundation board of directors at his home in McLean, Virginia, Tyrrell had pushed through a motion immediately removing Burr as publisher and electing Ted Olson in his place as the foundation's secretary-treasurer. All this was done amid expressions of "affection and respect for Mr. Burr and gratitude for his service," according to the board minutes.

If Burr agreed to abide by the agreement's confidentiality provision, he could walk away with a "generous severance package" worth a total of $350,000. He eventually took the deal and has never spoken publicly about the Arkansas Project or the *American Spectator* since.

Ron Burr's abrupt dismissal was not well received by the magazine's staff and supporters. Conservative humorist and author P. J. O'Rourke quit the editorial board in protest and canceled his appearance as master of ceremonies at the *Spectator's* upcoming thirtieth anniversary festivities. "The tendency of the magazine to do this Clinton-obsessive stuff, I don't get," O'Rourke told the *Washington Post.* "It seems strange and somewhat embarrassing." He wasn't alone in viewing Burr's treatment as "reprehensible."

The sacrifice of Burr didn't mollify Scaife and Larry. Two months later, after the *Spectator* ran a harshly negative review of Christopher Ruddy's book *The Strange Death of Vincent Foster,* it was reported that the angry billionaire called Tyrrell to say that he had cut the magazine off from his foundations' wealth.

If Scaife ever did learn the details of how that money had been squandered by Richard Larry's friends, he must have been truly appalled. Known for penny-pinching among his own employees, he could only have been outraged by the sums Henderson and Boynton were paying themselves, let alone the hefty checks they wrote Rex Armistead and others. According to the *Washington Post,* Scaife came very close to firing Larry over the Arkansas Project.

What had Scaife bought with all his money? For that matter, what had all of Clinton's foes accomplished after almost five years of partisan warfare? While they had failed to destroy his presidency, certainly they had succeeded in crippling his leadership. They had done so by staining him and his wife with a spatter of accusations that, if not provable, would nevertheless leave a permanent mark on their reputations. The lasting irony is that by the autumn of 1997, the Clintons were closer than they or their enemies knew to vindication, if not exoneration.

Although Kenneth Starr's prosecutors were in no rush to inform their friends in the Washington press corps, the independent counsel had for all practical purposes given up by then on charging Bill and Hillary Clinton with any wrongdoing involving the White House Travel Office, the FBI files fiasco, or, most importantly, Madison Guaranty Savings and Loan. The FBI files and Travel Office probes had been dormant for nearly a year, with no indictments filed and none contemplated.

The OIC had been more reluctant to give up on Whitewater. Earlier in 1997, according to Michael Isikoff's book, a Starr assistant named Stephen Bates had drafted an impeachment report to Congress that accused the president of lying under oath during the Tucker-McDougal trial when he denied meeting David Hale at Castle Grande or receiving a loan from Madison Guaranty.

The Bates draft would never reach Capitol Hill. Even the politically inept Starr was sufficiently astute to see that an impeachment referral relying upon the shaky testimony of David Hale and Jim McDougal would embarrass him more than it would endanger the president. There was one final piece of evidence—a certified check made out to Bill Clinton and found in the trunk of an abandoned Mercury outside a Little Rock transmission shop—that initially seemed to promise a breakthrough. Yet that very same piece of paper helped to prove that Jim McDougal, the OIC's newest witness against the Clintons, was lying again.

Associated Press reporter Pete Yost broke the story on November 4, 1997. "In a bizarre Whitewater discovery," he wrote, "a repair shop owner opened the trunk of a tornado-damaged car and found a cashier's check for more than $20,000 payable to Bill Clinton from his former business partner's savings and loan." It seemed that the vehicle's owner, a former Madison Guaranty employee named Henry Floyd, had been assigned to put some documents in storage ten years earlier but had simply forgotten they were in his car. Made out in the sum of $27,600 and dated November 15, 1982, the check had never been endorsed by Clinton.

It had been written on Madison Guaranty Savings and Loan and stamped twice for deposit: first at Madison Bank and Trust in Kingston, Arkansas (the tiny bank in the Ozarks also owned by Jim McDougal), and then at Union National Bank in Little Rock.

"They're going to hang them [the Clintons] with the documents they've got," Jim McDougal boasted to reporters. Interviewed at the federal penitentiary in Fort Worth, he contended that the check "certainly proves the chief executive perjured himself." In the *Washington Post* and elsewhere, the unearthed check was portrayed as possible evidence that the president had committed perjury.

The question no one asked was why Clinton would have lied about borrowing money from Madison Guaranty, which would have violated no law. The Clintons had borrowed and repaid loans from several Arkansas banks. Besides, if the president hadn't signed the check, why would anyone conclude that he had even seen it? Under normal circumstances, as several bankers explained to the *Arkansas Democrat-Gazette,* a cashier's check that large wouldn't be honored unless the payee endorsed it in a bank officer's presence.

The fact that Clinton's signature wasn't on the check eluded some reporters. Susan Schmidt's initial account in the *Washington Post* failed to mention his signature's absence, or that the check had been cashed at a McDougal-owned bank.

An obvious explanation of the Clinton check lay within the pages of the 1995 Pillsbury Report. The report showed that Jim McDougal himself, and not the Clintons, had owed $27,600 to McDougal's own tiny bank in the Ozarks back when that check had been drawn in November 1982. Without consulting his Whitewater partners, McDougal had borrowed $30,000 from his own bank in August 1981 for what the application called "Whitewater operating capital." Some of the loan proceeds went to pay valid Whitewater debts; the rest ended up in McDougal's pocket.

That same loan from Madison Bank and Trust had been satisfied on November 18, 1982, with what the Pillsbury Report called "a $27,600 payment from an unstated source." It appeared almost certain that the resourceful McDougal had simply drawn a cashier's check on his brand-new Madison Guaranty Savings and Loan to repay a bank loan he had made to himself a year earlier. When reporters from the *Democrat-Gazette* tried to locate the teller who had allegedly issued the $27,600 to Clinton, they were unable to find any such person.

But why would McDougal have written Bill Clinton's name as payee on the cashier's check? Possibly because that check, drawn on Madison Guaranty, ended up at Little Rock's Union National Bank—where McDougal also owed a quarterly payment on $548,186 debt used to finance his purchase of the savings and loan. The Union National loan offices wouldn't have been reassured to see their customer McDougal writing cashier's checks to himself from the thrift institution they had recently helped him purchase. How wise of McDougal to use the name of his very prominent business partner, who had just been reelected governor of Arkansas two weeks earlier.

In any case, there was something else about the check that had drawn FBI special agent Michael T. Patkus's attention immediately: the date.

After Jim McDougal "flipped" in August 1996, one of the first stories he told the OIC investigators was that Bill Clinton had indeed taken a $25,000 loan from Madison Guaranty—and thus had perjured himself by denying it. Agent Patkus had spent several months searching the Madison Guaranty records and interviewing its former employees, without finding any evidence for this assertion. According to McDougal, he had hand-carried a loan application to the state capitol, where Clinton had casually signed it while leaning against a doorframe in the governor's office.

The problem, as Patkus quickly realized, was that on November 15, 1982, Bill Clinton hadn't been in the governor's office—because the governor of Arkansas was still Frank White, Clinton's Republican foe. Therefore McDougal's story, with all its otherwise convincing detail, couldn't be true. Along with Hickman Ewing, Jr., Patkus had traveled to the federal penitentiary in Fort Worth to interview McDougal again. This time, wily Jim "remembered" asking Clinton to fill out a backdated application some months after the fact. McDougal also claimed to have destroyed all of the loan documentation.

Not surprisingly, the meticulous FBI agent didn't really believe McDougal anymore. Much later, at Susan McDougal's 1999 contempt trial, her attorney Mark Geragos put the issue to Patkus directly. "You still have those doubts as you sit here today," asked Geragos, "whether or not Jim McDougal had told you the truth. Isn't that correct?"

"On certain issues, yes, that's correct," Patkus answered. Digging a bit deeper, the FBI agent had also found an October 17, 1982, directive from state and federal bank regulators giving Madison Bank and Trust exactly thirty days to "clean up" its loan portfolio by removing insider deals like McDougal's $30,000 loan to himself. Under further questioning by Geragos, Patkus acknowledged that McDougal had been under pressure to get his own loan off the Madison Bank books, and might well have created a "phantom loan" to Clinton for that purpose. "Absolutely. That's possible," Patkus agreed. "I mean, just because there's a check to Bill Clinton from Madison Guaranty—and if it is a loan, which I believe it is—does not mean that Bill Clinton had knowledge regarding that check or that loan." He also agreed that without further confirmation of Hale's and McDougal's stories, he wouldn't have felt comfortable indicting anyone.

Presumably the FBI agent would have felt that same discomfort or considerably more if the person to be indicted happened to be the president of the United States. Not a single newspaper or television correspondent reported his testimony, but it almost certainly represented the OIC's own analysis of the Whitewater case in late 1997—as Starr himself confirmed in a 1999 interview on CNN's *Larry King Live*.

Asked to explain how the Whitewater investigation had ended up probing the president's sex life instead, the independent counsel told King that his office had "drafted a report to Congress on Whitewater . . . in December of 1997. But it was my assessment and an assessment shared within my office that the information did not reach what the statute requires, 'substantial and credible.' . . . It's got to be weighty, and it's got to have some believability to it— information that an impeachable offense may have been committed. We didn't think that the evidence was there."

Yet as Starr and his staff faced the likelihood at the end of 1997 that they would come up with no further indictments of Clinton associates—except for redundant prosecutions of Webster Hubbell and Susan McDougal—the independent counsel added another young associate to the OIC roster. His name was Paul Rosenzweig, and he had, for a brief period in 1994, flirted with the idea of helping Paula Jones. Two friends and fellow alumni of the University of Chicago Law School, Jerome Marcus and Richard Porter, had tried to bring Rosenzweig onto the Jones legal team—and when he joined Starr's office that November, he was still in contact with them.

With the departure of Gil Davis and Joe Cammarata as counsel of record for Jones in September, prospects for settling her case gradually faded. For an interim period during the weeks that followed, Bill McMillan took over as her counsel. At first Bob Bennett regarded Susan Carpenter-McMillan's lawyer husband with suspicion, but quickly came to regard him as a "savvy guy" who might sincerely want to reach a settlement. Any trust that might have been established between Bennett and McMillan, however, was lost in October when two other Jones supporters, George Conway and Ann Coulter, took it upon themselves to leak details of the supposed "distinguishing characteristic" of the president's genitals. With that humiliating disclosure, any attempted settlement agreement would surely be scuttled.

Just to be certain, Conway sent a confidential E-mail on October 8 to the *Drudge Report.* The New York lawyer refreshed Matt Drudge's memory by identifying himelf as a friend of Laura Ingraham. (Conway forwarded the same message to her the following morning.) This "exclusive" was being provided, Conway wrote, on the condition that Drudge would conceal its source. Among other problems, Conway's leak was a clear violation of Judge Wright's gag order covering all attorneys in the Jones litigation.

"The distinguishing physical characteristic that Paula Jones says she believes she saw is that Clinton's penis is curved when it is erect," he wrote. "If she is correct, then Clinton has a urological condition called Peyronie's disease. . . . It is caused by blockages in blood flow to the penis. . . . if blood is constricted on one side, the penis curves when it is erect. . . . Jones's former lawyers, Cammarata and Davis, attempted to find a urological expert witness before they resigned for [sic] the case. The idea was that the expert witness, a physician, would examine Clinton in a turgid state (induced by injection), and then would render an opinion as to whether it is possible that Clinton had the problem in 1991. . . ."

"Disgusting or what????" Conway had exclaimed over his forwarded message to Ingraham, and there he had a point. It later turned out that the president had no history of Peyronie's disease and that, like other shifting allegations by Jones, this canard failed to survive close examination. But truth or falsity of the allegation mattered little to Conway and Coulter. Their interest, as Coulter candidly admitted later to Isikoff, was to "humiliate" the president; she thought a settlement would be a "disaster." While Conway pushed the Peyronie's theory on Drudge, Coulter gave it to Richard Johnson of the *New York Post's* "Page Six" gossip column. When Johnson's editors refused to let him print it, the item turned up on the front page of the *Washington Times* and on Don Imus's radio show. Isikoff writes that it was offered to him as well, although he doesn't say by whom.

In any event, Bill McMillan was soon replaced by a group of attorneys who displayed no interest in a settlement. The new legal team was comprised of John Whitehead, president of the Rutherford Institute, a nonprofit legal foundation based in Virginia, and lawyers recruited by Whitehead from the Dallas firm of Rader, Campbell, Fisher & Pyke. The Rutherford president planned to raise hundreds of thousands of dollars via direct mail for the lawsuit, while the Dallas lawyers conducted the actual litigation.

The sudden entrance of Whitehead—a prominent member of the Council for National Policy—provided yet another sign of the religious right's determination to bring down Bill Clinton. Whitehead had formerly worked as an attorney for Jerry Falwell's Moral Majority Legal Defense Fund. In 1982, he and another Falwell associate named Jerry Nims had left the Moral Majority to create their own "civil liberties" group, naming it after an obscure seventeenth-century Scottish cleric. Samuel Rutherford's contribution to theology was a precursor of Christian Reconstructionism; he asserted that God's law must be placed above any temporal legal authority of nation or king. Whitehead rarely admitted any such leanings. He preferred blander statements, telling reporters that his involvement in the Jones case "stems from the fundamental principle that no person, not even the president of the United States, is above the law. . . . I'm not out to hurt President Clinton, but I am here to see that justice is done and Paula Jones has her day in court."

The Jones case scarcely fell within Rutherford's organizational mandate, which is to defend religious freedom against the secularizing tendencies of government. As defined by Whitehead, his criteria for accepting legal work excluded any matter that did not "principally involve a violation of religious liberty or parental rights." The Jones litigation had nothing to do with those issues, and until October 1997 the Rutherford Institute had not taken up a single case of sexual harassment. John Whitehead's eagerness to help Paula Jones derived from his own lifelong ideological commitment to the religious right.

In 1982, the same year he founded Rutherford, Whitehead published *The Second American Revolution,* a treatise on the fundamentalist-Christian mission that became a genre bestseller. "The Church has a mandate from the Creator," he wrote, "to be a dominating influence on the whole culture." In practice, this meant Christians "taking control" of political parties and an educational system "reinstilled with Christian theism." His vision was an American society in which "all of civil affairs and government, including law, should be based upon principles found in the Bible," with indeed "nothing untouched by the Bible" as interpreted by right-wing theologians. His mentor in this totalitarian project was R. J. Rushdoony, whose views are cited numerous times in Whitehead's book and whose library he used for research. Rushdoony was among the founding directors of Rutherford and spoke at the institute's conferences. Rushdoony's own literature boasted that the old theocrat had been "instrumental in establishing the Rutherford Institute."

In recent years, Whitehead has adopted a more ecumenical tone, and his associates have denied that he was ever an adherent of Christian Reconstructionism. Among Rutherford's log of hundreds of cases, there are certainly instances where it has defended the religious prerogatives of Orthodox Jews, Native Americans, and Hare Krishna followers. But the bulk of its work is devoted to advancing the Christian fundamentalist perspective on such issues as abortion, gay rights, and proselytizing in public schools.

Among the most forthright exponents of Rutherford's view of civil liberties is Donovan Campbell, Jr., recruited by his friend Whitehead to serve as lead attorney in the Jones case. A longtime member of the Rutherford board of directors and recently listed on its tax returns as the group's secretary-treasurer, Campbell made his mark in Texas as the leading advocate for more than a decade to uphold that state's 1974 law banning sodomy. When gay rights groups challenged the Texas statute in 1993, Campbell led the legal team that defended it before the state supreme court in Austin. Their brief argued that homosexuality was a "psychopathological condition . . . and a disorder from mental health," and that gays were responsible not only for the spread of sexually transmitted diseases but for deviant mass murderers like Jeffrey Dahmer and John Wayne Gacy. The grim, bespectacled Campbell betrayed no hint of irony when, in spite of his long history of opposing civil rights for homosexuals, he claimed to be representing Jones because hers was "a very significant constitutional and civil rights lawsuit. That's the type of work that my law firm does."

While the new Jones legal team professed complete faith in their client's truthfulness, they eventually discovered that she and her adviser Susan Carpenter-McMillan were less than forthcoming even toward them. Near the end of 1997, Jones signed a fund-raising letter sent out by Whitehead's direct-mail consultant. "I know many of you who are familiar with the work of the Rutherford Institute are wondering why this group is coming to my aid," she said in the letter. "It's because I'm speaking the truth and need help. . . . so please, in the name of freedom, send in whatever gift you can today to the Rutherford Institute to help them with my case."

Whitehead was puzzled and dismayed when the letter got almost no response. Rather than being a cash cow, the Jones case was draining his organization's resources. In a year-end plea to his regular donors, he wrote, "Our backs are against the wall. It is now do or die."

He might have understood his financial difficulties more clearly if he had known then what he learned later. Paula Jones was also raising money for her own legal fund, which she and her husband operated as a nonexempt family business. In November 1997, around the time that Whitehead realized her case had brought him virtually no new contributors, Jones signed a fund-raising agreement with a prominent Virginia fund-raiser named Bruce Eberle. In exchange for the right to use her name in a series of direct-mail appeals, Eberle promised Jones at least $300,000 for her proprietary Paula Jones Legal Fund. Upon inking the deal, Jones reportedly received $100,000 up front from Eberle's company.

Of course, she had always denied that money or politics were the motives behind her lawsuit. Early on she had vowed to donate any proceeds after expenses to charity. Her new lawyers learned differently in late November, when she instructed them to answer any overtures toward a settlement from Bennett with a stunning new demand. Rather than the $700,000 she had originally demanded in her legal papers, Jones said she would accept nothing less than $2.6 million—a blatant breach of good faith in any legal negotiation.

Rather than explain to her that they felt that such conduct was unacceptable and even possibly unethical, Campbell and his partners simply transmitted their client's message to Bennett, who could hardly believe what he was hearing. The president and his lawyer had always suspected that Jones's backers were pursuing a political vendetta. The ideological complexion of her new backers had reinforced that suspicion. Now there was no further reason for doubt.

Chapter Sixteen

"THE BASTARD SHOULD BE EXPOSED"

WHEN LINDA TRIPP PICKED UP the ringing telephone on the night of September 18, 1997, it was almost 10:30 P.M. Right away she recognized the distinctively deep female voice, roughened by cigarettes and whiskey, even though she hadn't heard from Lucianne Goldberg for well over a year. She had asked Tony Snow to contact the agent on her behalf again. Still embarrassed over their earlier aborted book deal, Tripp spoke haltingly at first.

"I've thought about you various times over the past year and . . ." She sighed. "I wanted to—to chat with you about something that is—is completely ridiculous. Um, last September a young lady, um, who shall remain nameless for the time being . . ."

"All right," said Goldberg patiently.

". . . again, took me in as her confidante and, as it turns out, she has been a, quote, girlfriend of the big creep . . ."

"Mmm," muttered Goldberg.

" . . . and is still."

"Mm-hmm."

"Uh, she was twenty-one and an intern when it started."

"After he was at the major address," Goldberg prompted.

"Uh, yeah, this was only two years ago. . . . It's been going on for two years."

"All right."

"She was given a job there, things got hot after six months in terms of others', uh, comments, and uh, one of the female head honchos, not the big one—but one of her people gave him an ultimatum: basically, get her the hell out or else." Tripp sighed again. "So he got her out—he put her in an agency, um, with a promotion, and it was still going on all this time. It's still going on, but he's in a state of paranoia. Uh . . ." Another sigh. ". . . and it's so sickening to me."

"But," asked the literary agent, trying to frame the scene in her mind, "where did they do this?"

"In—in, again, the same location, in the office," replied Tripp, evidently assuming that Goldberg still remembered Kathleen Willey's story, as recounted in Tripp's 1996 book proposal.

"Yikes."

Without revealing Monica Lewinsky's name, Tripp went on to describe the affair between the former intern and the president of the United States: its furtive Sunday-afternoon trysts in the Oval Office, its late-night phone-sex sessions, its exhausting emotional turbulence. Tripp had been keeping careful notes for months, she told Goldberg, about everything the younger woman confided.

As she listened, Goldberg was calculating how this stunning information could best be used. "Well, have you talked to her about going forward with this?" This young woman would never do that, Tripp explained, because "she doesn't want him harmed."

"Well, then what can you do with it?" asked Goldberg. No matter how many notes and records Tripp might produce, the agent warned, the press would "destroy" the young woman and portray Tripp, already known for her roles in the Kathleen Willey and Vince Foster cases, as "some kind of, uh, you know, nutcase."

Despite those caveats, Goldberg was hooked. "My tabloid heart beats loud," she laughed as she pondered Tripp's options. "Is there any way to have, uh, this Ms. X that we're talking about here, have her be, um, shall we say, reached by the Paula Jones people?"

Tripp didn't think so, but then she mentioned another potential avenue of exposure: "Listen, Mike Isikoff has been on my tail about this one for months."

Had Linda Tripp known Lucianne Goldberg a little better, she might have suspected that the literary agent was taping their conversation—a habit Goldberg had acquired during a long career of intrigue and gossipmongering (and one that, however obnoxious, was perfectly legal in New York, where Goldberg lived). While Tripp had happened upon Goldberg by chance through their mutual friend Tony Snow, she could hardly have selected a more dedicated companion in a scheme against the president. With her bitter determination and self-serving righteousness, Goldberg in many ways epitomized the professional Clinton adversary. She had much in common with Larry Nichols and Sheffield Nelson. But she also had a degree of wit and media savvy displayed by very few of Clinton's enemies.

Politically, she was a hard-bitten conservative of Nixonian vintage, with the same inclination to fight dirty that had always identified the late disgraced president and his circle. Her resentment sometimes sounded quite personal, less perhaps because Bill Clinton was a Democrat than because he represented the succession to power of the antiwar, pot-smoking generation that had rejoiced at Nixon's resignation. Clinton had demonstrated against the Vietnam War and worked in the McGovern campaign, while his feminist wife had researched impeachment for the Democrats on the Senate Watergate committee. For the aging, haunted Nixonites, Clinton's presidency renewed a desire for vengeance that had never been satisfied.

It also presented an attractive opportunity to make a buck. The sixty-two-year-old Goldberg had long been a player in the market for a certain kind of political literature. Her bestsellers in this popular genre included *Teddy Bare*, an exposé of the Chappaquiddick incident, and former Los Angeles police detective Mark Fuhrman's version of the O. J. Simpson murder investigation. In the literary agent's entanglement with Tripp, the boundary between business and politics became blurred. Goldberg would later proclaim that her motives had been purely patriotic, saying she had been "interested in a Clinton-bashing book since the day I laid eyes on him." But then there had always been a mercenary aspect to her activism.

Lucianne Goldberg's first brush with the art of the dirty trick came in a sideshow to the Watergate affair. In the sizable domestic-espionage apparatus set up by the Nixon White House, she played a very minor role, so insignificant that she is omitted from most histories of the great scandal.

Posing as a journalist and using the code name "Chapman's Friend," Goldberg spied on George McGovern's presidential campaign from August to November of 1972. She was paid $1,000 a week from a Nixon campaign slush fund to provide gossip about what she later termed "the really dirty stuff" going on among campaign staffers and reporters covering the Democratic nominee, "like who was sleeping with who, what the Secret Service men were doing with the stewardesses, who was smoking pot on the plane—that sort of thing." On the campaign trail there was enough "dirty stuff" to pique Nixon's voyeurism, although little that was of any practical use.

The White House spies had recruited her through her second husband, Sidney Goldberg, a news syndicate executive with ties to the Nixon entourage, notably with Victor Lasky, an unsavory right-wing journalist who specialized in red-baiting liberal Democrats. Lasky introduced Lucianne Goldberg to Murray Chotiner, the veteran California GOP operative whose pedigree dated back to Nixon's first congressional campaign in 1950, when Chotiner engineered the smearing of Democrat Helen Gahagan Douglas as "the Pink Lady."

Hiring journalists to spy on his political opponents was a favorite Chotiner tactic. (Chotiner's first operative in the McGovern campaign, a freelance reporter named Seymour Freidin, abruptly lost his cover during the summer of 1971, when the syndicated columnist Jack Anderson revealed that he was actually a CIA agent.) At Chotiner's urging, Lucianne obtained campaign press credentials with the Women's News Service, a feature agency which had occasionally published her articles. She convinced the McGovern people that she planned to write a book about the election. What she really did was phone intelligence reports every few hours to Chotiner, who promptly had them transcribed and sent over to the White House.

Goldberg was also involved in another of Chotiner's little stunts during the 1972 campaign, which involved the dissemination of a letter smearing a distinguished Greek journalist as a Communist agent. Elias P. Demetracopoulos had fled the Greek military coup in 1967 and devoted his considerable skills to the restoration of democracy in his country. As was later revealed during the Watergate investigation, the Greek junta was funneling hundreds of thousands in illicit cash to Nixon's campaign coffers. In a "Dear Elias" open letter to Demetracopoulos, Democratic presidential candidate George McGovern announced that if elected, he would cut off U.S. aid to the military government that he flatly termed a "dictatorship."

With Greek American vice president Spiro Agnew on the ticket, the Nixon campaign was portraying the junta as the only alternative to Communism in Greece. The Democratic mayor of Savannah, Georgia, John P. Rousakis, wrote an open letter to McGovern that was widely publicized in the Greek American press. Rousakis pronounced himself "shocked and appalled" not only by McGovern's position on military aid to Greece, but also by his having chosen to announce that policy through "an obscure Greek communist journalist."

Demetracopoulos, whose anti-Communist credentials could hardly have been better—the ultraconservative magazine *Human Events* once described him as "the foremost political editor in Greece"—demanded and belatedly got a retraction and apology. Later still, investigators for the Senate Watergate committee determined that the letter had in fact been written as part of a dirty tricks operation by Lucianne Goldberg.

Goldberg's cover as a member of the Women's News Service was part of the same game. The Women's News Service was a subsidiary of the North American Newspaper Alliance (NANA), a news agency whose top editors included Sidney Goldberg—and therein lies a curious coincidence. Like Forum World Features, the London-based news agency which was fronted and financed by Richard Mellon Scaife until 1975, NANA was exposed as a media conduit for the Central Intelligence Agency. (Among the columnists whose work it distributed was Goldberg's pal Lasky, a former employee of the CIA's Radio Liberty operation in Eastern Europe.)

So while Scaife and the Goldbergs moved in entirely different circles—and there is no evidence that they have ever met—it is nevertheless striking that during the early seventies they were simultaneously involved with the Nixon campaign and with CIA-connected press organizations. Such was the political milieu from which, twenty years later, two of Clinton's most dogged opponents emerged.

She was born Lucianne Steinberger, grew up in a middle-class Washington, D.C., suburb, dropped out of public high school, and married young and unwisely to William Cummings, her teenage sweetheart. For a while she drifted from one dull job to another, including a three-year stint as a clerk in the *Washington Post*'s promotion department. Her fortunes improved when, after separating from Cummings while still in her early twenties, she joined Lyndon Johnson's presidential campaign as a press assistant. Following the 1960 election, the fun-loving Lucy Cummings landed a job in the Kennedy White House press office despite her educational handicap. As she once remarked of her early career, "when you're tall, thin, blonde and have big boobs, you can have any job you want." That was certainly the impression she made on a former Lady Bird Johnson aide, who vividly recalled the low-level press staffer as "a very flashy blonde who wore short skirts, tight tops, and made goo-goo eyes at all the guys."

As a single woman in sixties Washington, the young Lucianne wasn't quite the stern moralist America later came to know through her televised scolding of Monica Lewinsky and Bill Clinton. "Lucy would claim that her entire social life took place Monday through Friday, because she only went out with married men," a former friend told *Newsday* in 1998. "On weekends they had to stay with their wives. She'd watch TV Saturday and Sunday."

With the change of administrations after President Kennedy's 1963 assassination, however, her bouncy sexuality may have been her undoing. According to Goldberg, she was frozen out of the White House in 1964 because of an adulterous romance with Dale Miller, an adviser to Lyndon Johnson. Miller's wife, a close friend of Lady Bird Johnson, evidently grew suspicious when she discovered that Lucianne possessed several "unexplained items" that had been billed to the Millers' account at Garfinckel's, a local department store. (Both Millers are since deceased, but their daughter told Knight-Ridder reporters Frank Greve and Ron Hutcheson that she believed there had been no affair and that the department store charges were "fraudulent"; Goldberg claimed that the Garfinckel's merchandize were gifts from her lover, who had given her "permission to charge.")

Among the items Lucianne took along as she departed the White House was a handwritten personal note sent by Jacqueline Kennedy to Lady Bird Johnson in 1960. That historic document caused a brief stir in 1965, after Mrs. Johnson's staff learned that Lucianne had brought it to a New York autograph broker for valuation. Unfortunately, not everyone believed her subsequent explanation that she had simply discovered it in a carton of "general debris" from the '60 Kennedy-Johnson campaign. The Secret Service ended up retrieving the note and returning it to the first lady.

While trying to set herself up as a public relations flack at the National Press Club building in Washington, she was first drawn into Republican circles after meeting Sidney Goldberg. In 1966, she married him at the Plaza Hotel and moved to Manhattan, where she worked briefly for a public relations firm run by the old Nixon hand William Safire.

By the time Goldberg's role as a Nixon spy was disclosed by the *Washington Star* in 1973, she was, like her husband, a confirmed Republican partisan. Publicly disgraced, both Goldbergs offered their resignations to the management of the Women's News Service. Lucianne's was accepted, and she soon embarked on a new dual career: as a literary agent specializing in politically tinged, sensationalized nonfiction, and as an author of cheesy contemporary fiction. What she once told an interviewer about her lifelong addiction to gossip could also be regarded as her professional motto: "I love dish. I live for dish." (She also later established a sideline selling items for a fee to publications owned by conservative press lord Rupert Murdoch, including the *New York Post*.)

Certainly she was no prude. Her most successful novel, *Madam Cleo's Girls*, was a soft-core tale of international prostitution. Her first nonfiction work, a leering critique of feminism titled *Purr, Baby, Purr*, suggested that every woman should consider herself "a switchboard with all sorts of lovely buttons and plug-ins for lighting up and making connections."

For several years her one-woman, low-overhead agency thrived, if mostly at the lower end of New York's literary hierarchy. But in 1982, Goldberg transformed an important asset into a controversial liability that almost drove her out of the book business. Her client Kitty Kelley, the celebrity biographer, had recently published *Elizabeth Taylor: The Last Star*, which was destined to become a major international bestseller. According to Kelley, however, she was puzzled when Goldberg seemed unable to sell foreign rights to the Taylor biography. It was only by luck, when her observant husband was traveling in Europe, that Kelley learned the book was in fact already being sold abroad without her knowledge or consent.

For more than a year, the frustrated author attempted to obtain royalty payments and straight answers from Goldberg. Finally, she was forced to file a lawsuit against her own agent in federal court in Washington, where Kelley lives. Her attorney charged Goldberg with civil fraud, breach of fiduciary responsibility, and failure to pay royalties. The jury didn't take long to find the defendant guilty, although the judge overturned both the fraud verdict and an award of punitive damages. In a recent interview, Kelley said that Goldberg wrote her a check for the full amount, about $50,000, before they left the courthouse. (In an ironic epilogue, Goldberg's lawyer soon found himself suing her to try to collect his fee; he won a judgment, but in 1998, twelve years after winning, still hadn't collected what Goldberg owed him.)

Lucianne Goldberg was not, to say the least, without her own history of peccadilloes. Her motivations as well as Tripp's would be questioned, as she seemed to know; and when that moment came, she would deny repeatedly that she and her client had even considered selling a book about Clinton and Lewinsky. Amazingly, Goldberg would tell FBI investigators working for Kenneth Starr that "there was no book deal mentioned during this time period," meaning the fall of 1997. She insisted that their sole aim was to protect Tripp from being labeled a nut or, worse, a perjurer.

Nobody would have known otherwise—except that the two tapes Goldberg made of her own telephone discussions with Tripp show that a book deal was their central concern in determining whether to cooperate with Isikoff. Many other matters came up, too: the gifts Clinton and Lewinsky had exchanged, their failure to consummate the relationship, Lewinsky's obsession with other alleged girlfriends of the president, Clinton's sexual proclivities, Isikoff's "manipulative" treatment of sources, and a strange invitation Tripp had received from a Clinton friend. What was barely mentioned on those tapes was any concern Tripp felt about being subpoenaed to testify in the Paula Jones lawsuit.

Clearly, something more personal than pure opportunism animated Linda Tripp's anger at the president. According to a *New Yorker* profile by Jane Mayer, Tripp's father repeatedly betrayed and finally left her mother. Tripp's own marriage had also ended in divorce. She was especially outraged by Clinton's lustful behavior toward the "beautiful young girl" (whose name she didn't mention to Goldberg during those initial September conversations).

"He plays to the world audiences as being a protector of women's rights," she complained.

"Oh, I know, yeah," said Goldberg.

"As being this—this sterling example of family values and—other than the fact that he's known to be a philanderer. But, I mean, beyond that, he's got a daughter five years younger than that . . ."

"Yeah," said Goldberg.

"I have a daughter five years younger, and I have a son her age."

"Right," said Goldberg.

"I—I find it appalling—and I think parents would find it appalling."

The literary agent wanted to talk business.

"Do you—um—how do you see your using this information, in a book or—"

"I don't know," Tripp replied. "I mean, I was working on—right now, my attorney has virtually all my files, but prior to that I had scrubbed the whole Maggie [Gallagher] product and started from scratch and had come up with a whole different spin. . . ." Tripp was already contemplating another book project about her White House experiences.

"Now, um, have you considered going to Isikoff and going off the record with him?" Goldberg asked.

"Oh, I could do that in a minute. But then he'd write the book, or he'd—he'd write the whole thing."

Goldberg thought not. "No. Uh, he only has a certain amount of space."

"Oh, no," Tripp fretted. "He's—working on a book deal. He's doing an all-the-president's-women kind of thing." Although Isikoff later tried to minimize his effort to sell a book in 1997, there is no doubt he tried to put together a book proposal on Clinton's scandals during that spring and summer.

Goldberg wasn't worried. "Well, then we make a deal with Isikoff that here's—here's the information we'll give you. Here is just enough documentation for you to do the story, but—but the rest of it belongs to Linda because she's doing a book. He would have to honor that if he wanted the story. . . . Um, the trick would be to get it out there, just enough of it to titillate the public."

Tripp explained that first she wanted to get a new job, one that wouldn't be vulnerable to an angry president. In leaving the White House for the Pentagon, she had given up the protections of the civil service for a more lucrative political appointment. A job change might take some time, but by early spring 1998, she told the agent, she could be ready for a book deal.

Again, Goldberg reassured her jumpy client about talking to *Newsweek*. "I think—just hearing it for the first time . . . I think we can make a deal with Isikoff that protects you totally, that gets the surface of this out, and then you stand back to fill in the pieces, and I get you a publisher that will be happy to do that."

"All right. Well, let's talk again," said Tripp. "I—my reservation about Isikoff is that he is known to her, uh, because of my involvement with him before."

There was no point in worrying about that, Goldberg pointed out. "If you're ready to go ahead with this, you have to be ready to lose her as a friend."

"Oh," said Tripp. "I've already made this decision."

In that case, Goldberg said, "Isikoff should not pose a problem." And, she added, "There's nothing wrong with going to Isikoff soon, and the deal that we would cut would be, 'You write nothing, but here's background so you can start piling up stuff.'" Before hanging up she instructed Tripp to "think about going to Isikoff and write a list of what demands you want to take to him . . . and then you and I will collude on it. . . ."

Then, she chuckled, they could all meet at her new and better "safe house" in Washington, a duplex apartment the Goldbergs had recently bought for their son Jonah.

The next time they spoke, about a week later, Goldberg and Tripp apparently discussed the possibility of cutting out Isikoff and selling their story to the *Star* or the *Globe*, supermarket tabloids where the down-market agent was already well connected. That conversation wasn't recorded by Goldberg, but she has acknowledged that she raised another sensitive subject that evening. Only by taping the constant calls from Lewinsky about her affair with Clinton, Goldberg insisted, would Tripp be able to compile sufficient proof that it was true.

A few days later they spoke again, and this time Goldberg's tape recorder was running. Their agenda was still how to break the story in *Newsweek* without spoiling Tripp's value as a tell-all author. Ever mindful of the aborted 1996 book deal, Tripp apologized for putting Goldberg "in a sore spot."

"It's not a sore spot," the agent said. "My ultimate goal in this is that the information become public, with you being protected—and your being able to step forward and tell an extraordinary story." She scoffed at Isikoff's doubts. "When he says no—[that] in this climate no publisher will touch it—I'm sorry, but the attitude in publishing now is 'We don't give'—even the liberals that were pro-Clinton—'We don't give a shit.' Nobody cares about him anymore. . . . The climate is extremely good for this kind of information."

"I would have absolutely no qualms going that way," said Tripp, referring to "the tabloid stuff."

"Yeah, but the problem with that," warned Goldberg, "is that you've gotta really rat and that you've gotta tape."

That night Goldberg placed Tripp in serious legal jeopardy. Evidently they had already discussed the legality of taping phone conversations with only one party's consent, as Goldberg herself was doing at that very moment. Now she told Tripp, "I checked that out. You can—one-party taping is fine. You checked it out too, but—it's fine. There's no problem with that."

There was a big problem, however, with one-party taping in the state of Maryland, where Tripp resided. There and in eight other states, it was illegal. Recording even one such tape could bring a felony conviction, with a penalty of up to five years in prison and a $10,000 fine.

They decided to ask Isikoff to a meeting where both women would be present. "Tell him that we, the three of us want to sit down, and I don't want him to be wired," instructed Goldberg. "'Cause I'll be wired," she joked. "Tell him . . . that I've been your agent for a long time. . . . And I am also keenly interested, as you are, in doing something with this information that protects you, but eventually leads to you doing a book about your entire experience."

"Okay. All right. I'll do that tomorrow morning."

Several months later, Tripp would testify before the OIC grand jury in Washington about her September 1997 conversations with Goldberg. When associate independent counsel Stephen Binhak asked whether she and the literary agent had talked about "putting together a book, another book proposal," Tripp said, "We both realized right away that this was coming to a head and this wasn't particularly what could be a book." Instead, she insisted, the "whole premise" of her renewed contact with Goldberg was her fear of being called to testify in the Jones case. "[A book] was not what we were looking to do and I say that with all candor. When I threw away the book idea in August of '96, I was completely finished with it." If Binhak ever listened to the Goldberg tapes—which were in the OIC's possession—he would have realized that her sworn testimony was false. Ostensibly terrified at the prospect of telling less than she knew in a civil deposition, Tripp appeared to have no difficulty at all lying to a federal grand jury.

Within days of Goldberg's suggestion that she tape Lewinsky, Tripp visited a nearby Radio Shack store and purchased a $100 recorder. (Reportedly, employees of that store later testified that they had advised Tripp about the illegality of one-party taping in Maryland, following a company policy that was reiterated in a warning on the tape recorder's packaging.) She set up the device on a little-used phone line in her study, and inaugurated her home wiretap on the evening of October 3 with a call to Lewinsky.

That maiden tape produced little useful dialogue. The two women fell into an argument over whether Lewinsky had been "having sex" with Clinton or whether they had just "fooled around." Lewinsky insisted that "blow jobs" were far less intimate than intercourse, a distinction Tripp mocked. "You've been around him too much."

Perhaps Tripp had been around Lewinsky too much, as Lewinsky's biographer, Andrew Morton, later theorized. Listening to Monica moaning about her heartaches with the "big creep" had grown tiresome. Over the course of a year, the sheer tedium of Lewinsky's whining may have hardened her "friend" for the manipulations Tripp used to gradually trap her.

On the morning of October 6, Tripp began to play on the emotions of the younger woman, informing her that "Kate"—a White House friend of Tripp's who worked for the National Security Council—had said there was no chance Lewinsky would be brought back into the White House. A successful job interview at the NSC and a strong recommendation from Tripp couldn't mitigate rampant rumors about her misbehavior. Deflecting Lewinsky's furious questions, Tripp would not say how "Kate" supposedly knew this. (Tripp's friend, NSC staffer Kate Friedrich, later testified that she had never discussed Lewinsky's bad reputation with Tripp—but Tripp can be heard on tape telling Lucianne Goldberg about the same alleged conversation with "Kate.")

Lewinsky had known for months that her chances of going back to the West Wing were not good. During the summer she had met with presidential aide Marsha Scott to plead her case, and had broken down in tears when Scott said that her reputation as a "stalker" had made her unemployable there. Scott would later explain to the grand jury how she had tried to counsel Lewinsky that returning to the White House would do her career more harm than good. A strikingly attractive woman whom the *American Spectator* had called Clinton's mistress, she had become furious when Monica had responded by naming a list of White House employees suspected of sleeping with the president whose careers were prospering. "I thought she seemed rather pathetic," Scott explained, ". . . but I was also very angry that she was going down this road. I thought it was very self-centered. It was like a little spoiled kid."

Nevertheless, it was Tripp's account of what "Kate" had supposedly said that finally ended Lewinsky's fantasy. From that moment, she became increasingly receptive to Tripp's insistence on an alternative course: She should demand that Clinton find her a suitably "substantive" and well-paid job in New York City. It was the least the big creep could do.

A few minutes after hanging up with Lewinsky, Tripp's phone rang again. It was Lucianne Goldberg calling from her son's apartment in Washington's Adams-Morgan neighborhood. She had arranged a meeting with Michael Isikoff, and had come down from New York the night before.

"What I have on tape is very little," Tripp cautioned. "I mean, I'll get more. Because this isn't over, in terms of what she'll want to rehash over and over again. But there are dates. She says some dates on there, and, you know, when he called her from the road and—"

"Well, that's enough," replied Goldberg. "You know, all you need is a snippet to—"

"Oh, I got snippets." Did Jonah have a cassette recorder so Tripp could play the snippets for Isikoff? He did.

"It's telling that in, I think, three conversations I went through a hundred-and-twenty-minute tape, and I think one side of [another], and, actually, what I'm trying to do is stall here, because I think she's going to call me from the Watergate and let me know what she's decided to do. . . . And I want to hear, if she's flipping out, I want to get that on tape."

Isikoff stopped off at Jonah Goldberg's apartment for an hour that evening on his way to appear on *Hardball with Chris Matthews,* a CNBC evening talk show. Sitting in the living room, he listened as Tripp told him she had been surreptitiously taping her recent conversations with the president's paramour. She had brought along a tape for him to hear.

First, said Isikoff, "I need to know this woman's name." Tripp glanced over at Goldberg, then replied, "Her name is Monica Lewinsky." As the reporter scribbled, Tripp gave the details on Lewinsky's background and family, her entrée to the White House through a Clinton contributor named Walter Kaye, and her current job at the Pentagon.

It was an interesting story, especially the parts about a presidential girlfriend on the public payroll. But when Tripp started to play the tape cued up on Jonah Goldberg's coffee table, Isikoff stopped her. As he explained in *Uncovering Clinton,* he felt queasy about hearing a tape made under such dubious circumstances. And something else bothered him too, he later wrote. "If I started to listen in on her conversations as she was taping them—as opposed to when she was finished—then I inevitably would have become part of the process." He didn't want to influence conversations that would become part of his story. (According to Tripp's testimony, however, the fastidious journalist "encouraged me to continue my taping.")

He needed more "documentation" than the tapes anyway, he told Tripp and Goldberg as he prepared to leave. "I had nothing particular in mind when I made this point." Yet he did say that he was particularly intrigued by Lewinsky's search for a new job.

When Tripp arrived home later that night, she dialed Lewinsky's number. The voice-activated recorder switched on automatically before Lewinsky answered. After chatting awhile, Tripp subtly guided her into a discussion of potential employment opportunities in New York. Whenever she grew despondent over Clinton's lack of attention to her, Lewinsky thought about joining her mother in Manhattan and finding a job there, perhaps at the United Nations. Months earlier, Lewinsky recalled, Betty Currie had spoken with Clinton about that idea on her behalf. According to Currie, the president had said, "Oh, that's no problem. We can place her in the UN like that." Now she and Tripp together composed a letter to Clinton, imploring him to make good on that implied promise by December 1.

"You don't have to limit yourself to the UN. There are a bazillion options in New York," urged Tripp, who also offered advice about how to send the letter. The quickest way would be delivery via a safe, bonded courier like Speed Service. Lewinsky hesitated, worrying that a messenger might open her letter or draw unwanted attention, but Tripp convinced her that no such danger existed. "Courier it tomorrow morning from work. What is more natural than something being couriered from the Pentagon to the White House?"

A mature woman trusted by Lewinsky almost as much as her own mother, the authoritative, experienced Tripp didn't have much difficulty directing the action. Lewinsky sent the letter to Betty Currie by courier from the Pentagon the following day, and continued to use Speed Service to deliver packages and letters to Clinton.

She couldn't have conceived the real reason Tripp had insisted on that particular Washington courier firm. Speed Service was managed by a relative of Lucianne Goldberg—and he had been instructed by her to keep the routing slips of every letter and package the young woman sent to the White House.

Goldberg later admitted that conning Lewinsky into using Speed Service had been her idea, although she also told the FBI she had suggested the firm to Tripp "in an offhanded way, with the only intention of steering some business" to her family. (Very considerate of her, even if the total was well under $50.) Within a few weeks, Tripp and Goldberg provided Isikoff with several routing slips from Speed Service as documentation of the Clinton-Lewinsky relationship.

On October 11, responding to Lewinsky's courier-delivered letter asking to see him, the president called her at home around 2:30 A.M. Her feelings of rejection and his mounting impatience quickly erupted into a "huge screaming match" that went on for well over an hour. She later recalled his saying that night, "If I'd known what kind of person you are, I would never have gotten involved with you." At these moments of emotional release, his relationship with Lewinsky sounded like a pairing of equally immature teenagers; and when the weeping and yelling subsided, he characteristically tried to reassure her that he really did care. He would prove it by helping her find a good job in New York.

Several hours later, Currie invited her to see the president in the Oval Office. In a warm and friendly Saturday-morning mood, they talked over her move to Manhattan, her mother's new apartment there, and her career possibilities at the UN and elsewhere. Giving her a farewell hug, he asked her to send him an employment "wish list."

It was either during that meeting or on the telephone the night before that Lewinsky first raised the name of Vernon Jordan, the suave Washington attorney, Clinton golf buddy, and adornment of various corporate boards. Would the president ask his influential friend to help her find work? "Good idea," Clinton agreed.

Good or bad, that idea had originated with someone else, as Lewinsky told Kenneth Starr's investigators after she received immunity and began talking. According to the transcript of her initial OIC interview on July 27, 1998, "Linda Tripp suggested to Lewinsky that the President should be asked to ask Vernon Jordan for assistance." Tripp told Starr's grand jury that it was neither she nor Lewinsky but the president who had proposed contacting Jordan. The tapes she provided offer no clue as to who told the truth.

Yet there is little question that Tripp was guiding Lewinsky's job search toward a snare. Toward the end of October, UN ambassador Bill Richardson invited the ex-intern to an interview with him at his Washington quarters, in the same Watergate complex where Lewinsky then lived. On the pretext that there was something improper about Lewinsky going to Richardson's hotel room, Tripp frantically tried to persuade her to insist that the meeting take place in Acquarelle, a restaurant downstairs. Lewinsky herself didn't feel altogether comfortable going to the ambassador's suite, and Tripp shrewdly played on her fears by suggesting that it was all "a setup" engineered by Clinton aide John Podesta, who had arranged the interview.

"Monica, please promise me you will not meet this guy in the hotel room," Tripp wheedled. "What if John Podesta thinks a good way to neutralize you is to put you in a compromising situation? Then if ever you decide to become a crazy woman, they can say, 'Oh please, she propositioned Bill Richardson at the Watergate.'"

Beneath this pulp-novel scenario lay another Tripp trap. She wanted Lewinsky to meet Richardson in a public place so they could be observed, and perhaps photographed, by *Newsweek*. Tipped off by Tripp, Isikoff knew that Lewinsky was scheduled to meet Richardson at the Watergate on the morning of October 31. According to Isikoff, one of his colleagues staked out the complex for several pointless hours. As *Newsweek*'s bored sleuth flipped through newspapers at the restaurant downstairs, Lewinsky and Richardson chatted briefly and demurely upstairs, in the presence of his assistants. But having already decided she didn't really want to work at the UN, she declined the position Richardson offered her a few days later.

Instead Lewinsky decided to rely upon the extensive contacts of Vernon Jordan, with whom she met for the first time on November 5—an appointment she had been trying to arrange through Currie for nearly a month. Offering him the "vanilla" version of her departure from the White House and her reasons for leaving Washington, she showed the charming attorney her employment "wish list" of New York firms. He looked it over, suggested a few additions, and assured Lewinsky he would line up some interviews soon. "We're in business."

While Tripp continued to tape Lewinsky on more than two dozen occasions in October and November, she was beginning to feel the pressure of her own deception. It offended her that Clinton, despite his efforts to end the illicit relationship, still appeared to her to be toying with Lewinsky's affections, and that the young woman still remained so lovestruck. The possibility that the president had grown genuinely fond of Monica and was letting her down easy while protecting their secret doesn't seem to have occurred to her. (As in all love affairs, the proportions of altruism and selfishness in this one remained a mystery—perhaps even to Clinton and Lewinsky themselves.)

Meanwhile, despite Tripp's frequent reports to "Harvey," the code name she had bestowed on Isikoff, he wasn't moving forward on her timetable. The reporter was listening and cooperating, but there was no way to know when he would have sufficient evidence. *Newsweek*'s institutional caution had delayed the Kathleen Willey story until after the *Drudge Report* broke it.

Besides, to whatever degree Isikoff shared Tripp's and Goldberg's contempt for the president, his enthusiasm for their methods was more restrained. The week before Thanksgiving, according to him, Tripp called with the remarkable news that Lewinsky had kept a dress bearing stains from Clinton's semen since the previous February. Now she and Goldberg were thinking about purloining this damning frock and turning it over to Isikoff.

"What am I supposed to do with it?"

"Have it tested," Tripp answered.

"What in God's name are you talking about?" He was sure Tripp had lost her mind, and more or less told her so.

Crazy she might have been, but crafty too. Through Goldberg, she had benefited from the forensic expertise of Mark Fuhrman, the former Los Angeles detective then working with the literary agent on his second book. Fuhrman explained that even a tiny sample of semen could remain viable as evidence for years. The only problem, as Isikoff pointed out, was the absence of a sample of Clinton's own DNA for laboratory comparison. Where was *Newsweek* supposed to get that?

It is safe to say Tripp was fascinated by the stained dress. She even attempted a ruse to gain access to Lewinsky's apartment so she could steal it. When Lewinsky casually mentioned in late November that she planned to have the navy blue Gap shift dry-cleaned for a family occasion, the older woman begged her not to. The evidence should be preserved, Tripp admonished her, just in case.

"And I feel this is what I would tell my own daughter. That's why I'm saying this to you. I would say to my own daughter, for your own ultimate protection, which mea culpa [*sic*], I hope you never need it . . ."

"What for, though?" Lewinsky wondered.

"I don't know, Monica. It's just this nagging, awful feeling I have in the back of my head."

When those elliptical arguments didn't work, Tripp remarked that the Gap dress made the plump, insecure Monica look "really fat." Monica decided to leave the soiled souvenir in a closet.

Waiting for a subpoena from the Paula Jones lawyers was also taking a psychological toll on Tripp. She was looking forward to testifying, "gleefully," as she later put it, yet she desperately wanted to control the circumstances. Tripp is strongly suspected of having made several anonymous telephone calls to the

Jones lawyers, urging them to subpoena both herself and Monica Lewinsky. (She has denied making those calls, but some of her best friends apparently don't believe her.) According to Tripp's grand jury testimony, she remembered telling Goldberg, "I don't mind being subpoenaed, but I just wish there was a way to do this without having to be deposed in the presence of Bob Bennett," the president's lawyer. "He will find out about the tapes because if he asks me under oath I'll have to say, you know, that, yes, I have proof, and I'm dead meat. At that point if they know what I've been doing, I'm dead meat." (Describing her feelings to Lewinsky, Tripp sputtered, "The biggest thing is, I hate Bennett. I think he's an arrogant asshole, and I think he's a sleaze—a sleaze-ball.")

More than once that fall, the pressures on Tripp became so intense that she blew up in rage at Lewinsky and broke off their false friendship. "From now on, leave me alone," she E-mailed at the end of October. "I really am finished, Monica. Share this sick situation with one of your other friends, because, frankly, I'm past nauseated about the whole thing."

"I will respect that," Lewinsky replied. "I would only like to ask that I have your assurance that everything I have shared with you remains between us. You have given me your word before, but that was when we were on good terms. Can I still trust that?"

Another blowup occurred in late November, just before Tripp's birthday on November 24. Lewinsky sent gifts with a conciliatory note, which Tripp rejected the next day with a plea for solitude. "I need a break." They reconciled again, but by then Tripp was already talking about Lewinsky to the lawyers for Paula Jones. By then, in fact, the Jones lawyers had sent their own birthday present to Tripp at the Pentagon, in the form of a subpoena.

The man who set up Tripp's long-awaited rendezvous with the new Jones attorneys from Dallas was Richard W. Porter, the conservative activist with an expanding résumé: former Bush White House aide, adviser to Vice President Dan Quayle, and Republican opposition researcher; fellow University of Chicago Law School alumnus and close friend of Jerome Marcus, with whom he had arranged continuing legal assistance for Paula Jones; law partner of Kenneth W. Starr at Kirkland & Ellis; lawyer and anti-Clinton researcher for investment banker Peter W. Smith, who talked to him about negotiations with the Arkansas state troopers in Troopergate; and now conduit to the Jones team for Linda Tripp and Lucianne Goldberg.

During the third week of November, the agitated Tripp had asked Goldberg to "get me subpoenaed" by the Jones camp. She correctly assumed that the literary agent would be able to make the necessary connections. And Goldberg either knew or guessed that Alfred Regnery, the right-wing, Chicago-based president of Regnery Publishing and a publisher with whom Goldberg dealt frequently, might offer a useful suggestion. Regnery said Goldberg should call his friend Peter Smith, which she did on November 18.

"I did tell him at the time, I told him why we needed some help," Goldberg recalled much later. "Smith said, 'I'll be glad to help you with whatever you need, I know the whole story anyway.'" Smith called back that day with Richard Porter on a conference call. After Goldberg finished telling Tripp's story, Porter promised to take care of the subpoena.

Then, according to Isikoff—who had his own sources among the clique of conservative lawyers helping Jones—Porter also contacted George Conway in New York via E-mail. "There's a woman named Lewisky," he typed, misspelling her name. "She indulges a certain Lothario in the Casa Blanca for oral sex in the pantry." (Isikoff notes that Porter mentioned that among those aware of this situation was "a certain reporter at *Newsweek*.") He sent along Lucianne Goldberg's telephone number, too. Conway called the lawyers at Rader, Campbell in Dallas that same afternoon.

Until they heard about Monica Lewinsky, the Dallas attorneys were not so eager to contact Tripp. They regarded her testimony as potentially damaging to the credibility of their star witness, Kathleen Willey. But when David Pyke called Tripp at her Maryland home on the evening of November 21, he discovered that she intended to help him, a scenario that Pyke described as a "Willey-type situation."

Goldberg had briefed Pyke earlier, and now Tripp filled in most of the blanks regarding Lewinsky's affair with the president, except for her name. "I told him that I had been documenting through tape recording this information." She was relieved to learn that Jones had just won a ruling permitting the deposition of Willey, and thus providing a plausible reason for subpoenaing Tripp. According to Tripp's testimony Pyke worded the subpoena with sufficient imprecision that Tripp would not have to surrender the tapes just yet, "because he, too, did not want them to fall into the hands of Bob Bennett." They tentatively agreed on a deposition date in December. She also had a warning for Pyke, however. He was not to advise her attorney, Kirby Behre, that they had spoken about the subpoena.

Behre, a Democrat, had been recommended to her years before by the White House, and she no longer fully trusted him. (Evidently Tripp felt she couldn't fire Behre just yet because doing so might alert the White House to her real sympathies.) Pyke served Tripp the subpoena by mail at the Pentagon three days later.

After getting the subpoena, Tripp brought it to Behre's office along with the tapes of Lewinsky. Aghast that Tripp had violated Maryland's privacy statutes, Behre took possession of the tapes and ordered her to stop taping if she wanted to avoid prosecution. If they were subpoenaed, she would be exposed. But when Tripp showed him the Pyke subpoena, Behre laughed at how poorly it had been drawn. He had no idea his client had listened to Pyke draft it over the phone a few nights earlier. By demanding "writings" rather than "documents" from Tripp, the lawyer explained, it permitted him to withhold her tapes. "Oh," she said. "Isn't that great?"

Acting on an instinct that something was wrong, Bob Bennett made an attempt in early December to discern the true dimensions of his adversaries in the Jones case. The aggressive Clinton attorney had known for some time that back in 1994, before Kenneth Starr took over as the Whitewater independent counsel, Starr and others at Kirkland & Ellis had worked on an amicus brief supporting Jones's argument against presidential immunity. More recently, however, Bennett had learned something that troubled him even more. In October, according to James Warren, the Washington bureau chief of the *Chicago Tribune,* a sealed affidavit in the Jones case had been faxed to the newspaper's office, in violation of Judge Susan Webber Wright's strict gag order, from the Chicago office of Kirkland & Ellis. In other words, someone in Kenneth Starr's law firm had access to sealed documents in the Jones case.

Bennett had no way of knowing how serious the implications of that small fact were about to become. What bothered Bennett at the time was just the whiff of collusion. He was also aware that the OIC had, like Jones's lawyers, been investigating the president's personal life. At the very least, he thought, Starr might have a significant conflict of interest. The OIC's power could not be used to promote the interests of Starr's law firm. And he wondered whether the reluctance to settle on Jones's part might have something to do with the independent counsel.

Pursuing his intuition, Bennett delivered a subpoena on December 2 to Kirkland's Washington office, seeking any documents concerning the Jones lawsuit as well as all attorneys, individuals, and groups associated with it, including the Jones legal fund, Eberle & Associates, Susan Carpenter-McMillan, the Rutherford Institute, and Cliff Jackson, among others, that might exist in the files of the Starr firm's Washington or Chicago offices.

That same week, Monica Lewinsky returned from a Thanksgiving visit to her father's home in Los Angeles, and she was again becoming impatient with Clinton and his friends. Vernon Jordan hadn't returned any of her telephone calls since their meeting in November. On the morning of Saturday, December 6, she tried to enter the White House with an armful of presents for Clinton, but was turned away at the gate. When a Secret Service officer told her that the president was visiting with the blond CBS News correspondent Eleanor Mondale, Lewinsky made a scene and walked away enraged. A flurry of phone calls ensued between her and Betty Currie and Clinton, who first scolded her for being a pest and then invited her to come by later in the day.

In the Oval Office, Clinton greeted her warmly. She gave Clinton the gifts she had brought, and then told him of her frustration with Jordan. The president agreed to speak with his friend again. What Lewinsky didn't know then, although Clinton probably learned it that morning, was that her name was on a witness list delivered to Bennett by the Jones lawyers the previous day. Jordan saw the president that weekend, and on Monday his secretary called Lewinsky to set up a lunch meeting for her on December 11.

As they ate turkey sandwiches in his office, Jordan jokingly urged her to take out her anger with the busy, neglectful Clinton on him. Later that day, after sending Lewinsky away with a renewed promise to help her find a job, Jordan called top executives at three major New York firms: American Express; the diversified holding company McAndrews & Forbes, which owns Revlon; and the worldwide advertising agency Young & Rubicam.

About a week later, Clinton called Lewinsky at home around 2 A.M. with bad news. Betty Currie's brother, the president told her, had died in a terrible car accident. Also, Monica's name had showed up on the Jones witness list. According to Lewinsky, the president said she might avoid testifying if she gave an affidavit. They talked about whether Clinton could settle the lawsuit, as Lewinsky wished he would. He asked her to contact Currie if she received a subpoena.

The subpoena arrived at Lewinsky's Pentagon office on December 19. It summoned her for a deposition in January and demanded all her written communications with Clinton and all the gifts she had received from him. The list of gifts covered by the subpoena included, of all things, "hat pins"—a clear reference to the first present that Clinton had given her, and a none too subtle sign of treachery.

A shocked and sobbing Lewinsky called Vernon Jordan, who smoothly took control. He told her to come over, and when she got to his office, he tried to calm her down by explaining that there was really nothing extraordinary about the subpoena, despite its unusual demand for a hat pin. Jordan said he knew a good defense lawyer, Frank Carter, who might be able to represent her. She stepped out of the office for a moment so he could make a phone call. At that point, Jordan called Clinton and assured the president that he would find Lewinsky a good lawyer. Then he called her back in and asked two questions. Did she ever have sex with the president? Had he ever asked her to have sex with him? She answered no to both. She wasn't certain whether Jordan understood the real nature of her relationship with Clinton, although she later tried to explain their "phone sex" encounters to him. Perhaps because erotic talk on the phone hardly constitutes a love affair, perhaps because he might not have believed her, Jordan brushed it off.

On December 22, Jordan took Lewinsky in a limousine to Frank Carter's office. He stayed briefly to introduce them and then left. Carter, too, asked whether Lewinsky had had sex with the president. She again denied it. She had brought along some but not all of the gifts Clinton had given her, saying she hoped these would be enough to "satisfy" the Jones lawyers. Carter emphasized that she had to produce any and all items covered by the subpoena, and even urged her to go home and look for anything else that might be relevant. She hadn't brought the hat pin.

When Lewinsky returned to the Pentagon that afternoon, she and Tripp went out into an alley, where the older woman could smoke. There, Tripp came as close to telling her friend the truth as she ever would. "Monica, don't ask me to lie. If I'm asked about you, I'm gonna tell."

Frantic to find a way to avert that disaster, Lewinsky had talked through various scenarios, trying to convince Tripp to come over "to Bennett's side," to fake an injury that would postpone her deposition, to consult with the president's lawyers and Kirby Behre so that she wouldn't have to testify. At several points in November and December, Tripp had encouraged Lewinsky to believe that she might cooperate in some such scheme.

But in the alleyway, and again that night when they spoke on the telephone, Tripp made her intentions, if not her real purposes, clear. "Hey, look Monica, we already know that you're gonna lie under oath. . . . If I have to testify, if I am forced to answer questions and I answer truthfully, it's going to be the opposite of what you say. . . . If they say, 'Has Monica Lewinsky ever told you that she is in love with the president or is having a physical relationship with the president?'—if I say no, that is fucking perjury. That's the bottom line."

Gratuitously she added, "I will do everything that I can not to be in that position," when she had actually done everything she could to ensure she would be a witness for the Jones lawyers. "I am being a shitty friend," she said with unusual understatement, "and it's the last thing I want to do, because I won't lie."

If, during the last hour she spent with Clinton, Lewinsky had alerted him to the obvious danger posed by Tripp, everything might have turned out differently. But she couldn't bring herself to do that. It would have meant admitting that she had betrayed their secret and thereby jeopardized him, his family, and his presidency. On a Sunday morning, December 28, she went to visit him at the White House to pick up his Christmas gifts for her. Her job at the Pentagon had ended on Christmas Eve with a farewell party—where a smiling Tripp had insisted they be photographed together—and Lewinsky was preparing to leave for New York.

When the topic of the Jones subpoena came up, the trusting Clinton mentioned that troubling "hat pin" reference. Had Monica mentioned the little gift to "that woman from last summer," meaning Tripp? No, Lewinsky replied. Should she get rid of his other gifts, or give them to Betty Currie? she later said she asked him. According to her, he said he would think about it. They parted with a farewell kiss.

Sometime later, Betty Currie called Lewinsky at home to talk about the gifts. Their accounts of that conversation conflict somewhat as to the exact time, although neither woman said that the president had encouraged their scheming. The end result was that the secretary picked up a box of Clinton's gifts to Lewinsky, took it home, and stored it under her bed.

Just over a week later, Clinton called Lewinsky. She told him she had agreed that afternoon to sign an affidavit drafted by Frank Carter—which, if properly worded, might allow her to avoid testifying in the Jones case. The president didn't have much to say about that, although he suggested a few ways she might evade damaging responses to questions about why she had left the White House. In retrospect, his casual attitude toward her testimony suggests his confidence that she would protect him as well as herself. Their final conversation was brief and somewhat curt, as Lewinsky would later recall with some sorrow.

If Bill Clinton appears to have been dangerously cocksure as the Paula Jones case moved forward in late 1997, he did have his reasons. With hindsight, Clinton's decision to lie about Monica Lewinsky to his own lawyers and closest advisers, Hillary among them, appears almost inexplicable—especially given that the president knew perfectly well that Kenneth Starr's investigators were poking around Arkansas for evidence of his legendary sexual exploits. Moral considerations aside, how could anybody so smart be so dumb? Even if accounts of the OIC's questioning of his former state trooper bodyguards hadn't been widely publicized, many of the women in question were Clinton loyalists and would have reported to the White House. Starr's interest in the president's amorous past had long been an open secret in Little Rock.

Clinton must have believed that the OIC's sleuthing into his intimate life hadn't yet given Starr any useful evidence. The Washington Post's revelation of Starr's prurience had damaged the independent counsel badly, and Troopergate had already done Clinton all the damage it was ever going to do. Interviewing the troopers was like reshuffling a worn deck of pornographic playing cards. More importantly, meanwhile, the Jones case was falling to pieces.

Unknown to the press and general public, Jones's incoherent performance during her November 12, 1997, deposition made it seem that in the unlikely event Judge Susan Webber Wright allowed the case to proceed, the trial would be sheer farce. Jones had her story about Clinton's alleged demand for oral sex down reasonably well, although there were some significant loose ends. Her initial pleadings had specified that the incident at the Excelsior Hotel had taken place after 2:30 P.M. No witnesses, however, placed Clinton at the hotel after late morning, when he had departed to attend a luncheon at the governor's mansion.

Her coworker Pamela Blackard, whom Jones had first told about Clinton's boorish pass, was uncertain about the time. Asked in her October 23 deposition if she remembered telling a reporter that the incident happened in the morning, Blackard answered, "I probably said it could have happened in the morning or the afternoon. I really don't remember. I thought it happened in the afternoon. It might have happened in the morning. . . . It could have happened close to lunch, or after we went in. And I just cannot remember."

"Did you talk with Mrs. Jones about what time of day this happened?"

"We might have had that conversation," Blackard said, "because I said, 'Paula, you know, when did this happen? I don't even remember.' And I don't remember what she told me. I still don't know. Someone would have to tell me, because I do not remember what time of day."

The timing was important because Jones insisted she'd been so shaken by Clinton's behavior that she had left work immediately. Blackard didn't recall any mention of the governor's dropping his pants and asking for oral sex, or of any "distinguishing" genital characteristics. Considering that Blackard's testimony had been cited by many journalists as greatly enhancing Jones's credibility, she seemed to know very little. "People ask me . . . on a daily basis, 'Did it happen?'" Blackard testified. "I don't know."

Jones's sworn legal pleadings also claimed that her career as a state employee had suffered tangible damage as a result of turning down the governor's advances. Legally, some counts in her complaint depended upon the claim that she had received no pay raises or promotions and was treated by her superiors "in a hostile and rude manner" following the alleged incident at the Excelsior. Based upon those claims, Judge Wright had granted the Jones attorneys broad discovery to ask about the president's sexual conduct with other state and federal employees like Gennifer Flowers and Kathleen Willey.

During her deposition, however, Jones was pressed to admit that those claims had no factual basis. Confronted with documentation, she conceded that she had gotten the same cost-of-living increases as everyone else in her agency. Personnel records obtained by the Clinton lawyers showed that Jones wasn't the state government's most brilliant employee. She had scored 45 percent on a grammar test, had missed eleven of thirty-four questions in an alphabetizing exercise, and was a poor typist. Even so, she had received satisfactory evaluations, and her salary during her sixteen months at the agency after May 1991 had risen from about $10,000 to about $12,000. But Jones denied being aware of two merit pay raises, and professed ignorance that she had been promoted from grade 9 to grade 11 within two months of the alleged incident at the Excelsior. "I don't really know how the grades went," she testified. "I don't know what I came in as, and I don't know what I left as. So I don't know."

Jones also admitted that she'd left her job to move to California in pursuit of her husband's acting career, not because she'd been shunted to a "dead end" job, as her legal pleadings claimed. She had made no transfer requests and filed no grievances. Her entire case appeared to rest on her complaint that she hadn't gotten flowers on Secretary's Day. "I'm the only one out there that did not get any flowers," she said. "And everybody noticed it and was coming around saying, 'That is so cruel of them. I cannot believe they did that to you.' Now what other reason would they do that? Just to leave me out intentionally knowing that I'm a secretary. . . . There had to be a reason for it. I know I wasn't doing anything wrong. So that's why I feel that there was things—somebody knew something."

Other AIDC employees, including director David Harrington, testified unanimously that they had heard only good things about her encounter with Clinton, and had never heard a word about Paula Jones from the governor or his staff. Her supervisor, Clydine Pennington, said that immediately after the conference at the Excelsior, "Jones told me that she had met Governor Clinton and had shaken his hand. She appeared genuinely excited about having met the governor . . . [and] expressed a desire to obtain a position in the governor's office, and expressed that desire on other occasions as well. At no time did Mrs. Jones ever indicate or imply that Mr. Clinton had acted improperly." According to Pennington, Jones told her that Clinton had shaken her hand and complimented her clothes and her hair. "She was very excited about it. It was a big day in her life."

Another acquaintance who said she had heard an innocuous version of the meeting at the Excelsior was Carol Phillips. A receptionist in the governor's office who had moved to Washington with Clinton, Phillips testified that Jones came by her desk at the capitol twice a day on courier rounds, and often spent thirty minutes or more exchanging gossip and small talk. She said Jones had told her "in a happy and excited manner" about meeting Bill Clinton at the Excelsior, describing him as a "nice looking man" and his demeanor as "gentle and sweet." She often called ahead to ask about Clinton's schedule in order to enhance her chances of encountering him. She had asked for and been given an autographed photo of the governor. Phillips said that Jones often asked for troopers Larry Patterson and Danny Ferguson, and spoke with them frequently. She spent so much time hanging around the vestibule outside the governor's office that her superiors at the AIDC reprimanded her about it.

Nor was Paula Jones the only witness called whose story was far from persuasive. With the exception of Larry Nichols, Larry Case, and Say McIntosh, virtually the whole cast of characters from the sexual side of the "Clinton scandals" either filed affidavits or gave depositions between October 1997 and January 1998. Juanita Broaddrick had done both, adamantly insisting that the allegations made in Phillip Yoakum's widely circulated letter claiming Bill Clinton had sexually assaulted her in a Little Rock hotel in 1978 were spurious. No copies of tape recordings Yoakum claimed to have made of her allegedly confirming the charge ever materialized. Nothing surfaced that hadn't previously been reported. None of the president's accusers had done very well.

Kathleen Willey had come across as vague and scattered. She couldn't recall, for example, whether the president had kissed her before supposedly placing her hand on his genitals. Asked by one of Jones's lawyers whether she had communicated with Clinton after the incident or sought a job from the White House, she said that to the best of her recollection she had not. (That was before the White House released evidence of nine letters and twelve phone calls to the president asking for a job, including an ambassadorship.)

Clinton's lawyers walked Gennifer Flowers through a detailed accounting of every dollar she had banked as a result of going public about her alleged twelve-year affair with the president. The total came to more than $500,000. As in her two books, however, Flowers was unable in hours of cross-examination to specify a single time and place where she and Clinton had ever been alone together. After claiming to have shacked up with him in several Little Rock hotels, for example, she was unable to name one.

Dolly Kyle Browning arrived with a handful of brief handwritten notes from the childhood neighbor she insisted on calling "Billy." Most thanked her for gifts she had sent, or apologized for missing her when she visited Little Rock. None proved anything scandalous. Had Clinton ever sexually harassed her? "Absolutely not," she answered.

The Jones lawyers also deposed several bickering Arkansas state troopers, all of whom were cross-examined about their financial and contractual arrangements with Cliff Jackson, Peter W. Smith, and the *American Spectator,* and no two of whom appeared capable of agreeing about anything of substance in *Jones v. Clinton.*

Danny Ferguson and Roger Perry disliked Hillary Clinton and had their suspicions about Bill's friendships with several women, but knew nothing to confirm them. Ferguson claimed that *Los Angeles Times* reporter William Rempel had badgered him to say that Clinton had promised the trooper a job in return for silence, and that Rempel had put words in his mouth when he refused.

L. D. Brown claimed to have hustled babes for Clinton all over the United States and to have benefited from what he called "residuals" himself. But when it came to particulars, Brown had no names, places, or dates to offer—only hearsay and rumors.

Buddy Young, a Clinton federal appointee, testified that L. D. Brown hated

Clinton for refusing him the state crime laboratory job, and had also gotten himself fired as president of the state troopers' association for spending its money partying with lobbyists and state legislators. Young also mentioned that Larry Patterson was obsessed with getting in women's "britches," to the exclusion of all other topics. Patterson's accusations against Clinton, Young said, reflected nothing more than the trooper's own dirty mind. Patterson said Clinton had confessed several affairs to him, and claimed to have seen the governor receiving oral endearments in parked cars. Other troopers called that a physical impossibility. The video surveillance camera through which Patterson allegedly monitored those titillating scenes hardly worked at all.

Clinton's attorney Bob Bennett grilled Patterson about Troopergate payola, about his rent-free living arrangements with Cliff Jackson, and about his multistate speaking tour with Larry Nichols on *The Clinton Chronicles* circuit. Specifically, what did Patterson, a sworn law enforcement officer, know about the president's involvement in drug smuggling and murder?

"Mr. Bennett," Patterson said, "at no time have I ever said that Bill Clinton's ever been involved in any murder, or at no time have I ever said that Bill Clinton has ever used or abused drugs. . . . I have no reason to believe that."

"Has Mr. Nichols ever said that on these trips?"

"I have heard him on occasion say things like that."

"Did you ever tell him to stop it?"

"Mr. Bennett," the trooper replied, "he's an adult."

By the time Monica Lewinsky's name showed up on a subpoena, the president had every reason to believe that *Jones v. Clinton* would never go to trial. The Supreme Court had cautioned Judge Wright to conduct the case with due regard for the institution of the presidency. More scholarly than partisan, Wright was a well-known stickler for procedure. The tone of her rulings made it clear that she had been angered and embarrassed by wholesale leaking of salacious details to the media in defiance of her stringent gag order. She was unlikely to allow her courtroom to be used as a platform to dramatize dubious evidence about the president's sex life, acquired by equally dubious means. Based on evidence and law, Wright was likely to dismiss the case.

Once again Bill Clinton's luck appeared to be holding. With both reckless arrogance and justifiable anger, Clinton may have imagined that all he needed to do was finesse Monica Lewinsky away from the White House and up to New York, and dance around the hard questions at his own January 17 deposition. Hillary would never know, and he would win a significant victory over his worst personal and political enemies.

In consultation with Carter and Jordan during the first week in January, Lewinsky worked out the wording of the affidavit, which would be filed under "Jane Doe #6." Its last paragraph contained the lies she had been prepared to swear to for months. "I have never had a sexual relationship with the President. . . . The occasions that I saw the President after I left employment at the White House in April, 1996, were official receptions, formal functions or events related to the U.S. Department of Defense, where I was working at the time. There were other people present on those occasions." In her own mind, Lewinsky had rationalized that "sexual relationship" meant "sexual intercourse." Over her signature, dated January 7, 1998, was a line that read: "I declare under the penalty of perjury that the foregoing is true and correct."

She flew to New York the next day for a second interview at McAndrews & Forbes, the holding company for the Revlon cosmetics company. The interview went well, but Lewinsky felt otherwise and called Jordan, a company director, to pull strings on her behalf. Obligingly, Jordan called McAndrews & Forbes chairman Ronald Perelman. Lewinsky probably would have gotten the public relations job she wanted there even without Jordan's last-minute intervention. The McAndrews executives liked the bubbly young woman and made her an offer following her third interview on January 9. After accepting it, she called Jordan to express her gratitude. Jordan duly informed both Currie and Clinton: "Mission accomplished."

That night, she talked to Linda Tripp for the first time in over a week. According to Lewinsky, she no longer trusted the older woman and misled Tripp about both her affidavit and her new job. Now she lied, claiming that Jordan hadn't yet found her a job, that she hadn't signed the affidavit, and that she hadn't seen Currie, Jordan, or the president since New Year's.

Ironically, Tripp didn't pick up on the deception at all. Having decided to bring her tapes and other evidence to Starr, she tried to draw Lewinsky into a trap that not only would implicate Jordan and Clinton, but would provide a perfect context for intervention by the independent counsel. Tripp wanted immunity for her felonious taping, but she also wanted to destroy Clinton.

"Monica, promise me you won't sign the affidavit until you get the job," she said in her well-rehearsed tone of maternal concern. This advice had nothing to do with Tripp's "protecting" herself, and everything to do with the prosecutorial agenda of her conservative friends. "Tell Vernon you won't sign the affidavit until you get the job." Still hoping that Tripp might somehow be swayed or neutralized, Lewinsky agreed.

According to the Starr Report eventually submitted to Congress by the Office of Independent Counsel, everything that followed went exactly by the rulebook. "On January 12, 1998," the report's narrative began, "this Office received information that Monica Lewinsky was attempting to influence the testimony of one of the witnesses of the Jones investigation, and that Ms. Lewinsky herself was prepared to provide false information under oath in that lawsuit. The OIC was also informed that Ms. Lewinsky had spoken to the President and the

President's close friend Vernon Jordan about being subpoenaed to testify in the Jones suit, and that Vernon Jordan and others were helping her find a job. The allegations with respect to Mr. Jordan and the job search were similar to ones already under review in the ongoing Whitewater investigation.

"After gathering preliminary evidence to test the information's reliability, the OIC presented the evidence to Attorney General Janet Reno. Based on her review of the information, the Attorney General determined that a further investigation by the Independent Counsel was required."

But that wasn't quite how it all happened. The January 12 date, for example, is deceptive. The OIC learned about Monica S. Lewinsky at least several days earlier than the report acknowledges, and from sources whose complicity with his investigation Kenneth Starr had powerful motives to conceal. In Michael Isikoff's version of the story in *Uncovering Clinton,* "it was not clear who first had the idea" of bringing the independent counsel into the Paula Jones case. Isikoff lists several possibilities: Lucianne Goldberg, Linda Tripp, Richard W. Porter, and Jerome Marcus. Additional candidates would be Ann Coulter and George Conway, two more of the so-called elves helping Jones.

But there is no doubt that all the members of this group were in contact with one another from September 1997 onward, and also that Goldberg, Tripp, Coulter, and Conway, at least, were regularly in touch with Isikoff. According to the *Newsweek* reporter (whose book expresses deep discomfort at his having become "a player—one of the acts in the scandal circus"), he never realized that he was being used as a cat's-paw in a conspiracy against Clinton. Although he had become aware of Conway, Coulter, and Marcus five months before writing his first story about Lewinsky, the existence of a group of high-powered conservative lawyers working behind the scenes for Paula Jones had never struck him as newsworthy.

"I had relied on the elves for information at critical junctures," Isikoff wrote, "even while they concealed from me their role in bringing the Lewinsky allegations to the Jones lawyers and later to Ken Starr."

Presumably alerted by Jill Abramson and Don van Natta Jr.'s pathbreaking investigation in the *New York Times,* Isikoff discusses a dinner party that took place in Philadelphia on January 8, 1998. Present were Porter, Marcus, and Paul Rosenzweig, the fellow Chicago alumnus who had joined Kenneth Starr's Washington OIC staff in November 1997. Exactly why Starr hired an ambitious young lawyer at a time when the Whitewater investigation and Filegate, Travelgate, and the Vince Foster investigation were near completion isn't clear. But during the intervening three months, the *Times* reported, Rosenzweig had spoken with Marcus about the Jones case several times by phone.

Rosenzweig traveled up from Washington for the January 8 dinner at the elegant Deux Cheminées restaurant in Philadelphia. Porter, Kenneth Starr's law partner and Lucianne Goldberg's conduit to the Jones lawyers, flew in from Chicago. "Largely for the hell of it," Isikoff reports, Conway came by train from New York. It was Conway whose timely leaks to the *Drudge Report* had helped prevent the Jones case from being settled several months earlier, and who had just that day helped find another Federalist Society lawyer to represent Linda Tripp. "Pure serendipity" is how Jerome Marcus later described the gathering—a casual meal enjoyed by four very busy lawyers from four different cities.

Before the others arrived that Thursday evening, according to Marcus, he had informed Rosenzweig "very briefly" about the tale of the president and the intern, Jordan's efforts to find Lewinsky a job, and Linda Tripp's tapes. "I don't know if it's real or not," he said. "But do you think this is something that your office would be interested in?"

Rosenzweig didn't know, but would make it his business to find out. On the following Monday, January 12, Lucianne Goldberg called Linda Tripp. From Washington, Rosenzweig had called Marcus in Philadelphia, who had called Porter in Chicago, who had called Goldberg in New York, who had relayed the message back to Tripp in Washington. A deputy independent counsel named Jackie Bennett was definitely interested. But Tripp would have to call him directly. For the sake of propriety, the information would have to come in by "the front door."

Even if the participants' accounts are taken at face value, it was surely no accident that the January 8 dinner was omitted from the Starr Report. For Rosenzweig to be meeting with a clique of attorneys who had helped the Jones team was bad enough. But the participation of Porter, as Starr's law partner, presented the OIC with ethical problems. Avoiding even the appearance of impropriety was the whole point of the Independent Counsel Act. It specifically states that "any person associated with a [law] firm with which such independent counsel is associated may not represent in any matter any person involved in any investigation or prosecution."

Moreover, as Clinton attorney David Kendall pointed out when Porter's role came to light, by law "a legal representation of a client by one partner is attributable to all partners."

While her story found its way to the OIC, Linda Tripp had been taking the measure of her new lawyer, James Moody. Through Conway and Porter, Lucianne Goldberg had set Tripp up with Moody on the recommendation of Ann Coulter, the ubiquitous TV commentator with whom Moody shared a passion for right-wing causes and the Grateful Dead. In subsequent testimony, Tripp portrayed herself as politically independent and somewhat put off by Moody's ideological zeal. Even though he offered to represent her pro bono, Tripp said, "I was concerned about this new attorney's zealous behavior on the phone. . . . I spoke to him for hours over that couple of days. . . . His behavior seemed to me to be [that of] someone with clearly a political agenda as opposed to just an attorney's advocacy role." By January 12, Tripp said, she was "hysterical and saying to Lucianne, 'I don't know where to turn. I don't know what to do. I can't protect myself. This man sounds nutty to me on the phone.'"

Whatever her misgivings, Tripp apparently overcame them. She retained Moody, who promptly worked out an agreement with the Jones lawyers that Tripp wouldn't need to be deposed immediately—and thus face the feared Bob Bennett—if she would agree to brief them in detail about Lewinsky prior to Clinton's January 17 deposition. Moody quickly contacted Kirby Behre, who reacted by warning Tripp that Moody was not a criminal lawyer.

Behre had urged Tripp to warn the president's lawyers about the Lewinsky tapes. He thought Clinton would be forced to settle the Jones case—thus keeping the tapes a secret and protecting Tripp from potential prosecution. Moody had a different plan. Taking possession of the tapes, he and Ann Coulter made high-speed dubbings that, according to Tripp, Coulter kept for her own purposes. Tripp later testified that they did so contrary to her instructions.

According to the *New York Times*, Jackie Bennett briefed Kenneth Starr about Rosenzweig's meeting with the "elves" on Monday, January 12. After Tripp called that evening, Bennett, two assistant prosecutors, and FBI agent Steve Irons came to her Maryland home around 11:15 P.M. They stayed for two hours. According to Agent Irons's 302 report, Tripp represented herself as a victim of circumstances. "Tripp did not seek out *Newsweek* magazine to provide information concerning Kathy Willey," the agent wrote. "*Newsweek* reporter Mike Isikoff contacted Tripp. . . . [S]he told him she believed President Clinton did not harass Willey during the episode. . . . Tripp felt Willey had been seeking a relationship with President Clinton."

Tripp appears to have told the eager prosecutors essentially the same story she had given Monica Lewinsky. Because of the Willey allegation, she had been subpoenaed against her wishes by the Jones lawyers. The subpoena put her in a terrible position with regard to her young friend. She advised the OIC that she and her lawyer had listened to one of her Lewinsky tapes earlier that day. She told them it contained the following dialogue:

TRIPP: I'm going to tell the truth. . . . You're going to lie.

LEWINSKY: If I lie and he lies and you lie, no one has to know.

While true enough in essence, that last sentence does not appear on Tripp's tapes. "TRIPP advised," the FBI agent wrote, "she did not realize that recording her own telephone conversations with LEWINSKY was a violation of state law at the time she did it, and that she was just trying to protect herself from the eventuality . . . that [she] would be attacked for telling the truth." Neither Tripp's dealing with Lucianne Goldberg nor any book deal were mentioned.

According to Irons's 302 the OIC told Tripp they didn't have the power to grant her immunity from the state of Maryland, but did guarantee her that she would not face federal charges for turning over her tapes. After she told them of a planned lunch with Lewinsky the next day, Tripp signed a form agreeing to wear a wire to assist FBI agents in what the 302 report, with unintended irony, called "the consensual monitoring of MONICA LEWINSKY."

If the Starr Report is accurate, the independent counsel's decision to wire Tripp was a bold gamble. Acting on no legal authority but his own, Starr had set out to investigate a crime potentially involving the president that not only hadn't yet happened, but might never happen. It wasn't just the "elves" working for Paula Jones whose activities were well known to OIC prosecutors. Linda Tripp was herself a known commodity; by the time she presented herself as Monica Lewinsky's unwilling confidante, Tripp had previously testified in four previous OIC probes—Filegate, Travelgate, the Vincent Foster suicide, and Whitewater. While peripheral, her testimony nevertheless had made her hostility to the Clinton White House amply clear.

Before she left to meet Lewinsky on January 13, Tripp phoned Lucianne Goldberg to alert her. Almost instantaneously, *Newsweek*'s Isikoff got a call from a confidential source telling him what was going down at the Ritz-Carlton. A quick call to Goldberg confirmed it. Someone didn't trust Kenneth Starr to act with bold resolution. Someone wanted the whole world to know.

For her part, by the time Lewinsky turned up at the Ritz-Carlton in Pentagon City she had grown even more deeply distrusting of her former confidante. Having signed an affidavit denying a sexual relationship with Bill Clinton on January 7, she had accepted a job with Revlon in New York two days later. Tripp knew nothing about either decision. As far as she knew, Monica was holding out until Vernon Jordan got her the job she wanted in exchange for her silence. From the beginning to the end of their three-hour luncheon, the two women were lying to each other like high-stakes poker players. The difference, of course, was that Tripp knew that she was wired. Lewinsky only suspected it.

At first they talked in code. Betty Currie was "the black woman." Clinton was unnamed.

"So when do you get your present?" Tripp asked.

Monica didn't know. "I'm sure I'll get over it. I don't want to talk to him. I don't want him—I don't want to look at him. I can't look at him on TV, can't anything."

"You're kidding."

Two months of silence from the big creep, Lewinsky said, had cured her. The truth was that she had visited with Clinton in the Oval Office as recently as December 28. Monica told Tripp she had informed the "black woman" how events were to unfold.

"So I talked to her this week, and I said to her, I said, 'Look, I'm supposed to sign something.' And I said, 'I'm supposed to sign something, and I'm not signing until I have a job.'"

Tripp thought that was terrific. But she still didn't see how she could bring herself to lie under oath to protect Bill and Monica's secret. It just wasn't her nature. Besides, what if she got caught? Lewinsky tried every manipulative argument she could muster, from fear that Tripp might end up like "Mary Jo Chappaquiddick" to pity for her to metaphysical doubt about whether she had ever had "sex" with Clinton. "I'm not trying to have an existential conversation with you. . . . But what is the truth? Linda, did you ever see anything?"

Tripp conceded that she had not, but said that carrying Lewinsky's secret was still a heavy burden. Lewinsky had Vernon Jordan and the president of the United States looking out for her interests, while Tripp had Kirby Behre. Having fired Behre already, what Tripp really had were James Moody, Kenneth Starr, and a roomful of prosecutors and FBI agents in an upstairs suite. They were getting terribly agitated because the radio transmitter in Tripp's bra wasn't working and they couldn't be sure of the backup tape recorder.

Waxing patriotic, Lewinsky even invoked a national security argument: "To me . . . it's for the country. Every president, every [bleeping] president we have ever had has always had lovers, because the pressure of the job is too much. Too much. Too much to always rely on your wife, with whom you have too much baggage—which you inevitably will, if you got to that point. I think it's [i.e., the truth is] bad for the country." Then she began to cry.

A few minutes later, Tripp went to the bathroom. Lewinsky quickly rifled through her purse, looking for a recording device. Even if she had found it, the OIC investigators had everything they needed to threaten the heartsick young woman with prison.

Starr's prosecutors spent much of Wednesday, January 14, reviewing the "sting" tape and debating whether or not they needed to ask the attorney general and Judge David Sentelle's three-judge panel for expanded jurisdiction to investigate the president's sex life. Some argued that they could tie the case into Whitewater by way of Vernon Jordan. They had never found any evidence to implicate Jordan in paying hush money to Webb Hubbell, but they did have a mandate to investigate him. Cooler heads realized that merging Whitewater with *Jones v. Clinton* would be a controversial, high-risk venture. The OIC would be well advised to seek jurisdictional authorization.

At the same time, Jackie Bennett was getting repeated phone messages from Isikoff. It didn't take the prosecutors long to determine that Tripp had been communicating with Lucianne Goldberg.

Tripp, meanwhile, appeared to have taken it upon herself to expand the probe. Prompted by an early-morning phone call from Tripp, Lewinsky later testified, she spent several hours writing at her computer. She drove by the Pentagon at the end of the day and offered Tripp a ride home. On the way, Monica handed her betrayer a three-page document headed "Points to make in affidavit." As soon as Tripp arrived at her Maryland home, she handed FBI agents what would later be touted as hard evidence of a White House plot to suborn perjury. Shortly after receiving the "talking points," Jackie Bennett paged Eric Holder, the deputy attorney general, at a Washington Wizards basketball game. They agreed to meet in Holder's office at the Justice Department on Thursday morning, January 15.

The talking points was among the first items to leak, and quickly generated reams of media speculation about a White House conspiracy—much of it preceded by phrases like "Starr suspects" or "sources in Starr's office." Vernon Jordan was an alleged possible author. Tripp hinted (and later testified) that the wording reminded her of White House counsel Bruce Lindsey, prompting the New York Times's William Safire to write accusatory columns based on that surmise. But to prosecutors familiar with Lewinsky and Tripp's lunch conversation, the document's origins should have been clear from the start.

Believing Tripp's lie that she was a reluctant witness in the Jones case, Lewinsky had seen one way out. Tripp could contact Bob Bennett, hire a new lawyer, and file a truthful affidavit concerning Kathleen Willey, Michael Isikoff, and Newsweek. As soon as the Jones lawyers realized how badly Tripp's testimony would damage their star witness Kathleen Willey, they would drop her from their deposition list. The question of Monica Lewinsky would never come up.

Unaware that Tripp had betrayed her to Isikoff six months earlier, Lewinsky sympathized with her friend's plight. "You saw what happened to me in Newsweek," Tripp complained. "I mean I got smeared in the national media."

"If I were in your shoes," replied Lewinsky, "having already had that article, you know, with Isikoff screwing you over—that whole setup, that whole thing, already—what I would do, what I would say, you know. . . . You did see Kathleen and those things. You did see her disheveled. You did see her lipstick smeared. You did see those things. But what . . . you could say that the article didn't describe was that . . . you don't know that it happened."

"Well, I wasn't in the room."

Lewinsky agreed. She reminded Tripp that Julie Hiatt Steele had said Willey had asked her to confirm a phony story to Isikoff. Why couldn't Tripp now emphasize her own doubts about Willey?

"The first thing I would say," urged Lewinsky, "is 'Well, I didn't see her come out of the Oval Office. But after she allegedly came out of the office what she told me was blah, blah, blah. . . .' Okay. They say, 'Do you believe?' or 'Did you believe what she said?' You could say, 'I now do not believe it to be true, but at the time I did.' That you now do not believe. Why do you not believe it to be true? 'Well because Kathleen— Because she's changing her story. So if she lied to me . . .'"

"She's calling it sexual harassment," Tripp said.

"Right. 'If she lied to me once, why wouldn't she have lied to me before?'"

"Well, and I could say that I talked to her after Michael Isikoff," Tripp said. "Which is true."

"Which is true," Lewinsky repeated.

"And that she gave an entirely different version."

"Exactly," Monica said.

Lewinsky returned to the theme relentlessly. "Let me try to be clear," she said. "Listen to me. . . . 'This is what the situation was. This is what she told me. I believed it at the time, because I had no reason not to believe it.' . . . Okay? And then you say, 'My concern now in the light of everything that's happened, with her switching her story, she called me, and her switching her story, I really don't believe it.' You know? 'I certainly don't believe that he sexually harassed her.'"

The two also discussed in some detail Monica's experience in helping her lawyer draft the affidavit she supposedly hadn't signed yet. After lunch, Lewinsky drove Tripp back to the Pentagon. With the OIC's tape recorder still running, Lewinsky insisted that they get together the next day to go over the Willey matter one more time. Given her understanding of the situation, Lewinsky's legal tactics were not only sound but legitimate. Aware of Tripp's attitude toward Willey, the Jones lawyers had no intention of surfacing her at this point in the case.

Before she got out of the car, Tripp gave Lewinsky every reason to believe she might go along with the affidavit scheme. Outside the Pentagon, she said thanks for the ride.

"Oh, I don't mind at all," Lewinsky said. "I'd drive you to the moon, my dear."

On Wednesday morning, Lewinsky testified, Tripp called and agreed to her plan. She told Lewinsky yet another lie. She was meeting with Kirby Behre later that day, and needed Monica's help in composing an affidavit. So Lewinsky sat down to work. The talking points merely reiterated Lewinsky's oral argument in a more systematic fashion: "The next you heard of her [Willey] was when a *Newsweek* reporter (I wouldn't name him specifically) showed up in your office saying she was naming you as someone who would corroborate that she was sexually harassed," the document read in part. ". . . As a result of your conversation with her and subsequent reports that showed that she had tried to enlist the help of someone else in her lie that the president sexually harassed her, you now do not believe that what she claimed happened really happened. You now find it completely plausible that she herself smeared her lipstick, untucked her blouse, etc."

In a remarkable footnote in *Uncovering Clinton,* Isikoff concedes that the ideas expressed in the talking points closely parallel the angry unpublished letter Tripp sent *Newsweek* after his original Willey article in August 1997—a letter Lewinsky had urged her to write. Expressing regret that his own reporting fueled subsequent speculation about the document—his January 21, 1998, story on *Newsweek*'s Web site would be the first to break the news of its existence—Isikoff claims that in all the excitement, he had simply forgotten about Tripp's letter. His January 21 article merely "reported—perfectly accurately— that Starr's prosecutors were investigating to determine if [the talking points] had been written by anybody associated with Clinton's legal team."

But since the talking points portrayed Tripp's actual opinions, it never mattered much who wrote them. By studiously ignoring the now available context—though it was known from the first that Lewinsky handed the document to Tripp—Isikoff avoids confronting the likelihood that whoever fed him that story intended to light a firestorm of media speculation. Far from suborning perjury, the document asked Tripp to affirm the same views that Starr's prosecutors knew she and Lewinsky had discussed for hours. Yet as late as July 1998, "sources close to the investigation," as the press described them, speculated that Bruce Lindsey was the mysterious author.

"No contacts w Paula Jones lawyers," read the notes of one OIC deputy about Jackie Bennett's meeting with Assistant Attorney General Eric Holder on Thursday, January 15. Like the Starr Report, Bennett saw no need to mention Paul Rosenzweig's dinner in Philadelphia with the elves a week earlier. He would later say that he was unaware of the "elves'" ties to the Jones lawyers. Rosenzweig himself has never said anything on the subject. Bennett's recollection also conflicts with that of another OIC deputy, John Bates, who had the distinct impression that Bennett did know the information Rosenzweig brought him came "directly or indirectly" from "the Jones legal team."

There were several other items the OIC did not confide to Holder and Attorney General Janet Reno. No mention was made of Rosenzweig's conversations with Jerome Marcus, who represented Paula Jones. Nothing was said about Richard Porter being Kenneth Starr's law partner. Whether or not the independent counsel would have thought that posed a conflict, there are signs that Porter had his concerns.

According to Gil Davis and Joe Cammarata, he consistently asked that his name not appear on any documents or letters. During Starr's November 1998 testimony before the House Judiciary Committee, Clinton's lawyer David Kendall asked the independent counsel about an entry in Lucianne Goldberg's notebook for January 15 that read: "Call from Richard [Porter] on mobile phone worried that Ken Starr might be hurt." Porter called Goldberg five times that day.

Nor did Starr inform Attorney General Reno about his own personal involvement with the Paula Jones case. That Starr had once considered writing an amicus brief for the Scaife-funded Independent Women's Forum supporting Jones's right to sue the president before his appointment as independent counsel was no secret. What Starr kept to himself, however, was the fact that he had also been consulted over the telephone by Jones's lawyer Gil Davis. The Virginia attorney had billed Jones $975 for consultations with the former solicitor general on six occasions in 1994.

The OIC also withheld mitigating evidence from the attorney general that day—specifically, that Vernon Jordan's involvement in Monica Lewinsky's New York job search had preceded her subpoena in the Jones case by two months. In addition, Jordan was an old friend of both Betty Currie and Lewinsky's mother's fiancé, Peter Strauss. Those facts considerably weakened the likelihood of Jordan's participation in a conspiracy to obstruct justice, Starr's linkage between Lewinsky and the Whitewater investigation. The only evidence favoring that theory was taped conversations with Tripp, in which investigators knew Lewinsky was lying about her affidavit.

Tripp's tapes also showed that Lewinsky had been offered a job at the United Nations on October 31, 1997, and had turned it down a few days later—several weeks before her subpoena in the Jones case. There's no sign that Janet Reno was told that salient fact, either, if indeed the OIC was aware of it by then. It may have been morally objectionable for the president to recommend his ex-mistress for a government job. But it wasn't illegal.

Had Reno known any of these facts, she would probably have chosen someone else to investigate Linda Tripp's allegations. The situation was rife with appearances of impropriety, exactly what the independent counsel statute was enacted to prevent.

But there was one important fact Jackie Bennett decided to share with Reno and Holder, and that was the involvement of Michael Isikoff. His appearance had dashed any hope the OIC might have entertained about keeping its investigation of the president's sex life a secret. As the *Newsweek* reporter tells the story, he had confronted Bennett with what he knew early on January 15 at the OIC's Washington headquarters. In regular contact with Lucianne Goldberg and the elves, Isikoff had already phoned Betty Currie to ask her about any presents President Clinton might have given to a certain Monica Lewinsky. The secretary had put him off with a promise to look into it.

According to Isikoff, he had faced down Jackie Bennett with a threat. "Look, you guys are the ones that need to cooperate with me, I said. You need to lay out your evidence, or at least your basis for starting this investigation. . . . It was, in a way, a form of blackmail." The reporter gave them a deadline of 4 P.M. Friday.

By passing Isikoff's threat along to Janet Reno, the OIC prosecutors turned it into their own weapon. Any further actions taken by Isikoff to report the story would alert the White House and ruin the Jones lawyers' surprise at Clinton's deposition. Starr's prosecutors had no interest in putting the president's girlfriend in jail for filing a false affidavit. They intended to let an unsuspecting Clinton walk into the deposition blind on Saturday, and then flip Lewinsky to testify against him.

For that to happen, there were two necessary elements: Clinton had to remain ignorant of his peril, and the Jones lawyers had to ask the right questions. If Clinton somehow escaped, Reno would be blamed, not the OIC and Kenneth Starr. Whether Isikoff realized it or not, the real target of his "blackmail" was the attorney general.

In her January 16 letter to the three-judge panel recommending that Starr be authorized to investigate possible obstruction of justice, Reno wrote that Monica Lewinsky "may have filed" a false affidavit. To a judge, her murky statement could have meant any of three things: The affidavit may have been filed, or it may have been false, or both. Why was Reno so vague? She had no way of knowing whether the affidavit had been either signed or faxed. The OIC had two sources of information telling them different stories about the affidavit. On the Ritz-Carlton tapes, Lewinsky had lied to Tripp, indicating she would sign no affidavit until she had gotten her New York job. The next day, Tripp told FBI agents that Monica said she might sign it on January 15.

Only a select few knew that Lewinsky had already signed an affidavit on January 7, denying a sexual relationship with Bill Clinton. Nearly all of those who knew were on the White House side—except for the Paula Jones lawyers.

Lewinsky's attorney, Frank Carter, had faxed them a copy of the affidavit on January 12. His cover letter stipulated that unless he heard from them by January 15, he planned to file the affidavit in support of his motion to quash their subpoena with Judge Wright in Little Rock. All the lawyers involved in *Jones v. Clinton* were under a strict gag order. Under penalty of contempt, they were forbidden to communicate anything substantive about the case to any unauthorized person. For the OIC to be given a copy of the Lewinsky affidavit would require a court order.

Judge Wright had issued no such order, but the OIC did possess a copy of Lewinsky's affidavit by January 15. Following the House Judiciary Committee hearings in November 1998, Starr admitted that Linda Tripp's lawyer James Moody had faxed a copy to his office. But who was Moody's source for the affidavit? There is no doubt that Moody was in touch with the Jones lawyers. Neither he nor the Dallas lawyers have commented on the affidavit's strange journey. In any event, showing Reno the affidavit might have raised inconvenient questions about collusion (and exposed the Jones attorneys to contempt proceedings). Failing to show the affidavit to the attorney general could be interpreted as evidence of intentional deceit by the OIC.

This precise matter became the subject of an investigation by the Justice Department.

Having submitted a proposed court order for Judge Sentelle to rubber-stamp, Starr's deputies wasted no time after receiving approval from the three-judge panel. One last time they used Linda Tripp to bait the trap. She lured Lewinsky back to the Pentagon City Mall, where FBI agents working for the OIC grabbed her in the food court around 1 P.M. on Friday, January 16, and ushered her upstairs to room 1012 in the Ritz-Carlton Hotel. Present were six deputy prosecutors, including Jackie Bennett and Michael Emmick, as well as private investigator Coy A. Copeland (who had worked for Hickman Ewing in Arkansas).

Tripp was there, too. Grasping the situation at once, according to *Monica's Story,* the terrified young woman hissed, "Make her stay and watch. . . . I want that treacherous bitch to see what she has done to me." The OIC had already rented Tripp a room at the hotel. If, as promised, she was going to brief the Jones lawyers before the president's deposition, Tripp needed to know what had happened.

The smooth, good-looking Emmick was chosen to give Monica the bad news. An experienced federal prosecutor in Los Angeles, Emmick enjoyed a reputation as a ladies' man. Lewinsky came to view him as "a revolting specimen of humanity," and would later insist that he leave the grand jury chambers so she could testify about how he had browbeaten her.

In the hotel room, Emmick told Lewinsky that the OIC was prepared to charge her with a laundry list of federal crimes including perjury, obstruction of justice, subornation of perjury, witness tampering, and conspiracy. Altogether, she could expect to spend upwards of twenty-seven years in jail. Unless she agreed to cooperate, by giving a full statement and wearing a body wire for "consensual monitoring" of her conversations with Betty Currie, Vernon Jordan, and Bill Clinton, they would have no choice but to prosecute her. They might even be forced to file charges against her mother, Marcia Lewis. Shaking with fear, she nevertheless had the presence of mind to ask to speak with her attorney, Frank Carter.

Department of Justice policy required that Emmick let her make the call, and do his negotiating with Carter. It also forbade "seeking to compel testimony of a witness" by squeezing "close family members." But Starr's prosecutors had no time for such niceties; they particularly couldn't afford to let her call Frank Carter. According to Lewinsky, the prosecutors looked at each other and said they didn't want her to tell anyone about the matter, as it was "time sensitive." She thought she knew what that meant: keeping her on ice until after the president's deposition in the Paula Jones case the following day. The OIC's dilemma was even more elementary. If Isikoff blew their cover by phoning the White House with any more questions about Monica Lewinsky, the president would have been warned before he walked into his deposition.

Anyone who listened to Lewinsky's tearful conversations on Linda Tripp's tapes knew that the passionate young woman was in a volatile state. Her book says she contemplated suicide after Starr's team picked her up. If she had really believed Tripp would betray her secret, would Monica have allowed "Handsome" to go into the Jones deposition without a warning? By not telling Clinton the truth, she appears to have been clinging to the last shreds of romantic illusion. His cold anger when he suspected her of blabbing to Tripp had made her fear that she would lose him for good. She had no wish, however, to humiliate him and destroy his presidency. There was a real danger that she would finally warn him.

Instead, the prosecutors badly wanted to flip Lewinsky. Through Moody, the OIC had obtained a copy of her affidavit. But they couldn't be sure that it had been filed with the court in Little Rock. Until it was, the affidavit meant little. As of Friday afternoon, January 16, Lewinsky had committed no serious crime, and had she been permitted to call Frank Carter that day, she never would have.

Still wanting to do some research on case law in the Eighth Circuit, Carter hadn't sent Lewinsky's affidavit to the Little Rock court on January 15 as he had told the Jones lawyers he would. Marking it for Saturday delivery, he had dropped it into a FedEx box at 2:00 A.M. on the morning of January 16. Since an affidavit is for all practical purposes just another piece of paper until it's date-stamped for receipt by the court, all Carter would have needed to do to protect his client would be to telephone FedEx and cancel delivery.

Every time the weeping young woman asked to call Carter, however, the prosecutors had a different answer. She could call him, they explained, but all negotiations would be off; the time to make a deal was now. They told her Carter was a civil lawyer and she needed a criminal attorney. (Carter had headed the public defender's office for the District of Columbia for six years.) They offered to fix her up with a criminal defense lawyer of their own choosing, which she declined. Lewinsky feared that if she left the room to call her lawyer, she would be arrested and jailed. At 5:23 P.M. an FBI agent finally phoned Carter's office, which was already closed for the three-day Martin Luther King holiday weekend. The answering service declined to furnish a forwarding number. (The U.S. District Court in D.C. eventually rejected Lewinsky's argument that her constitutional rights had been violated by Starr's agents in the hotel room.)

When Lewinsky asked to call her mother, as she later testified to a grand juror's question, the hulking Jackie Bennett—he had played defensive tackle on his college football team—told her: "You're twenty-four, you're smart, you're old enough. You don't need to call your mommy." After a few hours, however, she was permitted to call Marcia Lewis in Manhattan, although an FBI agent had his finger poised above the button to cut her off if she started to say anything the OIC didn't like. Lewis agreed to take the Amtrak Metroliner down to Washington, arriving at 11:30 P.M. When the two women were allowed to speak alone for a few minutes, Lewinsky told her mother what she later told the grand jury. To gain immunity, "I'd have to agree to be debriefed [about her love affair with the president] and that I'd have to place calls or wear a wire to see—to call Betty and Mr. Jordan and possibly the president."

Lewinsky also told her mother that regardless of what happened to her, she could not betray Currie and Jordan, decent people who had been kind to her. "I can't do this," she said. "I can't wear a wire. I can't tape-record phone calls. I can't do this to the president." They decided to call Monica's father in Los Angeles. He made the mistake of calling his friend William Ginsburg, a medical malpractice lawyer of considerable renown on the West Coast. Had Lewinsky stuck with Frank Carter that night, the OIC's strategy would have crashed.

Despite his lack of criminal experience, the much-maligned Ginsburg wisely demanded that the OIC put its immunity offer in writing. He also asked Emmick for a copy of Lewinsky's affidavit. When Emmick admitted that he couldn't produce either one, Ginsburg told his clients to go home. At 12:23 A.M., more than eleven hours after FBI agents confronted her, the young woman and her mother were allowed to leave.

Whatever else can be said about Monica Lewinsky, her courage that night—bolstered partly by personal loyalty, partly by her strong belief that government agents had no business investigating her intimate life—may have saved her duplicitous and inconstant lover's presidency.

Several months later, in November 1998, Kenneth Starr was questioned by Clinton lawyer David Kendall about Lewinsky's treatment at the hands of his prosecutors that winter day. Growing petulant and defensive, Starr denied that Lewinsky had been "held" by his prosecutors in what he insisted were the "commodious" surroundings of the Ritz-Carlton Hotel. His voice rising with indignation, he also denied that the OIC had planned to put a body wire on Lewinsky to lure the president into an incriminating conversation—directly contradicting her grand jury testimony.

Moreover, according to Monica's father, Bernard Lewinsky, and corroborated by an FBI 302 report dated January 16, he was told by Emmick that "telephone calls [and] body wires" would be one condition of an immunity deal. The same document said that Lewinsky had asked whether partial cooperation was a possibility, and paraphrased her mother as follows: "Marcia Lewis asked what would happen if Monica Lewinsky gave everything but did not tape anything?"

In keeping with the deal worked out by her new attorney, James Moody, Linda Tripp went directly from the Ritz-Carlton to her home, where she had an appointment that evening to meet with the Paula Jones lawyers. While there was later some controversy over whether or not the FBI actually drove her to Maryland, there is little doubt that Starr's agents knew of her plans to brief Wesley Holmes, one of the lawyers from Rader, Campbell, Fisher & Pyke. By then a witness in a federal investigation, Tripp was herself Starr's agent, having recorded several additional phone calls with Lewinsky on her home recorder at the FBI's direction. (While denying any collusion with the Jones attorneys, Starr later conceded that his office ought to have kept its key witness under tighter control.)

According to Isikoff, Holmes was quite disappointed when Moody said he was unable to provide the Jones team with copies of any of Tripp's tape recordings. Holmes vaguely recalled Moody's saying that the tapes were evidence in a federal investigation, and that he possessed no copies. Moody denied talking about the federal investigation; but he did, in fact, possess copies of the tapes. According to an affidavit by Starr assistant Stephen Bates, as reported in an article in the *Baltimore Sun* on December 14, 1999, by Del Quentin Wilber and Jonathan Weisman, two of Starr's deputies handed over copies of Tripp's December 22, 1998, tape to Moody at what the article described as a "midnight rendezvous in a Howard Johnson's in Washington" on the night of January 16–17. Also present with Moody during the exchange according to the Bates affidavit, was "elf" George Conway. The affidavit was given in connection with Linda Tripp's unsuccessful prosecution by Maryland officials for illegally taping her phone conversations with Lewinsky. Sometime after midnight, Moody went downtown to *Newsweek*'s Washington bureau to play the December 22 tape—which he described as "the most important tape" for Isikoff and his editors.

"Long after I thought the tapes had been turned over," Linda Tripp later said of Moody in the grand jury, "he played for *Newsweek* one of the tapes. At the time he said that the independent counsel wanted him to do that because—to preempt Mike Isikoff from going forward with the story. So I thought this was a help to the investigation."

So it was. Isikoff had been pestering the OIC with demands for information, lest he write what he already knew and blow the investigation's cover. The delivery of the tape by Moody placated *Newsweek*.

When Tripp testified that her lawyer Moody had played the tape at the independent counsel's behest for Isikoff, the OIC prosecutors in the grand jury room who heard that remark didn't contradict her. They registered no surprise, displayed no curiosity, and asked no follow-up questions.

By all accounts, Bill Clinton left his six-hour deposition at the downtown Washington offices of Skadden, Arps, Slate, Meagher & Flom on January 17 believing that he had done well. Toward the end he had finally admitted that, under the convoluted definition of "sexual relations" provided by the Jones lawyers, he had once done something sexual—exactly what they did not ask—with Gennifer Flowers in 1977. He had brushed aside Kathleen Willey's accusations as coming from a "very upset" woman who had misinterpreted a kindly embrace. He had repeatedly denied the allegations of Paula Jones, insisting that he didn't remember meeting or even seeing her.

He had prevaricated in his responses to the initial questions from Jones attorney James Fisher about his relationship with Monica Lewinsky, claiming not to remember the last time he had met with her or whether they had been alone in his office, not recalling the gifts he had given her. "Do you know what they were?" he had asked Fisher.

Taking full advantage of a peculiar definition of sexual activity adapted by the Jones lawyers from the criminal code—which, of course, deals largely with nonconsensual encounters—the president thought he had spotted a loophole. After the judge struck a couple of clauses so vague they could have applied to two people who brush against each other in an elevator, "sexual relations" was defined for the purposes of the deposition as "contact with the genitalia, anus, groin, breast, inner thigh, or buttocks of any person with an intent to arouse or gratify the sexual desire of any person." On that basis, he testified, "I have never had sexual relations with Monica Lewinsky. I've never had an affair with her."

There is no question that Clinton intended to deceive the court and Fisher, not to mention his own attorneys. Since the dictionary definition of "sexual relations" is "coitus" or "intercourse," his answer could be considered technically true, even though it did put him in the preposterous position of arguing that he was not having sex with Lewinsky at the very moment that she was having sex with him.

But Judge Wright's ruling made more sense than that. After lengthy quibbling among the lawyers, she threw the definitions out altogether. "Mr. Bennett has made it clear," she said, ". . . that embarrassing questions will be asked, and if this is in fact an effort on the part of Plaintiff's counsel to avoid using sexual terms and avoid going into great detail about what might or might not have occurred, then there's no need to worry about that. You may go into the detail."

As for Bob Bennett, he had made the naive mistake of trusting his client, the president of the United States. When Lewinsky's name came up, he had produced a copy of her affidavit, but the judge had permitted the questioning to go forward. At times, Clinton appeared to be enjoying this contest of wits. Asked if he'd ever talked to anyone about finding a job for Monica Lewinsky, he answered with a question.

"When she got the job in the legislative affairs office? No."

"Before she got that job?"

"No."

Had he tried to get her a job in the White House? Also no. If Fisher wasn't going to ask about the New York job search, Clinton wasn't going to tell him. When Fisher asked if he'd ever taken Lewinsky down the hallway into his private kitchen in the White House, Bennett interrupted. Although Clinton later claimed he hadn't really been listening, he gazed directly at his lawyer while Bennett spoke.

"I'm going to object to the innuendo," Bennett told Judge Wright. "I'm afraid this will leak. . . . Counsel is fully aware that Ms. Lewinsky has filed an affidavit which they are in possession of saying that there is absolutely no sex of any kind in any manner, shape or form, with President Clinton, and yet listening to the innuendo in the questions—"

But the judge allowed Fisher to proceed, without requiring him to show any basis for his questions. "Go ahead."

He resumed asking Clinton whether and where he might have been alone with Lewinsky in the White House.

"Well, let me try to describe the facts first, because you keep talking about this private kitchen," he began. "The private kitchen is staffed by two naval aides. They have total, unrestricted access to my dining room, to that hallway, to coming into the Oval Office. The people who are in the outer office of the Oval Office can also enter at any time. . . . After I went through a presidential campaign in which the far right tried to convince the American people I had committed murder, run drugs, slept in my mother's bed with four prostitutes, and done numerous other things, I had a high level of paranoia. There are no curtains on the Oval Office, there are no curtains on my private office. . . ." Then he said something clever which he could only have wished was fully true. "I have done everything I could to avoid the kind of questions you are asking me here today."

The president said he couldn't recall whether he had ever been alone with Monica Lewinsky—if being alone meant Betty Currie wasn't nearby. Had he talked with her about testifying in the lawsuit? The last time she'd come by to see Betty, he had teased Lewinsky about how "you all, with the help of the Rutherford Institute, were going to call every woman I'd ever talked to . . . and ask them that, and so I said [to her] 'you would qualify,' or something like that."

After a number of more pointed questions about gifts he and Lewinsky had exchanged—which Clinton parried by explaining that he exchanged a lot of gifts with people who visited him—Fisher finally got down to the nub.

"Did you have an extramarital sexual affair with Monica Lewinsky?"

"No."

"If she told someone that she had a sexual affair with you beginning in November, 1995, would that be a lie?"

"It would certainly not be the truth. It would not be the truth."

"So the record is completely clear, have you ever had sexual relations with Monica Lewinsky as that term is defined in Deposition Exhibit 1, as modified by the court?"

Bennett objected, and the judge permitted Clinton to reread the definition.

"I have never had sexual relations with Monica Lewinsky," he answered. "I've never had an affair with her."

There was another exchange about Vernon Jordan's role in finding Lewinsky a job. ("Vernon liked to help people," Clinton explained. "He was always trying to help people.") Fisher went off on a tangent, asking whether the president had paid off Lewinsky's debts. After he signaled he had no further questions on Lewinsky, Clinton posed one of his own.

"Mr. Fisher, is there something, let me just—you asked that with such conviction, and I answered with such conviction. Is there something you want to ask me about this? I don't even know what you're talking about, I don't think."

"Sir," Fisher said, "I think this will come to light shortly, and you'll understand."

It came to light within about twelve hours: Matt Drudge posted an item on his Web site a few minutes after 1 A.M. EST on Sunday, January 18:

"NEWSWEEK KILLS STORY ON WHITE HOUSE INTERN
BLOCKBUSTER REPORT: 23-YEAR-OLD, FORMER WHITE HOUSE INTERN,
SEX RELATIONSHIP WITH PRESIDENT
WORLD EXCLUSIVE

"The *Drudge Report* has learned that reporter Michael Isikoff developed the story of his career, only to have it spiked by top *Newsweek* suits hours before publication. . . . The *Drudge Report* has learned that tapes of intimate phone conversations exist."

As Isikoff would later explain, his magazine's top editors in New York had hesitated to run a story accusing figures like the president and Vernon Jordan of committing felonies with no stronger proof than a taped telephone conversation between third parties who might be lying or crazy. Isikoff was deeply frustrated, and his editors were troubled. Having been promised by James Moody that they would hear Lewinsky say Jordan instructed her to lie, they had heard no such thing. When he learned early Saturday evening that the story wasn't going to run, Isikoff had notified both Tripp's lawyer and Lucianne Goldberg, a "courtesy" he would soon regret.

The first alarm was sounded by Republican strategist and *Weekly Standard* editor William Kristol on the ABC Sunday morning news program *This Week*. An old friend of Richard Porter, whom he had once hired when he served as Vice President Dan Quayle's chief of staff, Kristol had somehow learned of the details behind the Drudge item. A bit mysteriously, he suggested that while the president's dispute with Paula Jones was his word against hers, another, hotter story was developing that might produce hard corroborating evidence.

"I also think the media is going to be an issue here," Kristol continued. "The story in Washington this morning is that *Newsweek* magazine was going to go with a big story based on tape-recorded conversations, which a woman who was a summer intern at the White House—"

George Stephanopoulos interrupted. "And where did that come from, Bill? The *Drudge Report*. . . ."

"There were screaming arguments at *Newsweek* magazine yesterday," insisted Kristol, who had once cautioned David Brock against writing the Troopergate exposé and perhaps damaging his career. "They finally didn't go with the story. There's going to be a question of whether the media [are] now going to report what are pretty well validated charges of presidential behavior [*sic*] in the White House."

By Tuesday night, January 20, the OIC's favorite correspondent, Jackie Judd, and her producer, Chris Vlasto, had scooped the world with reports on ABC radio, the network's overnight TV news broadcast, and the ABC Web site. The print journalism race was won by Susan Schmidt, another Starr favorite, whose Wednesday-morning headline dominated the *Washington Post*'s front page: "STARR INVESTIGATES WHETHER CLINTON TOLD INTERN TO DENY AFFAIR." In conversations on Linda Tripp's tapes, the *Post* reported, "Lewinsky described Clinton and Jordan directing her to testify falsely in the Paula Jones sexual harassment case against the president, according to sources. . . . She said that Clinton then told Lewinsky that Jordan would help figure out what to say, the sources said." Over at *Newsweek*, where "sources" had promised them the same illusory smoking gun, they couldn't help but wonder whether Sue Schmidt knew what she was talking about.

Possibly to console Michael Isikoff for having the biggest story of his life lifted from under his nose, someone slipped him a copy of the talking points. "*Newsweek* obtained what may be an important new piece of evidence," he wrote in the long article he posted on the magazine's Web site on the evening of January 21. "It is a written document allegedly given to Tripp by Lewinsky. The document coaches Tripp on 'points to make in affidavit' in order to contradict the account of . . . Katheen Willey. . . . It was Tripp who partly confirmed Willey's claims that she had had a sexual encounter with Clinton—as reported in a *Newsweek* story in August." Isikoff went on to state categorically that while it wasn't clear who wrote the talking points, "Starr believes that Lewinsky did not write them herself. He is investigating whether the instructions came from Jordan or other friends of the President."

Before Isikoff finally managed to get his exclusive version on the *Newsweek* Web site that night, the story itself had been superseded by the TV pundits and political soothsayers. Just after 8:00 A.M. EST, George Stephanopoulos appeared on ABC's *Good Morning America* to recant his skepticism of two days before. The young man who had once been so close to Clinton made a dire prediction. "If the allegations are true, it could lead to impeachment proceedings." Not to be outdone, Sam Donaldson, the network's White House correspondent, predicted that the remainder of Bill Clinton's presidency would henceforth be measured in days.

AFTERWORD

Until the remarkable events of January 1998, none of the efforts to bring about the political destruction of Bill and Hillary Clinton appeared to have any chance of succeeding. His enemies' relentless intrusion into the president's intimate life, the continuing examinations of his family and political finances, and the ever-expanding investigations of his administration had failed to find sufficient credible evidence to prevent his election and then his reelection, to bring about his impeachment, or to sustain a civil lawsuit against him. Similarly, Hillary Clinton's oft-predicted indictment was by that time little more than a partisan daydream.

Despite several years of effort and many millions of dollars expended by teams of investigative reporters, two independent counsels, and multiple congressional inquests, in addition to the probes privately financed by Richard Mellon Scaife and other political adversaries, no prosecutable offense had been found. Although independent counsel Kenneth Starr was still keeping that secret to himself for the time being, the most heavily investigated couple in the United States had emerged unscathed. Nearly four years of costly litigation by the Paula Jones legal team had produced a weak case that would not withstand summary judgment.

Yet the hunting of the president had inflicted a severe trauma on him, his family, his friends, his administration, and more broadly on the political culture of American democracy. It had perverted the law and debased the media, and in the months to come it would cost the nation still more.

Despite his reckless and foolhardy behavior, the looming threat of impeachment had not been created by Clinton alone—as his enemies, seeking to obscure their own complicity, would stridently insist. The separate strands of the rope with which those bitter foes had so long hoped to hang him—Paula Jones's civil lawsuit and Kenneth Starr's ever-expanding criminal prosecution—were each too weak to bear any such constitutional weight alone. But during the bleak early days of January those two threads had been cunningly twisted together to form a noose, which the president then pulled over his own head.

Most of the country's citizens refused to join the lynch mob. To the astonishment of Clinton's critics, public support for the endangered president actually grew in the weeks after the Lewinsky story was exposed. A poll commissioned by CNN and the *Wall Street Journal* in early February 1998 recorded an astonishing 79 percent of respondents favoring him. That level of support could not be sustained indefinitely, particularly not when Clinton was forced, after eight months of denials, to admit that he had been lying about his relationship with Monica Lewinsky. Yet even then his standing with the public still remained surprisingly high.

Lacking the legitimacy that would have been conferred by popular demand, the Republican right's anti-Clinton crusade was a lost cause months before the Congress actually voted articles of impeachment against the president. As the national consensus emerged and held firm, disgruntled pundits suggested that the American people had been lulled into moral decadence by years of prosperity. Perhaps Clinton's popularity would have plunged, too, had the stock market done the same. But clearly there were other significant cultural and political factors that served to protect him.

In 1992, when Gennifer Flowers got her first taste of national fame, more than two-thirds of the electorate had told pollsters that they didn't believe the media ought to be exploring politicians' sex lives. Six years later, despite their fresh disappointment in Clinton, there was never any indication that the voters had abandoned that preference for privacy. Instead it appeared that the more they thought about it, the more the great majority of Americans resented not just Clinton's misconduct, but everything about the Lewinsky affair: a young woman betrayed by an older friend; a zealous, puritanical, and clearly partisan prosecutor using illegal tape recordings to snare the young woman; the OIC's attempt to bully her into betraying her lover by threatening her family and feeding smutty leaks to an insatiable news media; and the delight of so-called conservatives in stripping the last vestiges of dignity from the president of the United States.

Many found the very idea of a federal sex investigation abhorrent; they feared that anything that might be done to Bill Clinton and Monica Lewinsky could certainly be done to them.

Even as millions of television viewers became engrossed in the nightly soap opera that Clinton had made of his own life, most of them wisely assessed the complexity of his character and rejected the shrill calls for his resignation or removal. The people who had reelected him continued to regard Bill Clinton as a flawed but highly capable and essentially decent man, with a bad weakness regarding women—a trait that hardly made him unique in the nation's capital or anywhere else.

Perhaps just as importantly, many Americans sensed the Lewinsky scandal's true origins even though very few knew anything specific about them. After nearly six years of confusing headlines and constantly shifting Whitewater accusations, they no longer took the scandal's premises very seriously. There had been far too many "critical phases" and false alarms in Starr's investigation. The legalistic maneuvering by which the independent counsel transformed his interminable probe of a twenty-year-old real estate deal into a sexual inquisition struck the majority as intrinsically suspect.

Hillary Clinton's remarks about a "vast right-wing conspiracy to undermine my husband" were initially mocked by pundits as a feeble defense of her husband's bad character. Yet subsequent revelations about OIC's behavior lent weight to her accusation. Rather belatedly, through reporting by Jill Abramson and Don van Natta, Jr., of the *New York Times,* and later *Newsweek*'s own Michael Isikoff, enough details emerged about the secretive machinations of Lucianne Goldberg, Linda Tripp, Richard Porter, George Conway, Ann Coulter, and Jerome Marcus to buttress the first lady's allegations. By then there was little argument about the existence of a "conspiracy," and still less about whether the plotters were "right-wing." Only the "vastness" of their enterprise remained in question.

Forced to answer questions most Americans felt he should never have been asked, Bill Clinton had lied to protect himself, his marriage, his daughter, Monica Lewinsky, and his "political viability"—to choose the meanest way of putting it—from the consequences of his all-too-human frailty. But his shame posed little danger to the republic; his falsehoods and evasions were no threat to the Constitution. His behavior was shameful but hardly felonious, most of his fellow citizens believed, and certainly not in the category of impeachable offenses.

As always, Bill Clinton was also fortunate in his enemies. If Kenneth Starr's legal judgment was imperfect—in the end, his office lost three out of four jury trials—his political instincts were yet worse, as were those of the independent counsel's most fervent supporters. Morally certain that Clinton was on the verge of ruin, they hurt their own cause more with each clumsy attempt to strike the fatal blow. Each successive decision was worse than the one that came before: the incessant leaks about the Tripp tapes and the Lewinsky grand jury; the obsessive prurience of the *Starr Report;* the insistence of congressional leaders on releasing the independent counsel's complete investigative files; the decision to televise the president's August 17, 1998, grand jury testimony; and finally the precipitous, party-line vote on articles of impeachment in the lame-duck House of Representatives. These tactics succeeded in damaging Clinton's personal reputation. Politically, however, the public sympathy they provoked only made him steadily stronger.

As the ideological motivation of Clinton's enemies became clearer, their isolation became inescapable. Americans of all persuasions were disturbed by Clinton's behavior, but the most insistent voices calling for his removal—and most often speaking in southern accents ironically like his own—were heard from the precincts of the religious right. Organizations such as Citizens for Honest Government, Citizens United, and the Council for National Policy received scant notice in the months leading up to the impeachment vote, while characters like "Justice Jim" Johnson remained discreetly out of sight. But Richard Mellon Scaife and the Arkansas Project gained considerable notoriety, and figures such as the Reverend Jerry Falwell and Georgia representative Bob Barr appeared on television nearly every night.

Barr did not serve his cause well when he characterized the effort to remove the president as a "civil war," nor when he lectured a distinguished black federal judge testifying before the House Judiciary Committee that "real Americans" favored impeachment.

Such incidents and personalities helped frame the impeachment debate in terms of earlier cultural and political clashes, ranging from the Scopes trial of the twenties to the civil rights movement of the sixties. Both the nature and the agenda of the forces aligned against Bill Clinton made most Americans determined to deny them a victory. Having at last instigated the "culture war" for which they had long been yearning, the theological warriors of the religious right were chagrined to find themselves decisively outnumbered.

What ordinary citizens seemed to distrust most, however, as the Lewinsky affair unfolded, was the blatant collusion between the Office of Independent Counsel and prominent members of the Washington press corps. It was hard not to notice that the same reporters and news organizations that had been most critical of Clinton in the Jones and Whitewater cases also routinely scooped their rivals during the frenzied weeks that followed the revelations of January 21. Starr's denials that he and his staff were illegally passing along grand jury evidence in order to put pressure on witnesses and gain political advantage were widely disbelieved. The likelihood that reporters, editors, television correspondents, and producers were repeatedly fabricating attributions like "sources in Starr's office" and "Starr's investigators" seemed vanishingly small.

"What makes the media's performance a true scandal," wrote media critic Steven Brill, "a true example of an institution being corrupted to its core, is that the competition for scoops so bewitched almost everyone that they let the man in power write the story—once Tripp and Goldberg put it together for him."

Perhaps the most telling moment in that performance received far less attention than it should have. During a legal battle with the president's lawyers over his office's alleged violations of the rule forbidding prosecutors from leaking confidential grand jury information, the Office of Independent Counsel invoked a doctrine of "informant's privilege" to shield its dealing with the press from judicial scrutiny. What Starr sought to hide wasn't merely information he had given to reporters; he rather sought to conceal information that reporters had given to him. The identities of his alleged journalistic accomplices were redacted from those portions of Starr's brief released to the public.

Scarcely a word of demurral was heard in the press about journalists gathering information from sources or colleagues ostensibly for their own purposes, and then handing that evidence over to a prosecutor for very different uses. Not only did no reporters or news organizations step forward to explain themselves, but the topic went almost unmentioned.

Nevertheless, most Americans intuitively understood exactly what was happening. As the most powerful and largely unaccountable institution in American public life, the Washington press appeared to have joined forces with a partisan prosecutor to void the results of two presidential elections. This overreaching was more bitterly resented than many in the media realized. Whatever the American people thought and felt about Bill Clinton's private behavior, they refused to forfeit their constitutional right to choose their chief executive to what they regarded as a ratings-driven coup d'état.

When that democratic consensus was ratified, against all expectations, during the midterm elections of November 1998, American politics began a gradual withdrawal from the terrible scorched terrain of the previous decade. The old hatreds would linger but, as the desultory impeachment trial in the Senate made clear, their force was almost spent.

Within a few months, the entire episode took on the feeling of a fading nightmare. The media would move on to other wars and tragedies. The Independent Counsel Act would be left to expire by both parties, whose leaders sought to erase the embarrassments of recent years. The scandal culture, feeding on the sins and sorrows of public figures, would probably endure. But after ten years the Clinton scandals, at least, were over.

SOURCES

IN REPORTING and writing this book, the authors have adhered to standard journalistic practices. For the sake of clarity and simplicity, we have endeavored to make as many attributions as possible within the text. We interviewed or attempted to interview most of the principal figures named, including the president and Mrs. Clinton—both of whom initially agreed to cooperate by sitting for extensive interviews but ultimately did not. Nearly everyone agreed to speak for the record; in those instances where a quotation is not attributed by name, the source asked not to be identified. Insofar as possible we strongly preferred to avoid the use of anonymous sources. Among the periodicals and news services we used most extensively are the *Arkansas Democrat-Gazette* (and the now-defunct *Arkansas Gazette*), the *Arkansas Times,* the Associated Press, the *Los Angeles Times,* the *Memphis Commercial Appeal,* the *Minneapolis Star-Tribune,* the *New York Times,* the *Washington Post,* the *Washington Times,* and the *Wall Street Journal;* also the *American Spectator,* the *Columbia Journalism Review,* the *Drudge Report, Harper's,* the *American Lawyer,* the *Nation,* the *New Republic, Newsweek,* the *New York Observer, Penthouse, Salon, Slate, Time, U.S. News & World Report, Washington Weekly,* and the *Washington Monthly.*

Preface

The contemporary oral and published attacks on Jefferson, Lincoln, and Roosevelt are detailed in every standard biography. On reactions to past political misbehavior and the "culture of scandal," see *Scandal: The Culture of Mistrust in American Politics,* by Suzanne Garment (New York: Random House, 1991). Michael Kelly's profile of Bill Clinton was published in the July 31, 1994, issue of the *New York Times Magazine.* Sally Quinn's article appeared in the *Washington Post* Style section on November 2, 1998.

Chapter One

The late Republican strategist is chronicled sympathetically but unsentimentally in *Bad Boy: The Life and Politics of Lee Atwater,* by John Brady (Addison Wesley, 1997). Except where otherwise noted, the account of the 1990 race for governor is drawn from news stories in the *Arkansas Democrat-Gazette,* the now-defunct *Arkansas Gazette,* the *Arkansas Times,* and the *Washington Post* in 1989 and 1990, as well as from David Maraniss's fine Clinton biography, *First in His Class* (New York: Simon & Schuster,

1995). The career of Tommy Robinson is also examined in *Widow's Web,* Gene Lyons's account of the Mary Lee Orsini murder case (New York: Ballantine Books, 1993). Sheffield Nelson has been profiled frequently in the Arkansas press, most recently in the *Arkansas Democrat-Gazette,* Jan. 18, 1998.

[p. 1] "the two political operatives from Arkansas . . ." The account of the autumn 1989 meeting with Atwater is from author's interview with Rex Nelson. Pleading "a bad memory," Mary Matalin said she didn't recall the specific meeting with Nelson and Vigneault but added that "it sounds like a very logical thing." She confirmed both Atwater's early involvement in the Robinson candidacy and his related concern about Clinton as a presidential challenger to Bush.

[p. 2] "he had brought Vigneault onto the RNC staff . . ." *Arkansas Democrat-Gazette,* Jan. 14, 1990.

[p. 3] "My friends in the Bush camp dismissed him . . ." *Bare Knuckles and Back Rooms,* Ed Rollins (New York: Broadway Books, 1996), p. 218.

[p. 3] "compulsive, reckless womanizing . . ." *Bad Boy,* pp. 153–157.

[p. 4] "A *Washington Post* reporter confronted him with photographs . . ." *Bad Boy,* p. 260.

[p. 4] "rumors that the Democratic nominee once suffered from clinical depression . . ." and "Atwater 'had been investigating . . .'" *Village Voice,* Aug. 23, 1988, p. 20.

[p. 5] "Clinton just wasn't a 'good, solid Southerner.'" *Arkansas Democrat-Gazette,* May 11, 1989.

[p. 6] "'Mary Ann's plan was to become the Pamela Harriman of the GOP' . . ." Soon after Robinson's defeat, Mary Ann and Jack Stephens divorced. She moved to Florida and married Don Shula, the pro football coaching great.

[p. 7] "Robinson's lurid and ultimately baseless accusations." The McArthur episode and its aftermath are the subject of *Widow's Web.* A deranged but calculating former client of Bill McArthur's named Mary Lee Orsini was convicted of hiring two junkies to kill the defense attorney's wife. Taken in by Orsini's bogus conspiracy stories, Robinson twice arrested the unfortunate and totally innocent McArthur.

[p. 8] "The specific accusations revolved around a 1982 deal . . ." The most lucid of many accounts of the Arkla-Arkoma deal were those by veteran political journalist Ernest Dumas, written for the op-ed page of the now-defunct *Arkansas Gazette,* Nov. 10, 1989, and Aug. 10, 1990.

[p. 10] "Nelson defeated Robinson by just over eight thousand votes . . ." His winning margin came from Pulaski County, which he won by 8,600 votes. John Brummett, an influential columnist for the *Arkansas Democrat* (which merged with the *Gazette* in 1990), wrote columns urging liberals to cross over and vote against Robinson. According to Brummett, nobody in the Clinton camp encouraged the idea.

[p. 10] "A man whom McRae declined to identify . . ." Author's interview with Tom McRae.

[p. 12] "Jones likewise boasted . . ." *King of the Cowboys: The Life and Times of Jerry Jones,* by Jim Dent (Holbrook, Mass.: Adams Media, 1995), p. 211.

[p. 12] "On the Sunday before Election Day . . ." *First in His Class,* p. 456.

Chapter Two

The *Arkansas Democrat-Gazette* reported extensively on Larry Nichols's firing from ADFA and its lengthy aftermath, and also on the Darryl Glascock flag fraud case. Valuable reporting on the Gennifer Flowers affair appears in *Anatomy of a Scandal* by James D. Retter (Santa Monica: General Publishing Group, 1998); in a November 1992 *Penthouse* profile by CNN correspondent Art Harris; and in the *Democrat-Gazette*. Transcripts and copies of the Flowers tapes were released by the *Star* in January 1992. She testified about the approach from Republican politician Ron Fuller (which he denied making) and her dealings with the *Star* during her *Jones v. Clinton* deposition on November 19, 1997. Many of Nichols's phone conversations with Larry Case were recorded by the Little Rock detective.

[p. 14] "When the governor's chief of staff, Betsey Wright, heard that Nichols had been hired . . ." Author's interview with Betsey Wright.

[p. 15] "The mercurial Robinson, no stranger to eccentricity, later warned aides . . ." Author's interview with Rex Nelson.

[p. 16] " 'But if I did sleep with that fat white boy . . .' " Author's interview with Deborah Mathis.

[p. 16] "Wright had heard . . ." Author's interview with Betsey Wright.

[p. 17] "Two days before Election Day, Nichols . . ." Author's interview with Mike Gauldin.

[p. 17] "an extremely dubious tape . . ." Nothing on this tape, recorded in the Garland County, Arkansas, lockup by a former nightclub owner named Bob Troutt with a grudge against both men, strikes the authors as remotely credible.

[p. 18] "On January 30, 1991, Flowers's attorney . . ." Copies of this letter and all of her correspondence with Clinton were released by the Arkansas governor's office in January 1992.

[p. 18] "Over the next few months, Gaddy sent . . ." Author's interview with Judy Gaddy.

[p. 19] " 'she said it was all bullshit anyway.' " From an interview with a confidential source by *Arkansas Times* editor Max Brantley.

[p. 19] " 'you will never be able to run' . . ." Author's conversation with Hillary Rodham Clinton.

[p. 20] "She brought up Vigneault's name . . ." Gennifer Flowers tapes and Flowers deposition in *Jones v. Clinton*.

[p. 20] "A widely mocked example . . ." *Arkansas Democrat-Gazette,* Sept. 8, 1989.

[p. 20] "several weeks working in Ron Fuller's . . ." *Arkansas Democrat-Gazette,* Jan. 29, 1992.

[p. 22] "Susie Whitacre denied . . ." *Star,* Feb. 4, 1992.

[p. 22] "By the time . . ." Flowers deposition in *Jones v. Clinton*.

[p. 24] "Having sat in the kitchen . . ." Author's interview with Hillary Rodham Clinton.

[p. 25] "investigative work by Arkansas journalists demolished . . ." Numerous articles quoting associates and coworkers questioning Flowers's credibility appeared in the *Arkansas Democrat-Gazette* and *Arkansas Times* in January and February 1992. The most comprehensive reporting was by Mark Oswald and Valerie Smith in Little Rock's *Spectrum Weekly,* Feb. 19–25, 1992.

[p. 26] "agreement between Flowers and the *Star* . . ." and "a specialist hired by KCBS-TV . . ." *Los Angeles Times,* Jan. 31, 1992

[p. 28] "In a 1998 interview, Nichols indicated . . ." *Anatomy of a Scandal,* p. 67.

[p. 29] "in a curious partnership . . ." Author's interview with Larry Case; Larry Case tapes.

[p. 29] "During the 1990 gubernatorial campaign . . ." and "Over the strenuous objections . . ." Author's interview with Betsey Wright.

[p. 29] "When the job predictably failed . . ." and "If people wanted derogatory material . . ." Author's interview with Larry Case.

Chapter Three

Arkansas Mischief (New York: Henry Holt, 1998), the posthumously published memoir of Jim McDougal, written with *Boston Globe* reporter Curtis Wilkie, provided useful material (and some self-serving fiction) about the colorful life of its late coauthor. The most accurate and complete account of the Whitewater Development Corporation may be found in the seven volumes of the *General Report on the Investigation of Madison Guaranty Savings & Loan and Related Entities: Prepared for Resolution Trust Corporation,* by Pillsbury, Madison & Sutro (GPO, 1995, 1996). In addition to this we also relied heavily on the *Final Report of the Senate Whitewater Committee* (Washington, D.C.: GPO, June 17, 1996), the volume of exhibits titled *Minority Document Production* (Washington, D.C.: GPO, 1997), and the committee hearing record. The Clinton passport matter was most extensively covered in the *Washington Post.*

[p. 31] "No way, Bassett Schaffer told . . ." Author's interview with Beverly Bassett Schaffer.

[p. 32] "It's an extraordinary event. It smells . . ." *Fort Worth Star-Telegram,* May 23, 1994.

[p. 32] "McDougal nevertheless sent worthless deeds . . ." and "McDougal wanted Tucker to return $59,000 worth of promissory notes . . ." Author's interview with Jim Guy Tucker, who provided documentation. One of McDougal's versions of the story appears in *Arkansas Mischief,* pp. 236–243.

[p. 33] "Gerth said he had noticed . . ." *American Journalism Review,* June 1994. McDougal's account is on pages 244–245 of *Arkansas Mischief.* A more detailed critique of Gerth's Whitewater reporting by Gene Lyons appeared in *Harper's* magazine (October 1994). An exchange between Lyons and *New York Times* executive editor Joseph Lelyveld appeared in the February 1995 issue of *Harper's* and was reprinted in *Fools for Scandal* (New York: Franklin Square Press, 1996).

[p. 33] "According to McDougal . . ." *Arkansas Mischief,* p. 248.

[p. 33] "Gerth was sharing piles of documents . . ." Author's interview with *Arkansas Times* editor Max Brantley.

[p. 34] "as Bassett Schaffer had pointed out in twenty pages . . ." Her letters to Gerth, along with the full texts of his original Whitewater reporting, are also reprinted in *Fools for Scandal*, pp. 155–188.

[p. 34] "'unmitigated horseshit'. . ." Author's interview with Lee Thalheimer.

[p. 35] "'I never saw her take any action'. . ." Author's interview with Walter Faulk.

[p. 35] "'I subsequently had . . .'" Author's interview with Jeff Gerth.

[p. 35] "unguarded comments to reporters could have consequences . . ." Author's interview with Jim Blair.

[p. 36] "Jeff Gerth was initially somewhat apologetic, she recalled." *Blood Sport*, p. 208.

[p. 36] "Gerth later denied . . ." Author's interview with Gerth.

[p. 37] "amid strong FBI suspicions . . ." Testimony of FBI special agents Pettus and Irons before the Senate Whitewater committee, Dec. 5, 1995. Their sworn depositions are also on file.

[p. 37] "the RTC's Tulsa field office got two calls . . ." *Final Report of the Senate Whitewater Committee*, p. 421. These matters, including attempts by Bush White House aides in October 1992 to push for a Whitewater investigation, were first written about by Mollie Dickenson in an article scheduled for publication in the *Washington Post* on January 21, 1998. Spiked by *Post* editors, her articles later appeared in *Salon* and *I.F. Magazine*.

[p. 38–40] "In 1985, without telling his partners . . ." This analysis is based upon the April 24, 1995, "Preliminary Report to the Resolution Trust Corporation" regarding Madison Guaranty Savings & Loan and Whitewater Development Company, Inc., prepared by the law firm of Pillsbury, Madison & Sutro.

[p. 40] "Everyone in Arkansas . . ." RTC Criminal Referral No. C0004, L. Jean Lewis, Sept. 1, 1992 (*Minority Document Production*, pp. 48–68).

[p. 40] "Irons spoke with Lewis by phone . . ." See Irons and Pettus testimony before the Senate Whitewater Committee, Dec. 5, 1995.

[p. 41] "taking a direct interest in Lewis's intrigue." *Final Report of the Senate Whitewater Committee*, pp. 427–429.

[p. 42] "it's just McDougal . . ." Assistant U.S. Attorney Fletcher Jackson testified before the Senate Whitewater Committee on December 1, 1995.

[p. 43] "It is the opinion of Little Rock FBI . . ." Teletype to FBIHQ, Oct. 7, 1992 (*Minority Document Production*, p. 83).

[p. 44] "'Neither I personally nor this office . . .'" Letter from Charles Banks to Pettus, Oct. 14, 1992 (*Minority Document Production*, p. 92), and author's interview with Banks. Also see *Final Report of the Senate Whitewater Committee*, pp. 425–427.

[p. 45] Among the reporters who wrote about the Bush sons' savings and loan dealings during that period was Jeff Gerth of the *New York Times*.

Chapter Four

Larry Case made dozens of taped conversations available to the authors, without asking or receiving any compensation. He placed no restrictions on their use. Case also gave extensive interviews about his attempt to investigate the private life of Bill Clinton and his dealings with Clinton and other political figures in Arkansas.

[p. 47] "When Betsey Wright talked . . ." Author's interview with Betsey Wright.

[p. 47] "Rempel felt . . ." Author's interview with William Rempel.

[p. 47] "A regretful Rempel . . ." Ibid.

[p. 51] "Regarded as kooky and unreliable . . ." Author's conversations with a former editor and a former publisher of the *Pine Bluff Commercial.*

[p. 52] "the Clinton campaign learned . . ." Author's interview with Betsey Wright.

[p. 52] "The New Alliance Party was . . ." *Village Voice,* June 1, 1982.

[p. 52] "a photocopy . . ." Case's "note" is reproduced in the appendix to Floyd G. Brown's *Slick Willie: Why America Cannot Trust Bill Clinton* (Annapolis-Washington Book Publishers, 1992).

[p. 54] "Nichols convinced him . . ." Case tapes and author's interview.

[p. 55] "Although Case pressed him . . ." Author's interview with Rempel.

[p. 56] "A Fulbright scholar . . ." Maraniss, pp. 154–157 (Touchstone paperback edition).

[p. 56] "(Jackson himself got a medical deferment.) . . ." Maraniss, *First in His Class,* p. 157.

[p. 57] "I told them . . ." Larry Case tapes.

[p. 58] "Jackson said he regretted . . ." Author's interview with Rempel.

[p. 59] "Peter Smith was . . ." *Chicago Sun-Times,* July 30, 1995.

[p. 59] "'when Peter W. Smith talks' . . ." *Crain's Chicago Business,* April 10, 1995.

[p. 59] "He enlisted Eddie Mahe . . ." Author's interview with Eddie Mahe; *New York Observer,* March 30, 1998; *Chicago Sun-Times,* March 31, 1998.

[p. 59] "Porter would go on . . ." *Directory of Lawyers,* Martindale & Hubbell, 1993.

[p. 59] Porter did not acknowledge author's request for an interview.

[p. 59] "'they should have just hired . . .'" Author's interview with Mahe.

[p. 60] "printed a retraction." *Arkansas Democrat-Gazette,* Jan. 30, 1998. Williams later claimed again that Clinton had fathered her son Danny. The *Star* caused a brief uproar in early 1999 with a paternity test comparing Danny's DNA to the president's DNA sample in the Starr report. The results were negative.

[p. 60] "in tandem with a Fayetteville businessman named Philip Yoakum . . ." Described in press accounts as a "Fayetteville businessman" and a "Republican partisan," Yoakum has no telephone listing in the area and is unknown to veteran reporters at the *Northwest Arkansas Times* and the *Springdale News.*

[p. 60] "an open letter Yoakum distributed . . ." *Washington Post,* Feb. 20, 1999; *New York Times,* Feb. 24, 1999.

[p. 60] "I was particularly distraught . . ." All quotes from Yoakum's letters to Juanita and David Broaddrick are from copies posted on the ABCNews.com Web site.

[p. 61] "the couple was involved in a long-running dispute . . ." Author's interview with Arkansas Department of Human Services spokesman Joe Quinn.

[p. 61] "A photo of Clinton . . ." This episode appears particularly curious in light of Juanita Broaddrick's February 19, 1999, statement to *Wall Street Journal* essayist Dorothy Rabinowitz that her husband once "grabbed Mr. Clinton hard, by the hand, and warned him: 'Stay away from my wife and stay away from Brownwood Manor.'"

[p. 61] "The Brownwood Manor event . . ." Author's interviews with campaign aides Nancy Hernreich, Kay Goss, Kathy Gifford, and Weldon Ramey.

[p. 62] "Clinton had commuted the death sentence of one Guy L. Kuehn . . ." *Van Buren Press Argus,* Feb. 26, 1981.

[p. 62] "he and Hillary drove 150 miles from Little Rock . . ." Author's interview with Garrick Feldman.

[p. 62] "(Kuehn served out his sentence and was released . . .)" Author's interview with Arkansas Prisons and Parole Board member Charles Chastain.

[p. 63] "Broaddrick had phoned him that morning . . ." Author's interviews with Ken Richardson and former *Van Buren Press Argus-Courier* editor Roy Faulkenberry.

[p. 63] "Photographer Kia Larsen also remembered . . ." Author's interview with Kia Larsen.

[p. 63] "Years later, Juanita Broaddrick denied . . ." Author's interview with Juanita Broaddrick.

[p. 63] "there were several things wrong with the story . . ." Author's interview with Bill Rempel.

[p. 63] "Author David Brock recalled . . ." Author's interview with David Brock.

[p. 64] "FBI agents working for the Office of Independent Counsel . . ." *New York Times,* Feb. 24, 1999.

[p. 64–66] Author's interview with Andrew Cooper; the *Wellington (N.Z.) Dominion,* Oct. 31, 1992.

Chapter Five

Jim Johnson's voluminous papers, letters, clippings, audio- and videotapes, and other memorabilia are on file at the Arkansas Historical Commission in Little Rock. An excellent history of the 1957 Central High crisis appears in *Faubus: The Life and Times of an American Prodigal* by Roy Reed (University of Arkansas Press, 1997). The story of the "Willie Horton ad" is well told in *Crime and the Politics of Hysteria* by David C. Anderson (Times Books, 1995). Other accounts of Case's dealings with Citizens United may be found in *Slick Willie* and in the *American Spectator,* March 1997. The Susann Coleman story is also recounted in *Slick Willie.*

[p. 68] "'Clinton boasted that . . .'" *Washington Weekly,* Feb. 20, 1995.

[p. 69] "Examples of the Johnson style . . ." Johnson Papers, Arkansas Historical Commission.

[p. 69] "'There wasn't any caravan . . .'" Reed, p. 213.

[p. 70] "To a college student . . ." Maraniss, p. 79 (Touchstone edition).

[p. 70] "Johnson was endorsed . . ." *Arkansas Gazette,* Oct. 30, 1966.

[p. 71] "' the vacuous demagoguery . . .'" *Arkansas Gazette,* Nov. 10, 1966.

[p. 71] "One afternoon, Clinton drove . . ." Maraniss, p. 116 (Touchstone edition).

[p. 71] "'a queer-mongering, whore-hopping . . .'" *Blood Sport*, p. 314.

[p. 72] "They had met . . ." Johnson interview with NBC News producer Charles Thompson II.

[p. 73] "the *New Republic* revealed . . ." *New Republic*, May 28, 1990. The author was Joe Conason.

[p. 73] "the FEC's Republican members . . ." *New York Observer*, March 30, 1992.

[p. 73] "Floyd Brown's background . . ." *St. Louis Post-Dispatch*, Aug. 10, 1992; *National Journal*, May 30, 1992.

[p. 74] "sidekick named David Bossie . . ." *Columbia Journalism Review*, May–June 1994.

[p. 74] "Johnson offered historical guidance . . ." *Blood Sport*, p. 314–316; also see *Slick Willie*, p. 186 (2nd ed.).

[p. 75] "Susann Coleman had been a student of Clinton's . . ." She was also a literature student of Gene Lyons's at the University of Arkansas–Little Rock. An intelligent and charming young woman, she suffered from manic-depressive illness.

[p. 75] "whose detective Jack Palladino had been monitoring . . ." *Slick Willie*, p. 85, and author's interview with confidential source.

[p. 75] "'an unusually brazen dirty trick' . . ." *CBS Evening News*, July 13, 1992.

[p. 76] "1000 Reasons Not to Vote for George Bush; No. 1: He Cheats on His Wife," *Spy*, July-Aug. 1992. The author was Joe Conason.

[p. 77] "only after Johnson vouched for him . . ." Author's interview with Larry Case.

[p. 77] "Georgetown 'titty bar' . . ." Author's interview with Case.

[p. 77] "She had been . . ." Associated Press, July 19, 1987; Oct. 20, 1996. Deborah Stone later became a producer for correspondent John Stossel at ABC News.

[p. 77] "devotee of Ayn Rand . . ." *Washington Post*, Oct. 6, 1997

[p. 78] "Fund later recalled . . ." Author's interview with John Fund.

[p. 81] "If that sumbitch knew me . . ." Larry Case tapes.

[p. 81] "Citizens United agreed to pay . . ." Author's interview with Case, and *American Spectator*, July–August 1997.

Chapter Six

Apart from the Fiske and Starr Reports, the most accurate, comprehensive account of the Foster suicide and its aftermath is *A Washington Tragedy: How the Death of Vincent Foster Ignited a Political Firestorm*, by Dan E. Moldea (Washington, D.C.: Regnery Publishing, 1998). The criminal allegations against David Hale are detailed in U.S. Attorney Paula Casey's original indictment (*United States v. Hale*, LR-CR-93-147) and his own trial testimony (*United States v. McDougal*, LR-CR-95-173). See also "Ken Starr's Secret: How He Knows That Whitewater Is Bunk," by Gene Lyons, *Slate*, June 21, 1997; "Character Witnesses," by John Haman, *Arkansas Times*, March 1996; and "Family Skeletons," by Ernest Dumas, *Arkansas Times*, July 15, 1996, for authoritative accounts of Hale's career and his extensive political ties with Democrats and Republicans in

Arkansas. A remarkable series by Murray Waas examining Hale's corrupt judicial career appeared in *Salon* magazine during 1998 (Salon.com archives). The steering of
Hale into the national media by Citizens United was first reported by Trudy Lieberman
in "Churning Whitewater," her important analysis in the May–June 1994 *Columbia
Journalism Review*. We also relied here as elsewhere on the records of the Senate Whitewater Committee.

[p. 84] "They failed to report allegations . . ." "Travelgate: The Untold Story," by Joe
Conason, *Columbia Journalism Review*, March–April 1996.

[p. 85] "FBI officials testified . . ." Moldea, pp. 258–259; also the Fiske Report on Foster.

[p. 88] "Hale would eventually proclaim . . ." *NBC News*, November 11, 1993.

[p. 89] "Coleman placed a call . . ." Randy Coleman's testimony of Dec. 1, 1995, and
William Kennedy's testimony of Dec. 5, 1995, before the Senate Whitewater Committee and the *Final Report*, pp. 196–198.

[p. 90] " 'buying a pig in a poke.' " Casey, Jackson, and Assistant U.S. Attorney Michael
Johnson testified before the Senate Whitewater Committee on December 1, 1995. They
also gave depositions that are on file with the Senate. Career prosecutor Donald
MacKay, of the Department of Justice's Fraud Division, who took over Hale's prosecution pending the appointment of independent counsel Robert Fiske, was also deposed
by Senate staffers.

[p. 90] " 'I have known his family . . .' " *Washington Weekly*, Feb. 20, 1995.

[p. 90] " 'David was a young man . . .' " *Arkansas Democrat-Gazette*, April 9, 1996.

[p. 91] " 'I told him . . .' " *Washington Weekly*, Feb. 20, 1995.

[p. 91] "Johnson called David Bossie . . ." *Blood Sport*, p. 314.

[p. 92] " 'The file on the $300,000 loan . . .' " Associated Press, Feb. 12, 1997.

[p. 92] " ' "The devil made me do all this" ' . . ." Jackson's deposition was taken by the
Senate Whitewater Committee staff on October 19, 1995; page 168.

[p. 92] "Back in November 1989 . . ." Senate Whitewater Committee *Final Report*,
p. 594.

[p. 92] "Such exculpatory facts . . ." But not from Hale's testimony in *U.S. v. McDougal*.

[p. 93] "The lawyer had invited Gerth . . ." Author's interview with Gerth.

[p. 93] "telephone records show . . ." Hale's telephone bills are in the trial record of *U.S.
v. McDougal*.

[p. 93] " 'I don't remember speaking . . .' " Interview with Gerth.

[p. 93] " 'Gerth alluded . . .' " Senate Whitewater Committee *Final Report*, p. 187.

[p. 94] " 'Coleman was using Gerth . . .' " Testimony of Gerald McDowell and John
Keeney before the Senate Whitewater Committee, Dec. 6, 1995. Nathan and MacKay
gave depositions.

[p. 95] "Lewis and her boss . . ." See Senate Whitewater Committee *Final Report*,
pp. 436–442.

[p. 95] "Lewis sent a peculiar E-mail . . ." *Blood Sport*, p. 337.

[p. 96] " 'indicted on charges of misleading . . .' " *New York Times*, Nov. 2, 1993.

[p. 96] "According to Mike Narisi . . ." Senate Whitewater Committee *Minority Document Production,* p. 560.

[p. 97] " 'Whitewater started to take off . . .' " Rose's Isikoff interview aired on July 17, 1995.

[p. 98] *"Columbia Journalism Review* later concluded . . ." *Columbia Journalism Review,* May–June 1994.

Chapter Seven

David Brock gave several long interviews to the authors about his dealings with Peter Smith, Cliff Jackson, and the troopers for the *American Spectator*'s "Troopergate" cover article. (Other former *Spectator* staffers also spoke about the magazine, although not for attribution.) Internal documents from the "Arkansas Project" and the American Spectator Educational Foundation—including accounting documents, expense ledgers, bills, correspondence, and handwritten notes—were provided to the authors by confidential sources. Background material on Richard Mellon Scaife appears in *The Mellon Family: A Fortune in History,* by Burton Hersh (New York: Harper & Row, 1978); in Karen Rothmyer's pathbreaking profile in the *Columbia Journalism Review* (July-Aug 1981); in *Forbes* magazine's annual feature on the four hundred wealthiest Americans; and in the archive of the *Pittsburgh Post-Gazette.* Contribution and other data concerning the Sarah Scaife Foundation, the Scaife Family Foundation, and the Carthage Foundation may be found in the annual "IRS Form 990-PF" documents filed with the Internal Revenue Service, which are public records.

[pp. 99–102] Author's interviews with Brock.

[p. 103] "The *American Spectator,* which began . . ." *Washington Post,* Dec. 3, 1992; *New York Times Magazine,* July 3, 1994; *Esquire,* June 1994.

[p. 104] "Rempel doesn't remember . . ." Author's interviews with Rempel.

[p. 105] " 'written assurance from Jackson . . .' " *American Spectator,* Jan. 1994.

[p. 105] "But Laurence Silberman . . ." Silberman confirmed that he had spoken with Brock about the Troopergate article in a fax to the authors.

[p. 106] "('We've fished together many times . . .')" Author's interview with Boynton. Boynton declined to discuss the meeting at Theodore Olson's office.

[p. 107] "In 1971, he handwrote 334 separate checks . . ." *Washington Post,* March 16, 1997.

[pp. 108] "the agency asked Scaife . . ." *Free Agent,* by Brian Crozier (New York: Harper-Collins, 1993), p. 90.

[p. 108] "a disillusioned British army intelligence officer . . ." The *Times* of London, Feb. 1, 1990. For more on the CIA's role in destabilizing the government of New York: Harold Wilson, see *The Wilson Plot,* by David Leigh (Pantheon, 1988).

[p. 108] "Scaife developed an intense . . ." Confidential 1998 interview with Scaife associate by Harrison Rainie of *U.S. News & World Report.* The authors also interviewed other Scaife associates and employees. None would speak for the record except Scaife's attorney Yale Gutnick, who denied that his client "hates" Clinton. Gutnick did not respond to questions about Scaife's former ties to the CIA.

[p. 109] "Boynton and Henderson attended . . ." Both men declined to answer detailed questions about the Arkansas Project. The late 1993 meeting in Olson's office was confirmed by several sources, including the attorney himself. But Olson insisted that the meeting "had nothing whatever to do with the Arkansas Project or anything that could be characterized as the Arkansas Project." Another source told the authors that the main topic was obtaining stronger legal representation for Hale.

[p. 110] "Boynton seemed . . ." *Washington Post,* March 29, 1979; *Des Moines Register,* Oct. 20, 1993; author's interview with Boynton.

[p. 110] "Boynton and Henderson had known Larry . . ." Author's interviews with Boynton and Henderson.

[p. 110] "Larry's boss Scaife had . . ." *Washington Post,* Feb. 28, 1985.

[p. 110] "Dozhier was among Johnson's . . ." *Arkansas Times,* May 22, 1998. According to an interview Johnson gave to CNBC producer Charles C. Thompson II, Dozhier worked on his 1968 Senate campaign.

[p. 111] "His bait shop's counters . . ." Author's interview with David Brock.

[p. 111] "They had grown even closer . . ." *Arkansas Democrat-Gazette,* June 17, 1990, and author's interview with Stephen Boynton.

[p. 111] "Henderson had known David Hale . . ." Author's interview with Henderson.

[p. 112] "After all, the Arkansas Project . . ." Author's interviews with Caryn Mann, David Brock, and confidential sources at the *American Spectator;* also managing editor Wladyslaw Plesczynski's internal memo, dated Sept. 30, 1997.

[p. 112] "Wright had anticipated . . ." Author's interview with Betsey Wright.

[p. 113] " 'Most of the conversations . . .' " Deposition of Buddy Young in *Jones v. Clinton.*

[p. 114] "A Little Rock AP reporter . . ." Author's interview with former AP reporter Bill Simmons.

[p. 114] "Some newspapers published . . ." Notably the *Los Angeles Times,* Dec. 26, 1993.

[p. 114] "They made and then withdrew . . ." *Arizona Republic,* Dec. 26, 1993.

[p. 114] "The story merely quoted Jackson . . ." The troopers' lawyer also acknowledged to Rempel and Frantz that his clients were interested in a book deal.

[p. 115] Lynn Davis did not respond to author's request for an interview.

Chapter Eight

Suzanne Garment's *Scandal* includes a useful discussion of the Independent Counsel Act, as does Lawrence Walsh's *Firewall* (New York: W. W. Norton, 1997), from a later and very different perspective. The best account of Fiske's brief tenure appears in Dan Moldea's *A Washington Tragedy.* Many profiles of Kenneth W. Starr have been published since 1994; among the best were those that appeared in the *Fort Worth Star-Telegram* on August 23, 1998, and *The Washingtonian* magazine, September 1998. An important source for this and later chapters was Paula Jones's former attorney Gilbert K. Davis, who gave extensive interviews to the authors.

[p. 116] "Faircloth, a very conservative . . ." *Congressional Record,* June 19, 1994.

[p. 116] "Bob Dole publicly accused . . ." NBC's *Meet the Press,* Jan. 2, 1994.

[p. 117] "Nussbaum, for one, vehemently opposed . . ." *All Too Human: A Political Education,* by George Stephanopoulos (Boston: Little, Brown, 1999), pp. 240–241.

[p. 118] " 'Any such counsel appointed . . .' " *Congressional Record,* July 1, 1994.

[p. 119] "While traveling in eastern Europe . . ." *All Too Human,* p. 241.

[p. 119] "reached agreement with Fiske . . ." *Los Angeles Times,* Jan. 21, 1994.

[p. 120] "Politically Fiske was . . ." Ibid.

[p. 120] "By packaging the troopers and Jones . . ." *New Yorker,* June 20, 1994.

[p. 121] "Perry and Patterson received . . ." Depositions of Roger Perry and Larry Patterson in *Jones v. Clinton.*

[p. 121] "On May 8, 1991 . . ." *Washington Post,* May 15, 1994.

[p. 122] "As Cook later explained . . ." Deposition of George Cook in *Jones v. Clinton.*

[p. 122] "Charlotte Brown would later tell . . ." *People,* May 23, 1994.

[p. 122] "She had grown up . . ." Ibid., and *Penthouse,* April 1998.

[p. 123] "his powerful animosity toward Clinton . . ." *People,* May 23, 1994.

[p. 124] "His superiors, however . . ." *Uncovering Clinton,* by Michael Isikoff (New York: Crown, 1999), p. 74.

[p. 124] "According to Ambrose Evans-Pritchard . . ." *The Secret Life of Bill Clinton,* by Ambrose Evans-Pritchard (Washington, D.C.: Regnery Publishing, 1997), pp. 355–358.

[p. 125] "Apparently word went out . . ." Author's interview with Caryn Mann.

[p. 125] "A more direct role . . ." Author's interview with Gilbert K. Davis.

[p. 125] "Lund also declined . . ." *Chicago Sun-Times,* May 15, 1994.

[p. 125] "Frank Dunham, a Republican lawyer . . ." interview with confidential source. Dunham later represented Stephen Boynton during the federal probe of alleged Arkansas Project payments to David Hale.

[p. 126] "Both were solo practitioners . . ." *Wall Street Journal,* May 12, 1994.

[pp. 126–127] "Included among these covert advisers . . ." Author's interview with Davis.

[p. 127] "In Washington, Starr . . ." *Chicago Tribune,* Aug. 14, 1994.

[p. 128] "Although Senate Republicans . . ." *Minneapolis Star-Tribune,* March 10, 1994.

[p. 129] "exacerbated by the harsh editorials . . ." Fiske, *Final Report on the Suicide of Vincent Foster, Jr.*

[p. 130] "the power to choose and supervise . . ." 28 U.S. Code, Section 49, Independent Counsel Act.

[p. 130] "from a western extremist milieu . . ." See David Savage, *Turning Right: The Making of the Rehnquist Supreme Court* (New York: John Wiley & Sons, 1992).

[p. 131] "A loophole in the Independent Counsel Act . . ." 28 U.S. Code, Section 49(c).

[p. 131] "Nixon trusted Sneed . . ." J. Anthony Lukas, *Nightmare: The Underside of the Nixon Years* (New York: Viking, 1976), p. 321.

[p. 131] "one of the federal judiciary's most extreme conservatives . . ." *New York Times,* Aug. 17, 1994.

[p. 133] "Eventually, however, Sentelle would admit . . ." Testimony of David Sentelle before House Committee on Governmental Affairs, *Congressional Record,* April 14, 1999.

[p. 133] "Explaining its decision . . ." Order, *In re Madison Guaranty,* U.S. Court of Appeals for District of Columbia Circuit, Aug. 5, 1994.

[p. 133] "He was that rare combination . . ." *Washington Post,* Nov. 2, 1998.

[p. 134] "the deference of the *Washington Post* . . ." Associated Press, March 14, 1987.

[p. 134] "Harding College, a church-affiliated institution . . ." Arnold Forster and Benjamin R. Epstein, *Danger on the Right* (New York: Random House, 1964), pp. 88–92.

Chapter Nine

Citizens for Honest Government (CFHG) and Jeremiah Films have produced an enormous amount of published and videotaped material, from the various editions of *The Clinton Chronicles* to a monthly newsletter that was formerly available on-line. The authors also obtained some CFHG internal documents, fund-raising letters, and correspondence from confidential sources. In researching the religious right and Christian Reconstructionism, we referred frequently to articles and books by Frederick Clarkson and Skipp Porteous. The Reverend Jerry Falwell and the movement he represents are ably profiled in *Under God* by Garry Wills (New York: Simon & Schuster, 1990); *Spiritual Warfare: The Politics of the Christian Right,* by Sara Diamond (Boston: South End Press, 1989); and *With God on Our Side,* by William Martin (New York: Broadway Books, 1996). Original reporting by Robert Parry on the Unification Church and Falwell in *I.F. Magazine* was indispensable, as was reporting by Murray Waas on Falwell's relationship with CFHG in *Salon* magazine. Warren Stephens and John Brown gave extensive interviews to the authors.

[p. 136] "(Actually, Citizens was set up . . .)" Internal documents of CFHG.

[p. 137] "Until 1993, Jeremiah Films produced . . ." Video catalog, Citizens for Honest Government Web site (www.cfhg.org).

[pp. 137–138] "tightly guarded political organization . . ." The Council for National Policy is among the least-reported national organizations of any importance. The Institute for First Amendment Studies provides membership lists and other significant data on its Web site (www.ifas.org).

[p. 138] "a California theologian (and CNP member) . . ." Rushdoony is profiled in Wills, *Under God.*

[p. 139] "a repudiation of our forefathers' covenant . . ." *New York Times,* July 5, 1994.

[p. 139] "They were introduced in late 1993 . . ." *New York Times Magazine,* Feb. 23, 1997.

[p. 140] "Indianapolis lawyer named Linda Thompson . . ." Ibid.

[p. 141] "Even more disturbing . . ." *I.F. Magazine,* Sept.–Oct. 1997.

[p. 141] "'the kingdom of Satan.'" Address by Rev. Sun Myung Moon, Oct. 4, 1985.

[p. 141] "Falwell's own right-wing sympathies . . ." Martin, pp. 57–72, 232–235, 278.

[p. 141] "After being forced to abandon . . ." Martin, p. 271; also *Roanoke Times,* Feb. 6, 1995.

[p. 142] "Carrie Rengers drew the assignment . . ." *Arkansas Democrat-Gazette,* Oct. 30, 1994.

[p. 142] "(which ran a correction) . . ." *New York Times,* April 20, 1994.

[p. 143] "A few of the more than two hundred TV stations . . ." *Richmond Times-Dispatch,* Aug. 18, 1994.

[p. 143] "The silhouette's voice . . ." *Salon* magazine, March 9, 1998.

[p. 144] "But the Stephens family . . ." *Fools for Scandal,* p. 19.

[p. 145] "The Council for National Policy bulk-ordered . . ." Internal documents of CFHG.

[p. 145] "On May 11, 1994, he spoke . . ." A transcript of a videotape of Nichols's speech to the Boulder (Colorado) Patriots was obtained by the authors.

[p. 145] "Eventually, the president . . ." *Washington Times,* June 25, 1994.

[p. 146] "Clintons were very 'thin-skinned.'" *New York Times,* June 26, 1994.

[p. 147] "a farcical episode . . ." *Fools for Scandal,* pp. 18–21.

[p. 149] "They didn't take long to find . . ." *Arkansas Democrat-Gazette,* March 28, 1994.

[p. 152] "Citizens for Honest Government ledgers . . ." See also *Salon* magazine, March 8, 1998.

[p. 153] "Jane Parks did quite a bit . . ." *American Spectator,* November 1996.

[p. 153] "Malak's verdict was eventually . . ." See Mara Leveritt, *The Boys on the Tracks* (New York: St. Martin's Press, 1999).

[p. 154] "Meanwhile, Brown was also engaged . . ." Author's interview with Brown and testimony of FBI agent Michael Smith in *Campbell and Lane v. Citizens for Honest Government, Inc., et. al.* (LR-C-97-0328).

[p. 156] "Ruddy had become nationally famous . . ." *New York Times Magazine,* Feb. 23, 1997.

[p. 156] "an average balance of over $3 million . . ." Printout of Citizens for Honest Government internal checking account records.

[p. 156] "his own addiction . . ." *Arkansas Democrat-Gazette,* Dec. 4, 1997.

[p. 157] "gobbling pills by the handful . . ." Author's interview with John Brown; *Arkansas Democrat-Gazette,* Dec. 4, 1997.

[p. 157] "he signed a contract to pay . . ." CFHG internal document.

[p. 157] "According to Waas . . ." *Salon,* March 11, 1998.

[p. 158] "Falwell's appearance had to be moved . . ." *Arkansas Democrat-Gazette,* Nov. 1, 1994.

[p. 158] "'the greatest day of financial advantage' . . ." *Roanoke Times,* Jan. 30, 1995.

[p. 159] "Clues to this mystery . . ." *I.F. Magazine,* Sept.–Oct. 1997.

[p. 159] Reber declined to discuss the $3.5 million grant when interviewed by Parry.

[p. 159] "Moms and Pops cashing in . . ." *I.F. Magazine,* Sept.–Oct.1997.

Chapter Ten

In addition to the Arkansas Project and *American Spectator* documents noted above, the authors had several interviews with Caryn Mann and Joshua Rand. Conspiratorial versions of the Mena airport affair appears in *Compromised: Clinton, Bush and the CIA,* by Terry Reed and John Cummings (New York: SPI Books, 1994); in *Boy Clinton,* by R. Emmett Tyrrell, Jr. (Washington, D.C.: Regnery Publishing, 1996); and in *The Secret Life of Bill Clinton: The Unreported Stories,* by Ambrose Evans-Pritchard (Washington, D.C.: Regnery Publishing, 1997).

[p.160] "the payments to Boynton were reported . . ." American Spectator Educational Foundation Form 990-PF reports to the IRS, 1994–1998.

[p. 160] "Nor did that include . . ." *American Spectator* financial documents obtained by authors.

[p. 161] "quarters for visiting *Spectator* personnel . . ." Author's interviews with Brock and other *Spectator* staff.

[p. 161] "In a confidential memorandum . . ." Plesczynski memo, Sept. 30, 1997, from Arkansas Project files.

[p. 162] "Hale boasted that he paid cash." Testimony in *U.S. v. McDougal,* LR-CR-95-173.

[p. 162] "FBI special agent David F. Reign, who . . ." Author's interviews with Caryn Mann and testimony in *U.S. v. Susan H. McDougal* (LR-CR-98-82).

[p. 162] "it was decided to add him . . ." Associated Press, March 5, 1998.

[p. 162] "an assertion that Dozhier . . ." In July 1998, the alleged payments to Hale became the subject of a year-long special investigation by former Justice Department official Michael Shaheen, who took grand jury testimony from Scaife, among others. Shaheen reported in late July 1999 that while Hale had apparently received "things of value" from the Arkansas Project, the investigation had found no provable criminal intention on the part of his benefactors to influence his Whitewater testimony. Beyond that, it was difficult to know exactly what the special probe had discovered, because Starr's July 28 press release quoted less than one paragraph of Shaheen's 168-page report. The OIC withheld the remainder of the report, citing grand jury secrecy.

[p. 163] "Testimony at Susan McDougal's . . ." Testimony of W. Hickman Ewing, Jr., *U.S. v. Susan H. McDougal.*

[p. 164] "Until he fell out with the Clintons . . ." *American Spectator,* May 1994, and author's interviews with Betsey Wright.

[p. 165] "the magazine paid Brown . . ." Travel expense accounting, Arkansas Project files.

[p. 165] "misused the magazine's tax-exempt funding . . ." Data from *Spectator* files; also see *Salon* magazine, June 9, 1998.

[p. 165] "Taki . . . had served three months . . ." *New York Times,* July 3, 1991.

[p. 167] "Brown said he possessed direct . . ." Tyrrell, *Boy Clinton,* p. 10.

[p. 167] "A central figure in this scenario . . ." The late Jonathan Kwitny reported on Seal's ties to the CIA in the *Wall Street Journal,* April 22, 1987.

[pp. 167–168] "Local law enforcement officials . . ." *Arkansas Democrat-Gazette,* March 7, 1996.

[p. 169] "his account of an alleged 1986 meeting . . ." Reed, *Compromised,* chapter 17.

[p. 170] "Armistead had acquired a high profile . . ." *Memphis Commercial Appeal,* May 25, 1998.

[p. 170] "They had met . . ." Interview with Johnson, *Washington Weekly,* Feb. 20, 1995.

[p. 171] "'Bring your flags . . .'" Taylor Branch, *Parting the Waters: America in the King Years 1954–63* (New York: Simon & Schuster, 1988), p. 656.

[p. 171] "referring publicly to the NAACP . . ." Kenneth O'Reilly, *"Racial Matters": The FBI's Secret File on Black America, 1960–72* (New York: Free Press, 1989), p. 169.

[p. 171] "Armistead was present . . ." *Memphis Commercial Appeal,* May 25, 1998. The report of the Scranton Commission on the shootings at Jackson State confirmed the complicity of the state highway patrol in covering up an unprovoked massacre.

[p. 172] "'this is his bag . . .'" *Jackson Daily News,* Oct. 30, 1983.

[p. 172] "Under questioning by Rivera . . ." *20/20,* Nov. 27, 1983.

[p. 172] "'If the man is a homosexual . . .'" *Jackson Daily News,* Oct. 30, 1983. Armistead had publicly challenged Allain to submit to a polygraph exam and said he would, too; Allain did (and passed), but Armistead did not.

[p. 172] "The short version . . ." Brock made his notes available to the authors.

[p. 175] "'absolutely no doubt . . .'" Interview with Johnson, *Washington Weekly,* Feb. 20, 1995.

[p. 175] "Leach's press secretary, Joe Pinder." *Blood Sport,* p. 381.

[p. 176] "Over the protest . . ." *Fools for Scandal,* pp. 94–96.

[p. 176] "'No facts can be identified . . .'" Senate Whitewater Committee *Minority Document Production,* p. 73.

[p. 177] "But Lewis, it turned out . . ." *Wall Street Journal,* Aug. 18, 1994.

[p. 180] "Golden had showed up . . ." *Blank Check: The Pentagon's Black Budget,* by Tim Weiner (New York: Warner Books, 1990), pp. 184–185.

[p. 181] "Golden later conceded . . ." Interview with Golden by CNBC producer Charles C. Thompson II.

[p. 181] "Rex Armistead's activities had . . ." *Salon,* April 17, 1998. Armistead also investigated the personal life and finances of Murray Waas, the reporter who authored several *Salon* stories about him.

[p. 182] "'I emerged with a huge dilemma . . .'" *Fools for Scandal,* p. 206.

[p. 182] "Camp showed him . . ." CNN, Dec. 4, 1994.

Chapter Eleven

Unless otherwise indicated, all quotes and references to witness testimony during the House and Senate Whitewater hearings are from hearing transcripts or depositions. All quotes and references to the *Pillsbury Report* are taken from one or more volumes of *General Report on the Investigation of Madison Guaranty Savings & Loan and Related Entities: Prepared for Resolution Trust Corporation,* submitted by the law firm of Pillsbury, Madison & Sutro on December 28, 1995, or from the *Supplemental Report* submitted by the same firm on February 25, 1996.

[p. 183] "the indictments had no connection . . ." *U.S. v. Jim Guy Tucker, et al.* (96-3268EALR).

[p. 184] "He and Clinton first crossed . . ." and "in a rough contest . . ." Maraniss, pp. 351, 401.

[pp. 185–186] "greeted with popping champagne corks . . ." Author's interview with Caryn Mann.

[p. 186] "a bitter foe of . . ." Transcript of Johnson interview by Charles C. Thompson II.

[p. 186] "voiding the notorious 'Johnson Amendment' . . ." Author's interview with U.S. District Judge Henry Woods.

[p. 186] "Wesley Pruden was . . ." Transcript of Johnson interview by Charles C. Thompson II.

[p. 187] "Pruden acknowledged . . ." Author's interview with Wesley Pruden.

[p. 187] "the judge summoned . . ." *Minneapolis Star-Tribune,* April 11, 1998.

[p. 188] "D'Amato would demand . . ." *New York Observer,* May 16, 1994.

[p. 188] "his own testimony was 'classified' . . ." *Power, Pasta and Politics,* by Alfonse M. D'Amato (New York: Hyperion, 1995), p. 317.

[p. 188] "Senator Shakedown . . ." *New Republic,* March 10, 1986.

[p. 188] "once appeared as a character witness . . ." and "twice approached Rudolph Giuliani . . ." "The Worst Senator in America," by Joe Conason and Jack Newfield, *Playboy,* July 1992.

[p. 188] "For years, as a town official . . ." *New York Observer,* May 15, 1996.

[p. 193] "a Scaife-supported outfit . . ." IRS documents (Form 990-PF) filed in 1994 and 1995 by the Carthage Foundation showed a total of $330,000 in contributions to the Western Journalism Center during those two years.

[p. 195] "Among the charges . . ." *Wall Street Journal,* Sept. 23, 1994.

[p. 195] "Starr's law firm . . ." See "Troubled Whitewater: The Dual Roles of Kenneth Starr," by Joe Conason and Murray Waas, *The Nation,* March 18, 1996.

[p. 198] "Senator D'Amato charged . . ." CNN, Dec. 21, 1995.

[p. 199] "The Pillsbury Report found . . ." Republicans on the Senate Whitewater Committee later pointed out that Pillsbury lawyers had not interviewed David Hale.

[p. 200] "Ewing enjoyed a well-earned reputation . . ." *Memphis Commercial Appeal,* Aug. 12, 1990.

[p. 201] "He sometimes said he blamed his father's criminality..." See "Clinton's Other Pursuer," by Jeffrey Toobin, *New Yorker,* April 6, 1998.

[p. 201] "asked the new president to seek Ewing's resignation..." *Memphis Commercial-Appeal,* Aug. 12, 1990.

[p. 201] "Sundquist eventually succeeded..." *Memphis Commercial Appeal,* Aug. 6, 1990.

[p. 202] "Ewing modestly protested..." *Memphis Commercial Appeal,* June 9, 1991.

[p. 202] "'such as the Rutherford Institute.'" *Memphis Commercial Appeal,* Oct. 7, 1991.

[p. 202] "They met at a McDonald's..." *Memphis Commercial Appeal,* July 10, 1995.

[p. 204] "On January 4, 1996, Huber found..." Senate Whitewater Committee *Final Report,* p. 660.

[p. 205] "FBI fingerprint analysts found..." Senate Whitewater Committee *Final Report,* p. 419.

[p. 205] "The records' contents..." Senate Whitewater Committee *Final Report,* pp. 661–664.

[p. 209] "'visiting her mother and father'..." *Blood Sport,* p. 29.

[p. 209 "Rodham had died three months earlier..." *Friends in High Places,* by Webster Hubbell (New York: William Morrow, 1997), pp. 230–231. Hubbell attended the funeral.

[p. 209] "Other errors are more significant..." Author's interview with former governor Frank White. Also see "Family Skeletons," by Ernest Dumas, *Arkansas Times,* July 15, 1996.

[p. 210] "Again Stewart was badly mistaken..." Senate Whitewater Committee *Final Report,* p. 476 n.

[p. 211] "Office of Independent Counsel had notified..." Author's interview with Beverly Bassett Schaffer.

[p. 212] "It was Helen Dickey who..." Senate Whitewater Committee *Final Report,* pp. 48–50.

[p. 212] "Telephone records obtained..." Senate Whitewater Committee *Final Report,* p. 50.

Chapter Twelve

All citations and quotes regarding *U.S. v. Jim Guy Tucker et al., U.S. v. Jim Guy Tucker, James McDougal and Susan McDougal,* and *U.S. v. Herbert Branscum and Robert W. Hill* are from the court records and trial transcripts, unless otherwise noted.

[p. 217] "Starr's deputies had been sharply divided..." *New Yorker,* July 26, 1999.

[p. 217] "But the clippings did include..." Supplemental appendix to appellant's brief, *U.S. v. Tucker et al.*

[p. 218] "fired off an angry letter..." Letter from U.S. Judge William Wilson to Richard S. Arnold, Chief Judge, Eighth Circuit Court of Appeals, May 13, 1996.

[p. 218] "Two years later . . ." Statement by Judge Henry Woods, April 10, 1998.

[p. 220] "Jahn would later testify . . ." Testimony of Ray Jahn, *U.S. v. Susan H. McDougal* (LR-CR-98-82).

[p. 220] " 'betrayal by one of my best friends . . .' " *Arkansas Mischief,* p. 236.

[p. 220] "Tucker made good . . ." Author's interview with Tucker, who produced documentation.

[p. 221] "allegedly looted its assets." *Salon,* Aug. 12, 1998.

[p. 221] "a letter Stodola had sent . . ." Author's interview with Mark Stodola, who provided a copy of the letter.

[p. 225] "Watt had suspected Hale was a crook . . ." Author's interview with Watt. Gene Lyons was among the columnists who had called for Watt to step down. When his immunity agreement permitted it, Watt contacted Lyons and volunteered documents, letters, receipts, and copies of polygraph examinations verifying his account of his dealings with both David Hale and the OIC. Lyons subsequently wrote two columns of apology to Watt in the *Arkansas Democrat-Gazette.*

[p. 226] " 'David would drop names . . .' " *Salon,* August 17, 1998.

[p. 226] "Watt had tried . . ." Author's interview with Watt.

[p. 226] "The documents kept . . ." Provided to authors by Watt.

[p. 227] "the OIC hadn't finished with him . . ." In the spring of 1998, the OIC again subpoenaed and threatened to indict Watt, despite his grant of immunity, but never did.

[p. 232] "Hale swore . . ." In December 1993, when Hale retained Olson, no independent counsel had been appointed yet. Starr would not be appointed by the Special Division until August 1994.

[p. 234] "Smith testified years later . . ." Testimony of Stephen Smith, *U.S. v. Susan H. McDougal* (LR-CR-98-82).

[p. 235] "an astringent article . . ." *Neiman Report,* Harvard University, winter 1997.

[p. 237] "A clogged carotid artery . . ." *Arkansas Mischief,* p. 274.

[p. 237] "Susan McDougal had seen . . ." Author's interviews with Susan McDougal.

[p. 238] "Everything she had feared . . ." Ibid.

[p. 241] "Behind the scenes . . ." Author's interviews with Susan McDougal and Pat Harris.

[p. 242] "Tucker and his lawyers thought . . ." Author's interview with Tucker.

[p. 245] "Juror Colin Capp . . ." Capp is the son of the late *L'il Abner* cartoonist and hard-line conservative Al Capp, whose Dogpatch theme park included Hale among its original investors.

[p. 248] "Kenneth Starr announced . . ." *Arkansas Democrat-Gazette,* Sept. 15, 1996.

[p. 248] "To his amazement . . ." Author's interview with Tucker.

[p. 249] "punching out a television producer . . ." *Arkansas Democrat-Gazette,* May 29, 1996.

[p. 250] "A recent review in *Harper's* . . ." By Gene Lyons, *Harper's*, July 1996.

[p. 251] "Vlasto, McDougal wrote in his book . . ." *Arkansas Mischief*, p. 291.

[p. 252] "He bragged to Susan . . ." Author's interview with Susan McDougal.

[p. 253] "Hawkins, once a federal bank examiner . . ." Author interviews with Sarah Hawkins and her attorney Rick Holiman. Holiman testified extensively about Hawkins's ordeal during Susan McDougal's 1999 trial.

[p. 253] "her legal problems in California." Susan McDougal was acquitted on all counts on November 23, 1998.

[p. 254] "You know who the investigation is about . . ." Testimony of Susan McDougal in *U.S. v. Susan H. McDougal* (LR-CR-98-82), March 25, 1999.

[p. 254] "(Under oath, Jahn emphatically denied . . .)" Testimony of Ray Jahn in *U.S. v. Susan H. McDougal*, April 5, 1999.

[p. 254] "'A lie isn't for that day . . .'" Author interviews with Harris and McDougal.

Chapter Thirteen

[p. 257] "the initiative of the Washington press corps . . ." See *Spin Cycle*, by Howard Kurtz (New York: Simon & Schuster, 1998) for a balanced account of the fund-raising scandal and its journalistic origins.

[p. 257] "The story did emerge in *Vanity Fair* . . ." In a Dole profile by Gail Sheehy, *Vanity Fair*, Aug. 1996.

[p. 258] "the OIC had found insufficient evidence . . ." See the surprisingly sober assessment of Starr's progress in the *American Spectator*, April 1998.

[p. 260] "Davis and Cammarata had decided early on . . ." Author's interview with Davis.

[p. 260] "William Lehrfeld, a tax specialist . . ." *Salon*, March 12, 1998.

[p. 261] "But other IRS records show . . ." Sarah Scaife Foundation IRS Form 990-PF, 1997, shows a $20,000 contribution to FLAG.

[p. 261] "Between 1988 and 1996 . . ." Analysis of Scaife Foundation tax documents by research department at *U.S. News & World Report*.

[p. 261] "Its roster of members . . ." Federalist Society Web site (www.fed-soc.org); also see "Right Place at the Right Time," by Jill Abramson, *American Lawyer*, June 1986, and *National Law Journal*, Sept. 8, 1997.

[p. 261] "At the urging of Conway . . ." See "Jerome's Secret," *Philadelphia*, April 1999.

[p. 261] "they brought Davis and Cammarata . . ." Author's interview with Davis.

[p. 264] "Starr said he had tendered . . ." Associated Press, Feb. 18, 1997.

[p. 266] "General Accounting Office records later showed . . ." See "Financial Audits of Independent Counsel Expenditures," Sept. 30, 1994, to March 31, 1998, plus accompanying documentation.

[p. 267] "Questions about Starr's partisanship . . ." See "How Independent Is the Counsel?" by Jane Mayer, *New Yorker*, April 22, 1996. On April 17, 1996, the *New York Times*, citing Starr's conflicts, published an editorial calling on him to resign.

[p. 268] "Well before his interview with Isikoff . . ." *Washington Post,* March 2, 1997.

[p. 269] "from an inquiring freelance journalist . . ." The White House had given a copy of the report to Philip Weiss, then writing an article on the "Clinton Crazies" for the *New York Times Magazine.*

[p. 269] "a tendentious article by Stuart Taylor, Jr. . . ." Left untold in the *Newsweek* cover story, which fulsomely praised the *American Lawyer* article, was how (and why) the frustrated Isikoff had briefed the legal analyst with his old interview notes. Isikoff tells the story in chapter 6 of *Uncovering Clinton.*

[p. 270] "An afternoon function . . ." Retter, *Anatomy of a Scandal,* pp. 98–100. After Retter's book appeared, Jones spokeswoman Susan Carpenter-McMillan claimed that Clinton had ducked out of a reception at the governor's mansion and "walked three blocks" back to the Excelsior for his meeting with Jones. But the mansion and the hotel are at opposite ends of downtown Little Rock, well over a mile apart and separated by a six-lane freeway.

[p. 270] "Jane Mayer of the *New Yorker* . . ." *New Yorker,* July 7, 1997.

[p. 271] "She told him . . ." Author's interview with Cammarata.

[p. 273] "Hillary Rodham Clinton had made headlines . . ." Associated Press, April 11, 1997.

[p. 273] "Subpoenas flew out . . ." *Friends in High Places,* by Webb Hubbell (New York: Morrow, 1997), pp. 324–325.

[p. 273] "Despite being encouraged to cooperate . . ." Author's interviews with Susan McDougal.

[p. 274] "'dragged on too long . . .'" *New York Post,* April 29, 1997.

[p. 276] "At a meeting in the Oval Office . . ." Referral from independent counsel Kenneth W. Starr (Starr Report), Sept. 11, 1998, p. 62.

Chapter Fourteen

Although the authors found much to quarrel with in *Uncovering Clinton,* Michael Isikoff is surely the leading authority on his own reporting; unless otherwise noted, references to him derive from his book and articles. Isikoff is also a primary source on Kathleen Willey, Linda Tripp, and Julie Hiatt Steele. Tripp told her own story in her grand jury testimony, published in Supplemental Materials to the Starr Report, Part 3, Sept. 28, 1998, and in transcripts of her 1995 deposition and public testimony before the Senate Whitewater Committee. Willey's accounts of the salient events appear in her sworn deposition in *Jones v. Clinton* and her testimony in *U.S. v. Steele.* Aside from her interviews with the authors, Steele offered her version of events in *Steele v. Isikoff et al.,* her complaint against the writer and *Newsweek.* Both John Brown and Larry Wood were extensively interviewed by the authors (and Brown also testified about his activities in *Campbell and Lane v. Citizens for Honest Government, Inc., et al.,* U.S. District Court, Eastern District of Arkansas, LR-C-97-0328).

Although she declined to be interviewed, Monica Lewinsky has recounted the events of her relationship with the president in her grand jury testimony, which appears in Appendices to the Starr Report, Part 1, as well as in *Monica's Story* by Andrew Morton (New York: St. Martin's Press, 1999).

[p. 277] "Isikoff had gone so far . . ." "The Fire This Time," by David Brock, *Esquire*, April 1998.

[p. 280] "Her federal civil service career . . ." Résumé of Linda R. Tripp, released by Department of Defense Public Affairs Office.

[p. 280] "By the summer of 1990 . . ." See "Portrait of a Whistleblower," by Jane Mayer, *New Yorker*, March 23, 1998.

[p. 281] "'During the Bush '92 campaign . . .'" Starr Report Supp. Part 3, p. 4037.

[p. 282] "'an inside White House source' . . ." *Slick Willie II: Why America Still Cannot Trust Bill Clinton*, by Deborah J. Stone and Christopher Manion (Annapolis-Washington Book Publishers, 1994), Appendix A.

[p. 283] "Three years later, Stone . . ." *Wall Street Journal*, Feb. 28, 1998.

[p. 283] "But her conservative fans . . ." *Washington Weekly*, Jan. 28, 1998.

[p. 285] "'took great care to conceal . . .'" *Washington Post*, Jan. 28, 1998.

[p. 285] "She confessed that . . ." FBI 302, Starr Report Supp. Part 3, p. 3995.

[p. 286] "Her last day ended . . ." Isikoff, *Uncovering Clinton*, p. 134.

[p. 287] "Tripp's portrait of Willey . . ." *Boston Globe*, Jan. 10, 1999.

[p. 288] "Her late husband's Richmond law practice . . ." *Richmond Times-Dispatch*, Feb. 1, 1998; *Time*, March 30, 1998.

[p. 289] "Willey had importuned . . ." The White House released Willey's correspondence with the president and his aides in March 1998, after her appearance on *60 Minutes*.

[p. 289] "Willey was simultaneously . . ." See "Starr & Willey: The Untold Story," by Florence Graves, *The Nation*, May 17, 1999.

[p. 291] "Willey's telephone records . . ." Defense exhibits in *U.S. v. Steele*.

[p. 292] "As Nesbit recalled . . ." Interview with Nesbit by Florence Graves, notes provided to authors.

[p. 292] "That day Hernreich . . ." Testimony of Nancy Hernreich, Starr Report Supp., Part 1, p. 1401.

[p. 292] "Isikoff's sudden silence . . ." Author's interview with Cammarata.

[p. 293] "Cammarata placed a call to John Brown . . ." Author's interviews with Joseph Cammarata and John Brown.

[p. 293] "his acquaintance named Larry Wood . . ." Author's interviews with John Brown and Larry Wood.

[p. 293] "He brought information and witnesses . . ." Author's interview with Larry Wood.

[p. 294] "Other journalists who acknowledged . . ." Author's interviews with John Crudele and Ambrose Evans-Pritchard.

[p. 294] "Expense reports submitted by Golden . . ." Invoices to *American Spectator* from T & P Associates (Tom Golden), obtained by authors.

[p. 294] "And Cammarata had no idea . . ." Ewing declined repeated requests to be interviewed on the subject.

[p. 296] "Obsessed with getting the story . . ." Author's interviews with Matt Drudge.

[p. 297] "Lewinsky was again summoned . . ." Starr Report, App. 1, p. 795–796.

[p. 298] "On July 25, Cammarata and Davis . . ." Author's interviews with Davis.

[p. 298] "The worst mistake . . ." Author's interviews with Davis; Davis and Cammarata time records in *Jones v. Clinton.*

[p. 299] "Marcus's own wife . . ." *Philadelphia,* April 1999.

[p. 300] "George T. Conway III was . . ." *New York Observer,* Feb. 2, 1998; *National Law Journal,* Oct. 19, 1998.

[p. 300] "On a Caribbean trip . . ." Author's interview with confidential source.

[p. 300] "In late June, she and David Brock . . ." Author's interviews with Brock.

[p. 302] "(Later still, in confirming the leak . . .)" *Hartford Courant,* June 25, 1999.

[p. 302] "On October 8, 1997, Conway sent . . ." E-mail dated October 8, 1997.

[p. 304] "That letter, which Tripp . . ." Starr Report Supp. Part 3, p. 3982.

[p. 304] "a twelve-page, painstakingly detailed letter . . ." Letter from Davis and Cammarata to Paula and Steve Jones, Aug. 16, 1997.

[p. 305] "Carpenter-McMillan had undergone . . ." See "The Political Pals of Paula Jones," by Joe Conason, *Penthouse,* April 1998.

Chapter Fifteen

The best reporting on Citizens for Honest Government, impeachment impresarios and producers of *The Clinton Chronicles* was done by Murray Waas and Jonathan Broder in *Salon* magazine. From confidential sources, the authors obtained some of CFHG's internal documents, records, and correspondence. But much of the organization's literature was available on its Web site (www.cfhg.org). Memos and financial records from the *American Spectator* and the Arkansas Project were also made available to the authors by confidential sources.

[p. 308] "an urgent telephone call . . ." Telemarketing script from Infocision, June 12, 1997.

[p. 309] "Matrisciana and his allies . . ." *Citizens' Intelligence Digest* newsletter, January 1997.

[p. 310] "the widow of the late former CIA director . . ." Letter of thanks on CFHG letterhead to Mrs. William J. Casey, Oct. 2, 1996.

[p. 310] "Together Ruddy and Matrisciana . . ." Letter from Matrisciana to Reed Irvine of Accuracy in Media, Jan. 20, 1997.

[p. 311] "Barr, too, had long-standing ties . . ." *Atlanta Journal-Constitution,* Oct. 20, 1994; IRS Form 990-PF, Sarah Scaife Foundation, 1988–1994.

[p. 311] "When the CNP met in June 1997 . . ." "The Clinton Contras' Smoke and Mirrors," by Frederick Clarkson, *In These Times,* May 3, 1998.

[p. 311] "Ed Meese's own career . . ." Garment, *Scandal,* p. 121.

[p. 312] "As Brown complained . . ." Letter on Citizens United Web site, July 1997.

[p. 312] "as early as the summer of 1994 . . ." Gannett News Service, Aug. 10, 1994.

[p. 312] "Bob Tyrrell was toiling . . ." *The Impeachment of William Jefferson Clinton,* by R. Emmett Tyrrell Jr. and "Anonymous" (Washington, D.C.: Regnery Publishing, 1997).

[p. 313] "After two years of investigation . . ." A spokesman for the House Banking Committee admitted to *Salon* magazine on March 11, 1998, that two years of exhaustive investigation had produced no credible information implicating Clinton in drug smuggling at Mena. "We engaged in an appropriate inquiry that uncovered valuable information about money laundering and other issues," said spokesman David Runkel. He added: "Regarding the president, we found no evidence of wrongdoing."

[p. 313] "At the meeting . . ." Letter from Ronald Burr to Richard Larry, July 14, 1997.

[p. 313] "Burr had been scrutinizing . . ." Internal accounting memoranda of *American Spectator.*

[p. 313] "He solicited proposals . . ." Sept. 11, 1997, engagement letter from L. M. Henderson & Co.; Sept. 17, 1997, audit proposal from Arthur Andersen, LLP.

[p. 314] Tyrrell did not return calls seeking comment on his relationship with Burr and other internal matters at the *Spectator.*

[p. 314] "On September 9, he sent Burr . . ." Memorandum from R. Emmett Tyrrell to Ronald Burr, obtained by authors.

[p. 314] "At a special meeting . . ." Draft minutes of meeting, Oct. 5, 1997.

[p. 314] "P. J. O'Rourke quit . . ." Author's interview with O'Rourke.

[p. 315] "the angry billionaire called . . ." Associated Press and *Pittsburgh Tribune-Review,* Dec. 5, 1997.

[p. 317] "Geragos put the issue to Patkus . . ." Cross-examination of Patkus, *U.S. v. Susan McDougal,* 1999.

[p. 318 "the independent counsel told King . . ." *Larry King Live,* CNN, April 14, 1999.

[p. 319] "The sudden entrance of Whitehead . . ." *Penthouse,* April 1998.

[p. 320] "until October 1997 . . ." Case docket of Rutherford Institute on its Web site, www. rutherford.org.

[p. 320] "'The Church has a mandate . . .'" John Whitehead, *The Second American Revolution* (Wheaton, Ill.: Crossway Books, 1982).

[p. 321] "In a year-end plea . . ." *National Law Journal,* Dec. 22, 1997.

[p. 321] "Jones signed a fund-raising agreement . . ." *Salon,* March 12, 1998. Eberle's firm had done significant fund-raising over the years for organizations associated with the Scaife foundations and Newt Gingrich's political apparatus.

[p. 321] "Upon inking the deal, Jones reportedly received . . ." *Chicago Tribune,* Feb. 27, 1998.

Chapter Sixteen

Copious documentation of the events surrounding the Lewinsky investigation can be found in the Starr Report's five volumes of appendixes and supplements—which include most testimony before the grand jury, the Tripp tapes, and hundreds of letters, E-mails, FBI reports, depositions, and other exhibits. The Goldberg tapes quoted here were not included in the Starr Report appendixes but were released separately by the

Office of Independent Counsel. Testimony in *Jones v. Clinton* is quoted directly from deposition transcripts.

[p. 323] "When Linda Tripp picked up . . ." Goldberg tape 001, OIC transcript.

[p. 325] "The sixty-two-year-old Goldberg . . ." Knight-Ridder Newspapers, Feb. 6, 1998; *U.S. News & World Report,* Feb. 23, 1998.

[p. 325] "Posing as a journalist . . ." Jack Anderson and Les Whitten, United Feature Syndicate, Aug. 28, 1973.

[p. 326] "actually a CIA agent." Jack Anderson, Sept. 4, 1973.

[p. 326] "Goldberg was also involved . . ." *National Herald,* May 2–3, 1998, and author's interview with Elias Demetracopoulos.

[p. 326] "NANA was exposed . . ." *U.S. News & World Report,* Feb. 23, 1998.

[p. 327] "She was born . . ." Knight-Ridder Newspapers, Feb. 6, 1998.

[p. 327] "Among the items . . ." Ibid.

[p. 328] "she worked briefly . . ." Ibid.

[p. 328] "*Purr, Baby, Purr,* suggested . . ." *Washington Post,* Nov. 17, 1998.

[p. 328] "Her client Kitty Kelley . . ." Ibid.

[p. 329] "Kelley said that Goldberg wrote . . ." Author's interview with Kitty Kelley.

[p. 329] " 'there was no book deal mentioned . . .' " Starr Report Supp. Part 1, p. 1229.

[p. 329] " 'He plays to the world audiences . . .' " Goldberg tape 001, OIC transcript, pp. 9–19.

[p. 331] "The next time they spoke . . ." Isikoff, *Uncovering Clinton,* p. 196.

[p. 331] " 'It's not a sore spot . . .' " Goldberg tape 002, OIC transcript, pp. 8–18.

[p. 332] " 'We both realized right away . . .' " Starr Report Supp. Part 3, p. 4286.

[p. 332] "Tripp visited a nearby Radio Shack . . ." Ibid., p. 4283. She testified that no one at the store warned her about the illegality of one-party taping in Maryland.

[p. 333] "Isikoff stopped off . . ." *Uncovering Clinton,* p. 203.

[p. 334] " 'You don't have to limit yourself . . .' " Starr Report Supp. Part 2, p. 2488.

[p. 334] " 'Courier it tomorrow morning . . .' " Ibid.

[p. 335] "Goldberg later admitted . . ." Starr Report Supp. Part 1, p. 1231.

[p. 335] " 'huge screaming match' . . ." *Monica's Story,* p. 137.

[p. 335] " 'Linda Tripp suggested . . .' " Starr Report App. Part 1, p. 1393.

[p. 336] "Tipped off by Tripp . . ." *Uncovering Clinton,* p. 211.

[p. 337] " 'What am I supposed to . . .' " Ibid. p. 222.

[p. 337] "Tripp admonished her . . ." Starr Report Supp. Part 2, p. 2580.

[p. 337] " 'gleefully . . .' " Starr Report Supp. Part 3, p. 4280.

[p. 338] " 'From now on . . .' " Starr Report Supp. Part 3, p. 3974.

[p. 338] "The man who set up . . ." Author's interview with Lucianne Goldberg.

[p. 339] "Porter promised . . ." Author's interview with Goldberg.

[p. 339] "Porter also contacted . . ." *Uncovering Clinton,* p. 231.

[p. 339] "Goldberg had briefed Pyke . . ." Starr Report Supp. Part 3, p. 4329–4330.

[p. 340] " 'Isn't that great?' " Starr Report Supp. Part 3, p. 4331.

[p. 340] "Bennett had learned something . . ." Author's interviews with Robert Bennett and James Warren.

[p. 340] "Bennett delivered a subpoena . . ." Defendant's Motion to Compel Compliance with subpoena on Kirkland & Ellis, *Jones v. Clinton,* Jan. 27, 1988.

[p. 340] "When a Secret Service officer . . ." *Monica's Story,* pp. 150–152.

[p. 341] "The subpoena arrived . . ." Ibid. pp. 158–159.

[p. 342] "Tripp came as close . . ." Ibid. pp. 160–161.

[p. 342] "On a Sunday morning . . ." Ibid. pp. 162–165.

[p. 344] "The timing was important . . ." In *Uncovering Clinton,* Isikoff expresses anger that Clinton aides including Betsey Wright, George Stephanopoulos, and Phil Price had misled him about this issue. After calling a "dozen" businessmen around the country who had attended the Excelsior conference, he found one who said he recalled seeing Clinton around 1:00 P.M. This man wasn't called as a witness by either side in *Jones v. Clinton.* Phil Price, as the governor's liaison to the Arkansas Industrial Development Commission, which sponsored the conference, was deposed. He said that if Clinton had returned to the hotel in the afternoon, he too would have returned—and he had not.

[p. 344] "Jones was pressed to admit . . ." In a footnote to his book, Isikoff states flatly that Paula Jones's claims of employment discrimination were "false" (a concession his *Newsweek* reports omitted). Although he notes that Jerome Marcus wrote her complaint (with help from Kenneth Starr's law partner Richard Porter), Isikoff blames this on Gil Davis and Joe Cammarata. Judge Wright's later dismissal of the lawsuit was based on Jones's inability to prove damages.

[p. 346] "L. D. Brown claimed . . ." The former trooper had tried to quash his subpoena, a motion rejected by Judge Wright.

[p. 347] "She was unlikely to allow . . ." On December 30, 1997, the judge warned Jones's attorneys, "I will not permit you to spend a lot of court time on this business of other women."

[p. 347] "Lewinsky worked out the wording . . ." *Monica's Story,* pp. 166–167.

[p. 348] " 'Monica, promise me you won't . . .' " *Monica's Story,* p. 169.

[p. 348] " 'On January 12, 1998, this Office . . .' " Starr Report, p. 3.

[p. 349] "a player—one of the acts in the scandal circus . . ." *Uncovering Clinton,* p. ix.

[p. 349] " 'I had relied on the elves . . .' " *Uncovering Clinton,* p. 357.

[p. 349] "pathbreaking investigation . . ." *New York Times,* Nov. 19, 1998.

[p. 350] "On the following Monday . . ." *Uncovering Clinton,* p. 269.

[p. 350] "Through Conway and Porter . . ." Author's interview with Goldberg, and Starr Report Supp. Part 3, pp. 4347–4348.

[p. 351] "an agreement with the Jones lawyers . . ." Starr Report Supp. Part 3, pp. 4347–4359.

[p. 351] "Coulter made high-speed dubbings . . ." Starr Report Supp. Part 3, p. 4365.

[p. 351] "Coulter kept for her own purposes . . ." Coulter declined to be interviewed but has publicly denied keeping copies of the tapes.

[p. 351] "Agent Irons's 302 report . . ." Starr Report Supp. Part 3, pp. 3753–3759.

[p. 352] "Isikoff got a call . . ." *Uncovering Clinton,* p. 286.

[p. 352] "At first they talked . . ." Starr Report Supp. Part 2, pp. 2759–2784.

[p. 354] " 'Points to make in affidavit' . . ." *Monica's Story,* pp. 173–174.

[p. 355] "Lewinsky returned to the theme . . ." Starr Report Supp. Part 2, p. 2792.

[p. 355] "On Wednesday morning . . ." Starr Report Supp. Part 1, p. 944.

[p. 355] "The talking points merely . . ." Starr Report Supp. Part 3, p. 3337.

[p. 356] "In a remarkable footnote . . ." *Uncovering Clinton,* pp. 383–384.

[p. 356] "Bennett's recollection also conflicts . . ." Ibid., p. 277.

[p. 356] "Nothing was said about Richard Porter's being Kenneth Starr's law partner." Starr's supporters argue that Kirkland & Ellis has hundreds of lawyers. But Porter was the public spokesman for a tort reform committee chaired by then solicitor general Starr under Vice President Dan Quayle's "Competitiveness Council." Having thus met many potential corporate clients, both lawyers joined Kirkland & Ellis in 1993.

[p. 357] "Tripp's tapes also showed . . ." Starr Report Supp. Part 2, pp. 2598–2601.

[p. 358] "the OIC did possess a copy . . ." Starr admitted this in a December 11, 1998, letter to the House Judiciary Committee, p. 13. "When we received the affidavit," Starr wrote, "we understood that it had been provided to us by Mr. Moody, who had received it in his capacity as Mrs. Tripp's attorney." Starr's letter begs the question of how Moody came into possession of the letter.

[p. 359] "they used Linda Tripp . . ." Starr Report App. 1, p. 1375.

[p. 359] "Emmick told Lewinsky . . ." *Monica's Story,* p. 176.

[p. 360] "all Frank Carter would have needed to do . . ." The Starr Report is characteristically opaque on this point. Footnote 1027 mentions that "although the motion (and affidavit) reached the Judge's chambers on January 17, the file stamp date was January 20, 1998." The OIC had seized Lewinsky too soon by twenty-four hours or more, a possible cause of mistrial had she ever actually been prosecuted.

[p. 360] "Every time the weeping young woman . . ." *Monica's Story,* pp. 177–178.

[p. 361] "His voice rising with indignation . . ." House Judiciary Committee impeachment hearings, Nov. 19, 1998.

[p. 362] "Moody went downtown . . ." *Uncovering Clinton,* p. 321. Although Isikoff's book says Moody delivered the Tripp tape to *Newsweek* "in late afternoon" on January 17, reviewers' galleys gave the time as after midnight the night before. Asked the reason for the discrepancy by *Baltimore Sun* reporters, Isikoff refused comment. Moving Moody's turnover of the tape until the next afternoon, however, had the effect of making it appear *Newsweek* got it after, rather than before, President Clinton's deposition in *Jones v. Clinton.*

[p. 362] " 'Long after I thought the tapes . . .' " Starr Report Supp. Part 3, p. 4365. The OIC's response to Tripp's remark may have come in the much-discussed footnote 126 to the Starr Report, hinting that Tripp herself is suspected of doctoring some tapes: "Ms. Tripp testified that she turned over the original recordings. . . . According to a preliminary FBI examination, several of the 23 tapes containing audible conversations exhibit signs of duplication, and one tape exhibiting signs of duplication was produced by a recorder that was stopped and re-started during the recording process [thus appearing to have been edited]. These preliminary results raise questions about the reliability and authenticity of at least one recording, which in turn raise questions about the accuracy of Mrs. Tripp's testimony regarding her handling of the tapes. The OIC is continuing to investigate this matter."

INDEX

Abbott, Josephine, 289
ABC
  Hillary Clinton's videotape,
    editing of, 203, 251
  Good Morning America,
    367
  Nightline, 24, 203, 208, 209,
    251
  Web site, 366
Abramson, Jill, 349, 371
Accuracy in Media, 270, 311
Adams, James Ring, 161, 181
Agnew, Spiro, 326
Ailes, Roger, 73
Ainley, Neal T., 247, 248
Aldrich, Gary, 283–84, 285
Allain, Bill, 181
Alliance for the Rebirth of an
    Independent America,
    56, 65–66
Altman, Roger, 127
American Civil Liberties
    Union, 172
American Justice Federation,
    140
American Lawyer, 269
American Spectator, 64, 99, 102,
    103, 107, 109, 113, 114,
    125, 259, 312, 333, 346
  and the Arkansas Project,
    111–12, 160–62, 178, 270,
    314–15
American Spectator Educa-
    tional Foundation, 103,
    110, 136, 165, 173–74,
    313
  and the Arkansas Project,
    105–6, 160–61
  audit of, 313–15

Americans for Bush, 5, 72–73
Anderson, Jack, 326
Anderson, Ronnie, 101, 275
Annapolis-Washington Book
    Publishers, 77, 282
Arkansas Democrat-Gazette,
    25, 26, 28, 29, 60, 71, 93,
    142–44, 149, 166, 184,
    186, 217, 225, 245,
    265–66, 317
Arkansas Development
    Finance Authority
    (ADFA), 14–15, 144, 157,
    168
Arkansas Faith (White Citizens
    Council publication), 69,
    70
Arkansas Merit System, 18–19
Arkansas Mischief (McDougal),
    33, 220, 251, 264
Arkansas Project, 105–6,
    109–12, 160–62, 169,
    172–73, 173–74, 174–76,
    181–82, 185–87, 270, 294,
    312–15, 372
  audit of, 313–15
  and the media, 218–19
Arkansas State Police Associa-
    tion, 112–13, 165
Arkansas State Police Criminal
    Investigation Division,
    69–70
Arkansas Times, 120
Arkla (Arkansas-Louisiana Gas
    Company), 8, 8–9
Arkoma, 8–9
Armey, Dick, 138
Armistead, Rex, 169, 170–72
  and the Arkansas project,

172–73, 173–74, 181, 294,
    315
Arthur Andersen LLP, 314
Associated Press, 176, 235–36
Atwater, Lee, 1–8, 10, 72

Baker, James, III, 59
Bakker, Jim, 141
Ballentine, Debra, 124
Banks, Charles, 42, 43, 43–44,
    89, 95, 176, 195, 196–97
Barbour, Haley, 257
Barnett, Ross, 68, 171
Barr, Bob, 311, 312, 372
Barr, William, 41, 42–43, 169
Bartley, Robert, 77–78, 149–50
Bassett Schaffer, Beverly, 31,
    34–35, 175–76, 178, 182,
    200, 210–11
Bates, John, 274, 275
Bates, Stephen, 315
Bauer, Gary, 138
Behre, Kirby, 298, 339, 342,
    351, 355
Bell, Griffin, 221
Ben-Veniste, Richard, 196–98
Bennett, Jackie, 225, 274, 350,
    351, 353–54
Bennett, Robert, 126, 132,
    262–63, 297, 298, 303,
    306, 318, 340, 347, 351,
    354, 356–58, 359, 363–65
Bentsen, Lloyd, 272, 279
Bernardin, Cardinal, 263
Binhak, Stephen, 332
Blackard, Pamela, 124, 344
Blair, Diane, 150
Blair, James, 35, 150–51
Blanton, Ray, 201

Blood Sport (Stewart), 205, 208–9, 209–10, 250–51, 265

Bone, Robert "Red," 150–51

Bork, Robert, 103, 261–62

Bossie, David

Bill Clinton, accusations concerning, 74, 75, 76, 79–80, 80, 91, 92, 96, 98, 121, 129, 174, 175, 178, 187, 191, 210, 230, 282

Bowers, Rodney, 265–66

Bowman, Pasco, 217, 218

Boxer, Barbara, 196

Boy Clinton (Tyrrell), 178

Boynton, Stephen S., 106, 125, 163, 187

and the Arkansas Project, 105–6, 109, 109–12, 165, 169, 172–73, 173–74, 313, 315

Braden, E. Mark, 59

Bradley, Bill, 2

Bradly Foundation, 100

Brady, John, 3

Branscum, Herbie, Jr., 245–48

Branscum-Hill trial, 245–48

Breslaw, April, 176, 177–78, 194, 195, 196, 197

Brill, Steven, 372–73

Broaddrick, David, 64

Broaddrick, Juanita, 60–64, 346

Brock, David, 59–60, 63–64, 103, 169, 172–73, 284

Bill Clinton, accusations concerning, 99–100, 101, 192, 277

and Troopergate, 104–5, 112–15, 213

Brown, Becky, 164

Brown, Charlotte, 122, 123

Brown, Darrell, 242

Brown, Floyd, 72, 73–74, 121, 138

Bill Clinton, accusations concerning, 74–75, 75–76, 76–77, 77, 79–80, 81, 92, 96, 98, 106, 129, 130, 132, 146, 169, 174, 282, 312

Willie Horton TV spot, 5, 72, 72–73

See also Citizens United; Presidential Victory Committee

Brown, Jerry, 36

Brown, John, 153–54, 154–56, 157, 293–95

Brown, Larry Douglas (L.D.), 164–65, 346

and the Arkansas Project, 166–67, 178–79, 181, 182

Brown, Mark, 122, 122–23

Browning, Dolly Kyle, 346

Brummett, John, 26

Bryant, Winston, 168

Buchanan, Pat, 139

Bumpers, Dale, 72, 152

Burger, Warren, 133

Burr, Ronald, 103, 109–12, 174, 313–15

Burton, Dan, 138, 145

Bush, George, 2, 4, 19, 40, 72–73, 141, 159, 168, 173, 201

alleged extramarital affairs, 76

Bush, Neil, 45

Bush campaign

and Bill Clinton, 45

Willie Horton TV spot, 5, 72, 72–73

Butler, Gary, 247–48

Butzner, John, 131

Byrd, Patricia, 181

C-SPAN, 180, 197

Calero, Mario, 15

Cammarata, Joseph, 125–26, 126–27, 260, 261, 262–63, 271, 278, 292, 293–95, 298–99, 304–5, 306–7, 356

Camp, John, 181–82

Campbell, Donovan, Jr., 320–21

Campbell, Jay, 154–55

Campobello Properties Ventures, 32

Capital Management Services (CMS), 86–87, 233–35

alleged loan, 85, 89, 91–92, 92–94, 94–95, 166–67

Capp, Colin, 245

Cardozo, Harolyn, 287

Cardozo, Michael, 287

Carpenter-McMillan, Susan, 305–6, 307, 318, 321, 340

Carter, Frank, 341–42, 343, 247–48, 358, 359–61

Carter, Jimmy, 119, 158, 186

Carthage Foundation, 106, 313

Carville, James, 267, 306

Case, Larry, 29, 57–58

Clinton, financial and political exploitation of, 46–47, 49–50, 52, 52–53, 54–55, 56, 64, 77–79,

79–80, 80–81, 81–82, 85–86, 136, 345

Casey, Albert, 42, 45

Casey, Paula, 89–90, 91, 92–94, 116, 163, 194–95

Casey, William, 169

Caudell, Louis, 221

CBS News, 24, 75–76, 127

Center for American Values, 282, 283

Chertoff, Michael, 211

Chotiner, Murray, 325–26

Christian Coalition, 175

Christian Heritage Foundation, 159

Christian Reconstructionism, 138–39, 320

Church & Institutional Facilities Development Corporation, 159

CIA

the far right and, 107–8

and the Mena Intermountain

Regional Airport, 167–68

North American Newspaper Alliance (NANA) and, 326

Circle of Power (video), 140, 143

Citizens for Honest Government, 136–37, 139–40, 140–41, 152–53, 153–54, 155–56, 157, 158, 193, 309–10, 311, 372

libel and defamation suit against, 154–55

See also Clinton Chronicles, The; New Clinton Chronicles, The

Citizens United, 72, 73, 74, 77, 81, 174, 175, 312, 372

Clintonwatch newsletter, 96

media manipulation, 96, 97, 98, 176

Clarkson, Frederick, 139

Clinton, Bill, 2, 5–8, 11–13, 51, 256–57

alleged drug use, 21, 153, 153–54

impeachment attempt, 308–9, 310, 311, 312, 315, 367

media and, 116–17, 147–48, 371

political expertise and career, 3, 19, 23–24, 27, 51, 71, 72, 81–82, 256–57, 263, 369–70

as target for negative political advertising, 11, 56
testimony, depositions and threats of indictments, 195, 239–41, 247, 343, 362–63, 363–65
Clinton, Bill (alleged sexual encounters and reputation for womanizing), 3, 11–12, 16, 47–50, 50–52, 53, 52–53, 54–55, 58, 59–60, 64, 164, 292, 346
Juanita Broaddrick, 60–64, 346
CBS *60 Minutes* Interview, 24
Susan Coleman, 74–75, 75–76, 76–77
Denise, 52–53, 79
endowment, alleged physical characteristics and distinguishing marks, 54, 55, 302, 319
Gennifer Flowers, 5, 16, 17–19, 19–21, 21–23, 23–24, 25, 25–27, 55, 79–80, 196, 197, 266, 275, 344, 346, 363
Connie Hamzy, 51
Paula Jones, 59, 120–21, 121–22, 124–26, 213, 259–61, 261–62, 262–63, 269–70, 271, 275.
See also Jones v. Clinton
Monica Lewinsky, 59, 213, 214–15, 276, 295, 297–98, 332–33, 335–36, 340–41, 342–43, 363, 375
Susan McDougal, 254, 264–65, 275
Michelle, 54–55, 79
Sally Miller Perdue, 51–52, 52
paternity allegations, 58, 75, 99–100, 248
Michelle Purdom, 47–50, 55
Kenneth Starr's OIC investigation of, 266, 266–67, 274
Kathleen Willey, 271, 271–72, 277–79, 279, 279–80, 286, 287–88, 288, 289, 290, 291–92, 295, 344, 346, 363
Bobbie Ann Williams, 58, 60
See also Wright, Betsey
Clinton, Bill (political scandals and allegations), 223–24, 230–31, 231–32, 236
Branscum-Hill trial, 245–48

campaign finance scandals, 256–57, 264
files and records. *See under* Clinton, Hillary Rodham
Green Forest sewage system, 151–52
Madison Guaranty Savings, 30, 30–31, 38, 38–39, 40, 44, 45
Master Marketing loan, 85, 89, 91–92, 92–94, 94–95, 117, 166–67
media (tabloid & mainstream) and, 46, 116–17, 123–24, 147–48, 150–52, 246, 371
Mena Airport (weapons and cocaine smuggling), 167–68, 168–69, 172–73, 174–75, 178–79, 179, 179–81
Larry Nichols lawsuit, 16–17,28
Resolution Trust Corporation criminal referrals, 40–41, 41–42, 43, 95, 96, 117, 175–76
Travelgate (White House Travel Office firings), 83–85, 257, 258, 283
Troopergate, 21, 54, 56, 67, 100–103, 104–5, 112–15, 120, 347
Tucker-McDougal trial. *See* Tucker-McDougal trial
Tyson loans, 150–51
Whitewater. *See* Whitewater; Whitewater Development Corporation
Clinton, Chelsea, 51
Clinton, Hillary Rodham, 12, 19, 24, 27, 51, 62, 163, 369–70
accusations against, 175, 189–90, 190–92, 194, 195, 236, 310
commodity futures trading, 150–51
and Vincent Foster, rumors concerning, 85–86, 102, 105, 112, 114, 164
law practice (Rose Law Firm), 34, 36, 38–39, 85
files and records, questions concerning, 97–98, 117, 189–90, 190–92, 204, 205, 257, 258
media and, 189, 190, 205–6, 208, 371

rumors concerning sexual preferences, 85, 112
testimony and threatened indictments, 164, 200, 202–5, 205–6, 294
Whitewater. *See* Whitewater; Whitewater Development Corporation
Clinton, Roger, 12, 21, 46–47, 78, 79, 153, 179
"Clinton Body Count: Coincidence or the Kiss of Death?, The" (Web site), 140
Clinton Chronicles, The (video), 140–41, 142, 144–45, 145–46, 157, 168, 179, 186, 308, 309
media and, 142–44, 146, 146–47
misrepresentations and revision, 142–44, 152–53
See also New Clinton Chronicles, The
CNBC, 333–34
CNN (Cable New Network), 46, 113, 181, 203
Coalition for Peace Through Strength, 15
Cole, Lance, 281–82
Coleman, Randy, 88–90, 92–93, 162, 166, 232
Collins, George, 228–29, 230–31
Compromised Clinton: Clinton, Bush and the CIA (Reed), 168–69
Conason, Joe, 267
Conservative Political Action Committee, 120
Conway, George T., III, 127, 260, 261, 262, 263, 298–301, 302, 319, 349–50, 371
Cook, George, 122
Cooper, Andrew, 65–66, 124
Coors family, 138
Corbin, Bobby Gene, 122
Corbin, Delmar, 122
Coulter, Ann, 302, 319, 349–50, 371
Council for National Policy (CNP), 137–39, 145, 157, 284, 309–10, 310–11, 372
Cranberg, Gilbert, 235
Crash: The Coming Financial Collapse of America, The (video), 137
Crozier, Brian, 108
Crudele, John, 180, 193, 294

Cummings, William, 327
Cuomo, Mario, 3
Current Affair, 46, 53
Currie, Betty, 297, 298, 334,
   335, 341, 343, 343, 357
Cutler, Lloyd, 285, 286

Dale, Billy, 84
D'Amato, Alfonse, 120, 128,
   175, 188–89, 193–94, 208,
   212–13, 238, 275
   See also Whitewater: Senate
      Banking Committee
      hearings
Dannemeyer, William, 137,
   140, 308–9, 310
Darden, Jean, 61, 63, 64
Dartmouth Review, 77
Davenport, David, 268
Davis, Gilbert, 125–26, 126–27,
   127, 260, 261, 262, 262–63,
   292, 298–99, 301, 302,
   304–5, 306–7, 356, 357
Davis, L. J., 147–48, 148–49
Davis, Lynn, 101, 104–5, 115,
   192, 212
"Deepwater," 282–83
DeLay, Tom, 138
Dellinger, Walter, 262–63
Demetracopoulos, Elias P., 326
Democratic Party campaign fi-
   nance scandals, 256–57,
   264
Denise (alleged abuse victim),
   52–53, 79
DeVos family, 138
Dickey, Helen, 192–93, 193–94,
   212–13
diGenova, Joseph, 45, 268
Direct Mail Communications,
   159
Dobson, James, 138
Dodd, Christopher, 189
Dole, Bob, 72, 74, 116–17, 118,
   120, 129, 257
   alleged extramarital affairs,
      257
   campaign finance impropri-
      eties, 257
Donaldson, Sam, 12, 84, 367
Dornan, Bob, 138
Douglas, Helen Gahagan, 325
Dowd, Maureen, 203
Dozhier, Parker, 106, 109, 109,
   125, 166–67
   the Arkansas Project, 110,
      110–11, 161, 161–62,
      162–64, 174, 186, 187,
      219, 294
   and Gennifer Flowers, 111

Drudge, Matt, 296, 300–301,
   301–2, 319, 365
Drudge Report, 295–97,
   300–301, 301–2, 319, 365,
   366
Duffy, David, 52, 57–58, 155
Dukakis, Michael, 4, 72–73
Dunham, Frank, 125

Eberle, Bruce, 321
Eberle & Associates, 340
Eisenhower, Dwight D., 68, 69
Emmick, Michael, 359, 360
Engberg, Eric, 75
Ervin, Sam, 312
Escobar, Pablo, 167
Espy, Mike, 211
Esquire magazine, 112
Evens, Rowland, 4–5
Evans-Pritchard, Ambrose,
   124–25, 146, 153, 162,
   173, 192–93, 212, 294,
   309
Evolution Conspiracy, The
   (video), 137
Ewing, Hickman, Jr., 164,
   200–202, 206, 213, 248,
   254, 266, 267, 274, 293,
   317

Faircloth, Lauch, 116, 118, 119,
   132, 138, 155, 175, 187,
   191, 217
Falwell, Jerry, 136, 138, 139,
   140, 140–41, 143, 146,
   152–53, 158, 158–59, 372
   Liberty University, 141, 144,
      158–59
   and Sun Myung Moon, 141,
      158–59
   *See also Clinton Chronicles,
      The*; Liberty Alliance;
      *New Clinton Chronicles,
      The*
Farrakhan, Louis, 52
Faubus, Orval, 5, 68, 69, 70,
   186
Faulk, Walter, 35
FBI, 40–41, 41–42, 43–44,
   86–87, 92, 93–94
Federal Home Loan Bank
   Board (FHLBB), 32,
   34–35
Federal Savings and Loan In-
   surance Corporation
   (FSLIC), 34
Federalist Society, 126–27, 261,
   261–62, 300
Fediay, Elizabeth, 73, 74
Fefferman, Susan, 159

Feldman, Garrick, 62
Ferguson, Danny, 101, 121–22,
   156, 345, 346
Ferguson, Kathy, 156
First in His Class (Maraniss),
   56
Fisher, James, 363, 364
Fiske, Robert B., 161
   and Vincent Foster's suicide,
      83, 129, 132, 193
   media and, 128
   Republicans and, 127–30,
      132–33, 140
   as Whitewater independent
      counsel, 119–20, 127–30,
      132–33, 178, 196
Flowers, Gennifer, 5, 16, 25–27,
   75, 111, 370
   and Bill Clinton, 17–19,
      19–21, 21–23, 23–24, 55,
      79–80, 196, 197, 266, 275,
      344, 346, 363
   media and, 23–24, 25,
      25–27, 67
Floyd, Henry, 316
Ford, Gerald, 119
Ford, Harold, 201
Fort Worth Star-Telegram, 32
Forum World Features, 108
Foster, Lisa, 85
Foster, Vincent, 36, 95, 97–98,
   153, 181
   and Hillary Clinton, rumors
      concerning, 85–86, 102, 105,
      112, 114, 164
   Clintons' legal files, 97–98,
      117, 189–90
   suicide, rumors concerning,
      83, 85–86, 106, 129, 156,
      174, 190–92, 192–93,
      193–94, 194, 198–99,
      204–5, 212, 213, 270,
      279–80, 282, 294, 310,
      315
   White House Travel Office
      firings, 83–84, 257, 258
Frantz, Douglas, 104
Freidin, Seymour, 326
Free Congress Foundation, 311
Frieden, Terry, 249
Friedrich, Kate, 332–33
Friendly, Andrew, 272
Friends in High Places
   (Hubbell), 85
Friess, Foster, 138
Fuhrman, Mark, 325, 337
Fulani, Lenora, 52
Fulbright, J. William, 41,
   41–42, 71, 237
Fuller, Karen, 181

Fuller, Ron, 5, 20, 25
Fund, John, 77–78, 79–80, 80,
81
See also Wall Street Journal
Fund for a Living American
Government (FLAG),
261

Gaddy, Judy, 18
Gallagher, Maggie, 290–91
Gately, Robert Gene, 108
Gauldin, Mike, 17, 269
Gay Rights, Special Rights
(video), 137
Gecker, Daniel, 278, 289, 295,
298, 302
Geragos, Mark, 317–18
Gerth, Jeff, 30, 33, 34, 35–36,
36–37, 38, 93–94, 95, 96,
142, 150, 176, 177, 207,
210, 220
Gingrich, Newt, 59, 107, 121,
125, 129, 158, 174, 193,
213, 263–64, 311
Ginsburg, William, 361
Giuffra, Robert, 282
Giuliani, Rudolph, 188
Glascock, Darrell, 15, 147
Globe newspaper, 58, 60, 99, 248
Godwin, Ronald N., 141
Golden, William T. "Tom,"
180–81, 294
Goldberg, Lucianne, 284, 290,
307, 323–25, 325–27,
327–28, 328–31, 331–32,
333, 333–35, 338–39, 339,
349–50, 352, 354, 357,
371, 373
Goldberg, Sidney, 325, 326,
327, 328
Goldwater, Barry, 107, 130
Good Morning America, 367
GOPAC, 99
Gore, Al, 116, 256, 309
Goss, Kay, 62
Gracen, Elizabeth Ward, 16
Graham, Katherine, 107
Graves, Florence, 292
Gray, C. Boyden, 42, 45, 105
Grecker, Danile, 272
Green Forest (Arkansas)
sewage system, 151–52
Greenfield, Jeff, 24, 203
Gregg, Donald, 179
Greve, Frank, 327
Guthrie, Dan, 247, 248

Hale, David, 7, 87–90, 184
alleged illegal loan, 85, 89,
91–92, 92–94, 94–95,

165, 166–67, 223, 223–24,
227–29, 229–30, 230–31,
231–32, 233, 253, 265
Arkansas Project and, 109,
110, 111, 161–62, 163,
174, 178, 219–22
Bill Clinton, accusations
concerning, 88, 91,
91–92, 92–94, 94–95,
96–97, 105–6, 117, 129,
217, 259, 265
FBI 302 form, 222, 223, 228,
265
Jim Johnson and, 90–91, 92,
106
legal problems, 85, 86–87,
88–90, 94–95
and the media, 94–95, 106,
116, 198
Tucker-McDougal trial tes-
timony, 217, 221–22, 222,
223, 224, 228–29, 229–30,
230–31, 231–32
See also Tucker-McDougal
trial
Halloween, Trick or Treat?
(video), 137
Ham, Everett, 65–66, 124
Hammonds, Bobby, 248
Hamzy, Connie, 51
Hard Copy, 46
Hardball with Chris Matthews,
333–34
Harmon, Dan, 154–55
Harper's magazine, 147, 182,
250
Harrington, David, 345
Harris, Art, 26, 55
Harris, Pat, 242, 254
Hart, Gary, 3
Hartford Courant, 302
Hawkins, Sarah, 253
Hayes, Charles Marvin, 248–49
Hayes, Renee Johnson, 248–
49
Hays, Cindy, 260
Helms, Jesse, 131, 132–33, 135,
138
Henderson, David W., 106
and the Arkansas Project,
109, 109–12, 125, 163,
165, 166, 169, 172–73,
173–74, 313, 315
Henry, Don, 153–54
Hernreich, Nancy, 272, 281,
288, 292, 297
Heuer, Sam, 35, 229–30, 237,
241, 241, 243, 251
Highland, Jim, 187
Hill, Anita, 99, 100

Hill, Robert W., 245–48
Hillyer, John, 139
Hofstadter, Richard, 142
Holder, Eric, 354, 356, 357
Holiday, Edith, 41, 42
Holmes, Wesley, 362
Holt, Frank, 70
Horne, Rex, 158
Horowitz, Michael, 109–12
Horton, Willie, 5, 72, 72–73
Howard, George, 219, 220, 222,
232, 235, 237, 242, 249,
252, 255, 2733
Hubbell, Webster, 36, 85, 143,
258, 285
the Clintons, pressures to
incriminate, 273–74
Huber, Carolyn, 204
Huckabee, Mike, 245, 249
Hudman, Doug, 159
Human Events magazine, 326
Humphrey, Hubert, 71
Hutchinson, Asa, 167
Hutcheson, Ron, 327
Hyde, Henry, 139, 308, 312

I.F. Magazine, 141
Ickes, Harold, 127
*Impeachment of William Jeffer-
son Clinton, The*
(Tyrrell), 312
Imus, Don, 319
Independent Counsel Act,
118–19, 130, 373
Special Division (three-
judge panel), 131–32,
133, 353
See also Fiske, Robert B.;
Starr, Kenneth W.
Independent Woman's Forum,
127, 357
Infocision, 308
Ingraham, Laura, 300, 319
Insight magazine, 141
Institutes of Biblical Law
(Rushdoony), 138
Integrity Films, 137
International Paper Co., 128,
132
Iorio, Richard, 38, 95
Irons, Steven, 40–41, 196,
351–52, 352–53
Isikoff, Michael, 50, 85, 86, 94,
97, 124, 204–5, 268,
269–70, 271, 272, 277–79,
286, 291–92, 295, 297,
302, 302–3, 304, 349, 354,
356, 357–58, 362, 367
and Linda Tripp, 289, 297,
303, 303–4, 324, 330,

Isikoff, Michael (*cont.*)
331–32, 333, 333–35, 336, 337
Ives, Kevin, 153–54

Jackson, Cliff, 53
Bill Clinton, accusations concerning, 56–58, 58, 67, 100–103, 104, 112, 125, 157
and Troopergate, 104–5, 114, 120–21, 192, 346, 347
Jackson, Fletcher, 42, 90, 92
Jackson, Robert, 185
Jackson *Clarion-Ledger*, 170
Jackson Daily News, 172
Jahn, LeRoy, 220
Jahn, Ray, 220, 222, 223, 223–24, 227, 228–29, 231–32, 238, 239, 241, 243–44, 251, 253, 254, 255, 259
Jeremiah Films, 137, 309
John Birch Society, 130, 134, 171
Johnson, Jim, 67–68, 169, 217, 218, 372
Bill Clinton, accusations concerning, 71, 74, 75, 77, 90–91, 92, 106, 110–11, 142, 153, 170–71, 174–75, 187, 310
politics of, 68–69, 70–71, 90, 98, 186–87, 219
See also White Citizens Council
Johnson, Lady Bird, 327, 327–28
Johnson, Lyndon, 327
Johnson, Mark, 74
Johnson, Paul, Jr., 171
Johnson, Richard, 319
Jones, Charlotte, 9
Jones, Jerry, 8–9, 12, 18, 32
Jones, Paula Corbin, 122–23
Bill Clinton, accusations concerning, 59, 120–21, 121–22, 124–26, 126–27, 153, 269–70, 275
Bill Clinton, lawsuit against. *See Jones v. Clinton*
media and, 123–24, 126, 269–70
Paula Jones Legal Fund, 260–61, 321–22, 340
Jones, Steve, 120, 122, 123, 153, 305
Jones v. Clinton, 213, 259–61, 261–62, 262–63, 271, 276,

276, 292, 298–301, 318–21, 321–22, 337–38, 339–40, 340, 342–47, 354, 362
Bill Clinton's deposition, 362–63, 363–65
the Office of the Independent Council and, 349–50, 356–58, 358–59
settlement, attempts to negotiate, 298–99, 301, 302, 303, 304–5, 306, 322
the Supreme Court and, 213, 259–61, 261–62, 262–63, 271, 276
Linda Tripp and, 337–38, 339–40, 362
Joo, Dong Moon, 141
Jordan, Vernon, 335, 336, 340, 341, 342, 247–48, 349, 357
Judd, Jackie, 366

Kakutani, Michiko, 208
Kantor, Mickey, 51
Kaye, Walter, 276
Keeney, John, 94
Kelley, Kitty, 328–29
Kelley, Virginia, 58, 116
Kelly, Michael, 151–52, 236
Lasky, Victor, 325
Kemp, Jack, 103
Kendall, David, 166, 178, 204, 274, 350, 357, 361
Kennedy, John F., 327
Kennedy, William, 89, 198, 200
King, Jim, 286
King, Larry, 318
King, Martin Luther, Jr., 263
Kirk, Dana, 201
Kirk, Lauren, 26
Kirkland, Carl, 54
Kirkpatrick, Jeane, 103
Kirkland & Ellis, 195–96, 220, 267
Klaidman, Daniel, 268
Klayman, Larry, 138
Klein, Joe, 312
Klein, Joel, 285
Kleindienst, Richard, 131
KMOX (St. Louis), 146
Koppel, Ted, 203, 208, 209
Kramer, Michael, 116–17
Kristol, Irving, 103
Kristol, William, 105
Kroft, Steve, 24
Ku Klux Klan, 69, 70–71, 98
Kuehn, Guy L., 62, 63
Kurtz, Howard, 266

Kyl, John, 138

Labaton, Stephen, 197, 200, 202–3, 207, 245, 273
Lader, Philip, 286
Lamb, Brian, 180
Landmark Legal Foundation, 125, 261
Lanasa, Anthony, 289
Lane, Kirk, 154–55
LaRouche, Lyndon, 4
Larry, Richard, 106, 109, 110, 125, 313, 315
Larry King Live, 318
Larsen, Kia, 63
Larson, Phil, 284
Lasater, Dan, 47, 79, 142, 168, 179, 182
Lassiter, Jack, 247
Latham, John, 203, 206, 207
Leach, Jim, 155, 180, 175–76, 177–78, 210–11, 238, 313
political influence on, 129, 155
See also Whitewater: House Banking Committee hearings Legal Affairs Council, 120–21
Legal Times, 125–26, 270
Lehrfeld, William, 260–61
Lerman, Bradley, 235
Leslie, Bob, 17, 82
Lewinsky, Bernard, 361–62
Lewinsky, Monica, 340
and Bill Clinton, 59, 213, 214–15, 276, 295, 297–98, 332–33, 335–36, 340–41, 342, 342–43, 363, 365
Jane Doe #6 affidavit, 347–48, 352–53, 360
and the Paula Jones lawsuit, 341, 343, 342–43, 347, 362
Office of Independent Council questioning, 359–61, 361–62
Office of Independent Council testimony, 335–36
the stained dress, 337
and Linda Tripp, 287, 289, 297–98, 304, 307, 324, 333–35, 335–36, 342, 342–43, 348, 351–52, 354–55, 355–56
the Linda Tripp tapes, 331, 332–33, 334–35, 336–37, 348, 352–53, 357, 362, 366
Lewis, Anthony, 208, 212

Lewis, L. Jean, 37–38, 39–41
  criminal referrals, 40–41,
    41–42, 43, 95, 96, 117,
    175–76
  Whitewater testimony,
    177–78, 194–96, 196–98,
    207
Lewis, Marcia, 361
Liberman, Lee, 105
Liberty Alliance, 140, 140–41,
  144
Liberty University, 141, 144
Liddy, G. Gordon, 121
Limbaugh, Rush, 103, 129, 140,
  213
Lindsey, Bruce, 246, 281, 285,
  286, 292, 298, 354
Lindsey, Lorna, 75
Livingston, Bob, 155
Livingston, Craig, 258, 310
London *Sunday Telegraph,*
  124–25, 192–93, 212
Los Angeles Times, 46, 47, 48,
  81, 218
  coverage of Bill Clinton,
    100, 102, 112–15
  See also Rempel, William
Lott, Trent, 137, 170
Lund, Nelson, 125
Lyons, James, 36

McAndrews & Forbes, 341
McArthur, Bill, 7
McAteer, Ed, 201
McClellan, John, 252
McCollum, Bill, 155
McConnell, John, 180
McCoy, Ann, 164
McCurry, Mike, 269
McDaniel, Bobby, 224, 233,
  243
McDougal, James, 30, 31, 38,
  71, 184, 237
  alleged illicit loan, 85, 89,
    91–92, 92–94, 94–95,
    129, 165, 166–67
  and the "cashier's check,"
    315–18
  and the Clintons, 31, 30–31,
    35–36, 45, 67, 150
  the Clintons, pressures to
    incriminate, 251–52,
    252–54, 259, 264, 273
  legal problems, 31, 32–33,
    39, 41, 43
  Madison Guaranty Savings
    and Loan, 31, 32, 34–35,
    39, 39–41, 166–67
  psychiatric history, 36–37,
    43

Tucker-McDougal trial tes-
    timony and sentencing,
    237–38, 238–241, 244,
    273, 274
  and Whitewater, 30, 30–31,
    41, 132, 177
  See also Pillsbury Report;
    Tucker-McDougal trial
McDougal, Susan, 34–35, 41,
  132, 163–64, 237–38
  alleged loan, 85, 89, 91–92,
    92–94, 94–95, 165
  Bill Clinton, alleged affair
    with, 254, 264–65, 275
  the Clintons, pressures to
    incriminate, 251, 252–54,
    273–74
  Tucker-McDougal trial tes-
    timony and sentencing,
    223–24, 237, 241–42, 244,
    255
  Nancy Mehta's charges,
    253–54, 264
  See also Tucker-McDougal
    trial
McDowell, Gerald, 94
McGovern, George, 325, 326
McIntosh, Robert "Say," 58,
  249, 345
Mack, Connie, 206
McKay, Donald, 94
McKenney, Tom, 155
McMillian, Bill, 307, 318
McRae, Tom, 10
Maddox, Lester, 68, 71
Madison Guaranty Savings
    and Loan, 31, 32, 34–35
  audits and criminal refer-
    rals, 32, 36, 37, 40–41,
    41–42, 43, 95, 96
  the Clintons and, 30, 30–31,
    38, 38–39, 40, 44
  Resolution Trust Corpora-
    tion (RTC) and, 37, 38,
    39–41
  See also Lewis, Jean; Rose
    Law Firm; Pillsbury Re-
    port; Tucker-McDougal
    trial
Mahe, Eddie, 59, 59, 60
Malak, Fahmy, 153–54
Manchester Union-Leader, 23,
  56
Manion, Christopher, 282–83
Mann, Caryn, 125, 162,
  162–64, 166–67, 174
Mann, Josh, 163, 164
Maraniss, David, 56
Marceca, Anthony, 258
Marcello, Carlos, 170

Marcus, Jerome, 127, 298–99,
  371
Mason, Louwanda Faye, 48–50,
  55, 79
Massey, Richard, 206–7, 298
Matalin, Mary, 2
Mathis, Deborah, 16, 22
Matrisciana, Pat, 137, 139–40,
  140–41, 143–44, 153, 153,
  154–55, 155–56, 157,
  309–10, 310–11
Mayer, Jane, 329
Meese, Edwin, III, 137, 311–12
Mehta, Nancy, 253–54, 264
Memphis Commercial Appeal,
  201–2
Mena Intermountain Regional
    Airport, 167–68, 168–69,
    172–73, 174–75, 178–79,
    179–80, 179, 179–81
Meredith, James, 171
Meyer, Jane, 270
"Michelle," 54–55, 79
Miller, David Lee, 53
Mills, Wilber, 252
Mintz, John A., 109–12
Mondale, Eleanor, 340
Monica's Story (Lewinsky), 359
Moody, James, 350–51,
  358–59, 360, 362
Moon, Sun Myung, 94, 141,
  158–59
Moral Majority, Inc., 141
Morgenthau, Robert, 267
Morrison, Alexi, 109
Morrison, Micah, 162, 163,
  173, 186, 187, 217
Morrison v. Olson, 109, 118,
  185, 218, 259
Mueller, Robert, 43
Murdoch, Rupert, 94, 328
Murkowski, Frank, 189

Narisi, Mike, 96
Nash, Bobby, 169
Nathan, Irv, 93–94
Nation magazine, 168, 174, 267
National Empowerment Tele-
    vision, 311
National Enquirer, 46, 48–49, 51
  coverage of Bill Clinton,
    57–58
National Security Political Ac-
    tion Committee
    (NSPAC), 73
National Taxpayers Union, 270
NBC News, 64
  coverage of Bill Clinton, 23,
    96–97, 106
  Whitewater coverage, 97

Nelson, Mary Lynn, 12
Nelson, Rex, 1, 2–3, 3
Nelson, Sheffield, 8–10, 10–11,
    12–13, 20, 23, 31, 32, 88,
    164, 220, 246
  Bill Clinton, accusations
    concerning, 12–13, 25,
    30–31, 33, 35–36, 45, 53,
    60, 61, 63, 67, 93, 96, 144,
    164, 184, 247
Nesbit, Lynn, 291, 292
Neuwirth, Steve, 190
New Clinton Chronicles, The
    (video), 154, 155–56, 157
New Republic magazine, 73,
    144, 147–48, 188
New York magazine, 291
New York Observer, 60
New York Post, 76, 180
New York Times, 27, 95, 96
  coverage of Bill Clinton,
    106, 146, 150
  Whitewater coverage, 30, 33,
    34–35, 35–36, 36–37, 38,
    93, 94, 95, 117, 128, 133,
    134, 135, 150, 176, 177,
    197, 198, 200, 202–3, 203,
    208, 245, 351
New York Times Magazine,
    151–53, 274
New Yorker magazine, 250,
    264–65, 329
Newsday, 327
Newsweek magazine, 94, 124,
    126, 268, 269, 291, 292,
    303, 362, 365, 366, 367
  Web site, 356
Newton, Hugh, 59
Nichols, Larry, 14–16, 168, 182,
    212, 222
  alleged drug use, 156–57
  Bill Clinton, accusations
    concerning, 46–47, 50,
    52, 52–53, 54–55, 56, 64,
    67, 77–79, 79–80, 81–82,
    85–86, 139–40, 142, 144,
    145, 153, 154, 155–56,
    157, 168, 179, 192, 345,
    347
  Bill Clinton, lawsuits
    against, 16–17, 28, 28–29,
    136
  and Gennifer Flowers,
    22–23
Nichols vs. Clinton (video), 192
Nickles, Don, 138
Nieman Report, 235
Nightline, 24, 208, 209
  Hillary Clinton's videotape,
    editing of, 203, 251

Nixon, Richard, 4, 71, 107, 131
Norris (FBI agent), 241
North, Oliver, 15, 120, 121,
    125, 128, 138, 159, 168,
    168–69, 169, 173, 179
North American Newspaper
    Alliance (NANA), 326
Novak, Robert, 4–5, 103, 221
Novak, Viveca, 200
Nussbaum, Bernard, 97, 117,
    130, 140, 190–91, 191,
    194, 279, 280, 281, 285,
    310

Oakley, Meredith, 233
Obstruction of Justice (video),
    154–55
O'Connor, Sandra Day, 263
Olin Foundation, 100
Olson, Theodore B., 109–12,
    118, 163, 231–32, 262,
    263,
    268
O'Rourke, P. J., 314–15

Palladino, Jack, 50, 53, 75
Panetta, Leon, 272, 279
*Paranoid Style in American Pol-
    itics, The* (Hofstadter),
    142
Parish, Paul, 170
Parks, Gary, 146
Parks, Jane, 153
Parks, Luther "Jerry," 310
Parry, Robert, 141, 159
Passion and Betrayal (Flowers),
    27
Patkus, Michael T., 235–36,
    317–18
Patterson, Larry, 49, 54, 86,
    112–13, 192, 212, 213,
    266, 345, 347
  Troopergate, 101–2, 104–5,
    113, 114, 115, 120–21,
    157
Paul, Dean, 224–25, 227, 229
Paula Jones Legal Fund,
    260–61, 321–22
Pennington, Clydine,
    345
Penthouse magazine, 26, 55,
    123
People magazine, 123
Pepperdine University, 268,
    270, 274
Perdue, Sally Miller, 51–52, 52
Perelman, Ronald, 348
Perot, H. Ross, 50, 52
Perry, Roger, 21, 112–13, 192,
    193, 212, 213, 266, 346

Troopergate, 101–2, 104–5,
    114, 115, 120–21, 157,
    275
Peter Smith & Company, 59
Pettus, Don, 44
Phillips, Carol, 345
Pillsbury Report, 176–77, 178,
    199–200, 202, 211, 236,
    258, 316–17
Pindar, Joe, 175, 178
Pittsburgh Post-Gazette, 108
Pittsburgh Tribune-Review,
    107, 108, 129, 193, 270
Plesczynski, Wladyslaw, 103,
    161, 163, 169
Polk, Davis, 128
Pollock, Ellen Joan, 176–77,
    200
Pope, Alexander, 30
Porter, Richard W., 59, 104–5,
    125, 127, 260, 261,
    298–300, 338–39, 349,
    356, 371
Potts, Larry, 43
Power, Pasta and Politics
    (D'Amato), 188
Presidential Victory Commit-
    tee, 73, 74, 75, 75–76, 80
Primary Colors (Klein), 312
Pro-Family Media Coalition,
    306
Pruden, Wesley, 219
Pryor, David, 72, 152,
    184
Publisher Weekly, 291
Purdom, Michelle, 47–50, 55
Pyke, David, 339–40

Quayle, Dan, 134

Raines, Howell, 36
Rand, Joshua, 162, 163, 164
Rawls, Wendell, Jr., 33
Reagan, Michael, 222
Reagan, Ronald, 43, 109, 131,
    141, 168, 173, 201
Real Anita Hill, The (Brock),
    99, 100
Reasoner, Stephen M., 128
Reber, Daniel, 141, 158, 159
Reed, Ralph, 138, 139
Reed, Roy, 69–70
Reed, Terry, 168, 173, 179
Regnery, Alfred, 290
Regnery Publishing, 283, 290,
    312, 338–39
Rehnquist, William, 45,
    130–31, 131, 262, 263
Reign, David F., 162, 222, 226
Rempel, William, 63

coverage of Bill Clinton, 100, 102, 104, 346
contacts with Case and Nichols, 47, 50, 54, 55, 57, 58, 80–81, 81, 112
Troopergate, 112–15, 192
Rengers, Carrie, 142
Reno, Janet, 116, 118, 119–20, 132, 133, 140, 349, 356, 357, 358
Republican National Coalition for Life, 80
Republican National Committee, 1, 159
Republican Party, 58
campaign finance scandals, 256–57, 264
Bill Clinton and impeachment, 308–9, 310, 311, 312, 315
Resnick, Faye, 291–92
Resolution Trust Corporation (RTC), 37, 38, 95
criminal referrals, 40–41, 41–42, 43, 95, 96
Pillsbury Report, 176–77, 178, 199–200, 202, 211, 236, 258, 316–17
Richardson, Bill, 226
Richardson, Ken, 62–63
Riley, Bob, 252
Riley, Claudia, 252, 254
Rivera, Geraldo, 172
Robertson, Pat, 138, 139, 140
Robinson, Tommy, 1–2, 3, 5–8, 15, 20, 25, 58
Rockefeller, Winthrop, 8, 70–71, 71
Rodriguez, Felix, 169, 179
Roelle, William, 42
Roosevelt, Franklin Delano, 32
Root, Stewart, 200
Rogers, Norma, 61, 63, 64
Rose Law Firm, 34, 36, 85, 148
and Madison Guaranty Savings, 36, 39, 202–4, 204, 205, 206–7
Rosenzweig, Paul, 349–50, 356
Rotunda, Roland, 127
Rousakis, John P., 326
Ruddy, Christopher, 129, 156, 193, 294, 310, 310–11, 315
Rushdoony, R. J., 138, 320
Rutherford, Samuel, 320
Rutherford Institute, 319–20, 321

Safire, William, 128, 130, 132, 189, 190, 203, 204, 206, 236, 246, 248, 267, 268, 328, 354
St. Eve, Amy, 234, 251
Sally Jessy Raphael, 51
Salon magazine, 218–19, 226, 261, 311
Sandquist, Don, 201
Sarah Scaife Foundation, 106, 268, 313
Sarbanes, Paul, 196–97, 213
Scaife, Richard Mellon, 107–9, 260–61
and the Arkansas Project, 106, 173–74, 219, 315, 372
CIA connection, 107–8
conservative causes, financial support of, 106, 107, 127, 156, 173–74, 193, 219, 268–69, 283, 310–11, 313, 315, 357, 369
and Kenneth Starr, 268–69, 270
See also Carthage Foundation; Sarah Scaife Foundation
Scalia, Antonin, 118, 185, 217, 262
Schaffer, Archie, 210
Schlafly, Phyllis, 80, 138
Schmidt, Susan, 94, 95, 96, 166, 176, 178, 190, 207, 221, 228, 275
Schnieder, Howard, 94
Schumer, Charles, 212
Scott, Marsha, 285, 333
Seal, Adler Berriman "Barry," 167, 168, 169, 179, 180, 182
Second Amercian Revolution, The (Whitehead), 320
Secret Life of Bill Clinton, The (Evans-Pritchard), 173
Segretti, Donald, 4
Seidman, William, 32, 131–32
Sentelle, David, 45, 131–32, 132–133, 261, 353
Seper, Jerry, 86
Shelby, Richard, 191
Shirley, Craig, 121
Siebert, Debbie, 288
Silberman, Laurence, 105
Silverman, Ira, 96, 230
Simon, Paul, 211
Simonello, Peter, 193
Singlaub, John, 15
"60 Minutes" Deception, The, 310–11
Slick Willie: Why America Cannot Trust Bill Clinton (Brown/Bossie), 74, 76, 76–77, 77, 78, 81, 146, 282
Slick Willie II: Why America Still Cannot Trust Bill Clinton (Stone/Manion), 282–83
Smith, Michael, 154
Smith, Peter W., 59, 59–60, 99–100, 104, 114, 115, 125, 192, 338, 346
Smith, Stephen, 233–35
Sneed, Joseph, 131
Snow, Tony, 284, 290, 307, 323
Southeastern Legal Foundation, 311
Speed Service, 335
Spell, William, Jr., 172
Spence, Gerry, 124
Spy magazine, 76
Star newspaper, 22–23, 25, 27, 46, 56
Starr, Kenneth W., 133–35, 142, 361–62, 369
conflicts of interest, appearance of, 134–35, 195–96, 232, 261, 338–39, 356–57
Vincent Foster suicide investigation, 83
and the Paula Jones lawsuit, 127
the McDougals, pressuring to incriminate the Clintons, 251–52, 252–54, 273–74
media and, 134–35, 264–65, 267, 267–68, 269–70, 274, 318
politics of, 134–35
as Whitewater independent counsel, 64, 133–35, 155, 163, 166, 183–85, 185–87, 197–98, 202, 204, 213, 221, 222, 225, 258
Whitewater independent counsel, resignation of, 264, 267–68, 270
See also Starr Report; Tucker-McDougal trial; Whitewater
Starr Report, 348–50, 352–53, 371
Steele, Julie Hiatt, 272, 278–79, 303, 354
Stengel, Richard, 205–6
Stephanopoulos, George, 84, 127–28, 176, 199, 366, 367
Stephens, Inc., 6, 7, 10–11, 14, 33, 144, 148, 149–50, 186

Stephens, Jack, 5–6
Stephens, Jackson T., 149–50
Stephens, Jay, 127–28, 176, 199
Stephens, Mary Ann, 5, 6, 7
Stephens, Warren, 144, 149–50, 186
Stephens, Witt, 5
Stevenson, Mabel, 61–62
Stewart, James B., 205, 208–9, 209–10, 236, 250–51, 264–65
Stodola, Mark, 163, 221–22
Stone, Deborah, 77, 78–79, 79–80, 80, 282–83
Strange Death of Vincent Foster, The (Ruddy), 315
Strauss, Peter, 357
Sullivan, Lencola, 16
Sutton, Buddy, 242–43
Swaggart, Jimmy, 141
Swillinger, Daniel, 59

Taylor, Danny, 125–26
Taylor, Stuart, Jr., 269–70
Theodoracopulos, Taki, 103, 165
Thomas, Clarence, 99
Thomas, Evan, 269
Thomas, Jimmy, 158
Thomases, Susan, 36, 190, 191, 194, 203
Thomason, Harry, 122
Thompson, Charles, 172
Thompson, Linda, 140
Thurmond, Strom, 4
Time magazine, 94, 116–17, 134, 205–6
Toobin, Jeffrey, 202, 217
Travelgate (White House Travel Office firings), 83–84, 257, 258, 283
media and, 84–85
Traylor, Danny, 121–22, 124
Treece, Brooks, 62
Tretham, Ray, 62
Tripp, Bruce, 280
Tripp, Linda, 280–81, 329–31, 373
book proposals, 284, 290, 307, 323, 324, 329–30, 331–32, 354
Bill Clinton, animosity toward, 284, 284–85, 285–86, 289–90, 371
and Michael Isikoff, 289, 297, 303, 303–4, 324, 330, 331–32, 333, 333–35, 336, 337
and the Paula Jones lawsuit, 337–38, 339–40, 362

and Monica Lewinsky, 287, 289–90, 297–98, 304, 324, 335–36, 342, 342–43, 348, 355–56
Monica Lewinsky's stained dress, 337, 354–55
the Monica Lewinsky tapes, 331, 332–33, 334–35, 336–37, 348, 352–53, 357, 362, 366
and the Office of Independent Council, 349–50, 350–51, 351–52, 352–53, 354–55
Senate Banking Committee testimony, 279–80, 280, 281
suspected of being "Deepwater," 282–83
and Kathleen Willey, 272, 279, 279–80, 285, 286, 287–88, 288, 290, 297, 339
Troopergate, 21, 54, 56, 67, 100–103, 104–5, 112–15, 347
media and, 113–14, 115
Troopergate Whistleblower Fund, 120
Tsongas, Paul, 27
Tucker, Betty, 193
Tucker, Jim Guy, 31–32, 32–33, 40, 41, 44, 89, 91, 92, 129, 163, 164, 184–85, 192, 216, 217, 242
resignation and appeal, 245, 248–49
Tucker-McDougal trial, 213–14, 219–22
alleged loans, 223, 223–24, 227–29, 229–30, 230–31, 231–32, 233, 265
Arkansas Project, 219–22, 232
Bill Clinton, accusations concerning, 223–24, 230–31, 231–32, 236, 239–41
closing arguments, 242–43, 243–44
David Hale, 217, 221–22, 222, 223, 224, 228–29, 229–30, 230–31, 231–32
FBI 302 form, 222, 223, 228, 265
indictments, 183–85, 185–87, 216–18
jurors, 245, 248–49
Jim McDougal, 237–38, 238–241, 244

Susan McDougal, 223–24, 237, 241–42, 244, 255
media and, 217, 219, 221–22, 225, 228, 233, 235–36, 244–45
Theodore Olson, 231–32
Michael T. Patkus, 235–36
Stephen Smith, 233–35
Jim Guy Tucker, 242, 244–45, 249
verdicts and sentences, 244–45, 249, 255, 273
Bill Watt, 224–26, 226–27
Tyrrell, R. Emmett, Jr., 103, 312
and the Arkansas Project, 153, 161, 165, 167, 168–69, 169, 181, 312–15
and Mena Airport accusations, 172–73, 178, 179–80, 180–81
Tyson, Don, 142, 151, 279
Tyson, Laura, 272
Tyson Foods, 150–51, 152

Uncovering Clinton (Isikoff), 271, 278, 286, 302, 334, 349, 356
Unlimited Access (Aldrich), 283–84

Van Buren Press Argus/Van Buren Press Argus-Courier, 61, 62–63
van Natta, Don, Jr., 349, 371
Vanity Fair magazine, 76, 257
Vigneault, J. J., 1, 2–3, 5, 20
Vlasto, Chris, 251, 273, 366

Waas, Murray, 143, 153, 157, 267, 311
Wade, Chris, 38–39, 239
Walker, Edwin, 171
Wall Street Journal, 77–78, 144, 147, 148–49, 149–50, 186, 193, 217
coverage of Bill Clinton, 146–47, 179–80
Whitewater coverage, 128, 129–30, 176–77, 178, 193, 200, 202
Wallace, George, 68, 71
Wallace, Lurleen, 71
Wallace, Mike, 310
Walsh, Lawrence, 118, 128, 217
Wardell, Mark, 201–2
Warren, James, 340
Washington Post, 17, 27, 50, 86, 94, 95, 107, 126, 257, 315

coverage of Bill Clinton, 106, 366

Whitewater coverage, 117, 134, 150, 176, 190, 197, 198, 200, 207, 225, 275, 316

Washington Star, 328

Washington Times, 86, 141, 186, 187, 217, 219

coverage of Bill Clinton, 60, 94, 97–98, 127, 166, 319

Washington Weekly, 91, 283

Watt, Bill, 224–26, 226–27

Wattenberg, Daniel, 164–65, 166, 179

Weekly Standard magazine, 94

Wellington (New Zealand) *Dominion*, 66

Welsh, Russell, 168

Western Journalism Center, 193, 270

Westmoreland, William, 110

Weyrich, Paul, 138, 311

Whitacre, Susie, 16, 22

White, Frank, 6, 15, 62, 88, 148, 152, 228, 317

White Citizens Council, 68–69, 70, 98, 171

Whitehead, John, 138, 319–21

Whitener, Freddie, 161

Whitewater

independent counsel, demands for and appointment of, 116–19, 130–31, 131–32

House Banking Committee hearings, 175–76, 177–78, 180, 313

Senate Banking Committee hearings, 188–89, 189–90, 190–92, 194–96, 198–99, 199–200, 210–11, 211–13

Senate Banking Committee hearings, Linda Tripp's testimony, 279, 280, 281

Whitewater (independent counsel hearings— Robert Fiske), 119–20, 127–30, 132–33

Whitewater (Office of the Independent Council hearings, Kenneth Starr), 64, 83, 133–35, 155, 163, 166

Branscum-Hill trial, 245–48

Bill Clinton's sexual behavior, investigating, 266, 266–67, 274, 318, 329,

340, 343, 349–50, 350–51, 351–52, 352–53, 359–61

Bill Clinton's testimony, 195, 343

Hillary Clinton, testimony of, 195, 202–5, 205–6

Clinton files and records, questions concerning, 97–98, 117, 189–90, 190–92, 257, 258

indictments and threatened indictments, 200, 202–5

and the Paula Jones lawsuit, 349–50, 356–58, 358–59

leaks of testimony, 166, 268, 274, 340, 354

and Monica Lewinsky, 335–36, 348–50, 352–53, 354–55

Monica Lewinsky, questioning of, 359–61, 361–62

the McDougals, pressuring to incriminate the Clintons, 251–52, 252–54, 273–74, 315–18

media and, 116–17, 128, 129–30, 176–77, 178, 189, 190–91, 193, 197, 198, 200, 202–3, 203, 204–5, 205–6, 208, 208–9, 212, 265–66, 264–65, 267, 267–68, 269–70, 318, 351, 354, 365–66, 371, 372–73

mock juries, 265–66

Pillsbury Report, 176–77, 178, 199–200, 202, 211, 236, 258, 316–17

polls and public opinion, 190–91, 370–71

Republican politics and, 116–17, 127–30, 132–33, 174–76, 190–92, 195–96, 216–18, 294

Kenneth Starr's resignation, 264, 267–68, 270

Travelgate (White House Travel Office firings), 83–85, 257, 258, 283

and Linda Tripp, 329, 350–51, 351–52, 352–53

Tucker-McDougal trial. *See* Tucker-McDougal trial

See also Fiske, Robert B.; Leach, Jim; Starr, Kenneth W.; *Starr Report*

Whitewater Development Corporation, 30–31, 39, 177

the Clintons and, 30, 30–31,

38, 38–39, 40, 44

See also McDougal, James

Whitney, John Hey, 108

Why Did Vincent Foster Die? (Center for American Values), 283

Williams, Bobbie Ann, 58, 60

Williams, John Bell, 170, 171

Williams, Maggie, 189, 190, 191, 194, 310

Willey, Edward, Jr., 271, 272, 278, 288, 288–89

Willey, Kathleen, 285, 286, 288, 289

Bill Clinton, accusations concerning, 271, 271–72, 277–79, 290, 303, 344, 346, 354, 363

Drudge Report and, 300–301, 301–2, 350

Michael Isikoff and, 271–72, 291–92, 295

and *Jones v. Clinton*, 298, 339

and Linda Tripp, 272, 279, 279–80, 285, 286, 287–88, 290, 297, 339

Wilson, Harold, 108

Wilson, William R., 218

Winter, Ralph, 300

Wirges, Gene, 66

Women's Federation for World Peace, 159

Woman's News Service, 326, 328

Wood, Larry, 293–95

Wood, Sandra, 245

Woods, Henry, 185, 185–87, 216–18, 218–19

Woodward, Bob, 134, 275

Worthen Bank, 148, 234

Wright, Betsey, 14, 15, 16, 29, 41, 47, 50, 50–52, 53, 112, 113, 340

Wright, Susan Webber, 213, 245, 260, 340, 342–47, 358, 363, 364

Yoakum, Philip, 60–61, 63, 64

Yost, Pete, 265, 316

Young, Buddy, 54, 113, 346–47

Young Americans for Freedom, 74

Youth Federation for World Peace, 141